INTERNATIONAL
Reading Association
800 BARKSDALE ROAD, PO BOX 8139
NEWARK, DE 19714-8139, USA
www.reading.org

Doug Buehl

Developing
READERS
in the Academic
DISCIPLINES

The International Reading Association attempts, through its publications, to provide a forum for a wide spectrum of opinions on reading. This policy permits divergent viewpoints without implying the endorsement of the Association.

Executive Editor, Publications   Shannon Fortner
Managing Editor   Christina M. Terranova
Editorial Associate   Wendy Logan
Design and Composition Manager   Anette Schuetz
Design and Composition Associate   Lisa Kochel

Cover   Design, Lise Holliker Dykes; Photographs (cover and interior), Doug Buehl; Radiolarian image, p. 48, Scott Camazine/PhotoResearchers, Inc.; Rocks image, p. 48, Randy Morse/SeaPics; Coal miners image, p. 49, Bettman/CORBIS; Illustrations, p. 51, Jeff Grunewald.

Library of Congress Cataloging-in-Publication Data
Buehl, Doug.
 Developing readers in the academic disciplines / Doug Buehl.
    p. cm.
 Includes bibliographical references and index.
 ISBN 978-0-87207-845-1
 1. Content area reading. I. Title.
 LB1050.45.B85 2011
 372.47'6--dc23

                          2011024017

Suggested APA Reference
Buehl, D. (2011). *Developing readers in the academic disciplines*. Newark, DE: International Reading Association.

This book is dedicated to the memory of Milt McPike, my principal, my colleague, my friend, and one of the true towers of Madison East High School.

CONTENTS

CHAPTER 4   120

Frontloading Instruction That Activates and Builds Academic Knowledge

CHAPTER 5   163

Building Inquiring Minds Around Disciplinary Texts

CHAPTER 6   216

Instructional Practices for Working Complex Texts

CHAPTER 7   263

Customizing Literacy Practices

 **Doug Buehl** is a teacher, professional development leader, and adolescent literacy consultant. During his 33 years in the Madison Metropolitan School District in Madison, Wisconsin, USA, he was a social studies teacher, reading teacher, and reading specialist at Madison East High School and a district adolescent literacy support teacher. In addition to presenting literacy workshops, his experiences include collaborating with teachers as a school literacy coach, teaching struggling readers, coordinating a schoolwide content area tutoring program, teaching college-preparatory advanced reading, and teaching night school students returning for their high school diplomas.

Doug is the author of the bestseller *Classroom Strategies for Interactive Learning,* of which the third edition was published by the International Reading Association (IRA) in 2009. He is a coauthor of *Reading and the High School Student: Strategies to Enhance Literacy,* of which the second edition was published in 2007 by Allyn & Bacon, and *Strategies to Enhance Literacy and Learning in Middle School Content Area Classrooms,* of which the third edition was published in 2007 by Allyn & Bacon. In addition, Doug was the first editor of the adolescent literacy newsletter *The Exchange,* published by the IRA Secondary Reading Special Interest Group.

Doug has been an active literacy professional at the local, state, and national levels. He was a founding member of the IRA Commission on Adolescent Literacy and was a member of the interdisciplinary task force that drafted the national *Standards for Middle and High School Literacy Coaches,* a joint collaboration among IRA, the National Council of Teachers of English, the National Council of Teachers of Mathematics, the National Science Teachers Association, and the National Council for the Social Studies. Doug served terms as president of the Wisconsin State Reading Association, the IRA Secondary Reading Special Interest Group, and the Madison Area Reading Council. He was the 1996 recipient of IRA's Nila Banton Smith Award and was inducted to the Wisconsin State Reading Association's Friends of Literacy Hall of Fame in 2000. Recently, Doug served as cochair of the Wisconsin Department of Public Instruction's Adolescent Literacy Task Force.

Doug is currently an educational consultant who works with school districts to provide professional development for teachers. He is an instructor of undergraduate- and graduate-level courses in adolescent literacy at Edgewood College in Madison and is the parent of two sons: Jeremy, a social studies teacher, and Christopher, a biochemist. He lives in the near east side of Madison with his wife, Wendy, a professional violinist and middle school orchestra teacher. Contact Doug at drbuehl@ sbcglobal.net.

FOREWORD

In *Developing Readers in the Academic Disciplines,* Doug Buehl examines why and how secondary school teachers should translate the content reading strategies first advanced by Harold Herber in the 1970s into meaningful subject-area literacy instruction in middle and high school classrooms of 2011 and beyond. This book should prove to be extremely useful to pre- and inservice teachers alike as they work to integrate literacy instruction in the service of subject-area learning into their daily routines. Offering theory and research-warranted teaching practices in a humorous, conversational voice, Buehl makes a clear case for teaching students how to read as an act of inquiry, a central requirement for disciplinary literacy.

Before he turns to a discussion of inquiry, however, Buehl situates disciplinary reading as an act of identity. He provides numerous examples of how people read for varied purposes in varied domains and of how people engage in particular practices associated with those purposes and domains. Buehl endearingly exemplifies these ways of reading and types of reading identities by showing readers the different ways he (a history teacher, literacy coach, and ardent Milwaukee Brewers fan) and his wife (a classically trained, practicing violinist and music educator) engage with texts. The examples nicely bring to life the connection between people's identities, their ways of readings, and the domains in which they spend most of their lives. These ways of reading are also, as Buehl suggests, following scholars such as Jim Gee (1996), ways of being certain kinds of people, but typical secondary school instruction rarely conceives of teaching and learning as apprenticing people in different ways of being who they are. Buehl, however, suggests that unless students are invited to become the type of readers associated with each academic subject-area domain, they will not identify with the subject and their learning of content concepts, as well as their reading and writing skills, will be likely to suffer as a result. The rest of the book offers detailed strategies—along with rationales—for helping readers become those kinds of people across multiple academic domains.

In offering teaching strategies, Buehl is careful to recognize the role knowledge plays in robust comprehension of complex texts (as well as in developing an identity associated with historical, scientific, mathematical, musical, artistic, or linguistic study). As a result, Buehl does not fall into the trap of offering secondary school teachers strategies that are empty steps or procedures to follow. Instead, he carefully links the use of various teaching strategies (what I might call *tools*, simply to distinguish them from cognitive reading strategies employed by individual readers) to key aspects of secondary subject-area learning: inquiry and knowledge development. This linking of strategies/tools, inquiry, and knowledge development makes good sense. Why do members of disciplines engage in the work that they do? To solve problems, address questions, or work out thorny puzzles. Do they engage in such inquiry in a vacuum? No, they seek out information (i.e., they develop knowledge), often via a range of texts, to guide them in their inquiry. Do they wander aimlessly through texts and investigations, or do they use the tools at hand strategically to advance their development? Clearly, there is a discipline to inquiry, and that discipline is shaped by the available tools for making and representing knowledge in each domain. In other words, what Buehl suggests for secondary school subject-area instruction is that teachers work to replicate the inquiry practices—including those involving written and other text forms—that members of the academic disciplines and associated professions engage in their daily work.

At the same time, however, Buehl reminds readers that we are working with young people—novices to the disciplines—who are developing their skills. In addition, their learning occurs in school classrooms, not laboratories, archives, publishing houses, orchestra halls, or nuclear power plants. As such, they need to be apprenticed into disciplinary practice. At times that apprenticeship may involve implicit teaching— legitimate peripheral participation, in the lexicon of Jean Lave and Etienne Wenger (1991)—and at other times it might involve explicit instruction. In still other moments, such teaching can be a mix of implicit and explicit instruction, with the popular acronym teaching tools that are familiar to many (e.g., K-W-L, RT, or QtA) serving as frames for instruction, rather than as steps to follow in a lockstep manner. What Buehl makes clear in the book, however, is that although employing these strategies and tools may help young people improve their general reading comprehension, the strategies and tools will not enhance disciplinary reading if they are not embedded in a framework that puts the essential questions—or as my colleague Bob Bain calls them, the *intellectual problems*—of the disciplines front and center. If reading is engaged to address questions and solve problems, then readers have a purpose for reading. Their reading comprehension is likely to improve even as their understanding of disciplinary concepts and practices also grows.

Reading this book reminds me of why I have long been a fan of Doug Buehl: He speaks from experience, with wisdom, theory, and research to guide him. Doug is a veteran and expert teacher and literacy coach who values theory and research in advancing his pedagogical practice. He identifies strongly with his own discipline of history while being committed to advancing the literacy and learning skills of his students (and his teaching colleagues). Thus, when Doug exhorts us to take on the challenge of disciplinary literacy teaching, he cannot be dismissed as a talking head who works outside the real world of classrooms. He cannot be seen as an elitist who privileges the disciplines over other ways of knowing the world. Moreover, Buehl has worked closely with struggling readers and their teachers to improve subject-area literacy skills; he does not reserve disciplinary reading instruction for those who already achieve at the highest levels. He is clear about his commitment to offering all youths opportunities to learn in deep and profound ways, across a range of domains—disciplinary and otherwise.

I thank Doug for his commitment to youths, to teachers, and to teacher education. I recommend this book to anyone who cares about improving the subject-area learning and literacy skills of all youths in the United States. Read on!

Elizabeth Birr Moje
Associate Dean for Research
and an Arthur F. Thurnau Professor
School of Education
University of Michigan, Ann Arbor
June 2, 2011

When I was a fledgling social studies teacher in the mid-1970s, the mantra throughout the Madison Metropolitan School District was "Every teacher a teacher of reading." I had arrived to teach at Madison East High School from a university preparation program that was outstanding in many respects but significantly had not prepared me for this ambitious undertaking. The message that we channeled through professional development workshops, department work, and schoolwide initiatives was unambiguous: The texts that we expected students to read presented significant challenges, many students struggled to learn our content because they needed guidance and support as readers, and we could no longer merely assign reading; we now had to integrate reading instruction into our daily routines.

For veteran teachers, these truisms presented a distinctly new message, a reframing of their classroom mission, and a serious and maybe unsettling step outside their established comfort zones. Spirited conversations ensued about what we should be able to expect of students as a condition of their arrival at the high school and what role we should assume in developing abilities that were still evolving in many of our students. Some teachers tried to keep the door closed and bypass attention to literacy practices, others bent a little and tried a few things, a number bought into the arguments and changed important facets of their instruction, and a handful became true believers who reconceptualized their work with students. I was one of the teachers who bought in; it was pretty difficult for me not to once I had daily, firsthand opportunities to observe students' struggles with learning effectively through reading. I was an eager participant at literacy workshops, I test-drove a number of literacy strategies in my classroom work, and gradually I began to see my role as a teacher in a different light. As a result, I went on to get my master's degree in literacy and worked the bulk of my 33 years in the Madison Metropolitan School District as a reading teacher, reading specialist, literacy coach, and professional development leader in literacy.

I wish I could narrate an upbeat story line and proudly relate the ongoing and inexorable progress in adolescent literacy that was achieved in my district. Yet, like most places, our growth was sporadic, sputtering at times (e.g., "We've *done* literacy and have new school goals to tackle this year"), with district attention to the reading development of middle and high school students periodically resurfacing, only to be followed by stretches of backsliding. Our communal talk about the need to focus on adolescent readers morphed along the way. We began with "reading in the content areas," which to many had the unfortunate connotation of an intrusion: teaching reading being parachuted into the unfriendly terrain of content practices and instruction where it was unwelcome and did not belong. Gradually, the references were upgraded to "content literacy," which encompassed reading, writing, speaking, and listening (and eventually viewing and creating) but also somewhat blurred distinctions between being literate in the knowledge of a discipline, science for example, and behaving as a reader and writer in science contexts. At times, our language was more global (e.g., "reading and writing across the curriculum") and sometimes more general in targeting teacher routines and individual student processing (e.g., "strategic teaching," "strategic reading"). In the past decade, we have settled on talking about the students themselves as the rallying emphasis: "adolescent literacy." When my older son entered the teaching profession in this last decade, he would also say that although his university preparation was outstanding in many respects, he too significantly did not arrive at the classroom prepared to address the literacy challenges of his students as a social studies teacher.

So, decades later, many of the same issues and concerns about the growth of adolescents as readers and writers as they engage as learners of academic subjects remain unresolved. This book represents a slice of that continuing effort to integrate effective literacy practices into the fabric of classroom instruction, especially at the middle and high school levels. The term that will be employed throughout the book is *disciplinary literacy*, which I hope will not merely be construed as the latest semantic shuffle in our ongoing conversations but a helpful reformulation of what it means to truly address the literacy development of our students in disciplinary contexts. The book is intended to be a companion volume to my International Reading Association publication, *Classroom Strategies for Interactive Learning* (Buehl, 2009a), now in its third edition, and to provide additional support to teachers of academic disciplines as they explore literacy practices that can intersect with the teaching of their curricular content.

Acknowledgments

A number of individuals deserve thanks for their roles in making this book possible. I have worked with teachers, literacy coaches, and instructional leaders in a host of school districts during the development of the ideas that form the basis of this book, and I would like to heartily thank them for involving me in their school and district work. In particular, two Wisconsin literacy coaches, Emily Huttenburg of Waunakee High School and Jill Larson of Middleton High School, deserve a special mention for their insightful commentary and thorough feedback as reviewers of this manuscript. Their thoughtful reactions and suggestions have improved the book considerably, and their enthusiasm and professionalism were infectious. I would also like to thank Jane Belmore, acting dean of the Education Department at Edgewood College, who brought her experiences as district literacy leader, principal, and assistant superintendent in the Madison Metropolitan School District to her review of this manuscript. I appreciate the suggestions and feedback from a number of my teacher colleagues, who reviewed at various stages the self-questioning taxonomies developed for reading through different disciplinary lenses. In particular, I am grateful for Laura Jensen's ideas for the mathematics taxonomies. Finally, my graduate students at Edgewood College, as first readers of the manuscript, deserve recognition for their thoughtful reactions to the book's ideas, focus, and structure.

This is the second book on which I have had the privilege of working with Corinne Mooney, my editor at the International Reading Association. I deeply appreciate Corinne's ideas and insights for the development of this book and her good-humored professionalism in shepherding this project to completion.

As always with everything that I write, the final fine-tuning followed a careful and perceptive reading of the manuscript by my wife, Wendy Buehl, who brings an indispensable critical eye to the clarity of my message. Over the years, I have thrived from the sometimes daily, invigorating, pedagogical conversations that naturally unfold as a regular dynamic of the Buehl household, and I am indebted in particular to

Wendy for her contributions to the refinement of the thinking that unfolds in this work. We are a family of teachers: Wendy is an orchestra teacher at Oregon Middle School, and my son Jeremy, a social studies teacher at Madison East High School, and his wife Mandi, a chemistry teacher at Watertown High School, represent the next generation of teachers in the family. I would like to thank Jeremy for his thoughts on portions of this manuscript and for his astute observations on literacy issues in today's classrooms. Finally, conversations with my son Christopher, a biochemist working on his doctorate at Michigan State University, have helped hone my thinking on the science-related segments of this book.

CHAPTER 1

Mentoring Students in Disciplinary Literacy

Essential Question: *Why is there a significant need for disciplinary literacy instruction?*

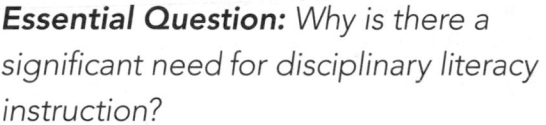

How would you describe yourself as a reader? That you are a reader is a given—you are reading this chapter, for example. So, if you talked about yourself as a reader, what kinds of things would you say? Some of your comments might be related to *what* you read: "I have several magazines I enjoy." "I never miss the sports section in my newspaper." "I prefer biographies." "I do a lot of on-the-job professional reading." "I have some favorite authors of popular fiction." "I am online several times a day, tracking the postings in some favorite blogs and websites." "I'm never without a book."

Some of your comments might concern *where* and *when* you read: "I read in bed every night before I go to sleep." "I always have something to read when I am traveling." "I read constantly throughout the school day." "I like to relax and do some reading with a cup of coffee when I get home from work." "I catch up on my leisure reading during the summers."

Some of your comments might detail *how* you read: "I get completely lost when I am reading something that really grabs me." "I have always been a slow reader." "I am one of those people who have to mark up a text when I need to do careful reading." "I am quite critical as a reader and tend to talk back to an author in my head." "I am a very methodical reader, pausing frequently to ponder what I have understood so far."

Some of your comments might express *why* you read: "I am very conscious of keeping up with the most recent findings in my discipline." "It is important to me to follow what is going on in the world each day." "I usually have a lot of student work to read." "I find that reading helps me unwind after a stressful day." "I would be bored if I did not have something with me to read." "Reading is just central to who I am. I cannot imagine my life without reading."

Reading and Identity

Your personal what, where, when, how, and why descriptions represent your reader profile. Obviously, when we talk to each other about our personal reading, we reveal reader profiles that may perhaps share some elements but differ dramatically with others. Let me use myself as an example. Recently, I embarked on a rather ambitious reading project: Francis Parkman's monumental seven-volume *France and England in North America*. It took Parkman nearly his entire adult life to recount the unfolding drama between the two European superpowers as they vied for supremacy on the North American continent. It looks like it will take me most of a year—reading Parkman interspersed with a variety of novels, periodicals, informational books, and professional material—to arrive at the climactic resolution in 1759 on the Plains of Abraham, as Volume 7 takes me to the decisive battle of Québec.

Does spending extended hours with a 19th-century historian who strived to contribute to our understanding of a critical but little known period of North American history sound interesting? Or, to ask it another way, would *you* choose to read a work such as this? And if so, why?

For me, the Parkman history allows me once more to slip into one of my identities, that of historian. I majored in history as a university undergraduate and began my career in education teaching high school social studies. I have always been an avid reader of history, even back to my years as an elementary school student, when I would page through volumes of the family *World Book Encyclopedia*, skipping everything but the entries that dealt with historical events and people. As a preteen, I checked out from our school and community libraries pretty much all of the Landmark series of histories written for adolescents (I was apparently about the only reader of some of them). I also was constantly on the lookout for articles that featured historical themes as I leafed through newspapers and magazines. By the time I was in high school, I had accumulated a personal library of several shelves of paperbacks on topics ranging from the genius of Hannibal to the grimness of Verdun.

I currently have an entire wall in my home devoted to my history hardcovers—but there I go, talking about myself as a reader.

Of course, my reader profile encompasses many other identities in addition to historian. For example, sometimes what, when, and why I read is sparked by my identity as a public school teacher. In addition, I have an identity as a literacy educator, which leads me to target the subset of texts written within the educational profession that emphasize reading and writing instruction. I have an identity as a voracious reader of fictional literature, with my tastes running from classical to contemporary works. Additional identities that intersect with my reading would include baseball fan, humorist, moviegoer, home improvement practitioner, traveler, adult male, family member, baby boomer, political liberal, and global citizen, to name a few.

Literacy theorist Gee (2000) describes identity as being "a certain 'kind of person'" (p. 99). Because we all display multiple identities, it can be helpful to elaborate a bit more on who we are. Gee subdivides identities into four categories:

1. Identities that are part of our *nature* and over which we have little control (e.g., I am white, European American, an adult male, and an oldest son)

2. Identities that are related to *positions* that we have attained and that may be confirmed by various groups or institutions (e.g., I am a college graduate, public school teacher, married person, U.S. citizen, and Wisconsin resident)

3. Identities that reflect personal *traits* or characteristics that others recognize in us and that define us as individuals (e.g., I have a good sense of humor, am handy with woodworking, and listen to classical music)

4. Identities that we share with others through our *associations* with them or through group memberships (e.g., I am a Milwaukee Brewers fan, Democrat, adolescent literacy advocate, and International Reading Association member)

My various identities very much influence my personal profile as a reader. Because of these identities, my reading profile includes the daily

New York Times, Yahoo! sports postings, Ward Just political novels, e-mails from family, *Newsweek* magazine, museum circulars, teacher union newsletters, the *Journal of Adolescent & Adult Literacy,* a myriad of other texts, and yes, histories like Francis Parkman's seven volumes. My reading is an extension of who I am, and my abilities as a reader allow me to extend who I am.

REFLECTION INTERLUDE

The term *reader* often presumes a connotation of book reader. Yet you can see that my reader profile encompasses a wide range of texts (that yes, do include books). Consider for a moment your profile as a reader, and the identities that most govern what, when, and why you read (see Figure 1.1).

Figure 1.1. What's Your Reader Profile?

Identity	So I read...

Our shared identities as teachers mark us as members of a community whose personal reader profiles often coincide. For example, we are all readers of the variety of texts encountered on the job in our schools, from e-mails to district directives. We all tend to read educationally relevant items in newspapers, magazines, and online. We all read materials that guide our professional growth, such as this book. We have examined standards documents, policy statements, and educational proposals, theories, and ideas. We read student work regularly in our role as classroom instructors. Our shared identity makes it likely that we have read, continue to read, and are interested in reading similar things.

Yet, obviously at many points, our identities diverge. Within the educational profession, some of you share an identity as mathematicians, scientists, language teachers, fitness experts, musicians, or technology specialists, as well as other identities. Your profiles as readers will look markedly different from mine and from each other's.

Fostering Academic Identities

Of course, not everything that I have read over the years has necessarily been a matter of choice. Like all of us, I have read many texts that I felt obligated to read. Sometimes, I felt personally obligated. For example, I recently felt obligated to carefully read the directions for assembling a table saw, obviously for pragmatic reasons. Sometimes, others have obligated me. Frequently, I am asked to read something to satisfy workplace expectations, such as material distributed at a faculty inservice meeting. Additionally, like our students, I have been obligated to read numerous nonchoice texts in my role as learner in school and college contexts.

REFLECTION INTERLUDE

Pause for a moment and revisit your personal reader profile. What are the arrays of written texts, from formal to informal, that you have read? Which of these would you call choice texts—things that you desired to read—and which would you consider obligation texts—things that you, or someone else, felt you needed to read. Next, reflect on your experiences reading obligation texts as you progressed through your years of education (see Figure 1.2).

Figure 1.2. Revisiting Your Reader Profile: Choice Texts Versus Obligation Texts

Choice Texts (I wanted to read...)	Obligation Texts—Personal (I felt obligated to read...)	Obligation Texts—Others (Someone else obligated me to read...)

It becomes increasingly clear that as readers, we do not read all texts with equal competence, need, interest, and enthusiasm. Obligation texts, in particular, can be problematic for us. What happens to us as readers when we are obligated to stray outside our identities to tackle texts that do not reflect our preferred ways of thinking and interacting with the world?

Student Identities

Coping with obligation texts is no different for our students than it has been for us. Consider the various identities that our students might bring to the classroom and how these identities could affect their personal reading profiles. First, like us, many of the students' identities do not necessarily seek out the kinds of reading that is expected in school and within academic disciplines. To use Gee's four identity categories, we will meet young people who have nature identities as teenagers, adolescent boys, African American females, Latina immigrants, students with learning disabilities, or English learners. Second, these young people occupy roles and positions in society that include identities as diverse as dependent children, high school sophomores, talented and gifted individuals, persons living in poverty, licensed drivers, restaurant employees, children of divorced parents, or adjudicated juveniles. Third, in terms of traits and characteristics, we will meet young people who see themselves, and are recognized by others, as the kinds of persons who text, listen to hip-hop, are shy, are athletic, are not good readers, are skilled at working with their hands, are vegetarians, aspire to be popular, are rebellious, and on and on and on. Finally, we will meet students who identify with others and display association identities as widespread as soccer teammates, Twilight readers, Spanish speakers, video game players, Comedy Central watchers, taggers, Lutherans, school band musicians, Facebook friends, gang members, and community volunteers.

During the past decade, researchers have been intrigued by the out-of-school literacies employed by young people (e.g., Alvermann, 2002; Alvermann, Hinchman, Moore, Phelps, & Waff, 2006). For example, students communicating through text messaging and online social networking, such as MySpace and Facebook, are displaying a host of literacy behaviors that may represent a significant segment of the students' personal reader profiles. Some researchers (e.g., Hagood, Alvermann, & Heron-Hruby, 2010) have suggested that educators need to explore ways to factor in the breadth and volume of reading and writing practices that are central to the reader profiles of many of our students, based on their out-of-school identities.

However, the emphasis in this book is on the honing of in-school, or academic, literacies. As literacy researcher Moje (2008) so cogently observes,

> Although literacy educators and researchers acknowledge the value and power of the knowledge, practices, and texts young people bring to school, it is also critical that we work to expand youth knowledge, practices, and texts as a function of education. Young people do not need to go to school to learn what they already know; content literacy instruction can help youth gain access to the accepted knowledge of the disciplines, thereby allowing them also to critique and change that knowledge. (p. 97)

Very likely, only a modest number of our students will have articulated association identities, such as future historian, future mathematician, or future scientist. A number of students will exhibit more vague inclinations as traits identities: the type of person who is good in math, likes science, is interested in history, enjoys reading fiction, or has a talent in art. Most students will articulate aspirations to more general and careerist position identities (e.g., "I am going to be a [doctor, business person, construction worker, computer technician, elementary school teacher, or police officer]"), tentative identities that may shift relatively frequently.

Identities and Literacy

Clearly, students' academic identities matter a great deal when we consider students' abilities and willingness to meet the literacy demands inherent in learning within content disciplines. As Moore and Onofrey (2007) conclude, "Students who enact claims as insiders to classroom reading and writing, who assert membership in particular classroom literacy communities, have an academic advantage" (p. 287). Some academic identities can empower students as learners: "I am the kind of student who likes to learn things." "I am the kind of student who gets my work done." "I am the kind of student who will be successful if I make the effort." "I am the kind of student who is a good reader." Other academic identities can undermine academic performance: "I am the kind of student who does not do homework." "I am the kind of student who does not get math." "I am the kind of student who probably will not understand even if I try." "I am the kind of student who avoids reading." "I am the kind of student who hates school."

As teachers, we can play a significant role in these dynamics of identity formation. Academic identities can be fluid rather than static, and the instructional context can make a dramatic difference for developing and shaping students' conceptions of themselves as readers and writers (McCarthey & Moje, 2002). Gee (2001) labels as discursive what I have referred to as traits identities because of the crucial role of language and dialogue in their development and maintenance: They are the things we tell ourselves about ourselves but are also the things others tell us about ourselves. Others can reinforce or challenge what we say about ourselves.

Our role as teachers and mentors is especially critical for developing students as readers, writers, and thinkers in the different academic disciplines studied in middle and high school classrooms. In *Choice Words: How Our Language Affects Children's Learning*, Johnston (2004) extensively examines the powerful relationships between what we as teachers tell students, the language we use, and the emerging academic identities of our students:

> Building an identity means coming to see in ourselves the characteristics of particular categories (and roles) of people and developing a sense of what it feels like to be that sort of person and belong in certain social spaces. As children are involved in classroom interactions, they build and try on different identities….Teachers' comments can offer them, and nudge them toward, productive identities. (p. 23)

Teachers may unintentionally reinforce problematic identities, such as "I am not any good at doing this," or "I am not a science person." Or, teachers can directly through their language encourage the creation of new identities: "As a person thinking like a scientist, what might you suggest?" "What did you notice as a reader when you read that passage?" Both of these statements explicitly position students as individuals who are perceived as scientist types and as readers. Ultimately, academic identities that empower learning begin to emerge: "I am able to do things I could not do before." "I can learn things by reading about them." "I am able to handle challenges in math."

Reading in Academic Disciplines

As teachers, each of us has academic identities that have evolved over our years of schooling and that have eventually centered on specific disciplinary preferences. Obviously, my interests in and experiences with reading history-themed material have led me to approach such texts with confidence and purpose. I certainly gravitate toward reading history as choice texts, but I have also been receptive, and frequently eager, to undertake the reading of history as obligation texts, even when such texts were difficult or not particularly motivating.

Over the years, I have internalized how to read history texts. When I read through a historian lens, I automatically shift my thinking in certain characteristic ways to examine what an author is saying. Questions occur to me that parallel what historians might want to know and care about: What does this author say happened and how did the author find out? Why does the author believe this happened? Why does the author think this matters? I track indicators of the author's personal beliefs, perspectives, and points of view as I weigh the author's explanations and conclusions. I focus on how this knowledge can inform my insights into who we are and how we have gotten to this point. Reading through a historian lens helps me prioritize what to look for and provides me with a mental template for cutting to the gist of a message and constructing the big picture of what an author is saying. Thinking this way as a reader comes naturally to me now. I just do it.

Personally, I also recognize that my historian lens has often been my default mode for many of the texts that I read. As a result, I might read, say, a newspaper article and come away with a take on what an author was saying that contrasts with what a colleague has understood. In our conversations, we discover that we read through different lenses; perhaps she read the article more like a scientist or focused on the literary qualities of the writing. Consequently, we may have asked ourselves different questions, noticed different aspects of the message, drew on different background knowledge, organized our thinking in different ways, and arrived at somewhat different conclusions. Yet we both read with comprehension.

I realize that there are times when reading through a scientific lens, a literary lens, a mathematical lens, or others is more appropriate for organizing my thinking and reaching understanding. As a learner, it became readily apparent to me that reading like a historian would not suffice when tackling an algebra textbook or studying chemistry chapters. Although mathematic or scientific modes of thinking may not be my preferred interaction with the world and with texts, I have over the years learned to adjust my thinking to match these needs as a reader more directly. I have developed the capacity to comprehend a range of texts that sometimes fall outside my immediate comfort zone. It may not always be my choice, but I can do it.

> **"**
> Readers engage in distinct thinking processes, colored by the human enterprises and habits of mind that shape academic disciplines.
> **"**
> —*Greenleaf, Cribb, Howlett, & Moore, 2010, p. 291*

Our students face these same challenges every time the bell rings during a typical school day. Like you, some students' academic identities may lean toward some disciplines, such as science or math, and away from others, such as history or literature. Yet, for many students, none of these academic identities predominate. Instead, students may enter our classrooms convinced that science is hard, social studies is boring, algebra is something they will never use, and the assigned novels are uninteresting and irrelevant to them. Some will have identities more geared to artistic, musical, hands-on, technological, athletic, or other directions. For some students, out-of-school identities will be more significant to them than their academic identities. As a result, the reading that students are asked to do in some classes will more closely approximate their strengths, interests, and personal outlooks than the reading they encounter in other courses. Yet, ultimately, our students are expected to develop as competent readers, writers, and thinkers in *all* academic disciplines.

A Model of Disciplinary Literacy

What, then, does it mean to be a reader in middle and high school content classrooms? Increasingly, researchers are referring to these more specialized applications of reading and writing as disciplinary literacy (Lee & Spratley, 2010; Moje, 2008; T. Shanahan & Shanahan, 2008). With instruction and guided practice, students gradually develop the capacity to read disciplinary-specific texts through an insider perspective (Buehl, 2009c). In other words, students need to be mentored to read, write, and think in ways that are characteristic of discrete academic disciplines.

Mentoring students as insiders means they gain the ability to talk the talk of an academic discipline; they can access communications in particular subject areas through reading and listening, and equally important, they develop the facility through writing and speaking to communicate in the ways that insiders such as historians, mathematicians, biologists, musicians, or accountants do. Students begin to develop personal disciplinary lenses for reading within different academic disciplines.

> **"**
> Each academic discipline or content-area presupposes specific kinds of background knowledge about how to read texts in that area, and often also requires a particular type of reading.
> **"**
> —*Lee & Spratley, 2010, p. 2*

Basic Literacy

Shanahan and Shanahan (2008) have offered a model that envisions literacy instruction as progressing in three phases (see Figure 1.3). During the initial phase of instruction, basic literacy, teachers of the primary grades work with beginning readers to build the foundation for reading and writing. Students learn to decode words, recognize high-frequency words from spoken language, understand conventions of print, and attend to meaning. Typically, when middle and high school teachers talk about reading instruction, they are visualizing this basic literacy phase, which happens, say, in a first-grade classroom. When teachers of adolescents are urged to integrate reading instruction into the teaching of content areas, the teachers often respond apprehensively that they were not trained to teach reading. Of course, most middle and high school teachers are obviously unprepared to deliver basic literacy instruction to students needing this foundational phase of development.

Intermediate Literacy

The middle phase of instruction, intermediate literacy, is emphasized as students move along from primary to upper elementary grades. This is a streamlining and multitasking phase of development, as students orchestrate their thinking routines to juggle several facets of reading at once. Students improve their reading fluency, expand their vocabularies, and encounter increasingly more sophisticated texts. Comprehension strategies become increasingly important, and students are exposed to a greater variety of text structures. Although teachers of adolescents

Figure 1.3. The Increasing Specialization of Literacy Development

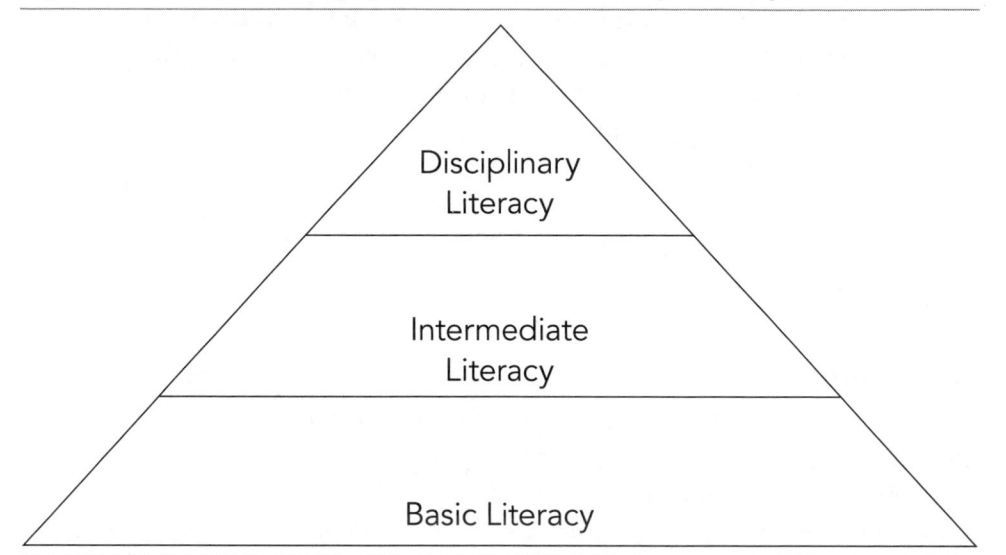

Disciplinary
Literacy

Intermediate
Literacy

Basic Literacy

Note. From "Teaching Disciplinary Literacy to Adolescents: Rethinking Content-Area Literacy," by T. Shanahan and C. Shanahan, 2008, *Harvard Educational Review, 78*(1), p. 44. Copyright 2008 by the President and Fellows of Harvard College.

generally encounter very few students still developing basic literacy, teachers do encounter struggling readers who are continuing to grow their capacities in this intermediate phase: students who are not automatic word decoders, read very slowly and perhaps word by word, read the words without difficulty but do not have satisfactory comprehension, or have limited vocabularies. Some of these students would benefit from literacy interventions taught by reading specialists that provide additional practice and instruction. Yet most of these struggling readers would be effectively served by classroom support, scaffolded lessons, and differentiated instruction. In a number of districts, literacy coaches assist disciplinary teachers in planning instruction that meets the needs of struggling readers still growing intermediate literacy.

Disciplinary Literacy

The third phase of literacy instruction, disciplinary literacy, predominates as students enter middle school and move on to high school. Students must navigate a curriculum that features arrays of texts from disparate and increasingly distinct academic disciplines. As learners, students are expected to fine-tune generic comprehension strategies to accommodate the demands of each of these different subject areas. As Heller and Greenleaf (2007) note,

> To become competent in a number of academic content areas requires more than just applying the same old skills and comprehension strategies to new kinds of texts. It also requires skills and knowledge and reasoning processes that are specific to particular disciplines. (p. 10)

Disciplinary literacy necessitates that we conceptualize reading and writing as contextually dependent practices; students are expected to become many different kinds of readers and writers (Gee, 2000). As a result, a student might be quite comfortable reading fictional works in a literature class, be less proficient reading biological texts, and feel helpless understanding the algebra textbook.

Figure 1.4 displays the complicated challenges facing adolescents as learners in different academic contexts. Unlike the foundational phase

Figure 1.4. The Contextualized Nature of Disciplinary Literacy

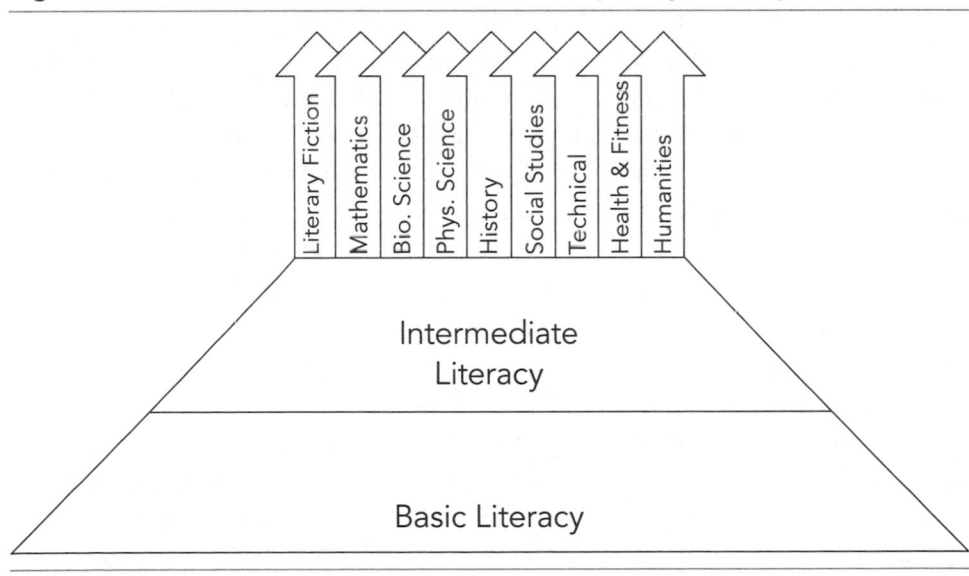

of basic literacy, and the continued general development during the intermediate literacy phase, disciplinary literacy is not one thing but many. Students are expected to gradually grow their capacities in each of the areas represented by the arrows in the figure. If, for example, students received rich literacy instruction in their English language arts classes, then we could expect them to become more competent readers of the materials emphasized in the English language arts curriculum, primarily literary fiction, such as novels and short stories, and to a lesser extent, some literary nonfiction, such as autobiography and essay. Yet what about their growth in the other towers of literacy represented in the figure? Because disciplinary literacy is contextualized, students will need similar rich literacy instruction within the disciplinary settings where other types of texts are emphasized: mathematics, biological science, physical science, history, other social studies (e.g., geography, civics, economics), technical texts, health and fitness, and humanities (e.g., art, music). In short, instruction that guides students in reading through a literary lens when interacting with authors of fiction will not prepare students to read an algebra chapter, an earth science passage, a segment of an auto mechanics manual, a recipe, a section of the U.S. Constitution, online software instructions, or information on using a heart rate monitor.

The reality is that for all of us, the figure's arrows in the disciplinary literacy phase would reveal an uneven, jagged profile, with some of the disciplinary arrows much higher than others (see Figure 1.5). All of us are more confident as readers in some disciplines and regard ourselves as less effective in others. The goal is not for all these disciplinary arrows to grow to equal heights. We know that our personal academic profiles lead us toward some disciplines and perhaps away from others. Instead, the goal is to mentor students so that they can access communications effectively in all disciplines, regardless of their personal preferences and interests. Otherwise, students' abilities to learn within a discipline become stalled, and students must rely on being told or shown what they need to know because they have not developed the capacity to independently access this knowledge as readers within the discipline.

I related earlier that I have a personal identity as a history-type person and that I am very comfortable reading texts within the discipline of history. I also have an identity as the kind of person who is a highly confident reader. Think about how these two identities intersect when

Figure 1.5. Example of a Disciplinary Literacy Profile

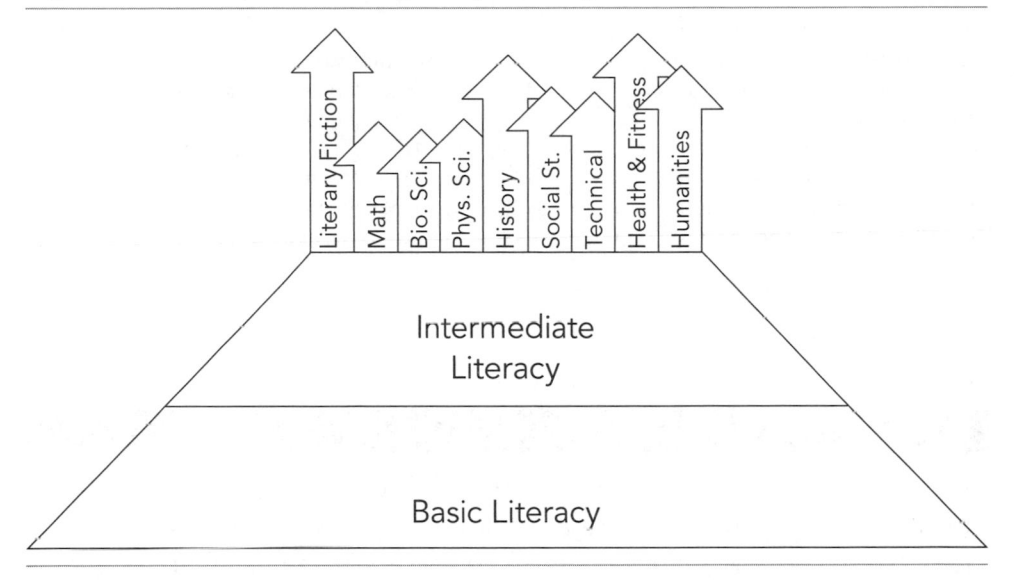

I am reading history texts and the likelihood that I would have a successful reading experience. I do not bring the same profile to my reading of science texts. Although I am still a highly confident reader, I am more of a science outsider and am less comfortable reading within the discipline of science. So, although I am receptive to learning about science, I may be less effective as a reader of science. Figure 1.6 displays the interplay between these two identities, with the arrow representing how they intersect for me personally. Where would you draw your arrow? Obviously, the most powerful scenario would be an arrow that extends straight across at the top, between "Is a highly confident reader" and "Is a science professional." The more your arrow dips downward one direction or the other, the more likely you will encounter struggles as a science reader. We could of course develop the same profile comparisons between reader identity and identity in any discipline (e.g., history, mathematics, literature, technical subjects). Where would many of our students draw their arrows, and what kinds of instruction would students need to support their success as readers in different disciplinary contexts?

Figure 1.6. Profile of a Science Reader

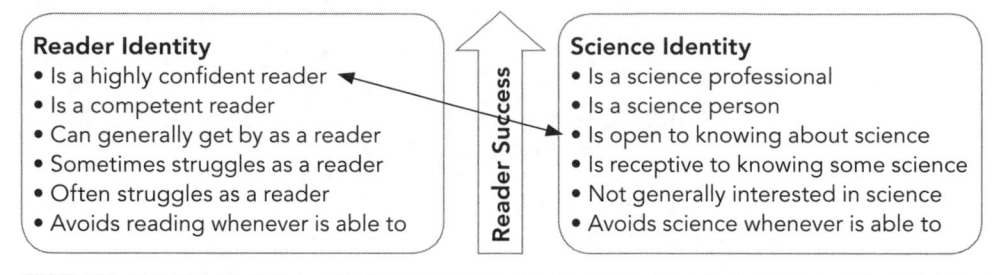

Reader Identity
- Is a highly confident reader
- Is a competent reader
- Can generally get by as a reader
- Sometimes struggles as a reader
- Often struggles as a reader
- Avoids reading whenever is able to

Reader Success

Science Identity
- Is a science professional
- Is a science person
- Is open to knowing about science
- Is receptive to knowing some science
- Not generally interested in science
- Avoids science whenever is able to

REFLECTION INTERLUDE

What is your disciplinary reader profile? Which disciplines are you most confident and accomplished in as a reader, and which are you least? Are there disciplines in which you do not feel that you are a particularly competent reader? Are there disciplines in which you would avoid reading if you could? Are there certain types of texts that you struggle with as a reader? Try your hand at creating your personal disciplinary literacy profile in Figure 1.7. Draw your "towers of literacy" that correspond to where you would place yourself as a reader in each of these disciplinary contexts.

Figure 1.7. What Is Your Profile as a Disciplinary Reader?

	Literary Fiction	Mathematics	Physical Science	Biological Science	History	Social Studies	Technical	Health & Fitness	Humanities
Highly Confident									
Generally Competent									
Can Get By									
Sometimes Struggles									
Often Struggles									
Avoids at All Costs									

The Need to Address Disciplinary Literacy

It is this third phase, disciplinary literacy, the goal of middle and high school literacy development, that is most neglected in our instruction. The RAND Corporation report on adolescent literacy (McCombs, Kirby, Barney, Darilek, & Magee, 2005) adopts deLeon's description of disciplinary literacy as an "orphaned responsibility" (p. iii); nobody takes care of it. As Shanahan and Shanahan (2008) conclude, "Although most students manage to master basic and even intermediate literacy skills, many never gain proficiency with the more advanced skills that would enable them to read challenging texts in science, history, literature, mathematics, or technology" (p. 45).

> **"**
> The need to guide adolescents to advanced stages of literacy is not necessarily the result of any teaching or learning failure in the preschool or primary years; rather, it is a necessary next step in normal reading development.
> **"**
>
> —McCombs et al., 2005, pp. 2–3

This concern about the lack of instruction at the disciplinary literacy level has been echoed again and again over the past decade by a series of influential research reports and policy documents. Historically, research investigations, policy initiatives, and public attention have targeted basic literacy instruction at the elementary school level. The prevailing attitude toward literacy development followed what some observers have termed an inoculation mentality: Provide excellent instruction to beginning readers, and they will be inoculated as readers, able to subsequently withstand increasingly more complex reading challenges without help or explicit teaching. The need to provide the necessary literacy instruction that supports students as readers and writers in academic disciplines was virtually ignored, as sporadic and short-lived efforts to teach reading in the content areas came and went. The decade since 2000 has witnessed an unprecedented shift in this attitude. As Frost, an advisor to the Clinton Administration's Department of Education, admits in the National School Boards Association (2006) policy statement on adolescent literacy, "We thought teaching every child to read well by the end of third grade would take care of the problem, but we were wrong" (p. 1).

A Shift Toward Disciplinary Literacy

Because disciplinary literacy has muddled along beneath the radar of public attention and policy concern, middle and high school teachers might be surprised to learn about the avalanche of recent action documents with unambiguous recommendations that have been released and are currently influencing education decision makers. The voices are an amazingly diverse assemblage, but the conclusions in policy document after document are in striking agreement: Middle and high school teachers need to integrate literacy practices into the instruction of their disciplines (see Table 1.1). What is most remarkable is that few of these organizations had previously regarded disciplinary literacy to be a significant policy concern.

Table 1.1. U.S. Policy Statements on Adolescent Literacy

Organization	Policy Statement
American College Testing Program	"Not enough high school teachers are teaching reading skills or strategies and many students are victims of teachers' low expectations. Another likely reason that high school students are losing momentum in readiness for college-level reading is that reading is simply not taught much, if at all, during the high school years, not even in English courses."[a]
Alliance for Excellent Education	"The idea is not that content-area teachers should become reading and writing teachers, but rather they should emphasize the reading and writing practices that are specific to their subjects, so students are encouraged to read and write like historians, scientists, mathematicians, and other subject-area experts."[b]
	"All content area teachers should know what is distinct about the reading, writing, and reasoning processes that go on in their discipline; they should give students frequent opportunities to read, write, and think in these ways; and they should explain how those conventions, formats, styles, and modes of communication differ from those that students might encounter elsewhere in school (Pearson, 1996)."[c]
Carnegie Corporation of New York	"Because of this need for ongoing literacy development, adolescent students need explicit instruction in reading and writing all the way through grade 12, as well as comprehensive forms of assessment and rigorously aligned standards detailing what they need to know and what they must be able to do both *within* and *across* content areas."[d]

(continued)

Table 1.1. U.S. Policy Statements on Adolescent Literacy (Continued)

Organization	Policy Statement
International Reading Association, in collaboration with National Council of Teachers of English, National Council of Teachers of Mathematics, National Science Teachers Association, and National Council for the Social Studies	"Middle and high school teachers need help to understand how they can develop content knowledge at the same time that they improve student literacy; that in fact, effective teaching in their subject areas will be boosted by complementary literacy instruction related to the texts (and the other communication demands) characteristic of their subjects."[e]
National Association of Secondary School Principals	"It becomes even more critical that secondary content area teachers better understand and teach specific literacy strategies to help students read and extract meaning from the written material used to teach the course content."[f]
National Association of State Boards of Education	"The importance of connecting reading and writing across the curriculum has never been more clear. Indeed, comprehension instruction that promotes strategic behaviors to encourage active and purposeful reading and writing (something which most struggling readers have trouble) should not only be taught explicitly, it should be incorporated into content area teaching, beginning in the early grades and continuing through high school."[g]
National Center for Education Evaluation and Regional Assistance	"Adolescent literacy is a complex concept because it entails more than the scores that students achieve on standardized reading tests. It also entails reading to learn in subjects that present their ideas and content in different ways. Students need to be able to build knowledge by comprehending different kinds of texts, mastering new vocabulary, and sharing ideas with others."[h]
National Council of Teachers of English	"In middle and high school, students encounter academic discourses and disciplinary concepts in such fields as science, mathematics, and the social sciences that require different reading approaches...(Kucer, 2005). These new forms, purposes, and processing demands require that teachers show, demonstrate, and make visible to students how literacy operates within the academic disciplines (Keene & Zimmermann, 1997; Tovani, 2000)."[i]

(continued)

Table 1.1. U.S. Policy Statements on Adolescent Literacy (Continued)

Organization	Policy Statement
National Governors Association Center for Best Practices	"Students need instruction beyond third grade to learn…how to employ reading strategies to comprehend complex texts about specialized subject matter. All students need such instruction, not just those who are struggling readers and writers."[j]
National School Boards Association	On students who meet state proficiency standards in literacy: "They can read simple texts such as newspapers or instruction manuals, but often can't understand specialized or academic materials. Researchers say these students desperately need help comprehending academic language and often benefit dramatically from having literacy instruction embedded in courses ranging from physical education to calculus."[k]
RAND Reading Study Group	"Research has shown that many children who read at the third-grade level in grade 3 will not automatically become proficient comprehenders in later grades. Therefore, teachers must teach comprehension explicitly, beginning in the primary grades and continuing through high school."[l]

[a]From *Reading Between the Lines: What the ACT Reveals About College Readiness in Reading* (p. 9), by ACT, 2006, Iowa City, IA: Author.
[b]From *Reading Next—a Vision for Action and Research in Middle and High School Literacy: A Report to Carnegie Corporation of New York* (p. 15), by G. Biancarosa and C.E. Snow, 2004, Washington, DC: Alliance for Excellent Education.
[c]From *Literacy Instruction in the Content Areas: Getting to the Core of Middle and High School Improvement* (p. 27), by R. Heller and C.L. Greenleaf, 2007, Washington, DC: Alliance for Excellent Education.
[d]From *Time to Act: An Agenda for Advancing Adolescent Literacy for College and Career Success* (p. 18), by Carnegie Council on Advancing Adolescent Literacy, 2010, New York: Carnegie Corporation of New York.
[e]From *Standards for Middle and High School Literacy Coaches* (p. 2), by International Reading Association (with National Council of Teachers of English, National Council of Teachers of Mathematics, National Science Teachers Association, and National Council for the Social Studies), 2006, Newark, DE: Author.
[f]From *Creating a Culture of Literacy: A Guide for Middle and High School Principals* (p. 1), by National Association of Secondary School Principals, 2005, Reston, VA: Author.
[g]From *Reading at Risk: The State Response to the Crisis in Adolescent Literacy* (Rev. ed., p. 5), by National Association of State Boards of Education, 2006, Arlington, VA: Author.
[h]From *Improving Adolescent Literacy: Effective Classroom and Intervention Practices: A Practice Guide* (NCEE 2008-4027, p. 6), by M.L. Kamil, G.D. Borman, J. Dole, C.C. Kral, T. Salinger, & J. Torgesen, 2008, Washington, DC: National Center for Education Evaluation and Regional Assistance, Institute of Education Sciences, U.S. Department of Education.
[i]From *A Call to Action: What We Know About Adolescent Literacy and Ways to Support Teachers in Meeting Students' Needs* (para. 3), by National Council of Teachers of English, 2004, Urbana, IL: Author.
[j]From *Reading to Achieve: A Governor's Guide to Adolescent Literacy* (p. 7), by National Governors Association Center for Best Practices, 2005, Washington, DC: Author.
[k]From *The Next Chapter: A School Board Guide to Improving Adolescent Literacy* (p. 1), by National School Boards Association, 2006, Alexandria, VA: Author.
[l]From *Reading for Understanding: Toward an R&D Program in Reading Comprehension* (p. xii), by C. Snow, 2002, Santa Monica, CA: RAND.

Middle and high school teachers tend to assume that if students have had adequate basic and intermediate literacy instruction, then they will automatically and on their own develop disciplinary literacy skills at that time when reading branches out into dramatically dissimilar texts during the learning of content subjects. Students are expected to comprehend texts dealing with complex concepts—and that are more abstract, ambiguous, and subtle—by applying sophisticated literacy skills that "are rarely taught" (T. Shanahan & Shanahan, 2008, p. 45). In its 2009 policy statement on adolescent literacy, the Southern Regional Education Board summarized these concerns:

> Few teachers have been asked to teach the reading skills that students need in each subject. They consider themselves responsible for teaching their subjects only—not for teaching students reading skills. Some teachers in various subjects have resisted efforts to incorporate reading instruction into their courses for fear that they are being asked to become "reading teachers." But asking a teacher to become a *reading teacher* is distinctly different from asking a teacher to *help students master texts within the teacher's own field.*
>
> In fact, subject-area teachers are best qualified to help their students master texts in each course. Subject-area teachers should not be expected to teach basic reading skills, but they can help students develop critical strategies and skills for reading texts in each subject. (p. 5)

The current Common Core State Standards Initiative reflects this significant shift in policy attention toward disciplinary literacy. A collaboration of the National Governors Association Center for Best Practices (NGACBP) and the Council of Chief State School Officers (CCSSO; 2010c), the Common Core State Standards for English Language Arts and Literacy were released in 2010 and adopted by the vast majority of states as their new state standards. For the first time, literacy expectations for teachers extend beyond solely English language arts. Emphasizing that the literacy development of students is a shared responsibility, the standards state,

> Just as students must learn to read, write, speak, listen, and use language effectively in a variety of content areas, so too must the Standards specify the literacy skills and understandings required for college and career readiness in multiple disciplines. Literacy standards for grade 6 and above are predicated on teachers of ELA, history/social studies, science, and technical subjects using their content area expertise to help students meet the

particular challenges of reading, writing, speaking, listening, and language in their respective fields. (para. 5)

For the first time, 10 reading standards for instruction by social studies teachers are explicitly articulated in the Common Core State Standards for Literacy in History/Social Studies for grades 6–12. Teachers of science, mathematics, and other subjects also are provided with 10 reading standards in the Common Core State Standards for Literacy in Science and Technical Subjects for grades 6–12. In addition, the Common Core State Standards include 10 writing standards for instruction by teachers of history/social studies, science, and technical subjects for grades 6–12. (The Common Core State Standards are available at www.corestandards.org/the-standards.)

Literacy Performance of Adolescents

There is a wealth of dispiriting assessment data that reveals that adolescents are not continuing to grow their capacities as readers and writers as they move through the middle and high school curricula. The National Assessment of Educational Progress (NAEP) has tracked reading progress since 1971, and while performance by fourth graders has achieved steady and impressive gains during this time period, eighth graders have shown only slight gains, and 12th graders' scores have declined 4 points since 1992. The 2009 NAEP data (National Center for Education Statistics, 2010a, 2010b) are illustrative: About three quarters of all eighth graders were able to handle general comprehension tasks, such as locating information, identifying main ideas, making some inferences, and interpreting word meanings. However, only one third were able to perform at a proficient level involving more sophisticated disciplinary comprehension expectations, and only 3% scored advanced. The 2009 NAEP results for 12th graders showed only 5% scoring at advanced levels, able to read specialized and complex texts. International studies, which compare students in the United States with their international counterparts, confirm this alarming trend. Fourth-grade U.S. students performed among the best in the world, but eighth graders scored considerably lower, and 10th graders ranked among the lowest of the nations studied. As the Carnegie Council on Advancing Adolescent Literacy (2010) concludes,

During the last twenty years our nation's educational system has scored some extraordinary successes, especially in improving the reading and writing skills of young children. Yet the pace of literacy improvement has not kept up with the pace of growth in the global economy, and literacy gains have not been extended to adolescents in the secondary grades. (p. 1)

In an extensive and much-cited study, the American College Testing Program (2006a) reveals similarly disturbing results. It concludes that the longer students were in school, the more they lost ground developing disciplinary literacy:

> Only 51 percent of 2005 ACT-tested high school graduates are ready for college-level reading—and, what's worse, more students are on track to being ready for college-level reading in eighth and tenth grade than are actually ready by the time they reach twelfth grade. (p. 1)

Particularly significant about the American College Testing Program analysis is the pinpointing of reading problems experienced by students beyond the basic and intermediate literacy levels and who have educational ambitions beyond high school. The report's lead recommendation is bluntly stated: "All courses in high school, not just English and social studies but mathematics and science as well, must challenge students to read and understand complex texts" (p. 23).

College Readiness

Finally, disciplinary literacy concerns are underscored by data on college readiness and success (Clark, 2009). Almost half of the 3 million people in the United States who start their first year of college will drop out before they earn their degree, and 30% will drop out after their first year. The problem is even more evident at the community college level, where out of 6 million students, 1 million will take remedial courses. Furthermore, college students who take remedial courses are highly likely to drop out. The College Board issued similarly disappointing findings in *The College Completion Agenda: 2010 Progress Report* (Lee & Rawls, 2010). The report notes that only 56% of students in the United States who enter institutions with the intention of earning a bachelor's degree persist to graduate in six years or less, and only 59% of those students entering a two-year college make it into their second year. Inadequate preparation is repeatedly cited as a central factor in the disappointing college success rates at two-year and four-year institutions.

The convergence of multiple, well-researched policy documents regarding adolescents and disciplinary literacy has dramatically shifted the landscape for middle and high school teachers. National, state, and local district conversations at these levels are transitioning from "what should teachers in the elementary grades be doing" to "what should *we* be doing." Although it may feel somewhat unsettling that so many varied constituencies are now "talking about us," it is also an opportunity to intensively explore effective practices for supporting and developing students as readers, writers, thinkers, and learners within our disciplines.

Apprenticing Readers, Writers, and Thinkers in Disciplinary Literacy

At this point, it would be useful to deconstruct the term *mentor* and examine how it can apply to instruction in disciplinary literacy. What images come to mind when you think of mentoring someone: an adult who is recruited to be a role model for youngsters in the community, an experienced hand who is assigned to be a mentor to a new employee, or an individual who is credited by a celebrity for providing help and encouragement on the way to the top? Who have been the significant mentors in your life?

For me, one person in particular stands out. Robert Hanson was the sawmill operator at a woodshop where I was employed for several summers during my college years. Although a sawmill was (at least for me) a fascinating place to spend my hours, my role as a tail sawer was quite unromantic. I was the person who guided the freshly sawed planks off the blade and onto the rollers and then lugged them to be stacked. I was the summer help who could be easily replaced. Robert was the craftsman.

As I worked alongside Robert, I observed him plying his trade. I learned how a master sawyer goes about his business: how to wield a cant hook, how to set the dogs into a log on the carriage, and how to feed boards into the edger. I could watch Robert's actions, of course, but I would have had to infer what he might be thinking as he made his decisions. Luckily for me, Robert was a garrulous man, determined to share the fine art of sawing logs with anyone who cared to listen. He talked as he worked, but mainly he explained his thinking: how to figure a series of cuts in advance to avoid waste, how to position a log for the most efficient first cut, and so forth. He would solve problems out loud and include me in the conversation. He would solicit my ideas and then provide feedback: why he would or would not act on my suggestions, what he would do instead, and why.

So, not only was I able to observe what a sawyer did, but I was also able to track the kind of thinking necessary to do this trade well. I realized that Robert had every cut figured even before a log hit the blade, had factored in exactly how much would be lost to sawdust each time the blade passed through a log, and had tallied in advance how many boards each log would yield. It may have seemed like magic to an onlooker, but Robert was a thinking man, and I was privileged to be treated like his apprentice.

After a couple summers, Robert would occasionally allow me to manipulate the controls and saw a log myself. It could be dangerous work, but he stood close by, offering supportive commentary and encouragement. Always, I would have to explain what I was planning and why. Also, when I had finished, we would always debrief. Maybe I would admit that my cuts resulted in too much waste that would be lost to the slab pile. Why, he would ask, did that happen? What had I misfigured or miscalculated? What should I have done differently?

Gradually, Robert ceded more opportunities to me to do some of the sawing. I might be allocated the last batch of logs of the day as my share, with Robert receding increasingly into the background. However, the conversation never ceased. We constantly conferred and always evaluated. Could I have gotten more out of that log? How might I have sawed it better?

The last summer I worked at the mill, I returned home from college to discover a new sawyer; Robert had moved on. The new man was injured in a mill mishap my first week on the job, leaving me as the only individual with any experience around a sawmill. The owner delegated me as the sawyer for that summer, a role I undertook with much trepidation. Yet, I soon discovered that the mentoring I had received over the years had positioned me, even though I had not realized it, as an individual capable of doing this work independently. So, I performed that summer as the sawyer, with Robert no longer nearby as my support and security blanket.

I have related this experience in some detail because the stages I went through as a learner were each significant and are often missing from our classroom instruction. Consider similar experiences that you have had in learning in the home, on the job, and while mastering a skill. Much of the most important learning that we have achieved in life—whether it is baking pastries, fishing for walleyes, driving a vehicle, learning to play a musical instrument, or throwing a pot on the wheel—has been in the role of apprentice to a master craftsman, an expert, an accomplished veteran. We learned by witnessing the expert engaged in an activity, we were invited to try our hand at doing it, and as we collaborated and received feedback on our performance, we gradually moved from novice status to independence. Notice how critical identity is to this process of growth. I could have easily assumed the identity of temporary employee. Instead, I was lifted to a different identity: apprentice sawyer. Each day, I was treated as the kind of person who is capable of doing this work alone. I am proud to say that in addition to all those identities I listed earlier in the chapter, I can add this one: sawyer.

Gradual Release of Responsibility

I realize now that during those summer days, under Robert's guidance and tutelage, I was being mentored in accordance with the classic model of learning theory attributed to the great Russian psychologist Vygotsky and articulated as the Gradual Release of Responsibility model by Pearson and Gallagher (1983). As you examine Figure 1.8, notice that the model envisions three phases of development, from a high-profile teaching phase, through an extended period of supported practice, to eventual independence with the student in charge. This model outlines an apprenticeship dynamic to literacy instruction (Schoenbach, Greenleaf, Cziko, & Hurwitz, 1999).

Modeling. The teacher-regulated phase assumes that many students do not know what doing a specific task well looks like, and they need explicit instruction to guide their thinking. For the purposes of this book, we are talking about what it means to read, write, and think through a disciplinary lens. This phase of mentoring means that students are provided with modeling and access to how experts think in order to build their own mental models of disciplinary thinking. When a history teacher engages in a think-aloud that talks through how historians interact with an author as they read, say, a primary document, the teacher is letting

Figure 1.8. Gradual Release of Responsibility Model

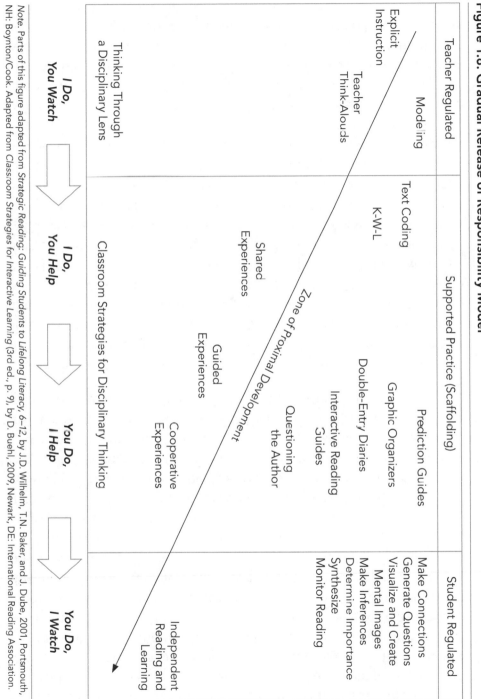

Teacher Regulated		Supported Practice (Scaffolding)			Student Regulated
Explicit Instruction	Modeling	Text Coding	Prediction Guides		Make Connections
		K-W-L	Graphic Organizers		Generate Questions
	Teacher Think-Alouds				Visualize and Create Mental Images
			Double-Entry Diaries		Make Inferences
			Interactive Reading Guides		Determine Importance
				Questioning the Author	Synthesize
					Monitor Reading
		Shared Experiences		Guided Experiences	Cooperative Experiences
Thinking Through a Disciplinary Lens		Classroom Strategies for Disciplinary Thinking			Independent Reading and Learning

I Do, You Watch ⇒ I Do, You Help ⇒ You Do, I Help ⇒ You Do, I Watch

Zone of Proximal Development

Note. Parts of this figure adapted from *Strategic Reading: Guiding Students to Lifelong Literacy, 6–12*, by J.D. Wilhelm, T.N. Baker, and J. Dube, 2001, Portsmouth, NH: Boynton/Cook. Adapted from *Classroom Strategies for Interactive Learning* (3rd ed., p. 9), by D. Buehl, 2009, Newark, DE: International Reading Association.

the students in on the secret, so to speak, of reading through a historian lens. When a mathematics teacher thinks out loud about how to carefully deconstruct sentences on a page of a geometry textbook, the teacher is demonstrating reading through a mathematics lens. When an English teacher publicly grapples with understanding a poem, the teacher is modeling reading through a literary lens. The most profound facet of this model is that students have access to something they cannot readily observe: thinking.

Teachers, of course, recognize this phase and will likely comment, "We already do this." Of course, we will find elements of such explicit instruction in many forms in classrooms, but we will rarely find it connected to mentoring students as readers and writers in disciplinary contexts. Students are given reading and writing assignments not reading and writing instruction. Again, the prevailing assumption tends to be that instruction from previous years is sufficient for students who must adjust to new disciplinary reading, writing, and thinking demands.

Scaffolding. The supported practice phase engages students in test-driving this thinking as they confront tasks of a discipline. This phase assumes that many students will not be particularly good at the task and that they will need extended practice, lots of support, and feedback from the expert and, most important, collaborators. Most of us prefer to have the assistance of others when we are doing something that we do not yet do well, especially when we might fumble around at times, fail perhaps regularly, and experience frustration and confusion. During this supported phase of learning, students need to be frequently granted what television quiz shows sometimes call a lifeline, someone students can work with as they try to resolve a challenging situation. Again, teachers will recognize this practice phase and note that "this is what homework is for." However, homework is predicated on independent behavior; when students are asked to independently do a task when they are not yet accomplished, they will likely fail. Of course, some students do have lifelines at home: parents, siblings, or friends who can help with homework that the students have not yet developed the ability to accomplish independently. Yet many of our students do not have access to such homework lifelines in their out-of-school lives.

This middle phase is where literacy strategies come into play. Researchers refer to these strategies as scaffolding: temporary instructional supports that guide students in their thinking as they strive to build their competency. The research is emphatic on this point: Students are not provided with adequate instructional scaffolds when they read disciplinary texts. When such texts are assigned, students are usually on their own and usually expected to read on their own outside of school and without support and feedback. Students are rarely engaged with collaborators as readers and writers, teamed to solve problems together to make sense of challenging disciplinary texts. Although we frequently conceptualize reading as a solitary act, researchers are increasingly examining the critical role that dialogue between students and also with the teacher plays in reading comprehension (Wilkinson & Son, 2011). Hence, an essential facet of scaffolding is fostering productive classroom student collaborations (Frey, Fisher, & Everlove, 2009). Vygotsky (1978) terms the scaffolding phase of learning as the zone of proximal development. Teaching in the zone is often the missing link in mentoring students as readers, writers, and thinkers through various disciplinary lenses in middle and high school classrooms.

Independent Reading and Learning. The third student-regulated phase, independence, is the condition that many middle and high school teachers expect: students who will arrive already able to read disciplinary texts independently. This phase involves readers confidently applying the fundamental processes of comprehension, which is discussed more thoroughly in Chapter 2. Many of our students, even those who have achieved basic and intermediate literacy, do not develop independence in reading disciplinary texts, not because these students are incapable but because they never received the appropriate instruction from appropriate mentors—disciplinary experts, the teachers who are accomplished readers, writers, and thinkers through their chosen disciplinary lenses.

PARTING THOUGHTS AND TALKING POINTS

- Disciplinary literacy refocuses attention at the middle and high school levels from "how well do you read?" to "what are you able to read well?"

- Teachers need to invite their students to expand the identities they bring to the classroom to include academic and specific disciplinary identities.
- Mentoring students as readers, writers, and thinkers is an integral and essential component of instruction within a discipline, enabling students to become increasingly more independent in accessing the communications of different academic disciplines.
- Disciplinary literacy instruction, embedded into the daily flow of the teaching of an academic subject, develops students' capacities to adjust their reading and writing so that they can engage an expanding array of different disciplinary lenses for thinking and comprehending.
- Disciplinary literacy is perhaps in many respects a reconceptualization of what it means to teach an academic subject. Disciplines are organized ways of thinking about the world, and learning within a discipline involves more than becoming merely knowledgeable. Learning must also encompass how scientists, mathematicians, historians, and others read, write, and think. This is the difference between covering a subject and teaching a discipline.

CHAPTER 2

Teaching Comprehension With Complex Texts

Essential Question: What does it mean to read, write, and think through a disciplinary lens?

"Let me get a read on it." How often has this phrase slipped into your conversation or thinking? Consider for a moment all the different situations in which you might try to get a read: how well your spouse appreciated a birthday gift; what exactly your principal or superintendent is up to; whether spring is finally here, and it is safe to plant your garden; whether you can squeeze another year out of driving your car before trading it in; which route would be the best option to avoid heavy traffic; how fit your body is for a 10-mile hike in the state park; how entertaining a particular movie will be; or which high-definition television best suits your needs and budget. Arguably, we are getting reads on something almost constantly. Reading is a very common human enterprise.

Later in the year, I ask my students at Madison East High School what the first thing was that they read when they entered my classroom back on that opening day of the semester. Some offer that it was the course syllabus, stacked on the table by the door waiting to greet them. Others are sure that it was the day's outline of activities, scrawled in my somewhat passable handwriting on the board. A few suggest some of the environmental print displayed about the room on the walls: posters, signs, and bulletin board items. A couple speculate that it was the covers of class texts, piled in front on my desk. No one ever mentions a first read that did not have something to do with the written word.

After the students have their say, I argue that the first read I saw most of them make was the class itself. As they walked into the room, they quickly did a read of the physical environment, sizing up how pleasant a setting this would be to spend time within and also getting a read on where they would be comfortable sitting. Almost simultaneously, they were doing a read on their classmates: Who else is taking this course? Who do I know in here? Who will be annoying? Who will be fun? What will it be like learning amid these fellow students? Of course, they also immediately got right down to the business of reading me, their teacher: What is this person like? How enjoyable will he be to work with? How demanding will he be? Does he seem to know what he is doing? Does he seem to have a sense of humor? How will I get along with him? Undoubtedly, that first day they were reading the course, too: Will I be successful in this class? How challenging will class expectations be? What will the daily workload be? How useful will this class be for me?

My point is not to trick my students or play semantic games. Instead, I want to emphasize what it truly means to read. Typically, we associate reading with the process of interacting with written language, deciphering the words on a page, and that mental translation we do to transform symbolic representations into a message from another person. Yet, in its larger usage, reading is what we do to make sense, to understand. We examine relevant information, think about what it might mean, decide on our understanding, and act accordingly. Ultimately, the goal of any act of reading is comprehension.

Comprehension Processes of Proficient Readers

However, it can become easy for students, and sometimes for their teachers, to lose sight of comprehension as the central purpose of reading. As students become immersed in the daily pipeline of school expectations, they may come to regard academic reading as merely completing assignments, looking over textbooks and other materials to fill out worksheets and answer questions, finding information to write down and study for tests. Unfortunately, the routines associated with middle and high school reading may replace the intention of reading in academic disciplines: comprehension of new concepts and ideas. As a result, many students *do* reading to get work done rather than *engage* in reading to understand.

Pseudoreading

Students who do reading frequently resort to behaviors that might be described as pseudoreading rather than reading for comprehension.

Teachers can readily spot students merely doing reading in the following classroom instances that are all too familiar (Buehl, 2009a).

Skimming for Answers. Students do not actually read the material at all but embark on a very superficial skim, searching for information that might qualify as acceptable answers to assigned questions. Although this is an efficient way to get work completed, skimming for answers has little to do with comprehension, and students frequently hand in written work that seems appropriate. However, in fact, they have not necessarily understood, or certainly learned, the content. Students who skim for answers frequently observe, "I don't have trouble with homework. I just have trouble with tests."

Surface Processing. Students read the material, or at least their eyes are indeed fixing on the words on the page. Yet they are not really thinking about what an author is saying. They may read an entire section and have little idea what it was about when they have finished. They were instructed to read it, so they dutifully did but not with a focus on comprehension. Their minds may have been drifting off to other topics while their eyes moved along, and sometimes they cannot recollect even seeing a paragraph they have just read. Students who do surface processing rely on their teachers to tell them what they need to know, commenting that "I read it, but I didn't understand it."

Reading and Forgetting. Students read, but they read to get done. They may regard the material as boring or difficult, but because they are not invested with truly understanding what an author is saying, they gain little from their reading. They do not engage with the kind of inner conversation with an author that involves a deeper processing of the material. They know that teacher presentations, classroom discussions, and other activities will fill in the gaps, so students accept a hazy and hurried trip through a text. They typically admit, "I read it, but I don't remember it."

Contrast these school-reading behaviors with the kind of thinking you do when you are immersed in reading comprehension. Suppose you chanced upon an article describing the 2010 volcano in Iceland that disrupted European air travel for a period of time. The photograph of the giant, billowing plumes of gray ash captures your curiosity, and you begin reading. Almost immediately, you may be reminded of events like the Mount St. Helens explosion in the Western United States and make mental comparisons of what you remember with details provided by the author. You wonder about the extent of the damage caused by the eruption and its impact on people, animals, and the terrain. The author addresses some of your questions while new ones surface, like why is there fluorine in the volcanic gases, and how deadly are these vapors. You find yourself imagining what local people were experiencing, with thick layers of black ash blanketing their countryside, their homes, their vehicles, and all the surrounding vegetation. You form a vivid mental picture of the glowing, red lava oozing from the volcanic fissures. Some segments you glance over quickly as of lesser importance to you, and you do not dwell on unfamiliar language, like the volcano's name, Eyjafjallajokull. Other portions you read more intently, especially details that relate to the extensive damage to bridges, roads, and local livestock, which relates to effects about which you were inquisitive. Author references to the melting of glacial ice, and information you can recall about Iceland in general, aid you in speculating about the climate in this area. Although the author does not mention it, you have a hunch that this landscape will be significantly altered for years to come. When you have completed the article, you ponder a few moments about what you have gained from your reading, and perhaps you carry on your thoughts later in the day in conversations with others.

What I have just described may seem like a commonplace reading experience for you, but such a thoughtful engagement while reading academic texts is not necessarily the norm in our classrooms. Instead, teachers witness the pseudoreading behaviors described earlier. Comprehension does not result from pseudoreading, and students do not develop the capacity to learn from disciplinary texts.

Seven Fundamental Comprehension Processes

Over 30 years of intensive research on reading comprehension has resulted in the identification of the characteristic modes of thinking that when bundled together during engagement with a text, result in comprehension. Literacy authorities such as Keene and Zimmermann (2007) have distilled from this research seven fundamental comprehension processes (see Table 2.1):

Table 2.1. Comprehension Processes Characteristic of Proficient Readers

Make Connections to Prior Knowledge	Reading comprehension results when readers can match what they already know (their schema) with new information and ideas in a text. Proficient readers activate prior knowledge before, during, and after reading, and they constantly evaluate how a text enhances or alters their previous understandings.
Generate Questions	Comprehension is, to a significant degree, a process of inquiry. Proficient readers pose questions to themselves as they read. Asking questions is the art of carrying on an inner conversation with an author, as well as an internal dialogue within one's self.
Visualize and Create Sensory Mental Images	Comprehension involves breathing life experiences into the abstract language of written texts. Proficient readers use visual, auditory, and other sensory connections to create mental images of an author's message.
Make Inferences	Much of what is to be understood in a text must be inferred. Authors rely on readers to contribute to a text's meaning by linking their background knowledge to information in the text. In addition to acknowledging explicitly stated messages, proficient readers read between the lines to discern implicit meanings, make predictions, and read with a critical eye.
Determine Importance	Our memories quickly overload unless we can pare down a text to its essential ideas. Texts contain key ideas and concepts amid much background detail. Proficient readers strive to differentiate key ideas, themes, and information from details so that they are not overwhelmed by facts.
Synthesize	Proficient readers glean the essence of a text (determine importance) and organize these ideas into coherent summaries of meaning. Effective comprehension leads to new learning and the development of new schema (background knowledge). Proficient readers make evaluations, construct generalizations, and draw conclusions from a text.
Monitor Reading and Apply Fix-Up Strategies	Proficient readers watch themselves as they read and expect to make adjustments in their strategies to ensure that they are able to achieve a satisfactory understanding of a text.

Note. From Buehl, D. (2007). A professional development framework for embedding comprehension instruction into content classrooms. In J. Lewis & G. Moorman (Eds.), *Adolescent literacy instruction: Policies and promising practices* (p. 200). Newark, DE: International Reading Association.

You will notice that each of these modes of thinking was employed during our Iceland volcano example. When our comprehension falters, it is likely that one or more of these modes of thinking are not clicking for us.

REFLECTION INTERLUDE

Pause for a moment to consider a text that you have recently read and analyze your thinking. How did each of these seven modes of thinking surface as facets of your comprehension? As you deconstruct your reading, try to identify an instance when you engaged in each comprehension process described in Table 2.1 (see Figure 2.1).

Figure 2.1. Analyzing Your Thinking While Reading

I noticed myself...	When I...
Making connections to prior knowledge	
Generating questions	
Visualizing and creating sensory mental images	
Making inferences	
Determining importance	
Synthesizing	
Monitoring reading	

The challenge for middle and high school teachers is to plan instruction that elicits and supports these seven fundamental comprehension processes. It may be tempting for teachers to adopt a rather fatalistic attitude toward reading comprehension: There isn't much we can do about it; it is inevitable that some of our students are going to get it and some are not. After all, teachers ask, we cannot really *teach* students how to comprehend, can we? To the contrary, research has provided teachers with an unequivocally affirmative answer: Yes, we can indeed teach comprehension. In the *Handbook of Research on Reading Comprehension*, renowned researcher Pearson (2009) summarizes two consistent findings from the deep vein of research on comprehension strategy instruction, noting that "when students are taught to apply strategies to text, their comprehension of those texts improves" (p. 21), and their ability to transfer those strategies to their comprehension of new texts can also improve. In other words, comprehension instruction leads to improved learning from current texts and builds the capacity to learn independently from future texts.

Current practices in content classrooms tend to focus on assigning reading and assessing performance but not teaching comprehension. A frequently heard complaint from teachers is "Shouldn't we be able to expect students to be effective readers of our materials by the time they enter middle and high school?" Chapter 1 outlined a different expectation for middle and high school students: the need for disciplinary literacy instruction as they advance into reading more complex and varied texts. A key component of this instruction involves the embedding of comprehension development into the daily classroom routines of learning content and reading disciplinary texts. As Wilkinson and Son (2011) observe in their analysis of comprehension instruction in Volume 4 of the *Handbook of Reading Research*, "strategies provide the tools to help students make sense of the content, and the content gives meaning and purpose to the strategies" (p. 367).

The Nature of Complex Texts

I use the term *text* frequently in this book, and it is probably time to pause and elaborate on exactly what qualifies as a text. I opened this chapter with a discussion about reading in a very general sense: the examination of some sort of relevant input to arrive at a desired comprehension.

Anything that we read might be considered a text in this general sense, such as a human face, a gesture, a landscape, an athletic formation, an interaction, a telephone conversation, a painting, a movie, a musical composition, and of course, written language.

In addition, texts that use written language could be relatively informal (e.g., a text message, a note, an e-mail, a list, a personal letter, a blog comment, a Facebook posting, a wall of graffiti) or more formal (e.g., a novel, a textbook, a scholarly article, a newspaper analysis, a magazine story, a poem, a proposal, a set of instructions, an advertisement, a legal document, a recipe, a website page, a set of song lyrics). Certainly, in our classrooms, students interact with a broad range of sources of information, including visual media, hands-on experiences, class presentations, lectures, online resources, software applications, and field trips. For the purposes of this book, *text* will be used in the narrower sense, to refer to written language that can be used in academic settings. Of course, *text* should not be merely construed as *textbook*. Obviously, students interact with many formats and genres of written language, both conventional print and hypertexts, as they learn within an academic discipline. Furthermore, written language may exist in texts that include multiple modalities of information that contribute to the communication of a message, especially with hypertexts.

In our discussion of disciplinary literacy in Chapter 1, we noted that as students advance through their years of schooling, they encounter increasingly more complex texts. The Common Core State Standards (NGACBP & CCSSO, 2010c) are predicated on students systematically gaining the capacity to independently and proficiently comprehend complex texts that are typical of college and careers. Just what is meant by a complex text? The American College Testing Program (2006a) outlines the following six characteristics of disciplinary texts that increase complexity for readers. As you examine each element of text complexity, consider how texts in your discipline exhibit these features.

> **The challenge of teaching reading comprehension is heightened in the current educational era because all students are expected to read more text and more complex texts.**
>
> —Snow, 2002, p. 15

What constitutes a written text in your discipline? What types of written text does a literate person need to have the capacity to read in your academic discipline? What are the various texts that students are expected to read, or could be reading, to access knowledge and understanding in your subject? (See Figure 2.2.) Extend your thinking to beyond the textbook.

Figure 2.2. What Constitutes a Written Text in Your Discipline?

Texts That Insiders in My Discipline Read	Texts That Students Could Read for Learning in My Discipline

Text Relationships

The relationships between ideas in informational texts or between characters in literary fiction become less basic and straightforward. Readers increasingly have to identify relationships that are implicit, sometimes subtle, more involved, and deeply embedded in the message rather than overtly presented. Consequently, complex texts place a greater load on the readers' abilities to make inferences and construct a meaning that is not always directly stated. In addition, complex texts may present multiple themes, multiple perspectives, or perspectives that are significantly unlike or even in opposition to those held by many readers.

Richness of Detail

As texts gain in complexity, more depth of background detail and conceptual information is provided. Readers have to navigate considerable and sometimes highly sophisticated material to construct an understanding. In addition, complex texts increasingly display information in multiple visual forms and graphic representations, requiring readers to move back and forth from prose language to sometimes elaborate visual displays, which must be examined and then synthesized into an overall understanding. In other words, such texts should perhaps be stamped, "Some assembly required for comprehension!"

Complex texts also exhibit higher intertextuality: Readers are expected to meaningfully connect to references and allusions to other texts or knowledge. Complex texts are likely to be more lengthy and demand more reader decisions on what are essential ideas and what are supportive details.

Text Structure

The way that ideas and information are organized becomes more elaborate and perhaps less conventional. Awareness of text structure and the ability to track how authors develop explanations, arguments, and ideas becomes a central facet of comprehension of complex texts.

Students must transition from texts that explicitly signal text structure to texts requiring a reader to recognize without being directly informed, for example, that a cause–effect organizational pattern is being followed. More than a single logical relationship between ideas might be present (e.g., an author might use argumentation, comparison, and causal developments all in the same section). Literary texts may adopt less straightforward methods of storytelling, such as unreliable narrators, and narration of events out of chronological order.

Writing Style

Complex texts feature more intricate writing styles. Certainly, such texts will offer fewer simple sentences and employ more lengthy and elaborate sentence structures, with subordinate clauses and extensive punctuation. Readers also need to track key connective language, like *but, however, therefore, such as,* and *consequently,* as they attempt to parse sentences that have a number of turns and signposts embedded in the language.

In addition, readers need to be sensitive to the author's tone as well as explicit statements and notice how the author's use of language and word choice influences an understanding of a particular text. For example, language might be figurative or ironic in tone, requiring readers to pick up undercurrents of meaning that are not literal. Also, writing styles may not mirror contemporary or familiar conventions.

Vocabulary Density

Clearly, a major facet of text complexity is the increase in challenging vocabulary. Complex texts strive for more precision and clarity in use of language, and as a result, they rely less on general conversational talk and more on academic discourse. Readers can expect to encounter unfamiliar words with greater frequency, especially disciplinary vocabulary that can be highly technical and is employed primarily within the context of learning the concepts of a discipline. Students are asked to read words in science, for example, that they will rarely meet outside of science contexts.

Author Purpose

Finally, complex texts may mandate that readers infer the author's purpose and intentions for writing the text. Such purposes may be clearly articulated sometimes but may be more ambiguous at other junctures. Or, there may be multiple purposes, some stated and some not. Furthermore, textbooks are generally written by hidden authors, as it may not be apparent who in actuality wrote various sections or chapters, which complicates the task of determining author intent. The conceptual load presented to readers becomes increasingly abstract and assumes deeper and more sophisticated disciplinary knowledge and reliance on previous learning. Ultimately, readers must determine "Why is the author telling me this?"

After examining the nature of complex texts, it might appear reasonable for teachers to decide to spare their students the frustrations of learning from these more challenging materials. Indeed, in their research synthesis on the role of text in disciplinary learning, Wade and Moje (2000) conclude that "students engage in little reading of any kind of published text, either in class or as homework" (p. 613) and that students rely predominantly on teacher telling and explanation for their learning of new content. If assigned, complex texts were frequently read *to* students, either by the teacher or through round-robin oral reading—an exercise in listening comprehension not reading comprehension. As a result, even students who have achieved basic and intermediate literacy abilities remain stalled as readers and do not develop the capacity to independently access the range of complex texts central to the communication of disciplinary knowledge.

In the NGACBP and CCSSO's (2010a) extensive review of the research on text complexity, the Common Core State Standards emphatically rebut the practice of reading avoidance in content learning:

> Being able to read complex text independently and proficiently is essential for high achievement in college and the workplace and important in numerous life tasks. Moreover, current trends suggest that if students cannot read challenging texts with understanding—if they have not developed the skill, concentration, and stamina to read such texts—they will read less in general. In particular, if students cannot read complex expository text to gain information, they will likely turn to text-free or text-light sources, such as video, podcasts, and tweets. These sources, while not without value, cannot capture the nuance, subtlety, depth, or breadth of ideas developed through complex text. (p. 4)

Talking the Talk of an Academic Discipline

Let me provide an example of a complex text that I faced as an adult reader. My wife Wendy, who is a classical violinist and middle school orchestra teacher, enjoys Renaissance music and a couple of years ago purchased a compact disc featuring several selections from this time period. Like many listeners, I picked up the CD booklet and referred to the liner notes in an effort to more deeply understand this music I was listening to. The following is a segment of those liner notes:

> One is always surprised to observe how Western music has for so long been divided into two areas of activity, so far removed from one another: learned vocal polyphony on the one hand and the instrumental playing of minstrels on the other. These two categories of musician did not belong to the same environment; they were contrasted in their very different social status as well as in their mentalities and divergent techniques....the *Musique de Ioye* marks an interesting stage, for it places in the hands of all instrumentalists, professional or not, on the one hand refined and complex works by the

greatest Venetian masters and, on the other, rudimentary but vividly coloured pieces by anonymous composers. Within the same publication two musical mentalities come face to face, and so were led to gradually transform each other. It is here that we find the beginnings of the prodigious flourishing of the art of Western instrumental music, the point at which a rapprochement was reached between learned composers principally writing complex contrapuntal works for vocal groups, and the practical experience of the minstrels, nourished on the techniques of ornamentation and improvisation and concerned with particular instrumental combinations. (Musique de Ioye, 1987, para. 1)

Whew! Clearly, this text exemplifies all six of the elements of complex texts that were outlined previously. In particular, it is densely packed with information, follows multiple text structures (e.g., compare and contrast, explanation, concept development), features very complicated sentence structures, and employs sophisticated vocabulary and unfamiliar terminology. Like many of you, I suspect, I found this to be a challenging text to comprehend. I had to read carefully and methodically, stopping frequently to ponder what the author was saying, and I reread some segments multiple times. Even then, I realized I was obtaining only an incomplete understanding.

However, Wendy found the liner notes to be a relatively comfortable reading experience. Interesting, although we are both strong readers and get plenty of daily practice reading texts that exhibit complexity, we were not equally proficient as readers of this complex text. In Chapter 1, we examined how identities influence reader profiles. One of Wendy's significant identities is musician, and unsurprisingly, she is a much superior reader through a musical lens than I am. Of course, we could isolate the insider language as a major impediment to my understanding. The liner notes are written in musicianspeak; orchestral players, composers, conductors, and people who study the classical repertoire would qualify as music insiders, and very likely, they are the intended audience of this text. These individuals can talk the talk of classical music, but the rest of us are outsiders of what Gee (1996) terms a *Discourse*, an accepted use of language that typically employs a prescribed pool of vocabulary. When Wendy reads through a musical lens, she is in effect demonstrating her capacity to read the discourse of classical music. She not only can read the symbolic notation arrayed on a sheet of music while performing on her instrument, but she can also read complex written texts that talk about music.

Discourse Insiders

Insiders in a discourse bring much more to reading than the recognition of meanings of the specialized words used to describe concepts, items, and procedures in their field. Over time, insiders have developed deep knowledge and logged extensive experiences that allow them to make numerous personal connections when reading within a familiar discourse. A musician like Wendy reading the Renaissance music liner notes has immediate understanding of rare terms like *polyphony* and *contrapuntal* and realizes that general words like *ornamentation, improvisation,* and *coloured* have very specific meanings in musical contexts. Yet she can also engage her imagination to actually hear what the author is describing. She has personally performed pieces that exhibit these musical properties, and she has previously learned a great deal about this musical genre. As she read, Wendy had accompanying music playing in her head, so to speak, whereas I would have to play the CD to have any chance of relating the author's words to a musical interpretation. Even then, I would not really know what exactly I should be listening for or how some facet of what I was hearing exhibited characteristics described as contrapuntal, ornamental, or polyphonic.

Communities of Insiders

Wendy and other music insiders can be seen as a community of individuals who are comfortable with the discourse of classical music. Any group of people who share a specific identity can be described as a discourse community. These people operate from a common knowledge base, draw on a shared set of experiences and beliefs, and are expected to adhere to accepted ways of interacting when assuming that identity.

A discourse community helps define the persona for a particular identity. Doctors, for example, are a discourse community, a group of people who share an identity, employ a common vocabulary, have comparable training, relate to similar experiences, display a certain outlook, and conform to expected types of deportment when acting as doctors. Lawyers, accountants, pharmacists, electricians, civil engineers, baseball players, automobile mechanics, computer programmers, classical musicians—all display the qualities of discourse communities. If you are a member, you know how to talk and how to act.

If you are not a member, however, you can quickly find the talk of a discourse unintelligible, aggravating, and even marginalizing. You may resent that people are communicating to you in a language that makes little sense, or you may make minimal effort to comprehend. You know full well that you are an outsider in that conversation with shop mechanics about repairing your automobile, with hockey enthusiasts as they comment about the events of a Stanley Cup matchup, with video players extolling the merits of various games, or with culinary experts swapping recipe combinations and techniques. You may have decided it was not worth it to you to really try to dig out an understanding of the liner notes passage provided at the beginning of this section. Indeed, you may have uttered the classic cry of frustration of the discourse outsider: "Why can't they just say this in English?" You may denigrate insider vocabulary as jargon. You may even regard folks who ensnare you in unfamiliar discourse as snobs who are trying to exclude others through their use of insider language. You may also find it irritating that I am using literacy discourse terminology like *discourse* in writing this section.

Identity and Discourse

Of course, all of us talk some forms of insider talk. Each of us is comfortable putting into play a variety of discourses. Our identities qualify us as members of a host of formal and informal groupings, from our immediate family, to associations that coincide with our interests, to our daily professional exchanges. People who have the identity of teachers are a discourse community. We can talk the talk of the education profession, and sometimes parents, who have outsider identities, feel we are speaking in a language that leaves them left out. Yet, we may share other identities with these same parents, enabling us to shift into a discourse that reflects a common ground. However, if we share no identities, then we are likely to have difficulty communicating with each other.

People who are insiders in many discourses become flexible in using and accessing language; we can code-switch, smoothly transitioning from one discourse to another. The specific discourse that we choose at any given moment depends on who is receiving our talk and the conditions of our interaction. A basketball coach, for example, engages in one type of discourse when conducting a workout with the team, a different discourse when conferring with an insurance representative, and a third when visiting a grandparent.

We also can quickly judge the appropriate discourse for a specific context. The discourse that you might use when casually talking with a group of close friends might contain language, references, and behavior that while tacitly agreed on as acceptable for your interactions with each other, would be highly inappropriate in other contexts, such as teaching a group of middle school students, chatting with the pastor of a church, or addressing the school board on live public access television. We can talk the talk, and we know when to talk it.

REFLECTION INTERLUDE

Take a moment and jot down a list of discourses for which you feel you would qualify as an insider (see Figure 2.3). When you get together with fellow members of these communities, you can hold your own in the conversation and are comfortable engaging in the groupspeak. A list for my father, for example, would include discourses based on identities such as dairy farmer, agricultural seed salesman, town board member, sportsman, amateur wine maker, Medicare recipient, and Wisconsin history enthusiast.

Then, jot down a list of texts that you read featuring your insider discourses. Which of these texts might be particularly troublesome for outsiders?

Figure 2.3. Are You a Discourse Insider?

My Insider Discourses	Texts I Read That Feature This Discourse

Complex Texts in Academic Disciplines

Discourse is a key concept in understanding disciplinary literacy. Not only do texts that students read in middle and high school increase in complexity, but also the types of texts begin to vary a great deal across the different academic disciplines. Certainly, adolescents are expected to read a wider range of text genres: textbooks, novels, short stories, newspaper and magazine articles, Internet sources, essays, primary documents, biographies and autobiographies, technical materials, and more. Yet, the specific texts that students read to access disciplinary knowledge are also markedly different from each other. As the Carnegie Council on Advancing Adolescent Literacy (2010) observes,

> Each content area in middle and high school demands a different approach to reading, writing, and thinking. Texts read in history class are different from those read in biology, which in turn are substantially different from novels, poems, or essays read in English language arts. (p. 13)

Do readers read texts of one academic discipline in ways that are substantially different from the texts of other disciplines? In Chapter 1, I referred to reading, writing, and thinking through a disciplinary lens. How is reading through a historian lens different from, say, reading through a scientific lens, a mathematics lens, or a musical lens? To address this question, we next take an introductory excursion through the world of a reader who is confronted with a typical ninth-grade curriculum.

If we delved into the overstuffed backpack of a high school freshman, what types of texts might we discover? Perhaps a biology textbook emerges first. As we quickly flip through it, our eyes settle on the following page: "Characteristics of Protists" (see Figure 2.4). Notice first the visual layout. About half the page is flowing text (three paragraphs and a caption), with the other half partitioned into visuals (a photograph and an illustration) and study support (key ideas, key terms, why it matters, and a reading check). A boldface statement stands out: "Protists are eukaryotic organisms that cannot be classified as fungi, plants, or animals." The section is very descriptive and packed with detailed information and biological terminology.

Next, we might lift out a U.S. history textbook, and thumbing through it, we end on a page entitled "The Drive for Reform" (see Figure 2.5). Again, the page is divided between flowing text (three paragraphs, a caption, and

Figure 2.4. Biology Textbook Page

Characteristics of Protists

Key Ideas	Key Terms	Why It Matters
❯ What types of organisms are classified as protists? ❯ What methods of reproduction do protists use? ❯ Why is the classification of protists likely to change in the future?	gamete zygote zygospore alternation of generations	Protists offer clues about the evolution of fungi, plants, and animals.

From tiny glass stars that float in the ocean to slimy green fuzz that carpets rocks on the shore, a wide variety of organisms make up the group we call *protists*.

What Are Protists?

The kingdom Protista is made up of organisms that do not belong in any of the other kingdoms. As a result, the members of this kingdom are quite diverse, as **Figure 1** shows. But all protists have one thing in common: they are eukaryotic. ❯ **Protists are eukaryotic organisms that cannot be classified as fungi, plants, or animals.**

Several important characteristics evolved in protists. These characteristics include membrane-bound organelles, complex cilia and flagella, sexual reproduction with gametes, and multicellularity. Organelles, including mitochondria and chloroplasts, allow single cells to perform a wide variety of functions. Complex cilia and flagella like those found in protists are also found in many other types of cells. For example, the cells that keep particles out of our lungs use the same type of cilia as is found in protists. Sexual reproduction allows for greater genetic diversity than reproduction by binary fission does. Multicellularity allows cells to specialize, which in turn allows for the development of tissues, organs, and organ systems.

❯ **Reading Check** *What important characteristics arose among protists during their evolution? (See the Appendix for answers to Reading Checks.)*

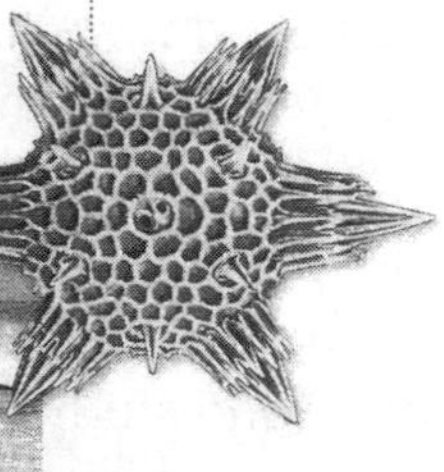

Figure 1 The radiolarian shown above is an example of a unicellular protist that captures and engulfs food. Algae, such as the kind growing on these rocks, contain chloroplasts and use photosynthesis to produce energy.

SECTION 1 Characteristics of Protists **497**

Figure 2.5. U.S. History Textbook Page

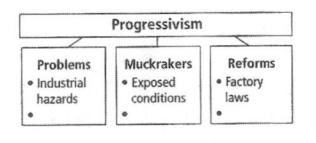

Children in the Coal Mines

Progressive reformers were appalled by the child labor that was common in coal mines, textile mills, and other industries. John Spargo, a union organizer and socialist, sadly described the terrible conditions endured by boys working in the coal mines.

❝The coal is hard, and accidents to the hands, such as cut, broken, or crushed fingers, are common among the boys. Sometimes there is a worse accident: a terrified shriek is heard, and a boy is mangled and torn in the machinery, or disappears in the chute to be picked out later smothered and dead. Clouds of dust fill the breakers and are inhaled by the boys, laying the foundations for asthma and miners' consumption. ❞

—John Spargo, *The Bitter Cry of the Children*, 1906

▲ These boys toiled in a West Virginia coal mine.

The Drive for Reform

Objectives

- Identify the causes of Progressivism and compare it to Populism.
- Analyze the role that journalists played in the Progressive Movement.
- Evaluate some of the social reforms that Progressives tackled.
- Explain what Progressives hoped to achieve through political reforms.

Terms and People

Progressivism	Jane Addams
muckraker	direct primary
Lincoln Steffens	initiative
Jacob Riis	referendum
Social Gospel	recall
settlement house	

NoteTaking

Reading Skill: Identify Details Fill in a chart like this one with details about Progressivism.

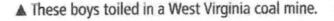

Progressivism		
Problems	**Muckrakers**	**Reforms**
• Industrial hazards	• Exposed conditions	• Factory laws
•	•	•

Why It Matters Industrialization, urbanization, and immigration brought many benefits to America, but they also produced challenging social problems. In response, a movement called **Progressivism** emerged in the 1890s. Progressives believed that new ideas and honest, efficient government could bring about social justice. Progressive ideas brought lasting reforms that still affect society today. **Section Focus Question: What areas did Progressives think were in need of the greatest reform?**

Origins of Progressivism

The people who made up the Progressive Movement came from many walks of life. They came from all political parties, social classes, ethnic groups, and religions. Many Progressive leaders emerged from the growing middle class, whose power and influence was rapidly spreading. Dissatisfied industrial workers also joined the Progressive Movement. So did a few wealthy Americans driven by a desire to act for the good of society.

Progressives Share Common Beliefs What the Progressives shared in common was a belief that industrialization and urbanization had created troubling social and political problems. Progressives wanted to bring about reforms that would correct these problems and injustices. They encouraged their state legislatures and the federal government to enact laws to address the issues faced by the poor. Progressives wanted to use logic and reason to make society work in a more efficient and orderly way. Many, motivated by religious faith, sought social justice.

---

two introductory paragraphs that feature a quotation), visual information (a photograph), and study supports (objectives, terms and people, a note-taking task with a graphic organizer, and a section focus question). We are informed why this section matters: "Industrialization, urbanization, and immigration brought many benefits to America, but they also produced challenging social problems." The section offers an exposition of events and features social science vocabulary.

We rummage a bit more and pull out an algebra textbook. The "Quadratic Graphs and Their Properties" section stops us (see Figure 2.6). There is much less flowing text on this page, with paragraphs consisting of one, two, or three precisely worded sentences. Study supports include lesson vocabulary, an objective, and a key concept box. The page also includes a graph and a problem to solve. An illustration accompanies the presentation of the problem to assist the reader in visualizing the scenario. The key concept is explained as follows: "A **quadratic function** is a function that can be written in the form $y = ax^2 + bx + c$, where $a \neq 0$." This section emphasizes explanation and, like our biology and history pages, employs a density of domain-specific terminology.

Our hands touch a slim volume next, a definite contrast to the three bulky textbooks that we have looked at. John Steinbeck's (1937/1963) classic novel *Of Mice and Men* emerges, a weathered paperback volume. Unlike the textbooks, this book is completely prose: no visual information, no study supports, just page after page of unbroken paragraphs. At the start of Chapter 3, you read,

> Slim and George came into the darkening bunk house together. Slim reached up over the card table and turned on the tin-shaded electric light. Instantly the table was brilliant with light, and the cone of the shade threw its brightness straight downward, leaving the corners of the bunk house in dusk. Slim sat down on a box, and George took his place opposite.
> "It wasn't nothing," said Slim. "I would of had to drowned most of 'em anyways. No need to thank me about that." (p. 42)

There is no technical vocabulary in the passage, although several references are made to life in a past time and place. This text also includes dialogue and dialect. Sentences are straightforward and not very elaborate. The entire work follows a storytelling pattern, as many of

Figure 2.6. Algebra Textbook Page

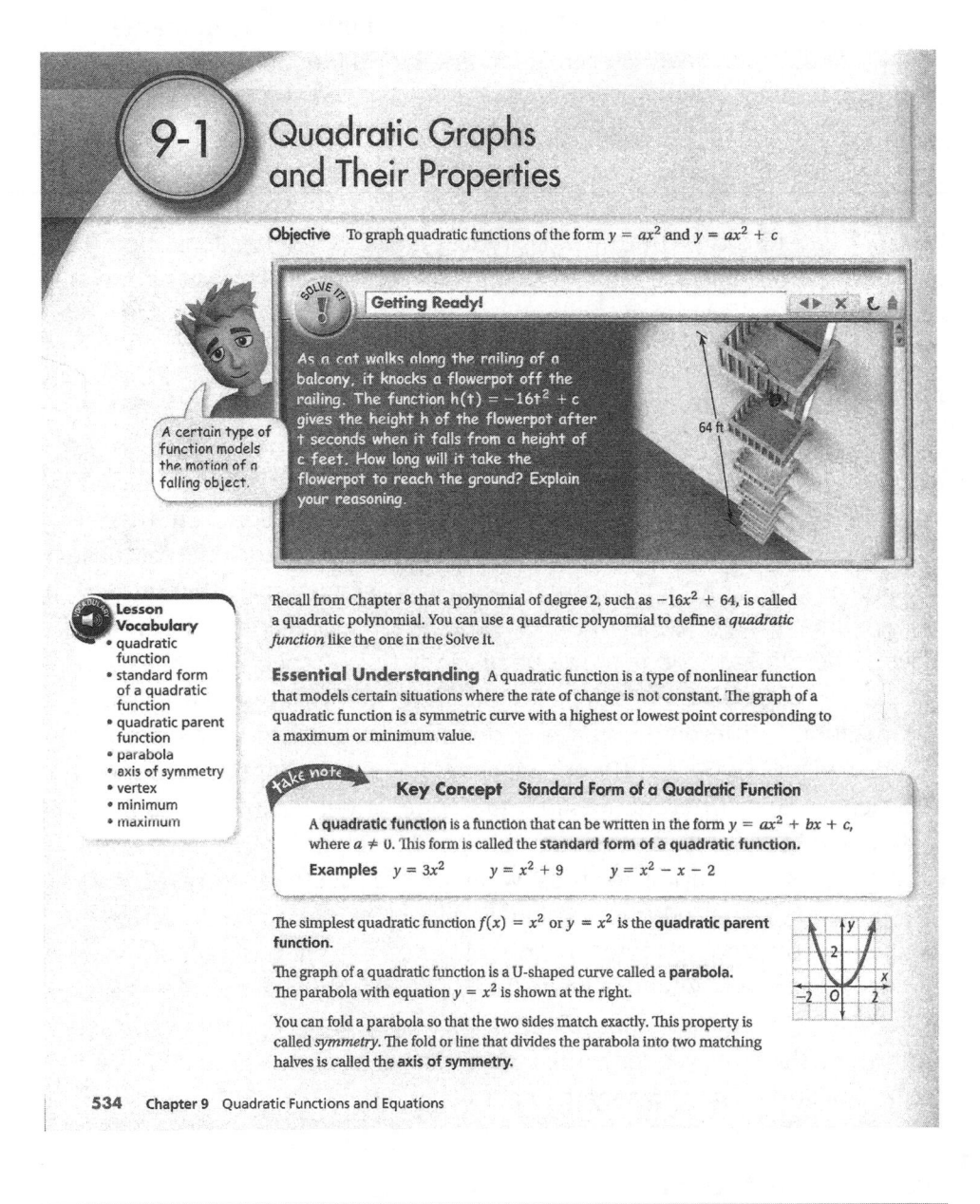

9-1 Quadratic Graphs and Their Properties

Objective To graph quadratic functions of the form $y = ax^2$ and $y = ax^2 + c$

Getting Ready!

As a cat walks along the railing of a balcony, it knocks a flowerpot off the railing. The function $h(t) = -16t^2 + c$ gives the height h of the flowerpot after t seconds when it falls from a height of c feet. How long will it take the flowerpot to reach the ground? Explain your reasoning.

A certain type of function models the motion of a falling object.

64 ft

Lesson Vocabulary
- quadratic function
- standard form of a quadratic function
- quadratic parent function
- parabola
- axis of symmetry
- vertex
- minimum
- maximum

Recall from Chapter 8 that a polynomial of degree 2, such as $-16x^2 + 64$, is called a quadratic polynomial. You can use a quadratic polynomial to define a *quadratic function* like the one in the Solve It.

Essential Understanding A quadratic function is a type of nonlinear function that models certain situations where the rate of change is not constant. The graph of a quadratic function is a symmetric curve with a highest or lowest point corresponding to a maximum or minimum value.

take note

Key Concept Standard Form of a Quadratic Function

A **quadratic function** is a function that can be written in the form $y = ax^2 + bx + c$, where $a \neq 0$. This form is called the **standard form of a quadratic function.**

Examples $y = 3x^2$ $\qquad y = x^2 + 9$ $\qquad y = x^2 - x - 2$

The simplest quadratic function $f(x) = x^2$ or $y = x^2$ is the **quadratic parent function.**

The graph of a quadratic function is a U-shaped curve called a **parabola.** The parabola with equation $y = x^2$ is shown at the right.

You can fold a parabola so that the two sides match exactly. This property is called *symmetry*. The fold or line that divides the parabola into two matching halves is called the **axis of symmetry.**

534 Chapter 9 Quadratic Functions and Equations

the same characters will be featured during the narration of the action throughout the book.

Of course, you are likely to find a number of other texts in that backpack: photocopied material, packets, a world language textbook, technical booklets, a health textbook, perhaps a trade book, and so forth. Our backpack analysis obviously does not factor in online hypertexts that this student will be reading as part of classwork. So, to return to our question, what does it mean to be a reader of such diverse and varied texts? What does this ninth-grade student face every time he or she transitions from one academic discipline to the next? What does it mean to read through a disciplinary lens?

Disciplinary Discourses

Certainly, you noticed with the four examples presented in this chapter that each text has a particularly unique way of talking to its readers. Vocabulary issues are definitely central to these distinctions, but there is more going on than use of discipline-specific terminology. Each of these texts relies on a different discourse. Each text assumes a discrete reservoir of disciplinary knowledge and asks students to gain insights about some facet of their lives through a unique disciplinary perspective. "These are different worlds: different purposes, different writing styles, different organizations, different language, different modes of communication, different visual layouts, different expectations of relevant background and experiences, and different uses of knowledge" (Buehl, 2009b, p. 230).

Each of these texts draws on established disciplinary traditions of what are useful materials to study, what are the accepted standards for locating and evaluating information, and what are the procedures to be used for examining and interpreting information to develop theories and explanations of what we know. How a reader thinks when trying to understand an author communicating through a historical text contrasts mightily with how a reader thinks when trying to understand an author communicating through a mathematics text.

Discourse Outsiders

Teachers need to realize that their subject disciplines are examples of discourse communities and that their students, who are predominately outsiders in these academic discourses, may feel overwhelmed or even alienated by all the academic jargon—the outsider's depiction of a discourse—in a biology text, a math lesson, a history passage, or a literary interpretation. People who are outsiders in a discourse need support and mentoring when encountering texts packed with insider knowledge.

In Chapter 1, I described literacy development as becoming increasingly specialized as adolescents move into the more compartmentalized studies of academic disciplines. We would agree that all four disciplinary texts featured in this chapter assume readers who have developed basic and intermediate literacy skills. Yet, because readers must also undertake qualitatively different approaches for understanding each of these distinctive texts, our students need the additional instruction that we have termed disciplinary literacy.

Let's take a closer examination of each of the four disciplinary texts presented in this chapter. A ninth grader reading these texts is confronted by four major variables in disciplinary learning.

1. Each text exhibits characteristics that we have identified as inherent in complex texts.

2. Each text represents a discrete academic discourse, which enhances text complexity.

3. Adolescents have to be receptive to expending the necessary effort to meet the challenge of reading and learning from each of these texts, which is an identity issue.

4. Adolescents must be sufficiently skilled to engage in the modes of thinking outlined earlier as essential reading comprehension processes.

Subsequent chapters detail instructional strategies that address these four key variables. The remaining pages of this chapter pinpoint some of the significant challenges awaiting readers in the four disciplinary areas of science, social studies, mathematics, and literature. At times, the discussion may feel overwhelming: We are talking about ambitious goals for our students, and many of them have certainly not yet reached these levels of performance. These are texts that will need to be worked to be comprehended, as explained in Chapter 6.

Touch base in your thinking with the Gradual Release of Responsibility model (see Chapter 1, page 27). What kinds of modeling, instructional support, and scaffolding would make it possible for students to gradually develop, grade by grade, the capacity to meaningfully interact with texts in these four disciplines?

Comprehension of Science Texts

The biology page presented earlier in this chapter (Figure 2.4) displays many of the issues that students must confront when reading science texts. This text will strike many readers, especially those who are not science insiders, as quite difficult. (Do those liner notes on Renaissance era music really seem so unfriendly in comparison?)

Vocabulary Load

The density of biological terminology is likely our first impression. The sample text provides a heavy dose of biological discourse that represents language used by biologists to describe and explain living things. New terms like *protists, gamete, zygote, zygospore,* and *alternation of generations* are introduced and defined, as are a host of other terms like *binary fission* and *cytokinesis* on subsequent pages in this chapter of the biology textbook. Yet, the text is rife with carryover terms, biological vocabulary that students have met previously and are expected to make meaningful connections to without elaboration. On the single sample page alone, these insider discourse terms are used: *organism, eukaryotic, membrane, organelle, cilia, flagella, multicellularity, unicellular, mitochondria, chloroplasts,* and *photosynthesis.* The reader is expected to fill in a sense of what each of these terms entails.

Assumed Knowledge

However, the discourse of science goes much deeper than biology words. When the author of this text refers to characteristics in the section title, readers must infer what scientists regard as essential characteristics in living things, why scientists focus on these characteristics, and how scientists find out. Readers must therefore make the adjustment to reading through a scientific lens. Likewise, the reference to classification represents a deep understanding of processes that scientists undertake to classify, in this case, living things, and implicit is the classification system used by biologists and why they use it. Readers are somewhat cued to this system of biological classification by mentions in the text of *kingdom, plant,* and *animal.* Several other deep scientific understandings are also assumed when the author drops in language like *genetic, sexual reproduction, organ systems, evolution,* and *specialize.* For example, how systems are conceptualized in biological science, how they work, how they interact with each other, and what the various systems are are subsumed beneath the appearance of the term *system* in this section. Each of these terms presumes an extensive network of science knowledge and experience. Finally, readers must recognize that general terms like *diversity, organ, tissue,* and *kingdom* have very significant and discrete meanings when used in science contexts (e.g., *diversity* means something very different when it crops up in social studies contexts).

Underlying the layer of information on this sample biology page, then, are not only how biologists communicate but also how biologists think and how they behave when investigating phenomena and developing biological knowledge. In the themed issue of *Science* on language and literacy, van den Broek (2010) summarizes this task facing readers of science materials: "Science texts differ greatly from narratives in their demands on working memory management, comprehension strategies, and the use of background knowledge" (p. 455).

> **"**
> Without systematic attention to reading and writing within subjects like science and history, students will leave schools with an impoverished sense of what it means to use the tools of literacy for learning or even to reason within various disciplines.
> **"**
> —*Pearson, Moje, & Greenleaf, 2010, p. 460*

Academic Language

These textual elements are also present in earth science, physical science, chemistry, and physics curricular materials. All tend to employ what researchers describe as academic language, which is more difficult for students when compared with more informal language or narrative structures such as fiction. Academic language can be recognized by the formal—and to many readers, distant and uninviting—tone, by the complexity of content, and by the impersonal stance. (Academic authors are not really noticeable, they exude little personality in their writing, and they just stick to the facts.) Academic language is well represented in sentences such as "Multicellularity allows cells to specialize, which in turn allows for the development of tissues, organs, and organ systems." Snow (2010) summarizes these textual qualities: "Among the most commonly noted features of academic language are conciseness, achieved by avoiding redundancy; using a high density of information-bearing words, ensuring precision of expression; and relying on grammatical processes to compress complex ideas into few words" (p. 450).

Visual Information

Another look at the biology page reveals additional elements of science texts, visual information—in this case, a photograph and an illustration. Science texts rarely depend on language alone to explain science concepts, and often as much as half a page is devoted to pictures, diagrams, drawings, models, figures, tables, and other graphic representations. Not only are visual literacy skills mandated (i.e., the ability to decipher a diagram or navigate a chart), but readers must also move back and forth between prose passages and visual information to make sense of an author's message. Consequently, readers must synthesize what an author is saying with how this might be visually represented, and they may indeed be compelled to reread a passage and reexamine a visual before they arrive at a satisfactory understanding.

Furthermore, because of the tight economics of producing written texts, publishers may adopt an either–or position, with information provided in either written prose or visual displays but not both. Hence, readers may have to infer what a science concept or process might look like, or infer how a visual might be described if discussed in written language. Finally, online texts may include video, simulations, and other multimedia, presenting readers with additional levels of processing and synthesizing information.

Mentoring Science Readers

Science teachers may underrate the challenge of science texts because of their deep familiarity with the concepts that these texts are presenting, although science teachers do tend to be aware that such texts can present a barrier to learning in science. As a result, complex science texts are often deemphasized or even sidestepped in the classroom, and teachers resort to imparting science information through telling and demonstrating. As Pearson et al. (2010) conclude,

> reading about science is replaced by listening to someone talk about science…. Avoiding the challenge of engaging students with texts may seem efficient, yet it ultimately undermines student learning. Instead of confronting reading problems head on, it breeds student dependence on the teacher for science knowledge and places the learner in a passive role. (p. 460)

Webb (2010) notes an emerging consensus within the science education community for the need to focus more on the facets of science literacy, which features two strands: fundamental science literacy, which emphasizes the language and thinking of science, and derived science literacy, which engages students in applying their understandings to their world and to societal issues that have science relevancy. Webb concludes,

> A number of researchers…believe that for someone to be judged scientifically literate in both the fundamental and derived senses, he or she must be first proficient in the discourses of science, which include reading, writing, and talking science. In order to achieve these goals, students must be helped to cross the borders between the informal language they speak at home and the academic language used at school, particularly the specialized language of science. (p. 448)

Science teachers will find ideas for mentoring students to read through a scientific lens in the following chapters.

Comprehension of Social Studies Texts

We now zero in on the history page entitled "The Drive for Reform" (Figure 2.5). Although the language in this text may seem less intense than on the sample biology page on protists that we just examined, readers are nevertheless immediately transported into a different realm of thinking and expression.

Conceptual Vocabulary

On our sample history page, the discourse of history predominates, with concept-laden terms like *industrialization, urbanization, immigration, Progressivism, ethnic groups, middle class, political parties, federal government, state legislatures, social classes, social problems, social justice,* and *society* constantly embedded into the flow of this narrative. Of these elemental social science terms, only Progressivism is presented as a new idea that will be discussed in this section of the history textbook. Readers are expected to make meaningful connections to the other terms on their own. Hugely significant overall concepts, such as reform, power, influence, and justice, are also referenced—each embodying extensive webs of relationships and prior knowledge that encompass not only history but also the disciplines of political science and sociology.

Historical References

In addition, proper nouns such as names of people (e.g., Jane Addams), places (e.g., West Virginia), events (e.g., the Triangle Shirtwaist Factory Fire, which appears on subsequent pages), or titles (e.g., *The Jungle* and *The Shame of the Cities,* which also follow) must be regarded as concepts and treated in many respects like meaningful vocabulary. For example, Jane Addams is emblematic of certain elements of Progressivism. Her contributions help readers develop a more nuanced understanding of this movement in U.S. history, and her name may conceivably be dropped into future discussions as an elaboration, illustration, or comparison. Readers must know more than who she was; they must develop an understanding of what she *means*. It is interesting that given all the history discourse identified on just this one page, only *Progressivism* appears in the "Terms and People" sidebar, which ostensibly highlights new learning to be detailed in this section of the chapter. The other targeted terms and people, including Jane Addams, are presented on ensuing pages.

Historian Perspectives

Readers will certainly feel that they are encountering a lot of stuff on these pages. Although the material may appear less esoteric than the description of the protists, the history text still may seem overwhelmingly jam-packed with facts. Many readers could possibly lose the strand of the narrative as they bounce along from one unfamiliar reference to the next. Again, comprehension necessitates that readers must shift into a particular disciplinary lens, in this case, reading like a historian.

Implicit on this sample page is an understanding of what types of past experiences are valued by historians, why historians are interested in these experiences, how they collect pertinent information about these experiences, what questions they entertain as they examine this information, and how they arrive at meaningful conclusions, explanations, or interpretations about these historical phenomena. Although the authors provide a "Why It Matters" explication, at a deeper level, readers must infer how the study of history helps them understand their lives and times and how the study of *this* history helps them make sense of some facet of their lives and times. Readers should rightfully ask of the authors of history, "Why are you telling me all this?" Readers should be able to construct possible answers through insights derived as readers through a historian lens.

Visual Information

Like science texts, history texts often provide information in multiple forms: There is both a photograph and a graphic organizer on this history page, and readers can also expect visual displays such as illustrations, maps, charts, political cartoons, graphs, and tables. Some of these visuals are intended to help readers imagine what is described in the prose segments, so they have a better feel for past times and events. The photograph of the children who worked in coal mines performs this function.

Other graphic information is presented to augment the text or provide information not specifically developed in the prose; these visuals must be examined more carefully and then be synthesized with written narration. Line graphs comparing children attending schools versus children employed in factories appear later in this section of the history textbook and are examples of this latter category of visual information.

In addition, primary source materials, such as quotations, personal letters, commentaries, and excerpts from historical documents, are frequently interspersed into the text. A quotation from a historical exposé introduces the Progressive movement on this page.

Mentoring History Readers

A number of these features also predominate in other texts that students read in history and other social studies classes: articles from magazines, newspapers and other periodicals, excerpts from biographies and autobiographies, secondary sources written by historians, primary documents, and a vast array of online content. Yet, as Lee and Spratley (2010) observe, the default experience for most students remains learning history through textbook reading, and students are not mentored to read such texts through a historian lens: "In contrast, schools typically socialize students into seeing history as a simple chronology of events and the explanations of social, political and economic phenomena offered in texts as a truthful and unexamined master narrative" (p. 7).

As a consequence, students tend to view the study of history as fact collecting, as Wineburg (1991) discovered in a study comparing how historians and high school students read historical texts. Students notice the whos, whats, and wheres of history, whereas historians are concerned primarily with the whys and hows: why events happened the way they did, how these events affected people and changed things, why the author of a text arrived at certain interpretations and conclusions, and how the author constructed and supported these explanations and perhaps theories. In particular, historians cue into the author of the texts they read. Historians critically examine the basis of the author's explanations and track possible author perspectives, beliefs, and even biases. In effect, historians read disciplinary texts as arguments, whereas students read these texts as truth statements.

> **66**
> **When reading history, students need to be able to understand what happened in a sequence of events as well as recognize the interpretation that an author inevitably incorporates.**
> **99**
>
> —*Schleppegrell, Greer, & Taylor, 2008, p. 176*

Like all textbooks, social studies textbooks are written to project an aura of authority, which is of course a natural tone for a useful classroom resource. Hynd, Holschuh, and Hubbard (2004) conclude, "The tradition in history textbook writing is to write a coherent, seemingly true story, even though the story relies on hypothesized cause/effect relationships and other interpretations of data" (p. 142). That social studies textbooks are written by hidden authors can obscure author voice and blur the lines between factual information and interpretative arguments. For example, two of the first three sentences on our sample history page qualify as arguments and not as fact statements: "Industrialization, urbanization, and immigration brought many benefits to America, but they also produced challenging social problems." "Progressive ideas brought lasting reforms that still affect society today."

Traditionally, we would identify such sentences as main idea statements, but in reality, these are arguments and must be read with an understanding of how historians might arrive at such conclusions. In addition, many sentences contain generalizations, which imply that the author examined specific factual information and could therefore confidently encapsulate such findings into statements such as "came from many walks of life," "growing middle class, whose power and influence was rapidly spreading," and "a few wealthy Americans driven by a desire to act for the good of society." In effect, the author is arguing that these statements reflect a justifiable reading of the evidence. Additionally, implicit in this entire chapter is the most transcendent argument: Of all the U.S. history that might be studied, the Progressive era is so particularly significant that it warrants extended time and consideration via an entire chapter.

This discussion focused primarily on history as the area of social studies most frequently taught in middle and high school. Yet the aforementioned issues with comprehension of social studies texts also apply to readers of civics and government, economics, cultural geography, psychology, and other social sciences. Each of these disciplines presumes a specific discourse and understanding of how knowledge is conceptualized, organized, and decided. Each also mandates a discrete disciplinary lens for reading, writing, and thinking. Social studies teachers will encounter a number of ideas for mentoring students as readers of the discipline in upcoming chapters.

Comprehension of Mathematics Texts

We now turn again to the sample algebra page on quadratic graphs (Figure 2.6). Once more, the discourse of mathematics is immediately striking to readers.

Mathematics Terminology

The new algebraic concept being presented is quadratic function, which is precisely defined and explained, with examples provided. Other new terms introduced are *parabola* and *axis of symmetry*. However, readers are assumed to be conversant with and knowledgeable of an embedded flow of mathematics terminology, such as *form, function, degree, rate, polynomial, nonlinear, property, equation,* and *value.* The term *graph* has a deep and significant meaning in mathematics contexts, which implies an understanding of what forms graphs might assume, why graphs might be used to illustrate relationships, and how various mathematics procedures can be followed to construct such graphs. Likewise, readers have to shift to an understanding of the mathematical usage of the term *models*: what is meant by a mathematic model, how mathematic models can be displayed, what types of phenomena can be modeled, and what we can learn from examining such models.

Furthermore, mathematics vocabulary can be especially deceptive because many key mathematics terms are also used in more common ways in general conversation, such as *model, property, form, line, function, divide,* and *value.* Readers have to become particularly adept at discourse code-switching from informal everyday usage to precise mathematical meanings.

Multiple Modes of Presentation

The other most obvious feature of mathematics text is the lack of extended prose. Mathematics texts typically communicate mathematics principles in multiple modes; pages display symbolic notations, graphic representations, drawings, illustrations, and examples of problem solutions, intertwined with a few conceptually deep, carefully worded sentences. On some pages, the only sentences that appear are embedded into problem discussions or word problems. Readers have to be flexible thinkers, able to adjust to these different informational modes constantly, and able to extract meaning from each. Comprehension is predicated on synthesizing insights from all these different informational forms and requires readers to go back and forth, from the sentences, to the symbolic notation, to the graphic representations, and so forth, to construct an understanding.

Compacted Prose

The terseness and density of the sentences require a reading (and sometimes rereading) that is careful and methodical. Consider the processing necessary to make sense of this sentence from the quadratic graphs page:

> A quadratic function [OK, this is the new concept I am learning. *Quad* means 4, so this has something to do with 4.] is a type of nonlinear [What do they mean by *nonlinear*: nonline, not a straight line?] function [What exactly is meant by *function*? Am I clear what a function is? What are other functions I have learned about?] that models [How do mathematicians model things? This connects to the cat and flowerpot example. They can show mathematically how the pot falls.] certain situations [Like the cat and flowerpot example, I wonder what other situations work here?] where the rate of change [What do I understand *rate* to mean? What are some things where the rate might change?] is not constant [What does *constant* mean: stays the same? So, if the rate or speed of something changes, then it doesn't stay the same rate while this change happens?].

In addition, readers have to be comfortable translating symbolic notation into prose language as they read; "$y = ax^2 + bx + c$, where $a \neq 0$" is translated into "y equals a times x-squared plus b times x plus c, where a does not equal zero." Of course, knowledge of the algebraic use of variables is assumed in this statement, as well as an implicit question of why a cannot be zero. In a real sense, readers of mathematics need to be bilingual as they constantly switch back and forth between reading math sentences and symbolic notation. As Moje and her colleagues (2011) observe, "Mathematics is a language, and algebra in adolescent classrooms, where symbolic notation may be confronted seriously for the first time, is as much about the language as the ideas expressed by it" (p. 469).

Reading Mathematically

Clearly, readers must read mathematics sentences differently and more intensely than they read sentences, and indeed paragraphs, in most other disciplines. For the majority of readers, one trip through a math sentence, and certainly a math page, will not result in satisfactory comprehension. Consider this sentence, for example: "The graph of a quadratic function is a symmetric curve with a highest or lowest point corresponding to a maximum or minimum value." This is a packed sentence with several meaningful parts and much deep conceptual language. It is unlikely that most readers will fully comprehend this sentence from a single reading at a relatively normal pace.

In their study investigating how historians, chemists, and mathematicians read the texts of their fields, Shanahan and Shanahan (2008) discovered that rereading is regarded as an essential strategy for mathematics:

> Students often attempt to read mathematics texts for the gist or general idea, but this kind of text cannot be appropriately understood without close reading. Math reading requires a precision of meaning, and each word must be understood specifically in service to that particular meaning. (p. 49)

Observers have noted that *text* in mathematics classes usually does mean *textbook*. There is ongoing conversation and sometimes spirited debate within math circles as to what constitutes most effective approaches for teaching mathematics and, as a corollary, what should be the nature of math textbooks.

Whatever the approach, all math textbooks introduce students to the discourse of mathematics and expect students to become increasingly comfortable receiving this discourse as readers and learners of the mathematics curriculum. Whether students are actually asked to *read* a mathematics textbook is another matter, however. Math teachers express concerns that reading the textbook can be a barrier to learning mathematics for struggling readers. Yet, many math teachers are also dubious that most of their students will successfully comprehend math texts, even in advanced mathematics courses.

A number of researchers describe traditional mathematics classroom routines as a review of previous instruction and homework, teacher explanation and demonstration of new material, interactions between teacher and students to check understanding through working of example problems, and seatwork as students tackle homework that provides further practice of new material (Draper, 2002). The textbook may be used solely as a source for model examples and practice activities; students may not actually be engaged in reading it to comprehend new material.

Mathematics teachers often maintain that reading in math is so unlike reading in other disciplines that many general literacy practices are not a particularly good fit for mathematics classrooms. When present, literacy instruction in mathematics typically is limited to a narrow focus on two areas: teaching mathematics vocabulary for obvious reasons and comprehension procedures for deciphering story problems (Siegel & Fonzi, 1995). At times, additional attention may be allocated to cueing students into textbook features (e.g., how a text is organized, how the textbook works), but as Draper (2002) comments,

> Learning to read and use the textbook for learning rather than simply as a repository for problems would be an advance over the lack of literacy instruction that currently exists in the typical mathematics classroom. However, more important than learning how to read the textbook is learning how to read, write, listen, speak, and think math texts. (p. 523)

In other words, learning to read through a mathematical lens.

Mentoring Mathematics Readers

Some mathematics programs explicitly guide teachers into mentoring their students as readers. In contrast to traditional instructional routines, students may work cooperatively to read and discuss textbook sections to work out their comprehension. In effect, students need to be mentored to think mathematically not only when occupied with solving math problems but also when reading about mathematical concepts and relationships. Students, and many adults, would react to mathematics texts such as the quadratic page displayed in this chapter by pleading, "This is too hard. You should just tell us what we need to know." The result is what many researchers term a pedagogy of telling. Teacher demonstration certainly plays a role in mathematics instruction, but when students do not develop the capacity to access mathematics understandings independently, students become mired in a continuing cycle of dependency on a knowledgeable other.

This cycle is depressingly familiar to math teachers:

1. A mathematical concept is explained and modeled.

2. Students seem to get it.

3. A day or so later, a number of students are unclear.

4. The teacher or an able student explains the concept again.

5. Students seem to get it.

6. A week or so later, a number of students are unclear again.

7. The teacher or a knowledgeable student explains once again.

Students who have not been mentored to think mathematically as readers tend to be students who struggle with retaining mathematical understandings over time. Many students, and adults, gradually adopt identities as the kind of people who cannot get math: "Students come to regard mathematics as a mysterious activity far removed from everyday life and reserved for an elite with special talents" (Siegel & Fonzi, 1995, p. 635).

> **"**
>
> Reading a wide array of mathematics-centric and mathematics-related texts in the classroom can generate lifelong interest and support learning to reason mathematically.
>
> **"**
>
> —Lee & Spratley, 2010, p. 15

Mathematics teachers justifiably tend to feel particularly singled out for the performance of their students because of No Child Left Behind testing and accountability. These pressures may lead math teachers to assert, "We have to do math. We don't have time to do literacy, too." Yet, literacy practices are inextricably linked to thinking mathematically, and the reasoning necessary to problem-solve comprehension of math texts is foundational to interacting with the world through a mathematical lens. Instructional ideas for reading through a mathematic lens are introduced in subsequent chapters.

Comprehension of Literary Texts

In comparison to the three disciplinary texts that we have just examined, the *Of Mice and Men* excerpt may seem remarkably less complicated. Readers are not navigating elaborate pages rife with varied informational displays and compacted sentences and paragraphs steeped in insider discourse. However, readers of literary fiction are presented with more novel challenges.

Indirect Communications

Unlike the science, history, and algebra examples, literary fiction such as Steinbeck's classic novel represent an indirect communication. Expository texts, such as the sample Progressives, protists, and quadratic pages, can be seen as direct communications: The author undertakes to tell readers directly what he or she feels is important for the readers to know. Of course, as pointed out in the previous sections, these texts also have significant implicit layers: unstated assumptions of knowledge, understanding, and perspective. However, the intention of authors of expository texts is to convey directly some sort of meaningful communication.

Literary fiction, however, depends on the reader's interpretation to achieve an understanding. Authors of literary fiction communicate to readers through the telling of a story, the behavior of characters, the use of language, and the craft of literary devices. Authors of literary fiction may grapple with ideas or project a point of view about some facet of life as a key element to their writing, as opposed to authors of popular fiction, whose main goal may be to tell an interesting story and provide entertainment to the reader. Did Steinbeck have something on his mind when he wrote *Of Mice and Men*? Was there something he wanted readers to understand about the Great Depression, the lives of displaced people, obligations to cognitively challenged individuals, friendship, loyalty, and morally ambiguous choices? If so, he does not directly tell us; it is left to the interpretations of his readers, using what he tells us and our own knowledge and experiences as guides for constructing our understandings.

Many individuals relish the experience of reading through a literary lens. However, other readers can become frustrated with this challenge of constructing meaning with competing possibilities, preferring instead expository texts and authors who come right out and tell us what they have to say. It is certainly acceptable for individuals to desire texts that exhibit direct communications.

In our schools, such individuals are frequently those who have math/science identities and may not see the point of reading literary texts. Another sometimes resistant group can be those students who are readers of popular fiction, sometimes voracious readers of a particular genre like fantasy or teen-centric novels, and expect fiction to be entertainment and deal with topics of high interest to them. These students revel in the vicarious experiences of their personal reading and may be stern judges of literary fiction as boring, disconnected from their lives, lacking in the imaginative flavor they seek, and too challenging for expending their time and energy. Many students, exasperated by their struggles with a work of literature, lobby to just be told what the book means, hoping for a CliffsNotes distillation from their teacher that they can settle on as their comprehension.

A Fictional Lens

However, unlike science and mathematics classrooms, students anticipate that they will be reading and writing for a significant portion of their learning in English language arts classes. Students will read from a variety of literary genres, from short stories, novels, plays, and poetry, to literary nonfiction such as essays, speeches, biographies, and autobiographies, to informational texts such as newspaper and magazine articles, to a myriad of online texts.

Literary fiction, whether delivered in literature anthologies or met in novels, can be especially problematic for students as they develop their capacity to read through a literary lens. First, because literary fiction is an indirect communication, readers need to be constantly aware of the author's voice and the author's moves in writing the work. Readers are called on to infer the author's perspective as they interact with the elements of a story. Furthermore, the craft of an author not only displays aesthetic value as a work of art but also is critical to the communication of a possible theme and ideas.

Second, novels, because of their length, require endurance, perseverance, and the ability to track events and ideas through extended story lines and details. Readers have to stay with it even if a work does not sparkle with the excitement and appeal of book-length popular fiction. Third, readers must engage their imaginations to re-create a world suggested by an author, a world that might focus on people, places, times, events, and cultural practices that are very distant from readers' lives or are unknown to readers. A common complaint by students is "Why do we have to read *this* book about people who are not like us?"

Our *Of Mice and Men* example illustrates these variables of literary fiction: a story set during a past historical period with people placed in a rural Western United States context that includes descriptive writing, dialogue between characters, and storytelling by an author skillfully employing literary devices in his craft. What this book might mean is something that student readers need to explore with their teacher.

Writing Conventions

In addition, literary fiction can contain a huge range of writing conventions and use of language. Students might read noncontemporary prose with more intricate and lengthy sentence structures by authors such as Nathaniel Hawthorne, Charles Dickens, or Edgar Allan Poe. Students might encounter unfamiliar dialects in works by Zora Neale Hurston or Mark Twain. Students might have to resolve unconventional narrative structures, such as stories told out of sequence or by multiple narrators. Students are also likely to be expected to infer meanings of unfamiliar general vocabulary, words infrequently used in conversation but which surface as the more precise language of written texts. A random stop on a page in *Of Mice and Men* reveals the words *lumbered, brusquely, pantomime, contemplated, imperiously,* and *terrier*—vocabulary that can be difficult for many students.

Literary Terminology

Unlike our science, social studies, and mathematics examples, however, the discourse of literature does not necessarily appear on the page of the novels and short stories read by students. Instead, the disciplinary discourse of English classes appears in the discussion and analysis of literary works. Terminology such as *figurative language, metaphor, simile, flashback, foreshadowing, satire, irony, parody, diction, allusion,* and *symbolism* are all vehicles for describing and explaining the author's craft as readers wrestle with developing an interpretation of a literary text. In effect, readers must pick up that an author is using irony even though the word *irony* is nowhere on the page. There is also the discourse of composition (e.g., *thesis statement, parallel structure, present tense*), the discourse of grammar (e.g., *noun, conjunction, adjective, complex sentence, modifier*), and so forth.

The discourse of literature provides a disciplinary tool for communicating recognition of an author's moves in writing a work and communicating understandings of that work. For example, readers should be aware that *Of Mice and Men* is an allusion to a line in the "To a Mouse, on Turning Her up in Her Nest With the Plough" poem by Robert Burns ("The best laid schemes of mice and men go often askew") as they consider possible ideas that Steinbeck is exploring through his story. Of course, many of our students would rather just read the story and not spend all that time delving into it using this disciplinary terminology.

Mentoring Literary Readers

Given that the reading of written texts is central to the English language arts curriculum, it is frequently assumed that it is the English language arts teachers who should shoulder the responsibilities for the development of adolescent readers and writers. Yet, English language arts teachers protest that they are not trained reading teachers either, and clearly the English language arts curriculum does not encompass the type of disciplinary texts that are prevalent in science, social studies, mathematics, and technical fields.

However, readers of literature also need mentoring. As Lee and Spratley (2010) observe,

> Just as there is little direct instruction about how to tackle the problems that disciplinary texts pose in history, science and mathematics classrooms, there is also insufficient attention in literature classrooms to the nuts and bolts of how to read a range of literary texts. (p. 9)

In a wonderful disciplinary literacy resource for English language arts teachers, Gallagher (2004) makes a strong distinction between assigning reading and teaching reading: "When it comes to reading challenging text, not enough attention has been paid to understanding the steps we can take to provide effective scaffolding for our struggling readers" (p. 7). He describes a series of classroom literacy practices that take readers through surface understandings to second-draft readings that engage readers in focused rereadings and collaboration to construct deeper understandings of complex literary works.

> **"**
> Our students CAN become readers if they are provided with consistent and explicit support to use strategies that they do not yet use on their own, and if these strategies are developed and then used with big purposes and relevant tasks in ready view.
> **"**
> —Wilhelm, Baker, & Dube, 2001, pp. 238–239

Smith and Wilhelm (2010) sum up mentoring students to read through a literary lens:

> It seems so obvious that we should teach students how to do what we want them to do, but sadly, many reviews of what and how we teach in our English language arts classes show that it is rarely done. In our experience, however, rather than focus on teaching students how to read literature, teachers often

substitute teaching two other foci: technical vocabulary and the details of a particular interpretation of a text. (p. 10)

Instructional ideas on reading through a literary lens are emphasized in subsequent chapters.

PARTING THOUGHTS AND TALKING POINTS

- Teachers can, and indeed need to, teach reading comprehension. Comprehension instruction emphasizes explicit modeling and support of fundamental comprehension processes: making connections to background knowledge, generating questions, creating visual and mental images, making inferences, determining importance, synthesizing, monitoring, and problem solving.

- Comprehension instruction must be embedded in the teaching of the discourse of an academic discipline to support learners as they increasingly assume some of the attributes of insiders. Content teachers, as masters of their disciplinary discourse, are the people best positioned to mentor their students as they experiment with using comprehension strategies to learn within specific academic disciplines.

- Reading through a disciplinary lens involves immersion into the discourse of a discipline. Students gain experience with reading, writing, hearing, and speaking the talk of an academic discourse and gradually adjust their thinking to correspond to the way scientists, historians, mathematicians, fictional authors, and other disciplinary experts think when engaged in reading and learning in their respective disciplines.

- Teachers need to examine the role that written texts need to play in the learning within their disciplines. Students who are not expected to read, or who can rely on being told or shown what they need to know, do not develop their capacities as readers of disciplinary complex texts.

CHAPTER 3

Teaching to the Match: Bridging Academic Knowledge Gaps

Essential Question: How do academic knowledge gaps affect the reading of disciplinary texts?

What would a reader have to know if the following passage is to make any sense? Obviously, you would need to know meanings of words, but what about deeper knowledge? As you read the following paragraph, make a mental inventory of all the knowledge a reader must bring to this text if comprehension is to occur:

> The key to much of Yemen's modern history lies just to the north in Saudi Arabia. The kingdom squats atop Yemen on the map like a domineering older brother with a rebellious sibling. Starting in 1962, the Saudi royal family viewed Yemenis' democratic aspirations with alarm and began paying hefty stipends to tribal sheiks throughout the country to reinforce its influence. Later, the Saudis began spreading their hard-line strand of Islam throughout the country, with help from some like-minded Yemenis. Hundreds of religious schools sprang up teaching Salafism, the puritanical sect that denounces all other sects as heresy. (Worth, 2010, p. 39)

What did you notice as necessary reader background knowledge? Clearly, there are language variables at play in the paragraph. A reader must be conversant with sophisticated general vocabulary (e.g., *squats, domineering, rebellious, sibling, aspirations, hefty, stipends, strand, denounces*), but it is certainly possible for a reader to be very comfortable using each of those words and still be mystified as to what the author might be talking about. Readers also must also be tuned into social science discourse (e.g., *democratic, tribal, sheiks, hard-line, puritanical, sect, heresy*), which involves extensive conceptual knowledge, as discussed in

Chapter 2. The author also does some name-dropping (e.g., *Yemen, Saudi Arabia, Islam*), expecting that readers will recognize that the first two references are countries and the third is a major religion.

Yet the complexity of this passage can hardly be ascribed to merely hard words. Beyond vocabulary, readers must activate several packets of considerable knowledge to facilitate an understanding of this paragraph:

- *Geography:* The part of the world the author is talking about and the proximity of these two countries to important geopolitical centers like Iraq, Iran, Israel, and Afghanistan
- *Political realities (historical and current):* From Arab–Israeli tensions to Al Qaeda activity
- *Regional culture, history, and politics:* Of Saudi Arabia, its royal family, and its connection to hard-line Islam
- *Governments:* How different governments are organized (e.g., kingdom, democratic, tribal sheiks) and how people might respond to these different governing structures
- *International relations:* The ways some countries attempt to influence other countries, including the propriety of one country making payments to potential dissident groups within another country
- *Religions:* How sects behave, what a puritanical sect would believe, what religions regard as heresy, and how a sect would act if it denounced heresy
- *The religion of Islam:* Awareness of schisms within Islam, conflict between different branches of believers, the role of Islamic fundamentalism in today's world, and the connotation of *religious schools*, which as used here by the author is dramatically different from religious-affiliated education, such as parochial schools that operate in the United States
- *Family dynamics:* The author's use of a simile for comparison ("like a domineering older brother"), how such a relationship might play out, and how each country might feel about its role in this ongoing interchange

Needless to say, there is a lot going on underneath this paragraph; what the author does not tell us is the most important variable in our comprehension of this passage as readers. Of course, this Yemen example is illustrative of any disciplinary text that students might be asked to read. As teachers, we may underestimate how critical prior knowledge is to reading comprehension. Our instructional role in addressing academic knowledge gaps is, without question, the starting point in mentoring students as readers, writers, and thinkers within our disciplines.

The Match Between Authors and Readers

How well you fared in your comprehension of the Yemen paragraph above was determined to a significant degree by what you knew before you even began reading. We tend to think of comprehension as the understanding of what an author tells us, but it is the implicit part—what is not on the page—that matters most. Consider for a moment whether you would have undertaken reading this article on Yemen if you had happened upon it. Your answer is partly an identity issue, as discussed in Chapter 1. Are you the kind of person who would elect to read an extended analysis about international affairs and events in other countries, in this case, about a relatively obscure place like Yemen? As we mentioned, identity has a huge impact on our reader profiles, especially personal selection of choice texts. A second possibility is that your interest might have been momentarily piqued by the author's teaser that appeared with the article: "Is this the next Afghanistan?" If a quick glance at the article had revealed an overload of unfamiliar references and terminology, then chances are good that you would have passed over this article and continued turning the pages of the magazine.

The ultimate question, then, is how well did you and the author match up. I decided that I was fairly well matched with the author when I encountered this article. My reader profile includes *The New York Times Magazine*, which was the forum the author used to communicate his ideas. My identity as a person interested in international affairs led me to want to know more about this part of the world. I felt reasonably well informed about the general topic areas. I caught a number of the references to specific people, places, ideas, and events (e.g., I know where the Arabian peninsula is, I remember the bombing of the USS *Cole*, and I know that Wahhabism is a radical Muslim sect). The author seemed to expect that while I would bring general knowledge about this region to my reading, I probably would not know all that much about Yemen, which was indeed accurate for me. So, I settled in and began to add more layers to my understanding of the political and cultural dynamics of a potentially important country. When a reader is well matched with an author, it seems that the reader is exactly whom the author had in mind when writing the text. This author was talking to me.

As readers, whether we consciously realize it or not, we are constantly scoping out the match with any text we read. When readers and authors match up, comprehension often seems to be a natural byproduct: We just read the text, and it makes sense. Of course, sometimes we are not well matched with an author: Some of what the author says makes sense, based on our prior knowledge, but some of the text escapes us. The author assumes that we know some things that we indeed do not know. My experience with the Renaissance music liner notes in Chapter 2 falls into this category of reading: I knew enough to figure out some of what the author was saying, but I was fully aware that my understanding was incomplete. My musician wife Wendy, however, was well matched with this author and came away with a deeper comprehension. When we are somewhat matched with an author, it seems like the author is mostly talking to someone else, and we are listening in, trying to pick up as much as we can but not totally getting it.

Finally, sometimes we as readers are mismatched. The author constantly refers to things that are unfamiliar to us, and we are soon overwhelmed by a text in which everything seems to be outside our knowledge and experiences. When we can make few, if any, connections to our prior knowledge, we struggle, we want to give up, we might even get angry, and we fail to comprehend. There seems to be no question that when mismatched, the author is definitely talking to someone else, and the conversation is totally going over our heads!

In our lives as readers, there are times when we have been well matched with authors, times when we have been unevenly matched, and times when we have been mismatched. That is of course true in our classrooms as well. When you sketched out your personal disciplinary profile in Chapter 1, you undoubtedly were thinking that the towers of literacy that revealed the shortest arrows were also probably those disciplines in which you felt least adequate with your background knowledge.

The central comprehension variable with any text that students might read in our disciplines is what this author assumes readers will already know. As teachers, we must then determine which of our students actually know what an author assumes and which do not. For our students who lack assumed knowledge, we face a critical teachable moment: How will our instruction address these knowledge gaps, and how will our instruction support readers who will struggle with comprehension without scaffolded assistance?

The Impact of Prior Knowledge on Reading Comprehension

In effect, a tacit agreement exists between authors and readers that underlies any act of reading comprehension. Authors have some obligations, and readers have some expectations. Authors have to decide just how much they need to say if a text is to make sense. They have to know to whom they are talking. Authors do not want to spend a lot of time telling readers things that the authors are fairly sure the readers already know. Otherwise, texts would become much too lengthy, and readers might soon become bored with the lack of newness or become frustrated with how much they have to wade through before they encounter something fresh. So, authors have to depend on their readers to fill in the unstated, implied knowledge while reading about what the authors anticipate will be the new stuff.

Assumed Knowledge

Authors try to trigger this process by dropping in references to assumed knowledge, but these references contain very little elaboration or discussion, which is where reader expectations come in. In Chapter 2, I described seven fundamental processes of comprehension. Paramount among these comprehension processes is making connections to prior knowledge. Proficient readers expect to make substantial contributions of their own when working to comprehend an author. Comprehension falls apart when readers cannot, or do not, connect their accumulated store of knowledge and experiences to what an author is saying.

With students, I have explained this dualism as overt knowledge and hidden knowledge. Overt knowledge is what an author directly tells readers; it is stated right on the page. Hidden, or assumed, knowledge is what readers are assumed to know; it is their prior knowledge and is not on the page. A reader needs both types of knowledge to comprehend. Readers who do not possess the necessary hidden knowledge to comprehend a text are thus stymied. They could read the text multiple times, and it still will not make adequate sense. What they are missing is not on the page; what they need is behind the words, hidden from view.

> **Knowledge begets comprehension begets knowledge.**
>
> —Pearson, 2011, p. 245

Of course, what I have described here as overt knowledge is the substance of our lessons, the new learning we have envisioned for our students. Overt knowledge tends to be the focus of our activities and the target of our assessments. Yet, the missing hidden knowledge undermines many reader efforts to comprehend disciplinary texts that present these new concepts, ideas, and information. In their seminal analysis of the research on learning from text, Alexander and Jetton (2000) draw a forceful conclusion: "Of all the factors considered in this exploration, none exerts more influence on what students understand and remember than the knowledge they possess" (p. 291). To state it another way, many of our students are unable to achieve satisfactory comprehension of disciplinary texts, not because they cannot read but because they lack the assumed knowledge that makes it possible for readers to make sense of the presumed new material. To return to our opening passage, our understanding of Salafism, the presumed new learning, is predicated on our assumed knowledge regarding religious sects that have puritanical beliefs and behavior.

Schema

Researchers (e.g., R.C. Anderson & Pearson, 1984) have referred to our prior knowledge banks as schema. Our schema represents networks of information, associations, and experiences that we activate and use when we interact with the world around us. So, when an author mentions Saudi Arabia and tosses in a few reminders about that country, in our minds as readers, we instantaneously touch base with our personal Saudi

Arabia schema, and all sorts of associations come rushing forth: oil, desert, sparsely populated, Middle East, Persian Gulf, monarchy, Mecca, and on and on. For many of us, however, Yemen may elicit relatively few prior knowledge hits in our memories. In this case, the author will need to directly tell us quite a bit more about Yemen if we are to achieve a satisfactory comprehension.

Figure 3.1 offers a dynamic representation of the fundamental comprehension processes outlined in Chapter 2. Prior knowledge (schema) is portrayed as the bedrock for comprehension. The questions we generate as we think about a text, the visual and sensory scenarios we create in our mind's eye through our imaginations, our ability to infer implicit layers of understanding, and our perceptions of the essence of a text—all involve a back and forth mental, and social, interaction with the knowledge we bring to a text as readers. Synthesis is what we make of a text, our take on it, our understanding which results in the creation of new schema: new learning, new prior knowledge that can be tapped for future

Figure 3.1. An Interactive Model of Comprehension Processes

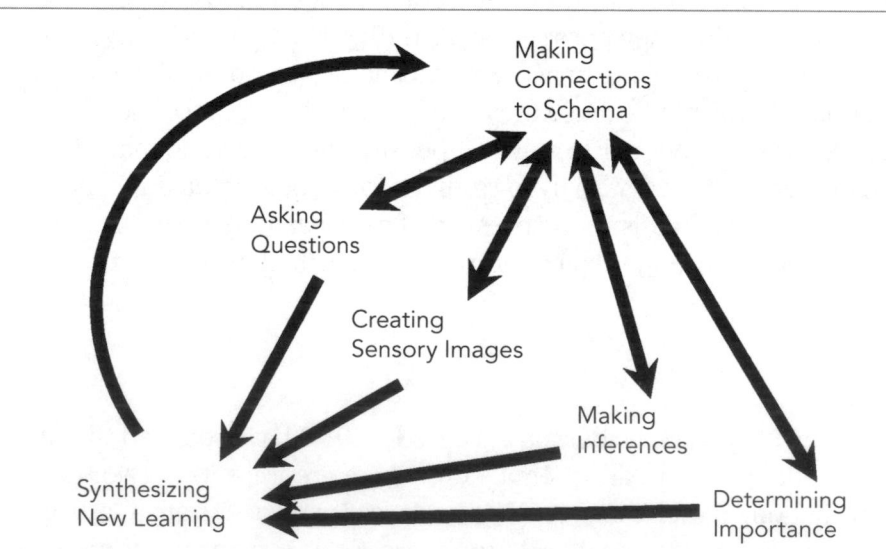

Note. From Buehl, D. (2007). A professional development framework for embedding comprehension instruction into content classrooms. In J. Lewis and G. Moorman (Eds.), *Adolescent literacy instruction: Policies and promising practices* (p. 204). Newark, DE: International Reading Association.

comprehension. To say this another way, comprehension starts with our knowledge base; the strands of thinking that comprise comprehension are extensions made possible by the knowledge we bring to a text. And comprehension may end with prior knowledge; if we are sufficiently mismatched by lack of knowledge, then we will be unable to question, imagine, infer, prioritize, and synthesize.

The Nature of Our Knowledge

It is useful to take a closer examination of our personal prior knowledge, or schema, that we rely on when engaged in comprehension. Once more, track the knowledge this second author assumes of readers as you read this short excerpt from an article from *The New York Times*:

> Nicotine provides a quick fix. With each inhalation, it is carried into the lungs, where it rapidly enters the circulation and moves quickly to the brain. There it binds to receptors and facilitates the release of various brain chemicals, especially dopamine, which induces feelings of pleasure that in turn reinforce the desire for more nicotine.
>
> [O]ver the course of a day, as the brain continues to be exposed to nicotine, partial tolerance develops and each subsequent cigarette produces less of an effect. But during sleep, nicotine comes off the receptors and smokers awaken with an intense craving for a cigarette. (Brody, 2010, p. D7)

Topic Knowledge and Domain Knowledge

As we examine the variety of prior knowledge assumed by this author, we can subdivide it into topic knowledge and domain knowledge (Alexander & Jetton, 2000). Topic knowledge represents a reader's background in and experiences with a particular idea or concept. As teachers, we are typically quite alert to what students might know about a topic that we are preparing to study. In this case, what did you know as a reader about smoking? You probably brought considerable knowledge about smoking, cigarettes, addiction to nicotine, links to lung cancer, development of emphysema, secondhand smoke, smoke-free workplaces, and so forth. Most readers of this excerpt will already possess a great deal of topic knowledge about smoking.

However, many readers will still find this complex text challenging to comprehend. In this case, the author wants to talk about some of the physiology of smoking, asking us to shift from a sort of general reading frame to reading through a scientific lens. Topic knowledge is insufficient. This is where domain, or disciplinary, knowledge comes in. Domain knowledge encompasses a reader's understanding of the vocabulary, concepts, processes, and thinking typical of an academic discipline. In Chapter 2, I extensively discussed domain knowledge as the discourse of a discipline. In this excerpt, the author employs science discourse (e.g., *receptors*, *dopamine*), but other implied domain knowledge includes some understanding of the chemistry of the brain, how systems work in our body, and how our body builds up tolerance to various substances that we ingest (e.g., foods, medicines, alcohol, drugs), which can lessen their effects. The amount of domain knowledge that you brought to this sample text determined the extent to which you could visualize the dynamics of nicotine binding to receptors and realize the implications of how nicotine stimulates a chemical response in the brain that results in a pleasurable yet addictive response for an individual.

Ways of Knowing

In addition, it is important to consider how you came to know what you know, in this case, your topic and domain knowledge related to smoking. It is helpful to look at three general ways of knowing (Harvey & Goudvis, 2007; see Table 3.1).

Text-to-Self Knowledge. First, you might have made text-to-self connections to the sample passage. To what extent does the author talk about things that have happened to you or that you have done? If you are, or have been, a smoker, then you would have been able to bring

Table 3.1. Ways of Knowing

Type of Knowledge	Source
Text-to-Self Knowledge	Direct knowledge accrued from one's personal life experiences
Text-to-Text Knowledge	Indirect knowledge resulting from one's reading and study
Text-to-World Knowledge	Vicarious knowledge based on our impressions of how things are, often obtained secondhand through others' interpretations and representations

substantial personal knowledge to your reading. As the author talks about inhaling cigarette smoke, the corresponding physical reaction of enjoyment, the continuing desire, the diminished impact of nicotine, and the morning craving for a cigarette, you can relate these comments directly to sensations that you have felt while smoking.

I have not been a smoker or lived with a smoker, so I bring very limited personal experience to this text. I can imagine what the author describes, but I will not understand it the way someone who has actually experienced it will. My wife grew up in a household with both parents who were smokers; she witnessed these dynamics close up, which influenced her comprehension of this paragraph. Text-to-self connections access knowledge that we have accrued through daily life; we know what we know because we have lived it.

Text-to-Text Knowledge. Luckily, we have other ways of knowing, although they may not be as powerful or evocative as life experiences. I made a number of text-to-text connections to knowledge about smoking that I had obtained over the years through my reading and learning. It is likely that we have all read numerous texts, in newspapers, magazines, books, or online, that gradually and incrementally have built our topic knowledge about this subject, and this passage represents just one more.

Yet, while we know things because we are readers, which can build topic knowledge, we also know things because we have been students, which is a primary way of building domain knowledge. For example, I can recall reading books and articles about the brain and remember descriptions of neurotransmitters, how these brain chemicals are stimulated and released, and how they influence the functioning of brain cells. Scientists could bring firsthand text-to-self laboratory experiences to their comprehension of the smoking passage, but many of us have read about and studied aspects related to this topic. Our habits of developing text-to-text knowledge through our schooling are critical to our abilities, and inclinations, to continue to add to our topic and domain knowledge as lifelong learners through reading. We can turn to text-to-text connections when we lack direct personal experiences; we know what we know because we have read about it and studied it.

Text-to-World Knowledge. Our third potential source of knowledge is text-to-world connections. This knowledge is more nebulous than the first two. We gradually gain impressions about how things are through an amalgam of sources: other media (e.g., television, movies, Internet sites), listening in on other people's talk about their experiences, visual and nonverbal outlets (e.g., photographs, works of art), and so forth. In other words, some of our knowledge is neither based on our direct experiences nor specifically on our reading and learning. Instead, some of our knowledge is a sort of secondhand knowledge, pieced together from multiple sources, frequently through our interpretations of other people's representations of reality.

We are constantly developing theories and ideas about how things are. We may not even be able to say how we have arrived at some of the knowledge we hold. When we say "I heard that..." or "I thought that...," we are probably negotiating the vast but often vague realm of text-to-world knowledge. Although a nonsmoker, I can dip into the deep reservoir of my ever-evolving, sometimes indistinct mass of thoughts, ideas, insights, attitudes, and understandings related to the topic of smoking. Much of the knowledge we bring to reading comprehension is text to world; we know what we know because that is how we have figured things out.

REFLECTION INTERLUDE

Revisit the chapter-opening excerpt. Try to identify six sources of knowledge that you bring to the topic of Saudi Arabia (see Figure 3.2). Enter how you know what you know under the categories of "Text-to-Self," "Text-to-Text," and "Text-to-World." For example, I have watched the classic movie *Lawrence of Arabia* several times; this source of knowledge, whether accurate or not, would be placed under "Text-to-World."

Figure 3.2. Considering How You Know What You Know

Text-to-Self Knowledge	Text-to-Text Knowledge	Text-to-World Knowledge

Of course, these knowledge categories play out very arbitrarily in real life; our knowledge types quickly merge, and blur, into those complex clumps of knowing that we term schema—prior knowledge. Yet, the implications for us as teachers are enormous. What our students know about a topic before they even start reading dictates to a large degree their ability to comprehend and learn from a text on that topic.

In addition to general knowledge about a topic, authors of disciplinary texts also expect students to bring some domain knowledge. Some of our students are comfortable with this disciplinary discourse, and some are not. Some of our students bring relevant personal experiences to the texts that we ask them to read, which will be highly advantageous to their comprehension, and some do not. Some of our students have previously read materials that have built foundational topic knowledge, and some have not. Some are quite adept at accessing previous learning, and some are not. Some have developed a sense of how things are that will provide logical stepping stones into our lessons, and some have not. Prior knowledge is a make-or-break variable for the comprehension of disciplinary texts, and some of our students bring much more of it to our classrooms than others.

Confronting Academic Knowledge Gaps

As you think about the students you work with daily, you would not be alone if you found the preceding discussion more than a bit daunting. We are well aware as teachers that our students arrive in our classrooms with dramatically different stores of prior knowledge. As discussed in Chapter 2, the temptation is sometimes great to bypass our students as readers, given their struggles with comprehension, and focus instead on telling, demonstrating, and interacting. However, we are not nurturing independent learners if we choose this path. Instead, we need to gear our instruction to addressing these knowledge gaps that are roadblocks to reading comprehension.

Informal Knowledge and Academic Knowledge

In their analysis on learning from text, Alexander and Jetton (2000) distinguish between unschooled or informal knowledge, and schooled or formal knowledge. As Marzano (2004) indicates, all of our students bring to the classroom an extensive store of informal knowledge. However, because students grow up in different circumstances and have lived different lives, the particulars of this general knowledge vary widely among individuals. For example, nearly all of our students know things about smoking; it is probably inevitable that smoking would have intersected with their lives in numerous although hardly identical ways.

It is also likely that many of our students know virtually nothing about Saudi Arabia from their out-of-school lives. The geographical, cultural, historical, and political knowledge that some of us have about this country is an example of schooled knowledge, or what many researchers term academic knowledge. Academic knowledge is central to the study of the various academic disciplines and is narrower and more prescribed than the more general informal knowledge.

Academic knowledge is comprised of both topic and domain knowledge. Marzano (2004), Hirsch (2006), and others have documented a significant disparity among our students in academic knowledge. Some students bring a wealth of academic knowledge accumulated from their out-of-school experiences, and others arrive in the classroom with very little to draw on that specifically relates to the content being studied. Many of the things that a number of our students do indeed know qualify as informal knowledge and do not surface in the school curriculum. Hence, their prior knowledge has significant holes when it must accommodate the new learning of academic disciplines. In contrast, some of our students are more fortunate in that their out-of-school knowledge features a rich mixture of both informal and academic knowledge. They arrive primed to add to what they already know.

Access to Academic Knowledge

To a large extent, these academic knowledge gaps can be attributed to a matter of access (Marzano, 2004). Some of our students have significant points of access to academic knowledge in their out-of-school lives, and some do not. One critical point of access is people: Some of our students have grown up around parents, family members, peers, community members, and other adults who regularly engage in conversations related to topics that will turn up in the school curriculum in the future. These students have observed individuals from their out-of-school lives reading and sharing about such topics and often have been invited to participate. The school focus on these topics becomes merely an extension of the conversations that these students have already been long engaged in.

The second major access point to academic knowledge is experiences: Some students have already seen and done things that will be part of disciplinary learning. As teachers, we know that field trips can provide text-to-self personal experiences for our students, but some individuals have been taking family versions of these field trips for as long as they can remember. These students have visited historical sites, regularly attended museums (starting perhaps with children's museums), taken part in library programs, viewed art in galleries, witnessed science fairs, benefited from enrichment programs, participated in specialty camps, and most important, have traveled. Students lacking these two access points—people and experiences—may have developed impressive informal knowledge but are constantly confronted with mastering academic knowledge that is totally new territory as they embark as learners in our disciplines.

Academic Knowledge Disparities

Marzano (2004) portrays these academic knowledge differences by describing nine students, each with a different profile and each of whom we are likely to meet in our classrooms each day. Figure 3.3 is a representation of Marzano's conceptualization, which displays the interaction of two key variables: academic background knowledge and processing ability.

Students With Matchup Assets. Let's start with Student 1, a quick study who already knows a substantial chunk of what we will be teaching. Student 1 is a fast learner who ironically has much less of the curriculum to master because of extensive prior academic knowledge established before the lesson from out-of-school experiences. Consider my oldest son, Jeremy, who developed an early and keen interest in history, just as I did. He thus had numerous interactions with a family member whose reading, conversations, activities, and travels often focused on historically related

Figure 3.3. Academic Knowledge Disparities

Out-of-School Academic Knowledge

High ← — — — — — — — — — — — — → Low

	High		
High	**Student 1:** • High academic knowledge • High processing ability	**Student 2:** • Moderate academic knowledge • High processing ability	**Student 4:** • Low academic knowledge • High processing ability
Processing Ability	**Student 3:** • High academic knowledge • Moderate processing ability	**Student 5:** • Moderate academic knowledge • Moderate processing ability	**Student 7:** • Low academic knowledge • Moderate processing ability
Low	**Student 6:** • High academic knowledge • Low processing ability	**Student 8:** • Moderate academic knowledge • Low processing ability	**Student 9:** • Low academic knowledge • Low processing ability

Note. Based on *Building Background Knowledge for Academic Achievement: Research on What Works in Schools*, by R.J. Marzano, 2004, Alexandria, VA: Association for Supervision and Curriculum Development.

topics. For example, I can vividly remember watching the 1990 Ken Burns public television series on the U.S. Civil War side by side with Jeremy. One memory in particular stands out: I had a meeting one evening and missed the first part of that episode. When I arrived home, I asked Jeremy what had transpired. My 9-year-old son looked up indignantly, made a gesture of futility, and snorted derisively, "McClellan!" His response was gratifying from a historian perspective because it revealed that he not only had obtained a meaningful association (i.e., McClellan was an exasperatingly indecisive Union general during the Civil War) but also understood what McClellan "means." Jeremy requested the series on videotape as a Christmas gift and watched it several more times while thumbing through my numerous books on the topic as well as those he checked out from the library. Do you really think he had much new to learn by the time he studied the Civil War in the eighth grade?

Students 2 and 3 also tend to be thriving in our classrooms, and although their performances in school look remarkably similar, these two students bring quite different profiles to their learning. Student 2 is acquainted with some academic knowledge but is able to pick up additional learning from the curriculum rather readily. Although highly able, Student 2 entered the lesson already less knowledgeable than Student 1, of course. Student 3 comes to lessons with a wealth of academic knowledge, which helps compensate for the extra time needed to absorb new learning. We are likely looking at the preponderance of A's and Bs in our grade books with these first three students, and the crucial variable is not our instruction but rather their out-of-school academic knowledge.

Students who arrive in our classrooms with extensive stores of academic knowledge because of rich out-of-school access points are highly likely to be treated, and labeled, as smart. Certainly, having an identity as the kind of person who is smart is a decided advantage, especially in school contexts. Yet, how much of what we regard as smartness is achieved through ready access lines to academic knowledge? Also, how many of our students evolve identities that being smart is either something you are or are not?

Students With Matchup Gaps. Students 4, 5, and 6 provide the most stunning contrasts. Again, they may look similar in their classroom performances, but they are vastly different individuals. Each is struggling with some elements of disciplinary learning. Student 4 is constantly discovering that there are few opportunities to make text-to-self connections to the curriculum. As classmates share how their life experiences link to curricular topics, Student 4 is clearly realizing that school has apparently little to do with his or her out-of-school realities. Student 4 will likely have extensive informal knowledge—interpersonal strengths, community-based know-how, popular culture savvy, skills with animals or agriculture, street smarts, and so forth—but is rarely able to capitalize on this knowledge in school. Student 4 is shrewd enough to realize that Students 1 and 2 do not have more ability, but they outperform him or her academically because of out-of-school academic knowledge. Therefore, it can become increasingly difficult for Student 4 to give top effort, especially when other similarly able classmates do not but still have more success with classroom tasks.

Student 4 is at risk for being demoralized and turning to out-of-school identities for direction and fulfillment. Student 4's performance may resemble Student 5's, who has to work at the curriculum but has somewhat less new material to master, and Student 6's, who struggles with learning but likely has a deep home support system and brings a lot of text-to-self academic knowledge to learning. Finally, there are indicators that Student 6 is more likely to attend college than Student 4, which is ultimately the cost of unattended academic knowledge gaps.

Students With Mismatches. Students 7, 8, and 9 must work hard to keep their heads above water in disciplinary learning. Students 7 and 8 perform at a similar level on classroom tasks, although Student 8 may have an Individualized Education Plan for exceptional educational needs. Student 9 is even more likely to have an Individualized Education Plan. It is interesting how much discussion on special education needs focuses on skill deficiencies when academic knowledge gaps are one of the most obvious barriers to learning for students who need a high degree of instructional support.

An additional variable comes into play with English learners, whose out-of-school and informal knowledge may lack cultural and societal knowledge. In addition, English learners may struggle to articulate in English the knowledge they do possess, or they may struggle with academic vocabulary (Short & Fitzsimmons, 2007).

REFLECTION INTERLUDE

It is easy for me to interject names and faces from my teaching career into each of the profile boxes displayed in Figure 3.3. Consider a class that you currently teach or have taught. As you think about these students, decide which ones exhibit the characteristics of each of these nine prototypes. Which students bring academic knowledge gaps to your classroom? What is your overall class profile in terms of academic knowledge?

Marzano (2004) sums up his research on background knowledge by isolating the critical role of poverty and the resulting limits to access of out-of-school academic knowledge. Students in poverty need schools and teachers as primary access points to academic knowledge. Yet, it is perplexing, even ironic if not sobering, that the most crucial academic access points for poor children—our schools—are places that may be ill equipped, and sometimes ill disposed, to teach these students. Our instruction may be best designed to serve Students 1, 2, and 3, who arguably need us the least, and be least hospitable to those students who need us the most.

I am reminded of a conversation I had years ago, as a school literacy coach, with one of our science teachers. As we talked about student troubles with reading biology, he remarked in frustration, "It's not that they can't read. They just don't know anything!" All hyperbole aside, in this case, at least, readers were lacking biological academic knowledge; they could read words, but many students truly struggled with making sense of the biology text. At this point, let's return to the essential comprehension question highlighted earlier in the chapter, what does an author assume readers already know? and the corollary question for us as teachers, which students have this assumed academic knowledge, and which do not? Finally, the instructional question, what do we as teachers do to address readers' academic knowledge gaps? How do we teach to the match?

Building Academic Knowledge Bridges

The research presented in this chapter underscores why, as teachers of adolescents, we cannot merely assign reading and hope for the best. The challenge for teachers is one of mediation: How can we be effective mediators between the academic knowledge demands of our curriculum and the out-of-school, often informal knowledge of our students? Sometimes, this dichotomy may starkly appear as an either–or choice. Either we plow resolutely ahead through our curriculum, heedless of crippling academic knowledge gaps, or we wallow in the predominantly informal knowledge brought by students and shortchange teaching the academic knowledge of our disciplines. I have managed, in the preceding sentence, to present both extreme alternatives in negative lights, but one could argue that many of us make good-faith attempts in our classrooms that unfortunately tilt heavily toward one end of this spectrum or the other.

Instead, our instruction needs to seek a middle ground, a teachable terrain between the extremes of academic knowledge and discourse, which is a considerable distance from many of our students, and student-centered approaches that honor everyday informal knowledge, which may be a considerable distance from our standards and curriculum. Moje and colleagues (2004) conceptualize this middle ground as a third space, where instruction acknowledges the informal knowledge capital that students bring as a bridge to the academic knowledge essential to disciplinary learning.

In Chapter 1, we explored the links between identity and reader profiles. Many of our students develop perceptions that the learning of our academic disciplines is not about them, that schooled knowledge does not intersect with the lives they lead and the identities they have established for themselves. Because their background and experiences may contrast considerably from school realities, the potential is high that some students will be confronted with the dissonance of competing knowledge and identities. Unlike students who have benefited from high access to academic knowledge in their out-of-school lives, students with academic knowledge gaps may actually have to face a significant identity change when engaged in disciplinary learning. These students may need to start to see themselves as the kind of people who can use academic knowledge in science, history, mathematics, literature, and other subjects to more deeply understand their lives and their world, as well as to expand their definitions of their lives and broaden their perspectives of their world.

If learning is to accomplish such identity changes, however, it somehow has to be intertwined with students' everyday realities. For students like my son, everyday realities and knowledge often meld seamlessly with academic realities and knowledge. However, for many students, instruction has to explore a third space that bridges these two realities. As Moje and her colleagues (2004) note,

> Building bridges is a necessary part of what makes third space because it helps learners see connections, as well as contradictions, between the ways they know the world and the ways others know the world.... Building bridges simply connects people from one kind of knowledge or Discourse to other kinds. (p. 44)

Consequently, instruction also needs to support students in navigating between these multiple knowledge bases and identities, and in challenging what they know (and what they study) as they strive to merge everyday knowledge resources with disciplinary learning.

As teachers, we may overlook everyday funds of knowledge available to our students in our preoccupation to meet our obligations to teach our curriculum. Yet, it is important to remind ourselves that in actuality, our charge is to meet our obligations to teach our curriculum to the students we meet each day in our classrooms. Such an approach emphasizes that we accentuate student knowledge assets rather than bemoan knowledge deficits. Especially for those students who arrive with alternative and competing knowledge bases, disciplinary learning needs to be predicated on sharing, connecting, and expanding knowledge rather than on exposing ignorance. Otherwise, students will come to recognize that the privileged knowledge in disciplinary learning is rarely the knowledge of their lives and world. Students will be at risk for feeling marginalized, become disconnected from academic tasks and texts, and be resistant to developing identities that are compatible with reading, writing, and thinking through different disciplinary lenses. The persistence of achievement gaps is one result.

Building these knowledge bridges is, of course, easier said than done. As Conley (2009) observes, regarding this emerging vision of disciplinary literacy, "it is not entirely clear what comprehension instruction might look like from a perspective balanced delicately between students' knowledge and literacies and academic texts and discourse" (p. 537). Yet, exploring potential common-ground knowledge is essential for disciplinary learning, especially for the reading of complex texts that build academic knowledge. Also, here is where the disciplines diverge in terms of how their academic knowledge intersects with out-of-school knowledge. What might bridge-building instruction look like in mathematics, science, technical subjects, literature study, or history? What possible topic knowledge, perhaps in a general and nonspecific sense, might students bring to the study of core concepts of a discipline, even when students lack domain knowledge? To answer these questions, teachers obviously need to get to know their students and to be sensitive to the out-of-school knowledge and literacies their students bring to the classroom.

What constitutes a third space in the discipline you teach? What are some areas in your curriculum that reveal significant academic knowledge gaps with many of your students? Focus on one topic area. Consider what knowledge capital students bring to the classroom that might represent ways of bridging out-of-school knowledge with academic knowledge.

Teaching to the Match in History and the Social Sciences

Some social science disciplines, notably psychology and sociology, lend themselves directly to the text-to-self knowledge of students' lives and identities. Others, such as cultural geography and political science, intersect with current events and times but may be distant from students' out-of-school experiences. History, the social science discipline most frequently taught, can be especially problematic.

Generational Knowledge

A key matchup variable in the study of the social sciences, especially the study of history, is generational knowledge. Understandably, the bulk of prior knowledge that students bring to social science disciplines is text-to-self generational knowledge: what students know related to their lives and times. Some of this knowledge is cultural and shared by us all; we all, regardless of our ages, are living during a current epoch that has seen wars in Iraq and Afghanistan, the Bush and Obama presidencies, Hurricane Katrina and the Gulf of Mexico oil spill, a serious economic downturn, and spirited national dialogue on issues such as immigration, health care, and gay rights. However, it is important to realize that a 17-year-old high school senior in 2011 was 7 when the September 11, 2001, terrorist attacks occurred, and the Clinton years are the stuff of history books.

Furthermore, much of the generational knowledge of our students can be subdivided into the various and often dissimilar slices of youth culture, much of which may not be shared by the rest of the population. What music do adolescents listen to? What video games are the current rage? What technologic applications are common practice? What movies, television, and online media are students watching? Who are the admired and emulated figures? What are the accepted social mores? This facet of generational knowledge can become quickly fragmented, as the wide range of student identities that I talked about in Chapter 1 will influence how individuals and subgroups of youths would weigh in on each of the items in these questions. While as teachers, we may wish to move quickly beyond generational knowledge in our disciplinary teaching, social scientists—historians, sociologists, psychologists, economists, and political scientists—are fascinated by all of this. Ironically, once such professionals have studied and digested the culture, practices, and behavior of this current generation, future students are likely to read about it in future textbooks.

So, a major issue of teaching to the match in the social sciences is how generational knowledge, in which our students are immersed and which is highly motivational, can be hooked into the specific disciplinary goals of the social studies curriculum. For students, especially when studying history, this discord between generational knowledge and the academic knowledge of history frequently leads to the challenge, whether blurted out loud or just quietly simmered, "So what?" "So what if this happened? So what if they did this, if they believed this, if they accomplished this? This is not us, so why should we care? Facts, facts, facts—so what?" Before you know it, the dreaded plea for relevance has reared its pesky head.

Topic Knowledge and Domain Knowledge

Generational knowledge is not the only matchup issue in history, of course. Topic knowledge and domain knowledge are also unequally distributed among a typical group of students. As discussed earlier in this chapter, some students have out-of-school lives that have included frequent and rich contacts with the academic knowledge of history, and some have not. Obviously, as adults, we have some text-to-self experiences within a narrow band of history that reflects our generational knowledge. I was a child in the 1950s and an adolescent during the 1960s. I can tell you where I was when President John Kennedy was assassinated. The Vietnam War was central to my daily life for many years, including the years when I was of draftable age. The Civil Rights movement was a daily story line in the newspapers and on television.

Yet, even though these were events of my times, I was not personally present in Dallas in 1963, I did not personally serve in Vietnam and witness the war upfront, and I was not on the bridge in Selma or in the throngs in Washington, D.C. to hear Martin Luther King, Jr.'s "I Have a Dream" speech. My topic and domain knowledge is mainly text-to-text (i.e., I read about these events) and text-to-world (i.e., I watched these incidents on television, saw them portrayed in movies, and heard others express their firsthand experiences). My text-to-self knowledge of much of this generational history was relatively modest; for example, I was a student at the University of Wisconsin–Madison during the era of fervent antiwar protests.

The same is true for our students, who bring limited text-to-self experiences to the study of history. Some of our students will have firsthand experiences with places associated with history through their travels and with artifacts of history encountered in museums and other historical sites. Yet those individuals who possess topic and domain knowledge will have gained most of it through text-to-text (i.e., personal reading) and text-to-world (i.e., conversations with others and learning from other media) experiences.

Text-to-World Knowledge

Text-to-world knowledge can be particularly problematic for the study of history, as stereotypes, common wisdom, and misinformation may all be packaged together as prior knowledge about topics under study. Lee and Spratley (2010) note that movies are a particularly powerful and pervasive source for the construction of text-to-world knowledge in history, yet movies are not especially reliable sources of historical academic knowledge. (Have movies like *Lawrence of Arabia* helped me develop a reasonably accurate understanding of the Arab world, a stereotypic perspective, or perhaps some of both?)

Movies are highly effective in evoking viewers' use of imagination to promote understanding, as watchers can imagine themselves having a text-to-self experience through the actions portrayed on the screen. Yet filmmakers bring a different intent and perspective to the stories of history than do historians. Were the stories developed in, say, *Saving*

Private Ryan or *Dances With Wolves* how things actually were or merely how the filmmaker chose to represent those times and those people? In addition, text-to-world knowledge is also intricately intertwined with the various individual student identities that interface with disciplinary learning. Students may believe what they believe because of who they are and how they see themselves and their lives.

Textual Allusions

Finally, text-to-text matchup discrepancies are significant for the study of history. First, history texts feature a great deal of name-dropping—textual references to the domain knowledge of names, events, locations, practices, ideas, and so forth. Many of these references are intratextual allusions, in which the author expects readers to connect a reference to things the author had told the reader previously in that section or earlier in the work. Readers are therefore expected to carry this domain knowledge after it was introduced, throughout their ongoing reading of the text. When I refer to domain knowledge in this section, I am asking you to think back to previous passages in this chapter that discussed this concept, compelling you to make an intratextual connection.

Second, historical works contain many intertextual allusions, which require the reader to make connections to other texts independent of the specific text an individual is reading. I referred above to Martin Luther King, Jr.'s "I Have a Dream" speech, which is not included in this book but about which I assume you have knowledge. Both King and his famous speech are intertextual allusions. Intertextual allusions are especially prevalent in primary documents and newspaper and magazine articles, in which authors assume that readers will make a number of connections that extend outside the text being read. Intertexual allusions are dependent on assumed reader knowledge, or what I termed hidden knowledge earlier in this chapter, another intratextual allusion. It is this domain knowledge of factual references that can be overwhelming to students who are encountering it all as substantially new learning and who almost never experience this type of name-dropping in their out-of-school lives.

> **"**
> Engaged readers negotiate textual understandings by linking information both within and outside of the text(s)... that they are reading.
> **"**
> —Hynd et al., 2004, p. 147

Essential Themes and Ideas

One highly effective tack for social studies teachers, especially teachers of history, is to identify essential questions that target transcendent themes and ideas of human experience and interactions. (Chapter 5 explores essential questions in more depth.) These themes and ideas can be connected to events and realities of students' lives as analogous relationships; students, too, have struggled with such circumstances.

For example, a central focus in world history during the study of feudalism could be who gets what and who decides. Adolescents are hugely interested in who gets what and who decides in their personal lives. During the unit on feudalism, students will see how these issues played out during this period of history, in effect studying feudal Europe as a case study of how people have resolved the question of who gets what and who decides. The factual details, the domain knowledge, become a means to study this dynamic in depth, as students examine how and why certain societal structures emerged, who benefited from these structures and who did not, and why and how such structures endured. Students can bring multiple insights from their personal lives as they track how the world worked for peasants and nobles, royalty and common folk.

Using the Past

The Thinking Like a Historian model, developed by Mandell and Malone (2007), pinpoints five focal points for mentoring students to read, write, and think through a historian lens. This model is explored more thoroughly in Chapter 5, but one of the five points of emphasis is using the past. Students are continually prompted to ponder how the past helps us make sense of the present.

As historians delve to understand the implications of studying the past, they constantly ask themselves, so what? Awareness of antecedents of current realities is one critical objective associated with using the past, as students come to perceive the backdrop behind life today and develop insights into how events leading to the present have unfolded. A second objective is examining the potential for using the past to inform future decisions.

However, not all history lends itself to the goal of using the past, as Mandell and Malone (2007) caution:

Using the past responsibly requires finding the useable past. In order to find the useable past we must be able to discriminate between those events and aspects of the past that are relevant to and those that are not relevant to the event under study. (p. 21)

For example, does studying some of the significant battles of World War II lend itself to using the past? Or, are these events that although they are part of the big picture and may be interesting, really do not particularly contribute to understanding how we have arrived at today, given what transpired during that tumultuous world period of upheaval? Time is always tight, and as teachers of history address standards, they are especially confronted with the need to narrow down what history (and actually which history and whose history, much more contentious territory) to target for instruction.

Teaching to the Match in Science

Part of the tenuousness of our personal knowledge base in science is that science knowledge does not tend to stay put. Instead, as lifelong learners, we, just like scientists, need to continuously evolve our understandings to reflect new evidence, new findings, new explanations, and new theories. Hence, a critical role of complex texts in science is to present ongoing evidence-based alternatives to unschooled conceptions of the physical and biological worlds.

Domain Knowledge

Text-to-text connections are highly significant in science reading. In particular, science texts present even more intense matchup challenges in terms of intratexual allusions than do history texts, as discussed earlier. Science authors expect readers to carry a great deal of domain knowledge from chapter to chapter. While a page of a science textbook, for example, is rife with the discourse and terminology of science, much of this technical vocabulary reflects assumed previous learning. Students with science academic knowledge gaps are particularly at risk for becoming overwhelmed by this mix of prior science learning with new concepts and information.

Unlike in history, students bring considerable text-to-self experiences to their study of science. They have all lived in the physical and biological worlds, and the study of science can be directly related to multifarious facets of their out-of-school lives. Whether instruction actually does so is another matter. Students often find science texts to be extremely esoteric and not much grounded in their life experiences. As Pearson and colleagues (2010) note, "Typical science textbooks are dense and disengaging to inexperienced science readers….Science teachers have little access to well-designed texts that readers can understand given their developing knowledge base and varying reading skill levels" (p. 460). Students are likely to bring some topic knowledge of the physical and biological worlds, whereas science texts tend to focus predominantly on domain knowledge, particularly the discourse and factual details of science. Many students may be at a loss to connect the discourse of science to their out-of-school topic knowledge and experiences.

Text-to-Self Experiences

Of course, there is great variety in the nature of scientifically relevant text-to-self experiences to which students would have had access. Some students will bring much richer connections to plants and animals, for example, than others. I grew up on a dairy farm and spent the days of my youth in woods, swamps, meadows, and fields. Although I lacked much of the domain knowledge of science, I brought considerable topic knowledge to the classroom. When my high school biology teacher told us that the vestiges of the old Wisconsin prairie remain intact on railroad rights-of-way, which were systematically burned off each autumn, I could personally connect to my frequent hikes along the Illinois Central tracks, waist deep in prairie wildflowers. I grew up on terrain located at the outer edge of the age of glaciation, and I had too many opportunities to recount for picking up rocks discarded by the retreating glaciers in our farm fields. I lacked the domain knowledge of *drumlin, kame, esker, kettle,* and *moraine,* but I could personally recognize each of these features from the landscape of our area of the state. I knew how floodplains worked, as our cow pasture was in a floodplain, although using nonscientific language, we referred to this land as river bottom.

Contrast what I have just described with students who have grown up in urban settings. While they too spend their lives in the physical and biological worlds, they will bring a different set of experiences to the classroom, and their topic knowledge may be primarily text-to-world experiences (e.g., television is a likely source of potential scientific knowledge), especially if students have not had introduction to science concepts through personal travel, proximity to knowledgeable others, and trips to repositories of science information like museums, science-oriented exhibits, nature centers, wildlife refuges, state parks, and community sites. As Krajcik and Sutherland (2010) conclude, "eliciting prior knowledge becomes especially important when concepts are abstract, when scientific principles seem distant from students' everyday lives, and when students' experiences lead them to develop inaccurate ideas" (p. 457).

Science Misconceptions

Text-to-world knowledge presents somewhat unique matchup issues with science texts. Not only do many students lack topic and domain knowledge, but they also frequently bring flawed understandings, naive interpretations, and misconceptions to their reading of science texts. (Some students, of course, will bring identities to the classroom predicated on interacting with the world through a religious lens. The dynamic described here is a different one: mistaken scientific reasoning.)

Gardner (1991), known primarily for his work in multiple intelligences, marshals the impressive array of research on misconceptions and misunderstandings in a fascinating analysis called *The Unschooled Mind: How Children Think and How Schools Should Teach*. He concludes that children develop naive and erroneous theories about how things are in the world (i.e., part of their text-to-world knowledge), and that in spite of education to the contrary, they tenaciously adhere to these misunderstandings throughout life. Even some of our most impressive students, Gardner observes, still view much of life through the lens of their 5-year-old minds. We all are apparently particularly prone to clinging to flawed notions of the scientific world, and such misconceptions are a frequent and powerful impediment to student learning in our classrooms.

When students' out-of-school knowledge conflicts significantly with the academic knowledge of a discipline, especially science, students are more likely to partition their understandings into "what I need to know while I'm in this class" and "what I really know about things."

Science Through Telling

Because many students struggle with the density of domain knowledge emphasized in science texts, science teachers have frequently, and justifiably, veered away from what some observers call text-centric science and instead overcompensated by one of two ways: teacher presentations, which essentially substitute telling for reading, or hands-on science, which engages students primarily in doing science. Teacher presentations, lectures, and demonstrations have the advantage of efficiency in covering content, and such an approach sidesteps student–text mismatches. Yet, as the new Common Core State Standards for Literacy in Science and Technical Subjects 6–12 (NGACBP & CCSSO, 2010) recognize, student proficiencies in accessing science learning through written texts are not developed with a telling approach. Reading Standard 10 of the Standards document explicitly states that middle and high school students will "read and comprehend science/technical texts in the grades 6–8, [9–10, or 11–12] text complexity band independently and proficiently" (p. 62) Students cannot meet this science reading standard, nor the other nine, in classrooms where telling is the predominant mode of accessing science knowledge.

The second default approach also tends to shift students away from reading science. The advantages of a hands-on, or inquiry, approach are obvious: Students are provided with daily text-to-self experiences while interacting with scientific concepts and phenomena. Science learning that can be highly abstract is instead translated into concrete applications. The disadvantages of a predominantly hands-on approach are that students do not receive adequate practice and instruction in reading complex texts in science. As Webb (2010) relates,

> The uncritical belief that hands-on science activities automatically lead to understanding has been replaced with the realization that this is a necessary, but not sufficient, approach. What is needed are minds-on experiences that include discussion, planning, reading, and writing, as well as deliberations and argumentation. (p. 448)

Reading and Inquiry

Researchers argue that science instruction should more closely mirror reading, writing, and thinking through a scientific lens. Scientists take an inquiry approach to engagement with scientific concepts and phenomena and certainly do science as they interact with materials and processes in laboratories, but they also read extensively to build a pertinent knowledge base, and they write about the results of their investigations. As Pearson and colleagues (2010) observe, "Scientists use texts to generate new research questions and to provide the background necessary for research design and investigation" (p. 460). These authors suggest a multimodal instructional model that addresses matchup issues in science by adopting an inquiry approach. This approach begins with significant questions and student hands-on experiences, then additional processing and discussion, followed by student reading of complex texts to deepen knowledge, culminating with student writing that synthesizes understandings, and then continuing on to the next inquiry phase. In this model, the reading of complex science is embedded in the inquiry approach, and reading follows initial classroom knowledge building.

Teaching to the Match in Mathematics

Matchup issues with reading mathematics texts rank among the most severe in disciplinary learning. At the heart of student difficulties with mathematics texts is the fatalistic perception carried by many students who are convinced that they are mismatched as math learners in general.

I witnessed many of these matchup issues in mathematics firsthand during the years I coordinated a high school tutoring program that offered support to students needing additional assistance with learning in their content classes. Our most frequent request for tutoring assistance was for algebra; students would arrive asking for some facet of algebra to be explained and modeled one more time. Although the students would invariably have their algebra textbooks in tow, they might as well have been carrying a rock, given how little they had developed their ability to work such texts to resolve confusions and lack of understandings. Instead, these students were solely preoccupied with being walked through problem-solving steps yet again, so they could tackle assigned problems and complete their homework. Yet, without internalizing the mathematical conceptual knowledge, the students would leave still dependent on being told what they will need to do when facing the next assignment.

Math Identities

In Chapter 1, I discussed how the span of multiple identities assumed by individuals influences personal reading profiles. It is certainly a truism of education that a disappointingly large number of students come to mathematics instruction with identities of people who are not good in math. Especially when it comes to the more advanced mathematics of middle and high school, most especially algebra and geometry, substantial numbers of students, and often their parents, feel no qualms about publicly announcing, "I just don't get math." In his analysis of research on mathematics learning, Willingham (2009) debunks this notion that some people just cannot do math, concluding, "Virtually everyone is fully capable of learning the numeracy content and skills required for good citizenship: an understanding of arithmetic procedures, algebra, geometry, and probability deep enough to allow application to problems in our daily lives" (pp. 14–15).

Text-to-Self Knowledge

The vast distance between many students' out-of-school mathematics experiences and the academic knowledge of mathematics disciplinary learning accentuates these feelings of math inadequacy. Many students do not perceive that reading and thinking through a mathematics lens has much to do with applications to problems in their daily lives. At best, students may see basic computational skills as the extent of their text-to-self real-world math applications, and of course, real-world computation may be viewed primarily as technology-assisted calculation. However, as to interacting with and understanding the continuous swirl of numbers that inundate our daily lives in almost every facet—to perceive the world at times through a mathematics lens—many students, and adults, fall short.

Observers such as Paulos (1988/2001), who has written extensively on innumeracy, have documented the struggles that people have in reasoning mathematically when trying to understand and act on the world around them. Mathematics textbooks may address this disconnect between out-of-school realities and mathematics academic knowledge through modeling by using realistic examples and problems that are constructed to simulate real-world scenarios. Yet, as Moje, Stockdill, Kim, and Kim (2011) observe, "The difference is subtle, but significant, and bears restating: Although 'mathematics' texts may be realistic, they are not typically real-life" (p. 468). They do not engage students in real-life text-to-self connections, yet students tend to adhere to a highly pragmatic point of reference for mathematics learning. Their text-to-world conceptualization of mathematics is that math is something you do, something you use. Quite frankly, many students do not see themselves doing or using mathematics classroom problem solving in their out-of-school, or real-life, existence, especially with the higher level applications in algebra, geometry, and beyond.

The National Mathematics Advisory Panel (2008) report, commissioned by the U.S. Department of Education, reviews the research on the use of real-world contexts for introducing and applying mathematics concepts. Although the number of studies was too small to justify policy recommendations, the panel notes that such an approach demonstrated a positive impact on certain types of problem solving.

Types of Domain Knowledge

Mathematics texts, of course, are heavily geared toward the domain knowledge of mathematics. Topic knowledge in mathematics seems more encompassed in the scenarios within which mathematics concepts are applied; students know something about situations within which thinking mathematically can be undertaken. The National Mathematics Advisory Panel (2008) report outlines three types of domain knowledge in mathematics: factual, procedural, and conceptual (see Table 3.2).

Procedural and conceptual knowledge are of particular importance to readers of mathematics. As discussed above, students tend to associate mathematics learning with procedural knowledge, the how-to methods for doing math. Mathematics texts ostensibly map out, section by section, various problem-solving routines, replete with examples, sample problems, and student applications. Generally, students will lobby for the teacher to tell them and show them this procedural knowledge rather than construct their own understanding through interactions with a mathematics text.

Table 3.2. Mathematics Domain Knowledge

Type of Knowledge	What It Is	Why It Is Critical
Factual Knowledge	In-memory and automatic access to basic math facts in addition, subtraction, multiplication, and division	Frees up thinking to engage in more extensive, higher order problem solving
Procedural Knowledge	Knowledge of and facility with the use of algorithms—series of problem-solving steps—that can lead to certain problem solutions	Focuses on how to use mathematics principles and presents systematic routines for problem solving
Conceptual Knowledge	Deep understanding of the logic behind factual and, most important, procedural knowledge	Centers on why specific mathematics relationships and processes make sense

However, significant issues with reading through a mathematics lens concern the domain area of conceptual knowledge. Students may endeavor to mimic the steps of an algorithm to solve designated problems without really internalizing why this is so. Much of mathematics conceptual knowledge is vocabulary driven; the discourse of mathematics is, of course, pervasive in mathematics texts. Yet students need to go beneath surface definitions of mathematics terminology; their understandings must extend to deep conceptual insights that are triggered by math terms. The National Mathematics Advisory Panel (2008) report concludes that although factual and procedural knowledge continue to need attention, conceptual knowledge is the area of mathematics domain knowledge that is particularly lacking. As Willingham (2009) reflects,

> Learning new concepts depends on what you already know, and as students advance, new concepts will increasingly depend on old conceptual knowledge.... If students fail to gain conceptual understanding, it will become harder and harder to catch up, as new conceptual knowledge depends on the old. Students will become more and more likely to simply memorize algorithms and apply them without understanding. (p. 18)

Lack of conceptual knowledge, arguably, leads to misconceptions as to what it means to think mathematically.

Role of Previous Learning

Failure to develop conceptual knowledge is arguably the crux of why so many students feel they cannot learn mathematics through reading math texts and must rely instead on their teachers to explain domain knowledge. Math texts, possibly more than in any other discipline, require readers to carry over significant previously encountered concepts and certainly language. The text-to-text knowledge demands of math texts are both heavily intertextual and intratextual. Authors of mathematics texts make constant references to foundational mathematical concepts that preceded a specific course of study, and of course, these authors refer regularly to mathematics concepts that were introduced in earlier sections and chapters of the current text that students are reading.

Students will frequently declare that math texts are hard, or indeed impossible, to understand because of all the difficult math terminology. Yet, for a given lesson, only a couple of new concepts are generally introduced and explained. What is challenging for readers, however, is that these new concepts, and terms, are defined and explained using the language of previously taught mathematics concepts. Students struggle to read mathematics texts in large part because such texts are predicated on what students have previously learned, and many students have not truly learned this conceptual knowledge at a deep and flexible level of understanding.

Text Features

When students comment that "we don't read in math," it is also due to the concise and compacted nature of mathematics prose. Students are least likely to read extended texts in mathematics; instead, they engage in very careful and analytical reading of precisely worded, conceptually deep sentences, which are illustrated and developed with examples, graphic displays, and mathematics notation. Such sentences have to be deconstructed, as readers verbalize their understandings of concepts from the past as they work out the logic of the new slice of mathematics knowledge. Readers literally have to hit the pause button after each sentence and work through the way past learning is being extended into deeper applications. As discussed in Chapter 2, mathematicians value rereading as a primary strategy for reading mathematics texts.

Teaching to the Match in Literature

In some respects, the "Reading is fun!" and "Enjoy reading!" messages that often permeate our libraries and language arts classrooms may also trigger potential mismatches with literary texts. Although these ubiquitous messages are intended to be inspirational and motivational, they also condition students to expect the stories and novels they read in English language arts classes to conform to these recreational reading standards of pleasurable ways to spend leisure time, perhaps comparable to television watching, movies, and video games. Certainly, devoted readers would maintain that their time spent in reading is as pleasant as, or indeed superior to, these other relaxing pastimes.

Yet, literary texts perform a deeper function than entertainment, and in our classrooms, such texts are more likely to be obligation texts rather than choice texts, as discussed in Chapter 1. As a result, students can be particularly harsh critics of literary works that present a challenge, and may regard reading such texts as anything but fun. Indeed, there is an ongoing tension in language arts classrooms between developing individual reading habits, which emphasizes helping students determine their tastes and preferences as readers as they build their general reading capacity, and introducing students to literature, which mentors students to perceive the world through a literary lens and builds their capacity to read complex literary texts. Both goals are examined in this section.

Reader Preferences

Certainly, developing readership is an important goal of education, and of English language arts classrooms in particular. In a frequently cited study, *To Read or Not to Read: A Question of National Consequence*, the National Endowment for the Arts (2007) concludes,

> There is a general decline in reading among teenage and adult Americans. Most alarming, both reading ability and the habit of regular reading have greatly declined among college graduates…. As Americans, especially younger Americans, read less, they read less well. Because they read less well, they have lower levels of academic achievement. (p. 3)

The National Endowment for the Arts (2007) study documents significant declines for 13- and 17-year-olds in daily reading habits from

1984 to 2004. Less than a third of 13-year-olds report daily reading activity, and nearly 20% of 17-year-olds are essentially nonreaders in their daily lives, a figure that doubled during the 20-year stretch of the study. The report criticizes schools for not developing a culture of daily reading habits and notes the impact on academics.

In addition, over the years, Guthrie and his associates have examined the potent role of student choice in motivation and engagement as readers. In particular, Guthrie (2008) argues, some measure of student choice of reading material is necessary to nurture self-directed readers and confront the following all-to-familiar reality for teachers of adolescents: "Students read too little, and they rarely read for deep understanding. They seldom read to expand their sense of who they are as people" (p. 1). (In Chapter 4, I detail the advantages of developing the habit of wide reading, which not only builds reading capital and is associated with vocabulary growth but also provides access to background knowledge that extends far beyond direct individual experience.)

Literature and Identity

Hence, a significant matchup issue for students as readers of literature is the contention between "texts I would want to read" and "literary texts that I am compelled to read." As Conley (2009) relates, there are distinct and divergent perspectives within English education that advocate different approaches to instruction and selection of texts that weigh into this dynamic, including the inevitable disagreements about a literary canon. Suffice it to say that identity is a critical variable when examining the match between authors and readers of literary fiction and that exploring that identity is a crucial function of reading literature.

In their research review on disciplinary literacy, Lee and Spratley (2010) note that although students may bring backgrounds and experiences that are far removed from the world being represented in a work of literature, students can use elements of their lives and interpersonal interactions to ponder this world and consider its implications for understanding themselves. "Overall, reading deeply complex literary texts offers unique opportunities for students to wrestle with some of the core ethical dilemmas that we face as human beings" (Lee & Spratley, 2010, p. 11). In other words, students' text-to-self knowledge is the springboard into the examination of the human condition that can be sparked by literary works.

Gallagher (2004) describes this necessity to be proactive in connecting readers to literary works as "framing the text" (p. 37). Framing a text is instruction that eases students into a mind-set for reading, as they do some prethinking about ideas and themes that surface in a work, and touch base with how elements of their personal lives may intersect with the work. Such prereading instruction contrasts with sending readers into a text cold and unprepared to navigate a challenging literary work. Instead, framing instruction attempts to forestall frustrations with specifics of a story that might be highly unfamiliar by focusing thinking on universal conditions to which students can relate. (Chapter 4 presents instructional practices that engage students in this prethinking before reading.)

Hypertexts

Complex literary texts, such as short stories, novels, and plays, are examples of extended texts, some of which are book-length. In addition to the factors mentioned previously, reading such texts mandate perseverance and reader stamina. Of course, in our classrooms, these literary works still primarily appear as print texts. Considerable scholarship has examined the nature of hypertexts, online reading, and new literacies. Although many of our students may not be spending much out-of-school time reading books, newspapers, and magazines, students are certainly increasingly engaged in interacting with a variety of forms of electronic texts, from websites to social networking, such as Facebook and texting. As a result, English language arts teachers face significant matchup issues with students who are tuned into the buzz of electronic reading and writing and who may regard print texts as "so 20th century."

In addition to the more subtle distinctions between reading a novel in print form versus reading it on a Kindle or iPad, students are accustomed to electronic texts that present stark contrasts to complex literary works. In his research review of meaning making within and across digital spaces, Tierney (2009) describes hypertext as a kind of labyrinth that must be navigated as readers pursue their purposes for reading, make decisions as to the route they will follow, and employ inferring, predicting, and evaluating as central comprehension processes. Hypertexts offer the possibility of integrating multiple modalities into digital communications, from visual links, to video clips, to ways that readers can interact with the technology, especially with gaming. Teacher responses to the digital text-to-self and text-to-world knowledge and experiences of our students range from embracing it to lamenting it, but for the purposes of this section, the main challenge for English language arts teachers is the need to mentor students on how to read complex literary texts.

Textual Allusions

Not only do authors of literary works assume that readers will access personal knowledge of the human condition and interpersonal interactions, but also readers are commonly also expected to bring insights into other times, other places, and other cultures that tap into sometimes considerable text-to-text and text-to-world knowledge. A persistent theme of Hirsch's (2006) criticisms is that academic knowledge gaps cause readers to miss these intertextual allusions and undermine readers' ability to understand complex texts. Literary authors may reference other texts (e.g., myths, Shakespeare, the Bible), drop names (similar to what historians do), and assume readers' general world knowledge that cuts across disciplines (e.g., a reference to psychoanalysis, Amazon rain forests, genocide, baroque music, or viral infections). Of course, we can build a considerable fund of this knowledge through our reading of literary works, but the load of unfamiliar knowledge references will also affect whether we are able to read such texts at a deep level or merely skim along superficially at the surface.

Domain Knowledge

The domain knowledge inherent in reading literature, unlike in other academic disciplines, is generally implicit. As discussed in Chapter 2, literary fiction functions as an indirect communication, which means that readers must develop an interpretation of an author's message, ideas, perspective, and purpose. Domain knowledge flows as an undercurrent through comprehension of literature and mainly centers on the author's craft and how literary fiction works. Readers are expected to recognize a number of literary genres, within and beyond the general categories of short story, novel, poetry, drama, and essay—for example, myth, memoir, fable, allegory, coming of age, satire, polemic, critique, and irony.

Much of the domain knowledge of literature study concerns the rhetorical tools employed by authors (e.g., symbolism, narrative point of view, figurative language). In effect, students need to be tuned into not only what the author says but also how the author says it; the way the author says it provides potential clues into what the author might mean. Many students, however, quickly lose patience with this analytical eye toward what is lurking beneath the words on the page, and instead beg to be allowed to just read the story, as they are accustomed to reading popular fiction. Clearly, developing an appreciation for seeing the world through a literary lens is a major matchup issue for many students.

In his manifesto *Readicide: How Schools Are Killing Reading and What You Can Do About It*, Gallagher (2009) decries a trend in English language arts classes away from teaching novels and more challenging works. He argues that underteaching, and sometimes overteaching, complex literary works lies at the core of the matchup problems that students encounter with these texts. Students need to be mentored to recognize the difference between liking a work of literature, which may or may not happen, and gleaning value from reading that work, which is why struggling with a complex text is so worthwhile.

Teaching to the Match in Technical Disciplines

A set of instructions to operate a piece of equipment, a recipe, a software help site, a blueprint, directions for assembling an item, a pattern, steps to follow in an exercise routine, a manual, an accounting textbook, nutrition guidelines—all are examples of texts that require technical reading. In an analysis of workplace literacy demands, the American College Testing Program (2006b) identifies a number of facets related to comprehension of technical texts, including

- Correctly use technical terms when describing the main idea and supporting details in a passage…
- Select important details to clarify meaning
- Apply straightforward instructions to new situations
- Apply complex instructions that include conditionals to situations described in a passage

- Figure out the correct meaning of a word based on how the word is used
- Understand the definitions of acronyms defined in a passage...
- Apply technical terms to stated situations
- Apply given information to new situations (pp. 4–5)

The American College Testing study concludes that students must attain a comparable level of readiness as readers of complex texts if they are to be successful at either the college level without remedial assistance or in workplace training programs that develop job-specific skills.

Hands-On Reading

I have referred to these types of nonfiction texts as hands-on reading because the intent behind comprehending such material is to act on your understanding in some way; you literally read and do when you engage in technical reading (Buehl, 2009a). As a result, technical reading is quite difficult to accomplish in a decontextualized environment. To fully comprehend, you need to have available all the items, and tools, referred to in the text, and you tend to read such texts in spurts—read a section, clarify your understanding, complete steps of the process or operation, return to the text, read another section, and proceed with accomplishing the task at hand—so reading comprehension is interspersed with action.

Many of our students, not to mention adults, find technical texts intimidating. A lot of us would greatly prefer that another person tell or show us what to do, rather than slogging through what sometimes seem to be inadequate or even inscrutable directions or procedures. It may seem that the only persons likely to make sense of some of the technical texts that we must decipher are exactly those people who already know what to do and hence do not need to carefully read these texts. Because technical texts are integral to hands-on activity, we may gamble that we can skip the reading entirely and tackle the hands-on part without benefit of the written instructions. Our task may degenerate to a trial-and-error, start-and-restart intuitive fumbling around rather than proceed as a self-directed, logically conceived sequence of steps guided by a technical text.

A personal anecdote illustrates this text-avoidance dynamic that represents a major matchup concern for technical reading. The first time my wife and I used a GPS navigation system was upon the purchase of a new car. We were becoming increasingly comfortable with the display options on the vehicle's computerized screen and managed to figure out how to program an address for the navigation system. The "GPS lady" kindly and emphatically guided our way to the target destination, but when we left, she became increasingly annoying as she tried to send us right back to where we had just left. We became frustrated with trying to reprogram and then disable the system, maneuvering through several screens, and finally my wife, who was driving, tensely ordered me "to get out the [expletive deleted—my homage to the Nixon tapes] manual." Even though it took some problem solving, as not everything stated in the manual was appearing on our screen, we deliberated, eventually discovered what we were doing wrong, and were finally able to quiet our imperious GPS companion. Both of us, who pride ourselves as readers, were frustrated with our initial inability to understand this text and act on our comprehension. Of course, we all live in an increasingly sophisticated technological environment, amid a wealth of computerized items for which we paid dearly and very likely underuse because of our reluctance to consult the technical texts that accompany them.

Assumed Knowledge

When one lacks prior knowledge, it is not only difficult to make something work but also difficult to read about how to make something work. As citizens of a technological world, many of us lack sufficient text-to-self experience, as well as the text-to-world knowledge, as to how things work and how things should be done. It is a truism today that if we cannot figure out how to accomplish a technological task, then we should ask a kid to do it for us. Yet our students are not necessarily any more inclined to engage in technical reading when their text-to-self knowledge fails them.

Text Features

Technical texts tend to be terse and get right to the point, without much in the way of introduction to or motivation for the reader. Completing the task successfully is regarded as sufficient motivation to interact with such complex texts. Authors of technical texts base their message on assumptions that readers will bring considerable domain knowledge, most particularly that readers will already have experience with doing the task.

These texts are typically packed with technical terminology, without much elaboration, and usually alternate between informative sentences and visual displays, such as diagrams and illustrations. Readers may have to infer meanings of such vocabulary, using definitions that may be steeped in technical language as well as the labeling in the pictorials. Of course, the domain knowledge is discipline specific, whether it is a computer context, an applied technology context, a family and consumer education context, a physical education context, or technical texts that might surface in other disciplines, such as the instructions for conducting an experiment in a science context.

Teaching to the Match in World Languages

Teachers of world languages have undoubtedly noticed that factors from several other disciplines intersect with instruction in language classrooms. An important slice of the curriculum in Spanish, French, German, or other world languages centers on building cultural awareness as well as facility with communicating a new language. Hence, many of the issues discussed in the Teaching to the Match in History and the Social Sciences section have relevance to world language teachers as well.

Cultural Knowledge

A handful of students will have experienced foreign travel and be able to draw on text-to-self connections to texts that address cultural aspects of people who speak a particular language. However, for most students, cultural knowledge will be text to world; what students know about a country or region will likely be heavily influenced by media such as television and movies. Often, these cultural perceptions may be simplistic or even stereotypic, an issue that can be compounded by the limits of world language texts that introduce cultural knowledge. Because such texts serve dual purposes—to also teach the structure of a language and key vocabulary—and because students have not yet developed the capacity to read more sophisticated, or nuanced, explications of culture, it is difficult to build text-to-text cultural knowledge unless supplemental texts in English are also sometimes used for this purpose.

Thus, teachers must mediate the tension between students' abilities to develop more in-depth cultural understandings with their lack of capacity to acquire such knowledge through reading texts in their new language. Because of the nature of world language texts, class efforts to augment text-to-self cultural knowledge through explorations of customs, cuisine, music, and perspectives have considerable value. Cultural artifacts brought to the classroom, guest speakers, field trips to area establishments and sites that hold cultural significance, interactions with local members of a language community, exchange programs, and ultimately foreign travel can affect the cultural knowledge variable.

Domain Knowledge

Likewise, world language teachers will find that a number of the observations in the Teaching to the Match in Literature section of this chapter are also relevant to teaching their discipline, especially as students become sufficiently accomplished to begin to read some literary texts in the new language. However, in addition, there is a great deal of domain knowledge that correlates with disciplinary learning in English language arts that is central to learning a second language, especially involving syntax. Language arts terminology, such as *noun, verb, direct object, nominative case, accusative, article, passive voice,* and *past participle*, are central to analysis of the structure of the language, as students gain insight into how a language works and how they can reproduce that language as speakers and writers.

We can intuitively pick up the usage of these language subtleties through long-term immersion within a language, as we did as we learned our first language, even though we may not have mastered the domain labels associated with these various facets of language. Yet, in school, we attempt to fast-track language learning. As a result, world language teachers often find that they must teach much of this analytical terminology themselves if they are to expect students to use such knowledge as tools for interacting with a new language.

Identity and Language Learning

Teaching to the match in a world language inevitably must take into account some significant identity factors that influence reading, writing, and thinking through a second-language lens. Certainly, some students will bring an identity of "I am the kind of person who picks up language quickly." Other students will bring heritage identities; for example, unsurprising given my surname, I have a German heritage. I brought at least a level of eagerness to learn more about the language of my people when I studied German in high school. In addition, some students will bring an already developed acquaintanceship with a language, perhaps because it is spoken by family members or in the community.

Yet the largest group of students will bring the identity of "I am the kind of person who needs a world language on my transcript for college." World language teachers attempt to convince students to at least entertain the notion of a bilingual identity: "I am the kind of person who is comfortable communicating in two languages." However, students' willingness to undertake language learning for achieving that ambitious goal is a constant issue, and language learning is often relegated to a lower priority status than mathematics, science, literature, or other subjects.

Finally, unlike teachers of other disciplines, world language teachers have to navigate all three levels of the model of increased specialization of literacy development, as described in Chapter 1, as a regular dynamic of instruction. Language teachers build basic literacy in the language (i.e., conversational vocabulary, introduction to syntax), intermediate literacy (i.e., the vocabulary of print texts; fluency in reading, writing, speaking, and listening; more sophisticated language structures), and disciplinary literacy (i.e., cultural knowledge, literary traditions).

Teaching to the Match in the Arts and Humanities

Although there is an extensive literature about art, music, and other humanities, students do not tend to associate the study of those disciplines with reading complex texts. This tends to be especially true in music performance classrooms (e.g., band, orchestra, chorus) and applied art classrooms (e.g., drawing, painting, ceramics, jewelry design). Both of these contexts are perceived to be hands-on experiences, and students tend to be resistant to reading about art and music, expecting instead that they will be told anything that they need to know.

Yet it is also important to realize that one of the four passages on the American College Testing entrance exam is always a humanities excerpt that may feature writing about art, music, architecture, dance, or some other facet of the fine arts, and the SAT for college entrance similarly includes such prose passages. Clearly the implication of these assessments is that students are not reading complex texts in the arts and humanities for the first time when taking these high-stakes tests on a Saturday morning.

Specialized Vocabulary

Of course, students do associate reading music with their music performance classroom experience, and both music and art, like other disciplines, rely extensively on insider discourse. In both disciplines, students are expected to respond with understanding to specialized vocabulary. Musicians are expected to adjust what they are doing based on language that is generally Italian in derivation, and in addition, singers must read and vocally communicate understanding of written lyrics. Likewise, disciplinary vocabulary in art, such as *form, line, shape, color, texture,* and *space,* have significant meanings in art texts that contrast with general usage; also, terms such as *value* and *proportion* contrast with their precise mathematics meanings, *harmony* and *rhythm* differ in art from their musical connotations, and *unity* is a different concept in art than in social studies.

Reading Short Texts

Yet there is also a place for interludes in the flow of the daily creation of art and music for deeper learning about art and music, facilitated by interactions with complex texts within each discipline. My wife, a middle school orchestra teacher, fairly bristles when adults, or fellow teachers or certainly her students, intimate that she represents a nonliterate discipline. Although most of the daily class minutes are spent developing the students as musicians, folding in the reading of short texts—excerpts elaborating on the music and pieces being studied as well as inquiry projects that engage students in deeper exploration—mentors students as readers of complex texts in the humanities. My wife argues that she is the portal to the rich tradition of writing about music—from background on composers and musical genres to reviews, concert program analyses, and CD liner notes—and if students do not access this disciplinary literature through her, then when will it ever happen?

Humanities texts such as in art and music, especially with art history and music history, share many characteristics described earlier for social science texts. In addition, some of the texts in these disciplines also qualify as technical texts, and the discussion in that section also applies here.

Teaching to the Match in Health and Fitness

Students also come to health and fitness classes with an expectation of physical involvement not the reading of complex texts. Yet an extensive literature on health, fitness, and wellness is central to the landscape of this discipline.

Explaining Why

Certainly, the modeling of exercise routines and recreational activities that provide physical tuning and general health receives primary emphasis in the physical education curriculum, but in addition to what to do and how to do it, students need a steady dose of why: Why is it important to exercise various muscle groups, why does cardiovascular activity matter, why do certain physical activities benefit the body, and why do our lifestyle choices affect our overall health and fitness? The why layer of understanding is probably the most difficult to establish and needs to go far beyond telling if it is going to stick and influence our students' physical health as they transition into adulthood and the rest of their lives. Complex texts in health and fitness play a central role in inculcating why our body thrives on certain physical routines and personal habits.

Vocabulary Knowledge

Students tend to read complex texts in the health curriculum, and these texts present many of the same issues as for biological science. Such texts are heavy with domain knowledge regarding how the body works and the relationship of certain behaviors to a person's health. Certainly, authors of health texts use some of the discourse of physiology and anatomy, and this discipline-specific vocabulary adds complexity and challenge to these texts. In addition, the health curriculum can draw on a daily store of health-related articles from newspapers, magazines, and websites. Popular-press texts are especially valuable to integrate into daily learning, as these articles tend to be written for the general population and are intended to raise awareness and encourage behavior change.

Personal Experiences

Students bring powerful text-to-self knowledge to health and fitness classrooms; students all have extensive knowledge of what it means to live in their bodies and have witnessed, or have indulged in, many of the behaviors that are addressed in the curriculum. Of course, this text-to-self knowledge also can manifest itself in denial: Although they may concede that something may be generally true for people, students may deny that it is true for themselves. Or, they may deny that something is true because it conflicts with their personal experience. You may hear comments like this: "My grandfather smoked two packs of cigarettes every day for over 70 years, lived to be 92 years old, and never got cancer. How do you explain that?" Although that statement happens to be true of my grandfather, I bring lots of domain knowledge to my reading about smoking that includes an understanding of risk factors, probability and inevitability, variations in the physical makeup of human beings, the impact of other lifestyle variables, and I guess, just plain luck. This example underscores why the physiology of health and fitness needs to be embedded into the learning about healthy choices and routines.

Text-to-World Knowledge

Students also receive conflicting messages about health and fitness through the media, especially television and movies, which results in problematic text-to-world knowledge. This is especially true of commercial messages, which are intended to repeat claims in order to influence consumers. Who is more believable, the health and fitness curriculum or the pervasive and often slickly conceived onslaught of competing representations of "truth"? As such, students may pay lip service to what they study in the health and fitness curriculum while "understanding" at a deeper level the misconceptions or misinformation that surrounds them in popular culture. Again, complex texts are a critical way to reinforce that the curriculum is more than "our opinion" and is based on sound scientific research and practices.

- Students may have learned effective comprehension strategies that structure their thinking about and understanding of written texts, but their success as readers may still be stymied by lack of academic knowledge.

- Authors assume that readers will already know part of what they will need to know to comprehend the message communicated. Readers who lack this assumed knowledge will falter in their comprehension, regardless of their general skills as readers.

- Many of our students come to our classrooms with low access to academic knowledge in their out-of-school lives. As a result, these students will face disciplinary texts that present a higher degree of unfamiliarity of assumed topic and domain knowledge.

- It is unlikely that individual students will be uniformly proficient or struggling readers across the curriculum; they are likely to be more successful in some content environments and less successful in others.

- Students need to become increasingly comfortable with the insider language of academic texts; students have to develop the facility to talk the talk of an academic discipline.

- Instructional strategies that build appropriate academic knowledge and encourage students to share relevant prior knowledge are essential for comprehension of complex texts in the various academic disciplines.

CHAPTER 4

Frontloading Instruction That Activates and Builds Academic Knowledge

Essential Question: What instructional practices should precede the reading of complex disciplinary texts?

As teachers, we realize that reading assignments are an important way for students to build background knowledge in our disciplines. Yet the research in Chapter 3 exposed limitations to this approach: If students lack prior academic knowledge, then they are less likely to build that knowledge through reading assignments. Teachers often compensate for these shortcomings in two ways. First, when students are assigned reading, teachers follow up with presentations that ensure that students are apprised of key material. In effect, as teachers, we hedge our bets; because we do not have faith that many of our students will get what they need to get on their own, we make sure that we also tell them what they need to know. The downside of this first approach is that students (i.e., all students not just struggling readers) very quickly figure out that they do not need to work a text to understand it; what they will be held responsible for learning will be handed to them in class presentations. As a result, students do not develop their capacity to independently access knowledge in the discipline.

Second, teachers may forgo reading assignments, as discussed in Chapter 2. Students do not even encounter complex texts in a discipline when this approach is followed, and they become totally dependent on someone else orchestrating their learning for them. Students very soon realize that effective listening, not competent reading, will be the pathway to acceptable classroom performance. It is apparent that the Common Core State Standards for reading in history and social studies, science, and technical subjects are a direct counterpoint to the tendency to avoid the reading of disciplinary texts.

Comprehension research suggests a different tack: Rather than expecting to build academic background *through* reading, we recalibrate our instruction to build academic background *for* reading. Rather than introducing concepts through reading, we introduce concepts before reading. Students then explore and develop these concepts more deeply as they engage as readers with complex texts. Frontloading—the teaching that addresses academic knowledge gaps—activates and builds hidden knowledge assumed by authors before students read. As teachers, we rearrange our instruction to frontload reading assignments so that the classroom flow evolves from "read about it and then we will talk about it" to "we will talk about it, read about it in more depth, and then talk about it some more."

Figure 4.1 presents a diagrammatic representation of frontloading disciplinary texts. New knowledge, the object of our lessons and the focus of disciplinary reading, is displayed in the box. Frontloading, the instruction preceding reading that addresses assumed academic knowledge, is portrayed as teaching outside the box. Although certainly a commonsensical way of proceeding, in our zest to move into the new material, we devote inadequate attention to frontloading instruction. Unfortunately, ineffective reading comprehension by many of our students is the result of our shortchanging the frontloading of instruction. By neglecting our teaching outside the box, we jeopardize the likelihood that many of our students will be able to obtain new knowledge through reading disciplinary texts. To underscore the importance of frontloading

Figure 4.1. Frontloading Disciplinary Texts

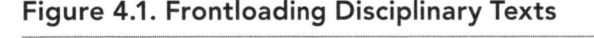

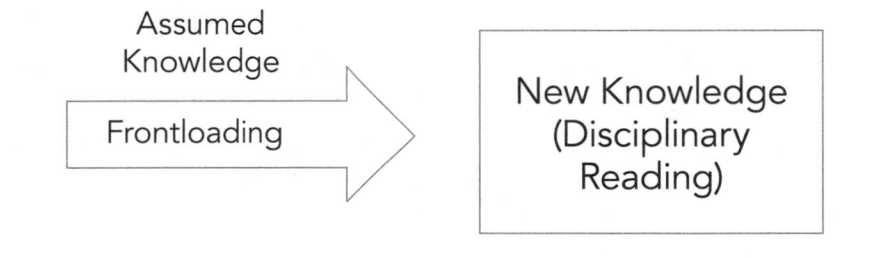

instruction, Alexander and Jetton (2000) refer to "knowledge" as "the scaffold for text-based learning" (p. 291).

REFLECTION INTERLUDE

What does teaching outside the box look like in your discipline? What would students already have to know to be successful readers of your disciplinary texts? Consider a specific unit of study. Try to list three or four packets of assumed knowledge that might be the focus of front-loading instruction to prepare students to read complex texts for that unit.

Three different frontloading scenarios may be considered as teachers address academic knowledge gaps in their disciplines: frontloading when students have had considerable access to assumed academic knowledge, frontloading when access to assumed academic knowledge is unequally distributed among students, and frontloading when many, or perhaps most, students lack academic knowledge. Detailed descriptions of a host of frontloading strategies, including those highlighted in the following sections, are provided in a companion volume to this book, *Classroom Strategies for Interactive Learning* (Buehl, 2009a). (For a complete listing of strategy references, see the Appendix.)

Frontloading With Much Knowledge

This first frontloading scenario in many respects flies under our radar as teachers, and although it is essential to disciplinary learning, frontloading with much knowledge is frequently overlooked. This is academic knowledge that we perhaps take for granted because we believe that students should already know this material. We assume that they will have access to this category of academic knowledge for good reason: We have personally taught it a unit ago, two months ago, or a semester ago, or our colleagues have taught it as part of the previous year's curriculum. This first frontloading scenario is predicated on review; as teachers, we need to ask to what extent authors assume that readers will need to review previous learning for comprehension.

However, although authors may assume that students are mentally reviewing previous learning, we cannot trust that this is actually transpiring as students read disciplinary texts. Students may quickly glide over references to prior knowledge without meaningfully connecting to past learning. Furthermore, if any class time is dedicated to review, chances are great that the only person in the room who does not need practice in revisiting prior knowledge, the teacher, is conducting the review. In his study of brain research and implications for memory, Sousa (2006) makes a distinction between teacher-centered review (i.e., the teacher or perhaps a couple of student volunteers restate previous learning) and cloture (i.e., every student is engaged in activating and verbalizing previous learning).

Many of our students will not automatically activate and process previously encountered academic knowledge unless classroom activities regularly prompt them to do so. As teachers, we are painfully aware that much of what students are expected to learn during units of study does not stand the test of time, and the temptation is great for students to view substantial portions of the curriculum as disposable knowledge, knowledge that only needs to be retained long enough to satisfy short-term assessments. Researchers are increasingly using the term *working memory* to refer to temporary storage that does not make it into permanent memory (e.g., Marzano, 2004). Hence, disciplinary instruction needs to continually factor in the necessity of reinforcing and utilizing learned knowledge.

The key dynamic of any of the following frontloading strategies is that students are conducting their own reviews, are engaged in reexamining their previous learning, and are gaining practice in continually verbalizing their understandings. Strategies within this first frontloading scenario provide ongoing reinforcement of domain knowledge and build a strong expectation that students remain conversant with previous learning. Review frontloading is especially beneficial for students who bring scant out-of-school knowledge to topics under study and who need repeat trips through material to learn it thoroughly.

> **"**
> The good reader knows to relate what is being read to prior knowledge, and he or she is aware that good readers predict what might be in upcoming text and relate ideas encountered in text to their prior knowledge.
> **"**
> —Pressley, 2002a, p. 304

Quick Writes

A number of frontloading strategies are effective tactics for immersing all students in touching base once more with acquired curricular knowledge. Particularly powerful are Quick Writes, which involves all students in verbalizing their understandings. A quick write is basically just that, a 1–3-minute informal written response, usually sparked by a prompt that the teacher provides to students for organizing their thinking as they reactivate previous learning (see Figure 4.2). Some examples of discipline-specific quick writes are the following:

- *History:* "One thing a person should know about the Reconstruction Era is...because..."

- *Physical science:* "A key term about plate tectonics is...because..."

- *Geometry:* "If I explained *congruent* so a person could really understand it, I would say..."

- *English language arts:* "Something that is ironic can be recognized by..."

- *Art:* "One thing particularly important about Impressionist painting is...because..."

- *Music:* "Something confusing about counting in 6/8 time is..."

Figure 4.2. Quick Write Prompts

• I learned...	• My definition of this is...
• I remember that...	• I can tell you that...
• I already know that...	• What really impressed me was...
• I was wrong to think...	• Something I should share about this is...
• I realized that...	• Some interesting information about...
• I would explain...	• I want to learn more about...
• I would describe...	• Something that people get wrong about...is...
• An important point is...	
• The confusing thing was...	• My learning answered my questions about...
• This helped me understand...	
• What made sense to me was...	• Since then, one thing I have thought about...
• I was surprised...	
• A person should know...	• One thing I understand now is...
• The first thing I think of is...	• I changed my thinking about...
• A key term about this topic is...because...	• A brief summary of...should include...

- *Health:* "Something I should share with others about high-sugar foods is...because..."
- *Technology:* "If I described the steps to follow, I would say, in order,..."

You can structure Quick Writes in a number of ways and use the strategy two or three times a week. You can integrate quick writes into notebook assignments, class journals, or learning logs; you can collect them as exit slips (i.e., students write for the last couple minutes of class and hand their writings to you as they leave the room) or assign them as entry slips (i.e., students write before class and hand their writings to you as they enter the classroom). I have counted quick writes as mini-assignments that are factored into students' grades; there is accountability, and these mini-assignments are not optional.

I have found using a timer to be an especially effective technique during Quick Writes time. (Online Stopwatch, available at www.online-stopwatch.com/full-screen-stopwatch/, is a great resource if you can project Internet sites in your classroom.) The teacher informs students of the time expectation for their quick writes. Students are expected to begin writing immediately and write steadily until the time has elapsed. The timer technique anticipates the perennial student query "How much do I need to write?" The answer is always "Write to fill the time."

A crucial dynamic of Quick Writes is student sharing; as a result, students not only reimmerse themselves into previous learning but also receive additional reminders from each other. Quick writes can be shared with partners or in small groups, can be written on index cards and passed several times around the classroom so that each student reads 8–10 different versions of responses, or written on sticky notes and posted on the board for students to peruse, rearrange, organize, and summarize.

(Quick Writes and many of the other strategies that appear throughout this book are more extensively described in *Classroom Strategies for Interactive Learning* [Buehl, 2009a]. In addition, the Appendix provides original sources for each strategy that appears in this book, should you need or want additional information on a particular strategy.)

Meaningful Associations

Association networking strategies are an additional way for you to stimulate student re-creation of past learning. These strategies are usually best accomplished by students working with partners or in teams to elicit meaningful connections to a topic and briefly elaborate on the nature of each connection. Knowledge Mapping, for instance, engages students in creating a concept map with the significant associations that they can recall about a topic previously studied. For example, students in world history are asked, "What are at least six meaningful associations you have to *feudalism* that are key to understanding that concept?" (See Figure 4.3.) When each team reports back to the class, ask them to briefly explain why each association contributes to an understanding of feudalism (e.g., "Land" is connected because the lords were granted tracts of land, and the peasants were required to stay on the land and work it).

Knowledge Maps could be displayed on chart paper, projected with overhead transparencies, or shared verbally as you solicit associations and construct a class Knowledge Map on the board. Within an entire class, it is likely that some of the discourse of the domain knowledge (e.g., *fief, manor, serf, vassal*) would surface on at least a few maps, providing a more comprehensive review for the entire class when these maps are shared and explained.

You can also use a variety of other association networking strategies that involve more extensive review. Alphabet Brainstorming charts, for example, provide students with a grid corresponding to the 26 letters of the alphabet. Student teams work to fill in as many of these boxes as they can, using the alphabet as first-letter prompts for meaningful associations

Figure 4.3. Feudalism Knowledge Map

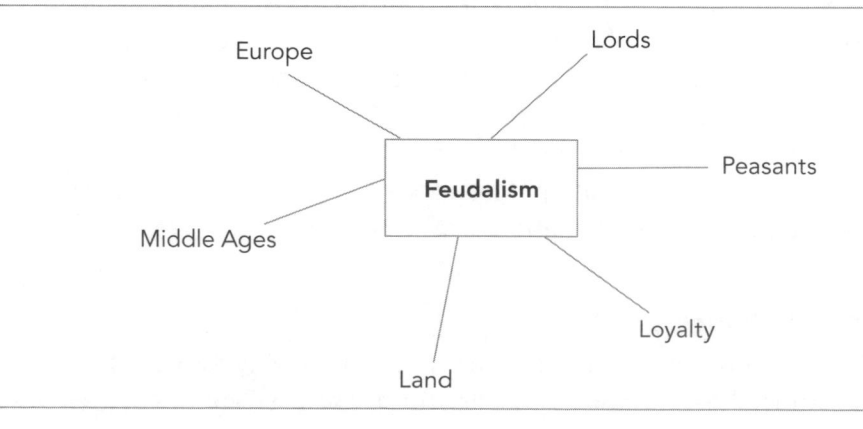

Figure 4.4. Students' Alphabet Brainstorming Chart on Genetic Traits

A	B	C	D	E	F	G
adaptations	baldness	chromosome cross	dominant DNA	eye color	female	Genes Gender Genotype
H heredity	**I** inherited traits inbreeding	**J**	**K**	**L**	**M** mutation meiosis Mendel	**N** natural selection
O offspring	**P** parents phenotype	**Q**	**R** recessive	**S** Sex-linked Traits	**T** Twins	**U**
V variation	**W** weight	**X** X-chromosome	**Y** Y-chromosome	**Z** zygote		

to a topic that has been studied. Figure 4.4 displays a biological science review on genetic traits; student teams were given between 7 and 10 minutes to probe their memories and jot down meaningful associations from prior learning on this concept. (A reproducible version of this chart is available in *Classroom Strategies for Interactive Learning* [Buehl, 2009a].) Most important, during sharing time, the student teams explain why each association is a meaningful connection to the concept, thus practicing verbalizing previous learning and providing a reminder to individuals who had perhaps forgotten some elements about the topic or needed additional explanation of the original learning.

Knowledge Ladders are a third variation of an association networking strategy. You array the prompt in this activity in a vertical column, and students use the letters as cues for meaningful connections to that topic. A letter can appear in any place in a word, unlike the first-letter trigger for the alphabet grid. A Knowledge Ladder created to review learning on the Holocaust that precedes the reading of literary works such as *Number the Stars* by Lois Lowry, *The Diary of Anne Frank*, or *Night* by Elie Wiesel in an English language arts class is presented in Figure 4.5.

Figure 4.5. Holocaust Knowledge Ladder

Gas c **h** amber

P **o** land

Hit **l** er

o vens

c oncentration camps

N **a** zis

Final Sol **u** tion

Jew **s**

Ghe **t** to

Assumed Knowledge Tracking

A third category of review strategies engages students in tracking assumed knowledge as they undertake a cursory first read of a disciplinary text. During this initial perusal, you prompt students to notice carryover items: author references to information and terminology that was previously introduced and discussed. As outlined in Chapter 3, these intertextual allusions assume that readers will be freshening up prior disciplinary learning and able to apply and expand their understandings of these concepts and connections. Basically, you ask students to track this information: "What have we already covered that this author expects us to know?" If students can mark the text, then you can have them highlight all terms and references that represent earlier learning, either during this course or previous courses. Highlighting is an especially vivid and colorful way of demonstrating how much of the understanding of a specific text is predicated on prior learning. Other options include students listing review items on sticky notes attached to the text, on a notebook page, or on an index card.

Of course, listing review items from a text is an awareness activity; students need to dig deeper and explain their understandings of these review items if comprehension is to be enhanced. Partner Shares are an excellent mechanism for verbalizations of prior learning. For example, one partner can be assigned one paragraph or section, and the other partner the next paragraph or section. After each has identified the review items from their assigned portion, they swap lists and study them before explaining each item to their partner. Or, teams can analyze a section, write the list on an overhead transparency or dry-erase board, and explain to the rest of the class. Another variation is for one team to explain a second team's review list and vice versa. Ultimately, however accomplished, students need to not only identify but also clarify their understandings of prior learning.

Review/New Charts are another example of an assumed knowledge tracking strategy, in this case tailored for mathematics reading. As discussed in Chapter 3, the comprehension of mathematics texts is highly dependent on deep conceptual knowledge that is triggered by mathematics terminology. Students first individually examine a chapter section of a math text to isolate review concepts as well as identify the new material that is being introduced. Initially, you might give students photocopied versions of the text and different colored highlighters (e.g., yellow for review concepts, pink for new concepts). The result will be pages highly colored in yellow, reinforcing how much mathematics reading is based on prior learning. Next, students meet with partners or in collaborative groups to chart review items side by side with the new learning. Figure 4.6 presents a Review/New Chart detailing concepts presented in an algebra chapter. After completing the chart, partners or group members then orchestrate their own review session by taking turns explaining each item in the review side of the chart, which are then shared with the entire class.

Frontloading With Diverse Knowledge

This second frontloading scenario represents a challenging daily classroom reality for disciplinary learning. Refer again to Marzano's (2004) descriptions of the disparities in academic knowledge among his nine prototypical students, as discussed in Chapter 3. Some of your students will bring high out-of-school access to topic and domain knowledge related to disciplinary units of study, some will bring spotty knowledge (i.e., they will know some things but lack other assumed knowledge), and some will arrive with significant academic knowledge gaps. Frontloading strategies in this scenario are more geared to building and sharing academic knowledge rather than merely activating prior classroom learning.

Figure 4.6. Review/New Chart of the Algebraic Concept Slope

Review	New
rate	rate of change
horizontal distance	slope
vertical distance	dependent variable
ratios	independent variable
quantity	run
variable	rise
unit rate	positive slope
constant	negative slope
ordered pair	
linear	
coordinates	
denominator	
numerator	

Note. Adapted from a strategy by Rita Crotty, Hempstead High School, Dubuque, IA.

Any classroom activity that engages students in exploring and sharing prior knowledge that can be subsequently expanded through the reading of disciplinary texts has high value when academic knowledge is diversely distributed among students. In addition to the strategies shared in this section, problematic situations (i.e., ask students to hypothesize solutions to a possible problem before reading a text that develops potential resolutions) and visual cueing (i.e., use illustrations or photographs to stimulate sharing of prior knowledge) are strategies that you can employ to address academic knowledge gaps when students bring unequal experiences and access to disciplinary learning.

Brainstorming

Brainstorming strategies are particularly conducive to this second frontloading goal. The intention behind these strategies is pooling academic knowledge. In this case, you, the teacher, are not the only potential access point to assumed academic knowledge; our classes offer multiple access points. Students who lack access to people who can introduce academic knowledge in their out-of-school lives have access to such people in our classrooms: you and their peers. Structure brainstorming activities to engage students in conversations related to topics of study, with the result being an extensive converging of what students know to create a class schema before students read more about curricular topics. Students access each other as knowledge sources and develop the habit of using each other to extend and clarify academic knowledge.

Several popular brainstorming strategies can be integrated into disciplinary instruction. LINK (List, Inquire, Note, Know), PReP (Prereading Plan), and a number of variations of the classic brainstorming strategy K-W-L (Know, Want to Know, Learned) Plus all have potential roles in disciplinary learning (for more detailed descriptions of these literacy practices, see Buehl, 2009a). To illustrate brainstorming as a frontloading activity, I outline a variation that I use with disciplinary texts, the Confirming to Extending grid. This frontloading strategy proceeds in five phases, each phase denoted in a sector of the student note-taking grid (see Figure 4.7).

Confirming: What We Know or Have Heard. The process starts with individual brainstorming, as students quickly jot down a list of things they think they know, or might have heard, in response to a topic prompt you provide. In this example, the strategy was used to prepare students for the study of pathogenic microbes. Initially, students were given three minutes to list as many meaningful connections as they could to the West Nile virus, a disease-causing virus that has appeared recently in various regions of the United States. All of the students responded individually to this first prompt, although out-of-school knowledge clearly varied. Some students had followed news reports or heard people talking about the virus, whereas other students could only think of generic comments related to previous learning about viruses in general (e.g., "It infects your body," "You could get sick," "Washing your hands prevents it from spreading"). The occasional student whose family kept horses, which are highly at risk to the virus, usually brought extensive topic and domain

Figure 4.7. Confirming to Extending Grid for the West Nile Virus

Confirming: What We Know or Have Heard ➤	Revising: What the Author Stated
✔ Is carried by mosquitoes	
✔ Is a disease that kills people	There are very few deaths from this disease in the United States.
✔ Crows can be infected.	
✔ They examine dead birds to see if they have it.	
Carried to the United States from Africa	
~~Is very contagious~~	Get it from mosquito bites not from other people
✔ You should use lots of mosquito spray.	Cities are not doing more spraying to control it.
✔ You can get a high fever.	
~~Washing hands controls the spread of the virus.~~	Virus is only carried through the blood.
✔ You get sick like you have the flu.	
✔ It is now in our state.	
~~It grows in stagnant water.~~	Virus does not live in stagnant water; mosquitoes breed there.
✔ It kills horses.	
✔ Is not a major threat to us	Officials are more worried about E. coli infections and bird flu virus.

Inquiring: What We Are Wondering ➤	Resolving: What the Author Stated
How deadly is this disease to humans?	1% of people get encephalitis (swelling of brain) and can die; hits elderly and people with weak immune systems; is a low risk to people; is rarely fatal.
Does the virus affect animals other than birds?	Infects birds, horses, people; 100 types of birds can get it.
What part of the United States or world has the most cases?	?
Is there an effective treatment or medicine?	No treatment
Is there a vaccine for it?	No vaccine for people but is being researched to find one
How can you tell which mosquitoes have it?	?
If you get it once, can you get it again?	?
Can you get it from touching a diseased bird?	Only spread by mosquitoes that feed on infected birds; you can't get it from infected animals.

(continued)

Figure 4.7. Confirming to Extending Grid for the West Nile Virus (Continued)

What are the symptoms?	Is like flu: high fever, headache, convulsions; symptoms can be like Parkinson's disease; 80% of infected people have no symptoms.

Extending: What Else Is Important to Know

Most people don't even know they have been infected and do not get sick.

May only feel tired and have headache or body aches

Could get skin rash

Can be spread through blood transfusions and organ transplants

Evidence that can be spread by infected mother to child at birth or through breast-feeding; not clear on this

Doesn't affect chickens or turkeys; poultry has natural antibodies.

First found in New York in 1999 and now found in 32 states

There is horse vaccine; horses should have vaccination; a third of unvaccinated horses die from West Nile.

Should wear long-sleeved clothes, use insect repellant, and avoid outdoors at dawn and dusk

knowledge to this personal inventory of information related to this microbe.

Students continue the brainstorming phase collaboratively as they share their lists with partners, talk about their connections, and augment their lists together. Finally, brainstorming culminates in a class sharing, as you create a baseline of class knowledge on the board or overhead by soliciting items from each set of partners. The emphasis of this first phase is to stimulate student conversation and sharing related to the topic and to provide students who bring low access to this academic knowledge with a heads-up on the material from their peers. Once a comprehensive class list is developed, students copy the items into the "Confirming" square of the note-taking grid.

Inquiring: What We Are Wondering. The second phase engages students in taking an inquiry mind-set into their reading. Each pair of partners considers the conversation at this point, and as they think about what has been revealed so far about the topic, they together generate two or three questions that a person might have about this virus. The pairs may even question some of the information that has been recorded in the first column, as students may know or have heard contradictory things. Partners share these questions with the class, and they are recorded as inquiry items in the second square, "Inquiring."

Revising: What the Author Stated. With their knowledge thus activated and primed, students read further on the topic. In this lesson, three short articles on the West Nile virus, each at different Lexile difficulty levels, were made available, and each set of partners selected one to read. As they read, students used text coding to compare what the author said with the class prior knowledge that they recorded in the "Confirming" square. They add a check mark in the text next to where the author confirms class prior knowledge, and an X next to where the author contradicts or disconfirms the class prior knowledge. In effect, students are being mentored to use texts to double-check the accuracy of their prior knowledge. Ensuing class discussion clarifies which prior knowledge was confirmed and which should be struck as being unsupported or inaccurate. A line is drawn through items inconsistent with the texts so that students have a visual reminder of which parts of the class prior knowledge is misinformation. Corrected knowledge from the texts is listed in the "Revising" square. Students have a visual, side-by-side representation of how their reading led to revisions in their understandings of this topic.

Resolving: What the Author Stated. Partners then return to the text for a second read to seek answers to the class questions recorded in the "Inquiring" square. Those addressed by their author are answered in the "Resolving" square. Questions not addressed by their author are identified by a question mark. Partners share their answers to the inquiry questions with the entire class. Because three articles were read, authors did not provide identical information. Some questions were addressed by all authors, some were talked about only in one or two articles, and some remained unresolved, as none of the authors dealt with them. This phase emphasizes reading to use texts to resolve questions that had piqued the interests of the class.

Extending: What Else Is Important to Know. The final phase involves a return once again to each text for a third examination to identify any information that seems important but did not surface in the confirming, revising, or resolving phases. These items represent new knowledge and are recorded in the "Extending" section at the bottom of the grid. When the process has been completed, students have filled in a note-taking grid that clearly indicates confirmed knowledge, revised knowledge, knowledge that resolved class inquiries, and new knowledge.

I have walked extensively through this frontloading strategy because brainstorming, while potentially powerful for addressing academic knowledge gaps, can also be problematic. Quite frankly, as every teacher is well aware, not everything that students feel they know or have heard will be accurate or consistent with disciplinary learning. In particular, our text-to-world connections by their very nature often contain prior knowledge that may be only partially accurate, hearsay, or erroneous. (See comments on science misconceptions in Chapter 3.) Students may also overgeneralize from or misinterpret personal experiences to bring flawed text-to-self connections. Whereas some of our students may know very little about a topic, others may "know" things that are untrue. Teachers fear, with good reason, that students may be just as apt to remember inaccurate information that emerges from class activities as they do the desirable content of our lessons. Yet, if prior knowledge is not examined and directly aligned with new learning, then students are also at risk for not making the necessary connections that would lead to refining or at times replacing their prior knowledge with the disciplinary learning of our curriculum. Brainstorming frontloading strategies should engage students in a side-by-side analysis of their prior knowledge as it compares with their reading and learning from disciplinary texts. Such strategies also encourage students to view knowledge as mutable, as incomplete and open to revision as they interact with it again and again over the course of their lives.

The teacher language used to introduce brainstorming activities therefore must be carefully considered. You will notice that for the initial stage of the West Nile virus lesson, I solicited things that students *might* know or have heard rather than things they categorically *do* know. The qualifying nature of this language is intentional; we all hold flawed understandings in some areas of our prior knowledge, and we all have heard things that we have not necessarily ascertained as to accuracy or from a credible source. Furthermore, students will be reluctant to openly share what they think they know about a topic if the classroom dynamic is structured to expose them as ignorant or ill informed. My response is generally, "If you have heard it, likely someone else has, too. Let's list it up here and test it with our further learning." To model, I emphasize with students that like anyone, I hold knowledge that is imprecise, erroronous, or in need of revision. One mark of intelligence is to recognize flawed understanding and rebuild knowledge that can claim a firmer basis in credibility and scholarship.

One other comment is necessary regarding brainstorming strategies. Teachers need to know their students and accurately predict whether they would be able to generate meaningful connections to a targeted prompt. "West Nile virus" was a workable prompt for my students in Wisconsin because of ongoing news reports and cautions about this disease. (Lyme disease, carried by deer ticks, would have been another probable winner for students in our apparently microbe-infested state.) However, if hardly anyone can say much of anything about the West Nile virus, then obviously as teachers, we would have miscalculated the extent of students' out-of-school knowledge about the topic and would need a more extensive frontloading activity, such as a video clip about the virus, as discussed in the third frontloading scenario.

Thought-Provoking Statements

A second group of frontloading strategies that engage students in pooling prior academic knowledge revolves around Lightning Rod Statements that serve as a springboard for discussion and sharing. An example of a Lightning Rod Statement in a foods class is "People in the United States can generally trust that the food they purchase is safe for their consumption." Students will bring text-to-self, text-to-text, and text-to-world knowledge to their thoughts on this statement. Any student who has contracted a food-borne pathogen will have some compelling personal experiences to share, but all will likely have read or heard something about this issue. After sharing perspectives, students are ready to read a disciplinary text, whether about food preparation techniques, laxly enforced regulations, the use of pesticides, the behavior of bacteria, historical developments in food safety, industry safeguards, food distribution in our world economy, or risk factors as to the prevalence of unsafe food. After reading, students revisit the statement and decide how they would respond now that they know more about the topic.

Anticipation and Prediction Guides. Popular variations of this type of frontloading are Anticipation Guides and Prediction Guides. Initially, you ask students to evaluate, agree or disagree, or predict based on their current knowledge about a topic by responding to a series of statements. The general intention of these guides is a before-and-after dynamic: "This is what I am thinking based on current knowledge" compared with "This is what I am now thinking based on my new understandings" after reading more about the topic.

Figure 4.8 presents a science Prediction Guide that engages students in conversation and sharing what they know about invasive species. Students first individually, then with partners or in small groups, talk about this topic by using their prior knowledge to predict which of these statements is supported by scientific evidence and which are not. After these conversations, groups share their comments with the whole class, again to pool the knowledge that students bring to this topic before reading. After this whole-class sharing, students then read further to compare what an author tells them to their prior knowledge and predictions. As students read, they annotate the text, either marking or using small

Figure 4.8. Prediction Guide on Invasive Species

What does the evidence say? Make some predictions about what scientists currently know about invasive species.

True	Prediction	False
	1. Invasive species are only plants.	
	2. Invasive species are destructive to an ecosystem.	
	3. Invasive species are introduced unintentionally into an ecosystem.	
	4. We really cannot stop invasive species from spreading.	
	5. Invasive species are usually introduced by humans.	
	6. Invasive species are always successful in host ecosystems.	
	7. Invasive species can kill humans.	

Note. Adapted with permission courtesy of Neil Rumney, Rhinelander High School, Rhinelander, WI.

sticky notes, to locate places in the text where the author has something to say about each statement. Students place a 1 in the margin where the author has said something relevant to statement 1, and so forth. Finally, to consolidate their understandings, ask students to marshal their findings from the text for each statement and summarize an accurate conclusion or generalization for each facet of knowledge related to invasive species.

Anticipation and Prediction Guides are a motivational and effective means to stimulate conversation and sharing that addresses assumed academic knowledge in a text. Figure 4.9 represents a Prediction Guide for U.S. history that engages students in thinking like a historian as they embark on learning more about the Reconstruction Era in the aftermath of the Civil War. Like the science guide, which was predicated on the scientific evidence for each statement, this activity asks students to wade into these topics the way a historian might. Students will learn, throughout this process, that historical evidence on these statements might be mixed and that establishing unequivocal answers to the statements is unlikely and, quite frankly, not what historians do. As students read after this frontloading activity, they begin to inventory evidence that supports or does not support each statement. Finally, as a synthesis activity, they develop their supported arguments on each statement, a much more nuanced process than may typically be followed in history classrooms.

Figure 4.9. Prediction Guide on the Reconstruction Era

What do historians think about the Reconstruction Era? Predict how likely *historians* would say each is true.

HL = Is highly likely to be true.   SU = Is somewhat unlikely to be true.
SL = Is somewhat likely to be true.   HU = Is highly unlikely to be true.

_____ 1. With the abolition of slavery, the lives of African Americans in the South improved.
_____ 2. Abraham Lincoln believed that "all men are created equal."
_____ 3. Most Americans held racist attitudes during this period in history.
_____ 4. The U.S. government did enough to support African Americans in the South after the Civil War.
_____ 5. The emergence of groups like the Ku Klux Klan in the South was inevitable.
_____ 6. The policies of the Radical Republicans were too radical and did more harm than good.

Figure 4.10. Prediction Guide on Bargaining

Rate each statement as either "L" for likely or "U" for unlikely.

_____ 1. Bargaining in Mexico is an enjoyable process for both the vendor and the customer alike.

_____ 2. Vendors deliberately price their goods above what they actually expect to get for the product.

_____ 3. Vendors think positively about the tourists who negotiate with them.

_____ 4. You will have better luck in the bargaining process if you act really interested in an item.

_____ 5. Merchants will frequently give discounts if you buy multiples.

_____ 6. Bargaining is not limited to handicrafts; you can also negotiate fruit, tacos, and other items in the produce markets.

Note. Adapted with permission courtesy of Barbara Davis, Oregon High School, Oregon, WI.

Figure 4.10 presents a Prediction Guide that deals with teaching cultural knowledge in a world languages curriculum. In this case, students in a Spanish class consider what they know about purchasing practices from merchants and vendors in Mexico. Students weigh in on a number of issues related to bargaining, an experience less frequent in the United States, where one generally expects to pay the price that is listed for a product. Then, students read a short article that talks about the daily theater of making purchases, the expectations of buyer and seller, the good-natured back-and-forth conversations, and the personable and enjoyable interactions. When students get to a statement in the article that defends or defies their guess, they write the number of the question in the margin of the article.

My wife Wendy created a Prediction Guide that accompanied a short article about possible microscopic infestations in the hairs of strings musicians' bows (see Figure 4.11). Although her middle school orchestra students had never heard of bow bugs, they brought extensive knowledge of microscopic creatures that provided a foundation for their understanding as they shared information about head lice, fleas, bedbugs, and other nefarious critters.

Finally, Figure 4.12 presents an Anticipation Guide that relates background knowledge on earthquakes to a newspaper article on an earthquake that occurred in the Midwest region of the United States. Students shared their perceptions and impressions about where

Figure 4.11. Prediction Guide on Stringed Instruments' Bow Bugs

Before reading, check the statements that you predict the author will confirm in the article. Then, after reading, check whether the author confirmed each statement.

Your Prediction	Confirmed by Author	Statement
		1. Bow bugs eat the bow hair on the bow.
		2. Bow bugs need light to survive.
		3. You will know if you have bow bugs because you can see them in the bow hair.
		4. The only way to get rid of bow bugs is to get a new bow and case.
		5. Bow bugs are a serious problem for strings players.
		6. You can actually get a disease from bow bugs.

Note. Courtesy of Wendy Buehl, Oregon Middle School, Oregon, WI.

Figure 4.12. Anticipation Guide on Earthquakes

Read each statement below and decide whether it could happen here.

I Agree	I Disagree	Statement
		1. Earthquakes have recently occurred in the midwestern United States.
		2. The Earth's crust in the Midwest is older and less fractured than in California.
		3. Quakes that occur in the Midwest are strong enough to damage buildings.
		4. Tremors from a quake in the Midwest are more deadly than those in California.
		5. The tremors of a quake in the Midwest reverberate differently than those on the West Coast.

Note. Adapted with permission courtesy of Janice Olson, Black Hawk Middle School, Gratiot, WI.

earthquakes generally happen and how severe earthquakes might be in certain areas. Of course, recent earthquakes in Haiti and Japan provided students with a wealth of text-to-text and text-to-world connections that were discussed before reading about midcontinent North American earthquakes. The newspaper article and Anticipation Guide prepared students to read a literary text by Jack London, who was an eyewitness to the 1906 San Francisco earthquake.

Point–Counterpoint Brainstorming. Another version of Lightning Rod Statements is presenting Point–Counterpoint scenarios to students as a brainstorming format. In this variation, you ask students to generate possible pros and cons, advantages and disadvantages, positives and negatives, of an idea, an action, or an event.

A useful format for Point–Counterpoint brainstorming is the Thumbs Up–Thumbs Down Chart. The topic for the language arts example in Figure 4.13 was teens and texting. The first phase proceeds with students individually generating positives and negatives of teens texting for the "Thumbs Up" and "Thumbs Down" boxes. These statements are then shared with partners before you solicit the statements for a whole-class inventory of pluses and minuses. Students are immersed in on-topic conversation that pools background knowledge and primes thinking for additional reading. As readers, they then compare their ideas with those articulated by an author, which are charted in the corresponding squares. It becomes readily apparent when the chart is completed where the author's arguments are tilted.

Point–Counterpoint scenarios are a good fit for many disciplines. Other examples of possible Point–Counterpoint brainstorming topics might include the following:

- *English language arts:* Ambition, self-interest, going out on your own
- *Family and consumer education:* Dieting, vegetarianism, divorce
- *Social studies:* Government regulation, foreign aid, free trade
- *Physical education:* Jogging, using steroids, weight training
- *Business education:* Credit cards, covenant not to compete laws
- *Mathematics:* Using a calculator, following a specific method to solve a problem
- *Science:* Protecting endangered species, using fertilizers, cloning, altering foods genetically
- *World languages:* Traveling to foreign countries, eating authentic foods

Figure 4.13. Thumbs Up–Thumbs Down Chart on Teens and Texting

Thumbs Up! Thumbs Down!

Topic: _____ Teens & Texting _____

Ideas/Arguments/Evidence For	Ideas/Arguments/Evidence Against
It is an easy way to be in touch. Can support relationships Is fun to text Can be answered when you want to You can figure out what you want to say before you send your answer. You can do it without interrupting what is going on. Can get a message to someone who can't take a phone call Is a good way to get a message out to a group of people Can do it practically anywhere	Could get to be expensive if you have a limited plan Could do it at inappropriate times, like when driving a car Could replace actually talking to people Might say something you wouldn't say if you were talking to a person Might do it too much Your parents could interfere and take your phone away Inappropriate stuff could get shared. A person might show messages to other people. Might do "sexting" Could use it to cheat in class Get used to spelling shortcuts
Author's Ideas/Arguments/Evidence	**Author's Ideas/Arguments/Evidence**
Offers companionship Helps teens feel connected to others Can help teens stay in touch with parents Can ask for feedback or suggestions from others Teens like to be a part of things and know what's going on. Have a 21st-century way of communicating Are doing written communications	Can become obsessive behavior Are doing it way too frequently: average of 80 messages a day Pressure to respond immediately, even if in bed at night; has become a distraction Anxiety of being out of the loop Interferes with developing independence Overreliance on getting in touch with parents, or parents getting in touch with teens Do it during classes in school and don't pay attention Repetitive action leads to thumb pain and injury Interruption; need times of peace and quiet Linked to falling grades

Vocabulary-Infused Predictions

Rather than provide students with a single-word topical prompt to cue thinking and brainstorming, you can use Vocabulary-Infused Predictions that present an array of key terms related to a topic. Ask students to share their connections as they piece together possible key ideas or themes. Students then read to clarify any terms and confirm or revise their predictions.

Possible Sentences. With Possible Sentences, you provide students with 12–15 key terms and phrases from a text that they will be reading. With partners, students examine the list and decide which words might logically fit with each other. Then, they put these words in play in a series of predictive sentences. In a sense, they are developing sentences that could appear in a text that features such an array of key terms and phrases. To do this activity, students need to review previously learned vocabulary and size up what they already know about the context of these words.

Figure 4.14 is a world history Possible Sentences activity about the ancient Mesopotamians. Students make predictions about unfamiliar names and places (e.g., *Hammurabi, Sumer*) by connecting these to items that are commonly known (e.g., *wheel, checkers, city-state*). Of course, students will recognize *Iraq* from the list, and some will be able to identify *Euphrates* from news stories on the war in that country. Is *Hammurabi* a person, a place, or a thing? Students will be especially alert for clarifying items such as this while they read.

Figure 4.14. Possible Sentences on Ancient Mesopotamians

Each of the terms below is used by the author to tell us something about the ancient Mesopotamians. Write five predictions about these important people. Each sentence should include at least two of the following terms:

Assyria	class	Iraq	stele
Babylon	cuneiform	king	Sumer
chariot	Euphrates	Nebuchadnezzar	Tigris
checkers	Gilgamesh	rivers	wheel
city-state	Hammurabi	soap	ziggurat

Note. Courtesy of Victoria Woodward, Spring Harbor Middle School, Madison, WI.

After sharing their predictions and engaging in conversation about what they currently know, students read the text to ascertain more accurate understandings of the identity and relationships of these items. Students then repair their sentences by rewriting predictive sentences that were not confirmed by the author into summary statements that are consistent with the text, again using the items from the list. Thus, a student predictive sentence (e.g., "Hammurabi was the inventor of the chariot," which is a reasonable prediction but inconsistent with the text) is rewritten after reading to reflect an accurate understanding (e.g., "Hammurabi was a king of Babylonia who issued laws that were displayed on a stone monument called a stele").

Figure 4.15 presents a mathematics example of Possible Sentences as students prepare to study data that are connected to their everyday lives. Partners might predict that they will learn that "Average is one of the measures of center." After reading, the partners revise their sentence to "Mean, median, and mode are all different measures of center" or "*Average* and *mean* are math terms that have the same definition."

Story Impressions. Story Impressions is another variation of Vocabulary-Infused Predictions. You offer students more clues about the interrelationships of items on a list by displaying them in the order they appear in the text to be read, so students can infer which items may be directly linked. Again, this activity is designed to promote conversation and knowledge sharing about a topic that will be studied in more depth. Figure 4.16 is an example of a Story Impressions activity for a health lesson on hearing damage. Relying on what they currently know, students work with partners using the terms to brainstorm a probable message in order

Figure 4.15. Possible Sentences on Data About Us

Write five mathematics predictions using the math words below. Each sentence should use at least two of the math words.

average	horizontal	median	stem-and-leaf plot
axis	line plot	mode	typical
bar graph	mean	outlier	vertical
data	measures of center	range	

Note. Courtesy of Sue Jackan, Toki Middle School, Madison, WI.

Figure 4.16. Story Impressions on Hearing Damage

What's your prediction? Write your version of what a newspaper article might tell us about this headline topic. Use each of the terms in the order they appear:

Headline: Hearing Damage

Terms:

decibel	preventable disability
movies	rising
MP3 player	sensory hair cell
noisy world	toys
pain threshold	volume
permanent damage	

to write a predictive paragraph. After reading, students work individually to use the same Story Impressions list to write a summary of the text.

Student-Directed Previewing

A cursory yet strategic first look at a text also provides students with opportunities to touch base with prior knowledge. Elements of a text, such as highlighted language, illustrations, photographs, and other visual displays, can serve as triggers to topic knowledge. Student-Directed Previewing, in which students undertake an initial overview of a text to identify elements that are familiar and that they already know something about, contrasts with previewing, which is more text-directed. Essentially, a Student-Directed Preview ignores anything in the text that is unfamiliar. Students bypass domain knowledge like the insider vocabulary of a discipline and instead scan the pages to search out anything that connects to text-to-self, text-to-text, or text-to-world personal knowledge. Essentially, students are sizing up the match with a disciplinary text, and they coordinate their own review of relevant prior knowledge.

The Science Connection Overview is an example of a Student-Directed Previewing activity. Because students can become quickly subsumed in insider vocabulary and content that appears esoteric, this student-directed activity concentrates attention on students locating text-to-self and text-to-world connections and stimulates general conversation about the topic before students become more deeply immersed in the domain knowledge of a chapter (for a completed example, see Figure 4.17). Because

Figure 4.17. Science Connection Overview on the Rock Cycle

What's Familiar?	***What's the connection?*** **Skim and survey the chapter for things that are familiar and that connect with your life or world. List them below.** quartz Hawaii volcanoes chalk Mount Rushmore granite coal mineral slate lava weathering marble statues rock salt volcanoes sandstone erosion limestone rock layers
What's It About?	***Read the summary:*** **What topic areas seem to be the most important?** the rock cycle sedimentary rocks igneous rocks metamorphic rocks
What Are You Wondering?	***Questions of interest:*** **What questions do you have about this material that may be answered in the chapter?** What do rocks have to do with volcanoes? Is coal a rock? How do fossils get into rocks? Do only certain kinds of rocks contain fossils? Why do we have the type of rocks in our region? What different materials could rocks be made up of? What are the best rocks for use in building? Is table salt essentially a rock we eat? What makes some rocks extremely hard and others easily crumble? Are there rocks in some parts of the world that we don't have in our region? How are rocks and minerals different?
What Will the Author Tell You?	***Chapter organization:*** **What categories of information are provided in this chapter?** The rock cycle and how rocks change from one to another The three categories of rocks: igneous, metamorphic, and sedimentary How each category of rock is formed How each category of rock is classified
Read and Explain.	***Vocabulary:*** **Use index cards or your notebook for recording your explanations.**

science textbooks are so heavily visual, this previewing strategy is a good fit for matchup issues in science. (A reproducible version of the Science Connection Overview is available in *Classroom Strategies for Interactive Learning* [Buehl, 2009a].)

The first phase is done individually, as students scan a section or chapter to quickly tag any familiar items. These are listed in the "What's Familiar?" box of the Science Connection Overview chart. The next phase involves scouting the chapter organization to get the big picture of the chapter for the "What's It About?" box; if available, a chapter summary is an excellent resource for this phase. Students then meet with partners to share connections and raise questions, which are recorded in the "What Are You Wondering?" box. These questions essentially serve as conversation starters, as students delve deeper into their topic knowledge, share experiences, and pool their knowledge. This activity is designed to prime the pump, so to speak, to center the initial stages of study on the familiar and the known before students embark as readers into the more rigorous examination of the domain knowledge presented in the text.

Frontloading With Insufficient Knowledge

The third frontloading scenario concerns those times when it appears that many, or even most, of your students will be mismatched with disciplinary texts. Because academic knowledge gaps seem endemic in these instances, this third scenario is the time when student reading of disciplinary complex texts is most likely to be sidelined. However, a rich menu of instructional options can be highly effective in building academic knowledge when pooling strategies are inadequate because not enough prior knowledge is available to be shared by students with each other. Your use of nonprint media, such as video, can be especially effective for building academic knowledge during this third frontloading scenario. Teacher read-alouds, hands-on and other interactive activities, guided imagery, visual previewing, and other teacher-led presentations can all be instrumental, not in displacing disciplinary learning from texts, which frequently happens, but in building sufficient academic knowledge for more in-depth learning through reading of complex texts.

Likewise, classroom text-to-self experiences, such as experiments, simulations, hands-on tasks, guest speakers, or even field trips, are often designed to follow reading, when they could instead be employed as frontloading to address academic knowledge gaps before students read complex texts.

Video and Other Media

In class routines, we often use video after reading, although it can have a more powerful knowledge-building impact before reading. Personally, I have at times been motivated to read a literary work *after* seeing it dramatized, whether it was the gripping novelization of events of the U.S. Civil War in *The Killer Angels* (read after viewing the movie *Gettysburg*), a revisiting of a play after seeing it performed live (a recent experience with *Waiting for Godot*), or even reading the text of a speech online after watching it on television (President Obama's inaugural address). Although I already know what happens, I still have useful purposes for engaging in reading the actual text.

For example, one of my former colleagues, a ninth-grade English teacher, experimented with frontloading strategies to counteract student frustrations with reading Shakespeare's *Romeo and Juliet*. Many of her students struggled with successfully reading the play as an independent expectation because of the complexity of the language, lack of background on the time period, unfamiliar cultural allusions, difficult vocabulary, and challenging dramatic literature text structure. The teacher did not wish to resort to a common but problematic practice, round-robin reading of the play out loud in class, in lieu of individual student interactions with the text. To preempt some comprehension roadblocks, she shifted to a viewing of the movie version of the play as a frontloading activity. Her students responded enthusiastically to the story as presented in the film adaptation (of course, Leonardo DiCaprio was probably a motivating asset as well), and they were much more eager to tackle reading the play once they realized what a compelling story was awaiting them. The archaic language and difficult text features were less problematic when students could connect the movie story line to what was happening in various scenes. She reported much more successful and engaged reading of the play after frontloading the story, and students now read for different purposes than for discovering what happened. The students were able to track character development, note Shakespeare's craft in writing the play, undertake scene studies, and otherwise examine significant elements of the play.

In some respects, this teacher treated the movie as a first read of the play; subsequently, students returned to the story by reading the actual text for more in-depth understandings. In classrooms, a movie version is typically used as a follow-up to reading a play or novel, although the instructional impact of this practice may be minimal. Quite frankly, at times, watching the movie may be equated as a class reward for surviving the reading of the play rather than as serving a central educational function in curricular learning. In this case, planning the movie as a frontloading activity made the subsequent reading of a complex text, Shakespeare's *Romeo and Juliet,* doable for many students who would have otherwise struggled.

The point being articulated here is not that we should always show a movie version of a literary work first, but there are times when doing so might be a valuable scaffold for texts for which many students might otherwise be mismatched. Of course, it is hardly necessary to show a movie-length video to frontload learning. Strategic use of video clips, segments of movies or programs, or YouTube snippets can be extremely advantageous in addressing academic knowledge gaps.

Short Texts and Alternative Texts

Finally, two other instructional options may factor into frontloading decision making when many students are mismatched with class texts. First, it is not always necessary to read all of a work to provide valuable interactions with complex texts. Although reading literary works (e.g., novels, short stories) in their entirety may be generally desirable, it may not be necessary, for example, to assign all of a physics textbook chapter on thermodynamics when that task may prove overwhelming to many students. If instead you have students work only a section of the chapter, or even seriously grapple with a few key pages, with appropriate frontloading and support, then they would still be developing a capacity to read the discourse of physics without always having to also be told the information.

Another instructional possibility is to assign teams of students to jigsaw different sections of a text, with each team responsible for working out their understandings and sharing with their classmates, who will reciprocate with their sections.

As a second instructional option, at some points, you may need to consider alternative texts that could be a better match for students. Given the wealth of potential texts available on valuable websites, as well as the current rich offerings of useful supplementary print materials, it may make sense to set aside a class textbook and provide students with texts that are more accessible. Again, you can jigsaw the reading, in this case providing the class with multiple texts, each containing some facets of learning on a disciplinary topic, and each at different Lexile levels of difficulty. Some student teams work a more accessible text and report their understandings, while other teams work more complex texts in order to share their contributions to class learning.

Putting It All Together: Frontloading Through Wide Reading

Regular daily reading is necessary if our students are to continue to mature as readers. Yet, Wide Reading is particularly instrumental in building the academic background knowledge that is a prerequisite for learning within the various content disciplines. In Chapter 3, research from the 2007 National Endowment for the Arts study was presented, which called for schools to do more to create a culture of personal reading to stem the slippage of reading habits of adolescents. Wide Reading in a disciplinary context establishes an inquiring mind-set toward learning that can provide bridges into the specific learning targeted by curricular standards.

> **"**
> Reading often and reading well are prerequisites for achievement in areas far beyond literature and literacy alone.
> **"**
> —National Endowment for the Arts, 2007, p. 91

Marzano (2004) advocated Wide Reading as a major strategy for building academic background knowledge for students who arrive at school lacking experiences with topics emphasized in the curriculum. In effect, Wide Reading—bringing a general disposition to include interactions with written texts as a way of learning about the world— is a significant access point to academic knowledge, especially for individuals who have had low access to academic knowledge through people and experiences in their out-of-school lives.

I consider myself an excellent example of how Wide Reading can trump lack of access to other sources of academic knowledge. I would rate myself as having entered my schooling as an individual with moderate access to people and experiences that paralleled my learning in disciplinary contexts (I would be Student 2 in Marzano's chart on page 86 of Chapter 3). I grew up on a dairy farm in Wisconsin (and no, I have never worn a cheesehead hat to a Green Bay Packers football game). As dairy farmers, our family was very much tied to the daily rhythms and routines of managing the farm, which most particularly meant milking the herd of 60 Holsteins twice a day, once at daybreak and once at nightfall. This was nonnegotiable work; it was done every day, whether or not it was a holiday or one of us was ill. Hence, we traveled very little, squeezing in short day trips on a Sunday, after chores and before evening milking. I relished those short visits to area historical sites, state parks, and other points of interest, but I experienced very few of the rich access points enjoyed by my sons as they traveled with me and my wife about the country, as our family took advantage of numerous cultural opportunities.

Most of the people I interacted with as a child were also farm folk or artisans and workers in the neighboring village. My parents were literate individuals who read the daily newspaper, talked about current events, and had subscriptions to *Prairie Farmer, The Farm Journal, Better Homes and Gardens,* and lucky for me, *The Saturday Evening Post* and *National Geographic.* I was fortunate to have intergenerational friendships with a couple of older adults who stretched my horizons (e.g., a retired farmer who had a passion for history and an especial expertise on the U.S. Civil War, and the assistant postmaster who was a curious and well-read fellow who initiated fascinating conversations and loaned me books). I was also a voracious reader, a youngster who according to my parents, always "had his nose in a book." My habit of Wide Reading permitted me access to academic knowledge that would not have been available for me in other ways. I related in Chapter 1 how my identity as a historian influenced *what* I read, but my identity as a reader influenced *that* I read. Stimulated by my reading, I traveled to many places in my imagination that I was unable to visit in person. It was not until I was well into adulthood that I finally set foot on some of the storied Civil War battlefields that I had so long imagined during my days as a farm kid and a reader. As a result, I entered my classrooms much more knowledgeable about topics of the curriculum than I would have been if I had not developed personal access points to academic knowledge through my personal reading.

What is a topic area from your out-of-school life that was enhanced by your personal reading? Can you think of a specific area of knowledge that you were able to accrue through personal reading of books, magazines, newspapers, online, or other texts? For example, readers of car magazines might cite knowledge in the automotive area, and readers of fantasy novels knowledge of medieval life and times.

Wide Reading is an especially critical strategy for students of poverty who arrive at school with low access to out-of-school academic knowledge. Some middle schools, and much more rarely high schools, initiate Sustained Silent Reading programs as vehicles to organize a school commitment to inculcate and encourage Wide Reading. Sustained Silent Reading time can be integrated into a school structure in a variety of ways, both within classes or subject areas, as well as across the curriculum. The intentions of these programs are to not only develop reading habits but also spread the benefits of expanding knowledge through Wide Reading. However, dedicating a portion of the scarce minutes of a school day or class period to Wide Reading is often a hard sell to teachers of adolescents, who do not necessarily perceive direct payoffs for disciplinary learning, feel it is more of a hassle than it is worth, or believe that supporting Wide Reading is really not their job as teachers of a specific academic discipline.

However, Wide Reading needs to be understood as an empowering strategy that allows individuals to expand their knowledge base dramatically beyond only text-to-self experiences. Teachers can seek ways to splice Wide Reading opportunities into their curriculum. For example, my son Jeremy, a high school social studies teacher, used Wide Reading as a central instructional strategy during a unit on the World War II years in his ninth-grade U.S. history course. He was teaching classes with a significant number of students who brought low or moderate access to out-of-school academic knowledge; he cotaught one section with a special education teacher and another section with an English as a Second Language teacher, because of the high percentage of English learners and students with disabilities. Working with the school literacy coach, he identified an ad hoc classroom library of texts that were connected in some way to the World War II years: books, magazines, articles, illustrated texts, graphic novels, and so forth, with a range of Lexile difficulty levels. Students spent the first 10 minutes of each 50-minute class period engaged in Wide Reading; they chose the texts they would read and regularly tracked their topics in their class notebooks. Students responded to their reading with daily quick writes, choosing from prompts such as "Something important I learned today is...." The intention behind this daily assignment was to build general foundational knowledge related to this important historical period, engage students in informing themselves more about the general topic, and develop possible text-to-text connections to unit themes. The Wide Reading assignment was a contrast to targeted reading assignments in class texts that specifically focused on the essential questions for learning for this unit.

> " The use of more than one text about a particular topic may actually facilitate gains in comprehension of that topic. The easier texts in the set could build the background knowledge that makes the more difficult texts easier to understand. "
>
> —C.H. Shanahan, 2008, p. 139

Considerations When Implementing Wide Reading

Marzano outlined several factors to be considered when integrating Wide Reading into curricular goals. A wealth of reading materials should be readily available to students in classroom libraries, the library media center, and other school sources. Wide Reading tends to be most successful when you connect materials to students rather than rely on students to locate materials on their own time. Because appeal is a key element of this strategy, you need to identify an array of materials that are of high personal interest and are at appropriate levels of difficulty.

Wide Reading within a disciplinary setting should be configured to pique personal interests within a topic area and not demonstrate a specific proficiency or knowledge to be gained by the reading. One of my former colleagues at Madison East High School required students in an advanced physics course to read a popular physics book of their choice as an out-of-class assignment. The point of this reading was not deep understanding of Stephen Hawking, for example; it was to begin to acquaint students with some of the wider literature in the field and encourage them to dip their toes into this literature. The goal was also, of course, to provide students with multiple contexts to hone their evolving abilities to read, write, and think through a physics lens.

In an important sense, you can use Wide Reading to frontload instruction and the subsequent use of complex texts that focus on unit goals, knowledge, and proficiencies. Follow-up activities are particularly important for mining the effectiveness of classroom Wide Reading experiences. You may ask students to interact with the material they are reading (e.g., "What is one thing you read today that you found especially interesting?") or interact with their peers about their reading. Design follow-up activities to deepen comprehension and spark conversation, as well as to insure accountability for using the designated class time to sample texts within a topic area.

Encouragement is a key variable, especially to plant the habit of continuing Wide Reading in out-of-school contexts. Conversing with individual students about their reading as a regular classroom dynamic not only reinforces building personal text-to-text connections but also demonstrates enthusiasm for this display of personal reading habits. You can encourage students in a multitude of ways to process what they are learning through their reading. You may ask students to interact with their texts by commenting in their journals or notebooks. You can provide prompts which ask students to talk about what they find particularly important or interesting to allow them to think through their learning in relatively nonthreatening ways. Nonlinguistic responses are equally beneficial; you can ask students to use visual displays, pictorial representations, or even dramatic responses to encourage the use of their imaginations to organize and synthesize their learning. Student–student sharing of interests and new knowledge through partner and small-group dialogue about the topics being investigated is especially valuable. Again, prompts such as "What is one thing you discovered today that you think others should know about your topic?" or "How has your thinking about your topic changed in some way?" can provide the basis for rich conversations about Wide Reading topics. This dynamic asks students to reformulate their learning into personal understandings as they explain to others, thus moving their new learning into permanent memory.

How could Wide Reading be integrated into facets of learning in the discipline that you teach? What are possible texts that could be employed to build general disciplinary knowledge and acquaint students with topics within a particular subject? Consider a specific unit of study that might be an appropriate context for folding Wide Reading into students' classroom routines. What might be some of the texts that you could make available (e.g., books, magazines, news articles, online sources, other texts)?

Mentoring Students to Inform Themselves

If you run across something that you do not know, and it matters, then what do you do? The standard answer today is "I'd Google it." Certainly, the ease of connecting to informed sources with a quick touch on our keyboard is one of the great advantages of life in the 21st century. Even given the potential dizzying array of informational options that may be compiled from your search, and the concomitant need for decision making and critical analysis, you have a high likelihood of informing yourself fairly readily. Knowledge of information is decidedly taking a backseat in many of our conversations involving disciplinary learning because the assumption has increasingly become that if we need to know something, then we can access it nearly immediately from the Internet. Yet, will we? When do we choose to inform ourselves, and when do we let unfamiliar references go by unresolved, thereby conceding an incomplete comprehension? Also, when do we decide to quit, to not continue reading, because we judge ourselves too uninformed to make sense of an author?

In Chapter 3, I talked about instances when we are well matched with an author, instances when we are somewhat matched, and instances when we are mismatched. We are mostly likely to inform ourselves in the first instance, when most of the text is familiar; a quick clarification of the infrequent unknown item would take little time, and we would be confident that informing ourselves would pay off in our comprehension. Yet, how about the second instance, when we are encountering a number of unknown references? How often will we really stop and check out what each of these might mean? We might do a lookup now and then, but really, how many such interruptions to our flow of reading will we tolerate? In all likelihood, this second situation is one when our incomplete prior knowledge will remain incomplete, and we will have to tolerate gaps in our understanding. Also, when we are mismatched with an author, informing ourselves would be too overwhelming; we might perceive the magnitude of the need as clarifying multiple items in each sentence. Sure, we can always Google these things, but when do we really take this step, and when do we let our lack of knowledge go by?

This places us at the crux of disciplinary learning, that transition from teaching to learning, the mentoring of students as they grow from teacher-directed responding to more self-directed independent learning. A key to this growth is inculcating in students an inquiry mentality to reading and learning. Chapter 5 focuses on developing an inquiring mind-set to disciplinary learning, but at a foundational level, an inquiry approach starts with "What do I not know that I need to know to understand, and what can I do about it?"

REFLECTION INTERLUDE

How well do you match up with the author of the following biological science passage, which appeared in an article in *National Geographic*? What do you as a reader need to know for this segment to make sense?

> Built to feed exclusively on corals like this spindly gorgonian, a translucent 1.7-inch-long (4.3-centimeter-long) *Phyllodesmium iriomotense* houses its branching digestive gland within tentacle-like cerata—outgrowths the animal can shed if under attack. This species is one of the few colorless nudibranchs. (Holland, 2008, p. 95)

Jot down the assumed knowledge that you brought to this text in the left column of the chart in Figure 4.18. Likewise, list the assumed knowledge that you lacked in the right column. What steps might you take to address the assumed knowledge that you were missing as a reader?

Figure 4.18. Comparing Assumed Knowledge to Actual Knowledge

Assumed Knowledge That I Know	Assumed Knowledge That I Lack

First, you very likely took stock of what the author actually tells you, in this case that what is being described is an animal known as a nudibranch and that this animal is quite small, under two inches long. The author also tells you that this creature is sometimes attacked and that most nudibranches are apparently quite colorful. Finally, the author introduces some technical scientific labels: In addition to *nudibranchs,* you are provided with a specific name (*Phyllodesmium iriomotense*), a type of coral (*gorgonian*), and a body part (*cerata*).

Yet what does the author *not* tell you? What does the author rely on you, the reader, to contribute toward a comprehension of this passage? An initial look confirms that this author expects a familiarity with some sophisticated general vocabulary. Your ability to conceptualize this animal is contingent on language such as *exclusively, spindly, translucent, houses, branching,* and *outgrowths.* The author also expects you to draw on some biological terminology: *corals* (which signals that this animal lives in the ocean but in shallower areas like coral reefs), *digestive gland, tentacle,* and *species.* Also, the author leaves it to you to infer why this nudibranch would be attacked; your knowledge of the dynamics of ocean life leads you to assume that another animal may try to eat this creature.

In Chapter 3, what an author assumes a reader will already know is referred to as hidden knowledge, knowledge cued by an author but not directly stated. How much of the hidden knowledge can a reader not know before comprehension breaks down? For many readers, the nudibranch example, rife with its complex terminology, would appear too forbidding, a mismatch. As readers, we do an automatic cost–benefit analysis and may determine that we do not know enough to satisfactorily comprehend this article. We may instead indulge in a quick and cursory look at the photographs on the adjoining pages and then skip on to friendlier territory.

Much of our focus in comprehension instruction has centered on student application of cognitive processes like self-questioning, creating visual and sensory images, predicting, inferring, determining importance, summarizing, and synthesizing. However, the baseline for comprehension remains the match (see the discussion in Chapter 3) between an author's assumptions of the reader's previous knowledge and the actual knowledge that a reader brings to the page.

Chapters 3 and 4 emphasize that as teachers, we must be proactive in our instruction to address such knowledge gaps in our lessons. Yet, our students must also develop a proactive habit of mind when their comprehension falters. Moore (2008) recommends explicit attention to informing yourself as a central comprehension strategy. When as a reader, you have engaged in all the appropriate strategies and your comprehension is still incomplete, you then need to inform yourself by reaching out beyond the text to seek the missing links in your knowledge.

Start by acknowledging with students that at times, effective reading strategies may not be sufficient for adequate comprehension. Occasionally students tell us, "I didn't try because nothing I could do would work anyway." Although it is frustrating to teachers when students throw in the towel without putting effort into attempting a challenging text, this is arguably reasonable behavior from a student perspective. Giving up is a justifiable response when students encounter mismatches with an author's demands: "Why keep digging at a reading when what I ultimately need is not on the page?"

Observe that even proficient readers sometimes make decisions that a text is too hard because they lack sufficient assumed knowledge. However, proficient readers also have developed a repertoire of routines that can diminish their knowledge gaps. For proficient readers, giving up translates into being denied access: access to necessary or useful information, access to others' ideas or perspectives, and access to learning opportunities that can open future doors.

Comprehension Checkdown

The Comprehension Checkdown (Buehl, 2008a) provides students with a protocol for isolating knowledge gaps within a text and systematically working through what students are able to understand and where they are stymied by lack of knowledge. The checkdown provides a series of questions that students should progressively ask themselves as they address mismatches with an author.

Figure 4.19 lists the checkpoints that make up the Comprehension Checkdown. The initial checkpoint is of critical importance. Because readers are strongly tempted to forgo tackling texts that present a mismatch, students need to begin with an asset rather than deficit mind-set. Instead of a preoccupation with what they are not getting, this step encourages students to verbalize what they *do* understand.

The second checkpoint is a fundamental comprehension strategy: inventorying personal knowledge that may have relevance to what the author is saying. Chapter 3 highlights text-to-self, text-to-text, and text-to-world knowledge. Students are cued to search their knowledge banks for anything that could be useful for supporting their comprehension.

The third checkpoint prompts students to examine the author's message for hidden knowledge. Some of the hidden knowledge will appear obvious because a reader is able to connect prior knowledge to things the author says. However, when the author assumes reader knowledge that an individual does not possess, comprehension grinds to a halt. Again, students are asked to verbalize exactly what is implicit in a passage that they do not know.

The fourth checkpoint cues readers to evaluate the risk of continuing with knowledge gaps. Some passages will generally make sense, even if

Figure 4.19. Comprehension Checkdown

1. What does the author tell me that I *do* understand?
2. What connections can I make to my personal knowledge?
3. What does the author expect me to already know?
4. How does not knowing affect my understanding?
5. What don't I know that I should know?
6. What hunches do I have about what something might mean?
7. What are some things that I might be able to figure out?
8. Where can I turn to get the information that I need to understand this author?

readers miss some of the author's references. Yet, in other spots, it will be evident that comprehension will be greatly compromised if the knowledge gaps are not addressed. Readers need to take notice of these spots, even if they decide that it is best to move on and look for clarification in the rest of the passage. Some spots will warrant a return sweep, a second read, for further deliberations.

The fifth checkpoint asks students whether they recognize the unknown information. Is the missing knowledge something that they have seen before? Two possible courses of action might present themselves. First, students may recognize that the author has previously covered this information, perhaps in an earlier section or chapter. A quick look back to review can rectify this knowledge gap. Second, a reader may have forgotten prior learning; the unknown material was previously learned but is no longer remembered. In this case, a reader will need to determine an accessible source for a quick revisit of this material.

The sixth and seventh checkpoints encourage inferential thinking. Inferences are possible when readers combine their prior knowledge with textual information to develop hypotheses about what an author might be saying. Clearly, understandings of these portions of a text may be imperfect, but inferential thinking represents readers doing the best they can with the knowledge they possess to figure out possible meanings. Some of the inferences may prove consistent with what an author subsequently tells, and some may unfold as inaccurate or improbable as readers encounter more of the text, and will need to be readjusted.

The final checkpoint takes readers outside the text, when they realize that they have exhausted all their text-based problem-solving strategies. This is the Inform Yourself phase, when readers decide where to turn to enhance their knowledge base. A second checkdown can guide them in their searching (see Figure 4.20). The Inform Yourself phase of comprehension monitoring alerts students to those times when they need to set a text aside and deepen their knowledge base in order to achieve a more acceptable understanding.

It is important that students recognize that all readers meet texts that are too hard given their current prior knowledge and that even proficient readers sometimes need to collaborate and take advantage of other routes to understanding. Mismatches are especially true with many of the texts that students encounter in disciplinary learning, which must be worked to

Figure 4.20. Inform Yourself Checkdown

1. *Use the text:* Are there additional features in the text that can help fill in missing knowledge, such as visual information, illustrations, glossaries, summary statements, and so forth?
2. *Locate a knowledgeable other:* Who might be available to provide a quick explanation or clarification, such as a peer, a teacher, a librarian, or a parent?
3. *Do an Internet search:* For many students, this may actually be their first step, as it now is with many adults. Many useful online resources, including Wikipedia, can assist readers in quickly building a baseline of related background knowledge.
4. *Use reference materials:* How might other available reference sources (e.g., dictionary, encyclopedia, almanac) fill in missing knowledge?
5. *Consult an easier text:* Again, the Internet presents many options for alternative texts, and students should develop the habit of seeking other versions of a topic that may better match their background knowledge.

be satisfactorily understood. Teachers cannot model this dynamic enough with the complex texts of their discipline. The danger is always that students may expend much effort in working a text and yet feel stranded in frustration because they did what they were supposed to do and still did not achieve adequate comprehension.

PARTING THOUGHTS AND TALKING POINTS

- A major recurring issue for teachers in the various academic disciplines is determining what students need to know to read the complex texts of their subjects and how instruction can compensate for gaps in assumed academic knowledge.

- Frontloading is instruction that fronts the reading of complex texts. Research continually indicates that insufficient attention is paid in disciplinary learning to frontloading, with the result being that students are frequently launched into the cold reading of complex texts and comprehend less than they may be capable of understanding.

- Frontloading is integral to teaching the topic and domain knowledge of a discipline. Teachers may be concerned with the classroom time needed to adequately frontload instruction, but if disciplinary learning is to culminate in the creation of new knowledge (referred to as schema in Chapter 2), then instruction must extend beyond covering the content and engage students in activities that support comprehension.

- Students need to be mentored in how to work a text and how to bring their knowledge to bear in comprehending complex disciplinary texts. In particular, this means helping students conceptualize reading as an act of inquiry that can lead to informing oneself.

CHAPTER 5

Building Inquiring Minds Around Disciplinary Texts

Essential Question: How can teachers mentor students as disciplinary readers, writers, and thinkers?

Albert Pujols. Joshua Bell. Does either of these names strike a meaningful chord for you? The first is arguably the preeminent baseball player of his generation, and the second is arguably the preeminent violinist of his generation. There is an excellent chance that you will get that argument from a serious baseball fan or a dedicated listener of classical music. What are the insider perspectives on Pujols and Bell? What do insiders look for when watching a baseball player during a game? What do insiders listen for when hearing a violinist during a performance? What questions would insiders ask when evaluating the greatness of a baseball player: batting average, home runs, yearly consistency? What questions would insiders ask when evaluating the virtuoso status of a violinist: smoothness of technique, quality of sound, difficulty of performed pieces? It would be much, much more than that.

My wife Wendy knows who Albert Pujols is, the magnificent first baseman of the St. Louis Cardinals, because of my frequent enthusiastic commentary, glancing up from the sports page. I know who Joshua Bell is, the brilliant young violinist, because of my wife's glowing admiration every time she slips one of his CDs into our compact disk player. Yet, in each circumstance, one of us is an insider, and one of us is an outsider. When we attend a baseball game together, what we see transpiring on the field are quite different things, even though we are watching the same series of plays. When we attend a symphony concert together, what we hear the musicians achieving are quite different things, even though we are listening to the same music. As a practicing classically trained violinist, Wendy actually has the insider edge on me, a former no-hit, weak-armed high school left fielder and insider wannabe. One of my great thrills was to sit alone for several minutes next to Hank Aaron's historic locker in the Baseball Hall of Fame in Cooperstown. One of Wendy's was to play violin just a couple of steps from Itzhak Perlman as he performed as a soloist for the Madison Symphony Orchestra.

Over the years, I have mentored my wife in baseball, and her insights into the game have grown. Over the years, Wendy has mentored me in classical music, and my appreciation of this music has been enhanced. In effect, we have both assisted each other in seeing some part of the world through a different disciplinary lens. Chapter 2 examines what it means to read, write, and think through a disciplinary lens—like a biologist, a historian, a mathematician, an artist, a novelist, a nutritionist, or a computer scientist. Such disciplinary lenses are predicated on knowledge and experiences; disciplinary insiders have extensive knowledge about the relevant topics of a discipline and have had numerous experiences interacting with the ideas, practices, phenomena, and tools of the discipline.

Wendy not only has studied classical music in considerable depth but also has spent over 30 years as a violinist performing symphonies, concertos, operas, sonatas, quartets, solos, and other musical forms from every period of classical music. Like her fellow music insiders, she brings deep text-to-self, text-to-text, and text-to-world knowledge to her disciplinary lens as a musician. She is able to talk the talk of her discipline, referred to in Chapter 2 as discourse. She can read, write, and think using the discourse of classical music (remember how challenging it was for us to comprehend the Renaissance music liner notes in Chapter 2 when we lacked familiarity with the music terminology used by the author). Yet, in addition, when thinking through a disciplinary lens like music, she knows what to look for, what information to seek, how to organize her thinking, and how she might act on, or react to, what she has read, seen, or heard. Most important, perhaps, she knows the right questions to ask when she is interacting with the world through a classical music lens.

Questioning Through a Disciplinary Lens

What does questioning through a disciplinary lens actually look like? An excellent glimpse into this mode of disciplinary thinking is the 2005 national nonfiction best seller *Freakonomics: A Rogue Economist Explores the Hidden Side of Everything* (Levitt & Dubner, 2005), coauthored by

University of Chicago economist Steven Levitt. The book's gimmick was to examine slices of modern life that are typically of no interest to traditional economists by asking the sort of questions about these phenomena that an economist would. The book is both playful and serious. Chapter titles such as "What Do Schoolteachers and Sumo Wrestlers Have in Common?" are quite whimsical, but the intent of the book is to mentor readers in recognizing that elements of our lives can be more deeply understood through thinking using an economist lens. As the authors state,

> Economics is above all a science of measurement. It comprises an extraordinarily powerful and flexible set of tools that can reliably assess a thicket of information to determine the effect of any one factor, or even the whole effect. That's what "the economy" is, after all: a thicket of information about jobs and real estate and banking and investment. But the tools of economics can be just as easily applied to subjects that are more—well, more *interesting*. (p. 13)

The authors proceed to untangle how incentives are the cornerstone of understanding modern life. If you are intrigued about the schoolteacher–sumo wrestler convergence, then you will have to pick up the book and try your hand at reading through an economist lens.

A number of other recent books also come to mind as outreaches of disciplinary questioning. Thomas Friedman's (2005) best seller *The World Is Flat: A Brief History of the Twenty-First Century* examines recent events and current times through a technological lens. He tracks the digitalization of information, and the resulting ripple effect on how work is done, who can do this work now, and how these changes affect local and global economies. His lens alerts readers to how digital technology is remaking the world around them in ways that they perhaps have not begun to realize. The questions that Friedman raises in his book concern how individuals, companies, educational systems, and countries will all need to adjust to this new technological reality.

Probably my favorite example of mentoring readers to reorient their thinking through a different disciplinary lens concerns, unsurprisingly, baseball. This disciplinary reformulation emerged about three decades ago in a manner that has revolutionized the understanding of baseball statistics. Baseball guru Bill James earned his revered standing among baseball fans by asking long-standing baseball questions (e.g., "What are the qualities of a good hitter?") and constructing answers through a mathematical lens. His formulas often arrived at answers that were dramatically different from the conventional wisdom (e.g., he discovered that batting average is much less significant than power).

Throughout the 1980s, my spring ritual necessitated purchase of the year's *The Bill James Baseball Abstract*, as he offered provocative fresh looks at about every facet of the game. He wrote wonderful essays tweaked with mathematical reasoning, each concerning an elemental baseball question: "What influence do ballpark characteristics have on performance?" "How does speed contribute to a player's offensive value?" and "Who really deserved to win the Cy Young Award last year?" Eventually, James discontinued his yearly publications because baseball statistics had shifted so dramatically, largely because of his influence, that the baseball establishment was now employing his methods. Everybody now understood baseball through this new lens, and we see the influence today in the way statistics are reported and discussed (e.g., on-base and slugging percentages are much more meaningful indicators of a hitter's value). Indeed, several baseball team front offices began looking more intently at players' contributions through a mathematical lens, much to the disgust of old-time, chaw-chewing traditionalists. In 2006, *Time* enshrined James as one of the 100 most influential people in the world for remarkably transforming a sport by asking questions through a different disciplinary lens.

Each of the examples in this section pinpoint the role that questioning plays in disciplinary thinking, even when applied to areas not necessarily considered part of a discipline. Questioning is also central to mentoring students as readers through a disciplinary lens.

Inculcating an Inquiry Mind-Set

As discussed in previous chapters, students tend to regard the reading of disciplinary texts as *doing* reading: taking care of a task that has been assigned, typically by a teacher. In contrast, disciplinary insiders approach the texts of their discipline with a *using* reading mentality: using reading as a point of personal access to knowledge and ideas that can inform actions and address questions. Although both students and insiders might be engaged in reading obligation texts, perhaps the primary distinction is that students usually perceive their disciplinary reading as obligated by others, whereas insiders tend to see their reading as obligated by themselves. As a result, insiders take an inquiring mind-set into their reading.

Reading as Inquiry

A critical facet of mentoring readers in the reading of complex disciplinary texts is nurturing the realization that reading is inquiry—of fostering a culture of reading to find out rather than reading to get done. As literacy researcher Wilhelm (2007) emphatically states,

> The work of academic disciplines is inquiry. And the most recent research in cognition shows that reading and writing are forms of inquiry, and are best learned in contexts of inquiry (Hillocks, 1999, 2002) and through the questioning and discourse that is central to it.... That means that students must be the ones asking the majority of questions and doing the bulk of classroom talk. They must shake off the passive role of receiving information and become apprentices who actually do the work of the disciplines they are studying. (p. 10)

Essential Questions

In their influential guidebook for curriculum planning, *Understanding by Design*, Wiggins and McTighe (2005) posit the central role of essential questions for disciplinary learning. Essential questions target the big ideas of a discipline and cut right to the core of why we study a discipline. When we ask, for example, "How does a novel work?" we are engaging in a serious examination of how authors employ a specific text genre—literary fiction—to communicate to others. We can then consider, "How does this particular novel work?" as an entry into "What does this author have to say to us?" and "How does this author say it?" James was so influential because he not only brought a unique disciplinary perspective to baseball but also asked essential questions. "What are the qualities of a good hitter?" is a question to which every manager and team wants the best possible answer. You will notice that each chapter of this book leads off with an essential question.

Coverage and Activities. Wiggins and McTighe (2005) are highly critical of two trends that frequently preoccupy disciplinary instruction: coverage and activities. Coverage places the primary emphasis on brief and often superficial introductions to the topics of a discipline, under the guise of needing to cover the curriculum, although much of this content is not retained over time.

Activities are attempts to motivate through the inclusion of fun activities and projects that may lead to an active classroom and a bustle of involvement but may not have much to do with deep learning. I am reminded of the colonial project that my sons undertook when they were in middle school, which culminated in an evening exhibition of the various projects completed by the students, and their apparently very talented parents. Some of the projects were thoughtful, some clearly showed meaningful research, and very likely students learned some things. Yet, I kept wondering as I strolled past the displays, how many students could provide insightful commentary to an essential question like "Why were the colonists so miffed at the British anyway?"

Characteristics of Essential Questions. Wiggins and McTighe (2005) instead argue for instruction that *uncovers* a discipline through essential questions that lead to deep and transferable understandings. The authors describe essential questions as

> doorways through which learners explore the key concepts, themes, theories, issues, and problems that reside within the content, perhaps as yet unseen: it is through the process of actively "interrogating" the content through provocative questions that students deepen their understanding. (p. 106)

In effect, an academic discipline is defined by its essential questions. Figure 5.1 presents examples of essential questions from several disciplinary perspectives.

Figure 5.1. Examples of Essential Questions for Disciplinary Learning

- What are the benefits and harms of altering an area's ecology?
- What does it mean to be fit?
- To what extent are people capable of governing themselves?
- What is the difference between music and noise?
- What is the impact of altering a recipe?
- How can stories about other people and times speak to my life?
- What makes a mathematical argument valid?
- What are the pitfalls of not following these directions as expressly stated?
- What influence can humans have on weather?
- What makes business practices ethical?
- Are there rules for art?

Consider a unit of study from the discipline that you teach. What are the enduring understandings—the big ideas that a literate person should still know after the passage of significant time, say, five years later? Now, frame these understandings as one or two essential questions that will guide students as readers and learners during this unit.

Essential questions exhibit a number of key characteristics. Obviously, they tend to elicit complex answers that result from concerted study within a discipline, and they are arguable. In fact, insiders within a discipline would have differing takes on how most of these questions might, or should, be answered. Essential questions are those that we come back to again and again throughout our life, as we keep working our understanding and responding to new knowledge; it seems that they are always under construction. Such questions offer bridges to our prior knowledge, as discussed in Chapter 3; an essential question should reach beyond the classroom and intersect with some elements of our out-of-school lives. Essential questions spark genuine inquiry into the topics of our disciplines and require deeper examination that involves weighing alternatives, evaluating evidence, and considering the case for multiple possible resolutions. Invariably, essential questions lead to more questions.

For example, "What should citizens expect from their government, and what should they provide for themselves?" is an essential question that has surfaced repeatedly in U.S. history and is still being heatedly debated today. This essential question might lead to the following points of inquiry:

- What is the sweet spot between individual initiative and government support?
- What are the advantages of tilting more toward individual initiative?
- What are the disadvantages?
- What are the advantages of more government support? What are the disadvantages?
- Who benefits in each possible scenario? Who does not?

- Whose voices should be heard on this issue?
- How should we as a people decide?
- How should changes be implemented?

Lots of questions, hard questions, that strike at the core of reading, writing, and thinking through a historian lens. These questions pop up again and again, from the early years of the republic, through the Populist, Progressive, New Deal, and Great Society eras in U.S. history, and on to today's contentious disagreements on national health care.

Leading Questions. Of course, essential questions are not leading questions, which tend to be the type of question most frequently aired in classroom settings. Leading questions imply an expected answer, and it is pretty clear to students that there are right and wrong responses to these questions. Leading questions have a sort of cut-and-dried quiz show dynamic about them: "Yes, you are correct" (a buzzer goes off), or "No, sorry, that is incorrect" (the audience sighs). A steady diet of leading questions conditions students to view reading, and learning in general, as the daily process of locating acceptable answers rather than thinking deeply within a discipline.

Essential questions instead lead to conversation—lots of it—and invite collaboration with others as we grapple with piecing together an understanding. To tackle such questions, we need to assemble and examine evidence that can support possible answers; we need to entertain sometimes conflicting interpretations of what the evidence might indicate; we need to continue to question, gather information, and refine our thinking; and finally, we need to be open to changing our understanding as time passes, and we gradually learn more. In other words, we need to behave the way insiders in an academic discipline behave. Harvey and Daniels (2009) contrast such an inquiry orientation with a coverage approach as the difference between "engaging in a discipline" and "hearing about a discipline" (p. 56).

Modeling Self-Questioning With Disciplinary Texts

That students should adopt a questioning disposition while learning disciplinary content is hardly a new notion for teachers. A wealth of research that echoes back to Durkin's (1978) landmark study on the dearth of classroom comprehension instruction reveals a pervasive imbalance in daily questioning routines. She concludes that classroom questions are used almost exclusively for assessment of comprehension but rarely for the purposes of comprehension instruction. Questions are used to assess if students got it, but rarely are designed to help students get it. In many cases, as discussed in Chapter 1, worksheet and textbook questions are the vehicle for skimming for answers, not comprehension. The classroom drill that students have been conditioned to expect is still predominantly that the teacher asks the questions, and the students provide the answers.

An extensive body of research confirms that teaching students to generate their own questions about texts can significantly improve their comprehension (e.g., Dole, Nokes, & Drits, 2009; Duke & Pearson, 2002; National Institute of Child Health and Human Development, 2000). Chapter 2 identifies question generating as one of the major comprehension processes; proficient readers pose questions to themselves and authors while engaged in making sense. An important function of disciplinary learning is to transfer the responsibility of raising good questions from the teachers to the students. Yet professional development sessions that I have attended as a teacher have typically focused on the need for us as *teachers* to ask better questions—to extend our questioning beyond literal-level responding to spark critical thinking and higher level reasoning. I can recall exiting those sessions feeling a tinge of guilt, and maybe some defensiveness, and resolving to upgrade the quality of my questions. Yet, while our questioning practices do deserve attention, we somehow miss the point if questioning remains a domain of teacher behavior rather than a key responsibility of student behavior.

Instead, we need to retool our questioning routines so that we model the kinds of questions that insiders would pose when thinking through a disciplinary lens. Rather than merely asking better questions, we need to consciously focus on modeling better questions as a key dynamic of the Gradual Release of Responsibility, as presented in Chapter 1. The next section presents an extended example of modeling self-questioning using a teacher think-aloud as an instructional strategy.

Practicing Self-Questioning

If students are to be mentored to think like disciplinary insiders, then they need the mental models of good questions to ask and ongoing deliberations as to why disciplinary insiders care about such questions. Students need plenty of practice engaged in questioning like disciplinary insiders as they read, share their thinking in conversation, interact with the processes of the discipline, complete assigned tasks, and synthesize their understandings, especially through writing. As a result, students will be able to progress from readers dependent on someone else's questions to independent readers who use their own questions to monitor their thinking and gauge their understanding of complex texts.

I can vividly recall my own painful adjustments as a reader when I encountered the reading demands outlined on college syllabi as an undergraduate at the University of Wisconsin–Madison. Like many of our students, I had experienced disciplinary reading in a highly orchestrated setting in middle and high school; I rarely read anything without the ever-present assigned set of questions, worksheets, study guides, or follow-up inquisitions. Someone else always did my questioning for me. What I got as a reader tended to be merely what I was asked for: often, low-level whos, whats, wheres, and whens. As a college reader, however, I was accorded virtually none of this teacher-directed questioning. I was completely on my own, staring down at the unaccustomed reading load that included extensive segments of complex disciplinary texts—often entire books—with the presumptions that I was totally independent, needed no scaffolding for my reading, could figure out exactly what I needed to achieve from my reading, and knew how to think when interacting with the authors of the various disciplines I was studying. I was expected to do the heavy lifting of comprehension unassisted, which meant that I had to generate my own questions about the texts I was reading.

I began my college career as a microreader: a slow, careful, laborious reader who tries to absorb everything. Had I majored in mathematics, this approach would have served me fairly well. However, I was a history and political science double major, and I could barely keep up with the voluminous reading expectations of my courses, even though I had always scored well above the 90th percentile on standardized reading tests. I was one of our best readers coming out of high school and had not been transitioned into independence; I was merely dropped into it. Gradually, I got the hang of how to read history, which was not the same as how to read political science. I began to question my texts, and by my junior year, I had become increasingly efficient at reading through a disciplinary lens.

I was fortunate that my grades did not suffer while I struggled, but I paid dearly in hours spent in laborious plodding, not quite knowing what to look for, so trying to retain everything. Of course, many college students experience frustrations as independent readers of complex disciplinary texts, their efforts culminating in disappointing grades or inadequate performance on college coursework.

REFLECTION INTERLUDE

I related my experiences adjusting to college-level reading demands, but how about yours? How do your experiences compare to mine? Can you think of instances when you really struggled with trying to figure out exactly what you should be looking for, what key disciplinary questions your reading should address? When did you begin to get a feel for reading through a disciplinary lens?

Questioning Disciplinary Texts

A major instructional shift for middle and high school teachers, then, is to empower students as active questioners who use the reading of complex texts to expand and refine their understandings of topics and ideas central to disciplinary learning. Such a shift begins with students tracking their own questions as readers of disciplinary texts. The baseline and ongoing question is "What are you wondering?" and the following are examples for extending this baseline question:

- …about cancer cells?
- …about Napoleon Bonaparte?
- …about cubism?
- …about the Pythagorean theorem?
- …about the movement of weather systems?
- …about cardiovascular activity?
- …about a toddler's interactions with playmates?
- …about starting your own business?
- …about the electoral college?
- …about Edgar Allan Poe's outlook on life?

It is perhaps a sad testimony to how far disciplinary instruction has strayed from an inquiry focus when teachers reply, "Nothing. My students will tell me they are wondering nothing." Wondering implies curiosity and inquisitiveness. Wondering is predicated on caring enough to engage in deeper thinking and further exploration. Wondering is an opening to a willingness to learn more. Wondering is an expectation that at least some of your questions will be entertained. Also, wondering is hitched to identity; what we wonder is intertwined with who we feel we are, what we feel we need, and what we expect to use. Wondering like an insider is an investment in disciplinary thinking; we are inviting students to be receptive to expanding their identities and understand some parts of their world through a new disciplinary lens. That students may be resistant is hardly surprising, but our disciplines have much to offer our students. "I'm not wondering anything" unquestionably needs to morph into "One thing I have a question about is...."

Questioning and Frontloading

Hence, we have our instructional opening. Chapter 4 presents several frontloading strategies that elicit question generating. For example, the modeled version of the Confirming to Extending strategy (see pages 131–136) dedicates one phase of the process to questions that surface for students, which are recorded by the class in the "Inquiring: What We Are Wondering" box. Students then use their reading to confirm or revise prior knowledge and attempt to resolve their questions. A key instructional tactic for ceding responsibility for question generating to students is accountability: For example, "Everyone must write down two questions that a person might be wondering about the topic" in order to receive credit for doing the thinking of this phase. Initially, I like structuring this phase with partners so that their conversation can lead naturally into potential questions. When students ask, "What if I'm not wondering anything?" I reply, not sarcastically, "Then, think about things another person might wonder." However, slipping into an inquiring frame of mind is nonnegotiable; every student needs to demonstrate having engaged in the important intellectual work of question generating.

You will notice that other frontloading strategies in Chapter 4 also directly elicit student questioning. The Science Connection Overview (see page 145) includes a phase for question generating. The Prediction and

Anticipation Guides (see page 137) are designed to spark curiosity and get students wondering about a topic so that they approach reading with an inquiring mind-set. The Possible Sentences and Story Impressions activities (see pages 143–145) cue students to start wondering about what an author will be telling them. The Comprehension Checkdown (see page 159) represents a set of monitoring questions that readers should be in the habit of asking themselves as they interact with an author.

Several other highly researched literacy practices for mentoring readers as self-questioners have been developed over the years and have application for disciplinary learning: Reciprocal Teaching (Palincsar & Brown, 1984), Question–Answer Relationships (Raphael, 1982, 1986; Raphael, Highfield, & Au, 2006), and Questioning the Author (QtA; Beck, McKeown, Hamilton, & Kucan, 1997). QtA in particular is an especially promising strategy for middle and high school learners.

Questioning the Author. This questioning routine is predicated on teacher modeling of queries directed to an author at various key junctures in a text (see Figure 5.2). These queries—questions targeting the author of a text—reinforce that reading is in many respects a dialogue between a reader and a writer. Students are constantly reminded that the author is a person who is talking to them, has certain expectations of them, and has obligations as a writer to fulfill. QtA prompts students to talk back and fully participate in the conversation.

Figure 5.2. Queries for Questioning the Author

- What is the author telling you?
- What does the author assume you already know?
- Why is the author telling you this?
- What is the point of the author's message?
- What does the author want you to understand?
- What does the author apparently think is most important?
- How does the author signal this?
- How does this follow with what the author told you before?
- How does this connect with your previous knowledge or experience?
- What does the author say that you need to clarify?
- What can you do to clarify what the author says?
- Does the author explain why something is so?

Note. Adapted from *Questioning the Author: An Approach for Enhancing Student Engagement With Text*, by I.L. Beck, M.G. McKeown, R.L. Hamilton, and L. Kucan, 1997, Newark, DE: International Reading Association. Copyright 1997 by International Reading Association.

These QtA queries reflect comprehension-monitoring questions that all readers, as a habit of mind, should ask of any text within any academic discipline. QtA encourages students to view reading as an act of communication with another person. I have consciously edited my language when talking with students about texts; instead of "what the book said" or "what the article stated," I now refer to "what the author said." Books, articles, and stories are all inanimate objects. It is the author, a fellow person, who is speaking to readers.

Teacher Modeling. To introduce this comprehension strategy, teachers model QtA queries as think-alouds to provide students with a window into the teachers' thinking as students work through an understanding of a text. The use of short texts that have relevance to the topics of disciplinary study is especially effective for modeling. Teachers can project a short text on a screen and proceed to demonstrate appropriate places to hit the pause button and consider a QtA query. For example, a science teacher might share a topical newspaper article and model the questioning process. The following is how a teacher think-aloud might unfold. Note the QtA queries that the teacher embeds throughout the think-aloud.

Questioning the Author Think-Aloud

Here is a 2010 article from *The New York Times* that I encountered recently: *They Crawl, They Bite, They Baffle Scientists* by Donald McNeil, Jr. Of course, I immediately have a question; I want to know, what is this author talking about? What is this nasty sounding creature that does these things and is baffling to scientists? I am also intrigued: What is the author going to tell me about why these creatures are confusing to experts like scientists? So, I take a quick look at the opening paragraph:

> Don't be too quick to dismiss the common bedbug as merely a pestiferous six-legged blood-sucker. Think of it, rather, as Cimex lectularius, international arthropod of mystery. (p. D1)

Ah, bedbugs! So, what does the author want me to understand about bedbugs? I am going to be looking for that. What is the author telling me here that seems important? OK, it looks like the author is cautioning me that although we think of them as common creatures, they really are quite mysterious. I wonder what makes them so mysterious? I will have to see what the author says about that. Is there anything the author says that I need to clarify? Well, there is a technical term here, *Cimex lectularius*, but that just looks like the science term for bedbug. There are a couple of other vocabulary words that people do not generally see. *Pestiferous* starts with pest, and considering that the author is talking about bloodsuckers who crawl and bite, it seems like this word means they are pests. *Arthropod* is another science term; the author says that these creatures are six-legged and that they are bugs, so *arthropod* is likely the classification term for this kind of insect. I'll read the next paragraph:

> In comparison to other insects that bite man, or even only walk across man's food, nibble man's crops or bite man's farm animals, very little is known about the creature whose Latin name means—go figure—"bug of the bed." Only a handful of entomologists specialize in it, and until recently it has been low on the government's research agenda because it does not transmit disease. Most study grants come from the pesticide industry and ask only one question: What kills it? (p. D1)

Well, I was right about *Cimex lectularius* being the technical term for bedbug; the author says it is Latin. What does the author assume I already know? The author mentions other insects but does not name them, so the author might figure that I know what some of these other insects are. Clearly, mosquitoes bite us, and I know some carry diseases. Flies walk on our food, and some also carry disease. Ticks bite both humans and animals and carry diseases. My cat once had ear mites, and many pets harbor fleas. I think also of ants walking across our food at picnics. I know that weevils and locusts eat crops. The author also seems to expect me to know who entomologists are. The author gives some clues, *specialize* and *study*, so these people must be scientists who study creatures like bedbugs. The author also assumes that I know what the pesticide industry is; *pest* again and *kills* tell me enough here. What does the author say that seems important here? Bedbugs do not carry diseases—that seems important—and I am inferring that it must be hard to kill them because that is what researchers want to find out. Maybe that is what is baffling to scientists: how to get rid of bedbugs. I will have to see if this hunch is correct.

Notice from this brief think-aloud transcript how a teacher models these periodic thinking interludes during reading to pose some of the QtA queries in order to work through an understanding. As teachers, we might take this thinking for granted, but many of our students just trudge on through a text and do not truly engage in a thoughtful conversation with an author. QtA queries stimulate an inquiring mind-set, as students are mentored to interrogate the author as they ponder their understanding. A teacher think-aloud needs to be fast-paced and engaging and tends to work best with short texts, such as excerpts from class materials or other topically relevant passages. Five minutes or so of intense modeling interspersed into the class routines provides students with the mental models for thinking as questioners of disciplinary texts.

Scaffolded Practice. The second stage of instruction engages students in the conversation; we are now teaching in the zone. It is now the students and the teacher who are working the text together. We ask students to read a short segment, and we pose appropriate QtA queries to them. As students verbalize what an author assumes they know, what an author regards as important, what an author wants them to understand, and what an author says that must be clarified, they receive the necessary guided practice to do this thinking independently. A brief example of teacher–student QtA work follows (note that you should mark an asterisk on the text where you, as the sample teacher, direct students to stop reading):

Questioning the Author Student Practice

Now it's your turn. Read the next segment and stop where you see the asterisk. Then, turn to your partners and talk about the question, What seems to be the author's point here?

> Ask any expert why the bugs disappeared for 40 years, why they came roaring back in the late 1990s, even why they do not spread disease, and you hear one answer: "Good question."* (p. D1)

[After partners deliberate] So, what are your ideas? What point does the author seem to want readers to get here?

The ensuing conversation becomes a give-and-take consideration of what students think the author is up to in this point of the text. The teacher needs to reinforce that this question does not have a categorical, expected right answer but that students should have some ideas about what the author is driving at. Students might offer that this passage provides some reasons for why these insects are so mysterious, leading to inferences that maybe we do not know much about bedbugs because they do not really harm us and that perhaps we stopped studying them because they seemed to be in decline. Students then are directed to read the next segment, stopping at your next placement of an asterisk, to entertain the next QtA query that you have chosen. We can eventually cede more of this thinking to students working in partner dyads as they begin to internalize the questions that one should ask when striving for understanding.

Independent Application. We can then transition this process to more independent application through the written tasks we provide to students. I found myself reworking my worksheets and study guides so that QtA questioning was predominant. (For example, examine the Interactive Reading Guide on the Solar System on pages 254–256, and notice the frequent QtA wording in the prompts for student thinking.) Harvey and Goudvis (2007) have termed such written tasks as think sheets rather than worksheets, a semantic adjustment that emphasizes the deeper processing intended from student reading.

REFLECTION INTERLUDE

Consider a segment of a complex text that you might use to teach some facet of your discipline. What could a think-aloud look like using QtA queries? Determine at least three stopping points where you could pause and interject one of the QtA queries for modeling. Then, select three following chunks of text that can be followed by a QtA query for students to consider. Try to use at least five different QtA queries from Figure 5.2 in your modeling and student practice.

If we want students to develop the habit of asking these valuable comprehension-monitoring questions themselves, then they need to see QtA queries frequently and have plenty of practice considering them as an integral facet of learning from disciplinary texts. Written tasks formatted with QtA questions not only check whether a student has comprehended but also actually model for students how to comprehend.

Self-Questioning Taxonomy

Over the years, teachers have heard a chorus of educational observers and researchers expressing concern about the depth and sophistication of classroom questioning practices (e.g., Duke & Pearson, 2002; Pressley, 2002b). Chapter 1 indicts low-level questions that encourage skimming for answers, a frequent student default behavior that does not lead to comprehension. Publishers have also been regular targets of criticism for the questions supplied in educational materials that we purchase. Students are disproportionately asked to name, identify, define, list, and state— what Raphael (1982, 1986) terms "right there" questions, as answers are expressly stated right there on the page and merely need to be located. In conversations with editors of educational materials (including an opportunity to serve as a contributing author of a literature series), I have been cautioned that text questions reflect feedback from teachers, who frequently complain about questions that are too difficult for students to complete as independent homework. The upshot of these concerns is that more thoughtful questions need to be entertained, and modeled, in supportive classroom settings rather than merely assigned as homework tasks.

Deeper Questioning

As teachers, we can all undoubtedly hearken back to our college days and our introduction to Bloom's Taxonomy of Educational Objectives (Bloom, Englehart, Furst, Hill, & Krathwohl, 1956). Bloom's Taxonomy offered us a blueprint for our instructional planning by helping us conceptualize how thinking at progressively more sophisticated levels might be integrated into our work with students. Although created with teachers as an audience, Bloom's Taxonomy can also be a powerful vehicle for mentoring student self-questioning. Table 5.1 displays an extension of the QtA strategy, which employs the revised Bloom's Taxonomy (L.W. Anderson & Krathwohl, 2001) as a framework for prompting a deeper level of self-questioning. (Notice that the 2001 revision of Bloom's has flipped the top two cognitive levels; Creating is now at the apex of the taxonomy.)

Table 5.1. Self-Questioning Taxonomy

Level of Thinking	Comprehension Self-Assessment	Focusing Questions	Comprehension Processes
Creating	I have created new knowledge.	How has this author changed what I understand?	• Synthesizing • Creating mental images
Evaluating	I can critically examine this author's message.	What perspective or authority does the author bring to what he or she tells me?	• Inferring
Analyzing	I can explore deeper relationships of the author's message.	How is this similar to (or different from) what I have heard or read before?	• Making connections • Determining importance
Applying	I can use my understanding in a meaningful way.	How can I connect what this author is telling me to understand something better?	• Making connections • Inferring
Understanding	I can understand what the author is telling me.	What does this author want me to understand?	• Determining importance • Inferring • Creating mental images
Remembering	I can recall specific details, information, and ideas from this text.	What do I need to remember to make sense of this text?	• Determining importance

Note. From "Modeling Self-Questioning on Bloom's Taxonomy," by D. Buehl, September 2007, retrieved April 20, 2011, from www.weac.org/news_and_publications/education_news/2007-2008/readingroom_modeling.aspx. Copyright 2007 by Doug Buehl. Adapted with permission.

Using author-directed queries, the Self-Questioning Taxonomy (Buehl, 2009a) cues thinking on all six cognitive levels:

1. Creating

2. Evaluating

3. Analyzing

4. Applying

5. Understanding

6. Remembering

In addition, each cognitive level is cross-referenced with the comprehension processes of proficient readers described in Chapter 2 (see Table 2.1, page 35). For example, thinking at the Understanding level invokes at least three comprehension processes: determining importance, inferring, and creating mental images.

Self-Monitoring

The Self-Questioning Taxonomy is an example of a metacognitive strategy; the focusing questions provide a protocol for students to monitor their own comprehension and trigger thinking that taps into deeper reading. The intention of the strategy is to prompt students to check in at all six cognitive levels with any text they are reading, using standard QtA queries such as "What does the author want me to understand?" "How can I connect what this author is telling me to understand something better?" and "How has this author changed what I understand?" The taxonomy questions are designed to transition students into independent readers who self-assess their comprehension and personally assume responsibility for expanding their thinking about an author's message.

So, if I modeled a personal comprehension self-assessment of my reading of the bedbug article discussed earlier, using the Self-Questioning Taxonomy, then I would demonstrate how to systematically check in at each level of thinking. The following is how a teacher think-aloud might unfold:

Self-Questioning Think-Aloud

Remembering: What should I remember from my reading? Two main ideas seem central: that bedbug infestation is on the rise and that we are not certain as to what to do about it.

Understanding: What does the author want me to understand? A major understanding seems to be that scientists need to learn much more about this insect, including why it has again become a major problem and how it can effectively be controlled.

Applying: How can I connect what this author is telling me to my personal understandings? An obvious area of connection for me is sanitary conditions of places where I might stay overnight, such as hotels or motels. One implication from the author is that I may need to adjust my personal behavior and be more vigilant and aware when lodging elsewhere.

Analyzing: How is what the author tells me similar to or different from what I have heard or read before? My analysis here is focused on comparison: how the author's message compares with my prior knowledge and experience. I had read that bedbugs are coming back, but I did not realize that it was to this extent. The author's comments on the regulation of potentially lethal pesticides reveal a familiar controversy. A major issue here seems to be the contention between controlling the insect and the use of toxins that could have far-reaching health repercussions.

Evaluating: What perspective or authority does the author bring to this topic? The author is apparently a journalist, but no other identification is offered. He cites an impressive number of scientists and references organizations such as the Environmental Protection Agency and the Centers for Disease Control. He showcases a wealth of expert testimony. The article appeared in the Science Times section of *The New York Times* newspaper, which is a reputable source.

Creating: How has the author changed what I understand? My major realization is that a creature that has always seemed distant to my life, and more relegated to highly unsanitary conditions, may quite possibly become a reality with which I must deal. Bedbugs are no longer necessarily someone else's problem!

Notice how by asking myself each of the six focus questions, I triggered some additional facet of my comprehension. The goal for our students is to be likewise able to articulate comprehensive self-appraisals of their reading and cue themselves to engage in thinking at all six cognitive levels. As such, the Self-Questioning Taxonomy is an instructional practice that provides a vehicle for combining two critical facets of comprehension: self-questioning and deeper questioning of complex disciplinary texts. The taxonomy can be posted in the classroom or even provided to students as personal bookmarks, as well as integrated into partner and whole-class discussions of written texts. Students need to develop as a habit of mind the asking of questions that plumb the sophistication of complex disciplinary texts.

Discipline-Specific Questioning

The six generic focusing questions in the Self-Questioning Taxonomy are valuable prototypes for self-questioning. However, these questions are general and do not necessarily reflect the extent of questioning that insiders within an academic discipline would pose about the texts they read. We know that insiders within a discipline would ask more pointed questions at each level, reflecting disciplinary priorities, ideas, and discourse. Examining a science text through the perspective of a biologist, for example, will generate a different set of relevant questions than those asked of a literary work. Generic questions are an important starting point, but they do not take students far enough into reading through a disciplinary lens.

> Expert readers use disciplinary knowledge to guide their reading—knowledge of the way individuals create, represent, and evaluate information, and this knowledge can guide reading even when topic knowledge is low.
>
> —C. Shanahan, 2009, p. 255

For example, consider the questions that would be germane to understanding a baseball game through the insider lens of a dedicated baseball fan. An insider seated in the stands who is engaged in understanding a game buzzes with relevant questions:

- How will the pitcher decide to handle this batter?
- Where should the fielders position themselves for this particular pitch? What are this batter's tendencies?
- How has this batter fared before against this pitcher?
- What should the next pitch be, given the previous pitches, at bats, and the immediate situation in this game?

A number of the questions would reflect baseball discourse:

- Will they call the hit and run on this pitch?
- Will they come inside with the high heat or go down and away?
- Would you instead go with a changeup?
- Can this batter hit to the opposite field?
- Given his low RBIs against southpaws, should they pinch-hit?
- Is it a good idea to take the extra base on the center fielder's arm?

Questions that would certainly be relevant from other perspectives are not pertinent to understanding the game the way a baseball insider sees it. For example, the following questions might be of great interest to a host of other individuals who are also enjoying the experience of an afternoon at the ballpark. Although worthy, these questions do not contribute to understanding the game of baseball through the lens of an insider:

- What type of fertilizer do the groundskeepers apply to ensure the durability of the ballpark grass?
- Who designed the team's logo?
- How do the variables of physics interplay with the trajectory of this fly ball?
- How much does the team mascot get paid?
- Why would players chew tobacco now that cancer risks are more evident?
- Is it more cost effective to schedule day or night games?
- What is the nutritional value of this bratwurst?

Although such questions would be tangential, irrelevant, or even laughable to a baseball insider, these sorts of queries potentially represent alternative ways of understanding the experience of a baseball game. The point is not that these questions are unreasonable but instead that these are not the right questions from an insider perspective. Insiders— knowledgeable and experienced observers within a specific domain of study—wonder about different things than outsiders do.

Using Discipline-Specific Taxonomies

An essential facet of thinking like an insider is question generating. Insiders within an academic discipline rely on posing a core of meaningful questions to guide their thinking and organize their understanding. For example, consider the following:

- What would be the questions that a doctor would ask to understand the state of a patient's health?
- What would be the questions that an auto mechanic would ask to understand the operating condition of a car?

- What would be questions that a meteorologist would ask to understand the coming weather?

- What would be the questions that a nutritionist would ask to understand a person's diet?

- What would be the questions that a financial consultant would ask when recommending investment options for a couple's retirement?

REFLECTION INTERLUDE

In Chapter 2, you identified several discourses of which you would qualify as an insider. Select one of your nonschool identities, such as a recreational identity (e.g., gardener, photographer). Jot down three or four insider questions that you would ask when you are engaged in thinking through this identity.

Following are several discipline-specific taxonomies that illustrate how a research-based generic literacy practice, QtA, can provide the foundation for questioning practices grounded in thinking through a disciplinary lens. Each adheres to the Bloom's Taxonomy framework, but each represents questioning through a different disciplinary lens. If students are to ask the kind of questions that insiders ask, then they need to be mentored by insiders—their teachers of academic disciplines—as they read, write, and think across the curriculum.

What does this process of mentoring look like? These taxonomy questions need to be infused into class conversations, activities, and assessments around the learning from disciplinary texts. Instruction should adhere to the Gradual Release of Responsibility progression toward independence discussed in Chapter 1.

- Disciplinary-specific questions need to be modeled through teacher think-alouds in conjunction with complex texts of a discipline.

- Students need frequent glimpses into these mental models of how insiders think when they engage in comprehension of the texts of their disciplines.

- Disciplinary-specific questions need to be the undercurrent of classroom questioning practices and need to surface constantly in class conversations and discussions of written texts.

- Disciplinary-specific questions need to permeate classroom written tasks, such as worksheets and study guides.
- Disciplinary-specific questions need to guide the assessment of student understanding of content concepts and topics.

Students become more accomplished with what is modeled and expected. If literal-level, location-of-information questions (i.e., get the facts) are emphasized, then that will be the extent of student comprehension. If disciplinary-specific questions are emphasized, then students will begin to exhibit reading, writing, and thinking through a disciplinary lens.

The taxonomies that follow provide teachers with questioning templates to foster student thinking as readers and learners within their disciplines. Obviously, not every question needs to be asked about every text; some questions will receive priority depending on the topic of study and the nature of the text. However, students should be cognizant of asking questions at all six levels about disciplinary texts that they are endeavoring to comprehend. Ultimately, the questions are intended to prompt and guide students into thinking through a disciplinary lens. If you are thinking like a historian, for example, then these are the questions that you are asking, and these are the understandings that you are seeking.

Clearly, not all disciplines arc directly represented in these taxonomies, but these are presented as models that can be further fine-tuned and adapted by teachers to fit the thinking demands of texts of their disciplines. For example, world language teachers will find elements of the history and literary fiction taxonomies useful. Art teachers will find the history taxonomy especially pertinent for reading art history, as well as the taxonomy for technical texts. A high school instrumental music teacher informed me that she found aspects of several of the taxonomies relevant to her work in a music performance context, including the taxonomies for literary fiction (story behind the music), history (influence of the times on the composition), physical science (the physics of proper playing position in relation to sound produced), and technical texts (language of practice materials), as well as the music taxonomy.

Chapter 6 presents a number of examples that illustrate questions from these taxonomies embedded in various literacy practices with disciplinary texts.

Self-Questioning Taxonomy for History Texts

Historians, like experts in other knowledge domains, know a lot of facts; they know the whos, whats, and whens. Yet, they are more focused on *using* facts, on examining pertinent information to help them understand historical events, actions, and phenomena. Insider questions guide historians, like other subject experts, into marshaling and organizing information so that they can make generalizations, develop interpretations, construct explanations, and draw conclusions. Historians broach questions to identify and evaluate the factual information. What do we know to be true, and how do we know it? What kinds of information would help us answer our questions, and how can we access it? Are we missing some information that could make a difference in our thinking? If so, where could we obtain this information? Are multiple interpretations of the information possible? If so, what might they be?

> " In the practice of history, texts are generally used in order to answer a question or analyze an historical problem, yet in classroom instruction the process is often reversed, with questions used to assess student comprehension of the text. "
>
> —Moje et al., 2011, p. 457

Mandell and Malone (2007) have developed a framework for guiding students into the disciplinary questioning practiced by historians. The authors identify five critical questioning themes that frame historical thinking: cause and effect, change and continuity, turning points, using the past, and through their eyes.

Cause and Effect. Perhaps the most elemental question in studying history is "why": What do we know to have happened, and why did this happen? "Why" questioning asks students to look for results, consequences, and effects and clarify reasons for these occurrences.

- What actions did people take, and what resulted from these actions?
- Did something change for people, and how did these changes affect them?
- Did people's actions turn out the way they expected, or were some effects unexpected?

Change and Continuity. Historians are particularly interested in the dynamics of change. Living conditions change. Populations change.

Ideas change. Technology changes. This focus area asks students to be vigilant in tracking any variables that do not remain constant for people:

- What changed, and what remained the same?
- Why do some things change and other things remain much as they are?
- Was a particular change positive for some and negative for others?

Turning Points. Some events in history are hugely influential in determining the course of future events. Historians are especially tuned into these turning points when the future unfolds in a certain direction because of particular actions or changes:

- How were people's lives different after this turning point?
- Were some people's options and choices expanded and others narrowed?

Using the Past. As discussed in Chapter 3, one compelling reason for studying history is to gain insight into our present circumstances. Our experiences of today, of course, have their antecedents in the past:

- What are some similarities between current situations and past times?
- How can these similarities help us understand the present?
- Are there lessons from the past that we can apply to decisions we need to make today?

Through Their Eyes. A common flaw of historical study is to evaluate people through the biases of modern values and conditions. As a result, students can become quite judgmental but not terribly insightful.

- How did the past actually look to the people alive at a point in history?
- How did the reality of their lives and times influence people's thinking and perspectives?
- How did people's ideas and beliefs intersect with their behavior and actions?

Table 5.2 displays a Self-Questioning Taxonomy that mentors students to read history texts through a historian lens. As teachers model these prototypical questions, teachers are inculcating the kinds of thinking

Table 5.2. Self-Questioning Taxonomy for History Texts

Level of Thinking	Comprehension Self-Assessment	Focusing Questions
Creating	I have created new knowledge about the past.	• How has this author changed what I understand? • Why does this matter to the author? To me?
Evaluating	I can critically examine this author's conclusions/ interpretations/ explanations.	• Who is the author and how has author perspective influenced the telling of this history? • What conclusions/interpretations/explanations does the author provide? • How did the author find out? What is the evidence? How can we evaluate this evidence? • What other conclusions/interpretations/ explanations could be justified by the evidence? • Does the author have an attitude, and if so, about what? • Whose viewpoints are not presented? What might be their perspective?
Analyzing	I can understand why.	• What happened? What caused it to happen? • What changed and what remained the same? Who benefited from the changes? Who didn't? • How does the author talk about the effect of past decisions or actions on future choices?
Applying	I can use my understanding to better understand how the past influences my life and world.	• How can I connect my experiences and knowledge to what this author is telling me? • How does studying the past help me understand my life and my world?
Understanding	I can understand what the author is telling me about the past.	• What does this author want me to understand about the past? • What questions does the author ask of the past? • How did people in this time period view their lives and world?
Remembering	I can recall specific details, information, and ideas from this text.	• What do I need to remember to make sense of the past?

Note. From "Reading Like an Insider," by D. Buehl, 2009, Exchange, 22(1), p. 5. Copyright 2009 by Doug Buehl. Reprinted with permission.

that are central to history insiders. Instead of becoming immersed, and perhaps lost, in historical details, students are prompted to ask questions that lead them to consult the information to develop an interpretation of what these facts might mean.

The Self-Questioning Taxonomy for History Texts mentors readers to regard historical facts as critical pieces that can be assembled to reveal a larger understanding, rather than details that must be remembered in and of themselves. Granted, some facts constitute historical literacy; students will encounter references to such facts and be expected to make some meaningful associations. This information is elicited by questions at the Remembering level. However, such facts are memorable only in the context of larger understandings of history. For example, a student who confidently remembers Franklin Roosevelt as the president who initiated the New Deal, but who has no sense of what the New Deal was intended to accomplish and how it changed our country, has not achieved satisfactory learning about this period of U.S. history at the Understanding level.

History teachers who model these questioning protocols take students beyond superficial questions about historical information. Instead, students are cued, especially at the Analyzing level, to strive to discern what a pattern of factual details might mean, and students are guided to approach historical study as an inquiry process rather than a discipline that merely emphasizes the memory of historical details. In addition, students are encouraged to study history by connecting past events to an understanding of their lives and world with the focus questions at the Applying level.

A critical realm of historical questioning centers on authority. Notice the number of focus questions at the Evaluating level. Students read history that is a reflection of the ideas and perspectives of specific historians. Therefore, students need to bring a critical literacy awareness to their study of history:

- Who is offering this version of history, and what perspectives does this interpretation reflect?
- Are other perspectives available?
- What information is used as a basis for this historical perspective?
- What information is not used or overlooked?

As discussed in Chapter 3, historians read history as arguments, not as truth statements.

I relate in Chapter 1 that as part of my personal reading profile, I am currently immersed in Francis Parkman's multivolume *France and England in North America*. The focusing questions for thinking like a historian aptly describe the thinking that I have been doing as a reader of this history. I am seeking his explanations for why things have turned out the way they have, and I am actively evaluating his case by tracking the impressive array of evidence that he provides. I am recognizing the significant changes that at this point in my reading, the French, the Algonquins, the Hurons, and the Iroquois experienced. Also, I am ever conscious of Parkman's voice as a historian, reflecting on how his apparent beliefs, experiences, and perspectives influenced how he understood this period of history. I recognize that I am reading Parkman, the historian, just as much as I am reading a work of history. I realize that I have, as a habit of mind, factored in all of the questions from the taxonomy into my insider reading of this historical work.

As students are cued to engage in the thinking represented by these focusing questions, they become less inclined to conceptualize the study of history as a static, cut-and-dried retelling of events and more likely to view history as dynamic and open to reinterpretation. In particular, students gain practice in using factual information to develop and support their own generalizations, interpretations, explanations, and conclusions.

A particularly powerful strategy at this stage is to provide students with opportunities to do their own historical research, especially through the use of targeted primary sources. As students examine authentic documents of history, they not only put their own questions into play but also become sensitive to the process followed by historians as they attempt to understand historical phenomena.

Self-Questioning Taxonomy for Literary Fiction

Two different questioning scenarios come to mind when many of us think about our experiences with reading literary fiction in school settings. The first line of questioning focused on the facts of the story: what happened, where and when it happened, who did what, and who said what. These questions directed attention to the basic story grammar of a literary work: plot, character, setting, and action. The intention behind these questions was apparently to assess our ability to follow the story line, although the questions often had the appearance of providing evidence to the teacher that students actually read the assignment. In particular, I recall chapter-by-chapter study guides that adhered to this approach as I waded my way through books like Mark Twain's *Adventures of Huckleberry Finn*.

The second line of questioning concerned theme and literary devices. These questions centered on what the story means and the hidden messages intricately positioned behind things that the author did or said. We were asked to notice the author in action and locate the use of language and literary devices, such as symbolism and point of view, to determine the author's theme. Yet, mostly we were asked to arrive at a standard interpretation and were guided toward or, even better, were explicitly taught *the* accepted understanding of a literary work. Hence, CliffsNotes appeal to many students; it saves time and struggle to just download someone else's understanding, allowing readers to rapidly skim over chapters to pick up the gist of the story line, or maybe not really read the book at all.

Yet the more essential questions focus on transcendent disciplinary considerations like the following:

- What can a reader get from reading a respected literary work such as *To Kill a Mockingbird* by Harper Lee?
- What advantages might there be in exploring our understandings of our world and our lives through a literary lens?
- How do we go about negotiating a meaning from texts that represent indirect communications, that are designed to be open to interpretation?
- What are questions that insiders ask to crack the meaning of literary fiction?

Table 5.3 represents a Self-Questioning Taxonomy for Literary Fiction that can be used by English and language arts teachers to mentor student questioning of short stories and novels. The questions for each level of the taxonomy are customized for thinking about how authors communicate through fictional literature.

Keep in mind that the focus questions of this self-questioning taxonomy are geared toward developing readers of literary fiction. Other

Table 5.3. Self-Questioning Taxonomy for Literary Fiction

Level of Thinking	Comprehension Self-Assessment	Focusing Questions
Creating	I have developed an interpretation of what this story means.	• Why is the author telling me this story? • What theme or idea might the author be exploring in this story? • What does this story mean to me? • How has this author changed what I understand?
Evaluating	I can critically examine this author's story.	• Who is the author, and how has the author's perspective influenced the telling of this story? • What does the author's choice of words indicate about what the author might be thinking? • What emotions is the author eliciting? • Does the author have an attitude, and if so, about what?
Analyzing	I can notice how the author wrote this story.	• What literary techniques does the author use? • What seems to be the purpose for using these literary techniques?
Applying	I can use my life experiences to understand the author's story.	• How can I connect this story to my life and experiences? • Why might the author have the characters say, or do, this? • What point might the author be making about the characters' actions? • Why might the author place the story in this setting?
Understanding	I can understand what the author is telling me.	• How does the author have the characters interact with one another? • How do the characters feel about one another? • How do the characters' feelings and interactions change? • How does the author use conflict in this story? • How does the author resolve this conflict?
Remembering	I can follow what happens in this story.	• Who are the characters? • Where does the story take place? • What are the major events of the story? • What is the sequence of these events? • What event initiates the action of the story?

Note. From "Questioning Literary Fiction," by D. Buehl, November 2007, retrieved April 19, 2011, from www .weac.org/news_and_publications/education_news/2007-2008/reading_room_literary.aspx. Copyright 2007 by Doug Buehl. Adapted with permission.

forms of literature, such as poetry, drama, or essay, would require teachers to tweak this taxonomy to make the questions relevant to the literary form. Biography, a related nonfictional genre that shares some of the attributes of story form, tends to feature direct statements of author conclusions and viewpoints. Thus, although biographies also usually follow a story line and a narrative structure, English and language arts teachers, as well as history teachers, would need to adapt this Self-Questioning Taxonomy to reflect those questions that are most appropriate for reading biographies or autobiographies.

Following the Story. The comprehension self-assessment for the Remembering level reflects the basic components of story structure (i.e., "I can follow what happens in this story"), which leads a reader to pose a series of questions appropriate for tracking story elements. Certainly, following the story is a precondition for comprehension, especially when the narrative structure unfolds out of sequence, when the narration omits parts of the story, which must be inferred by the reader, or when the narrator (or narrators) cannot be trusted or offer differing versions of what has transpired. I am reminded of my personal struggles with trying to reconstruct the story line in William Faulkner's *The Sound and the Fury*, which is told in three versions, by three different narrators, one of whom is cognitively disabled and does not understand what he is witnessing, and the other two are concealing things. Yet, Faulkner was skillfully mirroring how stories often come to us in real life, piecemeal and through multiple sources, forcing us to assemble, and reassemble and often adjust, our understandings of what happened as we encounter more of the pieces and points of view.

Following the Characters. Questions at the Understanding level prompt students to pay careful attention to the characters and notice how characters get along with one another, how they feel about one another, and whether dynamics between them change—or as Foster (2008) would argue, what the characters reveal. Readers are especially cued to notice how the characters face conflict and how the author chooses to resolve this conflict.

Reader Perspective. At the Applying level, the focus questions engage students in exploring how their lives and experiences with people can be used to understand what is happening in the story. In *How to Read Novels*

Like a Professor, Foster (2008) addresses essential questions about how novels work, why they work the way they do, and how readers can go about navigating this genre in a manner that is rewarding and perhaps even enjoyable. In contrasting novels with texts that directly aspire to inform, explain, or argue, he cautions not to expect "heavy-handed reminders about what's important. Overt message statements from the author" (p. 124). Instead, he notes, "That's what novels do: they reveal. They're not very good at explicating, at declaiming, or even at essaying. But they're excellent at revealing" (p. 124).

So, what is it that novels actually reveal? It depends. What is revealed is hugely influenced by the reader; the author sets a story into a motion, and the reader fleshes it out. Foster (2008) describes reading as "an interaction between two imaginations, that of the writer and that of the reader" (p. 44). He continues, in this instance referencing the character Pip from Charles Dickens's *Great Expectations*:

> We each bring a great deal of our own lives, our own perspective, our own reading of other works, to each new novel that we'll never see the same things. Your Pip can never be quite like mine, and not because I'm special. You and I know too many different things, entertain too many different thoughts, hold too many different beliefs to see Pip—or any character—in quite the same way. Same words, same pages. Different us. Sometimes, different me. (pp. 87–88)

We bring different life experiences to our reading, so our understandings will reflect different possibilities and interpretations. Literature also offers readers opportunities to extend from their life experiences and consider how they might react or respond—what some observers have called imaginative rehearsals for future life events. Literary fiction allows students to explore hard choices and sometimes harsh dilemmas through the safety of their imaginations.

Author's Craft. Although the focus questions at the Analyzing level look relatively modest, they are the tip of the iceberg in examining author's craft and lead students to be sensitive to how the author wrote the story. Although analysis questions are central to how literary fiction works, a word of caution is in order. Quite honestly, it is questions at the Analyzing level that have often driven many students to distraction when studying fictional literature, as they agonize over, for example, what a symbol means.

As both of my sons, who were devoted readers of choice fiction as high school students, complained, "Why can't we just *read* the book?" Both would say today, as adult readers of more complex texts, that they appreciate a more in-depth look at author's craft, but like many students, they felt analyzing could become a game of expected responses rather than a careful and open consideration of an author at work. Smith and Wilhelm's (2010), Gallagher's (2004), and Foster's (2003) books are excellent resources for deeper investigation of literary elements and author's craft at the analysis level. Teachers of literature will find numerous instructional applications from these sources that assist in questioning at the Analyzing level.

Author Perspective. Of course, literary fiction has much to reveal to authors as well as readers, which can make understanding a work of fiction a much trickier process for students. The focus questions at the Evaluating level help students continue to construct possible meanings of a literary work. Readers of literary fiction need to be conscious of the voice behind the keyboard, typewriter, pen, or quill and tune into perspectives, beliefs, and viewpoints that an author may be threading into the telling of the story. Readers of fiction need to be especially aware of emotional content that is displayed or elicited by an author. "Does the author have an attitude, and if so, about what, and how can you tell?" are especially useful questions to entertain at the Evaluating level. Did Harper Lee have an attitude about something when she wrote *To Kill a Mockingbird*? Did John Steinbeck have an attitude about something when he wrote *The Grapes of Wrath*? Did George Orwell have an attitude about something when he wrote *Animal Farm*? Students can readily relate to someone showing attitude.

Interpretations of Meaning. At the Creating level, the focus questions invite grappling with an author's possible message as well as articulating what a story means to an individual reader. We probably can all recall interviews with authors of literary fiction who cannot really express why they wrote a particular piece, but it is fair for readers to ask, Why is the author telling me this story? If the author did not intend for others to read the work, then the author would have not sought to have it published. Sometimes as readers, we end up speculating more about the author than about the actual work.

Clearly, much of what an author says is intentional: the decisions on word choice, the particular form of the work, the specifics of the story, and so on. Yet, once the process of writing begins, authors relinquish some of the control over where the story goes; as we tell our students, writing is an act of self-discovery. I certainly notice that my writing, which is not fiction, not only engages me in clarifying and probing my thinking but also leads me into deeper realizations about and insights into the topics I am exploring. (This book, for example, has led me into some unexpected directions in addition to what I had planned to say, and I have learned a lot through the writing.) To say this another way, writers do not totally own what a novel means. As Foster (2008) indicates, some authors obviously have specific ideas and themes that they examine through the telling of their stories, but for other authors, the stories emerge and do not necessarily intend to make significant statements about universal themes: "A lot of novels are happy merely to tell their story" (Foster, 2008, p. 114).

As a result, meaning cuts at least two ways. Presumably, a work of literary fiction was meaningful to the author, and searching for indicators of the author's meaning is part of the task of comprehension. However, as alluded to above, the reader also brings perspectives, beliefs, viewpoints, and experiences to the text, which necessitates a consideration of "What does this story mean to me?" At the Evaluating level, possible divergent interpretations of a literary work come into play in classroom conversations and other forms of booktalk.

Self-Questioning Taxonomies for Science Texts

A few years ago, shortly after I presented a literacy workshop for the teachers at my high school, one of the physics teachers visited me in my classroom. He arrived to take friendly exception to something I had said during the presentation: "thinking like a scientist." While agreeing that there are certainly significant similarities, and givens, among scientific folk, he argued that there are prominent differences between how physical scientists and biological scientists see, organize, and understand the world. "You should come to a science department meeting some time," he chuckled, "and see if you think there is great uniformity in thinking like a scientist."

Differences between the physical and biological sciences may be recognized through separate teaching licenses for teaching these disparate areas within science, especially at the high school level. Certainly, texts within these branches of science represent contrasting text structures, methods of organization, and most critically, discourse.

As a result, this section offers two questioning taxonomies, one designed for biological science texts and one for physical science texts. Table 5.4 presents the Self-Questioning Taxonomy to mentor students to read,

Table 5.4. Self-Questioning Taxonomy for Biological Science Texts

Level of Thinking	Comprehension Self-Assessment	Focusing Questions
Creating	I have created new knowledge about the biological world.	• How has this author changed what I understand? • How has this author corrected my previous misunderstandings?
Evaluating	I can critically examine this author's conclusions/theories/explanations.	• What conclusions/theories/explanations does the author provide? • How do we know? What is the evidence? • What other conclusions/theories/explanations could be justified by the evidence?
Analyzing	I can understand why.	• What happened? Why did it happen? How did it happen? • How does this [biological concept] work? • Why does this [biological concept] work the way it does? • What are its defining characteristics? • How is this similar to (or different from) other related biological concepts?
Applying	I can use my understanding to better understand the biological world.	• How can I connect my experiences to what this author is telling me? • How can I use what this author is telling me to better understand living things? • How is what the author is telling me different from what I previously understood?
Understanding	I can understand what the author is telling me about the biological world.	• What does this author want me to understand about living things? • How does the visual information help me understand what the author tells me? • What do I currently understand about what the author is telling me?
Remembering	I can recall specific information and ideas from this text.	• What biological concepts do I need to remember for future understandings? • What biological vocabulary do I need to become comfortable using?

Note. From "Questioning Biological Texts," by D. Buehl, May 2008, retrieved April 20, 2011, from www.weac.org/News_and_Publications/education_news/2007-2008/readingroom_tax.aspx. Copyright 2007 by Doug Buehl. Adapted with permission.

write, and think like a biologist. Table 5.5 presents the Self-Questioning Taxonomy for physical science texts.

Table 5.5. Self-Questioning Taxonomy for Physical Science Texts

Level of Thinking	Comprehension Self-Assessment	Focusing Questions
Creating	I have created new knowledge about the physical world.	• How has this author changed what I understand? • How has this author corrected my previous misunderstandings? • How do I see the world I live in differently now?
Evaluating	I can critically examine this author's conclusions/ theories/ explanations.	• What conclusions/theories/explanations does the author provide? • How do we know? What is the evidence? • How can we test these scientific principles? How can we collect our own evidence? • What do our observations tell us? • Are our observations consistent with the scientific principles we are examining? • What are possible limitations of our investigations? • What other conclusions/theories/explanations could be justified by the evidence?
Analyzing	I can understand why.	• What happened (or happens)? Why does it happen? How does it happen? • What process do objects go through? What happens at each stage of the process? • What are the relationships that cause each effect in this process? • How can we model this process? • How can these scientific principles be demonstrated?
Applying	I can use my comprehension to better understand the physical world.	• How can I connect my experiences to what this author is telling me? • How do these scientific principles explain the world I live in? • Where might I encounter these scientific principles in action? • How is what the author is telling me different from what I previously understood?
Understanding	I can understand what the author is telling me about the physical world.	• What does this author want me to understand about the physical world? • What do I currently understand about what the author is telling me? • Can I use my imagination to see what the author wants me to understand?
Remembering	I can recall specific information and ideas from this text.	• What scientific principles do I need to remember for future understandings? • What science vocabulary do I need to become comfortable using?

Conceptual Language. At the Remembering level, the biological and the physical science taxonomies both recognize the importance of deep conceptual understanding of recurring science vocabulary to comprehension of science texts. As discussed in earlier chapters, the discourse of science is usually a central variable in the difficulty that students have with understanding complex science texts. Both biological and physical science texts feature a great deal of carryover language, described in Chapter 3 as intratextual references. As a result, readers need to track incoming vocabulary that will be employed in communicating science concepts under study.

Science Misconceptions. A primary concern in science learning is the tenacity of student misconceptions, so both taxonomies prompt students to revisit their current understandings and revise these understandings as necessary. As van den Brock (2010) acknowledges, this is a particularly challenging enterprise:

> A reader's misconceptions are especially problematic. Not only do new elements and relations need to be added to the reader's knowledge base but conceptual change also needs to take place. Existing elements and relations need to be removed or adjusted (22). Modification of existing knowledge is often more difficult than acquisition of new knowledge (11, 23). (p. 455)

As a reader of science, I am personally very aware that my understandings are likely to be incomplete or even in error. This is especially true of my text-to-world knowledge base. I am highly conscious of the personal need to use my reading to refine my knowledge. This need is taken very seriously in both science taxonomies. Students check themselves on this issue at three of the levels of self-questioning. Questions at the Understanding level ask students to inventory their current understandings of specific biological or physical phenomena, whereas questions at the Applying level elicit comparisons of current understandings with the new learning. Questions at the Creating level ask students to verbalize how a text has transformed previous misunderstandings (i.e., almost literally, "I used to think...but now I understand..."). In effect, students are cued to remind themselves that they, like most people, often hold naive, incomplete, or erroneous ideas about the scientific world and that as learners, we need to constantly monitor the need to adjust or replace our current understandings.

Visualizing Abstract Texts. A distinction between the science taxonomies emerges at the Understanding level, which reflects research that indicates that visualizing and using visual representations of science concepts is central to comprehension of physical science texts (i.e., T. Shanahan & Shanahan, 2008). Transformation of the often abstract language of the prose into visual displays that are more concrete is especially important for physical science and is also elicited for this taxonomy at the Analyzing level, with questioning on how certain concepts or principles might be modeled to exemplify the processes involved.

Biological texts are even more extensively visual, often devoting as much as half a page or more to illustrations, photographs, and other visual information. For biological texts, students are prompted to use this vast array of visual communication to more deeply understand the science prose, to in effect go back and forth between what is said in the paragraphs, or even sentences, and what is presented in the visuals.

Cause and Effect. Both science taxonomies emphasize discerning cause–effect relationships at the Analyzing level, with questioning that revolves around explaining why and how. I have found that tracking cause–effect dynamics is a powerful tool for reading complex science texts. For example, when working with students preparing for the Science Reasoning subtest of the ACT college entrance test, a task many students do not fare well with and quite frankly dread, I have focused their thinking on cause and effect by looking for "What happens (or happened) and why?" or "What would happen if...?" I have also engaged them in coding the text, marking with a *C* every part of a sentence that represents a cause of something, and marking with an *E* every subsequent effect they can locate. Students are sometimes stunned to notice that they are marking cause–effect relationships in nearly every sentence, especially in physical science passages. (See page 234 in Chapter 6 for an example of science text coding.)

In contrast, biological science texts also emphasize concept/definition text structures, so that taxonomy cues students to establish the defining characteristics that identify a biological concept. Biological science engages readers in classifying and describing, in addition to establishing how an organism works and why it works the way it does (cause and effect).

Interpretations and Evidence. Both science taxonomies are concerned at the Evaluating level with how an author communicates a conclusion, theory, or explanation and what evidence is presented to justify these interpretations of biological life or physical phenomena. Readers need to monitor the logic of scientific claims given the evidence provided. Questioning for physical science texts also encompasses the frequent extensions from the text into experimentation. Hence, several questions for physical science ask students to evaluate experimental thinking: how principles in the text can be tested and observed. Of course, some portions of physical science texts are directly dedicated to describing and guiding experimental work by students.

Self-Questioning Taxonomies for Mathematics Texts

There is a basic irony afoot when talking about reading mathematics texts. On the one hand, as discussed in previous chapters, students do not necessarily think of engaging in reading in mathematics contexts, or certainly engaging in anything resembling extended reading. On the other hand, the reading of mathematics texts is usually an intense enterprise.

As discussed in Chapter 3, there is a significant disparity between conceptual and procedural knowledge for many students learning mathematics. As a result, students tend to regard mathematics texts primarily as problem-solving resources: As readers, students expect to encounter a series of prescribed steps that will enable them to successfully solve assigned problems. Thus, the main task of mathematics learning becomes for students merely an issue of remembering specific algorithmic routines to kick in when faced with problems of a certain nature.

> **"**
>
> Mathematics is not primarily a matter of plugging numbers into formulas and performing rote computations. It is a way of thinking and questioning that may be unfamiliar to many of us, but is available to almost all of us.
>
> **"**
>
> —*Paulos, 1995, p. 3*

However, the conceptual understanding of why the procedure makes sense mathematically may be hazy and not truly internalized, as the Common Core State Standards for Mathematics (NGACBP & CCSSO, 2010b) observe: "One hallmark of mathematical understanding is the ability to justify, in a way appropriate to the student's mathematical maturity, *why* a particular mathematical statement is true or where a mathematical rule comes from" (p. 4).

In other words, explaining why is an essential component of comprehension of mathematics concepts, although students may be preoccupied with grasping how to apply various mathematical procedures. Instead of reading, writing, and thinking through a mathematics lens, students may be immersed in determining the right steps to follow to arrive at the correct answer. Reading through a mathematics lens, however, expands far beyond acquiring the procedural knowledge involved in problem solving. As Battista (1999) observes,

> Mathematics is first and foremost a form of reasoning. In the context of reasoning analytically about particular types of quantitative and spatial phenomena, mathematics consists of thinking in a logical manner, formulating and testing conjectures, making sense of things, and forming and justifying judgments, inferences, and conclusions. (p. 428)

As a result, this section presents two Self-Questioning Taxonomies for reading mathematics: one for conceptual understanding (see Table 5.6) and one for procedural understanding (see Table 5.7). However, these two types of mathematics domain knowledge, conceptual and procedural, are often intertwined within mathematics texts. Some portions of a mathematics chapter, for example, may emphasize conceptual understanding, which may proceed to further elaboration that outlines the corresponding procedural knowledge. In a number of respects, readers must read mathematics through a dual set of lenses: understanding the mathematics at a conceptual level and applying the concepts using mathematics procedures. Hence, considerable teacher modeling of these Self-Questioning Taxonomies, especially through think-alouds directly applied to reading mathematics texts, will be necessary (e.g., the mathematics think-aloud presented in the Compacted Prose section of Chapter 2).

There is a constant interplay between the focus questions of these two taxonomies, and students will need much mentoring in determining which taxonomic question set is most appropriate for guiding their thinking at any particular point when reading mathematics texts. In essence, students need to realize when to emphasize *why* thinking and when to emphasize *how* thinking.

Table 5.6. Self-Questioning Taxonomy for Mathematics Conceptual Texts

Level of Thinking	Comprehension Self-Assessment	Focusing Questions
Creating	I have created new knowledge.	• What do I understand now that I did not understand before about mathematics? • How does this concept help me think mathematically?
Evaluating	I can critically examine this mathematics concept.	• Why is this definition needed? What can we do with this concept? • How does the author use the concept in mathematics problem solving? • What kinds of problems can I solve using my understanding of this concept?
Analyzing	I can follow the logic of what the author tells me.	• What are the defining characteristics of this concept? • How can I explain why this concept makes sense? • How does this concept relate to other mathematics concepts that I have learned?
Applying	I can use my mathematics understanding in some meaningful way.	• Where in my life might I encounter this mathematics concept? • What are some examples of this mathematics concept from my life? • How can I use this concept to describe, inform, or explain some part of my life?
Understanding	I can understand what the author is telling me.	• How can I explain the mathematics concept? In mathematics language? In everyday language? • How can I use visual information (e.g., diagrams, pictures, graphs) of the concept to understand its definition? • What examples of this mathematical concept does the author provide?
Remembering	I can recall specific terms and mathematics concepts presented by the author.	• What mathematics vocabulary does the author introduce? • What definitions does the author provide for new mathematics concepts? • What are the undefined terms (e.g., *whole number, point, line, plane, group operation, set*) in the definitions? • What previous mathematics learning do I need to review to make sense of the definitions? • What do the symbols and notation mean in the definitions?

Table 5.7. Self-Questioning Taxonomy for Mathematics Procedural Texts

Level of Thinking	Comprehension Self-Assessment	Focusing Questions
Creating	I have created new knowledge.	• How can my understanding be used to describe, inform, or explain information, objects, or situations in a mathematical way? • How have I expanded my ability to create solutions using mathematics?
Evaluating	I can monitor my effectiveness in applying this problem-solving procedure.	• Do the example problems make sense when I examine them? • What results have I obtained from applying the problem-solving procedure? • How close is the result to what I predicted or estimated? • What confusions did I encounter during problem solving? • What actions can I take to overcome any confusions that I might have?
Analyzing	I can follow the logic of what the author tells me.	• What is the logical reasoning justifying the mathematics statement? • How can I use this statement to explain mathematical facts that I already know to be true? How can I use this statement as proof? • How can I link this statement to similar mathematics statements that I have learned? • Is the converse of the statement (i.e., if B then A) true? • What predictions or estimations do I have when I am problem solving?
Applying	I can use my understanding for solving mathematical problems.	• What kinds of problems can I solve using this mathematics statement? • How can I apply this problem-solving procedure to a variety of problems? • What are similar mathematics statements that I have previously learned?
Understanding	I can understand what the author is telling me.	• How can I explain the mathematics statement in the form "if A then B"? • How can I rephrase the statement using other symbols or other notation without changing the meaning?
Remembering	I can recall specific terms and mathematics procedures presented by the author.	• What mathematics vocabulary does the author use? • What are the symbols, notations, and definitions of the terms used? • What mathematics statement (e.g., formula, theorem, rule, principle) does the author introduce? • What problem-solving procedure does the author introduce? • What are the steps I need to follow in this problem-solving procedure?

Previous Mathematics Learning. There is growing variation in the nature of mathematics texts that reflects different approaches to mathematics learning, from more traditional texts, to integrated mathematics programs, to texts that focus on mathematics investigations. When mentoring students as readers of most mathematics texts, self-questioning toward conceptual understanding, often the missing link in comprehension, should probably come first. Notice in Table 5.6 the number of questioning prompts at the Remembering level, which underscores how much of mathematics understanding is predicated on previous mathematics learning. Students are cued to pay careful attention to new vocabulary and be sensitive to undefined terms, which will represent assumed mathematics knowledge. New mathematics vocabulary tends to be defined and explained using previously learned terminology, which mandates clarifying all undefined terms. In addition, students frequently have to translate prose language into symbolic notation.

Explaining Understanding. Focus questions at the Understanding level engage students in verbalizing their understandings, both using mathematics discourse and paraphrasing conceptual understandings into more everyday language. Students not only need to talk the talk of mathematics but also engage in conversations about mathematics that reveal deeper understanding, not mere parroting of math talk. In addition, students are reminded to factor in visual information and relate diagrams, illustrations, graphs, or other visuals to the prose of the text. Students explore the new concepts at a deeper level at the Analyzing level, which asks readers to grapple with why: why this mathematic concept makes sense given logic and previous learning. Rather than focus merely on "this is what it is," students are asked to question why this might be so.

> **"** Researchers...recommend that students understand the logic of stipulated definitions [and] examine carefully how theorems and proofs are worked through in the examples to be sure they understand the underlying logic. **"**
>
> —Lee & Spratley, 2010, p. 14

Students are asked to seek ways to ground the concept in circumstances of their lives and world at the Applying level and asked to connect the concept to mathematics problem solving at the Evaluating level. Authors tend to signal how a specific concept relates to understanding some facet of the world around us through a mathematics lens, sometimes through explicit statements and other times through the contexts of application exercises and problems presented for students to put their conceptual knowledge into play. For example, Paulos (1995) examines typical newspaper fare, which he then dissects with the tools of mathematics in order to clarify, qualify, and sometimes offer alternative interpretations of reported information.

Assertions of Truth. The Self-Questioning Taxonomy for Mathematics Procedural Texts displays some similarities to the Self-Questioning Taxonomy for Mathematics Conceptual Texts, particularly with deconstructing mathematics language, but extends consideration into mathematics principles, formulas, rules, theorems, or other assertions of mathematical truths. Students are engaged in verbalizing mathematics statements at the Understanding level and explaining the logic of a statement, given previous mathematics concepts and principles at the Analyzing level. The focus questions in this taxonomy much more directly assume readers' interaction with the new ideas as they examine the procedural examples and explore using problem-solving procedures that are introduced in the text, especially at the Evaluating level. At the Creating level, students are asked very specifically to translate their new learning into thinking through a mathematics lens, as they are prompted to ponder how these understandings may describe, inform, or explain information, objects, or situations in mathematical ways.

Self-Questioning Taxonomy for Technical Texts

The increase in technology in our everyday lives has led to a corresponding increase in our exposure to technical texts, from do-it-yourself booklets, to software's help websites, to product manuals, to detailed instructions and other such resource materials. In Chapter 3, I refer to the reading that we must do when interacting with technical texts as hands-on reading; there is an assumption by the author that we will be actively engaged in applying our understanding to some task, literally *as* we read along. Our reading is presumed to be action directed. We read a portion of the text, stop and perform that facet of the task, read the next portion, complete the next function of the task, and so forth until we have completed the process and achieved our end result. There is a good chance that we have experienced impatience, frustration, and perhaps anger as we worked toward an understanding through technical texts with which we may be somewhat mismatched, as detailed in Chapter 3.

Table 5.8 is a Self-Questioning Taxonomy for Technical Texts, which could be used by teachers of applied technology, engineering, business, family and consumer education, physical education, and other related disciplines.

Table 5.8. Self-Questioning Taxonomy for Technical Texts

Level of Thinking	Comprehension Self-Assessment	Focusing Questions
Creating	I have created a product or completed a task.	• What have I been able to create or accomplish? • How can I use my understanding in future applications?
Evaluating	I can critically examine my completion of this task.	• To what extent have I been able to apply my understanding to complete the task? • To what extent have I been able to meet the author's expectations? • To what extent does my application of the author's instructions achieve the intended final outcome?
Analyzing	I can examine the text and determine what I need to do to accomplish the task.	• What is unclear to me? What can I do to problem-solve my lack of understanding? • What visual information does the author provide? • How does the visual information help me visualize (i.e., create a mental model) of what I need to do? • How do the visuals connect to written portions of the text? To unfamiliar vocabulary? • What might happen if I do not follow specified procedures?
Applying	I can use my previous experiences to understand procedures and instructions.	• How can I connect my previous experiences to performing this task? • What must I read especially carefully? • What help does the author provide for understanding key terms? • What can I do to develop an understanding of unfamiliar terms?
Understanding	I can understand how to follow the procedures and complete the task.	• What is the task that I need to accomplish? • What should the final outcome look like? • Can I imagine myself completing the procedures the author describes?
Remembering	I can follow the author's instructions.	• What steps do I need to follow? • What key terms are used? • What do I remember about these key terms?

Of course, not all of the texts of these disciplines are technical texts, but a number of these disciplinary texts will exhibit features of technical text. The Common Core State Standards for Literacy (NGACBP & CCSSO, 2010a) also include design and other workforce-related subjects, as well as the technical aspects of art and music, in their designations of technical texts.

Teachers in technical disciplines will frequently witness students attempting to complete the task with only a superficial read or without reading at all. In addition, students may lobby for the teachers to tell or show them what they need to know, without developing any capacity for independently accessing necessary technical information themselves. Therefore, teacher modeling using these taxonomy questions as a walk-through to thinking through a technical lens is an imperative with texts of this nature.

Visualizing Technical Language. At the Remembering level, students isolate key vocabulary that guides their actions, review their understanding of those terms, and gain an overview of the steps that they will be expected to follow to complete the task. This is a critical starting point, as lack of facility with technical terminology is a primary frustration when attempting technical reading. A key comprehension process at the Understanding level is visualizing; students have to be able to see themselves confidently undertaking the actions that are described or prescribed at each stage of the process. Students need to imagine what the end product or result will look like and to imagine themselves doing what they are reading. Usually, technical texts feature significant visual information to assist readers with imagining the process; students are directed at the Analyzing level to examine visual information and relate the diagrams, illustrations, or other visuals to the written portions of the text.

Knowledge and Experiences. Focus questions at the Applying level go beyond simply applying the text to the task. Readers are also cued to apply relevant background knowledge and experiences to their understanding. Authors of technical texts tend to assume that readers have already logged experiences with related tasks and are generally familiar with technical terminology; hence, these texts tend to be terse and all business, written in a straightforward manner and providing just enough concise language to help the reader complete the desired task. At the Evaluating level, students are asked to judge their results in comparison with their expectations and the author's instructions. At the Creating level, students track what they have been able to accomplish as well as acknowledge the procedural know-how that they have gained, which can be applied to future applications of the processes outlined in the technical text.

Self-Questioning Taxonomy for Music Performance Texts

Can you read music? At first glance, this strikes one as a fairly uncomplicated question; if handed a sheet containing lines of musical notation, could you translate the symbols into a melody? For most of us, reading music probably conjures up notes on a staff, flats and sharps, clefs and keys, accents and Italian commands, *accelerando* through *pianissimo*. However, to borrow a refrain from the legendary vocalist Peggy Lee, "Is that all there is...to music?"

A musician, of course, will tell you that there is a whole lot more to reading music than singing or playing the notes. Obviously, what is on the page matters, but how a musician understands a piece can elevate measures of symbolic notation into something more profound: a communication—music. Performance with understanding is predicated on a musician's knowledge about a particular musical work, its composer, and the context of the work's creation. Music performance classrooms, such as band, orchestra, and chorus, emphasize developing technical competence in music: facility with a musical instrument or one's voice, reading musical notation, and contributing as a member of an ensemble. Interpretation of a piece requires an additional layer of learning, developing an understanding that reaches beyond the notes and explores the story behind the music.

Students in music performance classrooms are quite naturally preoccupied with playing their instruments or singing. Typically, students do not associate reading and writing activities with becoming more accomplished musicians. The Comprehensive Musicianship Through Performance (CMP) model (O'Toole, 2003) offers a coherent framework for instilling in students that reading music involves getting a read on a piece that transcends reading notes: You can merely play notes, or you can play music.

Musical Selection. Initially, music teachers examine the role that a particular piece assumes in their curriculum. In addition to considering the quality, difficulty, and feasibility of a selection, the CMP model encourages teachers to decide how the piece contributes to a balance in the curriculum in terms of factors such as historical period, musical genre, and musical form. An orchestra teacher choosing Pyotr Tchaikovsky's

1812 Overture, for example, is selecting a work that will build student background about music from the Romantic Period and about the specific orchestral genre of concert overture. A vocal teacher, in choosing the spiritual "Nobody Knows the Trouble I've Seen," is focusing on an American work from the 19th century within the genre of gospel music.

Musical Context. A second component of the CMP model, analysis of the piece, engages teachers in fleshing out a story line for the music. Some of this analysis is contextual:

- What was the historical time period when the piece was written, and how might the times have influenced this music?
- What were prevailing musical forms, and to what extent was this piece consistent with them?
- What do we know about the composer, and was the piece characteristic of this individual's work?
- Why was the piece written, and for whom?
- What other cultural connections might be relevant for performing this piece with understanding?

Technical Analysis. Analysis also has a technical aspect: to encourage students to explore the musical decisions made by the composer to achieve a specific effect. At one level is awareness: How did the composer use the elements of music, such as form, rhythm, melody, harmony, timbre, texture, and expression? At another level is intent: Why did the composer make these particular musical choices?

Literacy Strategies. The CMP philosophy encourages instruction that integrates literacy strategies into the music performance curriculum as students examine the pieces that they are learning to perform. A band teacher, for example, interjects learning about the blues into the practice regime for rehearsing the "St. Louis Blues March." A short excerpt from a biography of W.C. Handy, the composer of this musical selection, introduces an important blues figure to the band students. A clip from a documentary about Beale Street in Memphis builds additional student background, as students begin to connect the song that they are learning to the experiences of black Americans over a century ago. Students listen to various ragtime recordings and reflect in their journals about the emotions that they discover in these pieces. Also, they investigate how the composer manipulated the elements of music—form, rhythm, melody, harmony, timbre, texture, and expression—to craft a musical communication.

The Self-Questioning Taxonomy for Music Performance Texts is infused with prompting thinking that emanates from the CMP model (see Table 5.9). Some of the questions, particularly at the Remembering and

Table 5.9. Self-Questioning Taxonomy for Music Performance Texts

Level of Thinking	Comprehension Self-Assessment	Focusing Questions
Creating	I have created an interpretation of this music.	• What might the composer be telling listeners through this music? • How can my performance communicate this music to my listeners?
Evaluating	I can critically examine my performance of this music	• What expectations does the composer have for the musicians playing (or singing) this piece? • How have I met the composer's expectations?
Analyzing	I can understand how the composer created the musical effects of this composition.	• How does the composer use the elements of music (i.e., form, rhythm, melody, harmony, timbre, texture, expression)? • Why did the composer make these particular musical choices?
Applying	I can use my understanding to perform and appreciate this music.	• How can I connect my experiences to performing this music? • What emotional responses to the music does the composer seem to be indicating?
Understanding	I can understand the background of this composition.	• When did the composer write this piece, and how might the times have influenced this music? • Why did the composer write this piece, and for whom? • What do we know about the composer, and was the piece characteristic of this individual's work?
Remembering	I can follow the composer's instructions.	• How has the composer indicated that this piece should be performed? • What attention do I need to pay to time signatures, key signatures, note values, dynamics, tempo markings, and pitches?

Note. From "Connecting Music to Literacy" (p. 300), by D. Buehl and W. Buehl, October 2008, paper presented at the Wisconsin School Music Association Conference, Madison. Copyright 2008 by Doug Buehl and Wendy Buehl. Reprinted with permission.

Analyzing levels, are targeted toward careful examination of the music; some of the questions, especially at the Understanding level, involve reading behind the music to gain insight into the composer, the genre, and the musical period; and some of the questions, generally at the Applying and Evaluating levels, monitor performance of the piece. At the Creating level, questions target music as communication, as students develop their interpretations of a piece, considering both composer intentions as well as their own choices as musicians to bring meaning to their performance.

The CMP model advocates that as students become more skilled in performing, they will become more knowledgeable about music. The Self-Questioning Taxonomy envisions a music performance classroom where most of the class time is occupied with rehearsal activities. Yet, the model also argues for interspersing throughout the rehearsal routine sidebars of instruction that engages students in developing the knowledge that will guide them in interpreting the music as well as effectively playing or singing the notes. The folk traditions inherent in the choral classic "The Water Is Wide," the confident outlook of imperial Great Britain embodied in an Edward Elgar Pomp and Circumstance march, the supernatural connections suggested by the Russian master Modest Mussorgsky in his eerie "Night on Bald Mountain"—all represent a rich vein of study as students become more insightful about the music that they are learning to interpret.

PARTING THOUGHTS AND TALKING POINTS

- Students need to be frequently provided with instructional activities that engage them in generating questions, rather than merely receiving questions, and in reading to use written texts to resolve their questions.

- The teacher role needs to evolve from question asker to question modeler. Teacher-generated questions, in both class interactions and student tasks, need to model the kind of questioning that we would like students to assume.

- Questioning the Author and the Self-Questioning Taxonomy are both promising instructional practices that model potent self-questioning routines for students; both are designed as general questioning strategies that facilitate the transition to independent reading and self-monitoring of personal comprehension.

- The deeper we study a discipline, the more our questioning is transformed from generic to disciplinary-specific queries; insiders within a discipline pose a line of questioning that has coherence and relevance according to the practices and ideas of that discipline. To a significant degree, thinking through a disciplinary lens is questioning from a disciplinary perspective.

- If students are to raise the kind of questions that disciplinary insiders ask, then they will need ongoing practice with exploring such questions. Students will need frequent modeling of the array of questions presented in the different Self-Questioning Taxonomies, demonstrated through teacher think-alouds, embedded in class conversations and discussions, emphasized in student tasks and written responses to texts, and gradually elicited from the students themselves, especially as readers.

Instructional Practices for Working Complex Texts

Essential Question: *How can instruction scaffold the reading of complex disciplinary texts?*

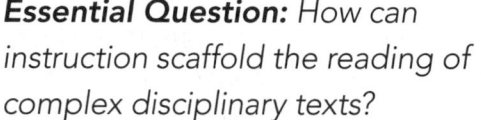

What do you do when you have to work a text, that is, when you *really* have to work a text? When you are unable to avoid reading it or cannot depend on someone else telling you what it says, what do you do to understand a problematic text? Take a moment and consider times when you were presented with this dilemma. I present a personal example in Chapter 2 of a complex text that I needed to work, the Renaissance music liner notes, but I can think of a multitude of times when I have been confronted with the need to work a text: digging into investment documents, picking through the legalese in an insurance policy, deciphering medical information such as medication stipulations, following unfamiliar procedures presented in a technical resource such as a cell phone booklet, and even crunching the occasional research article dripping with jargon and statistics-speak. I have at times dipped my toe into unfamiliar science terrain, such as sampling texts that describe how the brain functions. Sometimes, even my choice reads may need to be worked. I have tackled enticing but somewhat inscrutable-appearing

> **"**
> The message from [the] research is unequivocal: skilled readers know how to select and apply comprehension strategies where and when they need them to comprehend.
> **"**
>
> —*Conley, 2009, p. 531*

poetry and taken on authors who exhibit a more philosophical bent to their musings. I even had to work a recent Christmas present from my son Christopher, a bulky novel by the classic Russian author Fyodor Dostoevsky. Working a text means you do whatever you need to do to get whatever you need (or want) from the text.

Very likely, we would all prefer to pick up a text and just read it, without any nicks in our flow of understanding, without the thud of incomprehension, without the stark realization that what you have just read is not making any sense, and without that sinking feeling that this is going to take some serious work. Also, we undoubtedly have all experienced these sentiments during the progression of our lives as students, those times when we were faced with hard labor as readers.

I can vividly recall such a personal instance, one of my true epiphanies as a learner. As a high school junior, I found myself needing to upgrade my performance in my chemistry class. As mentioned in previous chapters, even in high school, I had an identity as a history-type person, and although I expected to do well in all of my classes, I did not necessarily look forward to studying science with the same eagerness that I displayed when learning social studies or even exploring literature. To some extent, I did not feel as confident in science contexts; I realized that I did not bring as much incidental background knowledge to support my science learning as I had in history. I was a nonscience person who was trying to operate successfully in science contexts. After the first couple of unit exams, it was clear to me that I had a solid but not comprehensive understanding of the topics that we were studying in chemistry. I could generally follow class conversations and at times contribute, but I was not the person to talk to if you needed an in-depth explanation. In other words, I was getting by with a B.

Almost daily, we were assigned sections to read in the chemistry textbook. The content of these sections provided the focus for class discussions and activities, but the teacher was not in the habit of repeating for us what we should have garnered through our reading. Instead, we were expected to display *our* understanding rather than listen to the teacher explain *his* understanding. He approached the topics of chemistry through a more Socratic line of questioning, preferring to ask us rather than tell us. I had been doing what I had always been doing with science reading: understanding only at the level necessary to complete the assigned questions. I was relying on surface reading to locate answers. It became increasingly evident to me that this reading behavior would not suffice if I was to obtain a deeper understanding of the topics of chemistry. I was going to have to undertake the necessary effort and work the chemistry text, and work it I did.

I started by resolving that nothing will go by without making perfect sense. I read carefully, with full attention and determination. I stopped frequently, almost after each paragraph, and summarized to myself what I had understood. I reread. I thoroughly examined visual information and related it back to the written prose. I found myself mumbling over and over again, "So this means...." I jotted down notes (this was before the advent of sticky notes; otherwise, my book would have been fluttering with colorful pennants of distilled knowledge and observation). I paged back to previous sections and revisited past concepts, connecting them to the current topics. At the end of each reading session, I explained. I explained as if I were an expert, as if I were a science guy, as if I knew what I was talking about. I talked to myself, talking the talk of chemistry.

I then walked into chemistry class with more of an attitude. I was determined to showcase my work, demonstrate that I had gotten the stuff, fully participate in the classroom dialogue, and exhibit my mastery of the discourse of chemistry. I discovered that I could respond to the class inquiries with assurance, perceive the implications of my new knowledge for class activities, and project my thinking through a scientific lens. Yet, what really struck me was my self-awareness of identity change; I had started to see myself as a science person, as a person in the know. I would not argue that I was the most stellar science student in the course, but I did become one of the individuals that others came to with questions to seek clarification. Here I was, a history guy, masquerading as a science insider, and I was now getting my A.

REFLECTION INTERLUDE

Think back to situations when you had to work a text. Try to recall a school context, like my chemistry example, when you were compelled to dig in and work a text to obtain a satisfactory understanding. You might even consider your experiences as a college student. What was the discipline? What was the nature of the text? What actions did you take to successfully work the text?

I have called this an epiphany because I had arrived at the empowering realization that I could truly understand material that may be outside my realm of preference and comfort by working it. It was surprising to me to discover that the more knowledgeable I became, the more I actually enjoyed learning chemistry. My identity shift was a significant variable in this reconceptualization of myself as a learner; I was no longer limiting my definition of who I was and what I was capable of doing. I was consciously reevaluating my possibilities of moving from outsider status to more of a chemistry insider. My willingness to embrace examining my life and world through a different disciplinary lens provided a huge impetus for working a text that did not come easily. As I realized, competence is a powerful motivator!

Perhaps many of you are thinking at this point, Nice story, but few of the students in our classrooms exhibit the kind of motivation you displayed with working your chemistry text. As research discussed in previous chapters suggests, in many of today's classrooms, students would not have to. They would not have to develop the capacity to read complex texts independently, as I did with my chemistry text, because they could count on the teacher telling them what they need to know. Because I am an excellent listener, and working the chemistry text was a tedious enterprise that took concerted time and effort, I am sure that I too would have preferred to have had the needed knowledge of chemistry handed to me if that had been an option. However, I was not given that option, and I am a more accomplished reader and thinker because of it. Of course, I am not advocating assigning reading without frontloading instruction—a sink-or-swim dynamic and my experience, which meant that I was constantly sent into the textbook cold and without preparatory work. Yet, I am certain that I would not have learned chemistry, or other sciences taken subsequently in college, with the depth of understanding that I was able to achieve if I had not engaged in the deep processing necessary to successfully work these texts.

A Reformulation of Study Skills

The strategies that I employed to work my chemistry text are traditionally lumped together under the umbrella of study skills; for example, I displayed mature study skills during my reading of the chemistry text. I showed motivation, managed my time well, and found a quiet, distraction-free spot in our farmhouse to give full attention to my exertions. I turned the radio off (these were pre-iPod days). I recited, I paraphrased, and I summarized. I used note-taking and would have marked the text, underlining or highlighting, if that had been permitted; I certainly used text marking and annotating a lot as a college student, when I was compelled to purchase the texts that I studied. Implicit in my actions were the use of text features provided by the author, especially visual information, to guide my thinking. In college, I sometimes took my verbalizations a step further, going public by linking up with other students in study groups, so we could practice our explanations, rehearse our understandings, and more deeply engage with the material. All of these actions are predicated on commitment, a commitment to do what is necessary when I have to work a complex text.

Identity and Habits of Mind

All of these actions are predicated on identity. Who is the kind of person who would use such study routines to work a text, and how do we as teachers nurture such disciplinary identities? This gets us into that nebulous territory that is encapsulated in the term *study skills*. The term *skill* is in and of itself diverting. For example, my wife Wendy is a skilled violinist. She got that way via certain attitudes and behaviors that she brought to practice routines as she worked her music. I do not know that we would term her practice routines as skills, however. We would more likely say she has excellent practice habits that have contributed to her development of skill on her instrument. Since her high school years, Wendy has sought an identity as a violinist, which has motivated her to adopt highly effective work routines that have enhanced her skill as a musician. When she practices, she demonstrates dedication, determination, perseverance, goal setting, attention to detail, adherence to proper technique, patience for incrementally gained mastery, and of course, frustration management—none of which we would necessarily term skills, but all are means to developing skill. These might be called habits of mind, a term I vastly prefer over study skills.

Goleman (1995) has introduced the term *emotional intelligence* to describe traits that are integral to these habits of mind. In his review of a wide range of research, he isolates a number of personality variables that affect performance, including the following:

- Resisting impulsivity
- Managing stress and frustration

- Handling failure
- Showing persistence
- Maintaining a positive outlook
- Collaborating effectively
- Delaying gratification

Linked to these traits is displaying an internal drive, an inclination to motivate oneself to meet valued personal goals. Goleman's (1995) central argument is that emotional intelligence factors are critical to achievement, perhaps more necessary than just talent alone, and that these are all traits that can be fostered by teachers in our students. It is easy to see how intricately such characteristics are woven into the kind of persona that can be successful in negotiating the rigor associated with disciplinary learning. We rarely pass a day with students without considering how motivation intersects with disciplinary learning.

Personal Systems

Teachers often refer to lack of study skills as a significant hindrance to student reading and learning in their disciplines. The conversation among teachers frequently veers into "Someone needs to teach these students study skills," or more rarely, "*We* need to teach our students study skills." When teachers mention study skills, they are generally speaking of student work routines and, in this case, the work that one must do to comprehend complex texts. Some of what we call study skills are personal systems that we employ to work at peak efficiency and effectiveness, and others are learning strategies that we use to successfully do the work of a specific task. For example, when we say students are disorganized, we are referring to personal systems for doing the general work of a student. Likewise, when we talk about students needing to schedule their time effectively, create a work environment at home that is conducive to studying, and manage competing demands to ensure that school tasks are completed properly, we are identifying personal systems. When we talk about actions like note-taking, text marking or annotating, previewing a chapter, reciting, or creating graphic representations like charts and concept maps, we are now referring to learning strategies that are appropriate for understanding and remembering.

When I think about personal systems for undertaking a task, I am immediately reminded of my father-in-law, who worked for 40 years as a mechanical expert and repair technician for the local Oscar Mayer food-processing plant. His life was maintaining and repairing the complicated and intricate machinery that kept the plant humming, and his personal systems for his work spilled over into other facets of his life, especially in home improvement projects. When we worked together, he insisted on clearing the area first and then unpacking and organizing his tools, each item allocated and returned to its place after each use. He always knew immediately where everything he needed was, and he proceeded to work methodically and carefully, never in a hurry and always rehearsing the steps that he would follow for a specific task. If my more sloppy routines, especially with handling tools, were not what he expected, then he kindly suggested that I should adhere to his methodology. I would stand by, sometimes impatiently, while he muttered aloud his problem solving and puttered about meticulously lining up materials and identifying necessary tools. My father-in-law had a very successful system for doing the work the "right" way; it was integral to his identity as a tradesman.

My family would tell you that although I had plenty of modeling and practice with my father-in-law's very precise and systematic routines, I have not really adopted them personally when I am engrossed in my own home improvement projects. I tend to jump into the work, fetch my tools as I need them, occasionally misplace them, waste time with searching for where I left an item, and generally operate in the midst of chaos. I am not careless, but I am not as efficient as I could be. My routines work well enough for me for my infrequent projects, and I tolerate work conditions that my father-in-law would never permit. Again, it is a matter of identity.

REFLECTION INTERLUDE

I have referred to my wife's personal system for practicing her violin and my father-in-law's personal system for projects that involve the use of tools. Who do you know who has a clearly articulated personal system for accomplishing tasks of a certain nature, perhaps yourself? Take a few moments and describe the elements and routines of this person's system. How does the personal system facilitate doing the targeted tasks efficiently and well?

Learning Strategies

Certainly, teachers have cause for concern with their students' personal study systems, from overstuffed backpacks and cluttered lockers to dilatory and dallying behaviors that result in rushed or shoddy efforts, late assignments, or uncompleted work. However, this chapter focuses on the second facet traditionally connected to study skills: learning strategies.

Several issues surface during a consideration of strategy use with complex texts:

- Teachers should neither assume that their students know how to effectively work a text nor that they have had the sufficient guided practice so that such strategies become internalized routines.

- Teachers should not regard study skills as generic practices but rather as disciplinary-specific strategies that will vary in form and application, depending on the nature of the text and the demands of the discipline. (Formulaic approaches, such as two-column note-taking, may overlook different challenges and needs with various disciplinary texts.)

- Teachers should not assume that students will choose to use particular learning strategies on their own, even if they have been introduced to them, or that students would be willing to work a text with the intensity that many of these strategies mandate.

This last issue, of course, directly involves developing student identities as readers, writers, and thinkers through specific disciplinary lenses.

In their research synthesis on cognitive strategy instruction, Dole and colleagues (2009) note the key role of motivation:

> Students must be persuaded to see that the goals of the strategies have personal relevance and meaning for them, that the various strategies have value and utility for them, and that self-managing their time and effort in using the strategies will aid them in achieving their reading goals. (p. 350)

Notice that this quotation centers on the word *persuaded*; mentoring students means we make a compelling case for the work rather than merely expect it to be done.

Researchers posit that students need to know the what, the how, and the when and why of using learning strategies to work complex texts (Paris, Lipson, & Wixson, 1983):

- *What* is declarative knowledge. Readers develop what Wilhelm and his colleagues (2001) have termed moves, which are actions to help readers understand and remember.

- *How* is procedural knowledge. Readers have experienced the necessary guided practice so that they are comfortable with the thinking involved in applying a learning strategy.

- *When* and *why* are conditional knowledge. Readers can scope out the conditions of a task and decide on the most appropriate actions to satisfy their challenges as a reader.

It is this conditional knowledge that can be the missing link in disciplinary learning, but conditional knowledge cannot be neglected if students are to become intentional agents of strategy use. As argued in previous chapters, the conditions are very context dependent and can vary dramatically from one disciplinary setting to the next. In other words, if students do not receive disciplinary-specific instruction in learning strategies, then they might become competent in applying learning strategies in some disciplines and not in others.

A common theme in the research on learning strategies is the lack of transfer; students learn strategies in one setting but do not transfer this knowledge to other settings (e.g., Conley, 2009; Dole et al., 2009). Often, learning strategies are introduced, and students receive practice applying them in decontextualized settings, such as a study skills unit or course. For a number of years, I taught an elective course for ninth-grade students that targeted the development of effective learning routines. It was not difficult to teach the declarative (what) and procedural (how) facets of learning strategies. Students could demonstrate effective strategy use with complex texts in my classroom, but the key variable was their comfort in transferring these actions to the study of other disciplines. Even though I modeled strategy use with the texts of their other disciplines, many students still had trouble making the jump to the when and why of conditional knowledge in those classes.

The most significant absent dimension was the context-specific modeling by their disciplinary teachers that reinforced strategy use in the service of understanding those disciplines, and the regular, ongoing guided practice within those disciplinary contexts. What I was proposing to my students was frankly more work than they were used to doing, especially when compared with skimming for answers. Students need to see that learning strategies are critical to unlocking learning in their disciplinary subjects and that expending such effort will be worthwhile. Students' motivation to do so hinges on fostering them to adopt identities that include interacting with the world through different disciplinary lenses.

Developing Reader Moves

Sports fans relish regaling each other with the fabled moves of their favorite players: the moves of hockey legend Wayne Gretzky as he swooped toward the net, the moves of tennis superstar Serena Williams as she shut down another opponent, the moves of silk-smooth NBA forward Kevin Durant as he outflanked a defender to slam home two more, and the moves of wily veteran NFL quarterback Peyton Manning as he marched through the defense for another touchdown. Children imitate the moves of admired athletes, and arguments abound as to whose "game" displays the best moves. (Will there ever be another baseball shortstop who can match the moves of the incomparable Wizard of Oz, Hall of Famer Ozzie Smith?)

As previously stated, Wilhelm and his colleagues (2001) coined the term *moves* to refer to the actions we take as readers when we engage with a text. The analogy to the effective moves developed by highly skilled athletes is a powerful one: Proficient readers have also established a repertoire of successful moves that enable them to handle a wide range of texts for a variety of useful purposes. Both accomplished athletes and proficient readers make moves that represent actions that are intentional, are undertaken to achieve success in one's efforts, are fine-tuned through considerable practice, are adaptable to varying situations or circumstances, can become a matter of habit, and can be personalized so that different individuals have their own preferred moves. Helping students identify the reader moves that enable them to work complex texts is a significant step in their development as independent readers and learners in disciplinary contexts.

Cognitive Strategies

Some reader moves can be described as orchestrated ways of thinking as a reader, identified in Chapter 2 as comprehension processes. These moves represent self-directing and planful thinking that becomes a habit of mind for accomplished readers. Some of these comprehension moves for readers are the following:

- I try to think about things I already know that are connected to what I am reading.
- I try to picture in my head what an author is saying.
- I raise questions to myself while I am reading.
- I try to decide what a person should know about what the author tells me.
- I look for implications of things that are not directly stated.
- I try to sum up what an author is saying in my own words.

These moves are sometimes referred to as cognitive strategies. Chapter 5 is dedicated exclusively to questioning moves that readers can make in different disciplinary contexts.

Metacognitive Strategies

Some reader moves can be categorized as metacognitive strategies. When readers are conscious of tracking their own thinking, they are behaving metacognitively. I would describe this dynamic to my students with the analogy that proficient readers behave as if they have a split personality, that there are of two of them engaged in the reading process. One personality does the direct work of comprehension: interacting with an author and the text. The other watches intently, monitoring to make sure everything is proceeding satisfactorily.

> "
> A good reader, then, should be one who questions what is read, re-reads confusing passages, and evaluates his or her understanding of what the author is trying to communicate.
> "
> —Baker & Beall, 2009, p. 380

The metacognitive voice is the one that periodically interjects, "Hold on there! This isn't making any sense." The metacognitive voice sometimes evaluates: "I know I didn't totally get that, but I probably understood well enough to meet my goals," or "Unacceptable! We're going to have to try something else here." The metacognitive voice is also analytical: "Hmm, tough vocabulary here, that's what's throwing me off," "Yeeks, I must have misread that previous part because this isn't what I was expecting," or "Pretty familiar stuff here, I'll just accelerate my rate to check for anything that might be new." Finally, the metacognitive voice is controlling: "OK, if this reading is going to end up making any sense, then there are some adjustments that we are going to need to make here." My students have shared that the metacognitive personality sounds a lot like a bossy backseat driver who really needs to be obeyed whether the driver likes it or not. The Comprehension Checkdown questions in Chapter 4 (see page 159) are an example of strategies to inculcate this metacognitive processing.

It is this metacognitive presence that needs to be awakened, or even ignited, for many of our students. For them, if there are any directives coming from the back seat, then they are in the teacher's voice not theirs. Otherwise, students drive merrily, or perhaps begrudgingly, along through the dense fog of a text, regardless of smashups in comprehension. You cannot work a text without this metacognitive self-guidance, and teacher modeling as well as classroom tasks around complex texts need to make explicit these metacognitive strategies. In Chapter 2, the comprehension process of monitoring one's reading and applying fix-up strategies sets into motion making metacognitive moves as a reader. Regular class debriefing sessions about *how* students are thinking are just as important as the discussions about *what* they are thinking. Schoenbach and colleagues (1999) call these debriefing sessions metacognitive conversations, periodic sharing and evaluating of the thinking and the strategies that students use as they work their comprehension.

Strategic Actions

This leads us to a third category of reader moves: strategic actions. Ultimately, these are actions that are initiated and directed by the reader to support comprehension and lay the groundwork for learning. Strategic actions contrast with the default reading behaviors often assumed by students: a sole focus on the completion of teacher-initiated tasks, such as filling out a worksheet or answering a set of questions. Strategic actions become internalized ways of responding to the demands of working a text. In their research review on learning strategies, Weinstein and Mayer (1986) subdivide these strategic reader actions into rehearsing, elaborating, and organizing moves. Each of these moves are examined in some detail in this chapter, with disciplinary-specific examples on instructional practices that mentor students in using these strategic actions.

Instructional Practices for Rehearsing

A rehearsing strategy emphasizes the comprehension process of determining importance. For example, highlighting and underlining are both moves that lift out portions of an author's message that are deemed by a reader to warrant some return time. Text annotating, such as inserting an asterisk next to places in the text that are judged important, is also a rehearsing strategy because it designates where in the text the reader needs to return for further deliberation. Jotting down verbatim notes and tagging spots in a text with sticky notes are further examples of rehearsing, both of which involve identifying segments of the author's message that will receive more work. Pausing periodically for reciting is a classic rehearsal strategy, a quick, on-the-spot return to verbalize some parts of a message. If you would pull out any of my old college texts, as well as most of the current professional books and articles that I have read, you would find ample evidence of me using nearly all of these rehearsal strategies.

Of course, as teachers, we can hardly take rehearsing moves for granted. When we engage in rehearsing as a reader, we are exhibiting a personal commitment to strive toward satisfactory comprehension and to use our reading to broaden and deepen our understanding. Rehearsing is in direct contrast to the drive-by reading preferred by many of our students, who hurry through a text merely to complete a task. Instead, when readers work a text, they pull over frequently for a more intense took, ponder what they are seeing, and come back repeatedly to view the highlights.

Students need a great deal of practice with rehearsing moves. Determining importance is a comprehension process that is particularly challenging. As mentioned a number of times in this book, students generally prefer tasks that allow them to quickly locate something that can be written down to satisfy an assignment demand. In contrast, rehearsing moves require judgment and decision making; readers must determine what is background information and what is essential for understanding. Rehearsing moves involve identifying those text elements that qualify for further study and learning. Otherwise, many disciplinary texts loom as overwhelming mazes of dense information and details.

Text Marking

Highlighting, underlining, and marginal annotating are the most efficient rehearsing moves, and when texts can be marked, these strategic actions should be integrated into any task assigned to accompany reading. However, much modeling and explicit instruction of the thinking behind determining importance need to be provided before eager students commence wielding their uncapped highlighters. Otherwise, "yellow marker syndrome" is likely to ensue, with overmarking, random marking, or outright coloring a probable result. During modeling, students need to tune into the teacher's thinking as these strategic marking choices are made, they need to see well-marked passages numerous times, and they need guided practice and frequent feedback on the intellectual work involved with determining importance. Sticky notes are certainly a workable option for achieving this purpose with any text, but they are a necessity with texts that cannot be marked.

For example, what would you target as important for marking in a work of literary fiction? Certainly, a number of highlighting or underlining choices could be made by a reader, but providing guidance to students as to what to be alert for can make marking a highly useful move. Edgar Allan Poe, that macabre presence in many literature anthologies, offers an outstanding opportunity for students to explore how the use of language

> **"**
> Providing students with even a limited amount of instruction in how to underline important main ideas and the need to review those ideas is important for enhanced performance.
> **"**
> —Caverly, Orlando, & Mullen, 2000, p. 113

establishes tone or mood of a passage. Two key evaluating questions in the Self-Questioning Taxonomy for Literary Fiction (see Table 5.3) are "What does the author's choice of words indicate about what the author might be thinking?" and "What emotions is the author eliciting?" The opening paragraph of Poe's (1839/1984) *The Fall of the House of Usher* provides an excellent practice text for marking emotional content in a literary work. In this case, students were instructed to mark all words and phrases that show emotion or stimulate an emotional response from a reader:

> During the whole of a <u>dull, dark, and soundless</u> day in the autumn of the year, when the clouds hung <u>oppressively low</u> in the heavens, I had been

passing <u>alone</u>, on horseback, through a <u>singularly dreary</u> tract of country; and at length found myself, as the shades of the evening drew on, within view of the <u>melancholy</u> House of Usher. I know not how it was—but, with the first glimpse of the building, a sense of <u>insufferable gloom pervaded my spirit</u>. I say <u>insufferable</u>; for the <u>feeling was unrelieved</u> by any of that half-pleasurable, because poetic, sentiment, with which the mind usually receives even the <u>sternest</u> natural images of the <u>desolate or terrible</u>. I looked upon the scene before me—upon the <u>mere</u> house, and the simple landscape features of the domain—upon the <u>bleak</u> walls—upon the <u>vacant eye-like windows</u>—upon a few <u>rank</u> sedges—and upon a few white trunks of <u>decayed</u> trees—with an <u>utter depression of soul</u> which I can compare to <u>no earthly sensation</u> more properly than to the after-dream of the reveller upon <u>opium</u>—the <u>bitter lapse</u> into everyday life—the <u>hideous</u> dropping off of the veil. There was an <u>iciness</u>, a <u>sinking</u>, a <u>sickening of the heart</u>—an <u>unredeemed dreariness</u> of thought which no <u>goading</u> of the imagination could <u>torture</u> into aught of the sublime. (p. 317, all underlining added)

Enough already! Poe goes on in this vein, but toss in some other opening details of the setting (e.g., autumn, when things begin to die; the isolated location, which could lead to feelings of vulnerability; the onset of evening, which foreshadows the coming darkness), and you have identified plenty of the spooky, menacing tone for what would surely be a Poe-like story to follow. In this instance, students were provided with explicit guidance in Text Marking, and as they inventoried the text elements that they identified as having emotional content, the students were prepared to talk about the mood created by Poe's choice of words and begin considering what this author might be up to here.

REFLECTION INTERLUDE

What could be a complex text from your discipline with which you could demonstrate appropriate text marking? Consider a short text, or a segment of a longer disciplinary text, for which you would like students to use text marking or highlighting as a rehearsing move. What would warrant attention as of key importance? How could you model your thinking as you decided what was deserving of marking versus what was merely secondary information or details?

Note-Taking

Note-Taking, the most laborious rehearsing strategy, may be the best strategic move with some texts, especially those that cannot be marked. Note-Taking is predicated on culling out key material that can be reviewed at a later time for learning and further application. Verbatim notes, the copying of identified key material, need to be thoughtfully and purposefully taken; obviously, Note-Taking needs to transcend the act of merely writing stuff down. The form that notes might take can be quite idiosyncratic, but regardless of format, notes function as personal reminders of elements of a text deemed important.

Online texts present special issues with rehearsing strategies, although at times, some texts can be printed and marked, which is my preference when that is an option, but it is often unworkable in a classroom setting. Students will need plenty of mentoring, with practice and feedback, in Note-Taking procedures for online texts.

> **Retrieval is not merely a read out of the knowledge stored in one's mind; the act of reconstructing knowledge itself enhances learning.**
>
> —*Karpicke & Blunt, 2011, p. 774*

Of course, rehearsing strategies ultimately must result in using the strategies' moves—Text Marking, highlighting, and Note-Taking—as a basis for rehearsing understanding. Karpicke and Blunt (2011) demonstrate the high level of effectiveness of intentional retrieval moves: reciting through free-recall note-taking (i.e., not looking at the text while listing what is important), repeated over multiple sessions. Deciding what deserves attention and then intending to remember it must go hand in hand.

Instructional Practices for Elaborating

Elaborating moves involve more in-depth processing of a text. The Self-Questioning Taxonomies presented in Chapter 5 are all examples of elaborating strategies; the reader begins to interact with an author, clarify understanding, and personalize a message. Questioning the Author (see page 175) is the epitome of a research-based elaborating move. In effect, all of the comprehension processes detailed in Chapter 2—making connections to prior knowledge, generating questions, creating mental images, making inferences, determining importance, and synthesizing—depend on elaborating moves by the reader.

Figure 6.1 presents an example from the health curriculum, as students are prompted to use the six levels of questioning discussed in Chapter 5 to elaborate on their understandings of an article that alerts readers to the dangers of hearing loss from MP3 players. Students use the Self-Questioning Taxonomy (see page 181) to walk their

Figure 6.1. Self-Questioning Response Chart on Hearing Damage

Level of Thinking	Comprehension Self-Assessment	Focusing Question	Sample Response
Creating	I have created new knowledge.	How has this author changed what I understand?	"Listening to my MP3 player too loud may not affect my hearing right away. I need to use the three-foot rule to protect my ears."
Evaluating	I can critically examine this author's message.	What perspective or authority does the author bring to what he or she tells me?	"An expert on hearing is likely to know what he's talking about, so I believe that listening to music too loud can hurt my hearing."
Analyzing	I can explore deeper relationships of the author's message.	How is this similar to (or different from) other texts that I have read?	"I've heard and read that the level of noise at rock concerts can cause temporary hearing loss."
Applying	I can use my understanding in a meaningful way.	How can I connect what this author is telling me to understand something better?	"I remember how my ears rang the day after I attended a rock concert last summer."
Understanding	I can understand what the author is telling me.	What does this author want me to understand?	"Listening to MP3 players on high volume with earbuds can contribute to hearing loss as much as rock concerts can."
Remembering	I can recall specific details, information, and ideas from this text.	What do I need to remember to make sense of this text?	"Exposure to loud noises can cause hearing loss."

Note. Courtesy of Jennifer Breezee, DeForest Area High School, DeForest, WI.

personal thinking through the article and express their understandings at each level of the taxonomy. In effect, the elaborating move is for students to question themselves as they consider what the author is telling them.

Text Coding

Text Coding is a powerful means for elaborating and also for talking back to an author and joining in the conversation. Figure 6.2 presents several widely used text codes that can be penciled into margins or onto sticky notes. Notice how each code signals the deeper processing that is involved with elaborating. The codes are entered with a brief notation—a question, a personal observation, or a comment—as the reader tracks a particular line of thinking while driving toward comprehension of a text. (For a more in-depth discussion of Text Coding, see Buehl, 2009a.)

Figure 6.2. Common Text Codes

Code	Mental Frame	Significance
R	"This reminds me of..."	A connection to background knowledge, experiences, or prior learning
V	"I can picture this..."	Creating mental images and sensory responses
E	"This makes me feel..."	An emotional response to the text
A	"The author feels..."	An attitude or view of the author
Q	"I wonder..."	A question triggered by the reading
I	"I figured out that..."	Making an inference, such as a prediction or an interpretation
*	"This is important..."	A need-to-know idea or information that needs to be remembered and revisited
!	"This is interesting..."	Something especially interesting or attention grabbing
?	"I don't understand this..."	A segment that is confusing and needs clarification
+	"I agree with this..."	A statement that elicits reader agreement
−	"I disagree with this..."	A statement that elicits reader disagreement

Note. Adapted from *Classroom Strategies for Interactive Learning* (3rd ed., p. 180), by D. Buehl, 2009, Newark, DE: International Reading Association. Copyright 2009 by International Reading Association.

Teacher think-alouds that model coding a text are a necessary instructional step, and students need practice using these codes as they work their understanding of disciplinary texts. Focusing on a particular comprehension process at one time is helpful to inculcate this thinking. For example, asking students to mark an asterisk next to three places in the text where the author talks about things that a person needs to know targets determining importance. Conversations then follow that engage students in sharing their thinking about why their choices deserve need-to-know status.

Figure 6.3 offers a disciplinary-specific variation of Text Coding, tailored for science reading. In this case, a chemistry teacher focused on questioning moves that students should make when working the chemistry textbook. Students were assigned a range of questioning codes to use, with the expectation that all of the framed questions were likely to surface in students' thinking during their reading. Obviously, the teacher was also prompting this thinking for students and raising awareness of using questioning moves to achieve comprehension. Following the reading, students turn to their think marking as discussion starters as they meet in groups, share their questions, and use one another to try to resolve as many of their questions as they can. Each group of students then reports

Figure 6.3. Chemistry Think Marks

Code	Purpose	Mental Frame	Significance
C	Clarifying	"What is the author saying here about...?"	A segment that is confusing and needs clarification
V	Explaining vocabulary	"What is the meaning of...?"	A chemistry term that is unclear
P	Predicting	"What does the author mean...?" or "Does this happen because...?"	Implications of the information being considered
T	Tying ideas together	"Is this related to...?" or "What did we learn before that relates to this?"	Connecting this section of the text with something learned earlier in the year
Q	Questioning	"I wonder if...?" or "I wonder whether...?"	Wondering how this material connects to some aspect of one's life and world

Note. Adapted with permission from a strategy by Katie Johnson, Madison, East High School, Madison, WI.

on their understandings and may ask for assistance from the rest of the class regarding unresolved questions and still problematic text sections.

Paraphrasing and Note-Taking

Paraphrasing actions are primary elaborating moves: stopping to paraphrase what an author has said, jotting comments in the margin or on sticky notes, or paraphrased note-taking, as opposed to merely writing down exactly what the author said, which are verbatim notes. Two-Column Notes, a widely popular note-taking system, is predicated on elaborating; the right column is reserved for the notes, either paraphrased or verbatim, and the left side is for elaborating (e.g., developing questions, generating key themes, summarizing). Figure 6.4 presents a two-column notes example taken from a psychology text; the left column represents questioning as an elaborating move, and the box at the bottom displays the culminating elaborating move of summarizing.

Two-Column Notes is sometimes adopted as a schoolwide literacy practice, as many teachers are concerned with student note-taking, or lack thereof, but note-taking initiatives often seem typically applied to capturing teacher talk, the verbal information from class presentations and lectures, rather than as an elaborating strategy for reading comprehension. Again, modeling, ongoing guided practice, and feedback are key variables in developing note-taking as an elaborating move.

Double-Entry Diaries are a variation of Two-Column Notes that are especially designed for elaborating moves. Students draw a line down the center of a sheet of paper and use the left side for recording textual ideas and information and the right side for elaborating. A teacher may solicit a range of elaborating moves for the right side: paraphrasing, questioning, connecting to prior learning, personal experiences and reflections, verbalizing why something the author says is important, and so forth. Harvey and Goudvis's (2007) and Tovani's (2000) books are excellent resources for a myriad of examples of using this instructional practice. Double-Entry Diaries are especially useful as a strategy for prompting elaborating moves when reading literary fiction. Figure 6.5 is an example of using a double-entry diary as an elaborating move in a literature class. Students jot down passages from the text that are particularly meaningful to them, and elaborate on the right side about how things the author said intersect with their lives.

Figure 6.4. Two-Column Notes on a Psychology Text About the Development of Habits

What Habits Are	1. Habits → patterns of Thinking, acting, + feeling Are repeated until are automatic 90% of our behavior habitual
Why Humans Need Habits	2. Habits are Survival Techniques Can do one thing when think of another (ex. talk while drive car) Helps humans adapt to change Calms body → reduces stress when can act automatically
How Habits start	3. 1st Habits → developed as a child Eating to feel good, not just for hunger
Why Practice is important in School + Sports	4. School Habits → from practice (Ex. Multiplication Tables from memory) Athletics - practice wrong, develop bad habits - also music instrument Not enough practice - not learned so can be automatic
Why Habits are Hard to Break	5. Break Habits → Hard to do Need to unlearn, brain cells already programmed Unlearning can be harder than new learning Fears are habits (ex. of snakes) Negative Habits hard to overcome (ex. overeating, smoking, biting nails)

Habits are necessary for human survival because we need to do multiple Things at once, without thinking about them. But getting rid of bad habits is hard because they are learned behaviors

Figure 6.5. A Student's Double-Entry Diary Page on Personal Connections to a Text

The book	My Connection
1) page 5 - "Don't humiliate us. You wouldn't like to be forgotten as if you had never been born. The villagers are watchful."	People of my nationality like to gossip a lot. Our parents are concerned about our family reputations, so they say things like this to make sure we behave.
2) page 11 - "Once my aunt found a freckle on her chin, at the spot that the almanac said predestined her for unhappiness. She dug it out with a hot needle and washed the wound with peroxide"	Hmong women do not think that birthmarks are attractive. My mother would heat a needle and remove our birthmarks when we were little girls.
3) p. 15 - "My Chinese brothers and sisters had died of an unknown sickness."	Both of my parents lost brothers and sisters from diseases in our home country.
4) p. 23 - "When we Chinese girls listened to the adults talking story, we learned that we failed if we grew up to be wives or slaves."	My parents believe very strongly in education and they want us to study and better ourselves. If we married before we finished school, we would not reach this dream, and we would be a disgrace to the family.

Note. Adapted with permission courtesy of Andrew McCuaig, La Follette High School, Madison, WI. Excerpts from Kingston, M.H. (1975). *The woman warrior: Memoirs of a girlhood among ghosts.* Vintage.

Summarizing

Summarizing strategies are essential elaborating moves and may take the form of summarizing orally to oneself (i.e., a more sophisticated variation of reciting) or actually condensing information into summary note-taking sheets that capture key material. Summarizing is challenging thinking for students because they must both determine importance and synthesize understanding. Table 6.1 compares three variations of reader interaction with a written text: retelling, paraphrasing, and summarizing. Summing up what an author says is not only paraphrasing but also engages a reader in establishing the gist of a message, the essence of what the author wants readers to take away from the text. Instructional practices that provide practice for students to verbalize their understandings, both orally with partners as well as in writing, are vital and need to occur on a regular basis during disciplinary learning. As Table 6.1 indicates, however, not all verbalizing actions represent summarizing.

Writing is obviously a more intense form of summarizing than are oral summations. Quick writes can be employed frequently to seed the process of regularly summing up understandings. Notice how Quick Write prompts from Chapter 4 (see page 124) also facilitate summarizing understandings. "One thing I understand now is..." and "A brief summary of...should include...because..." are examples of Quick Write stems that facilitate summarizing.

Table 6.1. Comparing Elaborating Moves

Retelling	Paraphrasing	Summarizing
Repeating what the author said	Restating what the author said	Condensing what the author said
Using the author's language	Using language different from the author's	Using key language from the author to develop a personal summary
Including secondary information	Possibly including secondary information	Focusing on need-to-know elements and eliminating secondary information
Rehearsing ("The author said...")	Personalizing the message ("How I would say it?")	Summing up the message ("Basically, the author said...")

In addition, providing students with some of the key language about a topic and asking them to create a summary of a few sentences built around this language is an effective way to support development of summarizing as an elaborating move. For example, the following is a prompt for summarizing understanding in an art classroom: "Write a three-sentence summary that explains your understanding of *Impressionism*. Use each of these terms in a meaningful way as you express your understanding: *light, brushstroke, France, outdoors, nature, perception, subjective, colors,* and *Monet*." This summarizing activity cues students toward key concepts and terms that should be folded into a comprehensive summary, and points them toward the central ideas of this concept. In addition, students receive practice personally putting the discourse of art into play in verbalizing their understandings.

A second variation of vocabulary prompting was used in a history context and provided a conceptual framework for the summarizing of key ideas. My son Jeremy and his colleagues constructed triplets for student summaries, each clustered around one of five central themes of U.S. history: opportunity, rights, equality, democracy, and liberty. For example, students studying the post–Civil War period might be provided with the instructions "What was the impact on opportunity? In a paragraph, identify and explain how each of these increased or decreased opportunity: the 15th Amendment, the Freedmen's Bureau, and sharecropping." This format provided students with a structure for formulating coherent summaries that connected factual information to general historical themes. Rather than asking for responses to isolated facts, this summarizing practice emphasized articulating cause–effect relationships, consistent with thinking through a historical lens, and using facts to explain understandings.

Figure 6.6 presents a more sophisticated version of a disciplinary-specific, scaffolded summarizing task. Students are provided with a menu of mathematics terminology and have to choose the most appropriate language to use to express their understandings. This version transitions students into becoming users of mathematics discourse by adding in the decision making of which insider mathematics terminology would be the best fit for summarizing in this instance.

Story Impressions, described in Chapter 4 (see page 144) is another instructional practice that scaffolds the critical process of summarizing text as an elaborating move. Figure 6.7 presents a Story Impressions template

Figure 6.6. Vocabulary Prompts for Summarizing "Data About Us"

Study the data display below. In a paragraph, explain your understanding of what the data tell you, using at least five of the math terms listed below.

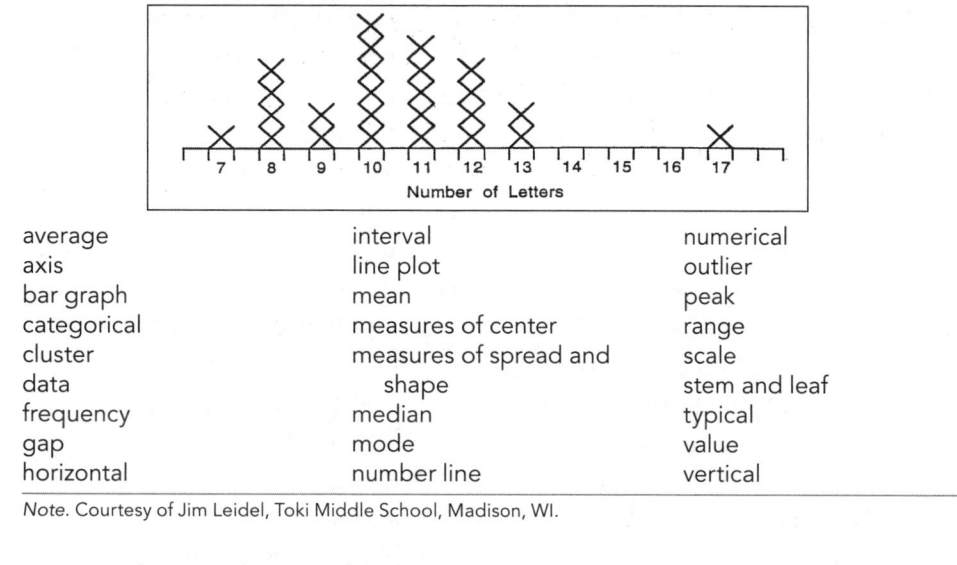

average	interval	numerical
axis	line plot	outlier
bar graph	mean	peak
categorical	measures of center	range
cluster	measures of spread and	scale
data	shape	stem and leaf
frequency	median	typical
gap	mode	value
horizontal	number line	vertical

Note. Courtesy of Jim Leidel, Toki Middle School, Madison, WI.

Figure 6.7. Story Impressions Summary on World War I

Cause and effect: Summarize how World War I began. Use all of the terms listed below in the order they appear. Your summary should be at least 10 sentences in length.

Headline: The Spark	The Europeans were optimistic about there would be no fighting. Then Francis Ferdinand, an Austrian leader, paid a visit to Serbia, when he got assassinated. Austria-Hungary issued Serbia an ultimatum to let Austro-Hungarians lead an investigation of the Archduke's murder. If Serbia didn't agree the Serbians would face war. Austria-Hungary didn't like the answer Serbia gave them, so Austria-Hungary declared war. After that both countries began mobilization of their armies. Russia supported Serbia. France was with Russia. Germany had Austria-Hungary's side. Some countries remained neutral and weren't on either side. On August 3 Germany invaded Belgium and the war was on. The European people had patriotic enthusiasm for the military forces of their respective nations.
Terms: optimism ↓ Francis Ferdinand ↓ Serbia ↓ assassination ↓ ultimatum ↓ war ↓ mobilization ↓ Russia ↓ France ↓ neutral ↓ invade ↓ patriotic	

Note. Adapted with permission courtesy of Jessica Hutchison, Lac Courte Oreilles Ojibwe School, Hayward, WI.

for world history, which asks students to summarize the cause-and-effect sequence of events that led to World War I. Story Impressions can also be integrated into essay assignments and exams as an excellent scaffold for verbalizing understandings through written assessments.

Instructional Practices for Organizing

Organizing moves expand on elaborating by reformulating an author's message in some coherent way. Implicit in organizing strategies is perceiving the structure of a message and using that structure to determine what is most important and to identify relationships between details, facts, and ideas. The comprehension processes of determining importance and synthesizing are especially central to organizing strategies. At a most basic level, jotting numbers (1, 2, 3, etc.) in the margin to identify a listing of key points or ideas is an organizing move.

Outlining

Outlining is a familiar, albeit intensive, method of organizing one's reading. The reader identifies superordinate and subordinate ideas and information and arranges them according to their relationships with each other. Classic outlining uses alternating Roman numerals, letters of the alphabet, and Arabic numbers, each layer indented to display interconnections of the material. Of course, outlines could follow more informal structures and still visually display relationships in a text. Word-processing programs offer a number of outlining options and have the advantage of liberating a student from the tedium of writing outlines; the computer versions also visually represent the relationships of entered information more precisely and certainly more legibly.

Power Notes, which employ a straightforward Arabic numbering system, is particularly easy for students to use. Figure 6.8 presents a portion of Power Notes created for a foods and nutrition class. A power 1 is a main idea or concept; a power 2 is an example, category, or elaboration of a power 1; a power 3 is an example or elaboration of a power 2; and so forth. (Power Notes are more extensively explained and modeled in Buehl, 2009a).

Figure 6.9 presents a second variation of Outlining, which follows a Structured Overview format. In this instance, students constructed a

Figure 6.8. Power Notes Outlining a Text Passage on Nutrients

1. Nutrients from foods
    2. Carbohydrates
        3. Body's main source of energy
        3. Mostly obtained from plants
            4. Simple: Sugars
            4. Complex: Starches
    2. Fats
        3. Body's source of stored energy
        3. Provides insulation for body
    2. Proteins

Figure 6.9. Structured Overview of Chemical Substances

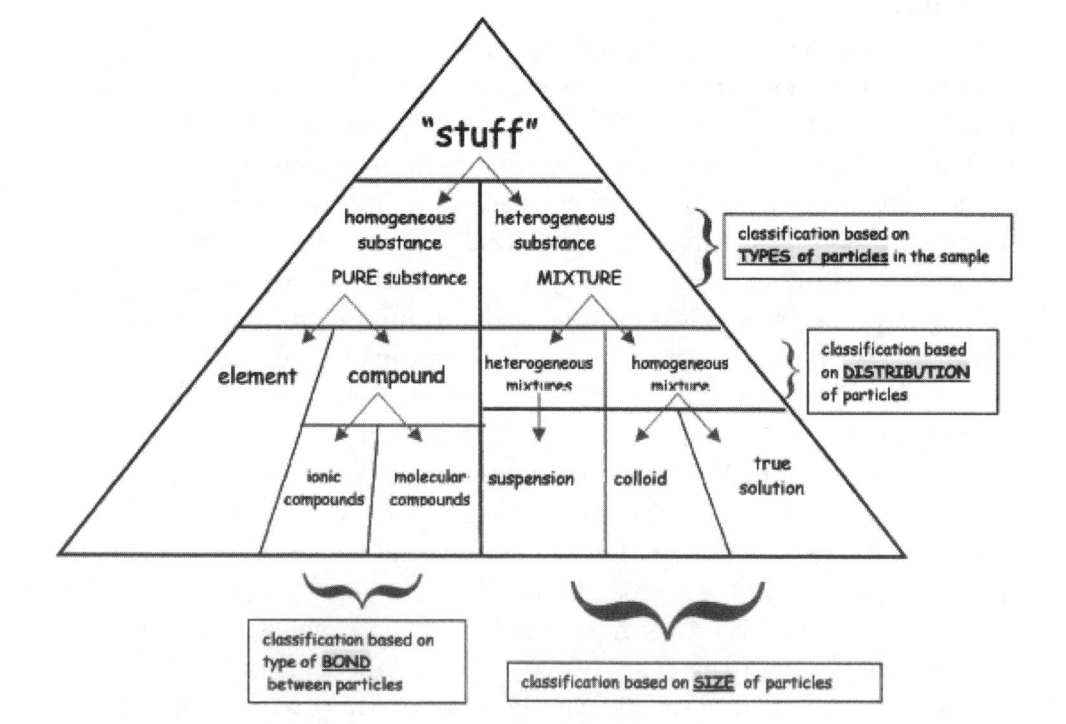

Note. Courtesy of Katie Johnson, Madison East High School, Madison, WI.

hierarchy of relationships among chemistry concepts, configured as a graphic representation. The visual display addressed the abstract nature of the text and guided students to clearly articulate to themselves how concepts are interconnected. You can see elements of outlining being applied in this process. Again, elaborating and organizing moves that support summarizing understanding are emphasized as students work their understanding.

Figure 6.10 combines outlining with note-taking and graphic representations. The pyramid notes in this fitness example are customized to walk readers through the organizational features of a specific textbook, spotlighting relationships among key information that should be integrated into students' notes.

The key element of using any outlining practice is thinking about the relationships among ideas and information. Asking students to copy

Figure 6.10. Pyramid Notes on Fitness

Chapter Title	Physical Activity + Fitness				
Section Title	Improving Your Body's Fitness				
Main Idea — Find on the first page of the Section	Different exercise activities can improve each element of your body's fitness.				
Supporting Details — Write the headings on the line & summarize the introductory paragraph	1 Cardiorespiratory Endurance	2 Muscular Strength	3 Muscular Endurance	4 Flexibility	5 ___
	The ability of your heart, lungs and blood vessels to send oxygen and fuel to your tissues during extended physical workouts.	The ability of your muscles to handle stress caused by lifting, pushing, or jumping.	The ability of your muscles to handle stress when doing tasks over an extended time period without getting fatigued.	The ability of your body to move all of its body parts through a full range of motion without straining or injuring them	___
Developing Details — Use the subheadings to explain the supporting details listed above	1 Regular aerobic exercise that raises heart rate and increases use of oxygen — Jogging Bike riding Swimming	2 Regular anaerobic exercise that works muscles hard without use of oxygen — Sprinting Weight Lifting Push-ups	3 Work outs that begin with lighter weights and gradually increase the weight amount until you get to your maximum — weight Lifting	4 Stretching exercise, done slowly for 10 to 30 seconds at a time, which also improves your circulation, coordination, eases stress - Stretching	5 ___

Note. Adapted from a strategy by Jada Callahan, Middleton High School, Middleton, WI.

a previously prepared outline that is projected on a screen or written on the board, however, is not an organizing move but rather a rehearsal action because students are not engaged in discerning the relationships themselves. Outlining may have generally fallen out of favor as a classroom practice for working a text, but the process certainly takes students deep into examining the relationships among textual information. I can recall spending a considerable chunk of time creating outlines of geography textbook sections during my middle school years. We were assigned to outline the material, in lieu of answering questions, which really involved us in closely examining the relationships among ideas and details. (Chicle, a type of tree sap, was a major export of Guatemala that was manufactured into chewing gum—a tenacious fact from one of these outlines that I will always remember.) A perennial central question is, What will students do with the outline once it is created? How will the outline be instrumental in helping students address essential questions and synthesize understanding? Otherwise, an awful lot of work has gone into merely lining up details on a page. Outlining is especially well suited for texts that are structured around classification and description of concepts, such as many science texts.

Text Frames

Organizing strategies based on text frames are particularly powerful (T.H. Anderson & Armbruster, 1984). Text frames represent how texts are tied together; they are the internal structure of ideas, information, and details of a text. Jones, Palincsar, Ogle, and Carr (1987) have presented six transcendent text frames, which are detailed in Table 6.2. Students may feel that many informational texts they read in disciplinary contexts are generally random disgorgements of stuff rather than discussions of key relationships that provide details and facts to flesh out these relationships. In Chapter 5, for example, I discussed how using cause–effect text frames in science leads to text coding the cause (C) and effect (E) relationships within a science text. (See the example presented in Figure 6.11.) Text coding based on text frames brings to the surface the cause–effect dynamics of text, a strong illustration of an organizing strategy. Likewise, annotating "problem," "cause of problem," "effect of problem," and "solutions" in the margin or on sticky notes next to appropriate text segments in a history text that displays problem–solution relationships is another strategic move that uses text frames for organizing understanding.

Table 6.2. Text Frames and Questions

Text Frame	Sample Questions to Ask
Problem–Solution Frame: The author emphasizes problem solving.	• What is the problem? • Who has the problem? • What is causing the problem? • What are the effects of the problem? • Who is trying to solve the problem? • What solutions are recommended or attempted? • What results from these solutions? • Is the problem solved? Do any new problems develop because of the solutions?
Cause–Effect Frame: The author emphasizes why something happened.	• What happens (or happened)? • What causes it to happen? • What are the important elements or factors that cause this effect? • How do these factors or elements interrelate? • Will this result always happen from these causes? Why or why not? • How would the result change if the elements or factors are different?
Goal/Action/Outcome Frame: The author emphasizes steps that are followed.	• What is the goal? What is to be accomplished? • Who is trying to achieve this goal? • What actions/steps are taken to achieve this goal? • Is the sequence of actions/steps important? • What are the effects of these actions? What happens? • Were these actions successful for achieving the goal? • Are there unexpected outcomes from these actions? • Would other actions have been more effective? Could something else have been done?
Compare/Contrast Frame: The author emphasizes similarities and differences.	• What is being compared and contrasted? • What characteristics are compared and contrasted? • What makes them alike or similar? • What makes them unalike or different? • What are the most important qualities that make them similar? • What are the most important qualities that make them different? • In terms of what is most important, are they more alike or more different?
Concept/Definition Frame: The author emphasizes conceptual understanding.	• What is the concept? • What category of things does this concept belong to? • What are its critical characteristics? • How does it work? • What does it do? • What are its functions? • What are examples of it? • What are examples of things that share some but not all of its characteristics?

(continued)

Table 6.2. Text Frames and Questions *(continued)*

Text Frame	Sample Questions to Ask
Proposition/ Support Frame: The author emphasizes developing an argument.	• What is the general topic or issue? • What viewpoint, conclusion, theory, hypothesis, or thesis is being proposed? • How is this proposition supported? • Are examples provided to support the proposition? • Are data provided to support the proposition? • Is expert verification provided to support the proposition? • Is a logical argument provided to support the proposition? • Does the author make a sufficient case for the proposition? • What are alternative perspectives to the author's proposition?

Note. Adapted from *Classroom Strategies for Interactive Learning* (3rd ed., pp. 23–24), by D. Buehl, 2009, Newark, DE: International Reading Association. Copyright 2007 by International Reading Association.

Figure 6.11. Text Coding Cause–Effect Relationships in a Physical Science Text

The region near the equator, extending about 20° north and south, is known as the tropics. The **C** Sun's rays hit Earth with the greatest intensity here. The tropics, which are predominantly **E** oceanic, absorb a lot of heat.

C Warm tropical water transfers energy to the air. The air **E** warms and expands. Hot **C** air is less dense and **E** rises into the atmosphere. Warm **C** air does not rise in only one place, like smoke from a fire. **E** Air rises like the smoke from thousands of fires all the way around the world in the tropics.

Note. Full Option Science System (FOSS) text selection from *Weather and Water Resources: Images, Data, and Readings* (p. 53), by Lawrence Hall of Science, 2004, Nashua, NH: Delta Education. Copyright 2004 by the Regents of the University of California.

246

Graphic Representations

Graphic representations are visual displays of key ideas and details, such as a table, flowchart, matrix, grid, concept map, cycle diagram, or hierarchy pyramid. To be effective, graphic representations must be more than chaotic webs or random arrays of geometric figures, such as circles and rectangles, into which details are recorded. Instead, graphic organizers are a means for selecting items deemed especially important and then displaying these items so that relationships are readily apparent. For example, creating a chart of the qualities and salient details of major characters in a novel allows for remembering who is who as well as setting up distinctions and comparisons between these characters, a strategy especially helpful with novels in which a multitude of characters pop up again and again (sounds suspiciously like the Dostoevsky book I read earlier this year).

Graphic organizers are the most widely implemented instructional strategy that uses text frames. Text frame relationships should be clearly prompted by graphic organizers that are created for student use. For example, Figure 6.12 shows a science graphic organizer that guides students in identifying problem–solution relationships as students locate science articles that involve some sort of problem-solving issue with science implications. In contrast, Figure 6.13 also targets problem–solution thinking but, in this case, is tailored for history texts. Notice that this graphic organizer guides students into perceiving and recording problem-solving relationships in history texts as students follow the story lines of different groups of people during a significant period of history. In addition, this history graphic organizer emphasizes change, one of the five key facets of the Thinking Like a Historian model presented in Chapter 5 (see pages 188–189). In this example, students track the story lines of three different immigrant groups in the United States. As the story lines are fleshed out, students are able to perceive how the immigrant experiences of these different groups contrasted with each other and notice the different change dynamics for each group. The graphic organizer prompts students to be sensitive to six categories of change that can affect people: population, technology, environmental, economic, political, and beliefs.

Graphic organizers are most effective as an organizing move when they are created by the readers themselves rather than provided by the teacher as a reading activity. However, students need plenty of

Figure 6.12. Problem–Solution Graphic Organizer for a Science News Report

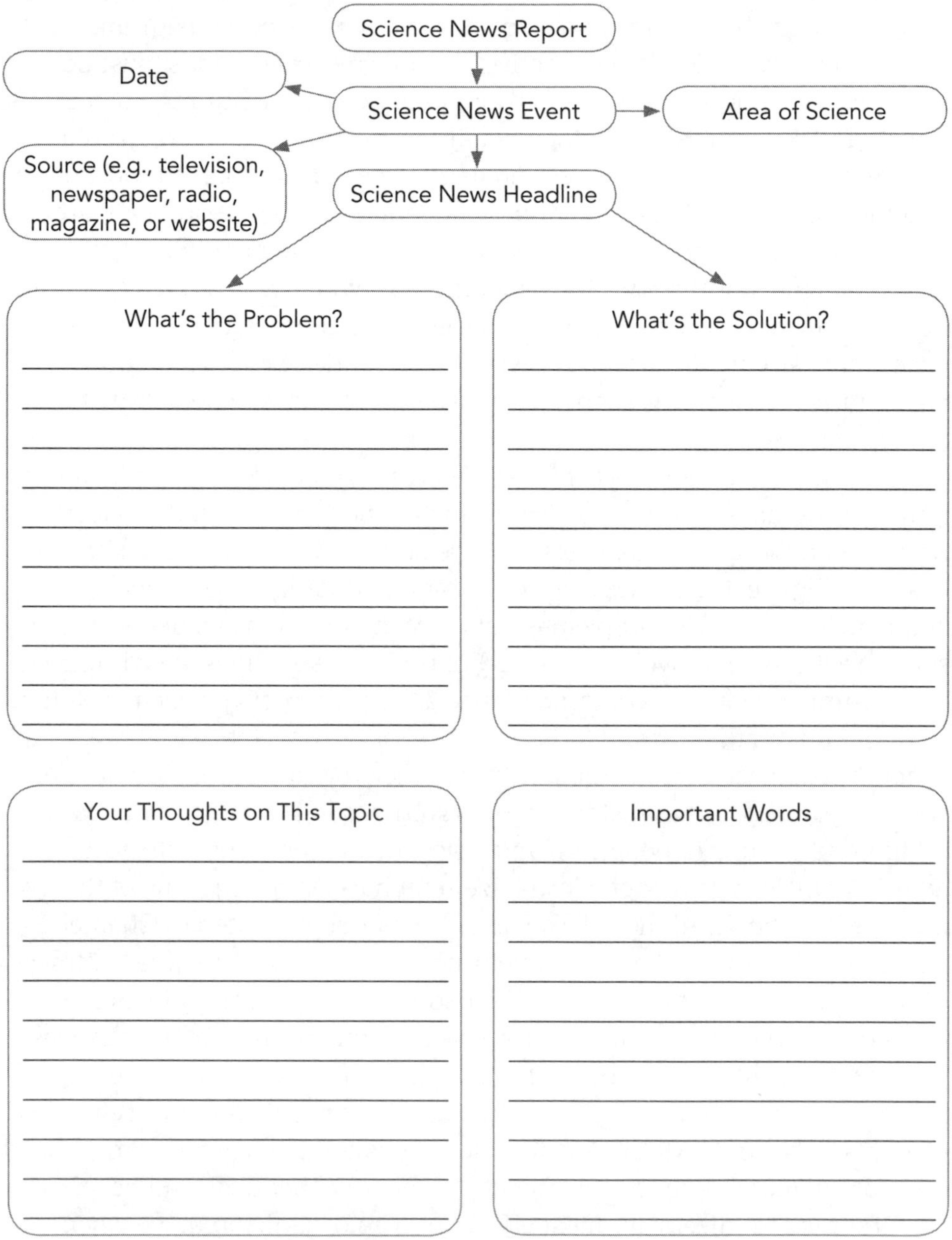

Science News Report

Date

Science News Event → Area of Science

Source (e.g., television, newspaper, radio, magazine, or website)

Science News Headline

What's the Problem?

_____
_____
_____
_____
_____
_____
_____
_____
_____
_____
_____

What's the Solution?

_____
_____
_____
_____
_____
_____
_____
_____
_____
_____
_____

Your Thoughts on This Topic

_____
_____
_____
_____
_____
_____
_____
_____
_____

Important Words

_____
_____
_____
_____
_____
_____
_____
_____

Note. Courtesy of Jim Leidel, Toki Middle School, Madison, WI.

Figure 6.13. Problem–Solution Graphic Organizer for a History Text

Who (Group)?	What Problems Did They Face?	What Changes Affected These People (Population [Pop], Technology [T], Environmental [En], Economic [Ec], Political [Pol], and Beliefs [B])?	What Did They Do to Solve Their Problems?
European Immigrants	• In Europe, overcrowding, lack of jobs, food shortages, not enough land, poverty, religious persecution • Were unskilled workers • Difficult passage to the United States in steerage section of ships • Subjected to medical inspections and legal interview • Could be detained and sent back • Little money and education • Not welcomed in the United States; nativist movement opposed them • Workers feared immigrants would take their jobs.	• Rapid population growth in Europe (Pop) • Lack of jobs and land in Europe (Ec) • More people wanted freedom and control over their lives. (B} • New industries in the United States made jobs available. (T) • Factories hired unskilled workers. (T) • Immigrants brought new ideas and beliefs to the United States. (B) • U.S. population growing, with many foreign languages and customs (Pop) • Quota laws passed (Pol)	• Left Europe to immigrate to the United States • Settled with others from home country and relatives • Many got jobs in factories. • Worked hard to get ahead • Lived in crowded areas of large cities, with many people sharing space in tenements • Received assistance from immigrant aid societies • Turned to political bosses for assistance in large cities • Became increasingly assimilated, learned English
Asian Immigrants	• In China, overcrowding, lack of jobs, food shortages, lack of opportunity, poverty • Were unskilled workers • Were mostly men not families • Usually detained, and 10% denied entrance and sent back • Little money and education • Prevented from becoming U.S. citizens • Subjected to mob violence, prejudice, hostility, discrimination, and segregation	• Rapid population growth in China (Pop) • Lack of jobs in China (Ec) • More people wanted freedom and control over their lives. (B) • Shortage of farm laborers in the United States (Ec) • Railroad hired unskilled workers. (T) • Encountered racist attitudes (B) • California economy falls into depression, and Chinese blamed. (Ec) • Chinese Exclusion Law passed (Pol) • Angel Island Immigration Station established for Asians (Pol)	• Settled in the West Coast of the United States • Worked on railroads, in mining, on farms; prospected for gold • Did work others refused to do, such as stoop labor harvesting on farms • Were willing to work for less money than were other workers • Lived together with others from home country • Tried to evade exclusion laws and come to the United States • Tried to cope with racism in communities, assimilated less

(continued)

Figure 6.13. Problem–Solution Graphic Organizer for a History Text *(continued)*

Who (Group)?	What Problems Did They Face?	What Changes Affected These People (Population [Pop], Technology [T], Environmental [En], Economic [Ec], Political [Pol], and Beliefs [B])?	What Did They Do to Solve Their Problems?
Mexican Immigrants	• In Mexico, lack of jobs, food shortages, lack of opportunity, poverty, civil unrest • Were unskilled workers • Little money and education • Treated as cheap labor • Kept in low-level jobs • Subjected to racism, prejudice, hostility, discrimination, and segregation • Commonly denied access to public facilities, such as restaurants	• Population growth in Mexico (Pop) • Lack of jobs in Mexico (Ec) • Mexican Revolution and conflict between political groups (Pol) • Shortage of farm laborers in the United States (Ec) • Irrigation expanded farming. (T) • Encountered racist attitudes (B) • Higher wages in the United States (Ec) • Chinese Exclusion Law passed, causing need for new laborers (Pol) • Railroads made travel to the United States easier and faster (T) • Length and isolation of border with the United States, hard to enforce laws (En)	• Settled in western United States, especially California and Texas • Worked on railroads, in mining, in canneries, and in construction • Became agricultural migrant workers for farms and citrus groves • Were willing to work for less money than other workers were • Crossed U.S. border unchecked • Settled in areas that were historically Spanish speaking • Built communities and spread their culture in the United States

well-designed models of useful graphic displays of information before they can be expected to develop coherent graphic reformulations of text that mesh with thinking through a disciplinary lens. Students need to transition from filling out graphic organizers designed by others to deciding how to visually represent their understanding themselves.

Other forms of visual representations also qualify as organizing strategies. Drawing a diagram, creating a structured overview that categorizes disciplinary vocabulary and information from a text, doing a quick sketch, or any other way of translating prose into a meaningful visual rendition engages readers in developing their personal moves that elaborate and organize. Figure 6.14 engages students in translating the abstract language of chemistry into a three-step film reel sequence as a

Figure 6.14. Quick Sketch of Chemical Reactions

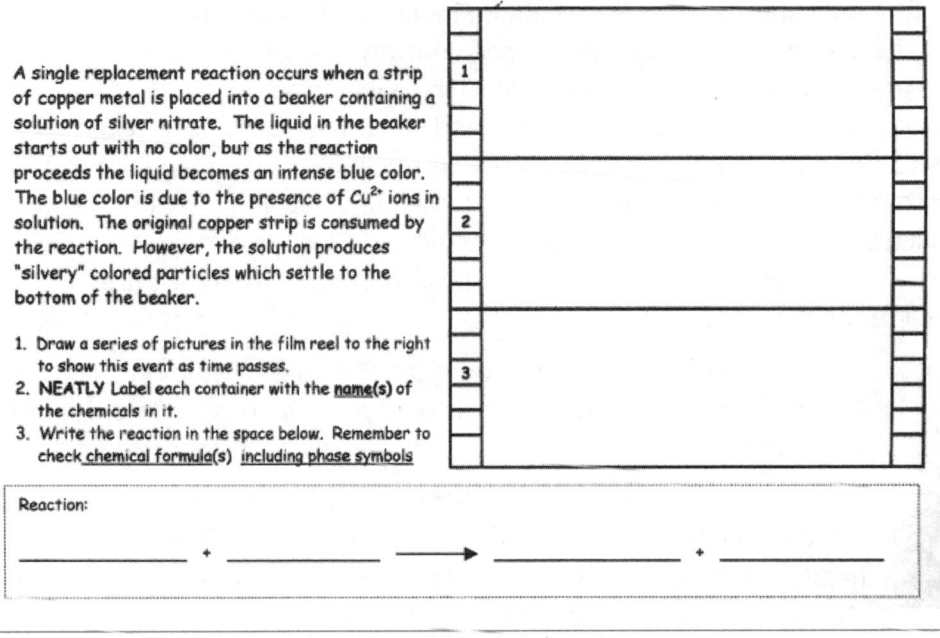

Visualizing Chemical Reactions

A single replacement reaction occurs when a strip of copper metal is placed into a beaker containing a solution of silver nitrate. The liquid in the beaker starts out with no color, but as the reaction proceeds the liquid becomes an intense blue color. The blue color is due to the presence of Cu^{2+} ions in solution. The original copper strip is consumed by the reaction. However, the solution produces "silvery" colored particles which settle to the bottom of the beaker.

1. Draw a series of pictures in the film reel to the right to show this event as time passes.
2. NEATLY Label each container with the name(s) of the chemicals in it.
3. Write the reaction in the space below. Remember to check chemical formula(s) including phase symbols

Reaction:

_____ + _____ ⟶ _____ + _____

Note. Courtesy of Katie Johnson, Madison, East High School, Madison, WI.

prelude for balancing the chemical reaction. In addition to determining importance and synthesizing, this literacy practice emphasizes the comprehension process of creating mental images.

Scaffolding Reader Moves Into Disciplinary Instruction

What are the preferred moves that insiders make to work texts in your discipline? To what extent are these insider moves central to the classroom tasks asked of readers of the texts of your discipline? Earlier in the chapter, we made the analogy to moves made by athletes as they work their "game." How can we mentor our students to work their game as readers, writers, and thinkers in different disciplinary contexts?

At this point, it is realistic to recognize the disconnect between the ambitious reader moves envisioned in this chapter that are the heart of working a complex text, and the preferences of many of our students, which are to read with as little exertion as possible with tasks that are easily accomplished, or not read complex texts at all, with the teacher telling and showing the predominant mode of encountering new content. Some of our students have developed cognitive and metacognitive strategic behavior, which guides their thinking as readers and informs their use of rehearsing, elaborating, and organizing actions to reach understanding. However, many students, including a substantial number of our college-bound learners, as discussed in Chapter 1, do not exhibit such a repertoire of internalized strategic moves as readers.

In Chapter 2, I presented three typical yet ineffective disciplinary reading behaviors:

1. *Skimming for answers:* The reader move is to do a quick surface scan for key textual indicators, such as bold print, to locate something to write down.

2. *Surface processing:* The reader move is to plow through without stopping, regardless of whether comprehension is occurring.

3. *Reading and forgetting:* The reader move is to rapidly finish without engaging in deeper processing.

If a task assigned to reading a text permits any of these three ineffective sets of reader moves, then the likelihood is high that many students will opt for moves that merely get them done with an assignment.

Guiding Thinking Through Interactive Reading Guides

Interactive Reading Guides explicitly cue the foundational comprehension processes—making connections to background knowledge, generating questions, creating sensory images, inferring, determining importance, and synthesizing—and are constructed with the assumption that this thinking will be challenging for many students to tackle independently as homework assignments, given the complexity of a specific text. In addition, rehearsing, elaborating, and organizing moves are integrated into the prompts on the guide.

Interactive reading guides (Buehl, 2009a; Wood, 1988) provide a scaffolded context for students to work a complex text as partners or perhaps teams of three or four. In effect, an interactive reading guide scripts a text and walks students through it, as if a tour guide was conducting their way through the material. The interactive reading guide borrows from the QtA strategy, described in Chapter 5, by pausing students after reading a short segment (e.g., a sentence, a paragraph, a couple of paragraphs) and prompts thinking that engages readers in working toward comprehension. Students are also directed toward visual and graphic information, such as photographs, illustrations, charts, and graphs.

In Chapter 5, I refer to think sheets as a contrast to the worksheets and study guides that students are often asked to complete as they read disciplinary texts. Table 6.3 offers a comparison between traditional worksheets and study guides, and interactive reading guides. A major difference is that an interactive guide is designed to be completed collaboratively, as students are working in the zone area of the Gradual Release of Responsibility process, where they need to problem-solve, engage in discussion, and construct an understanding of what an author is telling them. Obviously, not all of the texts that we use in our different disciplines need to be read as collaborative activities, but to mentor students as thinkers and support them as they read especially difficult but vital texts, interactive readings are a powerful option to merely telling students the information.

Figure 6.15 is an example of an interactive reading guide created for middle school students studying physical science. Notice that it was designed for partners and that the partners are assigned separate tasks during the working of the text. Comprehension processes are clearly indicated for each item to reinforce metacognitive awareness of the nature of the thinking being prompted. For example, the first item engages students with making connections to prior knowledge and learning by

Table 6.3. Comparing Traditional Study Guides and Interactive Reading Guides

Traditional Study Guides	Interactive Reading Guides
Literal focus on getting the facts	Stimulate thinking about information
Emphasis on content	Teach how to learn while learning
Individual centered	Collaborative problem solving
Discussion after reading	Discussion during reading
Look for answers	Consider author intent (why)
Memorization and answer questions	Synthesis: Construct knowledge

Figure 6.15. Interactive Reading Guide on the Solar System

1. ***Work together:*** *Make connections:* Think of what you already know about the solar system. Create a Knowledge Ladder by using each letter in the term *solar system* to complete a word or phrase that has a meaningful connection to the solar system.

    S
    O
    L
    A
    R
    S
    Y
    S
    T
    E
    M

2. Open your books to page 84: "The Solar System in a Nutshell." What a strange title! ***Work together:*** *Infer:* Make a prediction about what this section is likely to be about.

3. ***Both partners:*** Read the first paragraph on page 84 silently. *Determine importance:* Decide what the author's purpose is for this chapter. Write about what the author wants readers to get out of the text.

4. *Creating mental images:* The second paragraph is written to help readers visualize how the solar system began. ***Partner A:*** Read this paragraph aloud. ***Partner B:*** Use your imagination as you listen to your partner to see each stage that the author describes.

    The author uses descriptive words like *spin*, *carousel*, and *whirligig* in this paragraph. Both partners explain how these words help you imagine what matter was doing when the solar system was being formed.

    Both partners: *Determine importance:* List what happened during each of the four stages of the formation of the solar system.

    1st
    2nd
    3rd
    4th

5. ***Partner B:*** Read the third paragraph aloud. ***Partner A:*** As you listen to your partner, decide what a person should know from this paragraph. (*Hint:* It is usually not an exact fact!) Share what you were thinking. ***Both partners:*** *Determine importance:* Write one thing about the sun that a person should know.

6. The fourth paragraph starts with the statement "The sun rules." ***Both partners:*** *Infer:* Predict and write what the author means by this statement.

    The rest of the paragraph describes several cause–effect relationships that involve the sun. ***Both partners:*** Read silently. ***Work together:*** *Determine importance:* List four of the cause–effect relationships described by the author.

(continued)

Figure 6.15. Interactive Reading Guide on the Solar System *(continued)*

Cause	Effect

    Both partners: *Questioning:* Write down two things that you are wondering about the sun based on what the author has told you in this paragraph.
    1st Question:
    2nd Question:

7. **Both partners:** Read silently the first paragraph on page 85. *Making connections:* The author wrote this paragraph in 2001, but scientific knowledge has changed since then. Decide what knowledge needs to be corrected in this paragraph.

8. **Partner A:** Read the second paragraph on page 85 aloud. **Partner B:** Listen for clues for what the word *terrestrial* might mean. **Both partners:** *Infer:* There are details in this paragraph that hint at the meaning of *terrestrial*. Write down your explanation of the word. (*Hint:* The author will compare these planets with gas giants.)

9. **Partner B:** Read the third paragraph aloud. **Partner A:** Listen for how the terrestrial planets were formed. **Work together:** *Summarize:* Explain in a single sentence how these four planets were formed, using the following terms: *gravitational attraction, sun, collision, lighter materials, rocky matter,* and *objects.*

10. The next two paragraphs talk about atmosphere and how it changed. **Partner A:** Read the first paragraph silently. *Determine importance:* Look for the *before* conditions of the atmosphere. **Partner B:** Read the second paragraph silently. *Determine importance:* Look for the *after* conditions of the atmosphere. **Work together:** Share your understandings of the before and after and write them down.

Atmosphere Before	Atmosphere After

11. The first paragraph under "Gas Giants" introduces these planets. **Both partners:** Read silently. **Work together:** *Questioning:* Write one thing that you are wondering about the gas giants.

12. The next paragraph has a great deal of technical details. An important word is *volatile*, which the author has used before. It has something to do with these gases. **Partner A:** Look up the word *volatile* and read the definitions aloud. **Partner B:** *Infer:* Decide which definition makes the most sense in this paragraph and write it down.

(continued)

Figure 6.15. Interactive Reading Guide on the Solar System *(continued)*

> *Both partners:* Read this paragraph silently. *Work together:* Once again, this paragraph describes cause–effect relationships about the planets called gas giants. <u>Determine importance</u>: Locate and write down three cause–effect relationships.

Cause	Effect

involving the students in constructing a knowledge ladder around the concept of solar system (see page 127 of Chapter 4 for a description of the Knowledge Ladder strategy). The taxonomy questions for physical science (see Chapter 5) provide the basis for creating items for this guide, especially at identifying cause–effect relationships at the Analyzing level.

Partners will be hard-pressed to skim for answers as a task-completion strategy; instead, they collaborate to read (and reread), deliberate, and decide how to respond to the items. Teachers need only collect partner A's or partner B's interactive guide for evaluation, by choosing either "A" or "B" at the time guides are to be handed in. Because students collaboratively have decided on the best way of responding to each item, either completed guide should be equally representative of their joint efforts. Hence, all students are aware that their guide might be the one used to evaluate the partner work, so all students have the responsibility to personally complete their guide with their most complete agreed-upon responses.

Figure 6.16 presents an interactive reading guide created for a high school world history textbook section. Partners would spend multiple days in intensive reading of text segments, engaging in conversation and working out their understanding of the period of European history that is referred to as the Middle Ages. In addition to clear labeling of comprehension processes, this guide very explicitly mentors students on the Thinking Like a Historian model outlined in Chapter 5. Icons for the five facets of the Thinking Like a Historian model—cause and effect, change and continuity, turning points, through their eyes, and using

Figure 6.16. Interactive Reading Guide on the Middle Ages

1. **Both partners:** Read the paragraphs "the Big Picture" on page 320 silently. _Summarize:_ What did the Roman Empire leave behind as its legacy?

   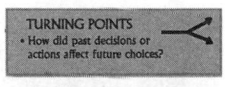

   Determine importance: Discuss all of the changes that Europe felt after the fall of the Roman Empire. List at least five of the changes that you discussed.
   1.
   2.
   3.
   4.
   5.

2. **Partner A:** Read the first paragraph on page 321 aloud. **Both partners:** _Visual representation:_ Draw a timeline from 600–1400. Add the date and the event in the 700s for when the Frankish Empire rose to power. (You will add five other events to this timeline as you continue this assignment.)

   Partner B: Read "A Powerful Ruler" aloud on page 321. **Both partners:** Add Charlemagne's biggest achievement to your timeline as well as the year it occurred.

   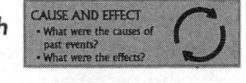

3. **Partner A:** Read aloud "The Growth of Towns" on page 324. **Both partners:** Add the events from 1000 to the 1200s to your timeline.

   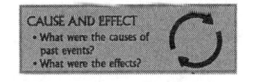

   Creating mental images: Draw three changes in Europe's economy and provide captions for each.

   Determine importance: List the advantages and disadvantages of town life.

   ADVANTAGES   DISADVANTAGES

4. **Partner A:** Read "Town Craftworkers" aloud. **Partner B:** Read aloud "European Cities" on pages 324–325.

   Creating mental images: Imagine that you are a 12-year-old serf. In a paragraph, explain four or more reasons why you might wish to be a carpenter's apprentice. Then, in a paragraph of at least five sentences, describe the house that you live in and the neighborhood that you would call home.

   (continued)

Figure 6.16. Interactive Reading Guide on the Middle Ages *(continued)*

5. **Both partners:** Read "Popular Songs" on page 325. *Infer:* Explain what a troubadour is in your own words. *Infer:* Explain what a minstrel is in your own words.

6. **Take turns:** Alternate reading page 326 aloud. **Both partners:** Add the dates and events for when the Normans invaded England and King John signed the Magna Carta to your timeline.
    Determine importance: Which of these events do you feel had the greatest effect on the greatest number of people, and why?

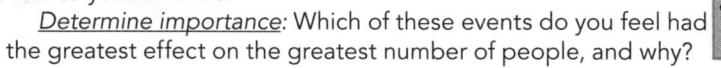

7. **Take turns:** Alternate reading "Many Voices" on page 327 aloud.
    Infer: Which liberty do you feel freed the most people? Explain why you think so.

8. **Partner A:** Read aloud "The Roman Church" on page 332.
    Visual representation: Draw a diagram to show the split in the Christian church. Add the names of these two churches after the split and the location where each church was based to your diagram.

9. **Partner B:** Read aloud "Magnificent Cathedral" and the captions by the pictures on pages 332–333.
    Infer: Explain why tourists would want to visit these cathedrals today.

10. **Both partners:** Read "The First Crusade " silently. *Creating mental images:* Draw a five-cell cartoon summarizing what you read and add captions to each cell.

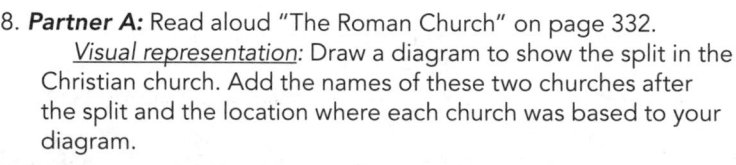

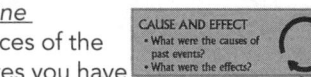

11. **Both partners:** Read pages 334–335 silently. *Determine importance:* List the positive and negative consequences of the Crusades and the Black Death. (Refer to the video notes you have on "The Black Death" and "Newscasts of the Past" for positive consequences.)

CRUSADES	BLACK DEATH
+	+
+	+
+	+
−	−
−	−
−	−

Note. Adapted courtesy of Julie Feltz, D.C. Everest High School, Weston, WI. Icons from Mandell, N., & Malone, B. (2007). *Thinking like a historian: Rethinking history instruction.* Madison, WI: Wisconsin Historical Society. Reprinted with permission of the Wisconsin Historical Society.

the past—are embedded into the guide, reinforcing which element of historical thinking is being elicited with each item in the study guide.

The intention behind Interactive Reading Guides is to provide a template for guiding students' thinking through a challenging text, so they are able to successfully work a reading without having to resort to being told by the teacher what the author said. The assumption is that certain texts would not be effectively read by many students as independent, out-of-class homework, but these texts could be understood if students worked them in collaborative teams. Obviously, interactive reading guides are a time-intensive literacy practice and are best used on occasions when students will struggle with specific texts that are particularly useful for disciplinary learning.

This instructional strategy provides a rich opportunity to mentor students' abilities to mine their understanding as they develop routines for working disciplinary texts. It is important to note that entire texts need not be assigned for this treatment. For example, an intensive examination of a section of, say, the physics text, or even an especially pertinent page or two that develops key concepts, can provide excellent practice for reading through a disciplinary lens without overwhelming readers.

Collaborative Reading

One final comment is in order regarding working complex texts. One of my most significant moves when I am mismatched with an author and struggling to understand is to seek collaboration. That collaborator could be a colleague, a fellow teacher, or another trusted coconspirator. In most cases, my most valued collaborator is my wife Wendy. We frequently ask each other to read something that one of us is working in order to gain additional expertise and another set of perspectives.

I am reminded of a perfect illustration of the two of us working in tandem to comprehend a complex text. We were engaged in one of our home improvement schemes, in this case removing some old windows (a snap with a reciprocating saw) and replacing them with new windows, which we had never done before. The directions for installation, however, were a prime example of an unfriendly technical text. The language careened from *nailing fin*, to *drip cap*, to *brick mould casing*, to *head jamb extrusion*. A straightforward reading did not lead to satisfactory comprehension for either of us, and a gaping opening in the side of the house beckoned. So, we got down to working the text. We read a sentence aloud and summarized what we thought the author was saying. We clarified terminology by examining the diagrams and inspecting the new window itself. We reread at times. We inferred and drew on previous experiences. We walked through the process, as we were able to understand it, so that we were able to decide exactly what each step entailed, and before we did any permanent or hard-to-undo acts with the hammer and nails. Of course, we also talked; our conversations were about problem solving and seeking understanding. (Well, there might have been a tinge of irritation sprinkled in, too.) We were behaving the way proficient readers behave when comprehension is essential. (For the record, our new windows open and shut, are plumb, and do not leak.)

Reading as a Social Act

If we consider once again the Gradual Release of Responsibility model outlined in Chapter 1, we can see that collaborative work is a central component of gradually developing competence, especially competence with challenging tasks for which support and feedback are essential. We tend to regard reading as solely a solitary behavior, but in so many respects, reading is a social act that extends beyond the interactions between author and reader. When we engage in conversation about a text, especially as we work through understanding, we extend our thinking, engage in concerted problem solving, and expand our capacity to do this work with increasing independence. As you have likely noticed, most of the literacy practices showcased in this book involve collaborative engagements with text, a necessary stage toward reader independence in disciplinary contexts.

Figure 6.17 presents a reader's protocol for mathematics texts that emphasizes collaborative problem solving as students work the math textbook. The Math Reading Keys strategy outlines for students the moves that mathematicians use to work their texts. Students are mentored to regularly apply moves that are particularly critical to reading mathematics texts: sentence-by-sentence reading, clarification of previously learned mathematics concepts, thinking actively with a pencil, and explaining understandings. The last step engages students in verbalizing the discourse of mathematics. The example in Figure 6.18 illustrates how to create flip cards for vocabulary; the front side is reserved for the precise mathematics definition, and the back side is the student explanation of this concept, which demonstrates his or her understanding. The math reading keys could be displayed as a classroom poster or provided as a laminated bookmark for the math text, as a resource reminder for moves that involve reading, writing, and thinking through a mathematics lens.

Figure 6.17. Math Reading Keys

1. *Read carefully* to make sure each sentence makes sense.
2. *Ask yourself* the following questions:
   a. What does the author assume I already know?
   b. What concepts are mentioned that I have learned in math before?
3. *Stop and summarize* each sentence in your own words. Explain all of the math concepts that you have learned before.
4. *Reread* parts that you are unable to summarize.
5. *Discuss* the following with a partner:
   a. Explain what you understand.
   b. Clarify what you do not understand.
6. *Read with a pencil:*
   a. Work any examples provided.
   b. Reread each section after working the examples.
7. *Explain new mathematics terms* in your notebook or on cards.

Figure 6.18. Translating Math Terms Into Student-Friendly Explanations

(front of flip card)	(back of flip card)
absolute value	**Explanation of *absolute value*:** Every number is a certain distance from 0, either in a + direction or a − direction. Absolute value is how far a number is from 0. $|7|$ and $|-7|$ have the same distance from 0, so they have the same absolute value: 7.
The absolute value of a number x is its distance from 0 on the number line.	
If x and y are two numbers, then the absolute value of (x − y), written as $|x - y|$, is the distance between the numbers x and y.	**Example:** $|7 - 2|$ and $|2 - 7|$ have the same absolute value: 5. This is because 2 and 7 are five units apart from each other on the number line. Both +5 and −5 are five units from 0, so the absolute value is 5.
Symbol for absolute value: $|x|$	

Note. *Absolute value* definition from *Algebra 1* (pp. 202–203), by Center for Mathematics Education, 2009, Boston: Pearson Education. Copyright 2009 by Pearson Education.

REFLECTION INTERLUDE

What is the repertoire of reader moves that are appropriate for reading the texts of your discipline? What might reading keys look like in your discipline? What might a series of insider moves look like for your discipline if they were provided as a protocol for reading various disciplinary texts (e.g., a poem, a primary document, a set of directions)?

PARTING THOUGHTS AND TALKING POINTS

- If we are to mentor students as readers, writers, and thinkers in our disciplines, then the use of cognitive strategies, metacognitive strategies, and strategic actions need to be integrated into our instruction.
- Modeling followed by scaffolded interactions with complex texts builds increasing independence as well as cognizance of what it takes to work a challenging text toward comprehension.
- Tasks that students complete in conjunction with their reading need to engage them in making strategic moves that parallel how insiders work texts of their disciplines.
- Working complex disciplinary texts often necessitates collaborative efforts between readers if they are to be expected to gain understanding without relying on teacher telling.
- Fostering a disciplinary identity in students is critical if they are to internalize the value of working complex texts and exhibit a willingness to expend the necessary effort to develop their capacities to access knowledge and understanding as readers of disciplinary texts.

CHAPTER 7

Customizing Literacy Practices

Essential Question: How can generic literacy practices be modified to meet the demands of readers and writers in disciplinary contexts?

About midpoint during a recent literacy workshop that I was conducting, one of the high school teachers participating commented, "So, what you are saying is that we need to force students to read in our classes." Implicit in his statement was that he felt that many of his students would not read unless forced, they would be very resistant to learning through reading, and he was dubious about attaining this objective. Setting aside the pervasive realms of compulsion in education in general—from compulsory attendance, to required subjects of study, to mandated testing, to behavioral codes, to assigned homework and other classroom tasks, and so forth—the issue of forcing students to read is an important one.

My response was to address the emotionally charged reference to force and reframe this action as "to expect." We need to expect our students to read, and our instruction needs to support this expectation. I am not all that optimistic about forcing students to develop as readers of complex disciplinary texts, especially if the classroom dynamic plays out to be one of powering students rather than empowering them. I would argue that we need to persuade students, indeed convince them, that the ability to independently access a variety of written communications is of considerable worth to them as their lives continue to unfold and as they explore the options that will be available to them in this 21st-century world.

In Chapter 1, I examined how our personal reader profiles have included both choice texts and obligation texts. Of course, many of the texts that students would be expected to read in disciplinary contexts fall under the obligation designation. Furthermore, these texts, as previously noted, become increasingly complex as students study deeper into our disciplines, which means that students will increasingly have to work these texts for comprehension. We can make reading such texts a curricular requirement, but requiring does not in itself guarantee successful fulfillment of a goal. Also, I think we can agree that we all tend to feel resentment when we are forced to do something that we would rather not do, and more important, we feel frustration or even anger if we are forced to do something that we are not prepared to do.

It feels different, however, when we are invited: invited to grow our capacities as learners, invited to investigate our worlds through the promise of different disciplinary perspectives, and invited to expand our sense of self. It also feels different when we are accorded some degree of choice within the requirements, when we are invited to choose some of the pathways that we might follow toward learning within a discipline. Many students, you are perhaps reflecting, are disposed to decline these invitations. Hence, we face a significant instructional undertaking as teachers: selling the value of reading, writing, and thinking through a disciplinary lens.

Once again, our conversation returns to identity. So much of what we endeavor in our work with students pursues the possibilities of extending who they are. We are essentially lobbying students to change, sometimes significantly, their identities—of being "the kind of person who...." We want these evolving identities to encompass the range of disciplines that students study: the kind of person who can think in a mathematics way, in an artistic way, in a historical way, in a musical way, in a literary way, in a scientific way, in a technical way, in a culinary way, and on and on. Of course, these identities include "I am the kind of person who can access written communications without having to be told what they say," and "I am the kind of person who can work challenging texts so that I can comprehend them."

It is important for students to realize that our purpose in disciplinary learning is not to transform them into minihistorians, miniscientists, or minimathematicians. Certainly, a handful of our students will develop aspirations in these directions. Yet although we all gravitate toward individual preferences—our default modes of perceiving, questioning, and organizing reality—the range of thinking that we might shift into through other disciplinary lenses is essential for all of us as we interact with and try to understand the world around us. As our students become more practiced in displaying disciplinary thinking as readers and writers, they gain insights not before available to them, which can be a profound invitation to continue to grow these capacities. As disciplinary insiders, teachers can provide accomplished and even inspirational models of examining the world through a variety of disciplinary perspectives.

What, How, and Why

Over the years, I have attended a number of workshop presentations that promised "practical strategies you can use with your students Monday morning." As a frequent workshop presenter, I tend to momentarily shudder if I am introduced in this manner. The subtext for this message is fairly clear: Teachers are uninterested in sitting through a lot of theory; they want to delve right into specific practices that might work with their students. In other words, teachers leave the workshop able to plunk pages from a handout directly onto the photocopy machine. (I am trying not to sound sarcastic here, but sometimes the innuendo seems to be that teachers are so desperate for something to do Monday morning that they need to be flooded with ready-to-use reproducibles.) Of course, I have been just as eager as anyone else to get my hands on new ideas for teaching that could improve student learning. However, the theory, informed by research, guides the practice. What (instructional practices) and how (the way these instructional practices are used with students) are intricately bundled into why (the thinking that is fostered by the instructional practices). This becomes an especially significant issue when we strive to mentor students as readers, writers, and thinkers in disciplinary contexts.

Generic Strategies = Instructional Prototypes

It is important for teachers to recognize that many of the literacy practices that they will experience in workshops or come across in professional resources will be generic strategies perhaps modeled in a discipline different from what they teach. Often, the modeled strategies may seem to have a language arts feel to them, given the texts used for presentation of the strategies—frequently literary texts and general nonfiction—and the thinking that is being elicited. This is unsurprising given that a high percentage of people who work with teachers on literacy practices have English language arts backgrounds and bring literary perspectives as their default lens for reading texts. This perspective does not negate the validity of such practices, but this can be a frustrating dynamic for teachers who teach through different disciplinary lenses and perceive that a specific instructional strategy does not necessarily engage students in scientific thinking, mathematics thinking, or technical thinking.

Of course, when literacy resources are presented to teachers across disciplines—science, technical education, social studies, music, family and consumer education, mathematics, literature, art, world languages, and so forth—there is a need to focus on general practices that many teachers might find useful. So, teachers are typically introduced to effective generic approaches to literacy instruction that may be modeled in a particular discipline or two. Teachers may not see how a strategy can be configured for instruction in the discipline they teach, or may conclude that the strategy does not mesh smoothly with their disciplinary instruction, although the practice may be seemingly well suited for other disciplines.

Yet, it is also evident that many of these highly effective generic literacy practices are not yet common knowledge to many teachers, and generic strategies do provide the foundation for deeper exploration into the reading and writing demands of their curriculum. In their excellent treatise *Literacy Instruction in the Content Areas: Getting to the Core of Middle and High School Improvement*, Heller and Greenleaf (2007) acknowledge that generic literacy strategies are indeed beneficial but are insufficient for developing readers, writers, and thinkers in the various disciplines. The authors argue that discipline-specific extensions are necessary:

> A sole emphasis on generic reading comprehension strategies may also lead students to believe that all academic texts are more or less the same, as though the reading that students do in math class were identical to the reading they do in history, or as though good writing in biology were identical to good writing in English. (p. 10)

Generic strategies can be understood as instructional prototypes, as models that illustrate how literacy practices can be embedded into disciplinary learning. However, prototypes are only starting points. Such practices will need to be fine-tuned and even reconfigured as teachers examine how generic literacy strategies can be customized to fit the unique demands of texts in their disciplines.

Modeling What and How

Teachers are obviously interested in the what: what strategies are available to use with students? Packets with lots of practical applications are always very welcome. Questions may also surface about how a strategy can be used effectively with students. We may need to see the process in action to truly get a feel for it, although sometimes teachers become impatient with experiencing strategy modeling ("Enough interaction, let's get onto the next strategy!"). I have observed, however, that the literacy strategies that teachers are most likely to be comfortable test-driving with their students are indeed those specific strategies that were adequately modeled for them in a workshop setting. The how is often trickier than it might seem, especially when being implemented with actual living, breathing adolescent learners.

Understanding Why

The why of the strategy takes teachers beyond the specific format design and prescribed steps to follow and instead deconstructs the underlying thinking prompted and supported by the strategy. The why of strategy instruction tends to be overlooked, but such analysis is absolutely necessary if teachers are to be able to extend beyond the structure of a literacy strategy to customize the practice to fit with specific disciplinary demands.

The why is the mentoring layer of instruction and is frequently the missing link with students. Students often do not internalize the thinking elicited by a strategy because this thinking is never explicitly revealed in class conversations. As a result, students do not become increasingly more independent with handling the reading, writing, and thinking demands in a discipline. Metacognitive conversations, as discussed in Chapter 6, are critical for effectively using literacy practices with students; these strategy debriefings are equally critical for teachers while they are occupied with grasping the workings of a strategy. The why facets of a literacy strategy must be clearly understood if teachers are to redesign a generic literacy strategy into a disciplinary-specific variation that engages thinking through a disciplinary lens.

This book examines disciplinary literacy predominantly from a why perspective to make explicit the intersections between literacy demands and disciplinary thinking. Several chapters also present examples of the what dimension: what form disciplinary-specific practices might assume. The how elements of a strategy are already available through other resources, in particular *Classroom Strategies for Interactive Learning* (Buehl, 2009a), which extensively outlines the steps to follow in using many of these literacy strategies with your students.

Adapting Practices

As disciplinary literacy receives increased attention from educators and researchers, resource materials will feature more discipline-specific models like those presented in this book. Yet, at this point, teachers still need to adopt a translator orientation to many literacy practices, to bring an expectation that they will regularly need to translate generic literacy practices into more discipline-specific variations that approximate what insiders do as readers and writers in their discipline. My wife Wendy, a music educator, relates that she never sees literacy practices modeled for use in her discipline. She recognizes that as a middle school orchestra teacher, she will need to probe how a generic literacy strategy might manifest itself in a music performance classroom. Her application of a strategy in the context of her academic discipline will take students deeper into thinking like a musician, and the variation of the strategy in a music context will likely look substantially different from how that same literacy strategy is reformulated to guide students across the hall into thinking, say, like a mathematician.

> **Without careful attention to what it means to *learn* in the subject areas and what counts as knowledge in the disciplines that undergird those subjects, educators will continue to struggle to integrate literacy instruction and those areas.**
>
> —Moje, 2008, p. 99

I was a member of the 2006 national task force that drafted the Standards for Middle and High School Literacy Coaches (International Reading Association, 2006). The standards recognize that literacy coaches are a critical resource for disciplinary teachers in their efforts to embed literacy practices into the instruction of their discipline. The standards are an initiative of five major professional educational organizations: the International Reading Association, the National Council of Teachers of English, the National

Council of Teachers of Mathematics, the National Science Teachers Association, and the National Council for the Social Studies. Conversations among the representatives of these organizations revealed the necessity to extend literacy practices into disciplinary variations that honor the unique natures of each discipline. Consequently, the national literacy coach standards are subdivided into sections for literacy coaching in each separate discipline to underscore the transition from general practices to disciplinary-specific literacy practices, to reading, writing, and thinking through discrete disciplinary lenses.

Transforming Generic Strategies Into Disciplinary Moves

In recent years, I have been involved in tweaking, or even substantially reconceptualizing, generic literacy practices, which are decontextualized, into versions that are disciplinary-specific, and are as a result contextualized. Although a strategy idea may strike me as very promising, I find that I am rarely satisfied with the generic structure, especially once I attempt to put the process into play in the service of disciplinary learning. In Chapter 4, for example, you see my version of the classic standby, the K-W-L Plus strategy, which for me morphed into the Confirming to Extending grid. Part of what is enjoyable for me is making literacy strategies my own and then helping my students also make these practices their own.

Many of the examples in this book demonstrate how disciplinary teachers have adjusted generic strategy formats to meet the needs of disciplinary thinking. Chapter 5 presents an extended examination of how an essential comprehension process, self-questioning, coupled with a generic literacy strategy, Questioning the Author, can be spun into a host of disciplinary-specific self-questioning taxonomies that can guide student reading and learning. The taxonomies are designed to be nongeneric; very likely, only science teachers will find the biological and physical science self-questioning taxonomies useful. Teachers of other disciplines will pay these two taxonomies only cursory attention, and science teachers will likely quickly bypass the other taxonomies in the chapter because these other variations are not configured as general literacy strategies and do not engage students in scientific thinking.

What is a promising literacy practice that you have encountered recently, or in this book, that was modeled on a different discipline from what you teach? What kind of tweaking could you do to customize this practice to be a better fit for your texts and disciplinary thinking?

Insider Moves

Key considerations for transforming generic literacy practices are the demands of texts in a discipline and the need for the literacy practice to guide student thinking through a specific disciplinary lens. Also, the strategy should approximate the moves that insiders make when reading the texts of their disciplines. For example, Shanahan and Shanahan (2008) relate their research with chemistry professionals and teachers, who felt that many of the literacy strategies presented to them seemed rather contrived; as a result, science teachers displayed some reluctance to integrating strategy instruction into the teaching of their discipline. This is probably unsurprising given that disciplinary literacy was a new notion to them and that they had not experienced such practices themselves when they were developing as science learners.

Yet, if their students were to develop the capacity to access chemistry texts, rather than depend on being told and shown what they need to know, then scaffolding practices in chemistry become necessary. When offered a disciplinary-specific literacy practice that mirrors what chemistry insiders would seek as readers—a graphic organizer that charts the properties of substances and their reactions—the attitude of these teachers shifted; this scaffolding practice seemed to be a chemistry strategy instead of a tangential literacy practice. Using this chart helped them read and think through a chemistry lens. Figure 7.1 presents a variation of that strategy used by a high school chemistry teacher to guide student reading. You can see that the chart elicits elaborating and organizing moves and engages students in the comprehension processes of determining importance and synthesizing. As students add to the chart, they are able to compare different chemical substances, and the chart especially facilitates summarizing the gist of what needs to be understood

Figure 7.1. Graphic Organizer on Chemical Substances

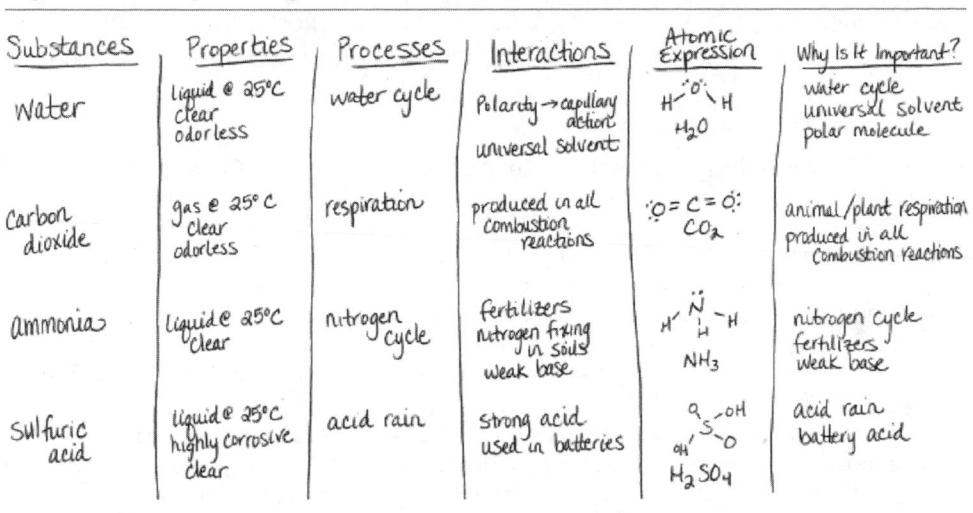

Substances	Properties	Processes	Interactions	Atomic Expression	Why Is It Important?
Water	liquid @ 25°C clear odorless	water cycle	Polarity → capillary action universal solvent	$H-\overset{..}{\underset{..}{O}}-H$ H_2O	water cycle universal solvent polar molecule
Carbon dioxide	gas @ 25°C clear odorless	respiration	produced in all combustion reactions	$\overset{..}{O}=C=\overset{..}{O}$ CO_2	animal/plant respiration produced in all combustion reactions
ammonia	liquid @ 25°C clear	nitrogen cycle	fertilizers nitrogen fixing in soils weak base	$H-\overset{..}{\underset{H}{N}}-H$ NH_3	nitrogen cycle fertilizers weak base
Sulfuric acid	liquid @ 25°C highly corrosive clear	acid rain	strong acid used in batteries	$\underset{OH}{\overset{O}{\underset{}{S}}}\overset{-OH}{\underset{-O}{}}$ H_2SO_4	acid rain battery acid

Note. Courtesy of Mandi Buehl, Watertown High School, WI.

about specific substances. This strategy takes a generic practice, graphic organizers, and customizes it to meet the demands of learning chemistry. The chart provides a blueprint for working a text through a chemistry lens.

Customizing a Generic Strategy

Figure 7.2 displays a substantial reworking of a generic literacy practice, again around a graphic organizer format. In this case, the disciplinary-specific variation targets reading through a historian lens. The generic strategy, the Facts/Questions/Response Chart (Harvey & Goudvis, 2007), was developed to prompt student questioning about information from their reading and synthesize understanding. When retooled to facilitate reading like a historian, the first column is relabeled as "Knowledge" to emphasize "What do I need to remember to make sense of the past?" from the Self-Questioning Taxonomy for History Texts (see Chapter 5, page 190) and to discourage random selection of individual facts just to fill in the grid. In the example from world history in Figure 7.2, students identify six need-to-know things about the Crusades, things a person should know long after the study of these historical events. Students are thus engaged in the comprehension process of determining importance.

What do historians regard as particularly important? The grid features the five facets from the Thinking Like A Historian model—cause and effect, change and continuity, turning points, through their eyes, and using the

Figure 7.2. Knowledge/Question/Response Chart on the Crusades

Knowledge		Question	Response
CE CH (TE) TP (UP)	Palestine was regarded as a holy land for three major religious groups: Christians, Muslims, and Jews.	Will there ever be peace in this region of the world given its emotional connections to these three major religions?	I can understand why there has been, and still is, so much conflict in the Middle East and why resolving this conflict has been so difficult.
CE (CH) TE TP UP	The Crusades were almost 200 years of multiple attempts by European Christians to take control of Palestine from the Muslims.	Why did the Europeans eventually give up on trying to take Palestine away from the Muslims?	I can see why Muslims living in this region today might feel that Christian countries are still trying to have control of the Middle East.
(CE) CH TE TP UP	The Crusades were violent and often brutal, with entire cities plundered and populations massacred.	Is religious intolerance why so much violence happened then, like it seems to happen today?	I can see this pattern happening over and over again in history, when groups with strong differences in beliefs came into conflict.
CE CH (TE) TP UP	Many Crusaders fought for religious goals, but others fought for land, riches, and personal gain.	How many of the Crusaders were motivated by sincere religious aims, and how many were looking for opportunity?	I understand that although religious goals were important for the Crusades, so were personal goals for self-advancement.
CE (CH) TE TP UP	The Crusades led to the exchange of much knowledge, ideas, and technology between the Christian and Arab worlds.	Who benefited more from this exchange, the Christian world or the Arab world?	I find it interesting that although this was a period of intense conflict, both sides were also able to learn from each other.
CE CH TE (TP) UP	The Crusades led to significant political changes in Europe, as nobles lost power, and feudalism began to break down.	How much longer would Europe have remained in the Dark Ages if the Crusades had not happened?	I understand that the Crusades caused significant changes in Europe, even though they were fought in distant lands.

Note. CE = cause and effect. CH = changes. TE = through their eyes. TP = turning point. UP = using the past.

past—as qualifiers for determining importance. For an item to qualify for need-to-know status, it must relate to at least one of these five facets, which is then circled. For example, the first need-to-know item on the Crusades grid is "Palestine was regarded as a holy land for three major religious groups: Christians, Muslims, and Jews," which connects to two facets of history: through their eyes (i.e., this was how people of these religions viewed this region) and using the past (i.e., this helps explain why there is so much religious discord in this region today). Notice the requirement that a need-to-know item must satisfy one of these five facets immediately engages students in making an argument (historians read history as arguments, as discussed in Chapter 3). Students need to be able to argue that their choices of need-to-know items are really things a person needs to know, using the criteria of thinking through a historian lens.

I have used this literacy practice, first by asking students to individually read to identify possible candidates for need-to-know status, by affixing sticky notes in the margins of the text as students do an initial reading. Next, they meet with partners or in cooperative groups to argue their final six choices, again paying attention to the five facets of historical thinking. These knowledge items are then solicited for discussion by the entire class, with groups offering one of their candidates until all possibilities have been listed on the board for the class to consider. The class then decides on the six that deserve need-to-know status, blank Knowledge/Question/Response Charts are handed out at this point, and all students fill in the first column with these items.

Notice how this process stimulates discussion of several of the history taxonomy questions. For example, the statement "The Crusades were violent and often brutal, with entire cities plundered and populations massacred" addresses the questions, "What happened?" and "What caused it to happen?"

Students then return to their partners or groups and work on the second column, "Questions." This phase of the strategy engages students in collaborative discussions about each need-to-know item as they talk over possible questions that surface for them about these key ideas. A possible question that a group might decide on for the third item might be: "Is religious intolerance why so much violence happened then, like it seems to happen today?" Each group gets to raise a question for deliberation by the entire class; the student-generated questions form the framework for continued class conversation about important ideas of this topic. Again, students are expected to carry the intellectual work of question generating during this phase.

The last phase, the "Response" column, is for individual student processing of this historical period. Each student summarizes personal understandings about each need-to-know item in this column. To follow along in Figure 7.2, a personal response for the third knowledge item might be "I can see this pattern happening over and over again in history, when groups with strong differences in beliefs come into conflict." Students are engaged in the comprehension process of synthesizing during this phase as they verbalize understandings in writing. This phase elicits thinking at the Creating level of the taxonomy: "How has this author changed what I understand?"

It is clear from this extended example that teacher decisions are critical to customizing a generic literacy practice so that it can be applied in the service of reading, writing, and thinking through a disciplinary lens. Although generic strategies have much to offer teachers of different disciplines, it remains likely that many of these strategies will need the fingerprints of disciplinary teachers in the strategies' specific structure or format if such strategies are to realize their potential for scaffolding literacy tasks in the respective contexts of different disciplines.

Embedded Literacy Practices

I recently participated in a literacy walk-through in a district where I had done extensive literacy work with teachers. I strolled about the building with the literacy coach, dropping in on classrooms just to get a snapshot in time of literacy practices in play. (We were most agreeably low key and nonthreatening, as this was not an evaluation excursion.) We saw plenty of literacy strategies in various guises being applied in classrooms across the disciplines, and we saw plenty of opportunities to do more with students. One classroom in particular struck me. As we entered, the teacher (middle school social studies) rather sheepishly apologized that unfortunately they were not using any literacy strategies that day, but we were welcome to partake in what was happening. It became abundantly clear almost immediately that a whole host of rich literacy practices were in operation in that classroom. Students were working collaboratively to review previous learning and brainstorm additional ideas. Students were engaged in constructing knowledge maps about culture. The assignment was jigsawed so that each group was working on a knowledge map related to a different facet of culture. Each group of students was then charged to summarize their understandings as they explained their knowledge map to the entire class, and the maps were subsequently displayed about the classroom as environmental knowledge cues. This work was all preparatory for students' reading of a passage in their eighth-grade textbook.

As we stepped back into the hallway, both the literacy coach and I snorted at the comment about not doing any literacy practices that day. We tallied at least eight different intentional instances of embedded literacy instruction, but the teacher had assumed that we were on the lookout for one of those typical labeled strategy prototypes, like Anticipation Guides, K-W-L, or Two-Column Notes. In other classrooms, students were indeed engaged in recognizable literacy activities, like completing graphic organizers; in this classroom, the literacy practices were totally integrated into the flow of teaching social studies. The practices were not extras tacked onto normal instruction; these literacy practices *were* normal instruction.

A number of years ago, I shared the responsibility of organizing a daylong literacy institute at an International Reading Association convention. One chunk of the program was to be spent modeling exemplary literacy strategies, and we had assembled a who's who of adolescent literacy notables for the presentations. Each presenter was asked to choose a particular strategy to model, and we had an impressive lineup of anticipation guides, concept mapping, structured overviews, semantic feature analysis charts, and other such favored strategies—about a dozen in all from which participants could pick. Our keynote presenter for the program was the venerable educator Harold Herber, recognized by many as the father of content reading practices. Herber, however, refused to model any labeled strategy; instead, he insisted on modeling "good teaching." Although at the time, we program organizers were a tad

> **"** As opposed to asking students to read for homework or as a classroom assignment and then simply answer questions when they finish reading, literacy rich content area classrooms include a variety of instructional routines that provide guidance to students before, during and after reading. **"**
>
> —Lee & Spratley, 2010, p. 17

irritated (after all, he *started* all of this), it was apparent that he was trying to send a strong message: Doing a prescribed literacy practice every once in a while in your classroom is not the point. Herber was telling us that doing effective teaching of one's discipline encompasses rich, ongoing literacy instruction as students are mentored as disciplinary readers, writers, and thinkers. This is good teaching—exactly what I had witnessed in that middle school social studies classroom.

Gradual Release in Practice

A final illustration is in order. I was privileged to be invited to spend a class period with a Spanish teacher, again in a district where I had done considerable literacy professional development. The class was Spanish III, with mainly sophomores and some juniors. Instruction centered on a short Spanish passage regarding barbecuing traditions in Argentina, a text with a great deal of unfamiliar vocabulary which loomed as a forbidding read for the students at this level of language learning. The teacher began instruction with a short think-aloud, modeling with a couple of paragraphs how he personally handled a challenging Spanish text as a college student, the Latin American classic *One Hundred Years of Solitude* by Gabriel García Márquez, and how he managed the onslaught of unknown vocabulary. Next, students met with partners to brainstorm words that might be used when describing a *parrillada* (Spanish for barbecuing or grilling). These were shared with the entire class and listed on the board. The teacher followed with a YouTube clip, in Spanish, featuring a *parrillada* event in Argentina. He played the clip twice, so students would have the opportunity to follow the language as they watched the barbecuing process.

Students next predicted key vocabulary, using familiar cognates, and completed the chart in Figure 7.3. The teacher modeled the process with a couple of words, then students tackled the new words using this strategy. Although I had studied both French and German, I know almost no Spanish; yet, I was stunned to discover that I was able to correctly predict all but one word from this list using familiar cognates—what a powerful strategy. (I was the only one in the room to correctly predict *las vísceras*, using my knowledge of the words *visceral* and *viscera*, which are internal organs. The students found this facet of barbecuing quite unsavory!)

Students then individually read the article detailing the Argentine *parrillada*, highlighting troublesome words that were interfering with

Figure 7.3. Spanish Cognate Brainstorming

Actividad 1: **¿Qué se necesita para hacer una parrillada?**
Tienes dos minutos para pensar en todas las palabras necesarias para describir una parrillada:

Actividad 2: **Los Cognados**

Vocabulary	Your Guess	What Other Words Can You Think Of?
los consejos		*aconsejar* (to advise) *el consejero* (advisor)
la fama		
el salado		
el carbón		
utilice		
las bolas		
las vísceras		
moderado		
constante		
la grasa		
paciencia		
porciones		

Actividad 3: **Una Parrillada**
Dibuja paso por paso una parrillada, en los espacios de abajo:

1.	2.	3.	4.	5.

Note. Courtesy of Jeff Haubenreich, Menomonee Falls High School, Menomonee Falls, WI.

comprehension. Students then engaged in a second reading, this time with a partner, and the two of them worked to explain the process of a *parrillada*, even if they did not figure out all of the words. This was done in lieu of merely looking up words in a Spanish–English dictionary. Finally, the partners decided on the five necessary steps of a *parrillada* and sketched each step, with a Spanish word or phrase identifying the process in each phase. The following day, students verbally summarized their understandings with partners, using their drawings and the vocabulary lists, which was a warm-up prelude for individually writing their summaries in Spanish.

Disciplinary literacy instruction permeated this lesson. As you deconstruct the embedded literacy components, you will notice all of the key ideas of this book on display. The foundational comprehension processes—connecting to prior knowledge, generating questions, inferring, creating mental images, determining importance, and synthesizing—were all integrated into the flow of learning. The application of the Gradual Release of Responsibility model was evident, with explicit modeling and collaborative problem solving, as students were mentored on how to read as a second-language learner. Students worked the text and told each other what the author was saying. Students verbalized their understandings. This was a model lesson of good teaching.

I currently teach a mandated disciplinary literacy class for future middle and high school teachers from across the curriculum at a small college in Wisconsin. My future teachers arrive very much like many of my former high school students at Madison East High School: They are in my class because someone is making them. The future teachers arrive excited about the prospects of teaching science, mathematics, literature, music, art, business, or social studies. They are not particularly enthralled with the idea of teaching reading. Yet, by the end of the course, a comment I consistently receive is, "We thought this class was just going to be about doing reading stuff, but it is really about how to teach." That is what disciplinary literacy practices should feel like in your hands: tools that can be folded into good teaching.

Disciplinary literacy has generally proceeded under the radar in our classrooms and has not been the tradition in university teacher preparatory programs, neither in subject area methods courses nor in supplementary literacy methods classes, which usually introduce generic strategies. As a result, teachers have not experienced many disciplinary-specific models of appropriate literacy practices for their subject areas. To customize generic strategies, teachers need to uncover literacy practices that underlie the thinking in their disciplines.

Insiders who have gradually become accomplished readers, writers, and thinkers in an academic discipline may take for granted the processes that have become second nature to them. As teachers carefully examine various literacy practices, they need to consider the moves that they, and professionals in their field, use when they engage with disciplinary texts. This process is especially fertile ground for collaborations between disciplinary teachers and literacy coaches.

PARTING THOUGHTS AND TALKING POINTS

- What does it mean to be a reader, writer, and thinker in your academic discipline?
- How are students developing the capacity to access communications in your discipline?
- To what extent are students actually expected to read within your academic discipline?
- What scaffolding is necessary to support students as they read complex texts in your discipline?
- How can generic strategies be customized into disciplinary-specific literacy practices?
- What continue to be challenges for students as readers, writers, and thinkers in your discipline?

References for Strategies

Strategies From *Classroom Strategies for Interactive Learning*

The following strategies are more extensively described in *Classroom Strategies for Interactive Learning* (Buehl, 2009a):

Alphabet Brainstorming

Ricci, G., & Wahlgren, C. (1998, May). *The key to know "PAINE" know gain.* Paper presented at the 43rd annual meeting of the International Reading Association, Orlando, FL.

Anticipation Guides

Herber, H.L. (1978). *Teaching reading in content areas* (2nd ed.). Englewood Cliffs, NJ: Prentice Hall.

Readence, J.E., Bean, T.W., & Baldwin, R.S. (2004). *Content area reading: An integrated approach* (8th ed.). Dubuque, IA: Kendall/Hunt.

Double-Entry Diaries

Harvey, S., & Goudvis, A. (2007). *Strategies that work: Teaching comprehension for understanding and engagement* (2nd ed.). Portland, ME: Stenhouse.

Tovani, C. (2000). *I read it, but I don't get it: Comprehension strategies for adolescent readers.* Portland, ME: Stenhouse.

Graphic Organizers

Armbruster, B.B., & Anderson, T.H. (1982). *Idea-mapping: The technique and its use in the classroom or simulating the "ups" and "downs" of reading comprehension* (Reading Education Report No. 36). Urbana: Center for the Study of Reading, University of Illinois at Urbana-Champaign; Cambridge, MA: Bolt Beranek & Newman; Washington, DC: National Institute of Education, U.S. Department of Education.

Jones, B.F., Pierce, J., & Hunter, B. (1988). Teaching students to construct graphic representations. *Educational Leadership, 46*(4), 20–25.

Smith, P.L., & Tompkins, G.E. (1988). Structured notetaking: A new strategy for content area readers. *Journal of Reading, 32*(1), 46–53.

Interactive Reading Guides

Wood, K.D. (1988). Guiding students through informational text. *The Reading Teacher, 41*(9), 912–920.

K-W-L Plus

Carr, E., & Ogle D. (1987). K-W-L plus: A strategy for comprehension and summarization. *Journal of Reading, 30*(7), 626–631.

Ogle, D.M. (1986). K-W-L: A teaching model that develops active reading of expository text. *The Reading Teacher, 39*(6), 564–570.

LINK

Vaughan, J.L., & Estes, T.H. (1986). *Reading and reasoning beyond the primary grades*. Boston: Allyn & Bacon.

Math Reading Keys

Buehl, D. (1998, October). *Making math make sense: Tactics help kids understand math language*. Retrieved April 25, 2011, from Wisconsin Education Association Council website: www.weac.org/news_and_publications/education_news/1998-1999/read_math.aspx

Possible Sentences

Moore, D.W., & Moore, S.A. (1986). Possible sentences. In E.K. Dishner, T.W. Bean, J.E. Readence, & D.W. Moore (Eds.), *Reading in the content* areas: *Improving classroom instruction* (2nd ed., pp. 174–179). Dubuque, IA: Kendall/Hunt.

Readence, J.E., Moore, D.W., & Rickelman, R.J. (2000). *Prereading activities for content area reading and learning* (3rd ed.). Newark, DE: International Reading Association.

Power Notes

Santa, C.M., Havens, L.T., & Valdes, B.J. (2004). *Project CRISS: Creating independence through student-owned strategies* (3rd ed.). Dubuque, IA: Kendall/Hunt.

Prediction Guides

Herber, H.L. (1978). *Teaching reading in content areas* (2nd ed.). Englewood Cliffs, NJ: Prentice Hall.

Nichols, J.N. (1983). Using prediction to increase content area interest and understanding. *Journal of Reading, 27*(3), 225–228.

Problem–Solution Graphic Organizer (for a History Text)

Buehl, D. (1992). A frame of mind for reading history. *The Exchange, 5*(1), 4–5.

Questioning the Author

Beck, I.L., McKeown, M.G., Hamilton, R.L., & Kucan, L. (1997). *Questioning the author: An approach for enhancing student engagement with text.* Newark, DE: International Reading Association.

Quick Writes

Fulwiler, T. (1980). Journals across the disciplines. *The English Journal, 69*(9), 14–19.

Rief, L. (1998). *Vision and voice: Expanding the literacy spectrum.* Portsmouth, NH: Heinemann.

Santa, C.M., & Havens, L.T. (1991). Learning through writing. In C.M. Santa & D.E. Alvermann (Eds.), *Science learning: Processes and applications* (pp. 122–133). Newark, DE: International Reading Association.

Science Connection Overview

Buehl, D. (1992). The connection overview: A strategy for learning in science. *WSRA Journal, 36*(2), 21–30.

Self-Questioning Taxonomy

Buehl, D. (2007, September). *Modeling self-questioning on Bloom's taxonomy.* Retrieved April 20, 2011, from Wisconsin Education Association Council website: www.weac.org/news_and_publications/education_news/2007-2008/readingroom_modeling.aspx

Self-Questioning Taxonomy for Literary Fiction

Buehl, D. (2007, November). *Questioning literary fiction.* Retrieved April 19, 2011, from Wisconsin Education Association Council website: www.weac.org/news_and_publications/education_news/2007-2008/reading_room_literary.aspx

Story Impressions

McGinley, W.J., & Denner, P.R. (1987). Story impressions: A prereading/writing activity. *Journal of Reading, 31*(3), 248–253.

Text Coding

Buehl, D. (2004, May). *Using graffiti as a reading tool.* Retrieved April 25, 2011, from Wisconsin Education Association Council website: www.weac.org/news_and_publications/education_news/2003-2004/read_graffiti.aspx

Harvey, S., & Goudvis, A. (2007). *Strategies that work: Teaching comprehension for understanding and engagement* (2nd ed.). Portland, ME: Stenhouse.

Tovani, C. (2000). *I read it, but I don't get it: Comprehension strategies for adolescent readers.* Portland, ME: Stenhouse.

Text Frames

Anderson, T.H., & Armbruster, B.B. (1984). Studying. In P.D. Pearson (Ed.), *Handbook of reading research* (pp. 657–679). New York: Longman.

Buehl, D. (1991). Frames of mind. *The Exchange, 4*(2), 4–5.

Jones, B.F., Palincsar, A.S., Ogle, D.S., & Carr, E.G. (1987). *Strategic teaching and learning: Cognitive instruction in the content areas.* Alexandria, VA: Association for Supervision and Curriculum Development; Elmhurst, IL: North Central Regional Educational Laboratory.

Additional Strategies

Comprehension Checkdown

Buehl, D. (2008, June). *Inform yourself.* Retrieved April 13, 2011, from Wisconsin Education Association Council website: www.weac.org/news_and_publications/education_news/2007-2008/readingroom_inform.aspx

Confirming to Extending

Buehl, D. (2011). *Developing readers in the academic disciplines.* Newark, DE: International Reading Association.

Inform Yourself

Buehl, D. (2008, June). *Inform yourself.* Retrieved April 13, 2011, from Wisconsin Education Association Council website: www.weac.org/news_and_publications/education_news/2007-2008/readingroom_inform.aspx.

Knowledge Ladders

Buehl, D. (2011). *Developing readers in the academic disciplines.* Newark, DE: International Reading Association.

Knowledge Mapping

Buzan, T. (1991). *Use both sides of your brain* (3rd ed.). New York: Plume.

Tierney, R.J., & Readence, J.E. (2004). *Reading strategies and practices: A compendium* (6th ed.). Boston: Allyn & Bacon.

Knowledge/Question/Response Chart

Harvey, S., & Goudvis, A. (2007). *Strategies that work: Teaching comprehension for understanding and engagement* (2nd ed.). Portland, ME: Stenhouse.

Point–Counterpoint

Buehl, D. (2011). *Developing readers in the academic disciplines.* Newark, DE: International Reading Association.

PReP (Pre-Reading Plan)

Langer, J.A. (1981). From theory to practice: A prereading plan. *Journal of Reading, 25*(2), 152–156.

Pyramid Notes

Burke, J. (2002). *Tools for thought: Helping all students read, write, speak, and think.* Portsmouth, NH: Heinemann

Review/New Charts

Buehl, D. (2011). *Developing readers in the academic disciplines.* Newark, DE: International Reading Association.

Self-Questioning Taxonomy for Biological Science Texts

Buehl, D. (2009). Mentoring literacy practices in academic disciplines. In S.R. Parris, D. Fisher, & K. Headley (Eds.), *Adolescent literacy, field tested: Effective solutions for every classroom* (pp. 228–238). Newark, DE: International Reading Association.

Self-Questioning Taxonomy for History Texts

Buehl, D. (2009). Reading like an insider. *The Exchange, 22*(1), 2–5.

Self-Questioning Taxonomy for Mathematics Conceptual Texts

Buehl, D. (2011). *Developing readers in the academic disciplines.* Newark, DE: International Reading Association.

Self-Questioning Taxonomy for Mathematics Procedural Texts

Buehl, D. (2011). *Developing readers in the academic disciplines.* Newark, DE: International Reading Association.

Self-Questioning Taxonomy for Mathematics Texts

Buehl, D. (2011). *Developing readers in the academic disciplines.* Newark, DE: International Reading Association.

Self-Questioning Taxonomy for Music Performance Texts

Buehl, D., & Buehl, W. (2008, October). *Connecting music to literacy.* Paper presented at the Wisconsin School Music Association Conference, Madison, WI.

Self-Questioning Taxonomy for Physical Science Texts

Buehl, D. (2011). *Developing readers in the academic disciplines.* Newark, DE: International Reading Association.

Self-Questioning Taxonomy for Technical Texts

Buehl, D. (2011). *Developing readers in the academic disciplines.* Newark, DE: International Reading Association.

Structured Overview

Barron, R. (1969). The use of vocabulary as an advance organizer. In H.L. Herber & P.L. Sanders (Eds.), *Research in reading in the content areas: First year report* (pp. 29–39). Syracuse, NY: Reading and Language Arts Center, Syracuse University.

Thumbs Up–Thumbs Down Chart

Buehl, D. (2011). *Developing readers in the academic disciplines*. Newark, DE: International Reading Association.

Two-Column Notes

Pauk, W. (2001). *How to study in college* (7th ed.). Boston: Houghton Mifflin.

Wide Reading

Marzano, R.J. (2004). *Building background knowledge for academic achievement: Research on what works in schools*. Alexandria, VA: Association for Supervision and Curriculum Development.

REFERENCES

Alexander, P.A., & Fox, E. (2011). Adolescents as readers. In M.L. Kamil, P.D. Pearson, E.B. Moje, & P.P. Afflerbach (Eds.), *Handbook of reading research* (Vol. 4, pp. 157–176). New York: Routledge.

Alexander, P.A., & Jetton, T.L. (2000). Learning from text: A multidimensional and developmental perspective. In M.L. Kamil, P.B. Mosenthal, P.D. Pearson, & R. Barr (Eds.), *Handbook of reading research* (Vol. 3, pp. 285–310). Mahwah, NJ: Erlbaum.

Alvermann, D.E. (Ed.). (2002). *Adolescents and literacies in a digital world*. New York: Peter Lang.

Alvermann, D.E., Hinchman, K.A., Moore, D.W., Phelps, S.F., & Waff, D.R. (Eds.). (2006). *Reconceptualizing the literacies in adolescents' lives* (2nd ed.). Mahwah, NJ: Erlbaum.

American College Testing. (2006a). *Reading between the lines: What the ACT reveals about college readiness in reading*. Iowa City, IA: Author. Retrieved April 13, 2011, from www.act.org/research/policymakers/pdf/reading_report.pdf

American College Testing. (2006b). *Ready for college and ready for work: Same or different?* Iowa City, IA: Author. Retrieved April 13, 2011, from www.act.org/research/policymakers/pdf/ReadinessBrief.pdf

Anderson, L.W., & Krathwohl, D.R. (Eds.). (2001). *A taxonomy for learning, teaching, and assessing: A revision of Bloom's taxonomy of educational objectives*. New York: Longman.

Anderson, R.C., & Pearson, P.D. (1984). A schema-theoretic view of basic processes in reading comprehension. In P.D. Pearson, R. Barr, M.L. Kamil, & P. Mosenthal (Eds.), *Handbook of reading research* (pp. 255–291). New York: Longman.

Anderson, T.H., & Armbruster, B.B. (1984). Studying. In P.D. Pearson, R. Barr, M.L. Kamil, & P. Mosenthal (Eds.), *Handbook of reading research* (pp. 657–679). New York: Longman.

Baker, L., & Beall, L.C. (2009). Metacognitive processes and reading comprehension. In S.E. Israel & G.G. Duffy (Eds.), *Handbook of research on reading comprehension* (pp. 373–388). New York: Routledge.

Battista, M.T. (1999). The mathematical miseducation of America's youth: Ignoring research and scientific study in education. *Phi Delta Kappan, 80*(6), 424–433.

Beck, I.L., McKeown, M.G., Hamilton, R.L., & Kucan, L. (1997). *Questioning the author: An approach for enhancing student engagement with text*. Newark, DE: International Reading Association.

Biancarosa, G., & Snow, C.E. (2004). *Reading next—a vision for action and research in middle and high school literacy: A report to Carnegie Corporation of New York*. Washington, DC: Alliance for Excellent Education.

Bloom, B.S., Englehart, M., Furst, E., Hill, W., & Krathwohl, D.R. (1956). *Taxonomy of educational objectives: The classification of educational goals. Handbook 1: Cognitive domain*. New York: Longman.

Buehl, D. (2007a). A professional development framework for embedding comprehension instruction into content classrooms. In J. Lewis & G. Moorman

(Eds.), *Adolescent literacy instruction: Policies and promising practices* (pp. 192–211). Newark, DE: International Reading Association.

Buehl, D. (2007b, September). *Modeling self-questioning on Bloom's taxonomy.* Retrieved April 20, 2011, from Wisconsin Education Association Council website: www.weac.org/news_and_publications/education_news/2007-2008/readingroom_modeling.aspx

Buehl, D. (2007c, November). *Questioning literary fiction.* Retrieved April 19, 2011, from Wisconsin Education Association Council website: www.weac.org/news_and_publications/education_news/2007-2008/reading_room_literary.aspx

Buehl, D. (2008a, June). *Inform yourself.* Retrieved April 13, 2011, from Wisconsin Education Association Council website: www.weac.org/news_and_publications/education_news/2007-2008/readingroom_inform.aspx

Buehl, D. (2008b, May). *Questioning biological texts.* Retrieved April 20, 2011, from Wisconsin Education Association Council website: www.weac.org/News_and_Publications/education_news/2007-2008/readingroom_tax.aspx

Buehl, D. (2009a). *Classroom strategies for interactive learning* (3rd ed.). Newark, DE: International Reading Association.

Buehl, D. (2009b). Mentoring literacy practices in academic disciplines. In S.R. Parris, D. Fisher, & K. Headley (Eds.), *Adolescent literacy, field tested: Effective solutions for every classroom* (pp. 228–238). Newark, DE: International Reading Association.

Buehl, D. (2009c). Reading like an insider. *The Exchange, 22*(1), 2–5.

Buehl, D., & Buehl, W. (2008, October). *Connecting music to literacy.* Paper presented at the Wisconsin School Music Association Conference, Madison, WI.

Carnegie Council on Advancing Adolescent Literacy. (2010). *Time to act: An agenda for advancing adolescent literacy for college and career success.* New York: Carnegie Corporation of New York.

Caverly, D.C., Orlando, V.P., & Mullen, J.L. (2000). Textbook study reading. In R.F. Flippo & D.C. Caverly (Eds.), *Handbook of college reading and study strategy research* (pp. 105–147). Mahwah, NJ: Erlbaum.

Clark, K. (2009). Solving the college crisis. *U.S. News & World Report, 146*(8), 26–39.

Conley, M.W. (2009). Improving adolescent comprehension: Developing comprehension strategies in the content areas. In S.E. Israel & G.G. Duffy (Eds.), *Handbook of research on reading comprehension* (pp. 531–550). New York: Routledge.

Dole, J.A., Nokes, J.D., & Drits, D. (2009). Cognitive strategy instruction. In S.E. Israel & G.G. Duffy (Eds.), *Handbook of research on reading comprehension* (pp. 347–372). New York: Routledge.

Draper, R.J. (2002). School mathematics reform, constructivism, and literacy: A case for literacy instruction in the reform-oriented math classroom. *Journal of Adolescent & Adult Literacy, 45*(6), 520–529.

Duke, N.K., & Pearson, P.D. (2002). Effective practices for developing reading comprehension. In A.E. Farstrup & S.J. Samuels (Eds.), *What research has to say about reading instruction* (3rd ed., pp. 205–242). Newark, DE: International Reading Association.

Durkin, D. (1978). What classroom observations reveal about reading comprehension instruction. *Reading Research Quarterly, 14*(4), 481–533.

Foster, T.C. (2003). *How to read literature like a professor.* New York: HarperCollins.

Foster, T.C. (2008). *How to read novels like a professor*. New York: HarperCollins.

Frey, N., Fisher, D., & Everlove, S. (2009). *Productive group work: How to engage students, build teamwork, and promote understanding*. Alexandria, VA: ASCD.

Gallagher, K. (2004). *Deeper reading: Comprehending challenging texts, 4–12*. Portland, ME: Stenhouse.

Gallagher, K. (2009). *Readicide: How schools are killing reading and what you can do about it*. Portland, ME: Stenhouse.

Gardner, H. (1991). *The unschooled mind: How children think and how schools should teach*. New York: Basic Books.

Gee, J.P. (1996). *Social linguistics and literacies: Ideology in Discourses* (2nd ed.). London: Taylor & Francis.

Gee, J.P. (2000). Discourse and sociocultural studies in reading. In M.L. Kamil, P.B. Mosenthal, P.D. Pearson, & R. Barr (Eds.), *Handbook of reading research* (Vol. 3, pp. 195–207). Mahwah, NJ: Erlbaum.

Gee, J.P. (2001). Identity as an analytic lens for research in education. In W.G. Secada (Ed.), *Review of research in education* (Vol. 25, pp. 99–125). Washington, DC: American Educational Research Association.

Goleman, D. (1995). *Emotional intelligence*. New York: Bantam.

Greenleaf, C., Cribb, G., Howlett, H., & Moore, D.W. (2010). Inviting outsiders inside disciplinary literacies: An interview with Cynthia Greenleaf, Gayle Cribb, and Heather Howlett. *Journal of Adolescent & Adult Literacy, 54*(4), 291–293. doi:10.1598/JAAL.54.4.7

Guthrie, J.T. (2008). Reading motivation and engagement in middle and high school: Appraisal and intervention. In J.T. Guthrie (Ed.), *Engaging adolescents in reading* (pp. 1–16). Thousand Oaks, CA: Corwin Press.

Hagood, M.C., Alvermann, D.E., & Heron-Hruby, A. (2010). *Bring it to class: Unpacking pop culture in literacy learning*. New York: Teachers College Press.

Harvey, S., & Daniels, H. (2009). *Comprehension and collaboration: Inquiry circles in action*. Portsmouth, NH: Heinemann.

Harvey, S., & Goudvis, A. (2007). *Strategies that work: Teaching comprehension for understanding and engagement* (2nd ed.). Portland, ME: Stenhouse.

Heller, R., & Greenleaf, C.L. (2007). *Literacy instruction in the content areas: Getting to the core of middle and high school improvement*. Washington, DC: Alliance for Excellent Education.

Hirsch, E.D., Jr. (2006). *The knowledge deficit: Closing the shocking education gap for American children*. Boston: Houghton Mifflin.

Hynd, C., Holschuh, J.P., & Hubbard, B.P. (2004). Thinking like a historian: College students' reading of multiple historical documents. *Journal of Literacy Research, 36*(2), 141–176. doi:10.1207/s15548430jlr3602_2

International Reading Association (with National Council of Teachers of English, National Council of Teachers of Mathematics, National Science Teachers Association, and National Council for the Social Studies). (2006). *Standards for middle and high school literacy coaches*. Newark, DE: Author.

Johnston, P.H. (2004). *Choice words: How our language affects children's learning*. Portland, ME: Stenhouse.

Jones, B.F., Palincsar, A.S., Ogle, D.S., & Carr, E.G. (1987). *Strategic teaching and learning: Cognitive instruction in the content areas*. Alexandria, VA: Association for

Supervision and Curriculum Development; Elmhurst, IL: North Central Regional Educational Laboratory.

Kamil, M.L., Borman, G.D., Dole, J., Kral, C.C., Salinger, T., & Torgesen, J. (2008). *Improving adolescent literacy: Effective classroom and intervention practices: A practice guide* (NCEE 2008-4027). Washington, DC: National Center for Education Evaluation and Regional Assistance, Institute of Education Sciences, U.S. Department of Education.

Karpicke, J.D., & Blunt, J.R. (2011). Retrieval practice produces more learning than elaborative studying with concept mapping. *Science, 331*(6018), 772–775.

Keene, E.O., & Zimmermann, S. (2007). *Mosaic of thought: The power of comprehension strategy instruction* (2nd ed.). Portsmouth, NH: Heinemann.

Krajcik, J.S. & Sutherland, L.M. (2010). Supporting students in developing literacy in science. *Science, 328*(5977), 456–459.

Lave, J., & Wenger, E. (1991). *Situated learning: Legitimate peripheral participation.* Cambridge, England: Cambridge University Press.

Lee, C.D., & Spratley, A. (2010). *Reading in the disciplines: The challenges of adolescent literacy.* New York: Carnegie Corporation of New York.

Lee, J.M., Jr., & Rawls, A. (2010). *The college completion agenda: 2010 progress report.* New York: College Board Advocacy & Policy Center.

Mandell, N., & Malone, B. (2007). *Thinking like a historian: Rethinking history instruction.* Madison: Wisconsin Historical Society Press.

Marzano, R.J. (2004). *Building background knowledge for academic achievement: Research on what works in schools.* Alexandria, VA: Association for Supervision and Curriculum Development.

McCarthey, S.J., & Moje, E.B. (2002). Identity matters. *Reading Research Quarterly, 37*(2), 228–238.

McCombs, J.S., Kirby, S.N., Barney, H., Darilek, H., & Magee, S. (2005). *Achieving state and national literacy goals, a long uphill road: A report to Carnegie Corporation of New York.* Santa Monica, CA: RAND Corporation.

Moje, E.B. (2008). Foregrounding the disciplines in secondary literacy teaching and learning: A call for change. *Journal of Adolescent & Adult Literacy, 52*(2), 96–107. doi:10.1598/JAAL.52.2.1

Moje, E.B., Ciechanowski, K.M., Kramer, K., Ellis, L., Carrillo, R., & Collazo, T. (2004). Working toward third space in content area literacy: An examination of everyday funds of knowledge and discourse. *Reading Research Quarterly, 39*(1), 38–70. doi:10.1598/RRQ.39.1.4

Moje, E.B., Stockdill, D., Kim, K., & Kim, H. (2011). The role of text in disciplinary learning. In M.L. Kamil, P.D. Pearson, E.B. Moje, & P.P. Afflerbach (Eds.), *Handbook of reading research* (Vol. 4, pp. 453–486). New York: Routledge.

Moore, D.W. (2008, May). *Advances in adolescent literacy instruction.* Paper presented at the annual meeting of the International Reading Association, Atlanta, GA.

Moore, D.W., & Onofrey, K.A. (2007). Fostering literate academic identities during the first days of school. In J. Lewis & G. Moorman (Eds.), *Adolescent literacy instruction: Policies and promising practices* (pp. 286–318). Newark, DE: International Reading Association.

National Association of Secondary School Principals. (2005). *Creating a culture of literacy: A guide for middle and high school principals.* Reston, VA: Author.

National Association of State Boards of Education. (2006). *Reading at risk: The state response to the crisis in adolescent literacy* (Rev. ed.). Arlington, VA: Author.

National Center for Education Statistics. (2010a). *The nation's report card: Grade 12 reading and mathematics 2009 national and pilot state results* (NCES 2011-455). Washington, DC: National Center for Education Statistics, Institute of Education Sciences, U.S. Department of Education.

National Center for Education Statistics. (2010b). *The nation's report card: Reading 2009: National Assessment for Educational Progress at grades 4 and 8* (NCES 2010-458). Washington, DC: National Center for Education Statistics, Institute of Education Sciences, U.S. Department of Education.

National Council of Teachers of English. (2004). *A call to action: What we know about adolescent literacy and ways to support teachers in meeting students' needs.* Urbana, IL: Author. Retrieved April 14, 2011, from www.ncte.org/positions/statements/adolescentliteracy

National Endowment for the Arts. (2007). *To read or not to read: A question of national consequence* (Research Report No. 47). Washington, DC: Author.

National Governors Association Center for Best Practices. (2005). *Reading to achieve: A governor's guide to adolescent literacy.* Washington, DC: Author.

National Governors Association Center for Best Practices & the Council of Chief State School Officers. (2010a). *Common Core State Standards for English language arts and literacy in history/social studies, science, and technical subjects: Appendix A: Research supporting key elements of the standards.* Retrieved April 15, 2011, from www.corestandards.org/the-standards/assets/Appendix_A.pdf

National Governors Association Center for Best Practices & the Council of Chief State School Officers. (2010b). *Common Core State Standards for mathematics.* Retrieved April 13, 2011, from www.corestandards.org/assets/CCSSI_Math%20Standards .pdf

National Governors Association Center for Best Practices & the Council of Chief State School Officers. (2010c). *The standards: English language arts standards.* Retrieved April 14, 2011, from www.corestandards.org/the-standards/english-language-arts-standards

National Institute of Child Health and Human Development. (2000). *Report of the National Reading Panel. Teaching children to read: An evidence-based assessment of the scientific research literature on reading and its implications for reading instruction* (NIH Publication No. 00-4769). Washington, DC: U.S. Government Printing Office.

National Mathematics Advisory Panel. (2008). *Foundations for success: The final report of the National Mathematics Advisory Panel.* Washington, DC: U.S. Department of Education.

National School Boards Association. (2006). *The next chapter: A school board guide to improving adolescent literacy.* Alexandria, VA: Author.

O'Toole, P. (2003). *Shaping sound musicians: An innovative approach to teaching comprehensive musicianship through performance.* Chicago: GIA.

Palincsar, A.S., & Brown, A.L. (1984). Reciprocal teaching of comprehension-fostering and comprehension-monitoring activities. *Cognition and Instruction, 1*(2), 117–175. doi:10.1207/s1532690xci0102_1

Paris, S.G., Lipson, M.Y., & Wixson, K.K. (1983). Becoming a strategic reader. *Contemporary Educational Psychology, 8*(3), 293–316. doi:10.1016/0361-476X(83)90018-8

Paulos, J.A. (1995). *A mathematician reads the newspaper.* New York: Basic.

Paulos, J.A. (2001). *Innumeracy: Mathematical illiteracy and its consequences.* New York: Hill & Wang. (Original work published 1988)

Pearson, P.D. (2009). The roots of reading comprehension instruction. In S.E. Israel & G.G. Duffy (Eds.), *Handbook of research on reading comprehension* (pp. 3–31). New York: Routledge.

Pearson, P.D. (2011). Toward the next generation of comprehension instruction: A coda. In H. Daniels (Ed.), *Comprehension going forward: Where we are and what's next* (pp. 243–253). Portsmouth, NH: Heinemann.

Pearson, P.D., & Gallagher, M.C. (1983). The instruction of reading comprehension, *Contemporary Educational Psychology, 8*(3), 317–344.

Pearson, P.D., Moje, E., & Greenleaf, C. (2010). Literacy and science: Each in the service of the other. *Science, 328*(5977), 459–463.

Pressley, M. (2002a). Metacognition and self-regulated comprehension. In A.E. Farstrup & S.J. Samuels (Eds.), *What research has to say about reading instruction* (3rd ed., pp. 291–309). Newark, DE: International Reading Association.

Pressley, M. (2002b). *Reading instruction that works: The case for balanced teaching* (2nd ed.). New York: Guilford.

Raphael, T.E. (1982). Question-answering strategies for children. *The Reading Teacher, 36*(2), 186–190.

Raphael, T.E. (1986). Teaching question answer relationships, revisited. *The Reading Teacher, 39*(6), 516–522.

Raphael, T.E., Highfield, K., & Au, K.H. (2006). *QAR now: Question answer relationships: A powerful and practical framework that develops comprehension and higher-level thinking in all students.* New York: Scholastic.

Savall, J. (Conductor). (1987). *Musique de ioye.* [CD]. Paris: Astrée.

Schleppegrell, M.J., Greer, S., & Taylor, S. (2008). Literacy in history: Language and meaning. *The Australian Journal of Language and Literacy, 31*(2), 174–187.

Schoenbach, R., & Greenleaf, C. (2009). Fostering adolescents' engaged academic literacy. In L. Christenbury, R. Bomer, & P. Smagorinsky (Eds.), *Handbook of adolescent literacy research* (pp. 98–112). New York: Guilford Press.

Schoenbach, R., Greenleaf, C., Cziko, C., & Hurwitz, L. (1999). *Reading for understanding: A guide to improving reading in middle and high school classrooms.* San Francisco: Jossey-Bass & WestEd.

Shanahan, C. (2008). Reading and writing across multiple texts. In K.A. Hinchman & H.K. Sheridan-Thomas (Eds.), *Best practices in adolescent literacy instruction* (pp. 132–150). New York: Guilford Press.

Shanahan, C. (2009). Disciplinary comprehension. In S.E. Israel & G.G. Duffy (Eds.), *Handbook of research on reading comprehension* (pp. 240–260). New York: Routledge.

Shanahan, T., & Shanahan, C. (2008). Teaching disciplinary literacy to adolescents: Rethinking content-area literacy. *Harvard Educational Review, 78*(1), 40–59.

Short, D.J., & Fitzsimmons, S. (2007). *Double the work: Challenges and solutions to acquiring language and academic literacy for adolescent English language learners.* Washington, DC: Alliance for Excellent Education.

Siegel, M., & Fonzi, J.M. (1995). The practice of reading in an inquiry-oriented mathematics class. *Reading Research Quarterly, 30*(4), 632–673.

Smith, M.W., & Wilhelm, J.D. (2010). *Fresh takes on teaching literary elements: How to teach what really matters about character, setting, point of view, and theme.* New York: Scholastic; Urbana, IL: National Council of Teachers of English.

Snow, C. (2002). *Reading for understanding: Toward an R&D program in reading comprehension.* Santa Monica, CA: RAND.

Snow, C.E. (2010). Academic language and the challenge of reading for learning about science. *Science, 328*(5977), 450–452.

Sousa, D.A. (2006). *How the brain learns* (3rd ed.). Thousand Oaks, CA: Corwin.

Southern Regional Education Board. (2009). *A critical mission: Making adolescent reading an immediate priority in SREB states: The report of the Committee to Improve Reading and Writing in Middle and High Schools.* Atlanta, GA: Author.

Tierney, R.J. (2009). The agency and artistry of meaning makers within and across digital spaces. In S.E. Israel & G.G. Duffy (Eds.), *Handbook of research on reading comprehension* (pp. 261–288). New York: Routledge.

Tovani, C. (2000). *I read it, but I don't get it: Comprehension strategies for adolescent readers.* Portland, ME: Stenhouse.

van den Broek, P. (2010). Using texts in science education: Cognitive processes and knowledge representation. *Science, 328*(5977), 453–456.

Vygotsky, L.S. (1978). *Mind in society: The development of higher psychological processes* (M. Cole, V. John-Steiner, S. Scribner, & E. Souberman, Eds. & Trans.). Cambridge, MA: Harvard University Press.

Wade, S.E., & Moje, E.B. (2000). The role of text in classroom learning. In M.L. Kamil, P.B. Mosenthal, P.D. Pearson, & R. Barr (Eds.), *Handbook of reading research* (Vol. 3, pp. 609–627). Mahwah, NJ: Erlbaum.

Webb, P. (2010). Science education and literacy: Imperatives for the developed and developing world. *Science, 328*(5977), 448–450.

Weinstein, C.E., & Mayer, R.E. (1986). The teaching of learning strategies. In M.C. Wittrock (Ed.), *Handbook of research on teaching* (3rd ed., pp. 315–327). New York: Macmillan.

Wiggins, G., & McTighe, J. (2005). *Understanding by design* (Expanded 2nd ed.). Alexandra, VA: Association for Supervision and Curriculum Development.

Wilhelm, J.D. (2007). *Engaging readers and writers with inquiry: Promoting deep understandings in language arts and the content areas with guiding questions.* New York: Scholastic.

Wilhelm, J.D., Baker, T.N., & Dube, J. (2001). *Strategic reading: Guiding students to lifelong literacy, 6–12.* Portsmouth, NH: Boynton/Cook.

Wilkinson, I.A.G., & Son, E.H. (2011). A dialogic turn in research on learning and teaching to comprehend. In M.L. Kamil, P.D. Pearson, E.B. Moje, & P.P. Afflerbach (Eds.), *Handbook of reading research* (Vol. 4, pp. 359–387). New York: Routledge.

Willingham, D.T. (2009). Is it true that some people just can't do math? *American Educator, 33*(4), 14–19, 39.

Wineburg, S.S. (1991). On the reading of historical texts: Notes on the breach between school and academy. *American Educational Research Journal, 28*(3), 495–519.

Wood, K.D. (1988). Guiding students through informational text. *The Reading Teacher, 41*(9), 912–920.

LITERATURE CITED

Brody, J.E. (2010, July 20). Not starting means never having to quit. *The New York Times*, p. D7.

DeSalle, R., & Heithaus, M.R. (2008). *Holt biology* (Student ed.). Austin, TX: Holt, Rinehart & Winston.

Friedman, T.L. (2005). *The world is flat: A brief history of the twenty-first century.* New York: Farrar, Straus & Giroux.

Holland, J.S. (2008). Living color. *National Geographic, 213*(6), 92–104.

Lapsansky-Werner, E.J., Levy, P.B., Roberts, R., & Taylor, A. (2008). *United States history: Reconstruction to the present* (Student ed.). Upper Saddle River, NJ: Pearson Education.

Lawrence Hall of Science. (2004). *Weather and water resources: Images, data, and readings.* Nashua, NH: Delta Education.

Levitt, S.D., & Dubner, S.J. (2005). *Freakonomics: A rogue economist explores the hidden side of everything.* New York: HarperCollins.

McNeil, D.G., Jr. (2010, August 31). They crawl, they bite, they baffle scientists. *The New York Times*, p. D1.

Poe, E.A. (1839/1984). The fall of the house of Usher. In P. Quinn (Ed.), *Poe: Poetry and tales* (pp. 317–336). New York: The Library of America.

Smith, S., Charles, R., Dossey, J., & Bittinger, M. (2009). *Algebra 1* (Student ed.). Boston: Pearson Education.

Steinbeck, J. (1963). *Of mice and men.* New York: Viking. (Original work published 1937)

Worth, R.F. (2010, July 11). The desert war. *The New York Times Magazine*, pp. 30–54.

AUTHOR INDEX

A

Alexander, P.A., 77, 79, 83, 88, 122
Alvermann, D.E., 6–7
American College Testing, 23, 38, 110
Anderson, L.W., 180
Anderson, R.C., 77
Anderson, T.H., 244
Armbruster, B.B., 244
Au, K.H., 175

B

Baker, L., 226
Baker, T.N., 70, 224, 225
Barney, H., 17
Battista, M.T., 204
Beall, L.C., 226
Beck, I.L., 175
Biancarosa, G., 20
Bittinger, M., 51f
Bloom, B.S., 180
Blunt, J.R., 231
Borman, G.D., 20
Brody, J.E., 79
Brown, A.L., 175
Buehl, D., 10, 33, 52, 111, 122, 131, 147,
    159, 181, 233, 253, 268

C

Carnegie Council on Advancing
    Adolescent Literacy, 22–23, 47
Carr, E.G., 244
Caverly, D.C., 229
Charles, R., 51f
Clark, K., 23
Conley, M.W., 91, 107, 216, 224
Council of Chief State School Officers
    (CCSSO), 21, 38, 42
Cribb, G., 10
Cziko, C., 26, 227

D

Daniels, H., 170
Darilek, H., 17
DeSalle, R., 48f
Dole, J.A., 20, 171, 223, 224
Dossey, J., 51f
Draper, R.J., 64, 65
Drits, D., 171, 224
Dube, J., 70, 224, 225
Dubner, S.J., 164–165
Duke, N.K., 171, 176, 180
Durkin, D., 170–171

E

Englehart, M., 180
Everlove, S., 29

F

Fisher, D., 29
Fitzsimmons, S., 88
Fonzi, J.M., 65, 66
Foster, T.C., 195, 196, 197, 198
Fox, E., 88
Frey, N., 29
Friedman, T., 165
Furst, E., 180

G

Gallagher, K., 70, 108, 110, 197
Gallagher, M.C., 26
Gardner, H., 99
Gee, J.P., 3, 6, 8, 13, 43
Goleman, D., 220, 221
Goudvis, A., 80, 179, 235, 271
Greenleaf, C.L., 10, 13, 26, 55, 57, 98, 101,
    227, 266
Greer, S., 60
Guthrie, J.T., 107

H

Hagood, M.C., 6–7

SUBJECT INDEX

Note. Page numbers followed by *f* and *t* indicate figures and tables, respectively.

mentoring and, 186–187; model of, 27f; modeling, 26, 28; practice of, 276, 277f, 278; scaffolding, 28–29

graphic representations: for history, 249–250f; overview of, 247, 250–251; for science, 248f, 251f, 270–271, 271f

H

habits of mind and identity, 220–221

Handbook of Reading Research, 37

Handbook of Research on Reading Comprehension, 37

hands-on, or inquiry, approach to science, 100–101

hands-on reading, 111–112

Hanson, Robert, 24–25

health and fitness: self-questioning taxonomy on hearing damage, 232f; teaching to match in, 117–118

Herber, Harold, 275–276

hidden knowledge, 77, 157

historian perspective, 58–59, 96–97. *See also* Thinking Like a Historian model

history textbooks: as complex texts, 47, 49f, 50; comprehension of, 57–59; generational knowledge and, 92–93; self-questioning taxonomy for, 188–192, 190t; topic and domain knowledge and, 93–94

How to Read Novels Like a Professor, 195–196

hypertexts, 108–109

I

identities: academic, fostering, 5–8; access to academic knowledge and, 90–91; categories of, 3; changing, 217–219; discourse and, 45–46; habits of mind and, 220–221; literacy and, 7–8; literature and, 107–108; as math students, 101–102; reading and, 2–5; as students, 6–7, 8, 263; world language studies and, 114–115

independence: in Gradual Release of Responsibility model, 29; in Questioning the Author, 179–180; self-directed independent learning, mentoring of, 155–161

Individualized Education Plans, 88

Inform Yourself Checkdown, 160, 161f

informal knowledge, 83–84, 89–91

informal texts, 38

informing self as comprehension strategy, 155–161

inoculation mentality of literacy instruction, 17

inquiry mind-set: inculcating, 166–170; self-questioning, modeling, 170–180. *See also* Questioning the Author; questions; self-questioning

insider moves, 270–271

insiders: communities of, 44–45, 52–53; in discourse, 44, 46f; mentoring students as, 10–11, 14

Interactive Reading Guides: on Middle Ages, 256, 257–258f, 259; overview of, 252–253, 256; on Solar System, 179, 253, 254–256f; traditional study guides compared to, 253t

intermediate literacy phase of instruction, 11–12

International Reading Association, 19t, 268, 275

intertextual allusions, 40, 95, 109, 128

intratextual allusions, 95

J

jigsawing reading, 149, 150

K

knowledge: background, handing to students, 120–121; conditional, 224; cultural, 113–114; declarative, 224; generational, 92–93; hidden, 77, 157; informal, 83–84, 89–91; of mathematics, 103–105, 104t, 203–204, 205t, 206t; overt, 77. *See also* academic

movies and text-to-world knowledge, 94–95

music performance texts, self-questioning taxonomy for, 211–214, 213*t*

N

O

P

purpose of author in complex texts, 41

pyramid notes, 243, 243f

Q

Questioning the Author (QtA): discipline-specific taxonomies for, 186; as elaborating strategy, 231; independent application, 179–180; interactive guides and, 253; overview of, 175–176; queries for, 175f; scaffolded practice, 178–179; self-questioning taxonomy, 180, 181t; teacher modeling, 176–178

questions: essential, 167–170, 168f; leading, 170; self-questioning, modeling, 170–171; through disciplinary lens, 164–166, 184–185

Quick Writes, 124–125, 238

R

RAND Reading Study Group policy statement, 20t

readers: match between authors and, 74–76; moves of, 225–228, 251–259; profiles of, 1–2, 4–5, 4f, 5f, 14–15, 15f, 16f; self-descriptions of, 1–2; strategic actions of, 227–228

readership, developing, 106–107

Readicide, 110

reading: in academic disciplines, 9; collaborative, 259–260; comprehension as goal of, 32; engagement while, 33–34; forgetting and, 33, 252; hands-on, 111–112; identity and, 2–5; as inquiry, 100–101, 167; jigsaw, 149, 150; in mathematics, 63–65; as social act, 260–261; wondering and, 174

references, historical, in textbooks, 58

rehearsing strategy, 228–231

relationships between ideas or characters in complex texts, 39

rereading of mathematics texts, 64, 105

reviewing previous learning, 122–129

Review/New Charts, 129, 130f

S

scaffolding: in Gradual Release of Responsibility model, 28–29; moves of readers into disciplinary instruction, 251–253, 253t, 254–256f, 256, 257–258f, 259; in Questioning the Author, 178–179

schema, prior knowledge as, 77–79, 78f

science curriculum: comprehension of textbooks, 47, 48f, 54–56, 199t; discipline-specific taxonomies for, 198–203, 199t, 200t; integrating strategy instruction into, 270; mentoring students in, 57; teaching to match in, 97–101; telling approach to, 100; textbooks, 98

self-descriptions of readers, 1–2

self-directed independent learning, mentoring, 155–161

self-questioning: modeling, 170–180; self-monitoring of, 182–183

self-questioning taxonomy: on hearing damage, 232f; for history texts, 188–192, 190t; for literary fiction, 192–193, 194t, 195–198; for mathematics texts, 203–204, 205t, 206t, 207–208; for music performance texts, 211–214, 213t; overview of, 180–183, 181t, 268; for science texts, 198–203, 199t, 200t; for technical texts, 208–211, 209t

skimming for answers, 33, 252

social studies curriculum, 50; mentoring students in, 60–61; teaching to match in, 92–97. *See also* history textbooks

Southern Regional Education Board, 21

special education needs, 88

Standards for Middle and High School Literacy Coaches, 267–268

Story Impressions, 144–145, 145f, 175, 239, 240f, 241

strategic actions of readers, 227–228

Betty Crocker

the big book of
weeknight
dinners

WILEY

JOHN WILEY & SONS, INC.

General Mills

Editorial Director: Jeff Nowak

Publishing Manager: Christine Gray

Editors: Diane Carlson and Grace Wells

Food Editors: Andrea Bidwell and Catherine Swanson

Recipe Development and Testing: Betty Crocker Kitchens

Photography: General Mills Photography Studios and Image Library

Photographer: Val Bourassa

Food Stylists: Carol Grones

John Wiley & Sons, Inc.

Publisher: Natalie Chapman

Associate Publisher: Jessica Goodman

Executive Editor: Anne Ficklen

Editor: Meaghan McDonnell

Production Editor: Marina Padakis Lowry

Cover Design: Suzanne Sunwoo

Interior Design and Layout: Holly Wittenberg

Manufacturing Manager: Tom Hyland

The Betty Crocker Kitchens seal guarantees success in your kitchen. Every recipe has been tested in America's Most Trusted Kitchens™ to meet our high standards of reliability, easy preparation and great taste.

FIND MORE GREAT IDEAS AT

This book is printed on acid-free paper. ∞

Published by John Wiley & Sons, Inc., Hoboken, New Jersey

Published simultaneously in Canada

For general information on our other products and services or for technical support, please contact our Customer Care Department within the United States at (800) 762-2974, outside the United States at (317) 572-3993 or fax (317) 572-4002.

Wiley publishes in a variety of print and electronic formats and by print-on-demand. Some material included with standard print versions of this book may not be included in e-books or in print-on-demand. If this book refers to media such as a CD or DVD that is not included in the version you purchased, you may download this material at http://booksupport.wiley.com. For more information about Wiley products, visit http://www.wiley.com.

Library of Congress Cataloging-in-Publication Data

Crocker, Betty.
  Betty Crocker, the big book of weeknight dinners.
    p. cm.
  Includes index.
  ISBN 978-1-118-13326-2 (pbk.), 978-1-118-19972-5 (ebk.), 978-1-118-19973-2 (ebk.), 978-1-118-19975-6 (ebk.)
  1. Cooking, American. 2. Entrées (Cooking) 3. Cookbooks. I. Title. II. Title: Big book of weeknight dinners.
  TX715.C9213845 2012
  641.5973—dc23

                                        2011031425

Manufactured in the United States of America

10 9 8 7 6 5 4 3 2 1

Cover photos: (clockwise) Mexican Chicken Pizza with Cornmeal Crust (page 70), Alfredo Chicken Pot Puff Pies (page 208), Spicy Chorizo-Stuffed Peppers (page 242), Chipotle Turkey Chili (page 76), Coleslaw-Topped BBQ Cheeseburgers (page 31), Bacon-Pepper Mac and Cheese (page 228)

Dear Friends,

It's time for dinner and everyone's hungry for a tasty meal but what should it be? There are many nights when this is the scenario but with *The Big Book of Weeknight Dinners* to guide you, it will be easy to answer that question. The book is filled with over 200 easy, delicious recipes chosen to please—you'll love the familiar but trendy flavors, easy preparation and fabulous variety in every one of them.

There are easy skillet meals and soups to make at the last minute, and satisfying casseroles to pop in the oven for later. Plus, a selection of sandwiches and pizzas can make dinner time fun and easy for the whole family. If you're in the mood for a great new salad idea, turn to the Suddenly Salad® contest-winning recipes in the Salads chapter for your dinnertime solution. Throughout the cookbook, there are even choices that can be made in 30 minutes or less for nights when you are really in a hurry—all marked with a FAST icon so you can locate them quickly.

And, be sure to check out Dinner Dilemma Solutions (page 6) for getting dinner on the table with ease. Included are shopping strategies, meal planning ideas and even some fun dinnertime ideas to help make it all easier. The Moment's Notice Meal Planner (page 8) provides some great ideas to reference and maybe it will spark some ideas of your own.

So don't let the "dinnertime dash" get you down. This book filled with great recipes, menus and tips is the perfect answer to the question "What's for dinner?"

Happy Cooking!
Betty Crocker

Contents

Dinner Dilemma Solutions

Getting dinner on the table with a minimum of fuss is not impossible, but it does take some thought. With the great recipes in this book and these strategies for simple pantry stocking, efficient meal planning and shopping savvy, you're well on your way to a delicious dinner. Also, be sure to check out the Moment's Notice Menu Planner on pages 8–9 for last-minute dinner inspiration.

Scratch Dinnertime Woes

With everyone on the go, it's hard to find the time to prepare a dinner that will please the whole family. Here are some quick tips to make the dash to dinner a little easier.

* Think ahead to the question that always comes up—what's for dinner tonight?
* Try to plan for foods that family members enjoy.
* Plan leftovers for quick meals.
* Plan a main dish for dinner and suggest that another family member stop at the deli for side dishes.
* Enlist the help of family members to get dinner ready and on the table.

Quick Cook's Pantry

In the midst of a busy week, you may not have time to think about dinner until shortly before sitting down to eat. A pantry stocked with items that you frequently use is a great solution for the last-minute dinner and can be a terrific meal-planning tool. Since we all like different foods and have different needs, no one pantry list works for everyone. Follow these tips as a starting point. As you make meals and discover new favorites, add those "staple" items to create your own custom-stocked pantry.

* Choose fresh fruits and vegetables weekly to have available for meals and snacks. Bagged salads, refrigerated potatoes and precut vegetables are easy choices. Items to simply slice and serve, like tomatoes, cucumbers, melons and pears, are all great to have on hand.
* Look for frozen fruits and vegetables that you like. Keep favorites in the freezer to serve often and to use when fresh varieties are not readily available.
* Keep favorite condiments on hand, such as ketchup, mayonnaise, mustard, Worcestershire sauce, vinegar and salsa.
* Dairy products like cheese, milk, eggs and sour cream are great items to have available.
* Meats such as ground beef, pork chops, steaks and chicken breasts are great to store in the freezer. Also look for frozen and refrigerated cooked chicken, meatballs, seafood and a variety of other convenience products.
* Packaged goods like pasta, rice, pasta sauce, soups, beans, broth, dried fruits and nuts and sauce mixes are perfect to have on hand for meals.

Meal Planning

A little time set aside for weekly meal planning pays off. No more frustrating last-minute dinner dashes or exasperated takeout splurges.

* Create a grocery list that you can update as necessary while meal planning.
* Keep the grocery list in a convenient place so family members can add items as they are used up.
* Create a chart sectioning off daily meals, including snacks and brown-bag lunches.
* Check the pantry to see what can be used for the meals in your chart.
* Scan your refrigerator for what needs to be used, such as leftovers or produce that might not last more than a few days. Plan immediate meals around these items.
* Fill in the rest of the week, adding needed recipe ingredients to the grocery list as you go.
* Take a final assessment to make sure you've considered the week's activities and the time you'll have to make each meal.

Smart Shopping

Be strategic about when and how you shop. The more you think and plan ahead, the easier and more efficient your shopping trips will be.

* Always shop with a list so you don't forget critical ingredients.
* Plan time to shop alone so you are not distracted and can allow a little browsing time.
* Read newspaper and online store ads. Clip or print coupons ahead of time.
* Bring your own bags because many stores offer a reusable bag discount.

* Have backup ideas in mind in case the store is out of an ingredient or product that's on your list.
* Consider seasonal items as you shop for peak freshness and the best price.
* Take a few moments when you arrive home from shopping to prepare ingredients for cooking ahead of time. Chop vegetables, wash fruit or cut up meat. You'll be glad you did on hectic nights when every extra minute counts.

Moment's Notice Menu Planner

Whatever night of the week it is, it's easy to put together a delicious meal with this selection of last-minute menu ideas. Easy deli choices, fresh sides and frozen favorites round out each meal for tasty dinner combinations any time.

Sandwich Special

Hearty Bacon-Steak Sandwiches (page 37)

French-fried potatoes

Creamy coleslaw

Chocolate ice cream

Pizza Night In

Loaded Baked Potato Pizza (page 69)
or Chicken Sausage, Spinach and Swiss Pizza (page 63)

Tossed green salad with Italian dressing

Chex® Snack Mix

Sliced watermelon and cantaloupe

Italian Restaurant Dinner

Italian Sausage and Vegetable Pasta (page 174)

Garlic bread

Gelato

Easy Does It Chicken Dinner

Chicken and Pasta with Creamy Basil Sauce (page 144)

Steamed baby carrots

Crusty French rolls

Cookies

Caribbean Salad Experience

Caribbean Jerk Chicken and Pasta Salad (page 272) or Gazpacho-Style Chicken Salad (page 281)

Sliced avocados and tomatoes

Warm flour tortillas

Down-Home Meatless Casserole Dinner

Cheesy Rigatoni with Eggplant Sauce (page 257)

Caesar salad

Sourdough bread

Apple pie

Easy Elegant Steak

Steak and Peppers in Chimichurri Sauce (page 192)

White or brown rice

Sliced tomatoes and cucumbers with balsamic vinaigrette

Fresh blueberries or raspberries with whipped cream

Soup and Wraps

Chunky Tomato-Bean Soup (page 110)

Veggie Wraps (page 60)

Apple and pear slices

Brownies

Chapter One
Hearty Supper Sandwiches and Pizzas

Buffalo Chicken Sandwiches

12 sandwiches   PREP TIME 15 minutes   START TO FINISH 7 hours 30 minutes

3¼ lb boneless skinless
      chicken thighs (about
      14 thighs)
1¾ cups Buffalo wing sauce
  1 English (seedless)
      cucumber
12 large sandwich buns, split
  ¾ cup crumbled blue cheese
      (3 oz)

1 Spray 3½- to 4-quart slow cooker with cooking spray. In slow cooker, place chicken. Pour 1 cup of the Buffalo wing sauce over chicken.

2 Cover; cook on Low heat setting 7 to 8 hours.

3 Remove chicken from slow cooker; place in medium bowl. Place strainer over another medium bowl. Strain juices from slow cooker; skim fat. Reserve 1½ cups juices. Stir chicken to separate into pieces. Return chicken to slow cooker; stir in reserved juices.

4 Increase heat setting to High. Cover; cook about 15 minutes longer or until thoroughly heated.

5 Meanwhile, cut cucumber in half crosswise. With vegetable peeler, cut 1 strip of peel lengthwise from 1 cucumber half; discard strip that is mostly peel. Continue cutting thin strips lengthwise from cucumber, making about 18 strips. Repeat with other half of cucumber.

6 Fill each bun with ½ cup chicken mixture, about 3 strips of cucumber, 1 tablespoon of the remaining Buffalo wing sauce and 1 tablespoon cheese.

1 Sandwich: Calories 400; Total Fat 15g (Saturated Fat 5g; Trans Fat 0.5g); Cholesterol 85mg; Sodium 1390mg; Total Carbohydrate 31g (Dietary Fiber 1g); Protein 34g **Exchanges:** 2 Starch, 4 Lean Meat, ½ Fat **Carbohydrate Choices:** 2

Quick Variation

For a quick appetizer, fill purchased mini fillo shells with the chicken mixture. Top with finely diced celery and a dollop of creamy dressing, such as blue cheese or ranch.

Caesar Chicken Subs

4 sandwiches   PREP TIME 15 minutes   START TO FINISH 15 minutes

FAST

4 submarine sandwich
    rolls (about 6-inch)
    or 1 baguette (8 oz)

⅓ cup Caesar dressing

½ package (3.5-oz size)
    sandwich sliced pepperoni

¾ lb deli rotisserie chicken
    (from 2-lb chicken),
    cut into ¼-inch slices

4 slices (1 oz each) Colby–
    Monterey Jack cheese
    blend

4 slices tomato, cut in half

4 lettuce leaves

½ medium red onion,
    thinly sliced

1 Cut rolls horizontally in half (if using baguette, first cut into fourths). Spread dressing over cut sides of rolls.

2 On roll bottoms, layer pepperoni, chicken, cheese, tomato, lettuce and onion. Cover with roll tops; press gently. Secure with toothpicks. Cut each sandwich diagonally in half.

1 Sandwich: Calories 620; Total Fat 35g (Saturated Fat 12g; Trans Fat 1g); Cholesterol 120mg; Sodium 1320mg; Total Carbohydrate 36g (Dietary Fiber 2g); Protein 41g **Exchanges:** 1½ Starch, ½ Other Carbohydrate, ½ Vegetable, 2 Very Lean Meat, 2 Lean Meat, 1 High-Fat Meat, 4 Fat **Carbohydrate Choices:** 2½

Time-Saver

You can make these sandwiches ahead, but add the tomato slices just before serving.

Chicken Caesar Sandwiches

12 sandwiches   PREP TIME 20 minutes   START TO FINISH 6 hours 55 minutes

2 lb boneless skinless chicken thighs

1 package (1.2 oz) Caesar dressing mix

1 can (10¾ oz) condensed cream of chicken soup

⅓ cup shredded Parmesan cheese

¼ cup chopped fresh parsley

½ teaspoon coarse ground black pepper

2 cups shredded romaine lettuce

12 mini burger buns (about 2½ inches in diameter)

1 Spray 3- to 4-quart slow cooker with cooking spray. Place chicken in slow cooker.

2 Cover; cook on Low heat setting 6 to 7 hours.

3 Using slotted spoon, remove chicken from slow cooker; place on cutting board. Discard liquid in slow cooker. Using 2 forks, pull chicken into shreds. In slow cooker, mix dressing mix (dry), soup, cheese, parsley and pepper; gently fold in chicken.

4 Increase heat setting to High. Cover; cook 30 to 35 minutes longer or until mixture is hot.

5 To serve, spoon ¼ cup chicken mixture onto lettuce in each bun. Chicken mixture can be kept warm on Low heat setting up to 2 hours; stir occasionally.

1 Sandwich: Calories 250; Total Fat 7g (Saturated Fat 2g; Trans Fat 0g); Cholesterol 55mg; Sodium 670mg; Total Carbohydrate 23g (Dietary Fiber 1g); Protein 23g **Exchanges:** 1½ Starch, 2½ Lean Meat **Carbohydrate Choices:** 1½

Quick Variation

Boneless skinless turkey thighs work great in this recipe, too. Just use the same amount of turkey as chicken.

Chicken Souvlaki Sandwiches

6 sandwiches PREP TIME 15 minutes START TO FINISH 15 minutes

FAST

3 cups chopped cooked chicken

1 cup chopped peeled cucumber

½ cup crumbled feta cheese (2 oz)

⅓ cup finely chopped red onion

⅓ cup sour cream

2 tablespoons chopped fresh dill weed

2 tablespoons mayonnaise or salad dressing

1 tablespoon red wine vinegar

¼ teaspoon salt

⅛ teaspoon pepper

6 pita fold breads (5 inch), heated

1 In medium bowl, place all ingredients except pita breads; toss until evenly coated.

2 Divide mixture evenly down center of each warm pita bread; fold in half. Serve immediately.

1 Sandwich: Calories 340; Total Fat 14g (Saturated Fat 5g; Trans Fat 0g); Cholesterol 80mg; Sodium 690mg; Total Carbohydrate 27g (Dietary Fiber 1g); Protein 26g **Exchanges:** 1½ Starch, ½ Vegetable, 3 Lean Meat, 1 Fat **Carbohydrate Choices:** 2

Time-Saver

You can substitute 1 to 2 teaspoons dried dill weed for the fresh dill in this recipe.

Easy Chicken Fajitas

4 servings (2 fajitas each)   PREP TIME 25 minutes   START TO FINISH 25 minutes

FAST

1   **medium onion, sliced**

1   **medium red bell pepper, thinly sliced**

2   **tablespoons Mexican seasoning**

1   **tablespoon vegetable oil**

2   **cups chopped deli rotisserie chicken (from 2-lb chicken)**

½   **cup chunky style salsa**

8   **flour tortillas for soft tacos & fajitas (6 inch; from 8.2-oz package)**

1   **large tomato, chopped (1 cup)**

1   **cup shredded Cheddar cheese (4 oz)**

1   **cup shredded lettuce**

½   **cup sour cream**

1 In large bowl, toss onion, bell pepper, Mexican seasoning and oil.

2 Heat 12-inch skillet over medium-high heat. Add onion mixture; cook about 4 minutes, stirring frequently, until onion is crisp-tender. Stir in chicken. Cook 1 to 2 minutes longer, stirring frequently, until thoroughly heated. Stir in salsa.

3 Divide chicken mixture among tortillas. Sprinkle with tomato and cheese. Add lettuce and sour cream. Roll up tortillas.

1 Serving: Calories 530; Total Fat 28g (Saturated Fat 12g; Trans Fat 0.5g); Cholesterol 110mg; Sodium 1430mg; Total Carbohydrate 37g (Dietary Fiber 2g); Protein 31g **Exchanges:** 1½ Starch, ½ Other Carbohydrate, 1 Vegetable, 3½ Lean Meat, 3½ Fat **Carbohydrate Choices:** 2½

Time-Saver

To substitute for the Mexican seasoning, use 1 teaspoon dried onion flakes, ½ teaspoon dried oregano leaves, ¼ teaspoon ground cumin and ¼ teaspoon garlic powder.

Quick Variation

Turn these into Easy Beef Fajitas. Use deli cooked roast beef instead of the chicken.
For a dash of extra flavor, add slices of fresh avocado to each fajita.

Teriyaki-Sesame-Chicken Wraps

12 wraps   PREP TIME 30 minutes   START TO FINISH 7 hours 45 minutes

3 **lb boneless skinless chicken thighs**
½ **cup teriyaki sauce**
1 **tablespoon finely chopped gingerroot**
4 **cloves garlic, finely chopped**
1 **tablespoon sesame seed**
1 **teaspoon toasted sesame oil**
½ **cup hoisin sauce**
12 **flour tortillas (10 inch)**
¾ **cup shredded carrots**
1 **medium bell pepper, cut into bite-size strips**
½ **cup sliced green onions (8 medium)**
¾ **cup chow mein noodles**

1 Spray 4- to 5-quart slow cooker with cooking spray. Place chicken in slow cooker. In small bowl, mix teriyaki sauce, gingerroot and garlic; pour over chicken.

2 Cover; cook on Low heat setting 7 to 8 hours.

3 Stir chicken mixture to break apart large pieces of chicken. Stir in sesame seed and sesame oil.

4 Increase heat setting to High. Cover; cook about 15 minutes longer or until thoroughly heated.

5 Spread 2 teaspoons hoisin sauce on each tortilla. Using slotted spoon, spread about ⅓ cup chicken mixture down center of each tortilla. Top chicken mixture with 1 tablespoon shredded carrot, a few bell pepper strips, 2 teaspoons onions and 1 tablespoon noodles. Roll up tortilla; cut diagonally in half.

1 Wrap: Calories 480; Total Fat 18g (Saturated Fat 5g; Trans Fat 1g); Cholesterol 80mg; Sodium 1170mg; Total Carbohydrate 47g (Dietary Fiber 2g); Protein 34g **Exchanges:** 3 Starch, 3½ Lean Meat, 1 Fat **Carbohydrate Choices:** 3

Quick Variation

Instead of using the tortillas, wrap the same ingredients in large lettuce leaves.

Smoky Chicken Melt Panini

4 servings (½ panini each)   PREP TIME 20 minutes   START TO FINISH 20 minutes

FAST

4   **large slices (½ inch thick) sourdough bread**

2   **tablespoons butter or margarine, softened**

4   **oz smoky Cheddar cheese, sliced**

1½   **cups shredded cooked chicken**

¼   **cup cooked real bacon bits (from 3-oz jar)**

6   **thin slices tomato**

2   **thin slices onion, separated into rings**

1 Heat panini maker or closed contact grill for 5 minutes. Spread 1 side of each bread slice with butter. On unbuttered side of 2 slices, arrange half of the cheese. Top evenly with chicken, bacon, tomato, onion and remaining cheese. Top with remaining 2 bread slices, buttered sides up.

2 Place sandwiches on panini maker or grill. Close maker or grill; cook 3 to 5 minutes or until bread is toasted and cheese is melted. Cut each sandwich in half to serve.

→ *Skillet Method: If you don't have a panini maker or closed contact grill, you can cook the sandwiches in a 10-inch nonstick skillet. Heat the skillet over medium heat; cook sandwiches for 2 to 3 minutes on each side or until bread is toasted and cheese is melted.*

1 Serving (½ Panini): Calories 570; Total Fat 22g (Saturated Fat 12g; Trans Fat 1g); Cholesterol 100mg; Sodium 1110mg; Total Carbohydrate 56g (Dietary Fiber 2g); Protein 36g **Exchanges:** 3 Starch, ½ Other Carbohydrate, 1½ Very Lean Meat, 1½ Lean Meat, 1 Medium-Fat Meat, 2 Fat **Carbohydrate Choices:** 4

Quick Menu Idea

Serve the sandwiches with deli coleslaw and fresh fruit.

Turkey, Bacon and Guacamole Wraps

4 wraps   PREP TIME 15 minutes   START TO FINISH 15 minutes

FAST

1 ripe avocado, pitted, peeled and mashed

1 tablespoon taco sauce

¼ teaspoon garlic salt

4 flour tortillas for burritos (8 inch; from 11.5-oz package)

½ lb thinly sliced cooked turkey

8 slices packaged precooked bacon (from 2.1-oz package)

4 leaves romaine lettuce

¼ cup drained roasted red bell peppers (from 7-oz jar), large pieces cut up

1 In small bowl, mix avocado, taco sauce and garlic salt. Spread about 1 tablespoon avocado mixture on each tortilla. Top with turkey; spread with any remaining avocado mixture. Top with bacon, lettuce and roasted peppers.

2 Roll up tortillas tightly; cut in half. Serve immediately, or wrap in plastic wrap and refrigerate up to 24 hours.

1 Wrap: Calories 370; Total Fat 19g (Saturated Fat 5g; Trans Fat 0g); Cholesterol 60mg; Sodium 680mg; Total Carbohydrate 26g (Dietary Fiber 3g); Protein 26g **Exchanges:** 1½ Starch, 3 Lean Meat, 2 Fat **Carbohydrate Choices:** 2

Turkey Salad Sandwiches

4 sandwiches   PREP TIME 20 minutes   START TO FINISH 20 minutes

FAST

1½ cups diced cooked turkey

½ cup diced unpeeled apple

½ cup mayonnaise or
    salad dressing

1½ teaspoons curry powder

¼ teaspoon ground ginger

¼ teaspoon pepper

1 medium stalk celery,
   chopped (½ cup)

2 green onions, chopped
   (2 tablespoons)

8 slices whole-grain bread

1 In medium bowl, mix all ingredients except bread.

2 Spread turkey mixture on 4 slices bread. Top with remaining bread slices.

1 Sandwich: Calories 460; Total Fat 28g (Saturated Fat 5g; Trans Fat 0.5g); Cholesterol 55mg; Sodium 510mg; Total Carbohydrate 31g (Dietary Fiber 5g); Protein 21g **Exchanges:** 2 Starch, 2 Lean Meat, 4 Fat **Carbohydrate Choices:** 2

Quick Variation

Skip the bread and serve this turkey salad on a lettuce-lined plate with cut-up fresh vegetables or fruits.

Healthy Twist

For less fat per serving, use fat-free or reduced-fat mayonnaise.

Toasted Philly Turkey Sandwiches

4 sandwiches   PREP TIME 10 minutes   START TO FINISH 10 minutes

FAST

2 **tablespoons butter or margarine, softened**

8 **slices (½ inch thick) rye or pumpernickel bread**

½ **lb thinly sliced cooked deli turkey or chicken**

4 **slices (1 oz each) mozzarella cheese**

1 Spread butter on 1 side of each bread slice. In 12-inch skillet, place 4 bread slices, buttered side down; top with turkey and cheese. Top with remaining bread slices, buttered side up.

2 Cover; cook sandwiches over medium heat 4 to 5 minutes, turning once, until bread is crisp and cheese is melted.

1 Sandwich: Calories 330; Total Fat 15g (Saturated Fat 8g; Trans Fat 0g); Cholesterol 60mg; Sodium 1200mg; Total Carbohydrate 27g (Dietary Fiber 2g); Protein 21g **Exchanges:** 2 Starch, 2 Very Lean Meat, 2½ Fat **Carbohydrate Choices:** 2

Quick Menu Idea

For a hearty meal combo, pair these sandwiches with tomato soup.

Ham and Egg Salad Sandwiches

4 sandwiches   PREP TIME 20 minutes   START TO FINISH 20 minutes

FAST

½ **cup chopped cooked ham**

½ **cup chopped fresh broccoli florets**

½ **cup chopped celery**

½ **cup mayonnaise or salad dressing**

1 **tablespoon chopped fresh chives**

2 **teaspoons chopped fresh or ¾ teaspoon dried marjoram leaves**

¼ **teaspoon onion salt**

3 **hard-cooked eggs, chopped**

Lettuce leaves

8 **slices herb or whole wheat bread**

1 In medium bowl, mix all ingredients except lettuce and bread.

2 Place lettuce leaf on each of the 4 bread slices. Spoon egg mixture onto lettuce. Top with remaining bread slices; cut each in half to serve.

1 Sandwich: Calories 440; Total Fat 29g (Saturated Fat 5g; Trans Fat 0g); Cholesterol 180mg; Sodium 840mg; Total Carbohydrate 29g (Dietary Fiber 4g); Protein 15g **Exchanges:** 2 Starch, 1½ Medium-Fat Meat, 4 Fat **Carbohydrate Choices:** 2

Pork Fajita Wraps

4 wraps   PREP TIME 20 minutes   START TO FINISH 35 minutes

¼   cup lime juice

1½ teaspoons ground cumin

¾   teaspoon salt

4   cloves garlic, finely
    chopped

½   lb pork tenderloin, cut into
    very thin slices

1   large onion, thinly sliced

3   medium bell peppers,
    thinly sliced

4   flour tortillas for burritos
    (8 inch; from 11.5-oz
    package)

1 In shallow glass or plastic dish, mix lime juice, cumin, salt and garlic. Stir in pork. Cover; refrigerate, stirring occasionally, at least 15 minutes but no longer than 24 hours.

2 Remove pork from marinade; reserve marinade. Heat 12-inch nonstick skillet over medium-high heat. Add pork; cook 3 minutes, stirring once. Stir in onion, bell peppers and marinade. Cook 5 to 8 minutes longer, stirring frequently, until onion and peppers are crisp-tender.

3 Place one-fourth of the pork mixture on center of each tortilla. Fold one end of tortilla up about 1 inch over pork mixture; fold right and left sides over folded end, overlapping.

1 Wrap: Calories 260; Total Fat 6g (Saturated Fat 1.5g; Trans Fat 0g); Cholesterol 35mg; Sodium 680mg; Total Carbohydrate 35g (Dietary Fiber 3g); Protein 18g **Exchanges:** 2½ Starch, 1½ Lean Meat **Carbohydrate Choices:** 2

Quick Menu Idea

These wraps are great for dinner with a side of refried beans and sliced tomatoes.

Peppered Pork Pitas with Garlic Spread

4 sandwiches   PREP TIME 20 minutes   START TO FINISH 20 minutes

FAST

⅓ cup fat-free mayonnaise
or salad dressing

2 tablespoons fat-free
(skim) milk

2 cloves garlic, finely
chopped

½ lb boneless pork loin
chops, cut into thin
bite-size strips

1 tablespoon olive or
canola oil

1 teaspoon coarse ground
black pepper

1 jar (7.25 oz) roasted red
bell peppers, drained,
sliced

4 pita fold breads (7 inch)

1 In small bowl, mix mayonnaise, milk and garlic; set aside.

2 In medium bowl, mix pork, oil and pepper. Heat 10-inch skillet over medium-high heat. Add pork; cook 5 to 6 minutes, stirring occasionally, until pork is lightly browned and no longer pink in center. Stir in roasted peppers; heat until warm.

3 Heat pita folds as directed on package. Lightly spread one side of each pita fold with garlic mixture. Spoon pork mixture over each; fold up.

1 Sandwich: Calories 340; Total Fat 9g (Saturated Fat 2.5g; Trans Fat 0g); Cholesterol 35mg; Sodium 560mg; Total Carbohydrate 45g (Dietary Fiber 2g); Protein 19g **Exchanges:** 2½ Starch, ½ Other Carbohydrate, 1½ Lean Meat, ½ Fat **Carbohydrate Choices:** 3

Quick Variation

Use thinly sliced chicken instead of the pork. Cook 5 to 6 minutes or until the chicken is no longer pink in center.

Healthy Twist

For extra fiber, texture and whole-grain goodness, use whole wheat pita bread instead of regular pita bread.

Coleslaw-Topped BBQ Cheeseburgers

4 sandwiches   PREP TIME 30 minutes   START TO FINISH 30 minutes

FAST

1 lb lean (at least 80%) ground beef

½ teaspoon Montreal steak grill seasoning

4 slices (1 oz each) Swiss cheese

2 cups coleslaw mix (from 14-oz bag)

2 tablespoons coleslaw dressing

4 ciabatta rolls, split

¼ cup barbecue sauce

1 In medium bowl, mix beef and grill seasoning. Shape mixture into 4 patties, about ½-inch thick.

2 Heat 10-inch nonstick skillet over medium heat. Add patties; cook 10 to 12 minutes, turning once, until meat thermometer inserted in center of patties reads 160°F. Top with cheese slice; cook 1 to 2 minutes longer or until cheese is melted.

3 Meanwhile, in small bowl, mix coleslaw mix and dressing.

4 Place patties on bottom halves of rolls. Top each with barbecue sauce and coleslaw. Cover with top halves of rolls.

→ *Broiling Method: Place on rack in broiler pan. Broil with tops 3 to 4 inches from heat 10 to 12 minutes, turning once, until meat thermometer inserted in center of patties reads 160°F.*

1 Sandwich: Calories 490; Total Fat 23g (Saturated Fat 10g; Trans Fat 1g); Cholesterol 95mg; Sodium 570mg; Total Carbohydrate 38g (Dietary Fiber 3g); Protein 32g **Exchanges:** 2 Starch, ½ Other Carbohydrate, 3½ Medium-Fat Meat, 1 Fat **Carbohydrate Choices:** 2½

Quick Menu Idea

Serve these tasty sandwiches with your favorite baked beans.

Pizza Joes

8 sandwiches PREP TIME 25 minutes START TO FINISH 25 minutes

FAST

1 lb extra-lean (at least 90%) ground beef

1 large onion, coarsely chopped (1 cup)

1 medium green bell pepper, coarsely chopped (about 1 cup)

2 cups pizza sauce (from two 15-oz jars or cans)

8 burger buns, split, toasted

1 cup shredded mozzarella cheese (4 oz)

1 Heat 12-inch nonstick skillet over medium-high heat. Add beef, onion and bell pepper; cook 7 to 9 minutes, stirring occasionally, until beef is thoroughly cooked.

2 Stir in pizza sauce. Reduce heat to medium; simmer uncovered about 5 minutes or until thoroughly heated.

3 Fill buns with beef mixture and cheese.

1 Sandwich: Calories 290; Total Fat 10g (Saturated Fat 4.5g; Trans Fat 0.5g); Cholesterol 45mg; Sodium 420mg; Total Carbohydrate 30g (Dietary Fiber 3g); Protein 20g **Exchanges:** 2 Starch, 1 Vegetable, 1 Lean Meat, 1 Fat Carbohydrate Choices: 2

Quick Variation

You can substitute 2 cups frozen diced onion and green bell pepper, or look for chopped fresh vegetables in the produce department.

Cheeseburger Sandwiches

12 sandwiches PREP TIME 20 minutes START TO FINISH 6 hours 20 minutes

1½ lb lean (at least 80%) ground beef

½ teaspoon garlic-pepper blend

1 package (8 oz) prepared cheese product loaf, diced (2 cups)

2 tablespoons milk

1 medium green bell pepper, chopped (1 cup)

1 small onion, chopped (¼ cup)

2 cloves garlic, finely chopped

12 burger buns, split

1 In 12-inch skillet, place beef; sprinkle with garlic-pepper blend. Cook over medium heat 8 to 10 minutes, stirring occasionally, until beef is brown; drain.

2 Spray 3- to 4-quart slow cooker with cooking spray. Mix beef and remaining ingredients except buns in slow cooker.

3 Cover; cook on Low heat setting 6 to 7 hours. Serve beef mixture in buns.

1 Sandwich: Calories 280; Total Fat 13g (Saturated Fat 6g; Trans Fat 0.5g); Cholesterol 50mg; Sodium 520mg; Total Carbohydrate 21g (Dietary Fiber 1g); Protein 17g **Exchanges:** 1½ Starch, 2 Medium-Fat Meat **Carbohydrate Choices:** 1½

Quick Menu Idea

These sandwiches are great for casual get-togethers or tailgating. Serve with chips and a tray of raw veggies and dip. Top off the meal with brownies.

Italian Country Sandwiches

4 servings   PREP TIME 10 minutes   START TO FINISH 10 minutes

FAST

1 uncut loaf (1 lb) Italian peasant-style rustic bread or ciabatta bread

⅓ cup olive oil or rosemary-flavored olive oil

¼ lb thinly sliced hard salami

¼ lb sliced provolone cheese

¼ lb thinly sliced prosciutto

1 small red onion, thinly sliced

1 Cut bread in half horizontally. Drizzle oil over cut sides.

2 On bread bottom, layer salami, cheese, prosciutto and onion; cover with bread top. Cut loaf into quarters.

1 Serving: Calories 730; Total Fat 42g (Saturated Fat 12g; Trans Fat 1g); Cholesterol 60mg; Sodium 1700mg; Total Carbohydrate 60g (Dietary Fiber 3g); Protein 29g **Exchanges:** 4 Starch, 2½ Lean Meat, 6½ Fat **Carbohydrate Choices:** 4

Quick Variation

If prosciutto isn't available, substitute very thinly sliced deli ham.

Hearty Bacon-Steak Sandwiches

4 sandwiches   PREP TIME 25 minutes   START TO FINISH 35 minutes

1 ripe large avocado,
   pitted, peeled

¼ cup chopped tomato

2 tablespoons prepared
   horseradish

1 tablespoon mayonnaise
   or salad dressing

1 beef flank steak, ¾ to 1 inch
   thick (1 lb)

1 teaspoon Montreal steak
   grill seasoning

4 kaiser rolls, split

8 slices bacon, crisply
   cooked

½ cup French-fried onions
   (from 2.8-oz can)

1 In medium bowl, mash avocado with fork. Stir in tomato, horseradish and mayonnaise until well blended; set aside.

2 Set oven control to broil. In both sides of beef, make cuts about ½ inch apart and ⅛ inch deep in diamond pattern. Sprinkle both sides of beef with grill seasoning. Place beef on broiler pan.

3 Broil with top about 4 inches from heat 4 to 5 minutes on each side for medium-rare or until desired doneness. Transfer beef to cutting board; cover with foil and let stand 10 minutes.

4 Thinly slice beef diagonally across grain. Divide beef onto bottom halves of rolls. Top each with about ¼ cup avocado mixture, 2 slices bacon and 2 tablespoons onions. Cover with top halves of rolls.

1 Sandwich: Calories 540; Total Fat 25g (Saturated Fat 6g; Trans Fat 1.5g); Cholesterol 100mg; Sodium 790mg; Total Carbohydrate 34g (Dietary Fiber 4g); Protein 45g **Exchanges:** 2½ Starch, 5 Lean Meat, 1½ Fat **Carbohydrate Choices:** 2

Hot Roast Beef Sandwiches au Jus

10 sandwiches   PREP TIME 20 minutes   START TO FINISH 6 hours 20 minutes

1 **beef eye of round roast (2½ lb), trimmed of excess fat**

6 **cloves garlic, peeled**

2 **teaspoons coarse ground black pepper**

1 **large onion, thinly sliced**

½ **cup condensed beef broth (from 10½-oz can)**

10 **kaiser rolls, split, toasted**

2 **large tomatoes, each cut into 5 slices**

1 Using sharp knife, make 6 evenly spaced deep slits in beef roast. Insert garlic clove into each slit. Sprinkle pepper evenly over entire beef roast; rub pepper into beef.

2 Spray 3- to 4-quart slow cooker with cooking spray. In slow cooker, place onion; pour broth over onion. Top with beef.

3 Cover; cook on Low heat setting 6 to 8 hours.

4 Remove beef from slow cooker; place on cutting board. Cut beef across grain into thin slices. Return beef to slow cooker to moisten. Fill each roll with beef, onion and 1 tomato slice. If desired, spoon small amount of broth from slow cooker over beef.

1 Sandwich: Calories 350; Total Fat 14g (Saturated Fat 5g; Trans Fat 1g); Cholesterol 60mg; Sodium 420mg; Total Carbohydrate 30g (Dietary Fiber 2g); Protein 25g **Exchanges:** 2 Starch, 2½ Medium-Fat Meat **Carbohydrate Choices:** 2

Time-Saver

Lightly spraying the inside of the slow cooker with cooking spray before using helps keep cleanup to a minimum.

Quick Menu Idea

Serve these hearty sandwiches with coleslaw or potato salad from the deli, or choose another favorite deli salad instead.

Root Beer Barbecue Beef Sandwiches

16 sandwiches   PREP TIME 30 minutes   START TO FINISH 10 hours 30 minutes

1   **boneless beef rump roast (4 lb)**

2   **cups barbecue sauce**

1   **cup root beer**

Dash salt and pepper, if desired

16   **sandwich buns, split**

1 In 3½- to 4-quart slow cooker, place beef. In 4-cup measuring cup or bowl, mix 1½ cups of the barbecue sauce and the root beer; pour over beef.

2 Cover; cook on Low heat setting 10 to 12 hours.

3 About 20 minutes before serving, remove beef from slow cooker; place on large plate. Pour juices from slow cooker into 12-inch skillet. Cook over medium-high heat about 15 minutes, stirring occasionally, until juices are thickened and reduced to about 3 cups. Meanwhile, using 2 forks, shred beef; return to slow cooker.

4 Stir remaining ½ cup barbecue sauce into reduced juices in skillet; pour over shredded beef in slow cooker. Stir in salt and pepper to taste. Spoon about ½ cup beef mixture into each bun.

1 Sandwich: Calories 310; Total Fat 5g (Saturated Fat 1.5g; Trans Fat 0g); Cholesterol 60mg; Sodium 570mg; Total Carbohydrate 36g (Dietary Fiber 1g); Protein 29g **Exchanges:** 1½ Starch, 1 Other Carbohydrate, 3 Lean Meat **Carbohydrate Choices:** 2½

Roast Beef and Bacon Wraps with Spicy Chili-Lime Mayo

4 wraps   PREP TIME 20 minutes   START TO FINISH 20 minutes

FAST

SPICY CHILI-LIME MAYO

⅓ cup mayonnaise or salad dressing

1 tablespoon lime juice

1 teaspoon chili powder

¼ teaspoon ground red pepper (cayenne)

¼ teaspoon salt

WRAPS

4 flour tortillas (10 inch), heated as directed on package

¾ lb thinly sliced cooked roast beef

8 slices bacon, crisply cooked

1 ripe avocado, pitted, peeled and sliced

4 small leaves romaine lettuce

12 thin red onion rings

1 In small bowl, stir together chili-lime mayo ingredients.

2 Spread one-fourth of the mayo over bottom half of each tortilla to within 1 inch of edge. Divide roast beef, bacon, avocado, lettuce and onion evenly over bottom half of each tortilla. Fold in sides of tortilla and roll up; cut in half.

1 Wrap: Calories 520; Total Fat 32g (Saturated Fat 7g; Trans Fat 1g); Cholesterol 65mg; Sodium 1790mg; Total Carbohydrate 29g (Dietary Fiber 3g); Protein 27g **Exchanges:** 2 Starch, 3 High-Fat Meat, 1½ Fat **Carbohydrate Choices:** 2

Quick Variation

For a smokier flavor, substitute chipotle chile pepper powder for the cayenne.

Dilled Shrimp and Egg Salad Wraps

4 wraps   PREP TIME 10 minutes   START TO FINISH 10 minutes

FAST

4 **hard-cooked eggs, chopped**

1 **cup chopped cooked shrimp**

1 **tablespoon chopped fresh dill weed**

2 **tablespoons finely chopped red onion**

3 **tablespoons creamy Dijon mustard-mayonnaise spread**

¼ **teaspoon salt**

4 **flour tortillas for burritos (8 inch; from 11.5-oz package)**

2 **cups shredded lettuce**

1 In medium bowl, mix all ingredients except tortillas and lettuce. Spread shrimp mixture evenly on each tortilla; top with lettuce.

2 Fold in sides of tortilla and roll up; cut in half. Serve immediately, or wrap in plastic wrap and refrigerate up to 24 hours.

1 Wrap: Calories 290; Total Fat 11g (Saturated Fat 3g; Trans Fat 1g); Cholesterol 335mg; Sodium 740mg; Total Carbohydrate 24g (Dietary Fiber 0g); Protein 22g **Exchanges:** 1½ Starch, ½ Vegetable, 1 Very Lean Meat, 1 Medium-Fat Meat, 1 Fat **Carbohydrate Choices:** 1½

Time-Saver

Shredding the lettuce makes rolling the wraps easier. To shred lettuce, cut the leaves into thin strips with a sharp knife. Or save time by buying bagged shredded lettuce.

Greek Tuna Salad Pita Sandwiches with Feta Cheese

6 sandwiches   PREP TIME 20 minutes   START TO FINISH 20 minutes

FAST

2   **tablespoons olive oil**

1   **tablespoon lemon juice**

1   **clove garlic, finely chopped**

¼   **teaspoon salt**

1   **medium cucumber, peeled, seeded and finely chopped**

1   **ripe medium tomato, seeded, diced**

½   **cup crumbled feta cheese (2 oz)**

12   **kalamata or other large ripe olives, pitted, coarsely chopped (¼ cup)**

2   **cans (5 oz each) tuna in water, drained, flaked**

3   **leaves romaine lettuce, torn in half**

6   **pita (pocket) breads (6 inch), cut in half to form pockets**

1 In small bowl, stir together oil, lemon juice, garlic and salt with whisk. In medium bowl, toss cucumber, tomato, cheese, olives and tuna. Pour dressing over salad; toss until coated.

2 Place 1 lettuce leaf half in each pita pocket; top each leaf with ½ cup tuna salad. Serve immediately.

1 Sandwich: Calories 310; Total Fat 8g (Saturated Fat 2.5g; Trans Fat 0g); Cholesterol 25mg; Sodium 600mg; Total Carbohydrate 38g (Dietary Fiber 3g); Protein 20g **Exchanges:** 2 Starch, 2 Vegetable, 1½ Lean Meat, ½ Fat **Carbohydrate Choices:** 2½

Quick Variation

It's easy to vary the flavor of these Greek sandwiches by substituting salmon for the tuna. Also look for different varieties of flavored feta cheese to spice up the flavor profile.

Lemon-Pepper Fish Fillet Sandwiches

4 sandwiches PREP TIME **15 minutes** START TO FINISH **15 minutes**

FAST

- 2 **tablespoons yellow cornmeal**
- 2 **tablespoons all-purpose flour**
- 1 **teaspoon seasoned salt**
- ½ **teaspoon lemon-pepper seasoning**
- 1 **tablespoon vegetable oil**
- 2 **walleye fillets (about 6 oz each), each cut crosswise in half**
- ¼ **cup tartar sauce**
- 4 **whole-grain or rye sandwich buns, toasted**
- 1 **cup shredded lettuce**

1 In shallow bowl, mix cornmeal, flour, seasoned salt and lemon-pepper seasoning.

2 In 12-inch nonstick skillet, heat oil over medium-high heat. Coat fish fillets with flour mixture. Cook in oil 4 to 6 minutes, turning once, until fish flakes easily with fork.

3 Spread tartar sauce on cut sides of toasted buns. Layer lettuce and fish fillets in buns.

1 Sandwich: Calories 310; Total Fat 14g (Saturated Fat 2g; Trans Fat 0g); Cholesterol 55mg; Sodium 870mg; Total Carbohydrate 25g (Dietary Fiber 2g); Protein 21g **Exchanges:** 1½ Starch, 2½ Lean Meat, 1 Fat **Carbohydrate Choices:** 1½

Quick Variation

Why not try another type of fish instead of the walleye? Tilapia is another mild white fish and is delicious cooked this way.

Salsa-Shrimp Tacos

6 servings (2 tacos each)   PREP TIME 15 minutes   START TO FINISH 15 minutes

FAST

¾ cup chunky style salsa

½ cup frozen chopped green bell pepper

¾ lb uncooked deveined peeled medium shrimp, thawed if frozen, tail shells removed

1 box (4.6 oz) taco shells (12 shells), heated as directed on box

¾ cup shredded Mexican cheese blend (3 oz)

¾ cup shredded lettuce

¼ cup taco sauce

1 In 10-inch nonstick skillet, heat salsa and bell pepper over medium-high heat, stirring frequently, until warm.

2 Stir in shrimp. Cook 3 to 4 minutes, turning shrimp occasionally, until shrimp are pink.

3 Fill each taco shell with about ¼ cup shrimp mixture. Top with cheese, lettuce and taco sauce.

1 Serving: Calories 190; Total Fat 9g (Saturated Fat 3.5g; Trans Fat 2g); Cholesterol 95mg; Sodium 400mg; Total Carbohydrate 16g (Dietary Fiber 1g); Protein 13g **Exchanges:** 1 Starch, 1 Vegetable, 1 Very Lean Meat, 1 Fat **Carbohydrate Choices:** 1

Quick Menu Idea

Serve the tacos with sliced cucumbers and Spanish rice.

Soft and Crunchy Fish Tacos

4 servings (2 tacos each)   PREP TIME 20 minutes   START TO FINISH 20 minutes

FAST

8 **flour tortillas for soft tacos & fajitas (6 inch; from 8.2-oz package)**

8 **taco shells (from 4.6-oz package)**

1 **bag (12 oz) broccoli slaw mix (about 4 cups)**

⅓ **cup reduced-fat lime vinaigrette dressing or vinaigrette dressing**

¼ **cup chopped fresh cilantro**

1 **package (1 oz) taco seasoning mix**

4 **tilapia or other mild-flavored, medium-firm fish fillets (about 1 lb)**

1 **tablespoon vegetable oil**

1 **cup guacamole**

1 **cup crumbled cotija or feta cheese (4 oz), if desired**

1 Heat tortillas and taco shells as directed on package. In medium bowl, toss broccoli slaw mix, dressing and cilantro; set aside.

2 In shallow dish, place taco seasoning mix. Coat both sides of fish with taco seasoning. In 12-inch nonstick skillet, heat oil over medium-high heat. Add fish; cook 6 minutes, turning once, or until fish flakes easily with fork. Divide fish into 8 pieces.

3 Spread each flour tortilla with 2 tablespoons guacamole. Place hard taco shell on center of flour tortilla. Using slotted spoon, spoon about ¼ cup slaw into each hard taco shell. Place 1 fish piece over slaw in each taco shell. Gently fold tortilla sides up to match taco shell sides. Top with 1 tablespoon cheese.

1 Serving: Calories 530; Total Fat 21g (Saturated Fat 4g; Trans Fat 2g); Cholesterol 60mg; Sodium 1630mg; Total Carbohydrate 54g (Dietary Fiber 5g); Protein 29g **Exchanges:** 3 Starch, ½ Other Carbohydrate, ½ Vegetable, 2½ Lean Meat, 2½ Fat **Carbohydrate Choices:** 3½

Tilapia Tacos

5 servings (2 tacos each)   PREP TIME 20 minutes   START TO FINISH 20 minutes

FAST

1 **box (8.8 oz) taco shells that stand on their own dinner kit**

1 **lb tilapia fillets, cut into 1-inch pieces**

2½ **cups coleslaw mix (from 16-oz bag)**

¼ **cup coleslaw dressing**

1 **ripe avocado, pitted, peeled and diced**

Lime wedges, if desired

1 Heat oven to 375°F. Spray large cookie sheet with cooking spray.

2 In large resealable food-storage plastic bag, place seasoning mix (from dinner kit) and fish pieces. Seal bag; shake to coat fish with seasoning. Place fish on one half of cookie sheet. Bake 8 to 10 minutes or until fish flakes easily with fork. For last 4 minutes of bake time, place taco shells (from dinner kit) on other half of cookie sheet.

3 Meanwhile, in medium bowl, toss coleslaw mix and dressing.

4 Divide coleslaw evenly among warmed taco shells. Top each with fish, avocado and 2 teaspoons taco sauce (from dinner kit). Serve with lime wedges.

1 Serving: Calories 220; Total Fat 11g (Saturated Fat 2g; Trans Fat 0g); Cholesterol 50mg; Sodium 350mg; Total Carbohydrate 11g (Dietary Fiber 3g); Protein 18g **Exchanges:** ½ Starch, 2½ Very Lean Meat, 2 Fat **Carbohydrate Choices:** 1

Quick Variation

Tilapia is a mild white fish available year-round. Other whitefish like cod, pollack or halibut would be a good substitute.

Create a Signature Grilled Cheese Sandwich

Here's how you can dress up grilled cheese sandwiches with just a few selected ingredients. Follow the easy directions for the sandwiches, then vary your sandwiches with different breads, cheeses and fillings from the choices below. For 2 sandwiches:

* Place 2 or 3 slices American or Cheddar cheese on each of 2 bread slices; top with 2 more bread slices.
* Spread 2 teaspoons softened butter over top of each sandwich.
* Place sandwiches in 12-inch skillet, buttered sides down. Spread 2 teaspoons butter over top of each one.
* Cook uncovered over medium heat 5 minutes or until golden brown. Turn; cook 2 to 3 minutes or until golden brown.

1 Apple Grilled Cheese Sandwiches: Spread raisin walnut bread with purchased apple butter, and top with slices of sharp Cheddar cheese.

2 Caramelized Onion Grilled Cheese Sandwiches: In 10-inch skillet, melt 1 tablespoon butter. Thinly slice 1 large sweet onion; cook uncovered in butter over medium-high heat 10 minutes, stirring 3 to 4 times. Sprinkle with ⅛ teaspoon salt; cook covered over medium-low heat 25 to 30 minutes, stirring every 5 minutes, until onions are deep golden brown. Top sourdough bread slices with onions and sliced smoked Gouda cheese.

3 Day-After-Thanksgiving Grilled Cheese Sandwiches: Spread slices of marble rye bread with cranberry mustard; top with sliced turkey, cranberry relish and Havarti cheese.

4 Gouda-Pear Grilled Cheese Sandwiches: Drizzle cinnamon swirl bread with honey; top with thin slices of pear and sliced aged Gouda.

5 Grilled "Hot" Ham and Cheese Sandwiches: Top pumpernickel bread with sliced pepper Jack cheese, sliced deli ham and well-drained pepperoncini slices.

6 Italian Country Grilled Cheese Sandwiches: Top sliced ciabatta bread with sliced fontina cheese, sliced tomato, sliced avocado and crisp bacon slices.

7 Mini Brie-Raspberry Grilled Cheese Sandwiches: Spread French bread slices with raspberry preserves, and top with thick slices of Brie cheese.

8 Spanish Grilled Cheese Sandwiches: Spread whole-grain rustic bread with fig jam, and top with sliced Manchego cheese.

Caesar Salad Wraps

4 wraps   PREP TIME 15 minutes   START TO FINISH 15 minutes

FAST

16 small leaves romaine lettuce, torn into bite-size pieces

¼ cup chopped red onion

2 tablespoons shredded Parmesan or Romano cheese

¼ cup Caesar dressing

4 garden vegetable–flavor or plain flour tortillas (6 to 8 inch)

4 hard-cooked eggs, sliced

2 plum (Roma) tomatoes, sliced

1 In large bowl, toss lettuce, onion, cheese and dressing to coat. Divide mixture evenly down center of each tortilla. Top with eggs and tomatoes.

2 Fold up one end of each tortilla about 1 inch over filling; fold right and left sides over folded end, overlapping. If necessary, secure with toothpicks. Cut each in half; serve immediately.

1 Wrap: Calories 330; Total Fat 18g (Saturated Fat 4.5g; Trans Fat 0.5g); Cholesterol 220mg; Sodium 570mg; Total Carbohydrate 28g (Dietary Fiber 2g); Protein 12g **Exchanges:** 1½ Starch, ½ Vegetable, 1 Medium-Fat Meat, 2½ Fat **Carbohydrate Choices:** 2

Cheese and Veggie Sandwiches

4 sandwiches   PREP TIME 10 minutes   START TO FINISH 10 minutes

FAST

4   hoagie buns, split

½   cup hummus (from 7-oz
    container)

4   slices (1 oz each) Cheddar
    cheese

4   slices (1 oz each) Swiss
    cheese

1   medium cucumber,
    cut into 16 slices

1   medium tomato, cut into
    4 slices

4   thin slices red onion,
    if desired

1 Spread bottom halves of buns with hummus. Layer with cheeses, cucumber, tomato and onion.

2 Cover with top halves of buns. Serve immediately.

1 Sandwich: Calories 480; Total Fat 23g (Saturated Fat 12g; Trans Fat 1g); Cholesterol 55mg; Sodium 650mg; Total Carbohydrate 44g (Dietary Fiber 4g); Protein 24g **Exchanges:** 3 Starch, ½ Vegetable, 2 High-Fat Meat, 1 Fat **Carbohydrate Choices:** 3

Quick Variation

Use your favorite cheese—provolone, Muenster, Monterey Jack or pepper Jack—or a slice of each.

Quick Menu Idea

Any fresh fruit is a good choice to serve with these quesadillas but you could also add refried beans or Spanish rice to the meal. A sliced fresh avocado is a tasty addition too.

Greek Quesadillas

8 servings (1 quesadilla and 4½ teaspoons sauce each)   PREP TIME 30 minutes   START TO FINISH 30 minutes

FAST

DIPPING SAUCE

- ⅔ **cup fat free plain yogurt (from 2-lb container)**
- 1 **tablespoon chopped fresh dill weed**
- 1 **teaspoon extra-virgin olive oil**
- 1 **teaspoon lemon juice**
- 1 **clove garlic, finely chopped**

QUESADILLAS

- 1 **cup crumbled feta cheese (4 oz)**
- 1 **cup shredded mozzarella cheese (4 oz)**
- 1 **small cucumber, peeled, diced (1 cup)**
- 1 **large tomato, finely chopped (1 cup)**
- ½ **cup chopped pitted kalamata olives**
- ⅛ **teaspoon salt**
- ⅛ **teaspoon pepper**
- 1 **package (11.5 oz) flour tortillas for burritos (8 tortillas; 8 inch)**

1 In small bowl, mix dipping sauce ingredients.

2 In large bowl, mix cheeses, cucumber, tomato, olives, salt and pepper. Sprinkle ½ cup cheese mixture onto half of each tortilla. Fold untopped half of tortilla over cheese mixture; gently press down with pancake turner.

3 Heat 12-inch nonstick skillet over medium heat. Cook 3 quesadillas at a time in hot skillet about 2 minutes on each side, gently pressing down with pancake turner, until tortillas are light brown and crisp and cheese is melted. Cut each in half; serve with dipping sauce.

1 Serving: Calories 240; Total Fat 10g (Saturated Fat 5g; Trans Fat 0g); Cholesterol 20mg; Sodium 560mg; Total Carbohydrate 28g (Dietary Fiber 2g); Protein 11g **Exchanges:** 2 Starch, ½ Medium-Fat Meat, 1 Fat **Carbohydrate Choices:** 2

Veggie Focaccia Sandwiches

4 sandwiches   PREP TIME 20 minutes   START TO FINISH 20 minutes

FAST

1   **round focaccia bread
    (8 inch)**

½   **yellow bell pepper,
    cut into strips**

½   **green bell pepper,
    cut into strips**

1   **small onion, sliced**

2   **tablespoons fat-free
    Italian dressing**

2   **plum (Roma) tomatoes,
    sliced**

2   **tablespoons chopped
    fresh basil leaves**

½   **cup shredded reduced-fat
    mozzarella cheese (2 oz)**

1 Heat oven to 350°F. Place focaccia on middle oven rack. Bake 5 to 7 minutes or until warm.

2 Spray 8- or 10-inch skillet with cooking spray; heat over medium-high heat. Add bell peppers, onion and dressing; cook 4 to 5 minutes, stirring occasionally, until peppers are crisp-tender. Stir in remaining ingredients; remove from heat.

3 Cut focaccia into 4 wedges; split each wedge horizontally. Spoon one-fourth of vegetable mixture onto each bottom half; top with other half of bread wedge.

1 Sandwich: Calories 260; Total Fat 9g (Saturated Fat 2.5g; Trans Fat 0g); Cholesterol 5mg; Sodium 670mg; Total Carbohydrate 35g (Dietary Fiber 3g); Protein 9g **Exchanges:** 2 Starch, 1 Vegetable, 1½ Fat **Carbohydrate Choices:** 2

Veggie Wraps

4 wraps   PREP TIME 20 minutes   START TO FINISH 20 minutes

FAST

- **4 oz (half of 8-oz package) cream cheese, softened**
- **1 teaspoon ground cumin**
- **½ teaspoon salt**
- **4 flour tortillas (10 inch), heated as directed on package**
- **4 small leaves lettuce**
- **1 medium red bell pepper, cut into thin strips**
- **1 cup sliced fresh mushrooms (3 oz)**
- **½ medium cucumber, cut lengthwise into thin strips**
- **4 medium green onions, chopped (¼ cup)**
- **½ cup shredded pepper Jack cheese (2 oz)**
- **Banana peppers, if desired**

1 In small bowl, mix cream cheese, cumin and salt until blended.

2 On each tortilla, spread 2 tablespoons cream cheese mixture. Layer remaining ingredients evenly over half of each tortilla. Tuck in sides of tortillas; roll up tightly to enclose filling. Cut in half to serve. Garnish with banana peppers.

1 Wrap: Calories 390; Total Fat 19g (Saturated Fat 9g; Trans Fat 1g); Cholesterol 45mg; Sodium 950mg; Total Carbohydrate 42g (Dietary Fiber 3g); Protein 12g **Exchanges:** 2 Starch, ½ Other Carbohydrate, 1½ Vegetable, ½ High-Fat Meat, 2½ Fat **Carbohydrate Choices:** 3

Quick Variation

Turn these into chicken veggie wraps by substituting chopped cooked chicken for the mushrooms.

Cheesy Chicken and Artichoke Pizza

4 servings (2 wedges each)   PREP TIME 20 minutes   START TO FINISH 30 minutes

FAST

1   **package (10 oz) prebaked thin Italian pizza crust (12 inch)**

¼   **cup reduced-fat mayonnaise**

¼   **cup grated Parmesan cheese**

1   **can (14 oz) artichoke hearts, drained, coarsely chopped**

1½   **cups shredded Monterey Jack cheese (6 oz)**

1   **cup chopped deli rotisserie chicken (from 2-lb chicken)**

3   **medium green onions, chopped (3 tablespoons)**

1 Heat oven to 450°F. Place pizza crust on ungreased cookie sheet. In medium bowl, mix mayonnaise, Parmesan cheese and artichokes.

2 Spread artichoke mixture over pizza crust to within 1 inch of edge. Top with 1 cup of the cheese, the chicken and onions. Top with remaining ½ cup cheese.

3 Bake 8 to 10 minutes or until cheese is melted and pizza is thoroughly heated. Cut into 8 wedges.

1 Serving: Calories 550; Total Fat 27g (Saturated Fat 12g; Trans Fat 0.5g); Cholesterol 85mg; Sodium 1250mg; Total Carbohydrate 43g (Dietary Fiber 7g); Protein 34g **Exchanges:** 3 Starch, 3½ Lean Meat, 3 Fat **Carbohydrate Choices:** 3

Quick Menu Idea

Serve pizza slices with a fresh green salad topped with your favorite dressing.

Chicken Sausage, Spinach and Swiss Pizza

4 pizzas   PREP TIME 20 minutes   START TO FINISH 30 minutes

FAST

4 **baked flatbreads (from 11.2-oz package)**

2 **tablespoons olive oil**

1 **bag (6 oz) fresh baby spinach leaves (about 3½ cups)**

½ **teaspoon garlic-pepper blend**

3 **cooked chicken sausage links (3 oz each; from 12-oz package), thinly sliced**

¼ **to ½ teaspoon crushed red pepper flakes**

½ **cup sliced green onions (8 medium)**

2 **cups shredded Gruyère or Swiss cheese (8 oz)**

1 Heat oven to 400°F. Place flatbreads on 2 large ungreased cookie sheets. Brush flatbreads with 1 tablespoon of the oil. Bake 5 minutes.

2 Meanwhile, in large bowl, toss spinach with remaining 1 tablespoon oil and the garlic-pepper blend.

3 Top each flatbread with spinach and sausage slices. Sprinkle each with pepper flakes, onions and cheese.

4 Bake 7 to 9 minutes longer or until cheese is melted.

1 Pizza: Calories 500; Total Fat 29g (Saturated Fat 12g; Trans Fat 0g); Cholesterol 95mg; Sodium 860mg; Total Carbohydrate 26g (Dietary Fiber 9g); Protein 33g **Exchanges:** 1½ Starch, ½ Vegetable, 4 Lean Meat, 3 Fat **Carbohydrate Choices:** 2

Chicken Taco Pizza

4 servings (2 wedges each)   PREP TIME 20 minutes   START TO FINISH 30 minutes

FAST

1 package (10 oz) prebaked thin Italian pizza crust (12 inch)

½ cup taco sauce

2 cups chopped deli rotisserie chicken (from 2-lb chicken)

1½ cups shredded mozzarella and Cheddar cheese blend (6 oz)

½ cup sour cream

1 cup shredded lettuce

1 medium tomato, seeded, chopped (¾ cup)

½ cup crushed nacho-flavored tortilla chips

1 Heat oven to 450°F. Place pizza crust on ungreased cookie sheet. In small bowl, stir together taco sauce and chicken.

2 Spread chicken mixture over pizza crust to within 1 inch of edge. Top with cheese. Bake 8 to 10 minutes or until cheese is melted and pizza is thoroughly heated.

3 Drop sour cream by teaspoonfuls over pizza. Top with lettuce, tomato and tortilla chips. Cut into 8 wedges.

1 Serving: Calories 580; Total Fat 29g (Saturated Fat 14g; Trans Fat 1g); Cholesterol 125mg; Sodium 1230mg; Total Carbohydrate 43g (Dietary Fiber 2g); Protein 38g **Exchanges:** 3 Starch, 4 Lean Meat, 3 Fat **Carbohydrate Choices:** 3

Quick Variation

Make this pizza your own by topping it with your favorite taco toppers. Try sliced olives, chopped avocado, fresh cilantro or pickled jalapeño slices.

Healthified Homemade Pizza

8 servings   PREP TIME 15 minutes   START TO FINISH 45 minutes

CRUST

1⅓ **cups all-purpose flour**

1 **teaspoon baking powder**

½ **teaspoon salt**

½ **cup fat-free (skim) milk**

2 **tablespoons olive oil**

TOPPING

1½ **cups shredded reduced-fat mozzarella cheese (6 oz)**

1 **can (14.5 oz) diced tomatoes, drained**

1 **cup fresh baby spinach leaves, coarsely chopped**

1 **cup yellow or green bell pepper strips**

¼ **teaspoon dried oregano leaves**

¼ **teaspoon garlic powder**

⅛ **teaspoon pepper**

2 **tablespoons freshly shredded Parmesan cheese**

1 Heat oven to 400°F. In medium bowl, mix flour, baking powder and salt. Stir in milk and oil until soft dough forms. (If dough is dry, stir in 1 to 2 tablespoons additional milk.) On lightly floured surface, knead dough 10 times. Shape dough into ball. Cover with bowl; let rest 10 minutes.

2 Place dough on ungreased cookie sheet; flatten slightly. Roll out to 12-inch round. Bake 8 minutes.

3 Sprinkle mozzarella cheese over crust; top with remaining topping ingredients. Bake 15 to 20 minutes longer or until crust is light golden brown and cheese begins to brown. Cut into wedges.

1 **Serving:** Calories 190; Total Fat 8g (Saturated Fat 3g; Trans Fat 0g); Cholesterol 10mg; Sodium 410mg; Total Carbohydrate 21g (Dietary Fiber 1g); Protein 10g **Exchanges:** 1½ Starch, ½ Lean Meat, 1 Fat **Carbohydrate Choices:** 1½

Ham and Gorgonzola Pizza

6 servings   PREP TIME 20 minutes   START TO FINISH 50 minutes

CRUST

2½ to 3 cups all-purpose flour

1 tablespoon sugar

1 teaspoon salt

1 package regular active or fast-acting dry yeast (2¼ teaspoons)

3 tablespoons olive or vegetable oil

1 cup very warm water (120°F to 130°F)

TOPPING

1 teaspoon olive oil

⅓ cup refrigerated Alfredo sauce

1 cup cubed cooked ham

½ cup crumbled gorgonzola or blue cheese (2 oz)

¼ cup sliced green onions (4 medium)

1 cup shredded mozzarella cheese (4 oz)

½ teaspoon dried oregano leaves

1 In large bowl, stir together 1 cup of the flour, the sugar, salt and yeast. Add 3 tablespoons oil and the warm water; mix well. Stir in enough remaining flour until dough is soft and leaves side of bowl. Place dough on lightly floured surface. Knead 4 to 5 minutes or until dough is smooth and springy. Cover loosely with plastic wrap; let rest 10 minutes.

2 Meanwhile, heat oven to 425°F. Spray large cookie sheet or 12-inch pizza pan with cooking spray.

3 Divide dough in half.* Press half of dough into 12-inch round on cookie sheet. Brush dough with 1 teaspoon oil. Bake 10 to 12 minutes or until crust is golden brown.

4 Spread Alfredo sauce on crust. Sprinkle ham, gorgonzola cheese and onions over sauce. Sprinkle with mozzarella cheese and oregano. Bake 9 to 11 minutes longer or until cheese is melted.

*Remaining pizza dough can be prepared and baked as directed above. Wrap baked crust tightly in plastic wrap and freeze for another use. Unwrap and thaw before topping and baking.

1 Serving: Calories 460; Total Fat 22g (Saturated Fat 9g; Trans Fat 0g); Cholesterol 45mg; Sodium 1060mg; Total Carbohydrate 45g (Dietary Fiber 2g); Protein 20g **Exchanges:** 3 Starch, 1 Medium-Fat Meat, 3 Fat **Carbohydrate Choices:** 3

Loaded Baked Potato Pizza

6 servings   PREP TIME 10 minutes   START TO FINISH 30 minutes

FAST

1   **package (14 oz) prebaked original Italian pizza crust (12 inch)**

½   **cup chive-and-onion sour cream potato topper (from 12-oz container)**

1   **cup refrigerated homestyle potato slices (from 20-oz bag)**

1   **tablespoon olive or vegetable oil**

¼   **teaspoon pepper**

8   **slices bacon, crisply cooked, coarsely chopped**

1   **small tomato, seeded, chopped (½ cup)**

1   **cup shredded Cheddar cheese (4 oz)**

2   **tablespoons chopped fresh chives**

1 Heat oven to 400°F. Place pizza crust on ungreased cookie sheet. Spread potato topper over crust to within ½ inch of edge.

2 In medium bowl, mix potatoes, oil and pepper; place over sour cream topper. Sprinkle evenly with bacon, tomato, cheese and chives.

3 Bake 18 to 20 minutes or until potatoes are thoroughly heated and cheese is melted. If desired, spoon additional sour cream topper over pizza. Cut into wedges.

1 Serving: Calories 410; Total Fat 21g (Saturated Fat 9g; Trans Fat 0g); Cholesterol 35mg; Sodium 830mg; Total Carbohydrate 38g (Dietary Fiber 1g); Protein 16g **Exchanges:** 2½ Starch, 1 Medium-Fat Meat, 3 Fat **Carbohydrate Choices:** 2½

Quick Variation

Vary your toppings based on what you have on hand, such as adding cooked broccoli florets and sprinkling with green onions instead of chives. Then, if you like, use chopped cooked ham instead of the bacon.

Mexican Chicken Pizza with Cornmeal Crust

6 servings   PREP TIME 20 minutes   START TO FINISH 50 minutes

1½ cups all-purpose flour

1 tablespoon sugar

1¼ teaspoons regular active dry yeast

¼ teaspoon coarse (kosher or sea) salt

¾ cup warm water (105°F to 115°F)

1 tablespoon olive oil

⅓ cup yellow cornmeal

Additional cornmeal

1½ cups Mexican cheese blend (6 oz)

1½ cups shredded cooked chicken breast

1 can (14.5 oz) fire roasted or plain diced tomatoes, drained

½ medium yellow bell pepper, chopped (½ cup)

¼ cup sliced green onions (4 medium)

¼ cup chopped fresh cilantro

1 Heat oven to 450°F. In medium bowl, stir together ¾ cup of the flour, the sugar, yeast and salt. Stir in warm water and oil. Beat with electric mixer on low speed 30 seconds; beat on high speed 1 minute. Stir in ⅓ cup cornmeal and remaining ¾ cup flour to make a soft dough.

2 On lightly floured surface, knead dough until smooth and elastic, about 5 minutes. Cover with bowl; let rest 10 minutes.

3 Spray large cookie sheet with cooking spray; sprinkle with additional cornmeal. On cookie sheet, press dough into 14×10-inch rectangle; prick with fork. Bake 8 to 10 minutes or until edges just begin to turn brown.

4 Sprinkle with ½ cup of the cheese blend. Top with chicken, tomatoes and bell pepper. Sprinkle with remaining 1 cup cheese. Bake 6 to 8 minutes longer or until cheese is melted and edges are golden brown. Sprinkle with onions and cilantro.

1 Serving: Calories 340; Total Fat 13g (Saturated Fat 6g; Trans Fat 0g); Cholesterol 55mg; Sodium 360mg; Total Carbohydrate 35g (Dietary Fiber 2g); Protein 22g **Exchanges:** 2 Starch, 1 Vegetable, 2 Lean Meat, 1 Fat **Carbohydrate Choices:** 2

Time-Saver

Purchase a deli rotisserie chicken and shred the meat for this pizza.

Quick Menu Idea

Toss a crispy salad of mixed greens and top it with ranch or Italian dressing to serve with this pizza.

Chapter Two

Soups, Chilies and Stews

Buffalo Chicken Chili

1 tablespoon vegetable oil

1 large onion, chopped
   (1 cup)

1 medium red or yellow bell
   pepper, chopped (1 cup)

2 cups cubed deli rotisserie
   chicken (from 2-lb chicken)

1 cup chicken broth
   (from 32-oz carton)

1 tablespoon chili powder

5 or 6 drops red pepper
   sauce

2 cans (15 oz each)
   pinto beans, drained

1 can (28 oz) fire roasted
   crushed tomatoes,
   undrained

1 can (14.5 oz) diced
   tomatoes, undrained

½ cup sliced celery

½ cup crumbled blue cheese
   (2 oz)

1 In 3-quart saucepan, heat oil over medium-high heat. Add onion and bell pepper; cook about 5 minutes, stirring occasionally, until crisp-tender.

2 Stir in remaining ingredients except celery and blue cheese. Heat to boiling. Reduce heat to medium-low; simmer uncovered 10 to 15 minutes, stirring occasionally. Serve topped with celery and blue cheese.

1 Serving: Calories 380; Total Fat 10g (Saturated Fat 3.5g; Trans Fat 0g); Cholesterol 50mg; Sodium 1060mg; Total Carbohydrate 43g (Dietary Fiber 13g); Protein 28g Exchanges: 2½ Starch, 1 Vegetable, 2½ Lean Meat, ½ Fat Carbohydrate Choices: 3

Quick Variation

Serve the chili over hot cooked spaghetti for Cincinnati-Style Buffalo Spaghetti.

White Chicken Chili

8 servings   PREP TIME 15 minutes   START TO FINISH 4 hours 35 minutes

6   **bone-in chicken thighs (1½ lb)**

1   **large onion, chopped (1 cup)**

2   **cloves garlic, finely chopped**

1¾ **cups chicken broth (from 32-oz carton)**

1   **teaspoon ground cumin**

1   **teaspoon dried oregano leaves**

½   **teaspoon salt**

¼   **teaspoon red pepper sauce**

2   **cans (15.5 oz each) great northern beans, drained, rinsed**

1   **can (11 oz) vacuum-packed white shoepeg corn, drained**

3   **tablespoons lime juice**

2   **tablespoons chopped fresh cilantro**

1 Remove skin and excess fat from chicken. Spray 3½- to 4-quart slow cooker with cooking spray. In slow cooker, mix onion, garlic, broth, cumin, oregano, salt and pepper sauce. Top with chicken.

2 Cover; cook on Low heat setting 4 to 5 hours.

3 Remove chicken from slow cooker. Using 2 forks, remove bones and shred chicken into pieces. Discard bones; return chicken to slow cooker. Stir in beans, corn, and lime juice.

4 Cover; cook on Low heat setting 15 to 20 minutes longer or until beans and corn are hot. Sprinkle with cilantro.

1 Serving: Calories 270; Total Fat 5g (Saturated Fat 1.5g; Trans Fat 0g); Cholesterol 35mg; Sodium 470mg; Total Carbohydrate 33g (Dietary Fiber 7g); Protein 23g **Exchanges:** 2 Starch, 2½ Very Lean Meat, ½ Fat **Carbohydrate Choices:** 2

Chipotle Turkey Chili

4 servings (1¼ cups each)   PREP TIME 30 minutes   START TO FINISH 30 minutes

FAST

¾ lb lean (at least 90%) ground turkey

1 medium onion, chopped (½ cup)

1 tablespoon finely chopped garlic

1 cup frozen whole kernel corn, thawed

1 can (15 oz) cannellini beans, undrained

½ cup chicken broth (from 32-oz carton)

¼ teaspoon salt

1 chipotle chile in adobo sauce (from 7-oz can), finely chopped

½ cup reduced-fat sour cream

½ cup chopped fresh cilantro

⅓ cup shredded Colby– Monterey Jack cheese blend

1 In 4-quart saucepan, cook turkey, onion and garlic over medium-high heat 4 to 6 minutes, stirring occasionally, until turkey is no longer pink; drain.

2 Stir in corn, beans, broth, salt and chile. Heat to boiling. Reduce heat to medium; cover and cook 10 to 15 minutes to blend flavors, stirring occasionally.

3 Stir in ¼ cup of the sour cream and ¼ cup of the cilantro. Serve with remaining ¼ cup sour cream, ¼ cup cilantro and the cheese.

1 Serving: Calories 350; Total Fat 7g (Saturated Fat 2.5g; Trans Fat 0g); Cholesterol 65mg; Sodium 760mg; Total Carbohydrate 40g (Dietary Fiber 7g); Protein 32g **Exchanges:** 2½ Starch, 3 Lean Meat **Carbohydrate Choices:** 2½

Healthy Twist

Like most beans, cannellini beans—also known as white Italian kidney beans—are a good source of fiber.

Turkey Mole Chili

6 servings (1½ cups each)   PREP TIME 15 minutes   START TO FINISH 8 hours 15 minutes

2 packages (20 oz each)
   lean (at least 90%) ground
   turkey

1 large onion, chopped
   (about 1 cup)

2 medium carrots, chopped
   (about 1 cup)

1 can (28 oz) diced
   tomatoes, undrained

1 can (15 oz) black beans,
   drained, rinsed

1 jar (8¼ oz) mole

1¾ cups chicken broth
   (from 32-oz carton)

½ cup sour cream

¼ cup crumbled cotija (white
   Mexican) cheese (1 oz)

1 In 12-inch nonstick skillet, cook turkey over medium-high heat 5 to 7 minutes, stirring frequently, until no longer pink; drain.

2 Spray 4- to 5-quart slow cooker with cooking spray. In slow cooker, mix turkey and remaining ingredients except sour cream and cheese.

3 Cover; cook on Low heat setting 8 to 10 hours.

4 Stir well before serving. Top each serving with sour cream and cheese.

1 Serving: Calories 740; Total Fat 40g (Saturated Fat 12g; Trans Fat 1g); Cholesterol 140mg; Sodium 1030mg; Total Carbohydrate 43g (Dietary Fiber 10g); Protein 51g **Exchanges:** 2 Starch, ½ Other Carbohydrate, 1 Vegetable, 6 Lean Meat, 4 Fat **Carbohydrate Choices:** 3

Time-Saver

You'll find cotija cheese in the dairy or cheese aisle of your grocery store. A hard cheese made from cow's milk, cotija tastes similar to Parmesan or feta cheese. It is white and usually sold in small rounds or large blocks.

Hearty Beef Chili

7 servings (1½ cups each)   PREP TIME 25 minutes   START TO FINISH 3 hours 25 minutes

CHILI

2½ lb beef stew meat, cut into 1-inch cubes

2 tablespoons quick-mixing flour

2 tablespoons vegetable oil

4½ teaspoons chili powder

2 teaspoons salt

2 teaspoons dried oregano leaves

2 teaspoons ground cumin

2 dried bay leaves

1½ cups beef flavored broth (from 32-oz carton)

1 can (28 oz) diced tomatoes, undrained

1 large onion, chopped (1 cup)

1 medium green bell pepper, chopped (1 cup)

3 cloves garlic, finely chopped

3 tablespoons cornmeal

1 can (15 oz) black beans, drained, rinsed

1 can (4.5 oz) chopped green chiles

GARNISHES, IF DESIRED

Shredded Monterey Jack cheese

Sour cream

Chopped fresh cilantro

Tortilla chips

1 In large resealable food-storage plastic bag, place half of the beef and 1 tablespoon of the flour; seal bag and shake to coat. Repeat with remaining beef and flour. In 4-quart Dutch oven, heat oil over medium-high heat. Add beef; cook until browned on all sides. Drain, if desired.

2 Stir in remaining chili ingredients except cornmeal, beans and chiles. Heat to boiling. Reduce heat to low; cover and simmer 3 hours or until meat is tender.

3 Stir in cornmeal; cook and stir about 1 minute to thicken. Add beans and chiles; cook until thoroughly heated. Remove bay leaves. Serve chili with garnishes.

1 Serving: Calories 440; Total Fat 22g (Saturated Fat 7g; Trans Fat 1g); Cholesterol 90mg; Sodium 1170mg; Total Carbohydrate 25g (Dietary Fiber 7g); Protein 36g **Exchanges:** 1½ Starch, 1 Vegetable, 4 Lean Meat, 2 Fat **Carbohydrate Choices:** 1½

Quick Menu Idea

If you like your chili spicy, add ¼ to ½ teaspoon crushed red pepper flakes with the other seasonings. Then serve the chili with crusty Italian rolls.

Quick Variation

Try this chili made with ground turkey and pinto beans instead of beef and kidney beans. It's a great way to easily adjust the recipe to what you like or have on-hand.

Taco-Corn Chili

5 servings   PREP TIME 30 minutes   START TO FINISH 30 minutes

FAST

1 lb extra-lean (at least 90%) ground beef

1 can (15 oz) kidney beans, drained, rinsed

1 package (1 oz) taco seasoning mix

1 can (10 oz) diced tomatoes with green chiles, undrained

1 box (9 oz) frozen whole kernel corn, thawed, drained

2 cups water

2 teaspoons sugar

1 Spray 4-quart Dutch oven with cooking spray; heat over medium-high heat. Add beef; cook 5 to 7 minutes, stirring occasionally, until thoroughly cooked. Drain.

2 Stir in remaining ingredients. Heat to boiling. Reduce heat; simmer uncovered about 18 minutes, stirring occasionally.

1 Serving: Calories 300; Total Fat 8g (Saturated Fat 3g; Trans Fat 0g); Cholesterol 55mg; Sodium 1030mg; Total Carbohydrate 36g (Dietary Fiber 6g); Protein 25g **Exchanges:** 2½ Starch, 2½ Lean Meat **Carbohydrate Choices:** 2

Time-Saver

To quickly thaw corn, cut a small slit in the center of the pouch; microwave on High 2 to 3 minutes or until thawed. Remove corn from pouch; drain on paper towel.

Texas Two-Meat Chili

6 servings (1½ cups each)   PREP TIME 25 minutes   START TO FINISH 7 hours 25 minutes

1 lb boneless beef chuck steak, cut into 1-inch pieces

1 lb pork tenderloin, cut into 1-inch pieces

¼ cup all-purpose flour

1 tablespoon vegetable oil

2 cans (10 oz each) tomatoes with green chiles, undrained

1 can (15 to 16 oz) pinto beans, undrained

1 can or bottle (12 oz) regular or nonalcoholic beer

½ cup chopped red onion

2 tablespoons chili powder

1 teaspoon ground cumin

½ teaspoon salt

½ teaspoon garlic powder

⅛ teaspoon ground cinnamon

Sliced green onions, if desired

1 In large resealable food-storage plastic bag, place beef, pork and flour; seal bag and shake until coated. In 12-inch skillet, heat oil over medium-high heat. Add beef and pork; cook 8 to 10 minutes, stirring frequently, until browned on all sides (cook in batches if necessary).

2 Spray 4- to 5-quart slow cooker with cooking spray. In slow cooker, mix meat and remaining ingredients except green onions.

3 Cover; cook on Low heat setting 7 to 9 hours.

4 Before serving, skim off fat; sprinkle with green onions.

1 Serving: Calories 380; Total Fat 14g (Saturated Fat 4.5g; Trans Fat 0g); Cholesterol 70mg; Sodium 520mg; Total Carbohydrate 27g (Dietary Fiber 8g); Protein 35g **Exchanges:** 2 Starch, 4 Lean Meat **Carbohydrate Choices:** 2

Time-Saver

Use a spoon to skim the fat, or place a slice of bread on top of the mixture to absorb the fat. You can do this with other soups and stews as well.

Quick Menu Idea

Sour cream and shredded Cheddar cheese make great toppings for this chili. And on the side, serve warm flour tortillas.

Quick Variation

Plan a "meatless" night to serve this hearty chili. Then for another meal, add some shredded cooked chicken and top with Cheddar cheese instead of Monterey Jack—you'll think it's a different recipe!

Black Bean Chili with Cilantro

5 servings (1⅓ cups each)   PREP TIME 30 minutes   START TO FINISH 1 hour 30 minutes

CHILI

¼ **cup dry sherry or chicken broth (from 32-oz carton)**

1 **tablespoon olive oil**

2 **large onions, chopped (2 cups)**

½ **cup chopped celery**

½ **cup chopped carrot**

½ **cup chopped red bell pepper**

3 **cans (15 oz each) black beans, drained, rinsed**

2 **cups chicken broth (from 32-oz carton)**

1 **large tomato, chopped (1 cup)**

2 **tablespoons finely chopped garlic**

2 **tablespoons honey**

2 **tablespoons tomato paste**

4 **teaspoons chili powder or to taste**

1 **teaspoon ground cumin**

½ **teaspoon dried oregano leaves**

¼ **cup chopped fresh cilantro**

Salt and pepper to taste

GARNISHES, IF DESIRED

Additional chopped onion

Shredded Monterey Jack cheese

Fat free plain yogurt (from 2-lb container) or sour cream

1 In 4- to 5-quart Dutch oven, heat sherry and oil over medium heat. Add onions; cook until softened. Add celery, carrot and bell pepper; cook 5 minutes, stirring frequently.

2 Stir in remaining ingredients except garnishes. Heat to boiling. Reduce heat to low; cover and simmer 45 to 60 minutes or until chili is desired thickness. Garnish individual servings with onion, cheese and yogurt.

1 Serving: Calories 400; Total Fat 5g (Saturated Fat 1g; Trans Fat 0g); Cholesterol 0mg; Sodium 560mg; Total Carbohydrate 70g (Dietary Fiber 23g); Protein 19g **Exchanges:** 3 Starch, 1 Other Carbohydrate, 2 Vegetable, 1 Lean Meat **Carbohydrate Choices:** 4½

After-Work Chicken Noodle Soup

4 servings PREP TIME 25 minutes START TO FINISH 25 minutes

FAST

2 cups cut-up deli rotisserie chicken (from 2-lb chicken)

2 medium stalks celery, chopped (1 cup)

2 medium carrots, sliced (1 cup)

1 medium onion, chopped (½ cup)

1 tablespoon chopped fresh parsley or 1 teaspoon parsley flakes

1 teaspoon dried thyme leaves

¼ teaspoon pepper

2 cloves garlic, finely chopped

7 cups chicken broth (from two 32-oz cartons)

1 cup uncooked wide egg noodles (2 oz)

1 In 3-quart saucepan, heat all ingredients except noodles to boiling. Stir in noodles. Return to boiling.

2 Reduce heat; simmer uncovered 8 to 10 minutes, stirring occasionally, until noodles and vegetables are tender.

1 Serving: Calories 260; Total Fat 8g (Saturated Fat 2g; Trans Fat 0g); Cholesterol 70mg; Sodium 2070mg; Total Carbohydrate 17g (Dietary Fiber 2g); Protein 30g **Exchanges:** 1 Starch, 4 Very Lean Meat, 1 Fat **Carbohydrate Choices:** 1

Time-Saver

Skip the step of chopping fresh garlic and use ¼ to ½ teaspoon garlic powder instead.

Cheesy Chicken Enchilada Soup

6 servings (1 cup each)   PREP TIME 20 minutes   START TO FINISH 20 minutes

FAST

- **2 cans (10¾ oz each) condensed 98% fat-free cream of chicken soup with 30% less sodium**
- **1 can (10 oz) enchilada sauce**
- **2 cups milk**
- **1 cup shredded reduced-fat Cheddar cheese (4 oz)**
- **1 package (9 oz) frozen cooked southwestern-seasoned chicken breast strips, thawed, chopped (2 cups)**
- **¾ cup crushed tortilla chips**

1 In 3-quart saucepan, mix all ingredients except tortilla chips. Cook over medium heat, stirring occasionally, until thoroughly heated and cheese is melted.

2 Top each serving with tortilla chips.

1 Serving: Calories 270; Total Fat 12g (Saturated Fat 3.5g; Trans Fat 0.5g); Cholesterol 35mg; Sodium 1150mg; Total Carbohydrate 22g (Dietary Fiber 0g); Protein 19g **Exchanges:** 1½ Starch, 2 Lean Meat, 1 Fat **Carbohydrate Choices:** 1½

Quick Menu Idea

This easy soup is a great choice for dinner any night. Serve bowls of the soup with warm breadsticks and cantaloupe wedges.

Chicken and Barley Soup

6 servings (1⅓ cups each)   PREP TIME 10 minutes   START TO FINISH 35 minutes

1 **carton (32 oz) chicken broth**

1 **can (14.5 oz) diced tomatoes, undrained**

2 **medium carrots, sliced (1 cup)**

2 **medium stalks celery, sliced (1 cup)**

1 **cup sliced fresh mushrooms (about 3 oz)**

⅓ **cup uncooked quick-cooking barley**

1 **teaspoon dried minced onion**

2 **cups chopped deli rotisserie chicken (from 2-lb chicken)**

1 In 3-quart saucepan, mix all ingredients except chicken. Heat to boiling over medium-high heat. Reduce heat to medium; cover and simmer 15 to 20 minutes or until barley is tender.

2 Add chicken. Cover; cook about 3 minutes longer or until chicken is hot.

1 Serving: Calories 180; Total Fat 4.5g (Saturated Fat 1g; Trans Fat 0g); Cholesterol 40mg; Sodium 1000mg; Total Carbohydrate 16g (Dietary Fiber 4g); Protein 19g **Exchanges:** 1 Starch, 2 Lean Meat **Carbohydrate Choices:** 1

Time-Saver

Save time with the quick-cooking barley used in this recipe. The regular type needs to cook longer than this recipe allows.

Chicken-Broccoli-Tortellini Soup

4 servings   PREP TIME 25 minutes   START TO FINISH 25 minutes

FAST

1 tablespoon olive or vegetable oil

1 small onion, chopped (⅓ cup)

1¾ cups chicken broth (from 32-oz carton)

½ cup water

½ teaspoon Italian seasoning

1 bag (12 oz) frozen broccoli & cheese sauce

1 package (9 oz) refrigerated cheese-filled tortellini

1 cup cubed cooked chicken

1 large plum (Roma) tomato, chopped (½ cup)

¼ cup shredded Parmesan cheese

1 In 2-quart saucepan, heat oil over medium-high heat. Add onion; cook about 2 minutes, stirring frequently, until crisp-tender.

2 Stir in broth, water, Italian seasoning, frozen broccoli & cheese sauce and tortellini. Heat to boiling, stirring occasionally and breaking up broccoli.

3 Stir in chicken. Cook about 4 minutes longer, stirring occasionally, until tortellini is tender. Stir in tomato. Top each serving with 1 tablespoon cheese.

1 Serving: Calories 370; Total Fat 14g (Saturated Fat 5g; Trans Fat 0g); Cholesterol 60mg; Sodium 1150mg; Total Carbohydrate 37g (Dietary Fiber 3g); Protein 25g **Exchanges:** 1½ Starch, ½ Other Carbohydrate, 1 Vegetable, 2½ Medium-Fat Meat **Carbohydrate Choices:** 2½

Quick Menu Idea

Serve this delicious hearty soup with warm slices of French bread.

Chicken and Pastina Soup

10 servings (1½ cups each)   PREP TIME 30 minutes   START TO FINISH 45 minutes

2   **lb boneless skinless chicken breasts**

2   **cartons (32 oz each) chicken broth (8 cups)**

1   **tablespoon olive oil**

1   **medium onion, chopped (½ cup)**

1   **medium carrot, diced (½ cup)**

1   **medium stalk celery, diced (½ cup)**

1   **cup fire roasted crushed tomatoes (from 14.5-oz can)**

½   **teaspoon gray salt or sea salt**

¼   **teaspoon freshly ground black pepper**

1   **dried bay leaf**

1   **cup uncooked acini di pepe pasta (8 oz)**

2   **cups chopped lightly packed mustard greens, spinach, Swiss chard or other greens**

⅓   **cup shredded Parmesan cheese**

Additional freshly ground black pepper, if desired

1 In 12-inch skillet, place chicken and 1 carton of the broth. Heat to boiling. Reduce heat; cover and simmer 20 minutes or until juice of chicken is clear when center of thickest part is cut (165°F).

2 Meanwhile, in 6-quart stockpot, heat oil over medium heat. Add onion, carrot and celery; cook 8 to 10 minutes, stirring occasionally, until tender.

3 Drain chicken, reserving broth; set chicken aside. Strain broth; add to vegetables. Stir in remaining carton of broth, the tomatoes, salt, pepper and bay leaf. Heat to boiling. Stir in pasta. Reduce heat; cover and simmer 15 minutes.

4 Shred or cut chicken into bite-size pieces; add to soup. Add greens; cook and stir just until wilted. Remove bay leaf. Top each serving with cheese and a sprinkle of additional pepper.

1 Serving: Calories 260; Total Fat 6g (Saturated Fat 2g; Trans Fat 0g); Cholesterol 60mg; Sodium 950mg; Total Carbohydrate 23g (Dietary Fiber 2g); Protein 28g **Exchanges:** 1 Starch, 1 Vegetable, 3 Very Lean Meat, 1 Fat **Carbohydrate Choices:** 1½

Quick Variation

You can use any variety of tiny pasta in place of the acini de pepe in this pastina ("little pasta") soup.

Chicken Soup Provençal

2 servings (2 cups each) PREP TIME 10 minutes START TO FINISH 25 minutes

FAST

2 **teaspoons olive oil**

½ **lb uncooked chicken breast strips for stir-fry**

½ **cup sliced leeks**

1 **can (14.5 oz) diced tomatoes with basil, garlic and oregano, undrained**

1¾ **cups reduced-sodium chicken broth (from 32-oz carton)**

2 **oz angel hair (capellini) pasta, broken**

Shredded Parmesan cheese, if desired

1 In 3-quart saucepan, heat oil over medium-high heat. Add chicken and leeks; cook 5 minutes, stirring frequently.

2 Stir in tomatoes and broth. Heat to boiling. Reduce heat; simmer uncovered 10 minutes.

3 Add pasta; simmer 3 to 5 minutes longer or until pasta is tender and chicken is no longer pink in center. Serve with cheese.

1 Serving: Calories 370; Total Fat 9g (Saturated Fat 2g; Trans Fat 0g); Cholesterol 70mg; Sodium 850mg; Total Carbohydrate 38g (Dietary Fiber 4g); Protein 34g **Exchanges:** 2 Starch, 1 Vegetable, 3½ Lean Meat Carbohydrate Choices: 2½

Curried Sweet Potato, Lentil and Chicken Soup

6 servings (About 1¼ cups each)   PREP TIME 30 minutes   START TO FINISH 30 minutes

FAST

1   large or 2 medium dark-orange sweet potatoes, peeled, cut into ½-inch cubes (2 cups)

⅓   cup chopped onion (1 small)

½   cup apple juice

½   cup water

2   cans (19 oz each) ready-to-serve lentil soup

1½   cups frozen cut green beans

1   cup finely chopped cooked chicken

2   to 3 teaspoons curry powder

1 In 3-quart saucepan, heat sweet potatoes, onion, apple juice and water to boiling over medium-high heat. Reduce heat to medium-low; cover and cook 5 minutes.

2 Stir in soup, beans, chicken and curry powder. Heat to boiling. Reduce heat to medium-low; cover and simmer 10 to 15 minutes, stirring occasionally, until vegetables are tender.

1 Serving: Calories 220; Total Fat 3.5g (Saturated Fat 1g; Trans Fat 0g); Cholesterol 20mg; Sodium 670mg; Total Carbohydrate 34g (Dietary Fiber 6g); Protein 14g **Exchanges:** 2 Starch, 1 Vegetable, 1 Very Lean Meat **Carbohydrate Choices:** 2

Quick Menu Idea

Serve this hearty soup with whole wheat pita bread and a green salad.

Chicken, Squash and Pasta Soup

6 servings (1⅓ cups each)   PREP TIME 40 minutes   START TO FINISH 40 minutes

1 **tablespoon olive or vegetable oil**

2 **medium stalks celery, coarsely chopped (1 cup)**

1 **medium onion, coarsely chopped (½ cup)**

1 **teaspoon dried sage leaves**

6 **cups chicken broth (from two 32-oz cartons)**

2½ **cups chopped deli rotisserie chicken (from 2-lb chicken)**

1½ **cups uncooked tricolor rotini pasta (about 5 oz)**

1½ **cups cubed (¾ inch) peeled butternut squash**

¼ **teaspoon salt**

⅛ **teaspoon pepper**

1 In 4½- to 5-quart Dutch oven, heat oil over medium-high heat. Add celery, onion and sage; cook 5 to 6 minutes, stirring frequently, until onion is softened.

2 Stir in remaining ingredients. Heat to boiling. Reduce heat to medium; cover and cook 12 to 15 minutes, stirring occasionally, until pasta and squash are tender.

1 Serving: Calories 270; Total Fat 8g (Saturated Fat 2g; Trans Fat 0g); Cholesterol 50mg; Sodium 1420mg; Total Carbohydrate 24g (Dietary Fiber 2g); Protein 25g **Exchanges:** 1 Starch, 1 Vegetable, 3 Lean Meat **Carbohydrate Choices:** 1½

Time-Saver

This recipe calls for the peanut-shaped butternut squash. Because it is hard to cut, this squash is often available precut, ready to cook.

Chicken-Vegetable Pot Pie Soup

6 servings (1⅓ cups each)   PREP TIME 1 hour   START TO FINISH 1 hour

1   **sheet frozen puff pastry (from 17.3-oz package), thawed**

2   **tablespoons butter or margarine**

6   **small red potatoes, cut into eighths**

1   **medium stalk celery, coarsely chopped (½ cup)**

1   **medium carrot, coarsely chopped (½ cup)**

1   **small onion, coarsely chopped (⅓ cup)**

5   **cups chicken broth (from two 32-oz cartons)**

¼   **cup quick-mixing flour**

1   **teaspoon poultry seasoning**

¼   **teaspoon salt**

⅛   **teaspoon pepper**

2½ **cups 1-inch pieces deli rotisserie chicken (from 2-lb chicken)**

1   **cup frozen sweet peas**

¼   **cup whipping cream**

1 Heat oven to 400°F. Cut 6 rounds from puff pastry with 3-inch round cutter. Place on ungreased cookie sheet. Bake 12 to 15 minutes or until puffed and golden brown. Keep warm.

2 Meanwhile, in 4½- to 5-quart Dutch oven, melt butter over medium-high heat. Add potatoes, celery, carrot and onion; cook 5 to 6 minutes, stirring frequently, until onion is softened.

3 With whisk, beat broth, flour, poultry seasoning, salt and pepper into potato mixture. Heat to boiling. Reduce heat to medium-low; cover and cook 15 to 20 minutes, stirring occasionally, until potatoes are tender and soup is slightly thickened.

4 Stir in remaining ingredients. Cover; cook 5 to 6 minutes longer, stirring occasionally, until chicken and peas are hot. Ladle soup into bowls; top each serving with pastry.

1 Serving: Calories 340; Total Fat 13g (Saturated Fat 6g; Trans Fat 0g); Cholesterol 75mg; Sodium 1310mg; Total Carbohydrate 32g (Dietary Fiber 4g); Protein 25g **Exchanges:** 2 Starch, 2½ Lean Meat, 1 Fat **Carbohydrate Choices:** 2

Time-Saver

For convenience, pick up the small amounts of carrot and celery at the salad bar in your grocery store.

Thai-Style Chicken Curry Soup

4 servings (1½ cups each)   PREP TIME 15 minutes   START TO FINISH 15 minutes

FAST

1 **carton (32 oz) chicken
   broth (4 cups)**

3 **tablespoons packed
   brown sugar**

2 **tablespoons soy sauce**

2 **tablespoons rice vinegar**

2 **teaspoons curry powder**

1 **small red bell pepper,
   coarsely chopped (½ cup)**

1 **small jalapeño chile,
   seeded, finely chopped
   (1 tablespoon)**

2 **cups chopped deli
   rotisserie chicken
   (from 2-lb chicken)**

2 **tablespoons chopped
   fresh cilantro, if desired**

1 In 3-quart saucepan, stir together all ingredients except chicken and cilantro. Heat to boiling over medium-high heat. Reduce heat to medium; simmer uncovered 3 to 5 minutes or until bell pepper is crisp-tender.

2 Stir in chicken. Cook 1 to 2 minutes longer or until chicken is hot. Just before serving, add cilantro.

1 Serving: Calories 210; Total Fat 7g (Saturated Fat 2g; Trans Fat 0g); Cholesterol 60mg; Sodium 1770mg; Total Carbohydrate 14g (Dietary Fiber 0g); Protein 25g **Exchanges:** 1 Other Carbohydrate, 3 Lean Meat **Carbohydrate Choices:** 1

Southwestern Chicken Rice Soup

3 servings (1½ cups each)   PREP TIME **25 minutes**   START TO FINISH **25 minutes**

FAST

2 **flour tortillas for burritos (8 inch; from 11.5-oz package)**

1 **cup cubed cooked chicken**

6 **medium green onions, chopped (⅓ cup)**

1 **can (19 oz) ready-to-serve tomato basil soup**

1¾ **cups chicken broth (from 32-oz carton)**

¾ **cup uncooked instant white rice**

1 **teaspoon chopped fresh cilantro**

2 **teaspoons lime juice**

1 Heat oven to 400°F. Cut tortillas into ¼-inch-wide strips; cut into 2- to 3-inch lengths. Place on ungreased cookie sheet. Bake 6 to 8 minutes or until browned.

2 Meanwhile, in 1½-quart saucepan, mix chicken, onions, soup and broth. Heat to boiling. Stir in rice; remove from heat. Cover; let stand 5 minutes.

3 Stir cilantro and lime juice into soup. If necessary, simmer 5 minutes to heat thoroughly, stirring occasionally. Top each serving with tortilla strips.

1 Serving: Calories 340; Total Fat 7g (Saturated Fat 2g; Trans Fat 0g); Cholesterol 40mg; Sodium 1160mg; Total Carbohydrate 48g (Dietary Fiber 2g); Protein 22g **Exchanges:** 2½ Starch, ½ Other Carbohydrate, 2 Lean Meat **Carbohydrate Choices:** 3

Time-Saver

The crispy flour tortilla strips that top this soup are delicious, but if you're in a hurry or don't want to heat the oven, you could top each serving with a few corn chips or broken tortilla chips instead.

Turkey–Wild Rice Soup

6 servings   PREP TIME 15 minutes   START TO FINISH 40 minutes

3 tablespoons butter
  or margarine

½ cup all-purpose flour

3½ cups reduced-sodium
  chicken broth (from
  32-oz carton)

1 package (8 oz) 98%
  fat-free oven-roasted
  turkey breast, cubed
  (about 2 cups)

2 cups water

2 tablespoons dried
  chopped onion

1 box (6 oz) original
  long-grain and wild rice
  mix (with seasoning
  packet)

2 cups fat-free half-and-half

1 In 5-quart Dutch oven, melt butter over medium heat. Stir in flour with whisk until well blended. Slowly stir in broth with whisk. Stir in turkey, water, onion, rice and contents of seasoning packet.

2 Heat to boiling over high heat, stirring occasionally. Reduce heat to medium-low; cover and simmer about 25 minutes or until rice is tender. Stir in half-and-half; heat just to boiling.

1 Serving: Calories 290; Total Fat 8g (Saturated Fat 4.5g; Trans Fat 0g); Cholesterol 40mg; Sodium 1200mg; Total Carbohydrate 40g (Dietary Fiber 1g); Protein 14g **Exchanges:** 2 Starch, ½ Other Carbohydrate, 1 Lean Meat, 1 Fat **Carbohydrate Choices:** 2½

Healthy Twist

Wild rice is really the seed of an aquatic grass and is considered a whole grain. It has a delicious nutty flavor and slightly chewy texture.

Asian Pork and Noodle Soup

5 servings   PREP TIME 30 minutes   START TO FINISH 30 minutes

FAST

1 **lb boneless pork loin, cut into ½-inch pieces**

2 **cloves garlic, finely chopped**

2 **teaspoons finely chopped gingerroot**

3½ **cups chicken broth (from 32-oz carton)**

2 **cups water**

2 **tablespoons soy sauce**

2 **cups uncooked fine egg noodles (4 oz)**

1 **medium carrot, sliced (½ cup)**

1 **small red bell pepper, chopped (½ cup)**

2 **cups fresh spinach leaves**

1 Spray 3-quart saucepan with cooking spray; heat over medium-high heat. Add pork, garlic and gingerroot; cook 3 to 5 minutes, stirring frequently, until pork is brown.

2 Stir in broth, water and soy sauce. Heat to boiling. Reduce heat; simmer uncovered 5 minutes.

3 Stir in noodles, carrot and bell pepper. Simmer uncovered about 10 minutes, stirring occasionally, until noodles are tender and pork is no longer pink in center. Stir in spinach; cook until hot.

1 Serving: Calories 230; Total Fat 6g (Saturated Fat 2g; Trans Fat 0g); Cholesterol 55mg; Sodium 1140mg; Total Carbohydrate 19g (Dietary Fiber 1g); Protein 25g **Exchanges:** 1 Starch, ½ Vegetable, 3 Very Lean Meat, 1 Fat **Carbohydrate Choices:** 1

Healthy Twist

This soup is nutrient-dense from the meat and all the vegetables. Plus green leafy vegetables such as spinach are a good source of vitamins and minerals.

Beef 'n Veggie Soup with Mozzarella

8 servings   PREP TIME 30 minutes   START TO FINISH 30 minutes

FAST

1 **lb lean (at least 80%) ground beef**

1 **large onion, chopped (1 cup)**

2 **cups frozen mixed vegetables**

1 **can (14.5 oz) diced tomatoes with green pepper, celery and onions, undrained**

4 **cups water**

5 **teaspoons beef bouillon granules**

1½ **teaspoons Italian seasoning**

¼ **teaspoon pepper**

1 **cup shredded mozzarella cheese (4 oz)**

1 In 4-quart saucepan or Dutch oven, cook beef and onion over medium-high heat 5 to 7 minutes, stirring occasionally, until beef is thoroughly cooked; drain.

2 Stir in remaining ingredients except cheese. Heat to boiling. Reduce heat; simmer uncovered 6 to 8 minutes, stirring occasionally, until vegetables are tender.

3 Sprinkle 2 tablespoons cheese in each of 8 soup bowls; fill bowls with soup.

1 Serving: Calories 200; Total Fat 9g (Saturated Fat 4.5g; Trans Fat 0.5g); Cholesterol 45mg; Sodium 790mg; Total Carbohydrate 13g (Dietary Fiber 3g); Protein 15g **Exchanges:** ½ Other Carbohydrate, 1 Vegetable, 2 Medium-Fat Meat **Carbohydrate Choices:** 1

Quick Variation

Make this soup your way with what's on hand. Use any frozen veggie, any variety of canned diced tomatoes, your favorite cheese and the herbs you like best.

Two-Potato Ham Chowder

5 servings (about 1¼ cups each)   PREP TIME 15 minutes   START TO FINISH 30 minutes

FAST

½ cup chopped leek or onion

2 cups reduced-sodium chicken broth (from 32-oz carton)

2 medium potatoes, peeled, each cut into 6 pieces

2 cups cubed (½ inch) peeled dark-orange sweet potatoes (about 2 medium)

1 cup diced cooked ham (from 8-oz package)

1 cup frozen sweet peas

2 tablespoons chopped fresh chives

½ teaspoon salt

¼ teaspoon pepper

1 cup half-and half or milk

1 Spray 3-quart saucepan with cooking spray; heat over medium heat. Add leek; cook and stir about 3 minutes or until softened. Increase heat to high. Add broth and white potatoes; heat to boiling. Reduce heat; cover and simmer 5 minutes.

2 Add sweet potatoes; cover and simmer about 10 minutes or until potatoes are tender when pierced with fork.

3 Using slotted spoon, remove white potatoes from saucepan; place in blender. With lid on saucepan, carefully drain off broth into blender, leaving leek and sweet potatoes in saucepan. Cover blender; puree potato mixture until smooth. Return mixture to saucepan.

4 Stir in remaining ingredients. Cook over medium heat about 8 minutes, stirring occasionally, until thoroughly heated.

1 Serving: Calories 240; Total Fat 8g (Saturated Fat 4.5g; Trans Fat 0g); Cholesterol 35mg; Sodium 900mg; Total Carbohydrate 28g (Dietary Fiber 4g); Protein 12g Exchanges: 1½ Starch, 1 Vegetable, ½ Very Lean Meat, ½ Lean Meat, 1 Fat Carbohydrate Choices: 2

Time-Saver

This is a great soup to take to work for lunch. Pour soup into microwavable containers. Cool slightly; cover and refrigerate. To eat, simply loosen the lid of the container and microwave until hot.

Bratwurst and Vegetable Soup

5 servings (about 1⅓ cups each)   PREP TIME 15 minutes   START TO FINISH 35 minutes

1   teaspoon caraway seed

1   medium baking potato, peeled, cut into ½-inch pieces (1 cup)

¾   cup fresh green beans (about 4 oz), cut into 1-inch pieces

1   cup ready-to-eat baby-cut carrots

¼   cup chopped fresh parsley

¼   teaspoon pepper

2   cups reduced-sodium beef broth

4   smoked beef bratwurst (from 12-oz package), cut into ½-inch-thick slices (about 1½ cups)

1   can (15.5 oz) great northern beans, drained

1   can (14.5 oz) organic diced tomatoes with garlic and onion, undrained

1 In 3-quart saucepan, cook and stir caraway seed 1 to 2 minutes over medium heat until toasted.

2 Stir in remaining ingredients. Increase heat to high; heat to boiling. Reduce heat; cover and simmer 15 to 20 minutes or until vegetables are tender.

1 Serving: Calories 320; Total Fat 13g (Saturated Fat 5g; Trans Fat 0g); Cholesterol 20mg; Sodium 1560mg; Total Carbohydrate 33g (Dietary Fiber 8g); Protein 16g **Exchanges:** 2 Starch, 1 Vegetable, 1 Medium-Fat Meat, 1½ Fat **Carbohydrate Choices:** 2

Quick Menu Idea

Pumpernickel bread or rolls would be perfect to serve with this German-inspired soup.

Italian Beef and Bean Soup

5 servings (about 1½ cups each)   PREP TIME 20 minutes   START TO FINISH 40 minutes

2 teaspoons all-purpose flour

¼ teaspoon salt

¼ teaspoon pepper

½ lb boneless beef round steak, cut into ½-inch cubes

1 tablespoon olive or canola oil

1 can (15 oz) cannellini beans, drained, rinsed

1 can (14.5 oz) diced tomatoes with basil, garlic and oregano, undrained

2 cups frozen Italian-blend vegetables (from 1-lb bag)

3 cups water

Grated Parmesan cheese, if desired

1 In 1-quart resealable food-storage plastic bag, place flour, salt and pepper; seal bag and shake until blended. Add beef; seal bag and shake until beef is evenly coated with flour mixture.

2 In 3-quart heavy saucepan or Dutch oven, heat oil over medium-high heat. Add beef; cook 4 to 5 minutes, stirring occasionally, until browned on all sides.

3 Stir in remaining ingredients except cheese. Heat to boiling. Reduce heat; simmer uncovered 15 to 20 minutes or until vegetables are tender. Serve with cheese.

1 Serving: Calories 230; Total Fat 5g (Saturated Fat 1g; Trans Fat 0g); Cholesterol 35mg; Sodium 260mg; Total Carbohydrate 25g (Dietary Fiber 6g); Protein 21g **Exchanges:** 1 Starch, 2 Vegetable, 2 Lean Meat **Carbohydrate Choices:** 1½

Healthy Twist

Lean cuts of beef (round steak, beef loin and sirloin) are lower in fat and saturated fat than fattier cuts such as rib-eye.

Quick Menu Idea

Add Italian breadsticks and a bagged salad for a quick and easy meal.

Old-Fashioned Beef-Vegetable Soup

14 servings (1½ cups each)   PREP TIME 30 minutes   START TO FINISH 4 hours

3 lb meaty cross-cut
   beef shank bones,
   cut into 3-inch pieces

10 cups water

3 tablespoons beef bouillon
   granules

1½ teaspoons salt

½ teaspoon pepper

½ teaspoon dried thyme
   leaves

2 dried bay leaves

4 cups vegetable juice

3 cups cubed potatoes
   (3 medium)

3 cups coarsely chopped
   cabbage

2 cups frozen small whole
   onions (from 1-lb bag)

2 cups cubed peeled
   rutabaga (1½ medium)

2 cups frozen cut green
   beans

4 medium carrots, sliced
   (2 cups)

3 medium stalks celery,
   sliced (1½ cups)

1 In 8-quart stockpot or Dutch oven, place beef bones and water. Heat to boiling. Reduce heat; cover and simmer 30 minutes. Skim off and discard any residue that rises to surface.

2 Stir in bouillon granules, salt, pepper, thyme and bay leaves. Heat to boiling. Reduce heat; cover and simmer 2 hours to 2 hours 30 minutes longer or until meat is tender.

3 Remove beef bones and bay leaves from broth. Skim and discard fat from broth. When bones are cool enough to handle, remove meat from bones; cut into bite-size pieces. Return meat to broth.

4 Stir in remaining ingredients. Heat to boiling. Reduce heat; cover and simmer 30 minutes or until vegetables are tender.

1 Serving: Calories 150; Total Fat 2g (Saturated Fat 0.5g; Trans Fat 0g); Cholesterol 35mg; Sodium 1030mg; Total Carbohydrate 17g (Dietary Fiber 3g); Protein 15g **Exchanges:** ½ Starch, 2 Vegetable, 1 Very Lean Meat, ½ Lean Meat **Carbohydrate Choices:** 1

Time-Saver

Serving soup to a crowd? Put the soup in a slow cooker to keep it warm, and set up a buffet so guests can serve themselves.

Chunky Tomato-Bean Soup

6 servings (1½ cups each)   PREP TIME 15 minutes   START TO FINISH 30 minutes

FAST

1   tablespoon olive or
    vegetable oil

1   large onion, chopped
    (1 cup)

2   medium carrots, chopped
    (1 cup)

⅓   cup oil-packed sun-dried
    tomatoes, cut into thin
    strips

2   cans (15 oz each)
    cannellini beans,
    undrained

2   cans (14.5 oz each)
    diced tomatoes with
    basil, garlic and oregano,
    undrained

1   carton (32 oz) chicken
    broth (4 cups)

¼   teaspoon dried thyme
    leaves

⅛   teaspoon pepper

½   cup shredded Asiago
    cheese (2 oz)

1 In 4-quart saucepan, heat oil over medium heat. Add onion and carrots; cook about 5 minutes, stirring occasionally, until softened.

2 Add remaining ingredients except cheese. Heat to boiling. Reduce heat; cook uncovered 10 to 15 minutes or until vegetables are tender. Top each serving with cheese.

1 Serving: Calories 330; Total Fat 8g (Saturated Fat 3g; Trans Fat 0g); Cholesterol 10mg; Sodium 1880mg; Total Carbohydrate 42g (Dietary Fiber 11g); Protein 21g **Exchanges:** 2½ Starch, 1 Vegetable, 1½ Medium-Fat Meat **Carbohydrate Choices:** 3

Healthy Twist

The cannellini beans make this a heartier soup and add some protein—it's a delicious meatless soup.

Quick Variation

This is an ideal quick meal for two but for four servings, just double the recipe—
be sure to use a 4-quart saucepan.

Creamy Southwestern Corn Chowder

2 servings (1¾ cups each)   PREP TIME 25 minutes   START TO FINISH 25 minutes

FAST

2 tablespoons butter
or margarine

1 medium onion, chopped
(½ cup)

¼ cup all-purpose flour

1¾ cups chicken broth
(from 32-oz carton)

½ teaspoon salt

¼ teaspoon black pepper

⅛ teaspoon ground red
pepper (cayenne)

½ cup half-and-half

1 can (11 oz) southwestern
style corn, undrained

2 tablespoons chopped
fresh chives

Additional fresh chives,
if desired

1 In 2-quart saucepan, melt butter over medium heat. Add onion; cook 3 to 5 minutes, stirring occasionally, until tender.

2 Stir in flour with whisk until well blended. Gradually stir in broth with whisk. Stir in salt, black pepper and red pepper. Heat to boiling. Reduce heat; cook about 5 minutes, stirring frequently, until thickened.

3 Stir in half-and-half, corn and 2 tablespoons chives. Cook until thoroughly heated. Garnish each serving with additional chives.

1 Serving: Calories 450; Total Fat 20g (Saturated Fat 12g; Trans Fat 0.5g); Cholesterol 55mg; Sodium 1980mg; Total Carbohydrate 58g (Dietary Fiber 4g); Protein 10g **Exchanges:** 3 Starch, 1 Other Carbohydrate, 3½ Fat **Carbohydrate Choices:** 4

Cuban Black Bean Soup

2⅔ cups dried black beans (1 lb), sorted, rinsed

2 tablespoons vegetable oil

1 large onion, chopped (1 cup)

3 cloves garlic, finely chopped

3 cups beef-flavored broth (from 32-oz carton) or vegetable broth

3 cups water

¼ cup dark rum or apple cider

1 teaspoon liquid smoke

1½ teaspoons ground cumin

1½ teaspoons dried oregano leaves

1 medium green bell pepper, chopped (1 cup)

1 large tomato, chopped (1 cup)

1 In 4- or 5-quart Dutch oven, place beans and enough cold water to cover beans. Heat to boiling; boil uncovered 2 minutes. Remove from heat. Cover; let stand 1 hour. Drain and discard liquid. Set beans aside.

2 In same Dutch oven, heat oil over medium heat. Add onion and garlic; cook, stirring occasionally, until onion is tender.

3 Stir in remaining ingredients and reserved beans. Heat to boiling; boil 2 minutes. Reduce heat to low; cover and simmer about 2 hours or until beans are tender.

4 Carefully pour soup into blender. Cover; blend until almost smooth.

1 Serving: Calories 360; Total Fat 6g (Saturated Fat 1g; Trans Fat 0g); Cholesterol 0mg; Sodium 520mg; Total Carbohydrate 54g (Dietary Fiber 19g); Protein 20g **Exchanges:** 3 Starch, ½ Other Carbohydrate, 1½ Very Lean Meat, ½ Fat **Carbohydrate Choices:** 3½

Quick Menu Idea

For an authentic garnish for this flavorful soup, sprinkle servings with diced red pepper and drizzle with sour cream.

Quick Variation

We like the peanuts and cilantro as a garnish but you can vary it to your taste. Cashews with fresh parsley are a nice option, or if you don't care for nuts, just sprinkle with chopped red and green bell pepper.

Curried Carrot Soup

6 servings (1 cup each)   PREP TIME 15 minutes   START TO FINISH 7 hours 25 minutes

SOUP

1⅔ cups chopped onions (about 3 medium)

1 tablespoon dried minced garlic

2 bags (1 lb each) frozen sliced carrots, thawed

1 to 2 tablespoons curry powder

⅛ teaspoon crushed red pepper flakes

¼ teaspoon salt

1 carton (32 oz) reduced-sodium chicken broth (4 cups)

1 cup half-and-half

GARNISHES, IF DESIRED

Chopped dry-roasted peanuts

Chopped fresh cilantro or parsley

1 Spray 3½- to 4-quart slow cooker with cooking spray. In slow cooker, mix all soup ingredients except half-and-half.

2 Cover; cook on Low heat setting 7 to 9 hours.

3 Strain cooked vegetables from cooking liquid, reserving liquid. In blender or food processor, place vegetables. Cover; blend until smooth. Return vegetable puree to slow cooker. Stir in 1½ cups of the reserved liquid and the half-and-half.

4 Cover; cook on Low heat setting about 10 minutes longer or until warm. Garnish each serving with peanuts and cilantro.

1 Serving: Calories 150; Total Fat 6g (Saturated Fat 3g; Trans Fat 0g); Cholesterol 15mg; Sodium 580mg; Total Carbohydrate 20g (Dietary Fiber 6g); Protein 4g **Exchanges:** ½ Other Carbohydrate, 2 Vegetable, 1½ Fat **Carbohydrate Choices:** 1

Time-Saver

Always use caution when blending any hot food in a blender or food processor. For either appliance, do not overfill. Blend vegetables in batches if necessary. For a blender, use the low speed and vent it by removing the center area of the cover so that any collected steam can escape. Or, try using an immersion blender to save time.

Edamame Corn Chowder

6 servings (1⅓ cups each) PREP TIME 25 minutes START TO FINISH 40 minutes

4 slices bacon, chopped

1 medium onion, chopped (½ cup)

2 tablespoons all-purpose flour

¾ teaspoon salt

¼ teaspoon pepper

4 cups milk

1 bag (12 oz) frozen shelled edamame (green) soybeans

1 can (14.75 oz) cream style corn

1 can (11 oz) whole kernel corn

4 cups frozen southern-style diced hash brown potatoes (from 32-oz bag), thawed

Chopped fresh parsley, if desired

1 In 4-quart saucepan, cook bacon over medium heat until crisp; drain on paper towel. Reserve 1 tablespoon drippings in saucepan. Cook onion in drippings about 2 minutes, stirring frequently, until soft.

2 Using whisk, stir in flour, salt and pepper. Cook and stir over medium-high heat. Stir in milk. Heat to boiling, stirring constantly; boil and stir 1 minute.

3 Stir in edamame, cream style corn, whole kernel corn, potatoes and cooked bacon. Heat to boiling. Reduce heat to low; cover and simmer 10 to 15 minutes or until potatoes are tender. Sprinkle each serving with parsley.

1 Serving: Calories 420; Total Fat 10g (Saturated Fat 3.5g; Trans Fat 0g); Cholesterol 20mg; Sodium 840mg; Total Carbohydrate 64g (Dietary Fiber 8g); Protein 19g **Exchanges:** 3½ Starch, 1½ Vegetable, 1 High-Fat Meat **Carbohydrate Choices:** 4

Greek Split Pea Soup

8 servings (about 1½ cups each)   PREP TIME 20 minutes   START TO FINISH 1 hour 30 minutes

- 1 bag (16 oz) dried split peas (about 2¼ cups)
- 2 large onions, coarsely chopped (2 cups)
- 3 medium stalks celery, coarsely chopped (about 1 cup)
- 8 cups water
- 2 medium red or yellow bell peppers, chopped (about 2 cups)
- ⅓ cup uncooked orzo or rosamarina pasta (about 2 oz)
- ¼ cup chopped fresh parsley
- 1 teaspoon salt
- 1 teaspoon dried oregano leaves
- ¼ teaspoon pepper
- ½ cup crumbled feta cheese (2 oz)
- ½ cup sliced ripe olives

1 In 5-quart Dutch oven, heat peas, onions, celery and water to boiling. Reduce heat to low; cover and simmer 1 hour to 1 hour 10 minutes or until peas are tender.

2 Puree pea mixture with immersion blender. (Or in blender, pour about 3 cups soup mixture into blender; cover and blend until smooth. Pour into heatproof pitcher or bowl. Repeat with remaining pea mixture; return to Dutch oven.)

3 Stir in bell peppers, orzo, parsley, salt, oregano and pepper. Cook over medium heat about 15 minutes, stirring frequently so orzo does not stick to pan, or until orzo is tender. Top each serving with cheese and olives.

1 Serving: Calories 260; Total Fat 4g (Saturated Fat 1.5g; Trans Fat 0g); Cholesterol 10mg; Sodium 500mg; Total Carbohydrate 41g (Dietary Fiber 17g); Protein 14g **Exchanges:** 2 Starch, 2 Vegetable, ½ Medium-Fat Meat **Carbohydrate Choices:** 3

Quick Menu Idea

The toppings really add to the flavor and seasoning level of this soup, so don't be tempted to add salt to the soup until you've tried it with the toppings first. A fresh fruit salad is a nice choice to serve with this hearty soup.

Harvest Vegetable Chowder

6 servings   PREP TIME 10 minutes   START TO FINISH 9 hours 10 minutes

2 large russet potatoes,
   cut into ¾-inch pieces
   (3 cups)

1 medium rutabaga or sweet
   potato, peeled, cut into
   ¾-inch pieces (2 cups)

3 medium stalks celery,
   cut into ½-inch slices
   (1½ cups)

1 large onion, coarsely
   chopped (1 cup)

4 cups water

4 teaspoons vegetable
   bouillon granules

2 cups any frozen vegetable
   blend (such as broccoli,
   cauliflower and carrots),
   thawed

1 can (10¾ oz) condensed
   Cheddar cheese soup

1 cup milk

1 teaspoon dried dill weed

2 cups shredded Colby or
   Cheddar cheese (8 oz)

   Freshly ground pepper,
   if desired

1 Spray 4- to 5-quart slow cooker with cooking spray. In slow cooker, mix potatoes, rutabaga, celery, onion, water and bouillon granules.

2 Cover; cook on Low heat setting 8 hours.

3 Stir in vegetable blend, soup, milk and dill weed. Cover; cook on Low heat setting 1 hour longer or until vegetables are tender and chowder is hot. Sprinkle each serving with cheese and pepper.

1 Serving: Calories 340; Total Fat 17g (Saturated Fat 10g; Trans Fat 1g); Cholesterol 45mg; Sodium 1310mg; Total Carbohydrate 30g (Dietary Fiber 4g); Protein 16g **Exchanges:** 1½ Starch, 2 Vegetable, 1 High-Fat Meat, 1½ Fat **Carbohydrate Choices:** 2

Time-Saver

To quickly thaw frozen vegetables, place in colander or strainer; rinse with warm water until thawed. Drain well.

North Woods Wild Rice Soup

6 servings   PREP TIME 20 minutes   START TO FINISH 6 hours 40 minutes

2   **teaspoons vegetable oil**

1   **medium onion, chopped (½ cup)**

2   **medium carrots, diced (1 cup)**

2   **medium stalks celery, diced (1 cup)**

1   **cup diced smoked turkey (6 oz)**

½   **cup uncooked wild rice**

1   **teaspoon dried tarragon leaves**

¼   **teaspoon pepper**

3½   **cups chicken broth (from 32-oz carton)**

1   **cup frozen sweet peas, thawed**

1   **can (12 oz) evaporated fat-free milk**

⅓   **cup all-purpose flour**

1 In 10-inch skillet, heat oil over medium heat. Add onion; cook about 4 minutes, stirring occasionally, until tender.

2 Spray 3½- to 4-quart slow cooker with cooking spray. In slow cooker, mix onion, carrots, celery, turkey, wild rice, tarragon and pepper. Pour broth over top.

3 Cover; cook on Low heat setting 6 to 8 hours, stirring in peas during last 15 minutes of cooking.

4 In small bowl, mix milk and flour; stir into soup. Cover; cook on Low heat setting about 20 minutes longer or until thickened.

1 Serving: Calories 230; Total Fat 2.5g (Saturated Fat 0g; Trans Fat 0g); Cholesterol 25mg; Sodium 630mg; Total Carbohydrate 32g (Dietary Fiber 3g); Protein 19g **Exchanges:** 1 Starch, 1 Other Carbohydrate, 1 Vegetable, 2 Very Lean Meat **Carbohydrate Choices:** 2

Quick Menu Idea

Serve with whole-grain rolls or assorted crackers for a simple, hearty meal.

Tortilla Soup

6 servings   PREP TIME 30 minutes   START TO FINISH 45 minutes

6 soft corn tortillas (6 inch)

¼ cup vegetable oil

1 small onion, chopped (⅓ cup)

2 cloves garlic, finely chopped

1 medium Anaheim, poblano or jalapeño chile, seeded, chopped

1 carton (32 oz) reduced-sodium chicken broth (4 cups)

1 can (14.5 oz) organic fire roasted diced tomatoes, undrained

½ teaspoon coarse (kosher or sea) salt

1½ cups shredded cooked chicken

1 ripe medium avocado, pitted, peeled and cut into 1-inch slices

½ cup shredded Monterey Jack cheese (2 oz)

Chopped fresh cilantro, if desired

1 lime, cut into wedges

1 Cut tortillas in half; cut crosswise into ¼-inch strips. In 3-quart saucepan, heat oil over medium-high heat. Add tortilla strips; cook, one-third at a time, until light brown and crisp. Remove with slotted spoon to drain on paper towels.

2 Heat oil remaining in saucepan over medium-high heat. Add onion; cook 2 minutes, stirring frequently. Add garlic and chile; cook 2 to 3 minutes, stirring frequently, until vegetables are crisp-tender. Stir in broth, tomatoes and salt. Heat to boiling. Reduce heat; cover and simmer 15 minutes. Add chicken; heat until hot.

3 Divide half of tortilla strips among 6 soup bowls. Ladle in soup. Top with avocado and cheese; garnish with remaining tortilla strips and cilantro. Serve with lime wedges.

1 Serving: Calories 330; Total Fat 20g (Saturated Fat 4.5g; Trans Fat 0g); Cholesterol 40mg; Sodium 730mg; Total Carbohydrate 20g (Dietary Fiber 5g); Protein 17g **Exchanges:** 1 Starch, ½ Other Carbohydrate, 2 Lean Meat, 2½ Fat **Carbohydrate Choices:** 1

Quick Variation

You can substitute another cheese for the Monterey Jack—try Cheddar, Colby-Jack or Chihuahua (Mexican melting cheese, also known as asadero or Oaxaca).

Chicken Taco Stew in Bread Bowls

3 servings   PREP TIME 35 minutes   START TO FINISH 35 minutes

1 **can (11 oz) refrigerated crusty French loaf**

1 **package (6 oz) refrigerated cooked southwest-flavor chicken breast strips, coarsely chopped**

1 **can (15 oz) dark red kidney beans, drained, rinsed**

1 **can (10 oz) diced tomatoes with green chiles, undrained**

1 **cup frozen corn**

1 **cup chicken broth (from 32-oz carton)**

1 **tablespoon cornstarch**

½ **cup shredded Cheddar cheese (2 oz)**

1 Heat oven to 350°F. Spray cookie sheet with cooking spray. Cut dough into 3 equal pieces. Shape each into a ball, placing seam at bottom so dough is smooth on top. Place dough balls, seam side down, on cookie sheet.

2 Bake 18 to 22 minutes or until golden brown. Cool 5 minutes.

3 Meanwhile, in 2-quart saucepan, mix remaining ingredients except cheese. Cook over medium heat, stirring occasionally, until mixture boils and thickens.

4 Cut off top of each bread loaf. Lightly press center of bread down to form bowls. Place each bread bowl in shallow soup plate. Spoon about 1 cup stew into each bread bowl. Sprinkle with cheese. Place top of bread bowl next to filled bowl.

1 Serving: Calories 620; Total Fat 12g (Saturated Fat 6g; Trans Fat 0g); Cholesterol 45mg; Sodium 1400mg; Total Carbohydrate 90g (Dietary Fiber 9g); Protein 36g **Exchanges:** 4 Starch, 1½ Other Carbohydrate, 2 Vegetable, 3 Lean Meat **Carbohydrate Choices:** 6

Cheesy Chicken-Pasta Stew

4 servings   PREP TIME **20 minutes**   START TO FINISH **20 minutes**

FAST

1 **tablespoon butter or margarine**

1 **lb boneless skinless chicken breasts, cut into 1-inch pieces**

1 **cup milk**

1 **package (3 oz) cream cheese, cut into cubes**

1 **bag (24 oz) frozen pasta, broccoli, carrots & cheese sauce**

2 **tablespoons chopped fresh chives**

1 In 12-inch nonstick skillet, melt butter over medium-high heat. Add chicken; cook 4 to 5 minutes, stirring occasionally, until browned.

2 Stir in milk and cream cheese. Cook, stirring frequently, until cheese is melted. Stir in frozen pasta and vegetable mixture. Heat to boiling, stirring occasionally. Reduce heat; cover and simmer 3 to 7 minutes or until pasta and vegetables are tender. Sprinkle each serving with chives.

1 Serving: Calories 450; Total Fat 18g (Saturated Fat 8g; Trans Fat 0g); Cholesterol 105mg; Sodium 910mg; Total Carbohydrate 37g (Dietary Fiber 2g); Protein 35g **Exchanges:** 2 Starch, ½ Other Carbohydrate, 4 Lean Meat, 1 Fat **Carbohydrate Choices:** 2½

Quick Variation

Chopped chives add a fresh taste and pretty color to this stew. If you don't have chives on hand, use chopped green onions or parsley instead.

French Peasant Chicken Stew

6 servings (1⅓ cups each)   PREP TIME 35 minutes   START TO FINISH 35 minutes

2   cups ready-to-eat baby-cut
carrots

1   cup sliced fresh mushrooms
(about 3 oz)

4   small red potatoes,
cut into quarters

1   jar (12 oz) chicken gravy

1¾ cups reduced-sodium
chicken broth (from
32-oz carton)

1   teaspoon dried thyme
leaves

½   cup frozen sweet peas

1   deli rotisserie chicken
(2 lb), cut into serving
pieces

1 In 4-quart saucepan, mix all ingredients except peas and chicken.

2 Heat to boiling over medium-high heat. Reduce heat to medium-low; cover and simmer about 20 minutes, stirring occasionally, or until vegetables are tender.

3 Stir in peas and chicken. Cover; simmer about 5 minutes longer or until peas are tender and chicken is hot.

1 Serving: Calories 290; Total Fat 10g (Saturated Fat 2.5g; Trans Fat 0g); Cholesterol 75mg; Sodium 920mg; Total Carbohydrate 22g (Dietary Fiber 4g); Protein 28g **Exchanges:** 1½ Starch, 1 Vegetable, 3 Lean Meat **Carbohydrate Choices:** 1½

Spicy Thai Pork Stew

6 servings (about 1 cup each)   PREP TIME **30 minutes**   START TO FINISH **1 hour 35 minutes**

⅓ cup all-purpose flour

½ teaspoon garlic-pepper blend

4 boneless pork loin chops, 1 inch thick (1½ lb), cut into 1-inch cubes

3 tablespoons vegetable oil

1 bottle (11.5 oz) peanut sauce

1 cup chicken broth (from 32-oz carton)

1 teaspoon crushed red pepper flakes

2 cups cubed (1 inch) peeled butternut squash (about ¾ lb)

1 medium red bell pepper, cut into 1-inch pieces (1¼ cups)

4 oz fresh snow pea pods (1 cup), strings removed, cut diagonally in half

Hot cooked white rice, if desired

1 In 1-gallon plastic bag, shake flour and garlic-pepper blend to mix. Add pork to bag; shake to coat.

2 In 5-quart Dutch oven, heat oil over medium heat. Add coated pork; cook, stirring occasionally, until pork is evenly golden brown.

3 Stir in peanut sauce, broth and pepper flakes. Heat to boiling. Boil 1 minute, scraping brown bits off bottom of Dutch oven. Reduce heat to low; cover and simmer 30 minutes.

4 Add squash; cover and simmer 30 minutes or until pork and squash are tender.

5 Stir in bell pepper and pea pods. Simmer uncovered 5 to 7 minutes or until bell pepper is crisp-tender. Serve over hot cooked white rice.

1 Serving: Calories 480; Total Fat 30g (Saturated Fat 7g; Trans Fat 0g); Cholesterol 70mg; Sodium 350mg; Total Carbohydrate 19g (Dietary Fiber 3g); Protein 34g **Exchanges:** 1 Starch, ½ Vegetable, 4 Lean Meat, 3½ Fat **Carbohydrate Choices:** 1

Quick Menu Idea

Top each serving with chopped dry-roasted peanuts and then add chopped fresh cilantro, if desired.

Beef-Barley Stew

6 servings   PREP TIME 15 minutes   START TO FINISH 1 hour 25 minutes

1   lb extra-lean (at least 90%) ground beef

1   medium onion, chopped (½ cup)

2   cups beef-flavored broth (from 32-oz carton)

⅔   cup uncooked barley

2   teaspoons chopped fresh or ½ teaspoon dried oregano leaves

¼   teaspoon salt

¼   teaspoon pepper

1   can (14.5 oz) whole peeled tomatoes, undrained

1   can (8 oz) sliced water chestnuts, undrained

2   cups frozen mixed vegetables

1 Heat oven to 350°F. Heat 10-inch nonstick skillet over medium heat. Add beef and onion; cook 7 to 8 minutes, stirring occasionally, until beef is brown. Drain.

2 In ungreased 3-quart casserole, mix beef mixture and remaining ingredients except frozen vegetables, breaking up tomatoes.

3 Cover; bake 30 minutes. Stir in frozen vegetables. Cover; bake 30 to 40 minutes longer or until barley is tender.

1 Serving: Calories 280; Total Fat 7g (Saturated Fat 2.5g; Trans Fat 0g); Cholesterol 45mg; Sodium 590mg; Total Carbohydrate 34g (Dietary Fiber 8g); Protein 20g **Exchanges:** 1½ Starch, ½ Other Carbohydrate, 1 Vegetable, 2 Lean Meat **Carbohydrate Choices:** 2

Family-Favorite Stew

6 servings   PREP TIME 15 minutes   START TO FINISH 40 minutes

1   lb lean (at least 80%) ground beef or lean turkey

2   cups water

2   cans (14.5 oz each) diced tomatoes in herbs and olive oil, undrained

1   can (6 oz) tomato paste

1   bag (1 lb) frozen cauliflower, carrots and pea pods

2¼   cups Original Bisquick® mix

⅔   cup milk

1   tablespoon chopped fresh parsley

1 Heat oven to 425°F. In 4-quart ovenproof Dutch oven, cook beef over medium heat 8 to 10 minutes, stirring occasionally, until thoroughly cooked; drain. Stir in water, tomatoes, tomato paste and vegetables. Heat to boiling, stirring occasionally.

2 In medium bowl, stir Bisquick mix, milk and parsley until soft dough forms. Drop dough by 6 spoonfuls onto boiling beef mixture.

3 Bake uncovered 20 to 25 minutes or until biscuits are golden brown and stew is bubbly.

1 Serving: Calories 460; Total Fat 19g (Saturated Fat 5g; Trans Fat 2.5g); Cholesterol 50mg; Sodium 1520mg; Total Carbohydrate 52g (Dietary Fiber 5g); Protein 20g **Exchanges:** 2½ Starch, 1 Other Carbohydrate, ½ Vegetable, 1½ Lean Meat, 2½ Fat **Carbohydrate Choices:** 3½

Ground Beef Stew over Garlic Mashed Potatoes

4 servings   PREP TIME 25 minutes   START TO FINISH 25 minutes
FAST

½ **lb lean (at least 80%) ground beef**

1 **small onion, chopped (⅓ cup)**

1 **cup frozen mixed vegetables**

1 **can (14.5 oz) diced tomatoes, drained**

1 **jar (12 oz) beef gravy**

¼ **teaspoon dried marjoram leaves**

¼ **teaspoon pepper**

1⅓ **cups water**

2 **tablespoons butter or margarine**

½ **teaspoon garlic salt**

⅓ **cup milk**

1 **cup mashed potatoes (dry)**

1 **tablespoon chopped fresh parsley**

1 In 12-inch nonstick skillet, cook beef and onion over medium-high heat 5 to 7 minutes, stirring frequently, until beef is thoroughly cooked; drain.

2 Stir in mixed vegetables, tomatoes, gravy, marjoram and pepper. Heat to boiling. Reduce heat to low; simmer uncovered 8 to 10 minutes, stirring occasionally, until vegetables are tender.

3 Meanwhile, in 2-quart saucepan, heat water, butter and garlic salt to boiling. Remove from heat; add milk. Stir in potatoes and parsley. Let stand about 30 seconds or until liquid is absorbed.

4 Fluff potatoes with fork. Serve stew over potatoes.

1 Serving: Calories 350; Total Fat 15g (Saturated Fat 7g; Trans Fat 1g); Cholesterol 55mg; Sodium 850mg; Total Carbohydrate 35g (Dietary Fiber 4g); Protein 18g **Exchanges:** 1 Starch, 1 Other Carbohydrate, 1 Vegetable, 2 Medium-Fat Meat, 1 Fat **Carbohydrate Choices:** 2

Quick Variation

Oregano can be used in place of the marjoram; both are mint-family herbs from the Mediterranean mountains.

Rigatoni Pizza Stew

4 servings   PREP TIME 30 minutes   START TO FINISH 30 minutes

FAST

1 lb Italian sausage links, cut into ¼-inch slices

1 can (14.5 oz) Italian-style stewed tomatoes, undrained

1¾ cups beef-flavored broth (from 32-oz carton)

1 cup water

¼ cup tomato paste with Italian herbs (from 6-oz can)

2 medium carrots, cut into ½-inch slices (1 cup)

1 medium onion, coarsely chopped (½ cup)

1½ cups uncooked rigatoni pasta (4½ oz)

1 medium zucchini, cut in half lengthwise, then cut crosswise into ¼-inch slices (2 cups)

½ cup shredded mozzarella cheese (2 oz)

1 Spray 4-quart saucepan or Dutch oven with cooking spray; heat over medium heat. Add sausage; cook, stirring occasionally, until no longer pink. Drain.

2 Stir in tomatoes, broth, water, tomato paste, carrots and onion. Heat to boiling. Reduce heat to medium-low; cook uncovered about 10 minutes or until carrots are tender.

3 Stir in pasta and zucchini. Cook uncovered 10 to 12 minutes, stirring occasionally, until pasta is tender. Sprinkle each serving with 2 tablespoons cheese.

1 Serving: Calories 560; Total Fat 27g (Saturated Fat 10g; Trans Fat 0g); Cholesterol 55mg; Sodium 2170mg; Total Carbohydrate 52g (Dietary Fiber 5g); Protein 28g **Exchanges:** 2½ Starch, 3 Vegetable, 2 High-Fat Meat, 2 Fat **Carbohydrate Choices:** 3½

Quick Variation

Turkey Italian sausage can be used in place of the regular sausage. Or for the pepperoni pizza lovers in your family, substitute sliced pepperoni; skip Step 1 and stir the pepperoni into the tomato mixture in Step 2.

Catfish Stew in Biscuit Bowls

8 servings   PREP TIME 35 minutes   START TO FINISH 35 minutes

1 can (16.3 oz) large refrigerated original or buttermilk flaky biscuits

2 slices bacon

1 medium onion, chopped (½ cup)

1 bag (12 oz) frozen mixed vegetables

1 jar (2.5 oz) sliced mushrooms, drained

½ cup milk

1 can (10¾ oz) condensed cream of celery soup

¼ teaspoon hot pepper sauce

½ teaspoon garlic powder

¼ teaspoon dried thyme leaves

¼ teaspoon pepper

1 lb catfish fillets, cut into 1-inch pieces

1 Heat oven to 350°F. On ungreased large cookie sheet, turn 8 (6-oz) custard cups upside-down; spray outsides of cups with cooking spray. Separate dough into 8 biscuits; press each to form 6-inch round. Press 1 round over bottom and around side of each cup, forming bowl.

2 Bake 15 to 18 minutes or until golden brown.

3 Meanwhile, in 3-quart saucepan, cook bacon over medium heat until crisp; drain on paper towel. Crumble bacon; set aside. Reserve 1 tablespoon drippings in saucepan. Cook onion in drippings 2 to 3 minutes, stirring occasionally, until tender.

4 Stir in all remaining ingredients except catfish and bacon. Heat to boiling. Reduce heat to medium; stir in catfish. Cook uncovered about 10 minutes, stirring occasionally, until fish flakes easily with fork.

5 Carefully remove biscuit bowls from custard cups; place on serving plates or in shallow bowls. Spoon stew into biscuit bowls. Garnish with crumbled bacon.

1 Serving: Calories 370; Total Fat 16g (Saturated Fat 3.5g; Trans Fat 3.5g); Cholesterol 45mg; Sodium 970mg; Total Carbohydrate 37g (Dietary Fiber 3g); Protein 19g **Exchanges:** 1½ Starch, ½ Other Carbohydrate, 1 Vegetable, 2 Medium-Fat Meat, 1 Fat **Carbohydrate Choices:** 2½

Quick Variation

You can substitute other fish fillets for the catfish in this stew, but choose one that is mild flavored and delicate to medium in texture, such as orange roughy or sole.

Chapter Three

Simple Skillet Meals

Bow-Ties with Chicken and Asparagus

6 servings (1½ cups each) PREP TIME 25 minutes START TO FINISH 25 minutes

FAST

3 cups uncooked bow-tie (farfalle) pasta (8 oz)

1 tablespoon canola oil

1 lb boneless skinless chicken breasts, cut into 1-inch pieces

1 lb fresh asparagus spears, trimmed, cut into 1-inch pieces

1 red bell pepper, sliced

2 cloves garlic, finely chopped

1 cup reduced-sodium chicken broth (from 32-oz carton)

1 tablespoon cornstarch

4 medium green onions, sliced (¼ cup)

2 tablespoons chopped fresh basil leaves

¼ cup finely shredded Parmesan cheese (1 oz)

Grated lemon peel

1 Cook and drain pasta as directed on package, omitting salt.

2 Meanwhile, in 12-inch nonstick skillet, heat oil over medium-high heat. Add chicken; cook 2 minutes, stirring occasionally. Stir in asparagus, bell pepper and garlic. Cook 6 to 8 minutes, stirring occasionally, until chicken is no longer pink in center and vegetables are tender.

3 In small bowl, gradually stir broth into cornstarch. Stir in onions and basil. Stir cornstarch mixture into chicken mixture. Cook and stir 1 to 2 minutes or until thickened and bubbly. If desired, season with salt.

4 Toss chicken mixture with cooked pasta. Sprinkle with cheese and lemon peel.

1 Serving: Calories 330; Total Fat 7g (Saturated Fat 2g; Trans Fat 0g); Cholesterol 50mg; Sodium 360mg; Total Carbohydrate 38g (Dietary Fiber 3g); Protein 27g **Exchanges:** 2 Starch, 2 Vegetable, 2½ Very Lean Meat, 1 Fat **Carbohydrate Choices:** 2½

Quick Variation

You could use frozen asparagus instead of the fresh. Use one 9- or 10-ounce package and you'll have just the right amount.

Breaded Chicken with Tomatoes

4 servings   PREP TIME 30 minutes   START TO FINISH 30 minutes

FAST

- **4 boneless skinless chicken breasts (1 lb)**
- **½ cup unseasoned crispy bread crumbs**
- **¼ cup grated Parmesan cheese**
- **½ teaspoon salt**
- **¼ teaspoon pepper**
- **3 tablespoons olive or vegetable oil**
- **3 large tomatoes, chopped (3 cups)**
- **2 medium green onions, chopped (2 tablespoons)**
- **1 clove garlic, finely chopped**
- **1 tablespoon balsamic vinegar**
- **1 tablespoon chopped fresh oregano leaves**
- **Fresh oregano sprigs, if desired**

1 Between pieces of plastic wrap or waxed paper, place each chicken breast smooth side down; gently pound with flat side of meat mallet or rolling pin until about ¼ inch thick. In shallow bowl or pie plate, mix bread crumbs, cheese, salt and pepper. Coat chicken with crumb mixture, pressing to coat well on both sides.

2 In 12-inch nonstick skillet, heat 2 tablespoons of the oil over medium-high heat. Add chicken; cook 6 to 10 minutes, turning once, until golden brown on outside and no longer pink in center. Remove chicken from skillet; cover to keep warm.

3 To skillet, add remaining 1 tablespoon oil. Add 2 cups of the tomatoes, the onions and garlic; cook and stir 2 minutes. Stir in vinegar; cook 30 seconds longer. Remove from heat; stir in remaining 1 cup tomatoes and the oregano. Serve over chicken. Garnish with fresh oregano sprigs.

1 Serving: Calories 350; Total Fat 17g (Saturated Fat 3.5g; Trans Fat 0g); Cholesterol 75mg; Sodium 490mg; Total Carbohydrate 17g (Dietary Fiber 2g); Protein 30g **Exchanges:** ½ Starch, ½ Other Carbohydrate, 4 Very Lean Meat, 3 Fat Carbohydrate Choices: 1

Chicken and Pasta with Creamy Basil Sauce

4 servings (1¾ cups each)   PREP TIME 30 minutes   START TO FINISH 30 minutes

FAST

3 cups uncooked bow-tie
(farfalle) pasta (6 oz)

2 cups fresh broccoli florets

1 tablespoon canola oil

1 lb boneless skinless
chicken breasts, cut into
1-inch pieces

½ teaspoon garlic-pepper
blend

1 cup chicken broth
(from 32-oz carton)

1 tablespoon cornstarch

1 teaspoon sugar

1 small red bell pepper,
chopped (½ cup)

¾ cup fat free plain yogurt
(from 2-lb container)

3 to 4 tablespoons chopped
fresh or 1 teaspoon dried
basil leaves

1 Cook pasta as directed on package, adding broccoli during last 4 minutes of cooking; drain.

2 Meanwhile, in 12-inch nonstick skillet, heat oil over medium-high heat. Sprinkle chicken with garlic-pepper blend. Add chicken to skillet; cook about 3 minutes, stirring occasionally, until no longer pink in center.

3 In small bowl, mix broth, cornstarch and sugar. Add broth mixture and bell pepper to skillet; cook about 3 minutes or until sauce is thickened. Stir in pasta, broccoli, yogurt and basil. Heat over low heat just until hot (do not boil).

1 Serving: Calories 640; Total Fat 10g (Saturated Fat 2g; Trans Fat 0g); Cholesterol 70mg; Sodium 760mg; Total Carbohydrate 93g (Dietary Fiber 6g); Protein 45g **Exchanges:** 5½ Starch, ½ Other Carbohydrate, ½ Vegetable, 2½ Very Lean Meat, 1 Lean Meat, ½ Fat **Carbohydrate Choices:** 6

Time-Saver

Look for packages of precut chicken in the meat department or with the frozen foods.

Quick Variation

Great substitutions for the recipe include frozen broccoli florets instead of fresh, rotini pasta instead of bow-tie pasta, and sour cream instead of yogurt. So go ahead and use what you have on hand!

Chicken Patties Parmigiana

4 servings (2 patties each)   PREP TIME 20 minutes   START TO FINISH 20 minutes

FAST

½ **cup Italian style dry bread crumbs**

1 **egg**

2 **tablespoons milk**

2 **tablespoons grated Parmesan cheese**

½ **teaspoon garlic salt**

2 **cups finely chopped deli rotisserie chicken (from 2-lb chicken)**

¼ **cup vegetable oil**

1 **cup tomato pasta sauce (from 25.5-oz jar), heated**

½ **cup shredded mozzarella cheese (2 oz)**

1 In medium bowl, mix bread crumbs, egg, milk, Parmesan cheese and garlic salt. Stir in chicken. Shape chicken mixture by about ¼ cupfuls into 8 (3-inch) patties.

2 In 12-inch nonstick skillet, heat oil over medium-high heat. Add patties; cook 4 to 5 minutes, turning once, until golden brown. Drain on paper towels.

3 Serve patties topped with pasta sauce and mozzarella cheese.

1 Serving: Calories 420; Total Fat 23g (Saturated Fat 6g; Trans Fat 0g); Cholesterol 125mg; Sodium 1140mg; Total Carbohydrate 23g (Dietary Fiber 1g); Protein 29g **Exchanges:** 1½ Starch, 3½ Lean Meat, 2½ Fat **Carbohydrate Choices:** 1½

Quick Menu Idea

Add a loaf of crusty bread, some pasta on the side and a tossed salad for a satisfying Italian-style meal.

Chicken and Ravioli Carbonara

4 servings   PREP TIME 30 minutes   START TO FINISH 30 minutes

FAST

2 **tablespoons Italian dressing**

1 **lb boneless skinless chicken breasts, cut into ½-inch strips**

¾ **cup chicken broth (from 32-oz carton)**

1 **package (9 oz) refrigerated cheese-filled ravioli**

½ **cup half-and-half**

4 **slices bacon, crisply cooked, crumbled**

   Shredded Parmesan cheese, if desired

   Chopped fresh parsley, if desired

1 In 10-inch skillet, heat dressing over high heat. Add chicken; cook 2 to 4 minutes, turning occasionally, until brown.

2 Add broth and ravioli to skillet. Heat to boiling. Reduce heat to medium; cook uncovered about 4 minutes or until ravioli are tender and almost all broth has evaporated.

3 Stir in half-and-half. Reduce heat; simmer uncovered 3 to 5 minutes or until chicken is no longer pink, and sauce is hot and desired consistency (cook longer for a thicker sauce). Sprinkle with bacon, cheese and parsley.

1 Serving: Calories 450; Total Fat 20g (Saturated Fat 8g; Trans Fat 0g); Cholesterol 125mg; Sodium 790mg; Total Carbohydrate 30g (Dietary Fiber 1g); Protein 38g **Exchanges:** 2 Starch, 4 Very Lean Meat, ½ Lean Meat, 3 Fat **Carbohydrate Choices:** 2

Quick Menu Idea

For a splash of vibrant color, cut one orange or red bell pepper into ¼-inch strips and add to the skillet with the broth and ravioli. Then serve the dish with a fresh green salad topped with Italian dressing.

Chicken Curry

FAST

1 **package (8.8 oz) microwavable long-grain white rice**

1 **package (10 oz) refrigerated cooked chicken breast cuts**

1 **cup frozen sweet peas**

1 **cup yellow or red curry sauce**

2 **teaspoons curry powder**

1 Cook rice in microwave as directed on package.

2 Meanwhile, in 10-inch skillet, cook remaining ingredients over medium heat about 5 minutes, stirring occasionally, until hot. Serve chicken mixture over cooked rice.

1 Serving: Calories 250; Total Fat 3.5g (Saturated Fat 0.5g; Trans Fat 0g); Cholesterol 55mg; Sodium 420mg; Total Carbohydrate 31g (Dietary Fiber 2g); Protein 23g **Exchanges:** 2 Starch, 2 Very Lean Meat, ½ Fat **Carbohydrate Choices:** 2

Easy Chicken Panfries

With just a few ingredients and in less than 20 minutes, you can have great-tasting chicken on the table—it's that easy and that quick.

✱ Start with 4 boneless skinless chicken breasts
✱ Flatten to ¼-inch thickness between sheets of plastic wrap or waxed paper using flat side of meat mallet or rolling pin.
✱ Use a 12-inch nonstick skillet and follow directions below using medium heat; chicken is done when juice of chicken is clear when center of thickest part is cut (at least 165°F).

1 Buffalo Chicken: Heat 1 tablespoon vegetable oil in skillet. Add chicken; brown both sides. Pour ½ cup buffalo-chicken-wing–flavored hot sauce evenly over chicken; turn to coat. Cook about 8 minutes, turning once. During last 2 to 3 minutes of cooking, sprinkle each breast with about 2 teaspoons crumbled blue cheese; cover skillet to melt cheese.

2 Caesar-Feta Chicken: Heat ¼ cup vinaigrette-style Caesar dressing in skillet. Add chicken; cook about 10 minutes, turning once. During last 2 to 3 minutes of cooking, sprinkle chicken with 1 cup cut-up seeded tomato and ½ cup crumbled feta cheese; cover skillet to soften cheese.

3 Fresh Herb Chicken: Heat 1 tablespoon butter in skillet. Add chicken; brown both sides. Add ¼ cup dry white wine or chicken broth, 1 tablespoon each chopped fresh basil, chives and dill and ¼ teaspoon garlic salt. Cook about 8 minutes, turning once.

4 Italian Chicken and Peppers: Heat ¼ cup vinaigrette-style Italian dressing in skillet. Add chicken; cook about 10 minutes, turning once. During last 5 minutes of cooking, add 2 small bell peppers (any color), cut into strips; stir once or twice.

5 Pecan-Maple Chicken: Melt 2 tablespoons butter with ½ teaspoon salt in skillet. Add chicken; brown both sides. Add 2 tablespoons pure maple syrup and ½ cup pecan halves. Cook about 8 minutes, turning chicken once and pecans twice.

6 Ranch Chicken: Heat 2 tablespoons vegetable oil in skillet. Brush chicken with ¼ cup ranch dressing; coat evenly with ⅓ cup Italian style crispy bread crumbs. Cook about 10 minutes, turning once.

Chicken Milano

4 servings   PREP TIME 25 minutes   START TO FINISH 25 minutes

FAST

2 **tablespoons all-purpose flour**

1 **cup unseasoned crispy bread crumbs**

1 **egg**

4 **boneless skinless chicken breasts (about 1¼ lb)**

3 **tablespoons olive or vegetable oil**

2 **teaspoons red wine vinegar**

⅛ **teaspoon salt**

4 **cups tightly packed arugula leaves**

½ **cup diced tomato**

1 **medium red onion, cut in half lengthwise, then cut into thin slices**

¼ **cup crumbled tomato-basil feta cheese (1 oz)**

1 On separate plates, place flour and bread crumbs. In medium bowl, beat egg with fork. Coat both sides of chicken with flour. Dip chicken into beaten egg, then coat well with bread crumbs.

2 In 12-inch nonstick skillet, heat 2 tablespoons oil over medium heat. Add chicken; cook 8 to 10 minutes, turning once, until juice is clear when center of thickest part is cut (at least 165°F) and coating is golden brown.

3 Meanwhile, in small bowl, beat remaining 1 tablespoon oil, the vinegar and salt with whisk. In medium bowl, mix arugula, tomato and onion. Pour dressing over salad and toss to coat.

4 Serve salad topped with chicken and sprinkled with cheese.

1 Serving: Calories 450; Total Fat 23g (Saturated Fat 3.5g; Trans Fat 0g); Cholesterol 145mg; Sodium 680mg; Total Carbohydrate 22g (Dietary Fiber 0g); Protein 37g **Exchanges:** 1½ Starch, 4½ Very Lean Meat, 4 Fat **Carbohydrate Choices:** 1½

Time-Saver

Short on time? Use 2 tablespoons purchased red wine vinaigrette dressing instead of making your own.

Chicken and Noodles Skillet

4 servings (1¼ cups each)   PREP TIME 40 minutes   START TO FINISH 40 minutes

1   **tablespoon vegetable oil**

1   **lb boneless skinless chicken breasts, cut into bite-size pieces**

1   **medium onion, chopped (½ cup)**

1   **cup ready-to-eat baby-cut carrots, cut lengthwise in half**

1   **cup frozen cut broccoli**

1   **cup uncooked egg noodles (2 oz)**

1¾ **cups chicken broth (from 32-oz carton)**

1   **can (10¾ oz) condensed cream of chicken soup**

   Chopped fresh parsley, if desired

1 In 12-inch nonstick skillet, heat oil over medium-high heat. Add chicken and onion; cook 6 to 8 minutes, stirring frequently, until browned and onion is just tender.

2 Stir in remaining ingredients except parsley. Heat to boiling. Reduce heat; cover and simmer 10 minutes. Uncover and simmer 5 to 8 minutes longer, stirring occasionally, until chicken is no longer pink in center and noodles are tender. Sprinkle with parsley.

1 Serving: Calories 340; Total Fat 13g (Saturated Fat 3.5g; Trans Fat 0g); Cholesterol 85mg; Sodium 1080mg; Total Carbohydrate 24g (Dietary Fiber 3g); Protein 32g **Exchanges:** 1 Starch, 2 Vegetable, 3½ Lean Meat, ½ Fat **Carbohydrate Choices:** 1½

Time-Saver

Using one 9-ounce package of frozen diced cooked chicken breasts will reduce the cooking time. Be sure to thaw the chicken first.

Easy Chicken with Tomatoes and Spinach

4 servings   PREP TIME 5 minutes   START TO FINISH 35 minutes

1 **tablespoon olive or vegetable oil**

4 **boneless skinless chicken breasts (about 1¼ lb)**

1 **clove garlic, finely chopped**

½ **teaspoon dried oregano leaves**

½ **teaspoon seasoned salt**

¼ **teaspoon pepper**

¼ **cup dry white wine or water**

2 **medium plum (Roma) tomatoes, sliced (about 1 cup)**

1 **bag (6 oz) fresh baby spinach leaves (about 3½ cups)**

1 In 12-inch nonstick skillet, heat oil over medium heat. Sprinkle chicken with garlic, oregano, salt, and pepper. Add chicken to skillet; cook 15 to 20 minutes, turning once, until juice of chicken is clear when center of thickest part is cut (at least 165°F).

2 Stir in wine. Top chicken with tomato slices. Cover; cook 2 to 3 minutes or until tomatoes are thoroughly heated.

3 Top tomatoes with spinach. Cover; cook 2 to 3 minutes longer or until spinach is wilted.

1 Serving: Calories 230; Total Fat 8g (Saturated Fat 2g; Trans Fat 0g); Cholesterol 90mg; Sodium 270mg; Total Carbohydrate 3g (Dietary Fiber 1g); Protein 33g **Exchanges:** ½ Vegetable, 2 Very Lean Meat, 2½ Lean Meat **Carbohydrate Choices:** 0

Quick Menu Idea

Brown rice is perfect to serve with this slightly saucy dish. Be sure to spoon some of the sauce over the rice. Then add a side of broccoli to finish the meal.

Creamy Asparagus-Chicken Bow-Ties

4 servings PREP TIME 30 minutes START TO FINISH 30 minutes

FAST

4 cups uncooked bow-tie (farfalle) pasta (8 oz)

8 oz fresh asparagus, cut into 1-inch pieces, or 1 box (9 oz) frozen cut asparagus

1 package (8 oz) sliced fresh mushrooms (3 cups)

1 container (8 oz) chive-and-onion cream cheese spread

¼ cup grated Parmesan cheese

⅓ cup milk

2 cups bite-size strips deli rotisserie chicken (from 2-lb chicken)

Additional grated Parmesan cheese, if desired

1 Cook pasta as directed on package, adding asparagus and mushrooms for the last 5 minutes of cooking. Drain and return to saucepan.

2 In small bowl, mix cream cheese, ¼ cup Parmesan cheese and the milk until smooth. Stir cheese mixture and chicken into pasta mixture.

3 Cook over medium heat about 2 minutes, stirring gently, until pasta is evenly coated with sauce and mixture is thoroughly heated. Serve with additional Parmesan cheese.

1 Serving: Calories 580; Total Fat 25g (Saturated Fat 13g; Trans Fat 0.5g); Cholesterol 120mg; Sodium 1070mg; Total Carbohydrate 52g (Dietary Fiber 5g); Protein 37g **Exchanges:** 3 Starch, 1 Vegetable, 4 Lean Meat, 2 Fat **Carbohydrate Choices:** 3½

Healthy Twist

Trim a bit of the fat by using reduced-fat chive-and-onion cream cheese.

Quick Variation

If you have cooked turkey on hand, go ahead and use it instead of chicken.

Easy Chicken and Garden Veggies

4 servings   PREP TIME 35 minutes   START TO FINISH 35 minutes

- **4 slices bacon, cut into ½-inch pieces**
- **4 boneless skinless chicken breasts (about 1¼ lb)**
- **½ teaspoon garlic salt**
- **¼ teaspoon coarsely ground pepper**
- **¼ cup water**
- **8 oz fresh green beans, trimmed (leave whole)**
- **1 medium yellow bell pepper, cut into ½-inch pieces**
- **2 medium plum (Roma) tomatoes, cut lengthwise in half, then sliced (about 1 cup)**
- **½ cup balsamic vinaigrette dressing or Italian dressing**

1 In 12-inch nonstick skillet, cook bacon over medium heat 3 to 4 minutes, stirring occasionally, until crisp.

2 Sprinkle both sides of chicken with garlic salt and pepper. Add chicken to bacon in skillet; cook 3 to 5 minutes or until browned on both sides. Discard excess bacon drippings if necessary.

3 Add water and green beans to skillet. Cover; cook over medium-low heat 8 minutes. Stir in bell pepper. Cover; cook 3 to 5 minutes, turning and stirring vegetables occasionally, until juice of chicken is clear when center of thickest part is cut (at least 165°F).

4 Stir in tomatoes and dressing. Cook uncovered about 2 minutes, stirring occasionally, until tomatoes are thoroughly heated.

1 Serving: Calories 400; Total Fat 25g (Saturated Fat 5g; Trans Fat 0g); Cholesterol 90mg; Sodium 550mg; Total Carbohydrate 10g (Dietary Fiber 3g); Protein 35g **Exchanges:** ½ Starch, 1 Vegetable, 4½ Lean Meat, 2 Fat **Carbohydrate Choices:** ½

Garlic Chicken and Broccoli Stir-Fry

4 servings (1½ cups each)   PREP TIME 20 minutes   START TO FINISH 20 minutes

FAST

2   tablespoons vegetable oil

4   cloves garlic, sliced
    (about 2 tablespoons)

4   cups fresh broccoli florets
    (about 1 lb)

½   cup ready-to-eat baby-cut
    carrots, cut lengthwise
    in half

1   can (8 oz) sliced water
    chestnuts, drained

¼   cup water

½   cup teriyaki baste and
    glaze (from 12-oz bottle)

2   cups bite-size strips
    deli rotisserie chicken
    (from 2-lb chicken)

    Hot cooked rice, if desired

1 In 12-inch nonstick skillet or wok, heat oil over medium-high heat. Add garlic; cook about 1 minute, stirring constantly and being careful that garlic does not burn, until golden brown.

2 Add broccoli, carrots, water chestnuts and water; cook 7 to 9 minutes, stirring occasionally, until vegetables are crisp-tender and water has evaporated.

3 Gently stir in teriyaki glaze and chicken. Cook 1 to 2 minutes or until chicken is thoroughly heated. Serve over rice.

1 Serving: Calories 310; Total Fat 12g (Saturated Fat 2.5g; Trans Fat 0g); Cholesterol 60mg; Sodium 1200mg; Total Carbohydrate 27g (Dietary Fiber 4g); Protein 24g **Exchanges:** ½ Starch, ½ Other Carbohydrate, 2½ Vegetable, 1½ Very Lean Meat, 1 Lean Meat, 1½ Fat **Carbohydrate Choices:** 2

Time-Saver

Pick up a bag of already-cut broccoli florets, or get broccoli at the grocery store salad bar to speed preparation. If the florets are large, cut them into 1- to 1½-inch pieces.

Italian White Beans with Chicken

4 servings   PREP TIME 25 minutes   START TO FINISH 25 minutes

FAST

1 **tablespoon olive or vegetable oil**

1 **tablespoon chopped fresh or 1 teaspoon dried basil leaves**

1 **clove garlic, finely chopped**

2 **cups chopped deli rotisserie chicken (from 2-lb chicken)**

½ **cup chopped drained oil-packed sun-dried tomatoes**

¼ **cup sliced ripe olives**

2 **cans (15.5 oz each) great northern beans, drained, rinsed**

1 In 10-inch skillet, heat oil over medium heat. Add basil and garlic; cook 3 minutes, stirring frequently.

2 Stir in remaining ingredients. Cook, stirring frequently, until hot.

1 Serving: Calories 450; Total Fat 12g (Saturated Fat 2.5g; Trans Fat 0g); Cholesterol 60mg; Sodium 460mg; Total Carbohydrate 48g (Dietary Fiber 12g); Protein 38g **Exchanges:** 3 Starch, 4 Lean Meat **Carbohydrate Choices:** 3

Pesto Chicken and Pasta

4 servings   PREP TIME 20 minutes   START TO FINISH 20 minutes

FAST

3 **cups uncooked bow-tie (farfalle) pasta (6 oz)**

2 **cups cubed deli rotisserie chicken (from 2-lb chicken)**

½ **cup basil pesto**

½ **cup coarsely chopped drained roasted red bell peppers (from 7-oz jar)**

Sliced ripe olives, if desired

1 In 3-quart saucepan, cook and drain pasta as directed on package. Return to saucepan.

2 Stir chicken, pesto and bell peppers into pasta. Heat over low heat, stirring constantly, until hot. Garnish with olives.

1 Serving: Calories 670; Total Fat 23g (Saturated Fat 5g; Trans Fat 0g); Cholesterol 65mg; Sodium 990mg; Total Carbohydrate 79g (Dietary Fiber 7g); Protein 36g **Exchanges:** 5 Starch, 3 Lean Meat, 2 Fat **Carbohydrate Choices:** 5

Healthy Twist

Look for reduced-fat pesto if you would like to shave off some fat grams from this recipe. Another way to cut back on the fat in pesto is to skim off some of the oil that rises to the top of regular pesto.

Lemon-Chicken Rigatoni with Broccoli

4 servings (1½ cups each)   PREP TIME 20 minutes   START TO FINISH 45 minutes

2   **tablespoons butter
     or margarine**

2   **cloves garlic, finely
     chopped**

2   **cups uncooked rigatoni
     pasta (6 oz)**

2   **cups chicken broth
     (from 32-oz carton)**

2   **cups frozen cut broccoli**

2   **cups chopped deli
     rotisserie chicken
     (from 2-lb chicken)**

1½ **teaspoons grated
     lemon peel**

¼   **cup shredded Parmesan
     cheese**

1 In 12-inch skillet, melt butter over medium heat. Add garlic; cook about 1 minute, stirring occasionally, until softened.

2 Stir in uncooked pasta and broth. Heat to boiling, stirring occasionally. Reduce heat to medium-low; cover and simmer 11 minutes. Stir well.

3 Spread broccoli and chicken over pasta. Cover; cook 12 to 14 minutes longer or until pasta is tender. Stir in lemon peel. Top with cheese.

1 Serving: Calories 410; Total Fat 14g (Saturated Fat 6g; Trans Fat 0.5g); Cholesterol 80mg; Sodium 1010mg; Total Carbohydrate 38g (Dietary Fiber 5g); Protein 32g **Exchanges:** 2½ Starch, 3½ Very Lean Meat, 2 Fat Carbohydrate Choices: 2½

Quick Variation

Replace the Parmesan cheese with crumbled feta for a delicious Greek flavor.

Speedy Mediterranean Chicken

4 servings   PREP TIME 30 minutes   START TO FINISH 30 minutes

FAST

1 tablespoon olive or vegetable oil

2 teaspoons curry powder

1 jar (16 oz) chunky style salsa

½ cup sliced green olives

¼ cup golden raisins

¼ cup honey

1 deli rotisserie chicken (2 lb), cut into 6 to 8 pieces, skin removed if desired

1 In 12-inch nonstick skillet, heat oil over medium heat. Stir in curry powder. Cook over medium heat 1 minute, stirring constantly.

2 Stir in remaining ingredients except chicken. Add chicken; turn to coat.

3 Cover; cook over medium-high heat 5 to 6 minutes, turning chicken occasionally, until sauce is bubbly and chicken is thoroughly heated.

1 Serving: Calories 430; Total Fat 15g (Saturated Fat 3.5g; Trans Fat 0g); Cholesterol 110mg; Sodium 1740mg; Total Carbohydrate 37g (Dietary Fiber 1g); Protein 36g **Exchanges:** 2½ Other Carbohydrate, 5 Lean Meat **Carbohydrate Choices:** 2½

Quick Menu Idea

These flavors are reminiscent of an exotic Moroccan tagine. Cooking the curry powder first gives an authentic taste, but if you're short on time, just skip that step. Then, serve with hot cooked couscous to make the most of the sauce.

Stir-Fry Chicken and Vegetables

4 servings   PREP TIME 25 minutes   START TO FINISH 25 minutes

FAST

1 tablespoon canola or vegetable oil

1 cup julienne (matchstick-cut) carrots

1 medium onion, sliced (about 1 cup)

1 lb boneless skinless chicken breasts (about 3), cut into 2×½-inch strips

1¼ cups water

4 oz uncooked vermicelli, broken in half

1 cup frozen sweet peas

½ cup stir-fry sauce

1 teaspoon garlic salt

1 In 12-inch nonstick skillet, heat oil over medium-high heat. Add carrots, onion and chicken; cook 6 to 7 minutes, stirring frequently, until chicken is no longer pink in center and vegetables are tender.

2 Stir in water and vermicelli. Heat to boiling. Cover; cook 3 minutes.

3 Stir in peas and stir-fry sauce. Cook about 2 minutes, stirring frequently, until peas are thoroughly heated. Remove from heat. Stir in garlic salt.

1 Serving: Calories 370; Total Fat 8g (Saturated Fat 1.5g; Trans Fat 0g); Cholesterol 70mg; Sodium 1730mg; Total Carbohydrate 40g (Dietary Fiber 4g); Protein 34g **Exchanges:** 1 Starch, 1½ Other Carbohydrate, ½ Vegetable, 3½ Lean Meat **Carbohydrate Choices:** 2½

Spicy Chicken and Vegetable Stir-Fry

4 servings   PREP TIME 15 minutes   START TO FINISH 15 minutes

FAST

2 **cups uncooked instant rice**

1 **bag (12 oz) frozen Asian style vegetable medley**

1 **package (10 oz) refrigerated grilled chicken breast strips**

½ **cup spicy stir-fry sauce**

⅓ **cup chopped dry-roasted peanuts**

Chopped green onions, if desired

1 Cook rice as directed on package. Meanwhile, in microwavable bowl, microwave vegetables uncovered on High 5 to 6 minutes.

2 Heat 12-inch skillet over medium-high heat. Add vegetables, chicken and stir-fry sauce; cook and stir until hot. Sprinkle with peanuts. Serve over cooked rice. Garnish with chopped green onions.

1 Serving: Calories 450; Total Fat 11g (Saturated Fat 2g; Trans Fat 0g); Cholesterol 55mg; Sodium 1650mg; Total Carbohydrate 59g (Dietary Fiber 4g); Protein 29g **Exchanges:** 3½ Starch, ½ Other Carbohydrate, 2½ Very Lean Meat, 1½ Fat **Carbohydrate Choices:** 4

Cajun Turkey Burger Skillet

5 servings   PREP TIME 25 minutes   START TO FINISH 25 minutes

FAST

1   **lb lean (at least 90%) ground turkey**

1   **small red bell pepper, chopped (½ cup)**

2   **teaspoons Cajun seasoning**

2   **cups hot water**

1   **cup milk**

1   **box (5.8 oz) Hamburger Helper® cheeseburger macaroni**

1   **cup shredded pepper Jack cheese (4 oz)**

1 In 10-inch nonstick skillet, cook turkey, bell pepper and Cajun seasoning over medium-high heat, stirring frequently, until turkey is no longer pink; drain.

2 Stir in hot water, milk and contents of pasta and sauce mix pouches (from Hamburger Helper box). Heat to boiling, stirring occasionally. Reduce heat; cover and simmer 13 to 15 minutes, stirring occasionally, until pasta is tender. Sprinkle with cheese.

1 Serving: Calories 350; Total Fat 13g (Saturated Fat 6g; Trans Fat 0g); Cholesterol 85mg; Sodium 1270mg; Total Carbohydrate 28g (Dietary Fiber 1g); Protein 29g **Exchanges:** 2 Starch, 2½ Medium-Fat Meat **Carbohydrate Choices:** 2

Quick Variation

Cajun seasoning is a blend of seasonings. If you don't have it, jazz up this skillet meal with chili powder for a different flavor.

Take-It-Easy Noodle Dinner

4 servings PREP TIME 20 minutes START TO FINISH 20 minutes

FAST

1 **lb ground turkey or lean (at least 80%) ground beef**

1 **medium onion, coarsely chopped (½ cup)**

1 **cup water**

1 **can (14.5) stewed tomatoes, undrained**

1 **box (9 oz) frozen sweet peas, thawed**

1 **package (3 oz) chicken- or beef-flavor ramen noodle soup mix**

1 In 12-inch nonstick skillet, cook turkey and onion over medium heat about 8 minutes, stirring occasionally, until turkey is no longer pink; drain.

2 Stir in water, tomatoes, peas and seasoning packet from soup mix. Break up noodles; stir into turkey mixture. Heat to boiling, stirring occasionally. Reduce heat; cover and simmer about 6 minutes, stirring occasionally, until noodles are tender.

1 Serving: Calories 310; Total Fat 13g (Saturated Fat 3.5g; Trans Fat 0.5g); Cholesterol 75mg; Sodium 740mg; Total Carbohydrate 22g (Dietary Fiber 4g); Protein 27g **Exchanges:** ½ Starch, ½ Other Carbohydrate, 2 Vegetable, 3 Lean Meat, ½ Fat **Carbohydrate Choices:** 1½

Quick Menu Idea

Toss a fruit salad and serve crunchy breadsticks to round out this simple supper.

Cheesy Scalloped Potatoes with Ham

6 servings (1 cup each) PREP TIME 50 minutes START TO FINISH 50 minutes

2 tablespoons butter
or margarine

1 clove garlic, finely
chopped

2 lb round white potatoes
(about 4 medium), peeled,
thinly sliced

½ lb cooked ham, cut into
½-inch pieces (about
2 cups)

1 cup shredded American-
Cheddar cheese blend
(4 oz)

3 tablespoons all-purpose
flour

¼ teaspoon pepper

1 pint (2 cups) half-and-half

1 In 4-quart Dutch oven, melt butter over medium heat. Add garlic; cook 1 minute, stirring occasionally, until softened. Remove from heat. Stir in potatoes, ham, cheese, flour and pepper.

2 Pour half-and-half over potato mixture. Heat to boiling over medium-high heat. Reduce heat to low; cover and simmer about 30 minutes, stirring occasionally, until potatoes are tender.

1 Serving: Calories 430; Total Fat 24g (Saturated Fat 13g; Trans Fat 0.5g); Cholesterol 85mg; Sodium 850mg; Total Carbohydrate 34g (Dietary Fiber 3g); Protein 20g **Exchanges:** 2 Starch, 2 Medium-Fat Meat, 2½ Fat **Carbohydrate Choices:** 2

Italian Sausage and Vegetable Pasta

6 servings   PREP TIME 35 minutes   START TO FINISH 35 minutes

2 cups uncooked ziti pasta
(7 oz)

2 cups bite-size fresh
broccoli florets

1 package (19.5 oz) lean
hot Italian turkey sausage,
cut into 2-inch pieces

1 tablespoon olive oil

1 large red bell pepper,
cut into bite-size strips

1 large yellow bell pepper,
cut into bite-size strips

1 medium sweet onion,
sliced (about 1 cup)

2 cans (14.5 oz each)
fire-roasted crushed or
diced tomatoes, undrained

1 cup shredded provolone
cheese (4 oz)

1 Cook pasta as directed on package, adding broccoli during last
2 minutes of cooking; drain. Return to saucepan; keep warm.

2 Meanwhile, in 12-inch nonstick skillet, cook sausage over medium-
high heat 8 to 10 minutes or until sausage is no longer pink. Drain;
remove sausage from skillet.

3 In same skillet, heat oil over medium heat. Add bell peppers and
onion; cook 3 to 4 minutes, stirring constantly, until vegetables are
crisp-tender.

4 Add pasta and broccoli, sausage and tomatoes to skillet; heat
to boiling. Reduce heat; simmer uncovered 4 to 5 minutes, stirring
occasionally. Sprinkle with cheese; cover and cook 1 to 2 minutes
or until cheese is melted.

1 Serving: Calories 470; Total Fat 18g (Saturated Fat 6g; Trans Fat 0.5g); Cholesterol 100mg; Sodium 1100mg;
Total Carbohydrate 43g (Dietary Fiber 4g); Protein 35g **Exchanges:** 2½ Starch, ½ Vegetable, 3½ Medium-Fat Meat
Carbohydrate Choices: 3

Ginger Pork and Snow Peas

4 servings (1 cup pork mixture and ½ cup rice each)   PREP TIME 20 minutes   START TO FINISH 20 minutes

FAST

1   package (8.8 oz) microwavable long-grain white rice

1   lb pork tenderloin, cut into ¼-inch slices

1   red bell pepper, cut into ¾-inch pieces

1   package (6 oz) fresh snow pea pods, strings removed

1   cup orange-ginger stir-fry sauce

1 Cook rice in microwave as directed on package.

2 Meanwhile, heat 12-inch nonstick skillet over medium-high heat. Add pork; cook 8 to 10 minutes, turning occasionally, until no longer pink. Remove pork from skillet; cover to keep warm.

3 Add 2 tablespoons water, bell pepper and pea pods to skillet. Cook and stir over medium-high heat 2 to 3 minutes or until crisp-tender.

4 Stir in stir-fry sauce. Return pork to skillet; heat until hot. Serve pork mixture over rice.

1 Serving: Calories 320; Total Fat 6g (Saturated Fat 1.5g; Trans Fat 0g); Cholesterol 50mg; Sodium 2140mg; Total Carbohydrate 42g (Dietary Fiber 2g); Protein 25g **Exchanges:** 1½ Starch, 1 Other Carbohydrate, ½ Vegetable, 2½ Very Lean Meat, 1 Fat **Carbohydrate Choices:** 3

Quick Variation

A bunch of fresh asparagus (cut into 2-inch pieces) or broccoli (cut into florets) can be substituted for the snow peas.

Pork, Broccoli and Noodle Skillet

5 servings (1½ cups each)   PREP TIME 30 minutes   START TO FINISH 30 minutes

FAST

4 cups uncooked dumpling
   egg noodles (8 oz)

1 bag (12 oz) frozen broccoli
   florets

1 tablespoon butter
   or margarine

1 lb pork tenderloin, cut
   crosswise into ¼-inch
   slices

1 cup sliced fresh
   mushrooms (3 oz)

1 clove garlic, finely chopped

1 jar (12 oz) mushroom
   gravy

1 tablespoon Worcestershire
   sauce

1 In 4-quart Dutch oven or saucepan, cook noodles as directed on package, adding broccoli during last 3 to 5 minutes of cooking time. Cook until noodles and broccoli are tender. Drain; return to saucepan. Cover to keep warm.

2 In 12-inch nonstick skillet, melt butter over medium-high heat. Add pork; cook 3 to 5 minutes, stirring frequently, until browned. Add mushrooms and garlic; cook 2 to 4 minutes, stirring frequently, until mushrooms are tender.

3 Stir in gravy and Worcestershire sauce. Cook over medium-high heat, stirring frequently, until bubbly and thickened. Add pork mixture to noodles and broccoli; toss gently to coat.

1 Serving: Calories 390; Total Fat 17g (Saturated Fat 6g; Trans Fat 0.5g); Cholesterol 80mg; Sodium 710mg; Total Carbohydrate 34g (Dietary Fiber 4g); Protein 25g **Exchanges:** 2 Starch, ½ Vegetable, 2½ Lean Meat, 1½ Fat Carbohydrate Choices: 2

Quick Variation

Use 2¾ cups mini lasagna (mafalda) noodles as a substitute for the egg noodles.

Pork Lo Mein

6 servings   PREP TIME 25 minutes   START TO FINISH 25 minutes

FAST

½ **lb boneless pork loin**

⅓ **cup chicken broth (from 32-oz carton)**

1 **tablespoon soy sauce**

2 **teaspoons cornstarch**

1 **teaspoon sugar**

2 **to 4 cloves garlic, finely chopped**

2 **teaspoons finely chopped gingerroot**

2 **cups fresh sugar snap peas**

1 **cup ready-to-eat baby-cut carrots, cut lengthwise into ¼-inch sticks**

½ **package (9-oz size) refrigerated linguine, cut into 2-inch pieces**

½ **cup thinly sliced red onion**

Toasted sesame seed, if desired

1 Trim fat from pork. Cut pork with grain into 2x1-inch strips; cut strips across grain into ⅛-inch slices. (Pork is easier to cut if partially frozen, about 1 hour 30 minutes.) In small bowl, mix broth, soy sauce, cornstarch, sugar, garlic and gingerroot; set aside.

2 In 3-quart saucepan, heat 2 quarts water to boiling. Add peas, carrots and linguine; return to boiling. Boil 2 to 3 minutes or until linguine is just tender; drain.

3 Spray wok or 12-inch skillet with cooking spray; heat over medium-high heat until cooking spray starts to bubble. Add pork and onion; cook and stir about 2 minutes or until pork is no longer pink. Stir in broth mixture. Add peas, carrots and linguine; cook and stir 2 minutes longer. Sprinkle with sesame seed.

1 Serving: Calories 160; Total Fat 3.5g (Saturated Fat 1g; Trans Fat 0g); Cholesterol 25mg; Sodium 270mg; Total Carbohydrate 20g (Dietary Fiber 2g); Protein 12g **Exchanges:** 1 Starch, 1 Vegetable, 1 Lean Meat **Carbohydrate Choices:** 1

Pork Medallions with Cherry Sauce

4 servings   PREP TIME 25 minutes   START TO FINISH 35 minutes

1 **pork tenderloin (1 to 1¼ lb), cut into ½-inch slices**

½ **teaspoon garlic-pepper blend**

2 **teaspoons olive oil**

¾ **cup cherry preserves**

2 **tablespoons chopped shallots**

1 **tablespoon Dijon mustard**

1 **tablespoon balsamic vinegar**

1 **clove garlic, finely chopped**

1 Sprinkle both sides of pork with garlic-pepper blend.

2 In 12-inch skillet, heat 1 teaspoon of the oil over medium-high heat. Add pork; cook 6 to 8 minutes, turning once, until pork is no longer pink in center. Remove pork from skillet; keep warm.

3 In same skillet, mix remaining teaspoon oil, the preserves, shallots, mustard, vinegar and garlic, scraping any brown bits from bottom of skillet. Heat to boiling. Reduce heat; simmer uncovered 10 minutes or until reduced to about ½ cup. Serve sauce over pork slices.

1 Serving: Calories 330; Total Fat 7g (Saturated Fat 2g; Trans Fat 0g); Cholesterol 50mg; Sodium 170mg; Total Carbohydrate 44g (Dietary Fiber 1g); Protein 23g **Exchanges:** 1 Starch, 2 Other Carbohydrate, 1 Very Lean Meat, 2 Lean Meat **Carbohydrate Choices:** 3

Time-Saver

For easy slicing, freeze the pork for 15 to 30 minutes before slicing.

Potato, Egg and Sausage Frittata

4 servings   PREP TIME 30 minutes   START TO FINISH 30 minutes

FAST

4 **frozen soy-protein breakfast sausage links (from 8-oz box), thawed**

1 **teaspoon olive oil**

2 **cups frozen country-style shredded hash brown potatoes (from 30-oz bag)**

4 **eggs or 8 egg whites**

¼ **cup fat-free (skim) milk**

¼ **teaspoon salt**

⅛ **teaspoon dried basil leaves**

⅛ **teaspoon dried oregano leaves**

1½ **cups chopped plum (Roma) tomatoes**

½ **cup shredded mozzarella and Asiago cheese blend with garlic (2 oz)**

Freshly ground pepper, if desired

Chopped green onion, if desired

1 Cut each sausage link into 8 pieces. Coat 10-inch nonstick skillet with oil; heat over medium heat. Add sausage and potatoes; cook 6 to 8 minutes, stirring occasionally, until potatoes are golden brown.

2 In small bowl, beat eggs and milk with fork or whisk until well blended. Pour egg mixture over potato mixture. Cook uncovered over medium-low heat about 5 minutes; as mixture begins to set on bottom and side, gently lift cooked portions with spatula so that thin, uncooked portion can flow to bottom. Cook until eggs are thickened throughout but still moist; avoid constant stirring.

3 Sprinkle salt, basil, oregano, tomatoes and cheese over eggs. Reduce heat to low; cover and cook about 5 minutes or until center is set and cheese is melted. Sprinkle with pepper and green onion.

1 Serving: Calories 280; Total Fat 12g (Saturated Fat 4.5g; Trans Fat 0g); Cholesterol 220mg; Sodium 590mg; Total Carbohydrate 26g (Dietary Fiber 3g); Protein 17g **Exchanges:** 1½ Starch, 2 Medium-Fat Meat **Carbohydrate Choices:** 2

Healthy Twist

If you haven't tried the newest soy products lately, you're in for a pleasant surprise. Soy sausage is a tasty alternative to higher-fat regular sausage and an easy addition to this fresh-tasting frittata.

Lamb and Potato Skillet

4 servings   PREP TIME 30 minutes   START TO FINISH 30 minutes

FAST

1   **lb ground lamb**

1   **medium leek, rinsed,
    cut in half lengthwise and
    chopped (about 2 cups)**

1   **clove garlic, finely
    chopped**

½   **cup beef flavored broth
    (from 32-oz carton)**

1   **tablespoon chopped fresh
    or 1 teaspoon dried
    dill weed**

½   **teaspoon salt**

¼   **teaspoon pepper**

3   **medium potatoes, cut into
    ¼-inch pieces (3 cups)**

1   **dried bay leaf**

2   **small tomatoes, coarsely
    chopped (1 cup)**

1 In 10-inch skillet, cook lamb, leek and garlic over medium heat, stirring frequently, until lamb is no longer pink; drain.

2 Stir in remaining ingredients except tomatoes. Heat to boiling. Reduce heat; cover and simmer about 12 minutes, stirring occasionally, until potatoes are tender. Remove bay leaf. Stir in tomatoes; cook until thoroughly heated.

1 Serving: Calories 360; Total Fat 16g (Saturated Fat 7g; Trans Fat 0.5g); Cholesterol 70mg; Sodium 470mg; Total Carbohydrate 33g (Dietary Fiber 4g); Protein 21g **Exchanges:** 1½ Starch, 1½ Vegetable, 2 Medium-Fat Meat, 1 Fat **Carbohydrate Choices:** 2

Asian Beef Noodle Bowls

4 servings (1¼ cups each)   PREP TIME **20 minutes**   START TO FINISH **20 minutes**

FAST

4 oz uncooked angel hair
(capellini) pasta, broken
in half

8 oz fresh sugar snap peas

5 teaspoons vegetable oil

1 lb boneless beef sirloin
steak, cut into ¼-inch
strips

1 medium carrot, thinly
sliced (½ cup)

½ cup teriyaki baste and
glaze (from 12-oz bottle)

4 medium green onions with
tops, sliced (¼ cup)

½ cup honey-roasted peanuts,
chopped

1 Cook pasta as directed on package. Meanwhile, snip off stem ends of sugar snap peas and remove strings, if desired. Drain pasta; cover to keep warm.

2 In 12-inch nonstick wok or skillet, heat 3 teaspoons of the oil over medium-high heat. Add beef; cook and stir 2 to 3 minutes or until no longer pink. Remove from skillet; keep warm.

3 In same skillet, heat remaining 2 teaspoons oil over medium-high heat. Add peas and carrot; cook and stir 3 to 4 minutes or until crisp-tender. Stir in cooked pasta, beef and teriyaki baste and glaze; toss until well blended.

4 Serve in bowls; sprinkle with onions and peanuts.

1 Serving: Calories 520; Total Fat 20g (Saturated Fat 4g; Trans Fat 0g); Cholesterol 75mg; Sodium 1500mg; Total Carbohydrate 41g (Dietary Fiber 5g); Protein 43g **Exchanges:** 1½ Starch, ½ Other Carbohydrate, 1½ Vegetable, 5 Lean Meat, 1 Fat **Carbohydrate Choices:** 3

Barbecued Beef and Bow-Tie Dinner

4 servings   PREP TIME 25 minutes   START TO FINISH 30 minutes

FAST

1   **lb lean (at least 80%) ground beef**

1   **medium red bell pepper, chopped (1 cup)**

1½ **cups uncooked mini bow-tie (mini farfalle) pasta (5 oz)**

2½ **cups beef-flavored broth (from 32-oz carton)**

½   **cup barbecue sauce**

½   **teaspoon salt**

¼   **teaspoon pepper**

1   **cup frozen whole kernel corn, thawed**

1½ **cups shredded Cheddar cheese (6 oz)**

1 In 12-inch nonstick skillet, cook beef over medium-high heat 5 to 7 minutes, stirring occasionally, until thoroughly cooked; drain.

2 Add bell pepper; cook and stir 1 minute. Stir in pasta, broth, barbecue sauce, salt and pepper. Heat to boiling. Reduce heat to medium-low; cover and cook 15 minutes, stirring occasionally, until pasta is tender.

3 Stir in corn and 1 cup of the cheese. Top with remaining ½ cup cheese. Cover; cook 3 to 4 minutes longer or until corn is hot and cheese is melted.

1 Serving: Calories 680; Total Fat 28g (Saturated Fat 14g; Trans Fat 1g); Cholesterol 115mg; Sodium 1470mg; Total Carbohydrate 66g (Dietary Fiber 4g); Protein 40g **Exchanges:** 4 Starch, ½ Vegetable, 3 High-Fat Meat, 1 Fat **Carbohydrate Choices:** 4½

Time-Saver

Buy a block of Cheddar cheese when it's on sale; shred and store, tightly sealed, in the freezer. It will be handy whenever you need shredded cheese for a recipe.

Beef and Kasha Mexicana

6 servings (1⅓ cups each)   PREP TIME 25 minutes   START TO FINISH 25 minutes

FAST

- 1 **lb extra-lean (at least 90%) ground beef**
- 1 **medium onion, chopped (½ cup)**
- 1 **cup uncooked buckwheat kernels or groats (kasha)**
- 1 **can (14.5 oz) diced tomatoes, undrained**
- 1 **can (4.5 oz) chopped green chiles, undrained**
- 1 **package (1 oz) 40% less-sodium taco seasoning mix**
- 2 **cups frozen whole kernel corn, thawed**
- 1½ **cups water**
- 1 **cup shredded reduced-fat Cheddar cheese (4 oz)**
- 2 **tablespoons chopped fresh cilantro, if desired**
- 2 **tablespoons sliced ripe olives, if desired**

1 In 12-inch skillet, cook ground beef and onion over medium-high heat 5 to 7 minutes, stirring occasionally, until beef is thoroughly cooked; drain. Stir in kasha until kernels are moistened by beef mixture.

2 Stir in tomatoes, chiles, taco seasoning mix, corn and water. Heat to boiling. Reduce heat to low; cover and simmer 5 to 7 minutes, stirring occasionally, until kasha is tender.

3 Sprinkle cheese over kasha mixture. Cover; cook 2 to 3 minutes or until cheese is melted. Sprinkle with cilantro and olives.

1 Serving: Calories 300; Total Fat 9g (Saturated Fat 3.5g; Trans Fat 0g); Cholesterol 50mg; Sodium 990mg; Total Carbohydrate 33g (Dietary Fiber 5g); Protein 23g **Exchanges:** 2 Starch, 2½ Lean Meat **Carbohydrate Choices:** 2

Beefy Rice Skillet

4 servings   PREP TIME 30 minutes   START TO FINISH 30 minutes

FAST

1   lb lean (at least 80%) ground beef

2½ cups hot water

¾   cup ready-to-eat baby-cut carrots, cut lengthwise in half

1   tablespoon butter or margarine

¼   teaspoon pepper

1   package (6.4 oz) four-cheese rice and pasta blend

1½ cups fresh broccoli florets

½   cup cherry or grape tomatoes, cut in half

1 In 12-inch skillet, cook beef over medium-high heat 5 to 7 minutes, stirring occasionally, until thoroughly cooked; drain.

2 Stir water, carrots, butter, pepper, rice mixture and contents of seasoning packet into beef. Heat to boiling. Reduce heat; cover and cook about 15 minutes or until rice and carrots are almost tender, stirring occasionally.

3 Stir in broccoli. Cover; cook 5 minutes or until crisp-tender. Stir in tomatoes. Cook uncovered about 1 minute or until heated.

1 Serving: Calories 420; Total Fat 20g (Saturated Fat 9g; Trans Fat 1g); Cholesterol 80mg; Sodium 700mg; Total Carbohydrate 35g (Dietary Fiber 2g); Protein 25g **Exchanges:** 2 Starch, 1 Vegetable, 2 Lean Meat, ½ Medium-Fat Meat, 2 Fat **Carbohydrate Choices:** 2

Time-Saver

Make this recipe even easier by simply purchasing already-cut veggies in the produce section or at the salad bar in the grocery store.

Quick Menu Idea

This is a great fuss-free family-pleasing skillet meal. Serve with your favorite bakery rolls, sliced tomatoes, sliced cucumbers and brownies.

Healthy Twist

Trim the calories and fat a bit by substituting low-fat soup and frozen cooked turkey meatballs.

Meatballs and Creamy Rice Skillet Supper

4 servings (1¼ cups each)   PREP TIME 30 minutes   START TO FINISH 30 minutes

FAST

¾ **cup uncooked regular long-grain white rice**

1 **can (10¾ oz) condensed cream of celery soup**

2 **cups water**

1½ **cups ready-to-eat baby-cut carrots, cut in half lengthwise**

1 **box (12 oz) frozen cooked Italian-style meatballs (12 meatballs), thawed**

Chopped fresh parsley, if desired

1 In 12-inch nonstick skillet, mix rice, soup and water: Heat to boiling. Reduce heat to medium-low; cover and cook 5 minutes.

2 Stir carrots and meatballs into rice mixture. Cover; cook 10 to 15 minutes, stirring occasionally to prevent sticking, until rice and carrots are tender and meatballs are hot. Sprinkle with parsley.

1 Serving: Calories 430; Total Fat 16g (Saturated Fat 6g; Trans Fat 1g); Cholesterol 90mg; Sodium 1070mg; Total Carbohydrate 50g (Dietary Fiber 3g); Protein 22g **Exchanges:** 3½ Starch, 1½ Medium-Fat Meat, 1 Fat **Carbohydrate Choices:** 3

Steak and Peppers in Chimichurri Sauce

4 servings   PREP TIME 25 minutes   START TO FINISH 25 minutes

FAST

½ cup basil pesto

1 tablespoon lemon juice

¼ teaspoon dried oregano leaves

⅛ to ¼ teaspoon crushed red pepper flakes

1 tablespoon olive oil

1 medium onion, thinly sliced (about 1 cup)

1 medium orange bell pepper, cut into bite-size strips

1 medium yellow bell pepper, cut into bite-size strips

1 lb boneless beef top sirloin steak, cut into 4 pieces

1 teaspoon garlic-pepper blend

½ teaspoon salt

1 In medium heatproof bowl, mix pesto, lemon juice, oregano and pepper flakes; set aside.

2 In 12-inch nonstick skillet, heat oil over medium heat. Add onion and bell peppers; cook 3 to 4 minutes, stirring frequently, until vegetables are crisp-tender. Stir in pesto mixture. Return mixture to same bowl; cover and set aside.

3 Sprinkle both sides of beef pieces with garlic-pepper blend and salt. Heat same skillet over medium-high heat. Add beef; cook on each side 5 to 6 minutes or until browned and medium-rare doneness.

4 Return onion-bell pepper mixture to skillet with beef. Cook 1 to 2 minutes, stirring occasionally, until peppers are hot and crisp-tender, and beef is desired doneness. Serve pepper mixture over beef.

1 Serving: Calories 380; Total Fat 22g (Saturated Fat 4.5g; Trans Fat 0g); Cholesterol 85mg; Sodium 610mg; Total Carbohydrate 11g (Dietary Fiber 2g); Protein 34g **Exchanges:** ½ Starch, ½ Vegetable, 4½ Lean Meat, 1½ Fat **Carbohydrate Choices:** 1

Skillet Lasagna

8 servings   PREP TIME 30 minutes   START TO FINISH 30 minutes

FAST

1   lb lean (at least 80%) ground beef

1   medium bell pepper, chopped (1 cup)

1   medium onion, chopped (½ cup)

3   cups uncooked mafalda pasta (6 oz)

2½ cups water

½   teaspoon Italian seasoning

1   jar (25.5 oz) tomato pasta sauce (any variety) or marinara sauce

1   jar (4.5 oz) sliced mushrooms, drained

1 In 12-inch skillet, cook beef, bell pepper and onion over medium heat 8 to 10 minutes, stirring occasionally, until beef is thoroughly cooked; drain.

2 Stir in remaining ingredients. Heat to boiling. Reduce heat; simmer uncovered 10 to 12 minutes, stirring occasionally, until pasta is tender.

1 Serving: Calories 210; Total Fat 8g (Saturated Fat 2.5g; Trans Fat 0g); Cholesterol 50mg; Sodium 580mg; Total Carbohydrate 22g (Dietary Fiber 3g); Protein 14g **Exchanges:** 1 Starch, 1 Vegetable, 1½ Medium-Fat Meat **Carbohydrate Choices:** 1½

Quick Variation

Mafalda pasta is also known as mini lasagna noodles. If you have leftover broken lasagna noodles, this recipe is a great way to use them up. Or for Skillet Pizza Lasagna, use two 15-ounce cans pizza sauce instead of the pasta sauce and add ½ cup diced pepperoni.

Spaghetti and Spicy "Meatballs"

6 servings   PREP TIME 25 minutes   START TO FINISH 25 minutes

FAST

1 box (1 lb) spaghetti

2 cups cooked white rice

½ cup quick-cooking oats

1 medium onion, chopped
   (½ cup)

¼ cup plain bread crumbs

¼ cup milk

1 tablespoon chopped fresh
   or 1 teaspoon dried basil
   leaves

2 teaspoons chopped fresh
   or ½ teaspoon dried
   oregano leaves

¼ teaspoon ground red
   pepper (cayenne)

1 egg, beaten

½ cup wheat germ

1 tablespoon vegetable oil

2 cups tomato pasta sauce
   (from 25.5-oz jar)

   Shredded Parmesan
   cheese, if desired

1 Cook and drain spaghetti as directed on package.

2 Meanwhile, in medium bowl, mix rice, oats, onion, bread crumbs, milk, basil, oregano, red pepper and egg. Shape into 12 balls; roll in wheat germ.

3 In 10-inch skillet, heat oil over medium heat. Add rice balls; cook about 10 minutes, turning occasionally, until golden brown.

4 Heat pasta sauce until hot. Serve rice balls and sauce over spaghetti. Sprinkle with cheese.

1 Serving: Calories 620; Total Fat 10g (Saturated Fat 2g; Trans Fat 0g); Cholesterol 35mg; Sodium 790mg; Total Carbohydrate 111g (Dietary Fiber 8g); Protein 20g **Exchanges:** 6 Starch, 1 Other Carbohydrate, ½ Vegetable, 1½ Fat **Carbohydrate Choices:** 7½

Szechuan Beef and Bean Sprouts

4 servings (1¼ cups each)   PREP TIME 20 minutes   START TO FINISH 30 minutes
FAST

1 lb boneless beef
   eye of round steak,
   trimmed of fat

¼ cup reduced-sodium
   chicken broth

1 tablespoon reduced-
   sodium soy sauce

1 tablespoon Szechuan
   sauce

⅛ teaspoon crushed
   red pepper flakes

4 plum (Roma) tomatoes,
   each cut into 8 pieces

2 cups fresh bean sprouts
   (4 oz)

1 tablespoon chopped
   fresh cilantro

1 Cut beef with grain into 2-inch strips; cut strips across grain into ⅛-inch slices. (Beef is easier to cut if partially frozen, 30 to 60 minutes.) In medium bowl, stir together broth, soy sauce, Szechuan sauce and pepper flakes. Stir in beef. Let stand 10 minutes.

2 Drain beef; reserve marinade. Heat 12-inch nonstick skillet over medium-high heat. Add half of the beef to skillet; stir-fry 2 to 3 minutes or until brown. Remove beef from skillet. Repeat with remaining beef. Return all beef to skillet.

3 Add reserved marinade, the tomatoes and bean sprouts to beef in skillet; stir-fry about 1 minute or until vegetables are warm. Sprinkle with cilantro.

1 Serving: Calories 200; Total Fat 6g (Saturated Fat 1.5g; Trans Fat 0g); Cholesterol 65mg; Sodium 340mg; Total Carbohydrate 6g (Dietary Fiber 1g); Protein 30g **Exchanges:** 1 Vegetable, 4 Very Lean Meat, 1 Fat **Carbohydrate Choices:** ½

Healthy Twist

For the leanest cuts of meat, look for the words "round" or "loin" in the name—think eye of round, top round, sirloin, or tenderloin.

Shrimp 'n Sugar Peas Lo Mein

4 servings (1 cup each)   PREP TIME 15 minutes   START TO FINISH 20 minutes

FAST

1   **tablespoon sesame oil**

¼   **cup chunky peanut butter**

1   **box (5.1 oz) Betty Crocker®
    Asian Chicken Helper®
    chicken lo mein**

1   **cup fresh sugar snap peas,
    strings removed if desired**

½   **lb cooked deveined peeled
    large shrimp, thawed if
    frozen, tail shells removed**

1 In 10-inch skillet, heat oil and peanut butter over medium heat just until peanut butter melts. Stir in noodles (from Chicken Helper box) until coated. Stir in 2¼ cups water and the sauce mix (from Chicken Helper box). Heat to boiling, stirring occasionally.

2 Reduce heat; stir in peas. Cover; simmer 6 minutes, stirring occasionally. Stir in shrimp. Cover; simmer 4 to 5 minutes longer or until noodles are tender.

1 Serving: Calories 350; Total Fat 13g (Saturated Fat 2.5g; Trans Fat 0g); Cholesterol 110mg; Sodium 740mg; Total Carbohydrate 34g (Dietary Fiber 4g); Protein 22g **Exchanges:** 2½ Starch, 2 Very Lean Meat, 2 Fat **Carbohydrate Choices:** 2

Skillet Coconut Shrimp with Apricot Sauce

4 servings   PREP TIME 30 minutes   START TO FINISH 30 minutes

FAST

½ **cup apricot preserves**

1 **teaspoon apple cider vinegar**

¼ **teaspoon crushed red pepper flakes**

1 **lb uncooked deveined peeled medium shrimp (21 to 25 count), thawed if frozen, tail shells removed**

½ **cup Original Bisquick mix**

½ **teaspoon ground red pepper (cayenne)**

2 **tablespoons milk**

1 **egg**

2 **cups flaked coconut**

About 1⅓ cups vegetable oil

1 In small bowl, mix preserves, vinegar and pepper flakes; set aside.

2 Pat shrimp dry with paper towels. In shallow dish, mix Bisquick mix, red pepper, milk and egg with fork until well blended. In another shallow dish, place coconut.

3 In 12-inch skillet, heat ¼ inch oil over medium heat. Working with half of the shrimp at a time, dip each shrimp into egg mixture, shaking off excess batter; lightly toss in coconut. Place in hot oil in single layer; cook 3 to 4 minutes, turning once, until coating is crisp and golden brown, and shrimp are pink. Serve with apricot sauce.

1 Serving: Calories 680; Total Fat 40g (Saturated Fat 18g; Trans Fat 0.5g); Cholesterol 215mg; Sodium 510mg; Total Carbohydrate 58g (Dietary Fiber 3g); Protein 21g **Exchanges:** 2 Starch, 2 Other Carbohydrate, 2 Lean Meat, 6½ Fat **Carbohydrate Choices:** 4

Quick Menu Idea

Serve the shrimp for dinner over cooked white rice. Or, they are great to serve as an appetizer or lunch served over baby lettuce greens. Drizzle the apricot preserves over the shrimp as a dressing.

Crispy Fish Fillets with Zesty Lime Sauce

4 servings   PREP TIME 20 minutes   START TO FINISH 20 minutes

FAST

FISH

3 **tablespoons all-purpose flour**

1 **teaspoon lemon-pepper seasoning**

½ **teaspoon salt**

1¼ **cups unseasoned crispy bread crumbs**

2 **eggs**

4 **tilapia or other medium-firm fish fillets**

¼ **cup canola oil**

SAUCE

1 **cup fat-free plain yogurt (from 2-lb container)**

1 **teaspoon grated lime peel**

2 **tablespoons lime juice**

¼ **teaspoon salt**

1 On plate, mix flour, lemon-pepper seasoning and salt. On second plate, place bread crumbs. In shallow bowl, beat eggs with fork. Coat fish fillets with flour mixture. Dip into eggs; coat well with crumbs.

2 In 12-inch nonstick skillet, heat oil over medium heat. Add fish; cook 3 minutes. Carefully turn fillets over; cook about 3 minutes longer or until fish flakes easily with fork. Meanwhile, in small bowl, mix sauce ingredients. Serve with fish.

1 Serving: Calories 450; Total Fat 21g (Saturated Fat 2g; Trans Fat 0g); Cholesterol 165mg; Sodium 760mg; Total Carbohydrate 34g (Dietary Fiber 0g); Protein 30g **Exchanges:** 2 Starch, ½ Other Carbohydrate, 2½ Very Lean Meat, 1 Lean Meat, 3 Fat **Carbohydrate Choices:** 2

Quick Variation

Cod, haddock and red snapper are other medium-firm fish fillets with a mild flavor that can be used instead of tilapia.

Quick Menu Idea
Serve these crispy fillets with green beans, crusty sourdough rolls and fresh fruit.

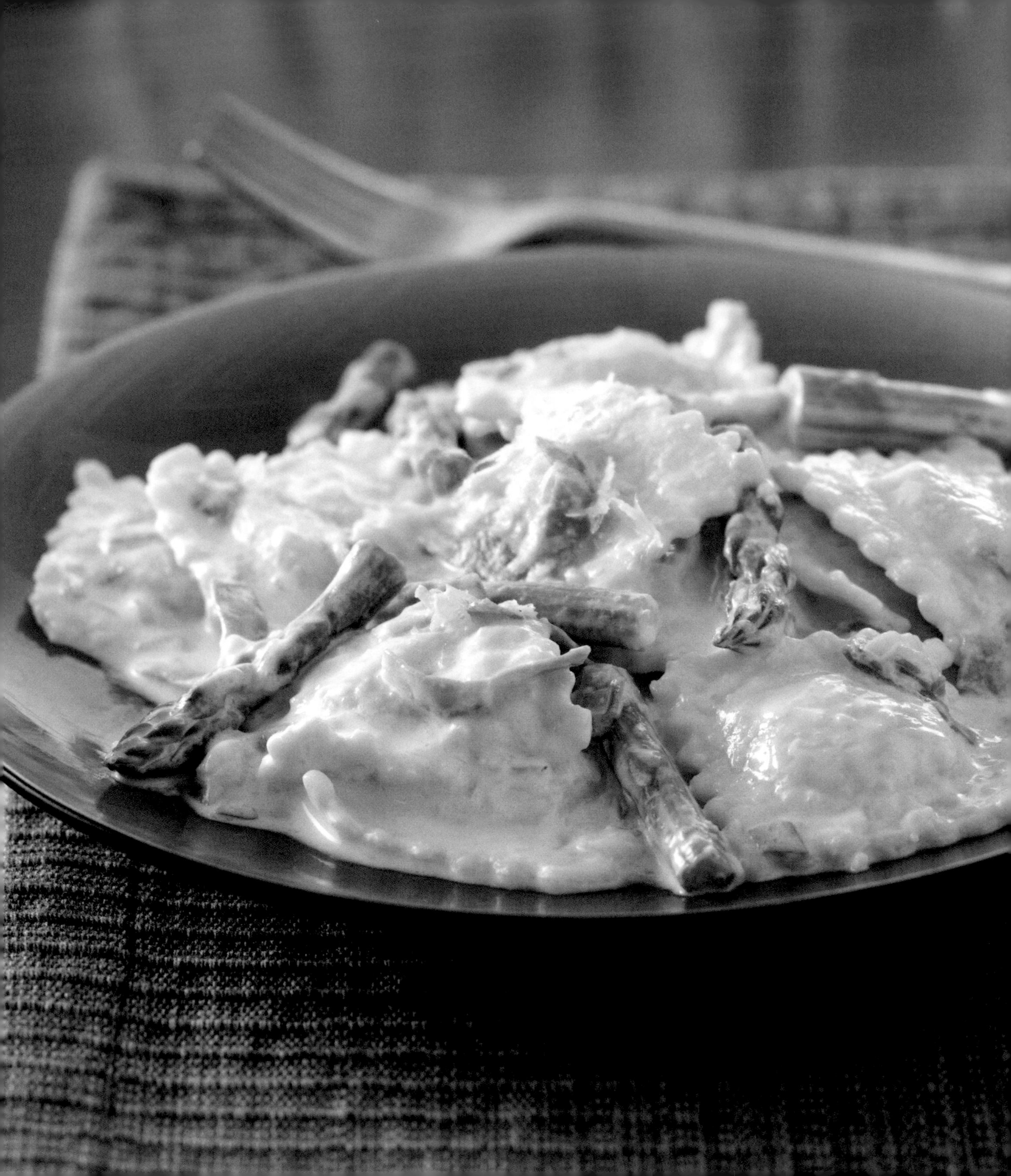

Lemony Asparagus-Prosciutto Ravioli

6 servings (1½ cups each)   PREP TIME 30 minutes   START TO FINISH 30 minutes

FAST

1 **package (9 oz) refrigerated cheese-filled ravioli**

10 **fresh asparagus spears (about ½ lb), trimmed, cut into 2-inch pieces (about 1½ cups)**

2 **tablespoons finely chopped shallots**

1 **package (3 oz) thinly sliced prosciutto, cut into thin bite-size strips (about 1 cup)**

1 **cup whipping cream**

3 **tablespoons white wine or chicken broth**

¼ **cup grated Romano cheese**

1 **teaspoon grated lemon peel**

1 Cook ravioli as directed on package, adding asparagus during last 4 minutes of cook time; drain and rinse.

2 Meanwhile, in 10-inch skillet, cook shallots and prosciutto over medium-high heat 2 to 3 minutes, stirring frequently, until prosciutto is slightly crisp. Remove from skillet; set aside. In same pan, cook whipping cream and wine over medium heat 4 to 6 minutes, stirring constantly, until slightly thickened.

3 Stir in ravioli with asparagus, prosciutto mixture and cheese. Cook 2 to 3 minutes or until thoroughly heated and cheese is melted. Stir in lemon peel.

1 Serving: Calories 300; Total Fat 19g (Saturated Fat 11g; Trans Fat 0g); Cholesterol 75mg; Sodium 370mg; Total Carbohydrate 22g (Dietary Fiber 1g); Protein 10g **Exchanges:** 1½ Starch, 1 Medium-Fat Meat, 2½ Fat **Carbohydrate Choices:** 1½

Quick Menu Idea

For a great early summer meal, serve this dish with fresh melon or clusters of grapes.

Southwestern Bean Skillet

4 servings   PREP TIME 20 minutes   START TO FINISH 20 minutes

FAST

1 cup fresh corn kernels or frozen whole kernel corn (from 12-oz bag)

2 tablespoons chopped fresh cilantro

½ teaspoon salt

1 small green bell pepper, chopped (½ cup)

1 small onion, chopped (⅓ cup)

1 can (15 oz) chili beans in sauce, undrained

1 can (15 oz) black beans, drained, rinsed

1 cup shredded Cheddar-Jack with jalapeño peppers cheese blend (4 oz)

2 medium tomatoes, chopped (1½ cups)

1 In 12-inch skillet, mix all ingredients except cheese and tomatoes. Heat to boiling. Reduce heat; cover and simmer 5 minutes.

2 Uncover; simmer 5 to 10 minutes, stirring occasionally, until vegetables are tender. Add cheese and tomatoes; stir until cheese is melted.

1 Serving: Calories 300; Total Fat 3.5g (Saturated Fat 1g; Trans Fat 0g); Cholesterol 0mg; Sodium 1400mg; Total Carbohydrate 53g (Dietary Fiber 16g); Protein 14g **Exchanges:** 3 Other Carbohydrate, 1½ Vegetable, 1 Very Lean Meat, ½ Medium-Fat Meat **Carbohydrate Choices:** 3½

Vegetarian Fried Rice

4 servings   PREP TIME 25 minutes   START TO FINISH 25 minutes
FAST

2 **cups uncooked instant brown rice**

2½ **cups water**

1 **teaspoon vegetable oil**

2 **eggs, beaten**

1 **tablespoon vegetable oil**

2 **medium carrots, sliced (1 cup)**

8 **medium green onions, sliced (½ cup)**

1 **clove garlic, finely chopped**

2 **cups fresh snow pea pods, strings removed, cut diagonally in half**

1 **cup fresh bean sprouts**

2 **tablespoons soy sauce**

1 Cook rice in water as directed on package.

2 Meanwhile, in 12-inch nonstick skillet, heat 1 teaspoon oil over medium heat. Pour beaten eggs over bottom of skillet; cook until firm. Remove from skillet; set aside. When eggs are cool, cut into small pieces.

3 In same skillet, heat 1 tablespoon oil over medium-high heat. Add carrots, onions and garlic; cook 1 minute. Stir in pea pods and bean sprouts; cook and stir 2 minutes or until bean sprouts are no longer crisp.

4 Stir in cooked rice and soy sauce. Reduce heat to medium; cook 2 minutes, stirring occasionally. Stir in eggs; cook until thoroughly heated.

1 Serving: Calories 490; Total Fat 10g (Saturated Fat 2g; Trans Fat 0g); Cholesterol 105mg; Sodium 1700mg; Total Carbohydrate 83g (Dietary Fiber 13g); Protein 16g **Exchanges:** 3 Starch, 1½ Other Carbohydrate, 3 Vegetable, ½ Medium-Fat Meat, 1 Fat **Carbohydrate Choices:** 5½

Quick Menu Idea

For an easy dessert, toss canned mandarin orange segments with chopped crystallized ginger, and spoon over orange or pineapple sherbet.

Chapter Four

Satisfying Casseroles

Alfredo Chicken Pot Puff Pies

4 servings PREP TIME 20 minutes START TO FINISH 55 minutes

1 **sheet frozen puff pastry (from 17.3-oz package), thawed**

1 **tablespoon butter or margarine**

2 **tablespoons finely chopped shallots**

2 **cups chopped cooked chicken**

2 **cups frozen peas and carrots (from 1-lb bag)**

1 **jar (16 oz) Alfredo pasta sauce**

1 **teaspoon dried thyme leaves**

1 **egg, beaten**

1 Heat oven to 400°F. Lightly spray 4 (10-oz) custard cups or ramekins with cooking spray. On lightly floured surface, roll puff pastry to 13-inch square. Cut into 4 squares. Lightly press 1 square in bottom and up side of each custard cup, letting corners hang over side.

2 In 10-inch skillet, melt butter over medium heat. Add shallots; cook about 3 minutes, stirring occasionally, until softened. Add chicken, frozen peas and carrots, and Alfredo sauce; cook 3 to 4 minutes longer, stirring occasionally, until vegetables are thawed and mixture is hot. Sprinkle with thyme; stir well.

3 Spoon chicken mixture into pastry-lined cups. Fold corners of pastry over filling, pinching to almost close tops. Brush pastry tops with egg.

4 Bake 25 to 30 minutes or until pastry is deep golden brown. Let stand 5 minutes. Serve in cups, or remove to individual serving plates.

1 Serving: Calories 730; Total Fat 50g (Saturated Fat 21g; Trans Fat 2.5g); Cholesterol 285mg; Sodium 1070mg; Total Carbohydrate 42g (Dietary Fiber 3g); Protein 28g **Exchanges:** 1½ Starch, 1 Other Carbohydrate, 1 Vegetable, 3 Lean Meat, 8 Fat **Carbohydrate Choices:** 3

Baked Chicken Panzanella

6 servings (1½ cups each)   PREP TIME 10 minutes   START TO FINISH 40 minutes

2 cups chopped cooked chicken

1 can (14.5 oz) diced tomatoes with garlic, onion and oregano, drained

4 medium green onions, sliced (¼ cup)

1 package (5 oz) Italian-seasoned croutons

¼ cup Italian dressing

¾ cup shredded Parmesan cheese (3 oz)

¼ cup sliced fresh basil leaves

1 Heat oven to 350°F. In ungreased 11×7-inch (2-quart) glass baking dish, layer chicken, tomatoes, onions and croutons. Drizzle with dressing.

2 Cover; bake 20 minutes. Uncover; sprinkle with cheese. Bake about 10 minutes longer or until hot and cheese is melted. Sprinkle with basil.

1 Serving: Calories 290; Total Fat 14g (Saturated Fat 4.5g; Trans Fat 1.5g); Cholesterol 50mg; Sodium 830mg; Total Carbohydrate 20g (Dietary Fiber 2g); Protein 21g **Exchanges:** 1 Starch, ½ Other Carbohydrate, 2½ Medium-Fat Meat **Carbohydrate Choices:** 1

Time-Saver

Any cooked chicken will work in this recipe. Use deli rotisserie chicken or refrigerated cubed cooked chicken. Or use leftover grilled chicken, which would give a slightly smoky flavor to the casserole.

Chicken Artichoke Casserole

6 servings (1⅓ cups each)   PREP TIME 15 minutes   START TO FINISH 50 minutes

1 **tablespoon olive oil**

1 **medium red bell pepper, chopped (1 cup)**

4 **medium green onions, sliced (¼ cup)**

3 **cups chopped cooked chicken**

1 **can (14 oz) artichoke hearts, drained, chopped**

1 **container (10 oz) refrigerated reduced-fat Alfredo pasta sauce**

1 **cup shredded Asiago cheese (4 oz)**

½ **cup reduced-fat mayonnaise**

1½ **cups Romano cheese croutons (from 5-oz bag), coarsely crushed**

   Additonal sliced green onions, if desired

1 Heat oven to 350°F. Spray 11×7-inch (2-quart) glass baking dish with cooking spray.

2 In 6-inch skillet, heat oil over medium heat. Add bell pepper and onions; cook 2 to 3 minutes, stirring occasionally, until vegetables begin to soften. In large bowl, mix bell pepper mixture and all remaining ingredients except croutons. Spoon into baking dish. Top with croutons.

3 Bake uncovered 30 to 35 minutes or until hot and bubbly. Sprinkle with additional sliced green onions.

1 Serving: Calories 460; Total Fat 28g (Saturated Fat 11g; Trans Fat 1g); Cholesterol 105mg; Sodium 890mg; Total Carbohydrate 20g (Dietary Fiber 4g); Protein 30g **Exchanges:** 1 Starch, 1 Vegetable, 3½ Medium-Fat Meat, 2 Fat **Carbohydrate Choices:** 1

Quick Variation

If refrigerated Alfredo sauce is not available, use about 1 cup of Alfredo sauce from a jar.

Quick Menu Idea

Spoon servings of the casserole onto individual plates and add steamed green beans to each serving.

Chicken and Broccoli Quiche

6 servings   PREP TIME 10 minutes   START TO FINISH 1 hour 25 minutes

1 refrigerated pie crust, softened as directed on box

1 cup chopped deli rotisserie chicken (from 2-lb chicken)

1 cup frozen chopped broccoli, thawed, drained

4 eggs

1¾ cups half-and-half

¼ teaspoon salt

½ cup garlic-and-herb whipped cream cheese spread (from 8-oz container)

1 Heat oven to 400°F. In 9-inch glass pie plate, place pie crust as directed on box for One-Crust Filled Pie. Bake 8 to 10 minutes or until light golden brown.

2 Sprinkle chicken and broccoli in partially baked crust. In medium bowl, beat eggs, half-and-half and salt with whisk until well blended. Pour into crust.

3 Drop cream cheese by teaspoonfuls on top. Cover crust edge with strips of foil to prevent excessive browning. Bake 10 minutes.

4 Reduce oven temperature to 300°F. Bake 35 to 40 minutes longer or until knife inserted in center comes out clean. Remove foil; let stand 15 minutes before cutting.

1 Serving: Calories 380; Total Fat 26g (Saturated Fat 12g; Trans Fat 0.5g); Cholesterol 205mg; Sodium 430mg; Total Carbohydrate 23g (Dietary Fiber 0g); Protein 15g **Exchanges:** 1½ Starch, 1½ Medium-Fat Meat, 3½ Fat **Carbohydrate Choices:** 1½

Chicken- and Spinach-Stuffed Shells

6 servings (3 shells each)   PREP TIME 30 minutes   START TO FINISH 1 hour 10 minutes

18 **large pasta shells (from 16-oz package)**

1 **container (15 oz) whole-milk ricotta cheese**

1 **egg, slightly beaten**

¼ **cup grated Parmesan cheese**

2 **boxes (9 oz each) frozen chopped spinach, thawed, squeezed to drain**

1 **cup chopped deli rotisserie chicken (from 2-lb chicken)**

1 **jar (25.5 oz) tomato pasta sauce**

2 **cups shredded Italian cheese blend (8 oz)**

1 Heat oven to 350°F. Cook and drain pasta as directed on package. Rinse with cool water; drain.

2 Meanwhile, in medium bowl, mix ricotta cheese, egg, Parmesan cheese, spinach and chicken.

3 Spread 1 cup of the pasta sauce in bottom of 13×9-inch (3-quart) glass baking dish. Spoon about 2 tablespoons ricotta mixture into each pasta shell. Arrange shells, filled side up, on sauce in baking dish. Spoon remaining sauce over stuffed shells.

4 Cover with foil; bake 30 minutes. Sprinkle with Italian cheese blend. Bake uncovered 5 to 10 minutes longer or until cheese is melted.

1 Serving: Calories 570; Total Fat 28g (Saturated Fat 15g; Trans Fat 0.5g); Cholesterol 120mg; Sodium 1330mg; Total Carbohydrate 48g (Dietary Fiber 4g); Protein 33g **Exchanges:** 3 Starch, 1 Vegetable, 3 Medium-Fat Meat, 2 Fat **Carbohydrate Choices:** 3

Time-Saver

Make this dish the night before. Cover and refrigerate until ready to bake. Add 5 to 10 minutes to the first bake time before topping with the cheese.

Green Chile–Chicken Lasagna

10 servings   PREP TIME 25 minutes   START TO FINISH 1 hour 35 minutes

1 **container (15 oz) ricotta cheese**

1 **egg**

1 **cup grated Parmesan cheese**

2 **cups chopped cooked chicken**

2 **cans (10 oz each) green enchilada sauce**

2 **cans (4.5 oz each) chopped green chiles**

1 **package (8 oz) oven-ready lasagna noodles (12)**

4 **cups shredded mozzarella cheese (16 oz)**

1 Heat oven to 350°F. In medium bowl, mix ricotta cheese, egg and ½ cup of the Parmesan cheese; set aside. In another medium bowl, mix chicken, enchilada sauce and chiles.

2 In ungreased 13×9-inch (3-quart) glass baking dish, spread 1 cup of the chicken mixture. Top with 3 uncooked lasagna noodles; press gently into chicken mixture. Spread with ⅔ cup of the ricotta mixture. Sprinkle with 1 cup of the mozzarella cheese. Repeat layers 3 times. Sprinkle with remaining ½ cup Parmesan cheese.

3 Cover; bake 45 minutes. Uncover; bake 10 to 15 minutes longer or until noodles are tender, cheese is bubbly and edges are lightly browned. Let stand 10 minutes before serving.

1 Serving: Calories 420; Total Fat 20g (Saturated Fat 11g; Trans Fat 0g); Cholesterol 90mg; Sodium 880mg; Total Carbohydrate 28g (Dietary Fiber 1g); Protein 33g **Exchanges:** 1½ Starch, ½ Other Carbohydrate, 4 Lean Meat, 1 Fat **Carbohydrate Choices:** 2

Time-Saver

The lasagna noodles won't cover the entire baking dish; they expand as they absorb liquid and cook, so when the dish is done, the lasagna will fill the pan. Look for oven ready lasagna with the rest of the dry pasta in the grocery store.

Home-Style Chicken Dinner

4 servings   PREP TIME 30 minutes   START TO FINISH 1 hour 20 minutes

2 **teaspoons dried basil leaves**

1 **teaspoon seasoned salt**

1 **teaspoon garlic-pepper blend**

2 **tablespoons olive oil**

1 **cut-up whole chicken (3 to 3½ lb), skin removed if desired**

6 **small unpeeled red potatoes, cut into quarters (2 cups)**

2 **medium dark-orange sweet potatoes, peeled, cut into 1-inch pieces (3 cups)**

1 **medium green bell pepper, cut into 1-inch pieces (1 cup)**

3 **plum (Roma) tomatoes, cut into quarters**

1 Heat oven to 400°F. Spray 13×9-inch (3-quart) glass baking dish with cooking spray.

2 In large bowl, mix basil, seasoned salt, garlic-pepper blend and oil. Brush about half of the mixture on chicken. Add remaining ingredients to bowl; toss to coat.

3 Place vegetables in baking dish. Place chicken on vegetables. Brush with any remaining oil mixture.

4 Bake uncovered 45 to 50 minutes or until vegetables are tender and juice of chicken is clear when thickest piece is cut to bone (at least 165°F). Serve with pan juices.

1 Serving: Calories 580; Total Fat 29g (Saturated Fat 7g; Trans Fat 0.5g); Cholesterol 140mg; Sodium 510mg; Total Carbohydrate 33g (Dietary Fiber 5g); Protein 46g **Exchanges:** 1½ Starch, ½ Other Carbohydrate, 6 Medium-Fat Meat **Carbohydrate Choices:** 2

Time-Saver

Keep frozen chopped onions and a jar of chopped garlic on hand to make prep quicker for recipes like this.

Italian Chicken Braciole

6 servings   PREP TIME 25 minutes   START TO FINISH 1 hour 40 minutes

4 slices bacon, chopped

1 medium onion, chopped (½ cup)

1 clove garlic, chopped

¼ cup Italian style dry bread crumbs

¼ cup grated Parmesan cheese

2 tablespoons chopped fresh rosemary leaves

1 egg

6 boneless skinless chicken thighs

1 tablespoon olive oil

1 tablespoon butter or margarine

1 can (14.5 oz) diced tomatoes with Italian herbs, undrained

3 tablespoons tomato paste

Hot cooked fettuccine, if desired

1 Heat oven to 350°F. Spray 11×7-inch (2-quart) glass baking dish with cooking spray.

2 In 12-inch skillet, cook bacon over medium-high heat, stirring frequently, until crisp. Reduce heat to low. Add onion and garlic; cook 2 to 3 minutes, stirring occasionally, until soft. Remove from heat; stir in bread crumbs. Add cheese, rosemary and egg; mix well.

3 Unfold chicken thighs so inside faces up. Spoon stuffing mixture over thighs, about 2 tablespoons each. Fold over; secure with toothpicks.

4 In same skillet, heat oil and butter. Add chicken; brown 2 minutes on each side. Place in baking dish. In medium bowl, mix tomatoes and tomato paste; pour over chicken.

5 Cover with foil; bake 1 hour to 1 hour 15 minutes or until thermometer inserted in center of stuffing reads at least 165°F. Serve chicken over hot cooked fettuccine.

1 Serving: Calories 250; Total Fat 14g (Saturated Fat 5g; Trans Fat 0g); Cholesterol 90mg; Sodium 500mg; Total Carbohydrate 9g (Dietary Fiber 1g); Protein 21g **Exchanges:** ½ Other Carbohydrate, 3 Medium-Fat Meat **Carbohydrate Choices:** ½

Quick Menu Idea

Braciole is the Italian term for roulade—a thin slice of meat rolled around a filling such as cheese, bread crumbs and vegetables. Serve the Braciole with a side of pasta and buttered baby carrots.

Layered Chicken-Black Bean Enchiladas

6 servings   PREP TIME 25 minutes   START TO FINISH 1 hour 15 minutes

2 **cups chopped deli rotisserie chicken (from 2-lb chicken)**

2 **tablespoons chopped fresh cilantro**

1 **can (15 oz) black beans, drained, rinsed**

1 **can (4.5 oz) chopped green chiles, undrained**

1 **can (10 oz) enchilada sauce**

8 **corn tortillas (5 or 6 inch)**

1½ **cups shredded Colby–Monterey Jack cheese blend (6 oz)**

1 **container (8 oz) sour cream**

1 Heat oven to 375°F. Spray 11×7-inch (2-quart) glass baking dish with cooking spray. In medium bowl, mix chicken, cilantro, black beans and chiles.

2 Spread 2 tablespoons of the enchilada sauce in bottom of baking dish. Place 4 tortillas over sauce, overlapping as necessary. Spoon half of the chicken mixture over tortillas; sprinkle with ½ cup of the cheese. Spoon half of the remaining enchilada sauce and half of the sour cream randomly over cheese. Repeat with remaining tortillas, chicken mixture, ½ cup cheese, the enchilada sauce and sour cream.

3 Cover with foil; bake 30 to 35 minutes or until hot. Sprinkle with remaining ½ cup cheese. Bake uncovered 5 minutes longer or until cheese is melted. Let stand 10 minutes before serving.

1 Serving: Calories 440; Total Fat 21g (Saturated Fat 11g; Trans Fat 0.5g); Cholesterol 90mg; Sodium 730mg; Total Carbohydrate 35g (Dietary Fiber 5g); Protein 28g **Exchanges:** 2½ Starch, 3 Lean Meat, 2 Fat **Carbohydrate Choices:** 2

Quick Variation

Pinto beans are a great substitute for the black beans in this recipe.

Swiss Chicken Casserole

8 servings   PREP TIME 15 minutes   START TO FINISH 1 hour 10 minutes

4 cups boiling water

2 boxes (6 oz each) sun-dried tomato Florentine long grain and wild rice mix

4 large boneless skinless chicken breasts

8 slices thick-sliced cooked deli ham (about 10 oz)

¼ cup diced red bell pepper

4 slices (1 oz each) Swiss cheese, cut in half

1 Heat oven to 350°F. Spray 13×9-inch (3-quart) baking dish with cooking spray. In baking dish, stir boiling water, rice and rice seasoning mixes.

2 Cut chicken breasts in half lengthwise; wrap ham slice around each chicken piece. Stir bell pepper into rice. Place wrapped chicken over rice.

3 Cover with foil; bake 40 to 45 minutes. Uncover; bake about 10 minutes longer or until liquid is absorbed and juice of chicken is clear when thickest part is cut (at least 165°F).

4 Top each chicken breast with cheese. Bake uncovered 3 to 4 minutes or until cheese is melted.

1 Serving: Calories 240; Total Fat 8g (Saturated Fat 4g; Trans Fat 0g); Cholesterol 75mg; Sodium 660mg; Total Carbohydrate 13g (Dietary Fiber 0g); Protein 28g **Exchanges:** 1 Starch, 3½ Very Lean Meat, 1 Fat **Carbohydrate Choices:** 1

Quick Menu Idea

Use other varieties of rice mixtures, such as chicken or mushroom to make this casserole. Then pair with steamed whole green beans to complete the meal.

Oven-Roasted Chicken and Vegetables

4 servings PREP TIME 10 minutes START TO FINISH 35 minutes

2 **cups ready-to-eat baby-cut carrots, cut in half lengthwise**

2 **cups frozen potato wedges with skins (from 24-oz bag)**

1 **cup frozen whole green beans**

1 **cup frozen bell pepper and onion stir-fry (from 1-lb bag)**

1 **cup grape tomatoes**

3 **tablespoons olive or vegetable oil**

½ **teaspoon seasoned salt**

1 **deli rotisserie chicken (2 lb), cut into pieces**

1 Heat oven to 475°F. In large bowl, toss all ingredients except chicken.

2 In 15×10×1-inch pan, arrange chicken and vegetables in single layer.

3 Roast uncovered 20 to 25 minutes or until vegetables are crisp-tender and chicken is hot.

1 Serving: Calories 440; Total Fat 20g (Saturated Fat 4g; Trans Fat 0g); Cholesterol 110mg; Sodium 820mg; Total Carbohydrate 27g (Dietary Fiber 6g); Protein 39g **Exchanges:** 1 Starch, 2 Vegetable, 4½ Lean Meat, 1 Fat **Carbohydrate Choices:** 2

Quick Menu Idea

A crisp green and mixed-vegetable salad is the perfect accompaniment for this hearty oven meal.

Quick Menu Idea

Toss a fresh Caesar salad together to serve with this casserole. Look for bags of ready-to-serve salads in the produce department.

Onion-Topped Turkey Divan

4 servings (1 cup each)   PREP TIME 15 minutes   START TO FINISH 1 hour 10 minutes

1 **bag (12 oz) frozen broccoli florets, thawed**

2 **cups diced cooked turkey**

1 **can (10¾ oz) condensed cream of chicken soup**

½ **cup mayonnaise or salad dressing**

½ **cup milk**

1 **cup shredded Cheddar cheese (4 oz)**

1 **cup French-fried onions (from 2.8-oz can), coarsely crushed**

1 Heat oven to 350°F. Spray 8-inch square (2-quart) glass baking dish with cooking spray. Layer broccoli and turkey in baking dish.

2 In medium bowl, mix soup, mayonnaise and milk; stir in cheese. Spread over turkey and broccoli.

3 Cover baking dish with foil; bake 30 minutes. Sprinkle with onions. Uncover; bake 20 to 25 minutes longer or until bubbly and broccoli is tender.

1 Serving: Calories 560; Total Fat 37g (Saturated Fat 12g; Trans Fat 2.5g); Cholesterol 110mg; Sodium 1130mg; Total Carbohydrate 22g (Dietary Fiber 3g); Protein 34g **Exchanges:** 1½ Starch, 4 Loan Meat, 5 Fat **Carbohydrate Choices:** 1½

Quick Variation

Diced chicken would be a good substitute for the turkey, and cream of celery or mushroom soup could be used instead of the cream of chicken soup.

Turkey and Green Chile Stuffing Casserole

6 servings   PREP TIME 25 minutes   START TO FINISH 1 hour 40 minutes

2 **tablespoons butter
   or margarine**

1 **medium onion, chopped
   (½ cup)**

1 **small red bell pepper,
   chopped (½ cup)**

4 **cups seasoned cornbread
   stuffing**

1 **cup frozen whole kernel
   corn**

1 **can (4.5 oz) chopped
   green chiles, undrained**

1½ **cups water**

2 **turkey breast tenderloins
   (about ¾ lb each)**

½ **teaspoon chili powder**

½ **teaspoon peppered
   seasoned salt**

1 Heat oven to 350°F. Spray 11×7-inch (2-quart) glass baking dish with cooking spray.

2 In 12-inch nonstick skillet, melt butter over medium-high heat. Add onion and bell pepper; cook 2 to 3 minutes, stirring frequently, until tender. Stir in stuffing, corn, chiles and water. Spread mixture in baking dish.

3 Sprinkle both sides of turkey tenderloins with chili powder and peppered seasoned salt. Place tenderloins on stuffing mixture, pressing slightly into mixture.

4 Spray sheet of foil with cooking spray; place sprayed side down over baking dish. Bake 1 hour. Uncover; bake 10 to 15 minutes longer or until juice of turkey is no longer pink when centers of thickest part is cut (at least 165°F).

1 Serving: Calories 360; Total Fat 7g (Saturated Fat 3g; Trans Fat 0.5g); Cholesterol 85mg; Sodium 990mg; Total Carbohydrate 43g (Dietary Fiber 3g); Protein 33g **Exchanges:** 3 Starch, 3½ Very Lean Meat, ½ Fat **Carbohydrate Choices:** 3

Bacon-Pepper Mac and Cheese

4 servings (1½ cups each)   PREP TIME 25 minutes   START TO FINISH 50 minutes

3 cups uncooked penne pasta (10 oz)

⅓ cup butter

1 red bell pepper, thinly sliced

4 medium green onions, sliced (¼ cup)

¼ cup all-purpose flour

½ teaspoon salt

¼ teaspoon pepper

1 teaspoon Dijon mustard

2¼ cups milk

10 slices precooked bacon (from 2.1-oz package), cut into ½-inch pieces

1 cup shredded sharp Cheddar cheese (4 oz)

4 oz Muenster cheese, shredded (1 cup)

2 oz Gruyère cheese, shredded (½ cup)

¼ cup Italian style bread crumbs

1 Heat oven to 350°F. Spray 2-quart casserole with cooking spray. Cook and drain pasta as directed on package, using minimum cooking time.

2 In 3-quart saucepan, melt butter over low heat. Reserve 1 tablespoon of the butter in small bowl. Stir bell pepper and onions into butter in saucepan. Increase heat to medium; cook and stir 1 minute. Stir in flour, salt, pepper and mustard. Cook and stir until mixture is bubbly. Increase heat to medium-high. Gradually add milk, stirring constantly, until mixture boils and thickens, about 5 minutes. Gently stir in bacon and pasta. Remove from heat; stir in cheeses until melted. Pour into casserole.

3 Stir bread crumbs into melted butter in small bowl. Sprinkle over pasta mixture.

4 Bake uncovered 20 to 25 minutes or until edges are bubbly.

1 Serving: Calories 1010; Total Fat 51g (Saturated Fat 29g; Trans Fat 1.5g); Cholesterol 145mg; Sodium 1790mg; Total Carbohydrate 91g (Dietary Fiber 5g); Protein 45g **Exchanges:** 5½ Starch, ½ Other Carbohydrate, 4 High-Fat Meat, 3 Fat **Carbohydrate Choices:** 6

Quick Variation

You can use elbow macaroni in place of the penne. You can also use Swiss cheese instead of the Gruyère, although Gruyère has a more pronounced nutty flavor than regular Swiss.

Beer-Cheese Mac and Sausages

8 servings   PREP TIME 20 minutes   START TO FINISH 1 hour

1 **box (7 oz) elbow macaroni (2½ cups)**

3 **tablespoons butter**

1 **small onion, finely chopped (⅓ cup)**

3 **tablespoons all-purpose flour**

2 **cups half-and-half**

1 **teaspoon ground mustard**

½ **teaspoon red pepper sauce**

¼ **teaspoon salt**

1 **cup regular or nonalcoholic beer**

2 **cups shredded Colby-Monterey Jack cheese blend (8 oz)**

1 **package (1 lb) cocktail-size smoked link sausages (about 48 sausages)**

2 **cups popped microwave popcorn**

1 Heat oven to 350°F. Spray 2½-quart casserole with cooking spray. Cook and drain macaroni as directed on package, using minimum cook time. Return macaroni to saucepan.

2 Meanwhile, in 3-quart saucepan, melt butter over medium heat. Add onion; cook 2 to 3 minutes, stirring frequently, until softened. Stir in flour; cook and stir 1 minute. Gradually stir in half-and-half, mustard, pepper sauce and salt; cook and stir until thickened and bubbly, about 5 minutes. Stir in beer. Remove from heat; let stand 2 to 3 minutes.

3 Stir in cheese until melted. Add sausages to cooked macaroni; stir in cheese sauce. Spoon macaroni mixture into casserole.

4 Bake uncovered 30 to 40 minutes or until bubbly and top begins to brown. Top with popcorn just before serving.

1 Serving: Calories 500; Total Fat 34g (Saturated Fat 16g; Trans Fat 1g); Cholesterol 80mg; Sodium 1130mg; Total Carbohydrate 30g (Dietary Fiber 1g); Protein 16g **Exchanges:** 2 Starch, 1½ High-Fat Meat, 4 Fat **Carbohydrate Choices:** 2

Quick Menu Idea

Serve this perfect football-game casserole with soft pretzels and fresh veggies, such as carrots, celery, pepper strips and cucumber slices.

German Pork 'n Cabbage Casserole

6 servings (1 rib and 1 cup vegetable mixture each)   PREP TIME 20 minutes   START TO FINISH 1 hour 5 minutes

3 slices bacon

6 country-style pork ribs

½ teaspoon salt

¼ teaspoon pepper

5 cups coleslaw mix
   (from 16-oz bag)

1 large onion, chopped
   (1 cup)

1 can (8 oz) sauerkraut,
   drained

1 apple, chopped

1 cup julienne-cut carrots
   (from 10-oz bag)

¾ cup apple cider

1 teaspoon caraway seed

1 Heat oven to 350°F. Spray 13×9-inch (3-quart) glass baking dish with cooking spray. In 12-inch nonstick skillet, cook bacon until crisp; remove from skillet and crumble into small bowl.

2 Sprinkle ribs with salt and pepper. In bacon drippings, cook ribs over high heat 3 to 4 minutes, turning once, until brown. Place ribs in baking dish, reserving drippings in skillet.

3 In same skillet, cook coleslaw mix and onion over medium heat about 3 minutes, stirring occasionally, until softened and wilted. Remove from heat. Add bacon, sauerkraut, apple, carrots, cider and caraway seed; mix well. Spoon on top of ribs.

4 Cover with foil; bake 30 to 45 minutes or until pork is tender and no longer pink next to bones.

1 Serving: Calories 280; Total Fat 13g (Saturated Fat 4.5g; Trans Fat 0g); Cholesterol 60mg; Sodium 610mg; Total Carbohydrate 18g (Dietary Fiber 4g); Protein 21g **Exchanges:** ½ Other Carbohydrate, 2 Vegetable, 2½ Medium-Fat Meat **Carbohydrate Choices:** 1

Time-Saver

Using the bag of coleslaw mix makes preparation of this casserole quick and easy but if you want to make your own, slice the cabbage very finely.

Ham and Cheese Ziti

8 servings (1⅓ cups each) PREP TIME 30 minutes START TO FINISH 55 minutes

1 box (16 oz) ziti pasta (5 cups)

½ cup butter or margarine

2 cloves garlic, finely chopped

½ cup all-purpose flour

1 teaspoon salt

4 cups milk

1 teaspoon Dijon mustard

4 cups shredded Colby cheese (16 oz)

8 oz sliced cooked deli ham, cut into thin strips

⅔ cup grated Parmesan cheese

1 Heat oven to 350°F. Cook and drain pasta as directed on package, using minimum cook time.

2 Meanwhile, in 4-quart saucepan or Dutch oven, melt butter over low heat. Add garlic; cook 30 seconds, stirring frequently. With whisk, stir in flour and salt. Cook over medium heat, stirring constantly, until mixture is smooth and bubbly. Gradually stir in milk. Heat to boiling, stirring constantly. Boil and stir 1 minute. Stir in mustard and Colby cheese. Cook, stirring occasionally, until cheese is melted.

3 Stir pasta and ham into cheese sauce. Pour pasta mixture into ungreased 13×9-inch (3-quart) glass baking dish. Sprinkle with Parmesan cheese.

4 Bake 20 to 25 minutes or until bubbly.

1 Serving: Calories 740; Total Fat 38g (Saturated Fat 23g; Trans Fat 1g); Cholesterol 120mg; Sodium 1470mg; Total Carbohydrate 62g (Dietary Fiber 3g); Protein 37g **Exchanges:** 3 Starch, 1 Other Carbohydrate, 4 High-Fat Meat, 1 Fat **Carbohydrate Choices:** 4

Italian Sausage Melt Casserole

4 servings (1 cup each)   PREP TIME 20 minutes   START TO FINISH 50 minutes

1¼ cups Original Bisquick mix

¼ cup butter or margarine, softened

2 tablespoons very hot water

½ lb bulk spicy Italian pork sausage

1 small green bell pepper, chopped (½ cup)

1 cup Alfredo pasta sauce (from 16-oz jar)

1 cup shredded mozzarella cheese (4 oz)

2 tablespoons grated Parmesan cheese

½ cup grape tomatoes, each cut in half

2 tablespoons fresh basil leaves, cut into strips

1 Heat oven to 400°F. Lightly spray bottom only of 8-inch square (2-quart) glass baking dish with cooking spray.

2 In medium bowl, stir Bisquick mix, butter and very hot water until dough forms. Press dough in bottom of baking dish.

3 In 10-inch skillet, cook sausage and bell pepper over medium-high heat 5 to 7 minutes, stirring occasionally, until sausage is no longer pink; drain if necessary. Spread sausage mixture over crust; spread Alfredo sauce over sausage. Sprinkle with cheeses.

4 Bake uncovered 25 to 30 minutes or until casserole is bubbly around edges and cheese is lightly browned. Sprinkle with tomatoes and basil.

1 Serving: Calories 710; Total Fat 53g (Saturated Fat 29g; Trans Fat 2.5g); Cholesterol 130mg; Sodium 1470mg; Total Carbohydrate 33g (Dietary Fiber 1g); Protein 24g **Exchanges:** 2 Starch, 2½ High-Fat Meat, 6½ Fat Carbohydrate Choices: 2

Quick Menu Idea

Serve this hearty casserole with a tossed green salad and apple crisp for dessert.

Cheesy Italian Pork Chops with Vegetables

4 servings   PREP TIME 10 minutes   START TO FINISH 50 minutes

4 **bone-in pork loin chops,
   ½ inch thick (about 1½ lb)**

1 **teaspoon dried thyme
   leaves**

½ **teaspoon garlic-pepper
   blend**

2 **tablespoons olive or
   vegetable oil**

3 **medium unpeeled Yukon
   Gold potatoes, cut into
   ½-inch cubes**

1 **red bell pepper, cut into
   bite-size strips**

⅔ **cup shredded Italian
   cheese blend**

1 Heat oven to 425°F. Spray 15×10×1-inch pan with sides with cooking spray. Place pork chops in half of pan.

2 In large bowl, mix ¾ teaspoon of the thyme, the garlic-pepper blend and oil; lightly brush tops and sides of pork with some of the oil mixture. In remaining oil mixture in bowl, toss potatoes and bell pepper to coat. Spread vegetables in other half of pan.

3 Bake 30 to 35 minutes or until pork is no longer pink in center. Sprinkle cheese and remaining ¼ teaspoon thyme over pork; bake 2 to 3 minutes longer or until cheese is melted.

1 Serving: Calories 440; Total Fat 20g (Saturated Fat 6g; Trans Fat 0g); Cholesterol 85mg; Sodium 210mg; Total Carbohydrate 30g (Dietary Fiber 3g); Protein 35g **Exchanges:** 2 Starch, 4 Lean Meat, 1½ Fat **Carbohydrate Choices:** 2

Time-Saver

Pre-shredded cheese is a definite time-saving product. Look for the Italian cheese blend in the dairy case near other shredded cheese products. Depending on the manufacturer, five or six cheeses are included in the blend. Either type will work in this recipe.

Roasted Pork Tenderloin with Vegetables

4 servings   PREP TIME 15 minutes   START TO FINISH 55 minutes

1 **tablespoon vegetable oil**

1 **pork tenderloin (1 lb)**

2 **teaspoons garlic-pepper blend**

2 **medium baking or Yukon Gold potatoes, peeled**

4 **small zucchini (1 lb)**

1½ **cups frozen small whole onions (from 1-lb bag)**

2 **tablespoons butter or margarine, melted**

½ **teaspoon dried thyme leaves**

¼ **teaspoon salt**

1 Heat oven to 425°F. Rub oil over pork; sprinkle with garlic-pepper blend. In ungreased 15×10×1-inch pan, place pork. Insert ovenproof meat thermometer horizontally into center of thickest part of pork.

2 Cut potatoes and zucchini in half lengthwise. Arrange potatoes, zucchini and onions around pork. Drizzle butter over vegetables; sprinkle with thyme and salt.

3 Roast uncovered 30 to 40 minutes or until thermometer reads 145°F. Let pork rest for at least 3 minutes. Cut pork into thin slices. Serve with vegetables.

1 Serving: Calories 320; Total Fat 14g (Saturated Fat 5g; Trans Fat 0g); Cholesterol 85mg; Sodium 250mg; Total Carbohydrate 21g (Dietary Fiber 4g); Protein 29g **Exchanges:** 1 Starch, 1 Vegetable, 3½ Lean Meat, ½ Fat **Carbohydrate Choices:** 1½

Quick Menu Idea

Pick up some creamy coleslaw at the deli to serve with this meat and vegetable dish. Then, add some soft, tender dinner rolls—they're always a great addition to a meal.

Smoked Pork Chops with Apple and Sweet Potato

4 servings   PREP TIME 20 minutes   START TO FINISH 1 hour

2 **tablespoons vegetable oil**

1 **teaspoon ground cinnamon**

½ **teaspoon ground cumin**

½ **teaspoon ground coriander**

1 **large peeled dark-orange sweet potato, cut into ½-inch slices, slices quartered**

1 **large unpeeled Granny Smith apple, cut into ½-inch pieces**

½ **small onion, cut into thin wedges and wedges separated**

1 **tablespoon packed brown sugar**

4 **fully cooked smoked boneless pork chops (about 2½ oz each)**

1 Heat oven to 425°F. Spray 15×10×1-inch pan with sides with cooking spray. In small bowl, mix oil, cinnamon, cumin and coriander.

2 In large bowl, combine sweet potato, apple and onion. Drizzle with 1 tablespoon of the oil-spice mixture; toss to coat. Spread mixture in pan.

3 Bake 30 minutes. Meanwhile, stir brown sugar into remaining oil-spice mixture (mixture will be thick). Rub mixture over one side of each pork chop.

4 Remove pan from oven. With spatula, move vegetable mixture to one side of pan. Place pork, coated side up, in other half of pan.

5 Bake 8 to 10 minutes longer or until pork is thoroughly heated, and sweet potato and apple are tender.

1 Serving: Calories 260; Total Fat 12g (Saturated Fat 3g; Trans Fat 0g); Cholesterol 45mg; Sodium 45mg; Total Carbohydrate 22g (Dietary Fiber 3g); Protein 16g **Exchanges:** 1 Starch, ½ Other Carbohydrate, 2 Lean Meat, 1 Fat Carbohydrate Choices: 1½

Time-Saver

Look for packages of smoked pork chops near the bacon at the grocery store. Since the chops are fully cooked, using them speeds up meal preparation because you only have to bake them until they are thoroughly heated.

Spicy Chorizo-Stuffed Peppers

8 servings   PREP TIME 15 minutes   START TO FINISH 1 hour 15 minutes

1⅓ cups water

⅔ cup uncooked regular long-grain white rice

2 smoked chorizo sausage links (3 oz each), diced (1¼ cups)

1 can (15 oz) black beans, drained, rinsed

1 can (14.5 oz) fire-roasted tomatoes with chipotle peppers, undrained

1½ cups shredded Mexican cheese blend (6 oz)

4 medium red and/or green bell peppers, each cut in half lengthwise, seeds and membranes removed

¼ cup chopped green onions (4 medium)

1 In 2-quart saucepan, heat water to boiling over medium-high heat. Stir in rice. Reduce heat to low; cover and simmer 15 minutes or until liquid is absorbed and rice is tender.

2 Heat oven to 375°F. In medium bowl, combine sausage, beans, tomatoes, 1 cup of the cheese and the cooked rice. Place pepper halves cut side up in ungreased 13×9-inch (3-quart) glass baking dish. Spoon about ⅔ cup rice mixture into each pepper half, mounding as necessary.

3 Cover tightly with foil; bake 35 to 40 minutes or until peppers are crisp-tender and filling is thoroughly heated. Uncover; sprinkle tops of peppers with remaining ½ cup cheese and the green onions. Bake uncovered 5 minutes longer or until cheese is melted.

1 Serving: Calories 340; Total Fat 15g (Saturated Fat 7g; Trans Fat 0g); Cholesterol 40mg; Sodium 540mg; Total Carbohydrate 34g (Dietary Fiber 7g); Protein 17g **Exchanges:** 2 Starch, 1 Vegetable, 1 Medium-Fat Meat, 2 Fat **Carbohydrate Choices:** 2

Quick Variation

Diced tomatoes with green chiles or plain fire-roasted tomatoes can be substituted for the fire-roasted tomatoes with chipotle peppers.

Make-Ahead Cheeseburger Lasagna

8 servings   PREP TIME 35 minutes   START TO FINISH 10 hours 5 minutes

1½ **lb lean (at least 80%) ground beef**

3 **tablespoons dried minced onion**

1 **can (15 oz) tomato sauce**

1½ **cups water**

½ **cup ketchup**

1 **tablespoon yellow mustard**

1 **egg**

1 **container (15 oz) ricotta cheese**

2 **cups shredded American-Cheddar cheese blend (8 oz)**

12 **uncooked lasagna noodles**

1 **cup shredded Cheddar cheese (4 oz)**

1 **cup shredded lettuce**

1 **medium tomato, sliced**

½ **cup dill pickle slices**

   Additional ketchup, if desired

1 Spray 13×9-inch (3-quart) glass baking dish with cooking spray. In 12-inch nonstick skillet, cook beef and onion over medium-high heat 5 to 7 minutes, stirring occasionally, until beef is thoroughly cooked; drain. Stir in tomato sauce, water, ketchup and mustard. Simmer 5 minutes, stirring occasionally.

2 Meanwhile, in medium bowl, beat egg with fork or whisk. Stir in ricotta cheese and 2 cups cheese blend.

3 Spread 1 cup beef mixture in bottom of baking dish. Top with 4 uncooked noodles. Spread half of the ricotta mixture over noodles; top with 1½ cups beef mixture. Repeat layers once with 4 noodles, remaining ricotta mixture and 1½ cups beef mixture. Top with remaining 4 noodles, beef mixture and 1 cup Cheddar cheese. Cover with foil; refrigerate at least 8 hours or overnight.

4 Heat oven to 350°F. Bake lasagna covered 45 minutes. Uncover; bake 25 to 35 minutes longer or until bubbly. Remove from oven. Cover with foil; let stand 5 to 10 minutes before cutting.

5 Just before serving, top with lettuce, tomato and pickles. Serve with additional ketchup.

1 Serving: Calories 590; Total Fat 32g (Saturated Fat 17g; Trans Fat 1g); Cholesterol 135mg; Sodium 1050mg; Total Carbohydrate 38g (Dietary Fiber 3g); Protein 39g **Exchanges:** 2 Starch, ½ Other Carbohydrate, 5 Medium-Fat Meat, 1 Fat **Carbohydrate Choices:** 2½

Time-Saver

Although this recipe is super to make ahead, you can bake it right away, too. Just cover the dish with foil and bake as directed.

Meat Lover's Pizza Casserole

8 servings (1½ cups each)   PREP TIME 20 minutes   START TO FINISH 1 hour

1 box (16 oz) ziti pasta
   (5 cups)

½ lb bulk Italian pork
   sausage

1 medium onion, chopped
   (½ cup)

1 medium green bell pepper,
   chopped (1 cup)

2 cloves garlic, finely
   chopped

2 cans (15 oz each) pizza
   sauce

8 slices bacon, crisply
   cooked, crumbled

½ package (3.5-oz size)
   sliced pepperoni

2 cups shredded Italian
   cheese blend (8 oz)

1 Heat oven to 350°F. Spray 3-quart casserole with cooking spray. Cook and drain pasta as directed on package, using minimum cook time. Return to saucepan.

2 Meanwhile, in 12-inch skillet, cook and stir sausage, onion, bell pepper and garlic over medium-high heat about 7 minutes or until sausage is no longer pink and onion is softened. Stir in pizza sauce, bacon and pepperoni.

3 Pour sausage mixture over cooked pasta; stir. Spoon half of pasta mixture (about 4 cups) into casserole. Sprinkle with 1 cup of the cheese. Spoon remaining pasta mixture on top.

4 Bake uncovered 30 minutes. Top with remaining 1 cup cheese. Bake 5 to 10 minutes longer or until hot in center and cheese is melted and bubbly.

1 Serving: Calories 540; Total Fat 21g (Saturated Fat 9g; Trans Fat 0g), Cholesterol 50mg; Sodium 1350mg; Total Carbohydrate 61g (Dietary Fiber 5g); Protein 27g **Exchanges:** 2½ Starch, 1 Other Carbohydrate, 1 Vegetable, 2½ High-Fat Meat **Carbohydrate Choices:** 4

Quick Variation

For authentic Italian flavor, use cooked crumbled pancetta instead of the bacon.

Swiss Steak Casserole

6 servings (1 cup each)   PREP TIME 20 minutes   START TO FINISH 2 hours 5 minutes

3 tablespoons all-purpose flour

1 teaspoon salt

1 teaspoon paprika

½ teaspoon pepper

1 lb boneless beef round steak, cut into ¾-inch cubes

2 tablespoons vegetable oil

2 cups sliced fresh mushrooms (about 5 oz)

1 cup frozen pearl onions

1 clove garlic, finely chopped

4 cups sliced carrots (8 medium)

1 can (14.5 oz) stewed tomatoes, undrained

1 Heat oven to 350°F. In medium bowl, mix flour, salt, paprika and pepper. Add beef; toss to coat.

2 In 12-inch skillet, heat 1 tablespoon of the oil over medium-high heat. Add beef, reserving remaining flour mixture; brown steak on all sides. Spoon into ungreased 2½-quart casserole.

3 In same skillet, heat remaining 1 tablespoon oil. Add mushrooms, onions and garlic; cook 2 to 3 minutes, stirring constantly, until browned. Spoon into casserole. Add carrots, tomatoes and reserved flour mixture; mix well.

4 Cover; bake 1 hour 30 minutes to 1 hour 45 minutes or until beef and vegetables are tender.

1 Serving: Calories 250; Total Fat 8g (Saturated Fat 2g; Trans Fat 0g); Cholesterol 55mg; Sodium 680mg; Total Carbohydrate 20g (Dietary Fiber 4g); Protein 25g **Exchanges:** ½ Other Carbohydrate, 2 Vegetable, 3 Lean Meat **Carbohydrate Choices:** 1

Time-Saver

Take some help from the grocery store. Look for packages of sliced carrots and mushrooms in the produce section to save time.

Beef Pot Pie with Potato Biscuit Crust

6 servings   PREP TIME 20 minutes   START TO FINISH 55 minutes

½ lb cooked deli roast beef, cubed (1½ cups)

2 cups frozen mixed vegetables

1 medium onion, chopped (½ cup)

1 jar (12 oz) beef gravy

⅔ cup mashed potatoes (dry)

⅔ cup hot water

1½ cups Original Bisquick mix

⅓ cup milk

1 tablespoon freeze-dried chives

1 Heat oven to 375°F. In 2-quart saucepan, heat beef, frozen vegetables, onion and gravy to boiling over medium heat, stirring frequently. Boil and stir 1 minute. Keep warm.

2 In medium bowl, stir potatoes and hot water until well mixed; let stand until water is absorbed. Stir in Bisquick mix, milk and chives until dough forms. Place dough on surface sprinkled with Bisquick mix; gently roll in Bisquick mix to coat. Shape into a ball; knead 10 times. Pat into 11×7-inch rectangle. Fold dough into thirds.

3 Pour beef mixture into ungreased 11×7-inch (2-quart) glass baking dish. Carefully unfold dough onto beef mixture.

4 Bake 30 to 35 minutes or until crust is golden brown.

1 Serving: Calories 310; Total Fat 11g (Saturated Fat 4g; Trans Fat 1.5g); Cholesterol 25mg; Sodium 740mg; Total Carbohydrate 38g (Dietary Fiber 4g); Protein 15g **Exchanges:** 2 Starch, 1 Vegetable, 1 Lean Meat, 1½ Fat **Carbohydrate Choices:** 2½

Quick Variation

For Chicken Pot Pie with Potato Biscuit Crust, use rotisserie chicken from the deli and chicken gravy in place of the beef and beef gravy.

Quick Menu Idea

This hearty dinner pie can be a meal just on its own but a crisp green salad is always a nice addition. Top the salad with your favorite dressing.

Herb-Crusted Tilapia with Lemon-Potatoes

2 servings PREP TIME 15 minutes START TO FINISH 40 minutes

1 **large unpeeled potato, cut into ½-inch pieces**

2 **teaspoons olive oil**

¼ **teaspoon salt**

2 **tablespoons all-purpose flour**

1 **egg**

¾ **cup unseasoned crispy bread crumbs**

¾ **teaspoon seasoning salt**

2 **tablespoons butter, melted**

2 **tilapia or other white fish fillets (5 to 6 oz each)**

1 **medium zucchini, cut into ½-inch slices**

2 **teaspoons chopped fresh thyme leaves**

2 **teaspoons grated lemon peel**

1 Heat oven to 425°F. Spray 15×10×1-inch pan with cooking spray. In medium bowl, toss potato, oil and salt to coat. Spread potato in half of pan. Bake 15 to 20 minutes or until potato is tender.

2 Meanwhile, place flour on plate. In shallow dish, beat egg with fork. In another shallow dish, mix bread crumbs, seasoning salt, and butter.

3 Coat tilapia with flour. Dip into egg; coat well with bread crumb mixture. Place fillets in other half of pan. Place zucchini over potatoes; toss to combine.

4 Bake 10 to 12 minutes or until fish flakes easily with fork and vegetables are tender. Sprinkle fillets with thyme; toss vegetables with lemon peel.

1 Serving: Calories 660; Total Fat 23g (Saturated Fat 10g; Trans Fat 0.5g); Cholesterol 210mg; Sodium 1360mg; Total Carbohydrate 71g (Dietary Fiber 6g); Protein 41g **Exchanges:** 4 Starch, 1½ Vegetable, 3½ Very Lean Meat, 4 Fat **Carbohydrate Choices:** 5

Roasted Tilapia and Vegetables

4 servings   PREP TIME 15 minutes   START TO FINISH 35 minutes

½ **lb fresh asparagus spears, trimmed, halved**

2 **small zucchini, halved lengthwise, cut into ½-inch pieces**

1 **red bell pepper, cut into ½-inch strips**

1 **large onion, cut into ½-inch wedges**

2 **tablespoons olive oil**

2 **teaspoons Montreal steak seasoning**

4 **tilapia fillets (about 1½ lb)**

1 **tablespoon butter or margarine, melted**

½ **teaspoon paprika**

1 Heat oven to 450°F. In large bowl, toss asparagus, zucchini, bell pepper, onion and oil. Sprinkle with 1 teaspoon of the steak seasoning; toss to coat. Spread vegetables in ungreased 15×10×1-inch pan. Place on lower oven rack; roast 5 minutes.

2 Meanwhile, spray 13×9-inch (3-quart) glass baking dish with cooking spray. Pat tilapia fillets dry with paper towels. Brush with butter; sprinkle with remaining 1 teaspoon steak seasoning and the paprika. Place in baking dish.

3 Place baking dish on middle oven rack. Roast fish and vegetables 17 to 18 minutes longer or until fish flakes easily with fork and vegetables are tender.

1 Serving: Calories 290; Total Fat 12g (Saturated Fat 3.5g; Trans Fat 0g); Cholesterol 100mg; Sodium 520mg; Total Carbohydrate 11g (Dietary Fiber 3g); Protein 35g **Exchanges:** 2 Vegetable, 4 Lean Meat, ½ Fat **Carbohydrate Choices:** 1

Quick Variation

Any firm or medium-firm fish fillets with mild flavor will work in this recipe. Try cod, haddock or red snapper. Baking time will vary depending on the thickness of the fillets.

Smoked Salmon–Potato Gratin

8 servings   PREP TIME 35 minutes   START TO FINISH 1 hour 15 minutes

CASSEROLE

2½ **lb Yukon Gold potatoes (6 medium), peeled, thinly sliced**

2 **tablespoons butter**

1 **cup thinly sliced leeks**

2 **tablespoons all-purpose flour**

3 **cups half-and-half**

4 **oz Gruyère or Swiss cheese, shredded (1 cup)**

2 **tablespoons chopped fresh dill weed**

½ **teaspoon salt**

¼ **teaspoon pepper**

12 **oz smoked salmon (not lox), cut or flaked into ½-inch pieces**

TOPPING

1 **cup unseasoned dry bread crumbs**

3 **tablespoons butter or margarine, melted**

1 Heat oven to 350°F. Spray 3-quart casserole with cooking spray. Fill 4-quart saucepan two-thirds with water; heat to boiling over high heat. Add potatoes; cook 6 to 9 minutes or until almost tender. Drain; return to saucepan.

2 In 12-inch nonstick skillet, melt 2 tablespoons butter over medium heat. Add leeks; cook about 5 minutes, stirring frequently, until softened. Stir in flour. Gradually stir in half-and-half. Heat to boiling. Remove from heat. Stir in cheese, dill, salt and pepper until cheese is melted.

3 Pour sauce over potatoes in saucepan. Spoon half of the potato mixture into casserole; top with half of the salmon. Repeat layers. In small bowl, mix topping ingredients; sprinkle over potato mixture.

4 Bake uncovered 30 to 40 minutes or until potatoes are tender and topping is golden brown.

1 Serving: Calories 490; Total Fat 25g (Saturated Fat 14g; Trans Fat 1g); Cholesterol 75mg; Sodium 720mg; Total Carbohydrate 47g (Dietary Fiber 4g); Protein 19g **Exchanges:** 2 Starch, 1 Other Carbohydrate, 2 Lean Meat, 3½ Fat **Carbohydrate Choices:** 3

Tuna and Broccoli Bake

6 servings   **PREP TIME 10 minutes**   **START TO FINISH 55 minutes**

2 **cups fresh broccoli florets**

2 **cans (5 oz each) tuna in water, drained**

2 **cups shredded Cheddar cheese (8 oz)**

¾ **cup Original Bisquick mix**

¾ **cup sour cream**

¾ **cup milk**

3 **eggs**

1 Heat oven to 350°F. Spray 8-inch square (2-quart) glass baking dish with cooking spray. Sprinkle broccoli, tuna and 1½ cups of the cheese in baking dish.

2 In large bowl, stir Bisquick mix, sour cream, milk and eggs with whisk or fork until blended. Pour into baking dish.

3 Bake 30 to 40 minutes or until knife inserted in center comes out clean. Sprinkle with remaining ½ cup cheese; let stand 5 minutes before serving.

1 Serving: Calories 380; Total Fat 24g (Saturated Fat 13g; Trans Fat 1g); Cholesterol 180mg; Sodium 610mg; Total Carbohydrate 15g (Dietary Fiber 1g); Protein 26g **Exchanges:** 1 Starch, 3 Medium-Fat Meat, 1½ Fat **Carbohydrate Choices:** 1

Cheesy Rigatoni with Eggplant Sauce

4 servings (2 cups each)   PREP TIME 20 minutes   START TO FINISH 50 minutes

2½ **cups uncooked rigatoni pasta (7½ oz)**

2 **tablespoons olive oil**

½ **cup chopped onion**

1 **small unpeeled eggplant, cut into ½-inch cubes (3 cups)**

1 **medium zucchini, halved lengthwise, cut into ¼-inch slices (1½ cups)**

1 **can (14.5 oz) diced tomatoes with basil, garlic and oregano, undrained**

1 **can (8 oz) tomato sauce**

1½ **cups shredded mozzarella cheese (6 oz)**

1 Cook and drain pasta as directed on package for al dente. Spray 12×8-inch (2-quart) glass baking dish with cooking spray.

2 Heat oven to 350°F. Meanwhile, in 12-inch nonstick skillet, heat oil over medium-high heat. Add onion, eggplant and zucchini; cook 5 to 7 minutes, stirring frequently, until crisp-tender. Stir in diced tomatoes and tomato sauce.

3 Spoon cooked pasta into baking dish. Spoon eggplant sauce over pasta.

4 Cover tightly with foil; bake 20 minutes. Uncover dish; sprinkle with mozzarella cheese. Bake uncovered 5 to 7 minutes longer or until cheese is melted.

1 Serving. Calories 540; Total Fat 17g (Saturated Fat 6g; Trans Fat 0g); Cholesterol 25mg; Sodium 1000mg; Total Carbohydrate 71g (Dietary Fiber 8g); Protein 25g **Exchanges:** 4 Starch, 2 Vegetable, 1 Medium-Fat Meat, 2 Fat **Carbohydrate Choices:** 5

Time-Saver

Put this together the night before. Then, bake it the next night for dinner. Since it will be cold, bake it about 10 minutes longer before topping with the cheese.

Easy Ravioli Bake

8 servings   PREP TIME 10 minutes   START TO FINISH 1 hour 20 minutes

1   **jar (25.5 oz) tomato pasta sauce (any variety)**

1   **package (25 to 27½ oz) frozen cheese-filled ravioli**

2   **cups shredded mozzarella cheese (8 oz)**

2   **tablespoons grated Parmesan cheese**

1 Heat oven to 350°F. Spray 13×9-inch (3-quart) glass baking dish with cooking spray.

2 Spread ¾ cup of the pasta sauce in baking dish. Arrange half of the frozen ravioli in single layer over sauce. Top with half of the remaining pasta sauce and 1 cup of the mozzarella cheese. Repeat layers once, starting with ravioli. Sprinkle with Parmesan cheese.

3 Cover with foil; bake 40 minutes. Uncover; bake 15 to 20 minutes longer or until bubbly and hot in center. Let stand 10 minutes before serving.

1 Serving: Calories 290; Total Fat 10g (Saturated Fat 6g; Trans Fat 0g); Cholesterol 30mg; Sodium 920mg; Total Carbohydrate 36g (Dietary Fiber 2g); Protein 14g **Exchanges:** 1½ Starch, 1 Other Carbohydrate, 1½ Medium-Fat Meat **Carbohydrate Choices:** 2½

Time-Saver

To make this super-easy recipe ahead of time, layer the ingredients in the baking dish, cover tightly with foil and refrigerate up to 24 hours. Bake as directed.

Four-Cheese Pasta

6 servings   PREP TIME 25 minutes   START TO FINISH 50 minutes

16 oz uncooked penne pasta
(5 cups)

½ cup butter or margarine

2 cloves garlic, finely
chopped

½ cup all-purpose flour

1 teaspoon salt

4½ cups milk

1 cup shredded provolone
cheese (4 oz)

1 cup shredded mozzarella
cheese (4 oz)

½ cup shredded Parmesan
cheese (2 oz)

½ cup shredded fontina
cheese (2 oz)

⅓ cup chopped fresh parsley,
if desired

1 tablespoon butter
or margarine

1 cup unseasoned crispy
bread crumbs

1 Heat oven to 350°F. Spray 13×9-inch (3-quart) glass baking dish with cooking spray. Cook and drain pasta as directed on package.

2 Meanwhile, in 4-quart saucepan or Dutch oven, melt ½ cup butter over low heat. Add garlic; cook 30 seconds, stirring frequently. With whisk, stir in flour and salt until smooth. Increase heat to medium; cook, stirring constantly, until mixture is smooth and bubbly. Gradually stir in milk. Heat to boiling, stirring constantly. Boil and stir 1 minute. Stir in cheeses. Cook until melted, stirring occasionally.

3 Stir pasta and parsley into cheese sauce. Pour mixture into baking dish.

4 In 6-inch skillet, melt 1 tablespoon butter over medium-high heat. Stir in bread crumbs. Cook and stir until crumbs are golden brown. Sprinkle over pasta mixture.

5 Bake uncovered 20 to 25 minutes or until bubbly.

1 Serving: Calories 850; Total Fat 39g (Saturated Fat 23g; Trans Fat 1g); Cholesterol 100mg; Sodium 1390mg; Total Carbohydrate 91g (Dietary Fiber 4g); Protein 35g **Exchanges:** 5 Starch, 1 Other Carbohydrate, 3 High-Fat Meat, 2 Fat **Carbohydrate Choices:** 6

Quick Variation

Panko (crispy) bread crumbs are Japanese-style bread crumbs that have a coarser texture and make a much lighter and crunchier casserole topping. Regular dry bread crumbs will also work, but you may want to use half the amount. The four cheeses in this recipe complement each other, but you can easily use any combination of shredded cheese that you prefer.

Loaded Baked Potato Casserole

8 servings   PREP TIME 15 minutes   START TO FINISH 1 hour

1   **package (30 oz) frozen extra-spicy and crispy potato wedges**

2   **cups chopped cooked ham (12 oz)**

8   **slices bacon, crisply cooked, crumbled**

1   **medium red bell pepper, chopped (1 cup)**

16   **medium green onions, chopped (1 cup)**

1   **jar (15 oz) cheese dip**

½   **cup sour cream**

1 Heat oven to 375°F. Spray 13×9-inch (3-quart) glass baking dish with cooking spray. Arrange potato wedges in baking dish; bake uncovered 10 to 15 minutes or until thawed and beginning to brown.

2 Top with half each of the ham, bacon, bell pepper and onions. Spread cheese dip over top. Sprinkle with remaining ham, bacon and bell pepper.

3 Bake uncovered 20 to 30 minutes or until cheese dip is melted and potatoes are tender. Top with sour cream and the remaining onions.

1 Serving: Calories 300; Total Fat 17g (Saturated Fat 8g; Trans Fat 0.5g); Cholesterol 60mg; Sodium 1270mg; Total Carbohydrate 18g (Dietary Fiber 3g); Protein 20g **Exchanges:** ½ Starch, ½ Other Carbohydrate, 2½ Medium-Fat Meat, 1 Fat **Carbohydrate Choices:** 1

Minestrone Casserole

6 servings   PREP TIME 25 minutes   START TO FINISH 1 hour 15 minutes

2 cups uncooked mini lasagna (mafalda) noodles (4 oz)

3 tablespoons olive oil

1 large onion, chopped (1 cup)

2 medium carrots, sliced (1 cup)

2 medium stalks celery, sliced (1 cup)

1 medium green bell pepper, chopped (1 cup)

1 medium zucchini or yellow summer squash, quartered lengthwise, sliced

2 cloves garlic, chopped

2 cans (15 oz each) dark red kidney beans, drained, rinsed

1 can (14.5 oz) diced tomatoes with Italian herbs, undrained

½ cup finely shredded Parmesan cheese (2 oz)

1 teaspoon salt

¼ teaspoon pepper

¼ cup refrigerated basil pesto

1 Heat oven to 350°F. Cook and drain noodles as directed on package, using minimum cook time.

2 Meanwhile, in 10-inch skillet, heat oil over medium heat. Add onion, carrots, celery and bell pepper; cover and cook 5 to 8 minutes, stirring occasionally, until carrots are just tender. Uncover skillet; stir zucchini and garlic into vegetable mixture. Cook and stir 1 minute longer.

3 Place noodles in ungreased 2½-quart casserole. Stir in carrot mixture, beans, tomatoes, ¼ cup of the cheese, salt, pepper and pesto.

4 Cover; bake 40 to 50 minutes or until hot in center. Top servings with remaining cheese.

1 Serving: Calories 440; Total Fat 16g (Saturated Fat 4g; Trans Fat 0g); Cholesterol 10mg; Sodium 840mg; Total Carbohydrate 54g (Dietary Fiber 11g); Protein 19g Exchanges: 3 Starch, 2 Vegetable, 1 Lean Meat, 2 Fat Carbohydrate Choices: 3½

Quick Variation

Minestrone is a classic dish that uses what the cook has on hand. Consider using up odds and ends of pasta packages instead of the mini lasagna noodles. Just make sure that they cook in about the same length of time.

Phyllo-Egg Breakfast Torta

8 servings   PREP TIME 50 minutes   START TO FINISH 3 hours 45 minutes

1   **lb bulk Italian pork sausage**

1   **medium red bell pepper, chopped (1 cup)**

1   **medium onion, chopped (½ cup)**

6   **eggs**

½   **teaspoon pepper**

30   **sheets frozen phyllo (filo) pastry (14×9 inch), thawed**

¾   **cup butter, melted**

2   **cups shredded Swiss cheese (8 oz)**

1   **box (9 oz) frozen chopped spinach, thawed, squeezed to drain**

2   **tablespoons chopped fresh basil leaves**

¼   **cup grated Parmesan cheese**

1 In 10-inch nonstick skillet, cook sausage over medium-high heat 6 to 8 minutes or until no longer pink. Remove sausage from skillet; place in bowl. Reserve 1 tablespoon drippings in skillet.

2 Reduce heat to medium. Cook bell pepper and onion in drippings 5 to 7 minutes until tender; add to sausage. In small bowl, beat eggs and pepper; add to skillet. Cook and stir over medium heat 3 to 5 minutes or until set.

3 Spray 13×9-inch (3-quart) glass baking dish with cooking spray. Cover phyllo with damp paper towel. Place 1 sheet in baking dish; brush with melted butter. Repeat 9 times.

4 Spread half of sausage mixture over phyllo. Layer with 10 more phyllo sheets, brushing each with butter. Sprinkle with cooked eggs, Swiss cheese, spinach and basil. Layer with 5 more phyllo sheets, brushing each with butter. Top with remaining sausage mixture. Sprinkle with Parmesan cheese. Layer with remaining 5 phyllo sheets, brushing each with butter. Cover tightly; refrigerate 2 to 24 hours.

5 Heat oven to 350°F. Uncover baking dish; bake 45 to 55 minutes or until top is golden brown.

1 Serving: Calories 560; Total Fat 38g (Saturated Fat 20g; Trans Fat 1g); Cholesterol 255mg; Sodium 640mg; Total Carbohydrate 31g (Dietary Fiber 2g); Protein 23g **Exchanges:** 2 Starch, 2½ High-Fat Meat, 3½ Fat **Carbohydrate Choices:** 2

Healthy Twist

Reduce the fat and calories a bit by using Italian turkey sausage instead of the Italian pork sausage.

Santa Fe Egg Bake

6 servings   PREP TIME 15 minutes   START TO FINISH 3 hours 15 minutes

4 cups frozen southern-style diced hash brown potatoes (from 32-oz bag)

1 can (15 oz) black beans, drained, rinsed

1 cup frozen whole kernel corn

1 cup frozen bell pepper and onion stir-fry (from 1-lb bag)

2 cups shredded Colby–Monterey Jack cheese (8 oz)

2 tablespoons chopped fresh cilantro

8 eggs

1¼ cups milk

½ teaspoon salt

¼ teaspoon ground red pepper (cayenne)

Sour cream, if desired

Salsa, if desired

1 Spray 13×9-inch (3-quart) glass baking dish with cooking spray. In baking dish, mix hash browns, beans, corn, and bell pepper and onion stir-fry. Sprinkle with cheese and cilantro.

2 In large bowl, beat eggs, milk, salt and red pepper with whisk until well blended. Pour evenly over potato mixture. Cover; refrigerate at least 2 hours but no longer than 24 hours.

3 Heat oven to 350°F. Uncover baking dish; bake 45 to 55 minutes or until knife inserted in center comes out clean. Let stand 5 minutes before cutting. Garnish with sour cream and salsa.

1 Serving: Calories 460; Total Fat 24g (Saturated Fat 10g; Trans Fat 2g); Cholesterol 240mg; Sodium 670mg; Total Carbohydrate 40g (Dietary Fiber 7g); Protein 20g **Exchanges:** 2½ Starch, 1½ Medium-Fat Meat, 3 Fat **Carbohydrate Choices:** 2½

Time-Saver

Frozen stir-fry bell peppers and onions is a great timesaving product, but if it is not available, substitute ½ cup each chopped onion and bell pepper.

Quick Menu Idea

Serve this easy dish with corn muffins and a variety of toppings, such as guacamole, salsa, sour cream, chopped fresh tomatoes and chopped fresh cilantro.

Chapter Five

Main Dish Salads

Asian Chopped Salad with Lime Dressing

4 servings   PREP TIME 25 minutes   START TO FINISH 25 minutes

FAST

DRESSING

⅓ **cup frozen (thawed) limeade concentrate**

¼ **cup vegetable oil**

1 **tablespoon rice vinegar or white vinegar**

1 **teaspoon grated gingerroot**

¼ **teaspoon salt**

SALAD

2 **cups chopped escarole**

1 **cup chopped cooked chicken**

1 **large papaya, peeled, seeded and chopped (2 cups)**

1 **small jicama, peeled, chopped (1 cup)**

1 **large yellow or red bell pepper, chopped (1 cup)**

½ **cup dry-roasted peanuts**

¼ **cup chopped fresh cilantro**

1 In tightly covered container, shake all dressing ingredients.

2 In large bowl, mix all salad ingredients except peanuts and cilantro. Pour dressing over salad; toss to coat. Top with peanuts and cilantro.

1 Serving: Calories 400; Total Fat 24g (Saturated Fat 4g; Trans Fat 0g); Cholesterol 30mg; Sodium 330mg; Total Carbohydrate 28g (Dietary Fiber 4g); Protein 15g **Exchanges:** ½ Fruit, 1 Other Carbohydrate, 1½ Vegetable, 1½ Lean Meat, 4 Fat **Carbohydrate Choices:** 2

Quick Variation

When papayas aren't available, you can substitute peaches or nectarines.

Balsamic-Mozzarella-Chicken Salad

4 servings (1¼ cups each) PREP TIME 15 minutes START TO FINISH 15 minutes

FAST

1 **container (8 oz) small fresh mozzarella cheese balls, drained**

1 **pint (2 cups) cherry tomatoes, cut in half**

1 **package (10 oz) refrigerated grilled chicken breast strips**

½ **cup balsamic vinaigrette dressing**

12 **leaves romaine lettuce**

Chopped fresh basil leaves, if desired

1 In medium bowl, gently stir mozzarella, tomatoes and chicken. Drizzle with dressing; toss lightly.

2 Line 4 plates with lettuce. Divide salad evenly among lettuce-lined plates; garnish with chopped fresh basil leaves.

1 Serving: Calories 370; Total Fat 19g (Saturated Fat 9g; Trans Fat 0g); Cholesterol 85mg; Sodium 990mg; Total Carbohydrate 13g (Dietary Fiber 3g); Protein 37g **Exchanges:** ½ Other Carbohydrate, 1 Vegetable, 5 Very Lean Meat, 3½ Fat **Carbohydrate Choices:** 1

Time-Saver

Leftover grilled chicken would be a great substitute for the purchased grilled chicken. Do a planned leftover and throw on an extra chicken breast next time you're grilling. Slice it and freeze.

Caribbean Jerk Chicken and Pasta Salad

[Suddenly Salad Contest Winner Melanie Gadzia Smith, Topeka, KS]

6 servings (1 cup each)   PREP TIME 25 minutes   START TO FINISH 1 hour 25 minutes

1   box Betty Crocker®
    Suddenly Pasta Salad®
    chipotle ranch pasta
    salad mix

⅓   cup mayonnaise

1   tablespoon packed
    brown sugar

1   tablespoon fresh
    lime juice

1   teaspoon grated
    gingerroot

½   teaspoon crushed
    red pepper flakes

2   packages (6 oz each)
    refrigerated grilled
    chicken strips, chopped

1½ cups chopped fresh
    pineapple

3   medium green onions,
    sliced

2   teaspoons chopped
    fresh cilantro

1 Fill 3-quart saucepan ⅔ full of water; heat to boiling. Empty pasta mix (from salad mix) into boiling water. Gently boil uncovered 15 minutes, stirring occasionally.

2 Meanwhile, in large bowl, stir together seasoning mix, mayonnaise, brown sugar, lime juice, gingerroot and red pepper flakes. Stir in chicken, pineapple, onions and cilantro.

3 Drain pasta; rinse with cold water. Shake to drain well. Stir pasta into salad mixture. Cover; refrigerate 1 hour to chill. Stir before serving.

1 **Serving:** Calories 300; Total Fat 13g (Saturated Fat 2g; Trans Fat 0g); Cholesterol 40mg; Sodium 670mg; Total Carbohydrate 30g (Dietary Fiber 1g); Protein 18g **Exchanges:** 1½ Starch, ½ Other Carbohydrate, 2 Lean Meat, 1 Fat **Carbohydrate Choices:** 2

Barbecued Chicken Salad

4 servings (about 1 cup each)   PREP TIME 30 minutes   START TO FINISH 30 minutes

FAST

4 slices thick-sliced bacon
   (about 5 oz), diced

½ cup mayonnaise or
   salad dressing

⅓ cup barbecue sauce

½ teaspoon salt

4 cups bite-size pieces
   deli rotisserie chicken
   (from 2-lb chicken)

½ cup finely chopped
   red onion

1 jalapeño chile, seeded,
   finely chopped

4 large Bibb lettuce leaves

2 tablespoons chopped
   fresh parsley

1 In 10-inch skillet, cook bacon over medium heat 7 to 9 minutes, stirring occasionally, until crisp. Drain bacon on paper towels.

2 In small bowl, beat mayonnaise, barbecue sauce and salt with whisk until blended.

3 In large bowl, stir chicken, bacon, onion, jalapeño chile and mayonnaise mixture until well mixed. Serve in lettuce leaves. Sprinkle with parsley.

1 Serving: Calories 380; Total Fat 29g (Saturated Fat 5g; Trans Fat 0g); Cholesterol 60mg; Sodium 1860mg; Total Carbohydrate 13g (Dietary Fiber 0g); Protein 18g **Exchanges:** 1 Vegetable, 3 High-Fat Meat, 1 Fat **Carbohydrate Choices:** 1

Chicken Pasta Salad with Poppy Seed Dressing

4 servings (1½ cups each)   PREP TIME 15 minutes   START TO FINISH 25 minutes

FAST

1   box Betty Crocker
    Suddenly Pasta Salad
    classic pasta salad mix

½   cup refrigerated poppy
    seed dressing

1½ cups cut-up cooked
    chicken

¾   cup halved seedless
    red grapes

½   cup thinly sliced celery

¼   cup slivered almonds,
    toasted*

1 Fill 3-quart saucepan ⅔ full of water; heat to boiling. Empty pasta mix (from salad mix) into boiling water. Gently boil uncovered 12 minutes, stirring occasionally.

2 Drain pasta; rinse with cold water. Shake to drain well.

3 In large bowl, stir together seasoning mix (from salad mix) and dressing. Add pasta and remaining ingredients; toss to combine. Serve immediately, or refrigerate until serving time.

*To toast almonds, cook in ungreased heavy skillet over medium heat 5 to 7 minutes, stirring frequently until almonds begin to brown, then stirring constantly until light brown.

1 Serving: Calories 520; Total Fat 22g (Saturated Fat 3.5g; Trans Fat 0g); Cholesterol 45mg; Sodium 1410mg; Total Carbohydrate 58g (Dietary Fiber 2g); Protein 23g **Exchanges:** 2½ Starch, 1½ Other Carbohydrate, 2 Lean Meat, 3 Fat **Carbohydrate Choices:** 4

Enjoy!

Chicken-Gorgonzola Pasta Salad

12 servings (1½ cups each) PREP TIME 30 minutes START TO FINISH 30 minutes

FAST

7 cups uncooked radiatore (nuggets) pasta (about 19 oz)

4½ cups cubed cooked chicken breast (about 20 oz)

1 package (2.1 oz) refrigerated precooked bacon (about 15 slices), cut into small pieces

1 can (14.5 oz) fire roasted diced tomatoes, drained

2 cups lightly packed fresh baby spinach leaves

1 jar (16 oz) refrigerated ranch dressing

1 cup crumbled Gorgonzola cheese (4 oz)

Bibb lettuce, if desired

1 Cook and drain pasta as directed on package.

2 In large bowl, mix chicken, bacon, tomatoes, spinach and cooked pasta. Pour dressing over mixture; toss until coated. Fold in cheese.

3 Line serving bowl with lettuce; spoon salad into lettuce-lined bowl.

1 Serving: Calories 630; Total Fat 29g (Saturated Fat 6g; Trans Fat 0g); Cholesterol 70mg; Sodium 590mg; Total Carbohydrate 62g (Dietary Fiber 4g); Protein 30g **Exchanges:** 4 Starch, 2½ Lean Meat, 4 Fat **Carbohydrate Choices:** 4

Time-Saver

Use cut-up deli rotisserie chicken for the cooked chicken breast. You'll need a 2- to 2½-pound chicken for 4½ cups.

Chipotle Ranch Chicken and Pasta Salad

4 servings   PREP TIME 20 minutes   START TO FINISH 20 minutes

FAST

1   box Betty Crocker
    Suddenly Pasta Salad
    chipotle ranch pasta
    salad mix

½   cup frozen whole kernel
    corn

3   tablespoons milk

⅓   cup mayonnaise

2   cups cubed cooked
    chicken

½   cup coarsely chopped
    tomato

4   medium green onions,
    sliced (¼ cup)

    Lime wedges, if desired

1 Fill 3-quart saucepan ⅔ full of water; heat to boiling. Empty pasta mix (from salad mix) into boiling water. Gently boil uncovered 15 minutes, stirring occasionally and adding corn during last 3 minutes of cook time.

2 Drain pasta with corn; rinse with cold water. Shake to drain well.

3 Meanwhile, in large bowl, stir together seasoning mix (from salad mix) and milk until blended. Stir in mayonnaise. Stir in pasta with corn, chicken, tomato and onions. Serve with lime wedges.

1 Serving: Calories 420; Total Fat 19g (Saturated Fat 3g; Trans Fat 0g); Cholesterol 65mg; Sodium 560mg; Total Carbohydrate 36g (Dietary Fiber 2g); Protein 27g **Exchanges:** 2 Starch, ½ Other Carbohydrate, 3 Lean Meat, 1½ Fat Carbohydrate Choices: 2½

Healthy Twist

For a lighter dressing, substitute reduced-fat mayonnaise.

Chicken-Thyme Penne Salad

8 servings (1½ cups each) PREP TIME 25 minutes START TO FINISH 4 hours 25 minutes

3 cups uncooked penne pasta (10 oz)

4 cups cubed deli rotisserie chicken (from two 2-lb chickens)

2 cups seedless red grapes, each cut in half

2 medium stalks celery, sliced (1 cup)

⅓ cup chopped onion

3 tablespoons olive or vegetable oil

2 tablespoons chopped fresh or 2 teaspoons dried thyme leaves, crushed

1¼ cups reduced-fat mayonnaise or salad dressing

1 tablespoon milk

1 tablespoon honey

1 tablespoon coarse-grained mustard

1 teaspoon salt

1 cup chopped walnuts, toasted*

1 Cook and drain pasta as directed on package. Rinse with cold water; drain.

2 In very large (4-quart) bowl, mix chicken, grapes, celery, onion and cooked pasta. In small bowl, mix oil and 1 tablespoon of the fresh thyme (or 1 teaspoon of the dried thyme). Pour oil mixture over chicken mixture; toss to coat.

3 In small bowl, mix mayonnaise, milk, honey, mustard, salt and remaining thyme. Cover chicken mixture and mayonnaise mixture separately; refrigerate at least 4 hours but no longer than 24 hours.

4 Up to 2 hours before serving, toss chicken mixture and mayonnaise mixture. Cover; refrigerate until serving time. Just before serving, stir in ¾ cup of the walnuts. Sprinkle salad with remaining walnuts.

To toast walnuts, heat oven to 350°F. Spread walnuts in ungreased shallow pan. Bake uncovered 6 to 10 minutes, stirring occasionally, until golden brown.

1 Serving: Calories 580; Total Fat 33g (Saturated Fat 5g; Trans Fat 0g); Cholesterol 75mg; Sodium 1090mg; Total Carbohydrate 44g (Dietary Fiber 4g); Protein 27g **Exchanges:** 2 Starch, 1 Other Carbohydrate, 3 Lean Meat, 4½ Fat **Carbohydrate Choices:** 3

Confetti Chicken 'n Couscous Salad

6 servings (1½ cups each)   PREP TIME 25 minutes   START TO FINISH 25 minutes

FAST

SALAD

1 box (10 oz) couscous

2 cups chopped cooked chicken

2 medium carrots, finely chopped (1½ cups)

1 medium red bell pepper, finely chopped (1 cup)

½ cup chopped fresh chives

DRESSING

½ cup olive or vegetable oil

⅓ cup fresh lemon juice

⅔ cup grated Parmesan cheese

1½ teaspoons salt

1 Cook couscous as directed on box.

2 In large serving bowl, mix chicken, carrots, bell pepper and chives. Add cooked couscous; fluff with fork until well mixed. Cool slightly.

3 In tightly covered container, shake dressing ingredients. Pour over salad; toss gently to coat. Serve immediately.

1 Serving: Calories 490; Total Fat 25g (Saturated Fat 5g; Trans Fat 0g); Cholesterol 50mg; Sodium 820mg; Total Carbohydrate 41g (Dietary Fiber 3g); Protein 24g **Exchanges:** 2½ Starch, 1 Vegetable, 2 Lean Meat, 3½ Fat **Carbohydrate Choices:** 3

Time-Saver

If you're going to make this recipe ahead of time and store it in the refrigerator, you may need to add a little more olive oil and/or lemon juice when ready to serve. When made ahead, the couscous will absorb these ingredients over time.

Gazpacho-Style Chicken Salad

2 servings   PREP TIME 25 minutes   START TO FINISH 25 minutes
FAST

SALAD

4 **cups packed torn green and/or red leaf lettuce**

1 **package (6 oz) refrigerated grilled chicken breast strips**

1 **medium tomato, chopped (¾ cup)**

1 **cup chopped peeled cucumber**

¾ **cup chopped yellow bell pepper**

⅓ **cup thinly sliced red onion**

DRESSING

½ **cup spicy Bloody Mary mix**

3 **tablespoons red wine vinegar**

2 **tablespoons olive oil**

½ **teaspoon salt**

¼ **teaspoon pepper**

¼ **teaspoon red pepper sauce**

1 **clove garlic, finely chopped**

1 Arrange lettuce on serving platter. Arrange chicken in center of lettuce. Place tomato, cucumber, bell pepper and onion on top of lettuce, around the chicken.

2 In tightly covered container, shake dressing ingredients. Spoon ¼ cup dressing over salad; gently toss to coat. Serve immediately. Reserve remaining dressing for another use.

1 Serving: Calories 240; Total Fat 8g (Saturated Fat 1.5g; Trans Fat 0g); Cholesterol 70mg; Sodium 720mg; Total Carbohydrate 13g (Dietary Fiber 3g); Protein 29g **Exchanges:** 3 Vegetable, 3 Lean Meat **Carbohydrate Choices:** 1

Quick Variation

Change up the flavor of the dressing by experimenting with different types of vinegar. Try white wine vinegar or cider vinegar.

Curry Chicken and Summer Fruit Salad

[Janet Roberts Camp Janet—Culinary Fun for Everyone www.campjanet.com]

6 servings (1 cup each) PREP TIME 20 minutes START TO FINISH 20 minutes

FAST

DRESSING

1 cup mayonnaise or salad dressing

1 tablespoon fresh lemon juice

1 teaspoon ground curry powder

1 teaspoon soy sauce

¼ teaspoon salt

¼ teaspoon pepper

SALAD

2 cups cubed cooked chicken

1 can (8 oz) whole water chestnuts, drained, quartered

1½ cups seedless red grapes, halved (about ½ lb)

1 cup honeydew melon cubes (about ½ lb)

1 cup cantaloupe melon cubes (about ½ lb)

6 lettuce leaves

⅓ cup sliced almonds, toasted*

1 In large bowl, mix dressing ingredients with whisk until smooth. Stir in all salad ingredients except lettuce leaves and almonds.

2 Place 1 lettuce leaf on each of 6 salad plates. Divide salad onto lettuce leaves. Top each salad with almonds.

To toast almonds, heat oven to 350°F. Spread almonds in ungreased shallow pan. Bake uncovered 6 to 10 minutes, stirring occasionally, until lightly browned.

1 Serving: Calories 450; Total Fat 35g (Saturated Fat 6g; Trans Fat 0g); Cholesterol 55mg; Sodium 410mg; Total Carbohydrate 18g (Dietary Fiber 2g); Protein 15g **Exchanges:** 1 Fruit, 2 Medium-Fat Meat, 5 Fat **Carbohydrate Choices:** 1

Quick Variation

Vary the fruit as you like; green grapes, strawberries or raspberries are all nice additions to the salad.

Lemon-Chicken Pasta Salad

4 servings (1½ cups each)   PREP TIME **25 minutes**   START TO FINISH **25 minutes**

FAST

1 **box Betty Crocker Suddenly Pasta Salad ranch & bacon pasta salad mix**

1 **cup mayonnaise**

2 **teaspoons grated lemon peel**

2 **tablespoons fresh lemon juice**

2 **cups cubed cooked chicken**

1½ **cups fresh snow pea pods, strings removed, cut diagonally into ½-inch pieces**

½ **cup sliced almonds**

 Lettuce leaves, if desired

1 Fill 3-quart saucepan ⅔ full of water; heat to boiling. Empty pasta mix (from salad mix) into boiling water. Gently boil uncovered 12 minutes, stirring occasionally.

2 Meanwhile, in large bowl, mix contents of seasoning pouch (from salad mix), mayonnaise, lemon peel and lemon juice.

3 Drain pasta; rinse with cold water. Shake to drain well. Stir cooked pasta, chicken, pea pods and almonds into mayonnaise mixture. Serve immediately in lettuce-lined bowl, or cover and refrigerate until serving time.

1 Serving: Calories 800; Total Fat 56g (Saturated Fat 9g; Trans Fat 0g); Cholesterol 80mg; Sodium 800mg; Total Carbohydrate 43g (Dietary Fiber 3g); Protein 31g **Exchanges:** 1½ Starch, 1 Other Carbohydrate, 1 Vegetable, 3½ Lean Meat, 9 Fat **Carbohydrate Choices:** 3

Time-Saver

Make this salad up to 24 hours before serving and store covered in the refrigerator. If needed, stir in a few drops of milk to make it creamy again.

Lemon Pepper–Chicken Salad

4 servings   PREP TIME 10 minutes   START TO FINISH 25 minutes

FAST

¾ **cup lemon pepper panko crispy bread crumbs**

1 **package (14 oz) uncooked chicken breast tenders (not breaded)**

1 **bag (9 oz) romaine lettuce (6 cups)**

2 **oranges, peeled, sectioned and chopped**

½ **cup tropical mango–olive oil vinaigrette dressing**

Sliced almonds, if desired

1 Heat oven to 400°F. Line cookie sheet with cooking parchment paper or spray with cooking spray.

2 In shallow dish, place bread crumbs. Add chicken tenders to dish; press crumbs into chicken to coat well. Place chicken on cookie sheet. Bake 12 to 15 minutes or until no longer pink. Cut chicken into 1-inch pieces.

3 Divide lettuce among 4 salad plates or shallow bowls. Top evenly with chicken and orange pieces. Drizzle each with 2 tablespoons dressing. Garnish with almonds.

1 Serving: Calories 320; Total Fat 13g (Saturated Fat 0.5g; Trans Fat 0g); Cholesterol 45mg; Sodium 750mg; Total Carbohydrate 27g (Dietary Fiber 3g); Protein 24g **Exchanges:** 1½ Starch, ½ Other Carbohydrate, 2½ Very Lean Meat, 2 Fat **Carbohydrate Choices:** 2

Time-Saver

Chicken can be panfried instead of baked. Spray a 12-inch skillet with cooking spray; cook chicken over medium-high heat 3 to 4 minutes on each side or until no longer pink.

Smoky BBQ Chicken Salad

[Suddenly Salad Contest Winner Felice Bogus Raleigh, NC]

6 servings (1 cup each)   PREP TIME 25 minutes   START TO FINISH 25 minutes

FAST

1   **box Betty Crocker Suddenly Pasta Salad ranch & bacon pasta salad mix**

½   **cup frozen whole kernel corn**

¼   **cup mayonnaise**

¼   **cup barbecue sauce**

2   **cups shredded deli rotisserie chicken (from 2-lb chicken)**

1   **cup cherry or grape tomatoes, halved**

12 **leaves butter lettuce**

4   **medium green onions, chopped (¼ cup)**

1 Fill 3-quart saucepan ⅔ full of water; heat to boiling. Empty pasta mix (from salad mix) into boiling water. Gently boil uncovered 12 minutes, stirring occasionally and adding corn during last 2 minutes of cook time.

2 Meanwhile, in large bowl, stir together seasoning mix (from salad mix), mayonnaise and barbecue sauce.

3 Drain pasta; rinse with cold water. Shake to drain well. Stir cooked pasta, corn, chicken and tomatoes into mayonnaise mixture.

4 Line 6 serving plates with lettuce leaves. Top each with salad mixture; sprinkle with onions.

1 Serving: Calories 330; Total Fat 12g (Saturated Fat 2g; Trans Fat 0g); Cholesterol 45mg; Sodium 680mg; Total Carbohydrate 36g (Dietary Fiber 2g); Protein 19g **Exchanges:** 1½ Starch, ½ Other Carbohydrate, 1 Vegetable, 1 Very Lean Meat, 1 Lean Meat, 1½ Fat **Carbohydrate Choices:** 2½

Time-Saver

This salad can be made ahead and chilled 1 hour. Spoon onto lettuce leaves just before serving.

Southwestern Chicken Taco Salad

4 servings   PREP TIME 15 minutes   START TO FINISH 15 minutes

FAST

DRESSING

½ **cup chunky style salsa**

½ **cup sour cream**

2 **teaspoons taco seasoning mix (from 1-oz package)**

SALAD

1 **bag (10 oz) romaine and leaf lettuce blend**

1 **cup shredded Mexican cheese blend (4 oz)**

1½ **packages (9 oz each) frozen cooked southwestern-seasoned chicken breast strips, thawed**

1 **can (2¼ oz) sliced ripe olives, drained**

4 **plum (Roma) tomatoes, cut into quarters**

1 **cup chili-flavored corn chips, slightly crushed**

1 In small bowl, beat dressing ingredients with whisk until well blended.

2 In large bowl, mix all salad ingredients except corn chips. Add dressing; toss until coated. Sprinkle with corn chips.

1 Serving: Calories 450; Total Fat 27g (Saturated Fat 12g; Trans Fat 0g); Cholesterol 115mg; Sodium 1290mg; Total Carbohydrate 20g (Dietary Fiber 3g); Protein 30g **Exchanges:** 1 Other Carbohydrate, 1 Vegetable, 4 Very Lean Meat, 5 Fat **Carbohydrate Choices:** 1

Quick Variation

Cheddar, Colby or Monterey Jack cheese can be used instead of the Mexican cheese blend. Also, you can use halved cherry tomatoes instead of the quartered plum tomatoes.

Supreme Chicken Salad

4 servings PREP TIME 20 minutes START TO FINISH 20 minutes

FAST

8 cups packed torn romaine
  lettuce

2 cups chopped cooked
  chicken

2 large mangoes, seed
  removed, peeled and
  cut up (2 cups)

1 cup fresh raspberries
  (6 oz)

½ cup crumbled goat cheese
  (2 oz)

¼ cup roasted salted
  sunflower nuts

½ cup raspberry vinaigrette
  dressing

1 Place 2 cups lettuce on each of 4 serving plates.

2 Evenly arrange chicken, mangoes, raspberries, cheese and sunflower nuts on lettuce. Drizzle with dressing. Serve immediately.

1 Serving: Calories 430; Total Fat 24g (Saturated Fat 6g; Trans Fat 0.5g); Cholesterol 70mg; Sodium 930mg; Total Carbohydrate 27g (Dietary Fiber 6g); Protein 26g **Exchanges:** 1 Fruit, 2 Vegetable, 3 Lean Meat, 3 Fat **Carbohydrate Choices:** 2

Time-Saver

A mango slicer/pitter makes chopping up this delicious tropical fruit super-easy and quick.

Smoked Turkey–Jarlsberg Salad Supreme

8 servings (1 cup each)   PREP TIME 20 minutes   START TO FINISH 20 minutes

FAST

1½ lb smoked turkey breast, cut into 1×¼-inch strips (5 cups)

8 oz Jarlsberg or Swiss cheese, cut into 1×¼-inch strips (2 cups)

2 cups seedless red grapes, whole or halved

1½ cups slivered almonds, toasted*

⅔ cup mayonnaise or salad dressing

⅔ cup sour cream

2 to 4 tablespoons milk

Salt and pepper to taste, if desired

Lettuce, if desired

1 In very large (4-quart) bowl, mix turkey, cheese, grapes and almonds.

2 In medium bowl, mix remaining ingredients except lettuce. Pour over turkey mixture; mix gently. Serve immediately, or cover and refrigerate until serving time. Serve on lettuce-lined plates.

To toast almonds, cook in ungreased heavy skillet over medium heat 5 to 7 minutes, stirring frequently until almonds begin to brown, then stirring constantly until light brown.

1 Serving: Calories 550; Total Fat 37g (Saturated Fat 11g; Trans Fat 0g); Cholesterol 115mg; Sodium 360mg; Total Carbohydrate 14g (Dietary Fiber 3g); Protein 38g **Exchanges:** 1 Other Carbohydrate, 3 Very Lean Meat, 1½ Lean Meat, 1 High-Fat Meat, 4½ Fat **Carbohydrate Choices:** 1

Time-Saver

Make the salad the night before. Just before serving, stir in a small amount of milk to make the dressing creamier.

Easy Club Salad

4 servings   PREP TIME 15 minutes   START TO FINISH 15 minutes

FAST

6 cups bite-size pieces
   lettuce

1½ cups cut-up cooked
    chicken

1 medium tomato, cut into
   eighths

⅓ cup Thousand Island
   dressing

⅓ cup bacon flavor bits
   or chips

   Hard-cooked egg slices,
   if desired

1 In large bowl, toss lettuce, chicken, tomato, dressing and bacon bits.

2 Garnish with egg slices.

1 Serving: Calories 210; Total Fat 12g (Saturated Fat 2.5g; Trans Fat 0g); Cholesterol 50mg; Sodium 370mg; Total Carbohydrate 7g (Dietary Fiber 2g); Protein 19g **Exchanges:** 1 Vegetable, 2½ Lean Meat, 1 Fat **Carbohydrate Choices:** ½

Time-Saver

In a hurry? Just use 2 cans (4.5 ounces each) chunk chicken, drained, for the cooked chicken.

Turkey-Chutney Pasta Salad

[Suddenly Salad Contest Winner S. Averett Westminster, MD]

4 servings (1¼ cups each)   PREP TIME 25 minutes   START TO FINISH 25 minutes

FAST

1 box Betty Crocker Suddenly Pasta Salad Caesar pasta salad mix

¼ cup mayonnaise

¼ cup sour cream

2 tablespoons mango chutney

2 teaspoons curry powder

2 cups cubed cooked turkey breast

¼ cup chopped cashews

2 tablespoons golden raisins

1 green onion, finely chopped

¼ cup chopped fresh cilantro

1 Fill 3-quart saucepan ⅔ full of water; heat to boiling. Empty pasta mix (from salad mix) into boiling water. Gently boil uncovered 12 minutes, stirring occasionally.

2 Meanwhile, in large bowl, stir together seasoning and crouton blend (from salad mix), mayonnaise, sour cream, chutney and curry powder. Stir in turkey, cashews and raisins.

3 Drain pasta; rinse with cold water. Shake to drain well. Stir pasta into salad mixture. Spoon onto serving platter. Top with onion and cilantro. Serve immediately, or cover and refrigerate 1 hour to chill.

1 Serving: Calories 480; Total Fat 19g (Saturated Fat 4g; Trans Fat 0g); Cholesterol 70mg; Sodium 780mg; Total Carbohydrate 48g (Dietary Fiber 2g); Protein 28g **Exchanges:** 2½ Starch, ½ Other Carbohydrate, 3 Lean Meat, 2 Fat **Carbohydrate Choices:** 3

Italian Chopped Salad

6 servings (1½ cups each)   PREP TIME 20 minutes   START TO FINISH 20 minutes
FAST

1 bag (5.5 oz) 50/50
   lettuce blend of spring mix
   and baby spinach (about
   5 cups)

⅓ cup drained mild banana
   pepper rings

1 medium tomato, seeded,
   chopped (about 1 cup)

3 oz salami, chopped
   (about ¾ cup)

4 oz provolone cheese,
   cut into ½-inch cubes
   (about ¾ cup)

1½ cups Caesar-flavored
   croutons (from 5.5-oz bag)

⅓ cup red wine vinegar
   dressing

1 In large bowl, place all ingredients except dressing.

2 Pour dressing over top; toss to thoroughly coat. Serve immediately.

1 Serving: Calories 180; Total Fat 11g (Saturated Fat 5g; Trans Fat 0.5g); Cholesterol 30mg; Sodium 590mg; Total Carbohydrate 10g (Dietary Fiber 2g); Protein 10g **Exchanges:** ½ Starch, ½ Vegetable, 1 Medium-Fat Meat, 1 Fat **Carbohydrate Choices:** ½

Roasted Pepper and Pepperoni Tossed Salad

6 servings   PREP TIME 30 minutes   START TO FINISH 30 minutes

FAST

1   **medium red bell pepper**

1   **package (5 oz) pepperoni links, diced**

1   **bag (10 oz) romaine lettuce (6 cups)**

½   **cup grape tomatoes**

1   **can (15 oz) chick peas, drained, rinsed**

3   **tablespoons olive or vegetable oil**

2   **tablespoons sherry vinegar**

½   **teaspoon garlic salt**

1 Set oven control to broil. Line broiler pan with foil. Cut bell pepper in half; remove seeds. Place halves, skin side up, on broiler pan. Broil 3 to 4 inches from heat about 5 minutes or until skin blackens. Place pepper in plastic bag; let stand 10 minutes to steam.

2 Meanwhile, line microwavable plate with microwavable paper towels. Spread diced pepperoni on plate; cover loosely with microwavable paper towel. Microwave on High 2 minutes to remove excess fat.

3 Peel skin from roasted pepper. Cut pepper into thin bite-size pieces. In large bowl, toss roasted pepper, pepperoni, lettuce, tomatoes and chick peas.

4 In small bowl, beat oil, vinegar and garlic salt with whisk until well blended. Pour over salad; toss to coat.

1 Serving: Calories 310; Total Fat 19g (Saturated Fat 4.5g; Trans Fat 0g); Cholesterol 25mg; Sodium 580mg; Total Carbohydrate 22g (Dietary Fiber 6g); Protein 12g **Exchanges:** ½ Starch, 3 Vegetable, 1 Very Lean Meat, 3 Fat **Carbohydrate Choices:** 1½

Seaside BLT Pasta Salad

[Suddenly Salad Contest Winner Mary Shivers Ada, OK]

6 servings (1⅓ cups each) PREP TIME 20 minutes START TO FINISH 1 hour 20 minutes

1 box Betty Crocker Suddenly Pasta Salad ranch & bacon pasta salad mix

¾ cup mayonnaise

2 tablespoons milk

2 tablespoons lemon juice

3 cans (6 oz each) lump crab meat, drained, rinsed

¼ cup thinly sliced green onions (4 medium)

4 slices bacon, crisply cooked, crumbled (¼ cup)

2 cups thinly sliced iceberg lettuce

2 medium tomatoes, chopped, drained (1½ cups)

1 Fill 3-quart saucepan ⅔ full of water; heat to boiling. Empty pasta mix (from salad mix) into boiling water. Gently boil uncovered 12 minutes, stirring occasionally.

2 Meanwhile, in large bowl, stir together seasoning mix (from salad mix), mayonnaise, milk and lemon juice. Stir in crab meat, onions and bacon.

3 Drain pasta; rinse with cold water. Shake to drain well. Stir pasta into salad mixture. Cover; refrigerate 1 hour to chill. Just before serving, gently toss with lettuce and tomatoes to coat.

1 Serving: Calories 490; Total Fat 26g (Saturated Fat 4g; Trans Fat 0g); Cholesterol 100mg; Sodium 850mg; Total Carbohydrate 38g (Dietary Fiber 2g); Protein 25g **Exchanges:** 2 Starch, ½ Other Carbohydrate, 3 Lean Meat, 3 Fat **Carbohydrate Choices:** 2½

Healthy Twist

Slim down this salad a bit by using fat-free mayo and turkey bacon.

Deli Beef and Bean Tossed Salad

6 servings   PREP TIME 10 minutes   START TO FINISH 10 minutes

FAST

1 **bag (10 oz) mixed salad greens**

1 **can (15 oz) three bean salad, chilled, or 1 pint (2 cups) three-bean salad (from deli)**

¼ **lb cooked roast beef (from deli), cut into julienne strips (¾ cup)**

1 **cup shredded Cheddar or Swiss cheese (4 oz)**

12 **cherry tomatoes, halved**

1 In large bowl, toss all ingredients to combine.

2 Serve immediately or refrigerate until serving time.

1 Serving: Calories 160; Total Fat 7g (Saturated Fat 4g; Trans Fat 0g); Cholesterol 30mg; Sodium 600mg; Total Carbohydrate 14g (Dietary Fiber 3g); Protein 11g **Exchanges:** ½ Starch, 1½ Vegetable, 1 Medium-Fat Meat, ½ Fat **Carbohydrate Choices:** 1

Quick Variation

You can substitute deli or leftover cooked ham or turkey instead of the beef. Also, feel free to use reduced-fat cheese, if you prefer.

Ground Beef Fajita Taco Salad

6 servings   PREP TIME 30 minutes   START TO FINISH 30 minutes
FAST

CREAMY GUACAMOLE DRESSING

1 **medium ripe avocado, pitted, peeled and cut into chunks**

¼ **cup sour cream**

3 **tablespoons milk**

2 **tablespoons lime juice**

2 **tablespoons chopped fresh cilantro leaves**

2 **tablespoons olive or vegetable oil**

½ **teaspoon salt**

½ **teaspoon ground cumin**

⅛ **teaspoon ground red pepper (cayenne)**

SALAD

2 **teaspoons vegetable oil**

2 **medium bell peppers (any color), cut into bite-size strips**

1 **medium onion, cut into thin wedges**

1 **lb lean (at least 80%) ground beef**

1 **package (1 oz) taco seasoning mix**

⅔ **cup water**

6 **cups torn romaine lettuce**

1 **medium tomato, chopped (¾ cup)**

1 **cup shredded Cheddar cheese (4 oz)**

2 **cups crushed tortilla chips (about 4 oz)**

1 In blender, place dressing ingredients. Cover; blend on medium speed 30 seconds or until smooth. Pour into small bowl. Cover; refrigerate until serving time.

2 In 12-inch nonstick skillet, heat 2 teaspoons oil over medium heat. Add bell peppers and onion; cook 6 minutes, stirring occasionally, until tender. Remove vegetables from skillet; set aside.

3 In same skillet, cook beef over medium-high heat 5 to 7 minutes, stirring occasionally, until thoroughly cooked; drain. Add taco seasoning mix and water; heat as directed on package.

4 Place 1 cup lettuce on each of 6 plates. Top with beef mixture, vegetables, tomato, cheese and chips. Serve with dressing.

1 Serving: Calories 470; Total Fat 31g (Saturated Fat 10g; Trans Fat 1g); Cholesterol 75mg; Sodium 890mg; Total Carbohydrate 25g (Dietary Fiber 5g); Protein 21g **Exchanges:** 1½ Starch, ½ Vegetable, 3 High-Fat Meat, 1 Fat **Carbohydrate Choices:** 1½

Steak and Feta Spinach Salad

4 servings   PREP TIME 30 minutes   START TO FINISH 30 minutes

FAST

1   **boneless beef sirloin steak, 1½ inches thick (1 lb)**

⅔   **cup balsamic vinaigrette dressing**

1   **bag (6 oz) fresh baby spinach leaves**

1½ **cups halved cherry tomatoes**

¾   **cup crumbled tomato and basil feta cheese (3 oz)**

1 Set oven control to broil. Spray broiler pan with cooking spray. Place steak on broiler pan; brush with 1 tablespoon of the dressing. Broil with top 4 to 6 inches from heat 10 minutes. Turn steak over; brush with another 1 tablespoon of dressing. Broil 5 to 10 minutes longer or until meat is desired doneness (145°F for medium-rare). Cover; let stand 5 minutes.

2 Meanwhile, on each of 4 serving plates, evenly divide spinach and tomatoes.

3 Cut steak across grain into thin slices; arrange over salads. Top with cheese. Drizzle each salad with remaining dressing.

1 Serving: Calories 360; Total Fat 19g (Saturated Fat 4g; Trans Fat 0g); Cholesterol 80mg; Sodium 810mg; Total Carbohydrate 14g (Dietary Fiber 2g); Protein 35g **Exchanges:** ½ Starch, ½ Other Carbohydrate, 4½ Lean Meat, 1 Fat **Carbohydrate Choices:** 1

Quick Variation

Not a spinach fan? There are so many great salad mixes in the produce department—you could use mixed field greens, romaine or arugula instead.

Steakhouse Salad

4 servings (2 cups each)   PREP TIME 35 minutes   START TO FINISH 35 minutes

12 **small red potatoes,
    quartered**

 2 **tablespoons olive or
    vegetable oil**

 2 **teaspoons kosher (coarse)
    salt**

½ **teaspoon pepper**

 1 **lb beef flank steak**

 1 **bag (6 oz) fresh
    baby spinach leaves**

 1 **medium tomato, cut into
    bite-size pieces**

¼ **cup tangy tomato-bacon
    dressing**

1 Heat oven to 375°F. In large bowl, toss potatoes, 1 tablespoon of the oil, 1 teaspoon of the salt and ¼ teaspoon of the pepper. Spread on ungreased 15×10×1-inch pan. Roast 20 to 25 minutes, stirring occasionally, until tender.

2 Meanwhile, sprinkle beef with remaining 1 teaspoon salt and ¼ teaspoon pepper. In 12-inch nonstick skillet, heat remaining 1 tablespoon oil over medium heat. Add beef; cover and cook 8 to 10 minutes, turning once, until desired doneness. Remove beef from skillet to cutting board; cover with foil and let rest 5 minutes.

3 Cut beef into thin bite-size pieces. In large bowl, toss beef, potatoes, spinach, tomato and dressing.

1 Serving: Calories 790; Total Fat 40g (Saturated Fat 8g; Trans Fat 0g); Cholesterol 55mg; Sodium 1440mg; Total Carbohydrate 71g (Dietary Fiber 10g); Protein 36g **Exchanges:** 3 Starch, ½ Other Carbohydrate, 3 Vegetable, 3 Medium-Fat Meat, 4½ Fat **Carbohydrate Choices:** 5

Time-Saver

Start the steak about 5 minutes after you start roasting the potatoes; they'll be done at about the same time.

Cinnamon-Maple Glazed Salmon Salad

4 servings   PREP TIME 35 minutes   START TO FINISH 35 minutes

DRESSING

⅓ **cup real maple or maple-flavored syrup**

⅓ **cup canola or vegetable oil**

2 **tablespoons plus 1 teaspoon balsamic vinegar**

½ **teaspoon ground cinnamon**

SALAD

1 **salmon fillet (1¼ lb), cut into 4 pieces**

6 **cups spring greens (from 5-oz bag)**

⅓ **cup coarsely chopped pecans, toasted**∗

⅔ **cup crumbled feta cheese (2⅔ oz)**

⅓ **cup dried cherries**

1 Heat oven to 400°F. Line 15×10×1-inch pan with foil. In small bowl, beat dressing ingredients with whisk until blended. Place 3 tablespoons dressing in small bowl; reserve for brushing on salmon. Set remaining dressing aside for salad.

2 Place salmon pieces, skin side down, in pan. Bake 10 to 14 minutes, brushing with reserved 3 tablespoons dressing twice during last 5 minutes of baking, until salmon flakes easily with fork. Discard any remaining dressing used for salmon.

3 In large bowl, toss greens with reserved dressing for salad. On each of 4 individual plates, evenly divide greens. Sprinkle each with one-fourth each of pecans, feta cheese and dried cherries. Lift pieces of salmon from skin with metal spatula; top each salad with salmon. Discard skin and foil.

∗*To toast pecans, cook in ungreased heavy skillet over medium heat 5 to 7 minutes, stirring frequently until browning begins, then stirring constantly until golden brown. Remove immediately from hot skillet to prevent overcooking.*

1 Serving: Calories 630; Total Fat 39g (Saturated Fat 7g; Trans Fat 0g); Cholesterol 100mg; Sodium 400mg; Total Carbohydrate 35g (Dietary Fiber 3g); Protein 34g **Exchanges:** 2 Starch, 1 Vegetable, 3½ Lean Meat, 5½ Fat **Carbohydrate Choices:** 2

Mediterranean Tuna Salad

5 servings   PREP TIME 15 minutes   START TO FINISH 15 minutes

FAST

5 large tomatoes

2 cans (4.5 oz each) light tuna in olive oil, undrained

1 can (15.5 oz) great northern beans, drained, rinsed

¼ cup chopped fresh Italian (flat-leaf) parsley

2 tablespoons capers, drained

3 tablespoons fresh lemon juice

2 teaspoons finely chopped garlic

1 teaspoon salt

¼ teaspoon pepper

5 sprigs fresh Italian (flat-leaf) parsley, if desired

1 Cut very thin slice from bottom of each tomato so it will stand upright. Cut thin slice from top of each tomato; scoop out tomato flesh, leaving tomato shell. Remove seeds from tomato flesh; chop enough tomato flesh to measure 1 cup.

2 In medium bowl, toss chopped tomato with all remaining ingredients except parsley sprigs.

3 Spoon tuna mixture into hollowed-out tomatoes. Garnish with parsley sprigs.

1 Serving: Calories 310; Total Fat 10g (Saturated Fat 1.5g; Trans Fat 0g); Cholesterol 10mg; Sodium 1020mg; Total Carbohydrate 30g (Dietary Fiber 8g); Protein 23g **Exchanges:** ½ Starch, 1 Low-Fat Milk, 2 Vegetable, 2 Lean Meat **Carbohydrate Choices:** 2

Orzo and Tuna Salad

4 servings (about 1¼ cups each) PREP TIME 25 minutes START TO FINISH 25 minutes

FAST

1 cup uncooked orzo or rosamarina pasta (6 oz)

1 package (3 oz) cream cheese, softened

1½ cups diced cucumber (about 1 medium)

2 medium stalks celery, thinly sliced (1 cup)

3 tablespoons cider vinegar

1 tablespoon olive or vegetable oil

2 cans (5 oz each) albacore tuna in water, drained

2 tablespoons chopped fresh dill weed

½ teaspoon salt

¼ teaspoon pepper

1 In 3-quart saucepan, cook pasta as directed on package. Drain; rinse with cold water to cool.

2 Meanwhile, in food processor, place cream cheese, 1 cup of the cucumber, the celery, vinegar and oil. Cover; process until smooth.

3 In large bowl, stir cooked pasta, cream cheese mixture, remaining ½ cup cucumber and remaining ingredients until well mixed.

1 Serving: Calories 380; Total Fat 13g (Saturated Fat 6g; Trans Fat 0g); Cholesterol 45mg; Sodium 920mg; Total Carbohydrate 40g (Dietary Fiber 3g); Protein 27g **Exchanges:** 1½ Starch, ½ Low-Fat Milk, 2 Vegetable, 2 Lean Meat, 1 Fat **Carbohydrate Choices:** 2½

Peppered Shrimp and Mango Salad

4 servings (about 2 cups each)   PREP TIME 20 minutes   START TO FINISH 20 minutes

FAST

20 uncooked large shrimp,
     thawed if frozen, peeled
     (tail shells removed),
     deveined (about ¾ lb)

½ teaspoon salt

½ teaspoon pepper

1 tablespoon sesame
    or vegetable oil

1 bag (5 oz) mixed salad
    greens

1½ cups diced mangoes
    (about 1½ medium)

½ cup sliced radishes
    (about 5 medium)

⅓ cup Asian sesame
    dressing

1 Toss shrimp with salt and pepper. In 10-inch skillet, heat oil over high heat. Add shrimp; cook about 3 minutes, stirring frequently, until pink. Remove from heat.

2 In large bowl, toss salad greens, mangoes, radishes and dressing. Divide salad among 4 serving plates; top each with 5 shrimp.

1 Serving: Calories 110; Total Fat 4g (Saturated Fat 0.5g; Trans Fat 0g); Cholesterol 60mg; Sodium 380mg; Total Carbohydrate 12g (Dietary Fiber 2g); Protein 7g **Exchanges:** ½ Starch, ½ Other Carbohydrate, ½ Very Lean Meat, ½ Fat Carbohydrate Choices: 1

Time-Saver

Purchase quick-peel shrimp to speed up prep time. The shells are already split and the shrimp deveined, so the shells come off easily.

Shrimp Salad with Zesty Dressing

4 servings   PREP TIME 20 minutes   START TO FINISH 20 minutes

FAST

DRESSING

⅓ **cup ranch dressing**

⅓ **cup zesty cocktail sauce**

SALAD

1 **bag (10 oz) torn romaine lettuce (about 7 cups)**

1 **cup thinly sliced English (seedless) cucumber**

1 **cup halved cherry tomatoes (about ½ pint)**

24 **cooked deveined peeled large shrimp, thawed if frozen, tail shells removed (about ½ lb)**

1 **tablespoon chopped fresh chives**

1 In small bowl, beat dressing ingredients with whisk until blended.

2 On each of 4 plates, layer one-fourth each of lettuce, cucumber and tomatoes. Arrange 6 shrimp on top of each. Drizzle with dressing; sprinkle with chives.

1 Serving: Calories 190; Total Fat 11g (Saturated Fat 1.5g; Trans Fat 0g); Cholesterol 85mg; Sodium 510mg; Total Carbohydrate 12g (Dietary Fiber 3g); Protein 11g **Exchanges:** ½ Starch, 1 Vegetable, 1 Very Lean Meat, 2 Fat **Carbohydrate Choices:** 1

Time-Saver

Need a new kitchen gadget? A mandoline works well for quickly slicing vegetables thinly.

Sesame Singapore Shrimp Salad

[Suddenly Salad Contest Winner Roxanne Chan Albany, CA]

4 servings (1½ cups each)   PREP TIME **25 minutes**   START TO FINISH **25 minutes**

FAST

- **1 box Betty Crocker Suddenly Pasta Salad classic pasta salad mix**
- **⅔ cup Asian toasted sesame salad dressing**
- **½ teaspoon crushed red pepper flakes**
- **2 cups angel hair or regular coleslaw mix**
- **1½ cups coarsely chopped cooked peeled shrimp**
- **¼ cup chopped dry-roasted peanuts**
- **¼ cup finely chopped basil leaves**
- **1 mango, seed removed, peeled and cut into ½-inch cubes (1 cup)**
- **1 green onion, chopped**
  Black sesame seed

1 Fill 3-quart saucepan ⅔ full of water; heat to boiling. Empty pasta mix (from salad mix) into boiling water. Gently boil uncovered 12 minutes, stirring occasionally.

2 Meanwhile, in large bowl, stir together seasoning mix (from salad mix), salad dressing and pepper flakes. Add coleslaw mix, shrimp, peanuts, basil, mango and green onion; toss gently to coat.

3 Drain pasta; rinse with cold water. Shake to drain well. Stir pasta into salad mixture. Sprinkle with sesame seed. Serve immediately, or cover and refrigerate until serving time.

1 Serving: Calories 550; Total Fat 20g (Saturated Fat 3g; Trans Fat 0g); Cholesterol 180mg; Sodium 1580mg; Total Carbohydrate 64g (Dietary Fiber 3g); Protein 28g **Exchanges:** 2 Starch, ½ Fruit, 1½ Other Carbohydrate, ½ Vegetable, 3 Lean Meat, 2 Fat **Carbohydrate Choices:** 4

Time-Saver

Buy peeled and precut mango in the produce section of your supermarket. You may need to chop more finely.

Spicy Coconut-Surimi Salad

6 servings   PREP TIME 15 minutes   START TO FINISH 15 minutes

FAST

1 **cup mayonnaise or salad dressing**

1 **to 2 teaspoons red curry paste (from 4-oz jar)**

1 **tablespoon fresh lemon juice**

2 **packages (8 oz each) refrigerated chunk-style imitation crabmeat (surimi)**

2 **cups fresh sugar snap peas, trimmed, cut in half diagonally**

1 **cup shredded coconut**

8 **medium green onions, sliced (½ cup)**

6 **cups thinly sliced Chinese (napa) cabbage**

1 In small bowl, beat mayonnaise, curry paste and lemon juice with whisk until blended.

2 In large bowl, stir imitation crabmeat, peas, coconut, onions and mayonnaise mixture until well mixed.

3 On each of 6 serving plates, place 1 cup cabbage. Top evenly with salad.

1 Serving: Calories 450; Total Fat 36g (Saturated Fat 9g; Trans Fat 0g); Cholesterol 35mg; Sodium 970mg; Total Carbohydrate 19g (Dietary Fiber 2g); Protein 14g **Exchanges:** 1 Other Carbohydrate, ½ Vegetable, 2 Very Lean Meat, 7 Fat **Carbohydrate Choices:** 1

Southwest Pasta Salad

[Suddenly Salad Contest Winner Bonnie St. Denis Spencerport, NY]

12 servings (1 cup each) PREP TIME 30 minutes START TO FINISH 30 minutes

FAST

2 boxes Betty Crocker Suddenly Pasta Salad classic pasta salad mix

½ cup cold water

⅓ cup olive oil

2 tablespoons cider vinegar

1 tablespoon chopped fresh cilantro leaves

1 to 2 tablespoons red pepper sauce, if desired

½ teaspoon ground cumin

1 can (15 oz) black beans, drained, rinsed

1 can (14.5 oz) diced tomatoes with jalapeño peppers, drained

1 can (11 oz) vacuum-packed whole kernel corn with red and green peppers, drained

½ cup sliced ripe olives

½ cup chopped red, yellow or green bell pepper

1 medium avocado, pitted, peeled and cut into ½-inch cubes

8 oz pepper Jack cheese, cut into ½-inch cubes (2 cups)

Lettuce leaves, if desired

1 Fill 3-quart saucepan ⅔ full of water; heat to boiling. Empty pasta mix (from salad mix) into boiling water. Gently boil uncovered 12 minutes, stirring occasionally.

2 Meanwhile, in large bowl, mix contents of seasoning pouches (from salad mix), cold water, oil, vinegar, cilantro, pepper sauce and cumin.

3 Drain pasta; rinse with cold water. Shake to drain well. Add pasta, beans, tomatoes, corn, olives, bell pepper, avocado and cheese to seasoning mixture; toss gently to coat. Serve immediately on lettuce-lined platter, or cover and refrigerate until serving time.

1 Serving: Calories 340; Total Fat 14g (Saturated Fat 4g; Trans Fat 0g); Cholesterol 15mg; Sodium 920mg; Total Carbohydrate 42g (Dietary Fiber 5g); Protein 11g **Exchanges:** 2½ Starch, ½ Other Carbohydrate, ½ High-Fat Meat, 1½ Fat **Carbohydrate Choices:** 3

Time-Saver

Make this salad up to 24 hours before serving. Give it a stir before serving.

Antipasto Curly Pasta Salad

[Suddenly Salad Contest Winner Francis Blackwelder Grand Junction, CO]

6 servings (1 cup each)   PREP TIME 30 minutes   START TO FINISH 30 minutes

FAST

1   box Betty Crocker
    Suddenly Pasta Salad
    classic pasta salad mix

3   tablespoons cold water

2   tablespoons vegetable oil

1   teaspoon Dijon mustard

1   cup cubed salami

4   oz provolone cheese,
    cut into ½-inch cubes

½   cup finely chopped
    red onion

1   jar (6 oz) marinated
    artichoke hearts, drained,
    chopped

1   can (6 oz) pitted small
    ripe olives, drained

1   jar (4 oz) sliced pimientos,
    drained, chopped

½   cup shredded or grated
    Parmesan cheese

1 Fill 3-quart saucepan ⅔ full of water; heat to boiling. Empty pasta mix (from salad mix) into boiling water. Gently boil uncovered 12 minutes, stirring occasionally.

2 Meanwhile, in large bowl, mix contents of seasoning pouch (from salad mix), water, oil and mustard. Add salami, provolone cheese, onion, artichokes, olives and pimientos; toss gently to combine.

3 Drain pasta; rinse with cold water. Shake to drain well. Add pasta to salad mixture; toss gently. Sprinkle with Parmesan cheese. Serve immediately, or cover and refrigerate until serving time.

1 Serving: Calories 420; Total Fat 23g (Saturated Fat 8g; Trans Fat 0g); Cholesterol 40mg; Sodium 1560mg; Total Carbohydrate 37g (Dietary Fiber 5g); Protein 17g **Exchanges:** 1½ Starch, 1 Other Carbohydrate, 1½ High-Fat Meat, 2 Fat **Carbohydrate Choices:** 2½

Time-Saver

This salad can be made a day ahead, but wait until just before serving to top with the Parmesan cheese.

Dilled Potato-Bean Salad

4 servings (1¾ cups each)   PREP TIME 30 minutes   START TO FINISH 35 minutes

2   **lb small red potatoes**

⅔   **cup olive or vegetable oil**

⅓   **cup white wine vinegar**

1   **teaspoon salt**

½   **teaspoon pepper**

½   **cup chopped celery**

¼   **cup chopped fresh dill**

2   **tablespoons sliced green onions (2 medium)**

1   **can (15 oz) dark red kidney beans, drained, rinsed**

4   **hard-cooked eggs, halved lengthwise, sliced**

1 Place potatoes in 3-quart saucepan with 4 cups water. Heat water to boiling over medium-high heat. Reduce heat; simmer uncovered 8 to 10 minutes or until potatoes are tender. Drain.

2 Meanwhile, in small bowl, beat oil, vinegar, salt and pepper with whisk until blended.

3 In large bowl, place potatoes, celery, dill, onions, beans and 3 of the eggs. Pour dressing over salad; stir gently to coat. Garnish with remaining egg. Let stand 5 minutes. Serve warm.

1 Serving: Calories 720; Total Fat 42g (Saturated Fat 7g; Trans Fat 0g); Cholesterol 210mg; Sodium 680mg; Total Carbohydrate 65g (Dietary Fiber 11g); Protein 20g **Exchanges:** 3½ Starch, 2 Vegetable, 1 Medium-Fat Meat, 7 Fat **Carbohydrate Choices:** 4

Spinach and Caesar Pasta Salad

[Suddenly Salad Contest Winner Thelma Babin Houma, LA]

8 servings (2 cups each)   PREP TIME 25 minutes   START TO FINISH 25 minutes

FAST

1 box Betty Crocker
   Suddenly Pasta Salad
   Caesar pasta salad mix

¼ cup sugar

⅓ cup ketchup

¼ cup cider vinegar

¼ cup vegetable oil

1 tablespoon water

1 package (12 oz) turkey
   bacon, cooked, cut into
   small pieces

1 bag or container (10 oz)
   fresh baby spinach leaves

1 package (8 oz) sliced
   fresh mushrooms
   (about 3 cups)

5 hard-cooked eggs, sliced

1 Fill 3-quart saucepan ⅔ full of water; heat to boiling. Empty pasta mix (from salad mix) into boiling water. Gently boil uncovered 12 minutes, stirring occasionally.

2 Meanwhile, in small bowl, stir together seasoning and crouton blend (from salad mix), sugar, ketchup, vinegar, oil and water.

3 Drain pasta; rinse with cold water. Shake to drain well. In large bowl, gently toss together cooked pasta, bacon, spinach, mushrooms and eggs. Just before serving, gently toss salad ingredients with seasoning mixture. Serve immediately.

1 Serving: Calories 340; Total Fat 18g (Saturated Fat 4g; Trans Fat 0g); Cholesterol 155mg; Sodium 1040mg; Total Carbohydrate 31g (Dietary Fiber 1g); Protein 16g **Exchanges:** 1½ Starch, ½ Other Carbohydrate, 1½ Medium-Fat Meat, 2 Fat **Carbohydrate Choices:** 2

Metric Conversion Guide

Volume

U.S. UNITS	CANADIAN METRIC	AUSTRALIAN METRIC
¼ teaspoon	1 mL	1 ml
½ teaspoon	2 mL	2 ml
1 teaspoon	5 mL	5 ml
1 tablespoon	15 mL	20 ml
¼ cup	50 mL	60 ml
⅓ cup	75 mL	80 ml
½ cup	125 mL	125 ml
⅔ cup	150 mL	170 ml
¾ cup	175 mL	190 ml
1 cup	250 mL	250 ml
1 quart	1 liter	1 liter
1½ quarts	1.5 liters	1.5 liters
2 quarts	2 liters	2 liters
2½ quarts	2.5 liters	2.5 liters
3 quarts	3 liters	3 liters
4 quarts	4 liters	4 liters

Measurements

INCHES	CENTIMETERS
1	2.5
2	5.0
3	7.5
4	10.0
5	12.5
6	15.0
7	17.5
8	20.5
9	23.0
10	25.5
11	28.0
12	30.5
13	33.0

Temperatures

FAHRENHEIT	CELSIUS
32°	0°
212°	100°
250°	120°
275°	140°
300°	150°
325°	160°
350°	180°
375°	190°
400°	200°
425°	220°
450°	230°
475°	240°
500°	260°

Weight

U.S. UNITS	CANADIAN METRIC	AUSTRALIAN METRIC
1 ounce	30 grams	30 grams
2 ounces	55 grams	60 grams
3 ounces	85 grams	90 grams
4 ounces (¼ pound)	115 grams	125 grams
8 ounces (½ pound)	225 grams	225 grams
16 ounces (1 pound)	455 grams	500 grams
1 pound	455 grams	0.5 kilogram

Note: The recipes in this cookbook have not been developed or tested using metric measures. When converting recipes to metric, some variations in quality may be noted.

Index

Recipe Testing and Calculating Nutrition Information

RECIPE TESTING:

* Large eggs and 2% milk were used unless otherwise indicated.

* Fat-free, low-fat, low-sodium or lite products were not used unless indicated.

* No nonstick cookware and bakeware were used unless otherwise indicated. No dark-colored, black or insulated bakeware was used.

* When a pan is specified, a metal pan was used; a baking dish or pie plate means ovenproof glass was used.

* An electric hand mixer was used for mixing only when mixer speeds are specified.

CALCULATING NUTRITION:

* The first ingredient was used wherever a choice is given, such as ⅓ cup sour cream or plain yogurt.

* The first amount was used wherever a range is given, such as 3- to 3½-pound whole chicken.

* The first serving number was used wherever a range is given, such as 4 to 6 servings.

* "If desired" ingredients were not included.

* Only the amount of a marinade or frying oil that is absorbed was included.

Complete your cookbook library with these *Betty Crocker* titles

Betty Crocker 30-Minute Meals for Diabetes

Betty Crocker 300 Calorie Cookbook

Betty Crocker Baking Basics

Betty Crocker Baking for Today

Betty Crocker's Best Bread Machine Cookbook

Betty Crocker's Best-Loved Recipes

Betty Crocker The Big Book of Cupcakes

Betty Crocker The Big Book of Slow Cooker, Casseroles & More

Betty Crocker Bisquick® II Cookbook

Betty Crocker Bisquick® Impossibly Easy Pies

Betty Crocker Bisquick to the Rescue

Betty Crocker Christmas Cookbook

Betty Crocker's Cook Book for Boys and Girls

Betty Crocker Cookbook, 11th Edition— *The* **BIG RED** *Cookbook*®

Betty Crocker Cookbook, Bridal Edition

Betty Crocker's Cooking Basics

Betty Crocker's Cooky Book, Facsimile Edition

Betty Crocker Country Cooking

Betty Crocker Decorating Cakes and Cupcakes

Betty Crocker's Diabetes Cookbook

Betty Crocker Easy Everyday Vegetarian

Betty Crocker's Easy Slow Cooker Dinners

Betty Crocker's Eat and Lose Weight

Betty Crocker Fix-with-a-Mix Desserts

Betty Crocker Grilling Made Easy

Betty Crocker Healthy Heart Cookbook

Betty Crocker's Indian Home Cooking

Betty Crocker's Italian Cooking

Betty Crocker's Kids Cook!

Betty Crocker Living with Cancer Cookbook

Betty Crocker Low-Carb Lifestyle Cookbook

Betty Crocker's Low-Fat, Low-Cholesterol Cooking Today

Betty Crocker Money Saving Meals

Betty Crocker More Slow Cooker Recipes

Betty Crocker's New Cake Decorating

Betty Crocker One-Dish Meals

Betty Crocker's Picture Cook Book, Facsimile Edition

Betty Crocker's Quick & Easy Cookbook

Betty Crocker's Slow Cooker Cookbook

Betty Crocker Ultimate Bisquick® Cookbook

Betty Crocker's Ultimate Cake Mix Cookbook

Betty Crocker's Vegetarian Cooking

Betty Crocker Why It Works

AIRPLANE FLYING
HANDBOOK

checklists

Trim Rudder
         ON/OFF
Bored: find
         landing field
smoke hoods?
personal measures
Icing
         No autopilot

1999

survival Bag

cell phone
matches
mirror
Blanket
Food/Water
knife

11/26/00
Scanning 10° 1sec
Clearing turns prior to practice
Dip wing to see
Right rudder on take-off
Ground effect 1/4 wingspan
off center wearing at night
Landings: think Go Around
Narrow Temp/Dewpoint
         = Fog
Victor (low altitude) airways
RNAV = Area Navigation
         electronically setting VORs
VOR/DME/vortac
Beware desire to save
         airplane over
         safety

↓
80% errors in preflight
(that occur late)

✱ Lose Vision > 5,000 ft
(Anti authority
(Invulnerability   p. 18-2

U.S. DEPARTMENT OF TRANSPORTATION
FEDERAL AVIATION ADMINISTRATION
Flight Standards Service

PREFACE

This Airplane Flying Handbook introduces the basic pilot skills and knowledge that are essential for piloting airplanes. It provides information on transition to *other* airplanes and the operation of various airplane systems. It is developed by the Flight Standards Service, Airman Testing Standards Branch in cooperation with various aviation educators and industry.

This handbook is developed to assist student pilots learning to fly airplanes. It is also beneficial to pilots who wish to improve their flying proficiency and aeronautical knowledge, those pilots preparing for additional certificates or ratings, and flight instructors engaged in the instruction of both students and certificated pilots. It introduces the future pilot to the realm of flight and provides information and guidance in the performance of procedures and maneuvers which have specific functions in various areas of operation.

This handbook conforms to pilot training and certification concepts established by the Federal Aviation Administration (FAA). There are different ways of teaching as well as performing flight procedures and maneuvers, and many variations in the explanations of aerodynamic theories and principles. This handbook adopts a selective method and concept to flying airplanes. The discussions and explanations reflect the most commonly used practices and principles. Occasionally, the word *must* or similar language is used where the desired action is deemed critical. The use of such language is not intended to add to, interpret, or relieve a duty imposed by Title 14 of the Code of Federal Regulations (14 CFR).

It is essential for persons using this handbook to also become familiar with and apply the pertinent parts of 14 CFR and the Aeronautical Information Manual (AIM). Performance standards for demonstrating competence required for pilot certification are prescribed in the appropriate airplane practical test standard.

This handbook supersedes AC 61-21A, Flight Training Handbook, dated 1979 (revised 1980 with Errata Sheet). This handbook also supercedes related portions of AC 61-9B, Pilot Transition Courses for Complex Single Engine and Light Twin-Engine Airplanes, dated 1974; and AC 61-10A, Private and Commercial Pilots Refresher Courses, dated 1972. It can be purchased from the Superintendent of Documents, U.S. Government Printing Office (GPO), Washington, DC 20402-9325, or from U.S. Government Bookstores located in major cities throughout the United States.

The current Flight Standards Service airman training and testing material, and subject matter knowledge codes for all airman certificates and ratings can be obtained from the Regulatory Support Division, AFS-600, home page on the Internet.

The Regulatory Support Division's Internet address is: http://www.mmac.jccbi.gov/afs/afs600

Comments regarding this handbook should be sent to U.S. Department of Transportation, Federal Aviation Administration, Airman Testing Standards Branch, AFS-630, P.O. Box 25082, Oklahoma City, OK 73125.

AC 00-2, Advisory Circular Checklist, transmits the current status of FAA advisory circulars and other flight information and publications. This checklist is free of charge and may be obtained by sending a request to U.S. Department of Transportation, Subsequent Distribution Office, SVC-121.23, Ardmore East Business Center, 3341 Q 75th Avenue, Landover, MD 20785. The checklist is also available on the Internet at http://www.faa.gov/abc/ac-chklst/actoc.htm

CONTENTS

CHAPTER 1

INTRODUCTION TO FLIGHT TRAINING

INTRODUCTION

Before beginning flight training, it is important to have a basic understanding of the responsibilities, safety regulations, and issues applicable to such an endeavor. This includes choice of a flight school, selected study materials, study habits, and the role of the instructor, student, and Federal Aviation Administration (FAA). Safety, proper decision making, good habits, and collision avoidance are emphasized from the very beginning to ensure one gets started in the right direction.

CHOOSING A FLIGHT SCHOOL

Once a person has decided to become a pilot, the next consideration is where to attend flight school. Part of this consideration should be whether he or she is learning to fly for personal reasons, or planning to pursue a career in aviation.

Some sources for selecting a flight school may consist of the yellow pages in the telephone directory, aviation trade or flying magazines, or local airports. Many flight schools, colleges, and universities advertise in aviation magazines and offer excellent programs.

Some flight schools are referred to as "FAA-approved schools." An FAA-approved school is certificated by the FAA and is required to meet certain standards regarding airplanes, personnel, and curricula. Another advantage of an approved school is that it may offer some courses of training with fewer flight hours.

There are also many excellent flight schools and independent flight instructors that meet or exceed the same high standards as an FAA-approved school.

INSTRUCTOR/STUDENT RELATIONSHIP

The FAA has adopted an operational training concept that places the full responsibility for student training on the authorized flight instructor. In this role, the instructor assumes the total responsibility for training the pilot to meet the standards required for certification within an ever-changing operating environment.

The flight instructor will provide guidance, and arrange for academic and flight training lessons. These lessons are presented in a logical manner to achieve desired goals. After each flight, the flight instructor will review the day's lesson. This will be the time to clear up any questions because it is important that misconceptions be clarified while the subject is still fresh in mind.

This handbook provides the background and explanations of the academic principles and recommended flight training procedures needed to complete flight training. This handbook is an important tool in developing a sound background of knowledge and judgment needed to be a competent and safe pilot.

For example, a basic knowledge of aerodynamic principles helps the pilot to better understand what is needed to properly perform maneuvers, such as straight and level, turns, climbs, and descents.

ROLE OF THE FAA

Congress empowered the FAA, among other things, to promote aviation safety by prescribing safety standards for civil aviation. This is accomplished through the Code of Federal Regulations (CFR's).

Title 14 of the Code of Federal Regulations (14 CFR) part 61 pertains to the certification of pilots, flight instructors, and ground instructors. 14 CFR part 61 prescribes the eligibility, aeronautical knowledge, flight proficiency, experience, and limitations required for each type of pilot certificate issued.

General Operating and Flight Rules

14 CFR part 91 prescribes the rules for operation of civil aircraft. The regulation is broad in scope and provides general guidance in the areas of general flight rules, visual flight rules (VFR), instrument flight rules

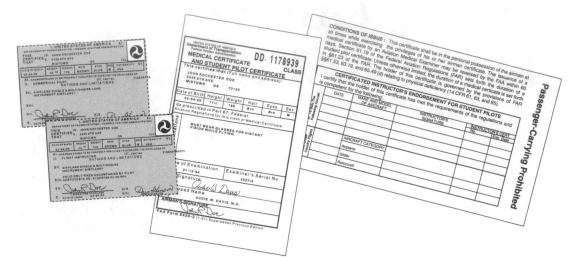

FIGURE 1-1.—*Instructor and student certificates.*

(IFR), maintenance, and preventive maintenance and alterations.

Practical Test Standards (PTS's)

The flight proficiency maneuvers listed in 14 CFR part 61 are the standard skill requirements for certification. They are outlined in the practical test standards (PTS's) as AREAS OF OPERATION. These AREAS OF OPERATION are phases of the practical test arranged in a logical sequence within the standard. They begin with Preflight Preparation and end with Postflight Procedures. Roman numerals preceding each AREAS OF OPERATION relate to the corresponding AREAS OF OPERATION contained in the regulation.

Each AREA OF OPERATION contains TASKS, which are comprised of knowledge areas, flight procedures, and/or flight maneuvers appropriate to the AREA OF OPERATION. For most pilot certificates, an applicant will be required to demonstrate knowledge and proficiency in all TASKS.

Each pilot applicant should obtain a copy of the PTS appropriate to the pilot certificate that he or she plans to acquire. This will enable the applicant to know exactly what is expected on the practical test.

Medical Certification

All pilots except those who fly gliders or free air balloons, must possess a valid medical certificate in order to exercise the privileges of their airman certificates. [Figure 1-1]

The periodic medical examinations required for medical certification are conducted by designated aviation medical examiners, which are physicians with a special interest in aviation safety and training in aviation medicine.

The standards for medical certification are contained in 14 CFR part 67. The requirements for obtaining medical certification are contained in 14 CFR part 61.

Prior to beginning flight training, a flight instructor should interview the prospective student about any health conditions and determine the ultimate goal of the student as a pilot. Good advice would be to obtain the class of medical certificate required before beginning flight training. Finding out immediately whether the student is medically qualified could save time and money.

Students who have physical limitations, such as impaired vision, loss of a limb, or hearing impairment may possibly be issued a medical certificate valid for Student Pilot Privileges Only. This kind of medical certificate will allow them to continue flight training and to prepare for the pilot certification practical test. During pilot training, flight instructors should ensure that students can safely perform all required TASKS to the required standards. Special devices may be necessary to allow students to manipulate the flight controls. If unable to perform certain TASKS, the student may have a limitation placed on his or her pilot certificate. For example, hearing impairment would require the limitation "Not Valid for Flight Requiring the Use of Radio." Another limitation may allow the pilot to only operate a certain make and model airplane, such as one without rudder pedals.

When a student with a physical limitation meets all of the knowledge, experience, and proficiency requirements, a letter should be written to the FAA Regional Flight Surgeon requesting a special medical flight test. Upon receipt of the letter, the student's medical file is reviewed, and a Letter of Authorization (LOA) or Denial is issued to the student. If the test is authorized, the student will be instructed to contact the nearest Flight Standards District Office (FSDO) and request a test. After demonstrating that the airplane can be operated within the normal level of safety, a waiver or statement of demonstrated ability (SODA) is issued. This waiver or SODA is valid as long as the student's physical impairment does not worsen. Additional information can be obtained on this subject at the local FSDO. Unless otherwise limited, medical certificates are valid for a period of time specified in 14 CFR part 61.

A private pilot certificate requires a third-class medical certificate, which is valid for 3 years for those who are under 40 years of age, and for those over, it is valid for 2 years.

A commercial pilot certificate requires at least a second-class medical certificate, which is valid for 1 year.

A airline transport pilot certificate requires a first-class medical certificate, which is valid for 6 months.

A pilot should note that the class of medical certificate required applies only when exercising the privilege of the certificate for which it was required. This being the case, a first-class medical certificate would be valid for 1 year if exercising the privileges of a commercial certificate, and 2 or 3 years, as appropriate for exercising the privileges of a private certificate. The same applies for a second-class medical certificate.

FLIGHT STANDARDS DISTRICT OFFICES (FSDO's)

Throughout the world, the FAA has approximately 100 Flight Standards District Offices and International Field Offices, commonly referred to as "FSDO's" and "IFO's." Through these offices, information and services are provided for the aviation community. In the United States, FSDO phone numbers are listed in the blue pages of the telephone directory under United States Government Offices, Department of Transportation, Federal Aviation Administration.

STUDY HABITS

The use of a training syllabus is an effective way to lead a student pilot through the proper steps in learning to fly safely.

When beginning flight training, the development of good study habits includes the practice of visualizing the flight instructor's explanation plus those of the textbook.

Study habits include time spent with cockpit familiarization. This includes reviewing checklists, identifying controls, and learning the cockpit arrangement.

STUDY MATERIALS

The FAA develops and makes available to the public various sources of aeronautical information. Some of this information is free; other information is available at a nominal cost. Of particular interest and value to those persons getting started in flying is: AC 61-12, Student Pilot Guide; AC 61-23, Pilot's Handbook of Aeronautical Knowledge; Aeronautical Information Manual (AIM); and practical test standards (PTS's). In addition, many aviation publications are available from commercial sources. [Figure 1-2]

FIGURE 1-2.—Selected study materials.

Complete listings and instructions for ordering airman training publications are contained in the latest issue of AC 00-2, Advisory Circular Checklist, which can be obtained from:

U.S. Department of Transportation
Subsequent Distribution Office (SVC-121.23)
Ardmore East Business Center
3341 Q 75th Ave.
Landover, MD 20785

This checklist is also available on the Internet at:

http://www.faa.gov/abc/ac-chklst/actoc.htm

Collision avoidance

14 CFR part 91 has established right-of-way rules, minimum safe altitudes, and VFR cruising altitudes to enhance flight safety. The pilot can contribute to collision avoidance by being alert and scanning for other aircraft. This is particularly important in the vicinity of an airport.

Effective scanning is accomplished with a series of short, regularly spaced eye movements that bring successive areas of the sky into the central visual field. Each movement should not exceed 10°, and should be observed for at least 1 second to enable detection. Although back and forth eye movements seem preferred by most pilots, each pilot should develop a scanning pattern that is most comfortable and adhere to it to assure optimum scanning.

If another aircraft is close enough to create a hazard, give way instead of waiting for the other pilot to respect the right-of-way.

Clearing Procedures

The following procedures and considerations should assist a pilot in collision avoidance under various situations.

• **Before Takeoff**—Prior to taxiing onto a runway or landing area in preparation for takeoff, scan the approach area for possible landing traffic, executing appropriate maneuvers to provide a clear view of the approach areas.
• **Climbs and Descents**—During climbs and descents in flight conditions which permit visual detection of other traffic, execute gentle banks left and right at a frequency which permits continuous visual scanning of the airspace.
• **Straight and Level**—During sustained periods of straight-and-level flight execute appropriate clearing procedures at periodic intervals.
• **Traffic Patterns**—Avoid entries into traffic patterns while descending.
• **Traffic at Very High Frequency Omnidirectional Range (VOR) sites**—Due to converging traffic, maintain extra vigilance in the vicinity of VOR's and intersections.
• **Training Operations**—Maintain vigilance and do clearing turns prior to a practice maneuver. During instruction, the pilot may be asked to verbalize the clearing procedures (call out "clear left, right, above, and below").

High-wing and low-wing aircraft have their respective blind spots. High-wing aircraft should momentarily raise their wing in the direction of the intended turn and look for traffic prior to beginning the turn. Low-wing aircraft should momentarily lower the wing.

CHAPTER 2

PREFLIGHT, POSTFLIGHT, AND GROUND OPERATIONS

INTRODUCTION

This chapter discusses the basic procedures and techniques for proper preflight, postflight, and safe ground operations of an airplane. Proper preflight preparation is the foundation for safe flight operations. The manufacturer's Airplane Flight Manual (AFM) and/or Pilot's Operating Handbook (POH) should be used as the final authority for airplane operation.

PILOT ASSESSMENT

Perhaps the best place for pilots to begin a preflight is with themselves. Pilots will need to determine that they:

- are physically fit to make the flight;
- are in possession of a current medical certificate appropriate to the operation being conducted;
- are in possession of a valid pilot certificate appropriate to the operation being conducted; and
- meet the applicable currency requirements of Title 14 of the Code of Federal Regulations (14 CFR), part 61.

The I'M SAFE checklist can be helpful to pilots in evaluating if they are in condition to conduct a flight safely. In doing this, pilots can ensure that they are not being impaired by:

Illness	I
Medication	M
Stress	S
Alcohol	A
Fatigue	F
Eating	E

PREFLIGHT PREPARATION AND FLIGHT PLANNING

Whether the flight is to be local or cross-country, certain preflight items need to be reviewed and accomplished. 14 CFR part 91 requires that before each flight, the pilot shall become familiar with all available information concerning the flight.

For all flights, this includes runway lengths, and takeoff and landing distances.

For flights not in the vicinity of an airport, the pilot must be familiar with:

- weather reports and forecasts;
- fuel requirements;
- alternate/diversion plans; and
- known traffic delays.

The best sources of information for airplane performance data are the AFM/POH. The best sources for preflight weather and Notices to Airmen (NOTAM's) information are FAA Automated Flight Service Stations (AFSS) or direct user access terminal systems (DUATS). Airport, navigation, and communication information can be derived from the Airport/Facility Directory.

Based on a review of this information, particularly the weather conditions, fuel requirements, and pilot qualifications, a decision can be made on whether to begin the flight, or to cancel and reschedule.

Airplane Preflight Inspection

The accomplishment of a safe flight includes a careful preflight inspection of the airplane. The preflight inspection is conducted with a checklist and helps determine if the airplane is in an airworthy condition for the intended flight.

Certificates and Documents

Airworthiness of the airplane is determined, in part, by the following certificates and documents, which must be on board the airplane when operated.

- Airworthiness certificate.
- Registration certificate.
- Radio Station License issued by the Federal Communications Commission (FCC), if the radio transmitter is to be operated outside of the United States.
- Operating limitations. These may take the form of an FAA-approved AFM/POH, placards, and instrument markings, or any combination of the above.

A complete preflight inspection includes a review of the airplane logbooks. These are not required to be kept in the airplane when it is operated, and most owners keep them in a secure location. There will be maintenance records for the airframe and engine. Most owners also maintain additional propeller records.

At a minimum, there should be an annual inspection within the preceding 12-calendar months. When the airplane is operated carrying persons for hire or giving flight instruction for hire, a 100-hour inspection is required by 14 CFR part 91. An annual inspection may be performed in lieu of a 100-hour inspection.

If the transponder is to be used, it is required to be inspected within the preceding 24-calendar months. If the airplane is operated under instrument flight rules (IFR) in controlled airspace, the pitot-static system also is required to be inspected within the preceding 24-calendar months.

The emergency locator transmitter (ELT) should also be checked. The ELT is battery powered, and the battery replacement or recharge date should not be exceeded.

Airworthiness Directives (AD's) have a variety of compliance intervals and are usually tracked in a separate area of the appropriate airframe, engine, or propeller record.

Maintenance status boards or other maintenance tracking systems used in many operations are useful inspection interval reminders, but official airworthiness and inspection status can only be determined from the records themselves.

Visual Inspection

The visual inspection should include potential obstructions in the parking area. Upon reaching the airplane, all tiedowns, control locks, window covers, cowling plugs, pitot covers, tow bars, and chocks should be removed. The general condition of the airplane should be checked for signs of damage and for fuel, oil, and hydraulic fluid leaks. Then, the preflight inspection should be performed in accordance with the printed checklist provided by the airplane manufacturer. While the battery master switch should not be on during the entire preflight, at one point it should be turned on briefly to ensure operation of landing-gear down lights, landing lights, taxi lights, strobes, rotating beacon, fuel gauges, and the stall warning device. If the flight is to be conducted at night, all lighting systems, both interior and exterior should be inspected.

Ice and frost may be factors during the winter months. There is no amount of safe ice for takeoff. Even a thin layer of frost can have a dramatic effect on a wing's ability to produce lift. The best solution for deicing is a heated hangar. If such facilities are not available, aircraft deicing fluid can be used. Deicing fluids may be applied in a variety of concentrations and temperatures. Guidance and information on the use of deicing fluids can be found in the AFM/POH.

Under certain meteorological conditions, ice can reform after initial removal; therefore, a careful check of the airplane's surfaces must be made just prior to takeoff.

Unless the airplane has been stored in a heated hangar, preheating the engine is advisable when temperatures are below freezing. The colder the temperature, the more a preheat becomes essential. Significant engine wear and even damage may occur from attempting to start a cold-soaked reciprocating engine in temperatures of approximately 20 °F or colder without a thorough preheat.

To ensure optimum visibility and collision avoidance, the windshield should be clean before flight. Plastic windows should be cleaned only with cleaners specifically approved for use on plastics. Do not use glass cleaners, gasoline, alcohol, or deicing fluids.

Particular attention should be paid to the fuel quantity, type and grade, and quality. Many fuel tanks are very sensitive to airplane attitude when attempting to fuel for maximum capacity. Nosewheel strut extension, both high as well as low, can significantly alter the attitude, and therefore the fuel capacity. The airplane attitude can, also be affected laterally by a ramp that slopes, leaving one wing slightly higher than another. Always confirm the fuel quantity indicated on the fuel gauges by visually inspecting the level of each tank.

The type, grade, and color of fuel are critical to safe operation. The only widely available aviation gasoline (AVGAS) grade in the United States is low lead 100 octane, or 100LL. AVGAS is dyed for easy recognition of its grade and has a familiar gasoline scent. Jet-A, or jet fuel, is a kerosene-based fuel for turbine powered airplanes. It has disastrous consequences when inadvertently introduced into reciprocating airplane engines. The piston engine operating on jet fuel may start, run, and power the airplane, but will fail because the engine has been destroyed from detonation. [Figure 2-1]

Product	Color Tint
Grade 80/87 AVGAS	Red
Grade 100LL AVGAS	Blue
Jet fuel (Jet A or A1)	Clear or straw

FIGURE 2-1.—Aviation fuel types, grades, and colors.

Jet fuel has a distinctive kerosene scent and is oily to the touch when rubbed between fingers. Jet fuel is clear or straw colored although it may appear dyed when mixed in a tank containing AVGAS. When a few drops of AVGAS are placed upon white paper, they evaporate quickly and leave just a trace of dye. In comparison, jet fuel is slower to evaporate and leaves an oily smudge. Jet fuel refueling trucks and dispensing equipment are marked with JET-A placards in white letters on a black background. Prudent pilots will supervise fueling to ensure that the correct tanks are filled with the right quantity, type, and grade of fuel. The pilot should always ensure that the fuel caps have been securely replaced following each fueling.

Engines certificated for grades 80/87 or 91/96 AVGAS will run satisfactorily on 100LL. The reverse is not true. Fuel of a lower grade/octane, if found, should never be substituted for a required higher grade.

Detonation will severely damage the engine in a very short period of time.

Automotive gasoline is sometimes used as a substitute fuel in certain airplanes. Its use is acceptable only when the particular airplane has been issued a supplemental type certificate (STC) to both the airframe and engine allowing its use.

Checking for water and other sediment contamination is a key preflight element. Water tends to accumulate in fuel tanks from condensation, particularly in partially filled tanks. Because water is heavier than fuel, it tends to collect in the low points of the fuel system. Water can also be introduced into the fuel system from deteriorated gas cap seals exposed to rain, or from the supplier's storage tanks and delivery vehicles. Sediment contamination can arise from dust and dirt entering the tanks during refueling, or from deteriorating rubber fuel tanks or tank sealant.

The best preventive measure is to minimize the opportunity for water to condense in the tanks. If possible, the fuel tanks should be completely filled with the proper grade of fuel after each flight, or at least filled after the last flight of the day. The more fuel there is in the tanks, the less opportunity for condensation to occur. Keeping fuel tanks filled is also the best way to slow the aging of rubber fuel tanks and tank sealant.

Sufficient fuel should be drained from the fuel strainer quick drain and from each fuel tank sump to check for fuel grade/color, water, dirt, and smell. If water is present, it will usually be in bead-like droplets, different in color (usually clear, sometimes muddy), in the bottom of the sample. In extreme cases, do not overlook the possibility that the entire sample, particularly a small sample, is water. If water is found in the first fuel sample, further samples should be taken until no water appears. Significant and/or consistent water or sediment contamination are grounds for further investigation by qualified maintenance personnel. Each fuel tank sump should be drained during preflight and after refueling.

The oil level should be checked during each preflight and rechecked with each refueling.

Reciprocating airplane engines can be expected to consume a small amount of oil during normal operation. If the consumption grows or suddenly changes, qualified maintenance personnel should investigate. If line service personnel add oil to the engine, the pilot should ensure that the oil cap has been securely replaced.

MINIMUM EQUIPMENT LISTS (MEL's) AND OPERATIONS WITH INOPERATIVE EQUIPMENT

The Code of Federal Regulations (CFR's) requires that all aircraft instruments and installed equipment is operative prior to each departure. When the FAA adopted the minimum equipment list (MEL) concept for 14 CFR part 91 operations, this allowed for the first time, operations with inoperative items determined to be nonessential for safe flight. At the same time, it allowed part 91 operators, without an MEL, to defer repairs on nonessential equipment within the guidelines of part 91.

There are two primary methods of deferring maintenance on small, non-turbine powered airplanes operated under part 91. They are the deferral provision of 14 CFR part 91, section 91.213(d) and an FAA-approved MEL.

The deferral provision of section 91.213(d) is widely used by most pilot/operators. Its popularity is due to simplicity and minimal paperwork. When inoperative equipment is found during preflight or prior to departure, the decision should be to cancel the flight, obtain maintenance prior to flight, or to defer the item or equipment.

Maintenance deferrals are not used for inflight discrepancies. The manufacturer's AFM/POH procedures are to be used in those situations. The discussion that follows assumes that the pilot wishes to defer maintenance that would ordinarily be required prior to flight.

Using the deferral provision of section 91.213(d), the pilot determines whether the inoperative equipment is required by type design, the CFR's, or AD's. If the inoperative item is not required, and the airplane can be safely operated without it, the deferral may be made. The inoperative item shall be deactivated or removed and an INOPERATIVE placard placed near the appropriate switch, control, or indicator. If deactivation or removal involves maintenance (removal always will), it must be accomplished by certificated maintenance personnel.

For example, if the position lights (installed equipment) were discovered to be inoperative prior to a daytime flight, the pilot would follow the requirements of section 91.213(d).

The deactivation may be a process as simple as the pilot positioning a circuit breaker to the OFF position, or as complex as rendering instruments or equipment totally inoperable. Complex maintenance tasks require a certificated and appropriately rated maintenance person to perform the deactivation. In all cases, the item or equipment must be placarded INOPERATIVE.

All small, non-turbine powered airplanes operated under part 91 are eligible to use the maintenance deferral provisions of section 91.213(d). However, once an operator requests an MEL, and a Letter of Authorization (LOA) is issued by the FAA, then the use of the MEL becomes mandatory for that airplane. All maintenance deferrals must be accomplished in accordance with the terms and conditions of the MEL and the operator-generated procedures document.

The use of an MEL for a small, non-turbine powered airplane operated under part 91 also allows for the deferral of inoperative items or equipment. The primary guidance becomes the FAA-approved MEL issued to that specific operator and N-numbered airplane.

The FAA has developed master minimum equipment lists (MMEL's) for airplanes in current use. Upon written request by an airplane operator, the local FAA Flight Standards District Office (FSDO) may issue the appropriate make and model MMEL, along with an LOA, and the preamble. The operator then develops operations and maintenance (O&M) procedures from the MMEL. This MMEL with O&M procedures now becomes the operator's MEL. The MEL, LOA, preamble, and procedures document developed by the operator must be on board the airplane when it is operated.

The FAA considers an approved MEL to be a supplemental type certificate (STC) issued to an aircraft by serial number and registration number. It therefore becomes the authority to operate that aircraft in a condition other than originally type certificated.

With an approved MEL, if the position lights were discovered inoperative prior to a daytime flight, the pilot would make an entry in the maintenance record or discrepancy record provided for that purpose. The item is then either repaired or deferred in accordance with the MEL. Upon confirming that daytime flight with inoperative position lights is acceptable in accordance with the provisions of the MEL, the pilot would leave the position lights switch OFF, open the circuit breaker (or whatever action is called for in the procedures document), and placard the position light switch as INOPERATIVE.

There are exceptions to the use of the MEL for deferral. For example, should a component fail that is not listed in the MEL as deferrable (the tachometer, wing's flaps, or stall warning device, for example), then repairs are required to be performed prior to departure. If maintenance or parts are not readily available at that location, a special flight permit can be obtained from the nearest FSDO. This permit allows the airplane to be flown to another location for maintenance. This allows an aircraft that may not currently meet applicable airworthiness requirements, but is capable of safe flight, to be operated under the restrictive special terms and conditions attached to the special flight permit.

Deferral of maintenance is not to be taken lightly, and due consideration should be given to the effect an inoperative component may have on the operation of an airplane, particularly if other items are inoperative. Further information regarding MEL's and operations with inoperative equipment can be found in AC 91-67, Minimum Equipment Requirements for General Aviation Operations Under FAR Part 91.

COCKPIT MANAGEMENT

After entering the airplane, the pilot should first ensure that all necessary equipment, documents, checklists, and navigation charts appropriate for the flight are on board. If a portable intercom, headsets, or a hand-held global positioning system (GPS) are used, the pilot is responsible for ensuring that the routing of wires and cables does not interfere with the motion or the operation of any control.

Regardless of what materials are to be used, they should be neatly arranged and organized in a manner that makes them readily available. The cockpit and cabin should be checked for articles that might be tossed about if turbulence is encountered. Loose items should be properly secured. All pilots should form the habit of good housekeeping.

The pilot must be able to see inside and outside references. If the range of motion of an adjustable seat is inadequate, cushions should be used to provide the proper seating position.

When the pilot is comfortably seated, the safety belt and shoulder harness (if installed) should be fastened and adjusted to a comfortably snug fit. The shoulder harness must be worn at least for the takeoff and landing, unless the pilot cannot reach or operate the controls with it fastened. The safety belt must be worn at all times when the pilot is seated at the controls.

If the seats are adjustable, it is important to ensure that the seat is locked in position. Accidents have occurred as the result of seat movement during acceleration or pitch attitude changes during takeoffs

or landings. When the seat suddenly moves too close or too far away from the controls, the pilot may be unable to maintain control of the airplane.

14 CFR part 91 requires the pilot to ensure that each person on board is briefed on how to fasten and unfasten his or her safety belt and, if installed, shoulder harness. This should be accomplished before starting the engine, along with a passenger on proper use of safety equipment and exit information. Airplane manufacturers have printed briefing cards available, similar to those used by airlines, to supplement the pilot's briefing.

USE OF CHECKLISTS

The importance of consistent use of the checklist cannot be overstated in pilot training. A major objective in primary flight training is to establish habit patterns that will serve pilots well throughout their entire flying career. Checklists provide a logical and standardized method to operate a particular make and model airplane. Following a checklist reinforces the use of proper procedures throughout all major phases of flight operations. For normal operations these phases include:

- Preflight Inspection.
- Before Engine Starting.
- Use of External Power.
- Engine Starting.
- Before Taxiing.
- Before Takeoff.
- Climb.
- Cruise.
- Descent.
- Before Landing.
- Balked Landing.
- After-landing.
- Shutdown.
- Postflight/ELT Check.

Additional procedures are provided for abnormal and emergency operations, as appropriate to the airplane. Supplemental information, such as performance data or optional equipment operation, may also be contained in the checklist.

Some general aviation airplanes have checklists for certain phases of flight on panel-mounted placards or printed on sun visors. Regardless of the format, the checklist should be an integral part of the pilot's operation of the airplane.

There are two primary methods of checklist usage, "read and do" and "do and verify."

The read and do method is when the pilot picks up a checklist, refers to an item, and sets the condition. The items for any particular phase of flight would all be accomplished before the checklist is set aside.

Another acceptable method is to set the condition of the items for a particular phase of operation from memory or flow pattern. Then the checklist is picked up and read to verify that the appropriate condition for each item in that phase has been set. It is not wise for a pilot to become so reliant upon a flow pattern that he or she fails to verify with a checklist. Checking important items solely from memory is not an acceptable substitute for checklists.

GROUND OPERATIONS

It is important that a pilot operates an airplane safely on the ground. This includes being familiar with standard hand signals that are used by ramp personnel. [Figure 2-2]

Starting the Engine

The specific procedures for engine starting will not be discussed here since there are as many different methods as there are different engines, fuel systems, and starting conditions. The before engine starting and engine starting checklist procedures should be followed. There are, however, certain precautions that apply to all airplanes.

Some pilots have started the engine with the tail of the airplane pointed toward an open hangar door, parked automobiles, or a group of bystanders. This is not only discourteous, but may result in personal injury and damage to the property of others. Propeller blast can be surprisingly powerful.

When ready to start the engine, the pilot should look in all directions to be sure that nothing is or will be in the vicinity of the propeller. This includes nearby persons and aircraft that could be struck by the propeller blast or the debris it might pick up from the ground. The anticollision light should be turned on prior to engine start, even during daytime operations. At night, the position (NAV) lights should also be on.

The pilot should always call CLEAR out of the side window and wait for a response from persons who may be nearby before activating the starter.

When activating the starter, one hand should be kept on the throttle. This allows prompt response if the engine falters during starting, and allows the pilot to rapidly retard the throttle if revolutions per minute (RPM) are excessive after starting. A low RPM setting (800 to 1,000) is recommended immediately following engine start. It is highly undesirable to allow the RPM to race immediately after start, as there will be insufficient lubrication until the oil pressure rises. In freezing temperatures, the engine will also be exposed to potential mechanical distress until it warms and normal internal operating clearances are assumed.

As soon as the engine is operating smoothly, the oil pressure should be checked. If it does not rise to the manufacturer's specified value, the engine may not be receiving proper lubrication and should be shut down immediately to prevent serious damage.

Although quite rare, the starter motor may remain on and engaged after the engine starts. This can be detected by a continuous very high current draw on the ammeter. Some airplanes also have a starter engaged warning light specifically for this purpose. The engine should be shut down immediately should this occur.

Starters are small electric motors designed to draw large amounts of current for short periods of cranking. Should the engine fail to start readily, avoid continuous starter operation for periods longer than 30 seconds without a cool down period of at least 30 seconds to a minute (some AFM/POH specify even longer). Their service life is drastically shortened from high heat through overuse.

Hand Propping

Even though most airplanes are equipped with electric starters, it is helpful if a pilot is familiar with the procedures and dangers involved in starting an engine by turning the propeller by hand (hand propping). Due to the associated hazards, this method of starting should be used only when absolutely necessary and when proper precautions have been taken.

An engine must never be hand propped unless two people, both familiar with the airplane and hand propping techniques, are available to perform the procedure. The person pulling the propeller blades through directs all activity and is in charge of the procedure. The other person, thoroughly familiar with the controls, must be seated in the airplane with the brakes set. As an additional precaution, chocks should be placed in front of the main wheels. If this is not feasible, the airplane's tail should be securely tied down. Never allow a person unfamiliar with the controls to occupy the pilot's seat when hand propping. The procedure should never be attempted alone.

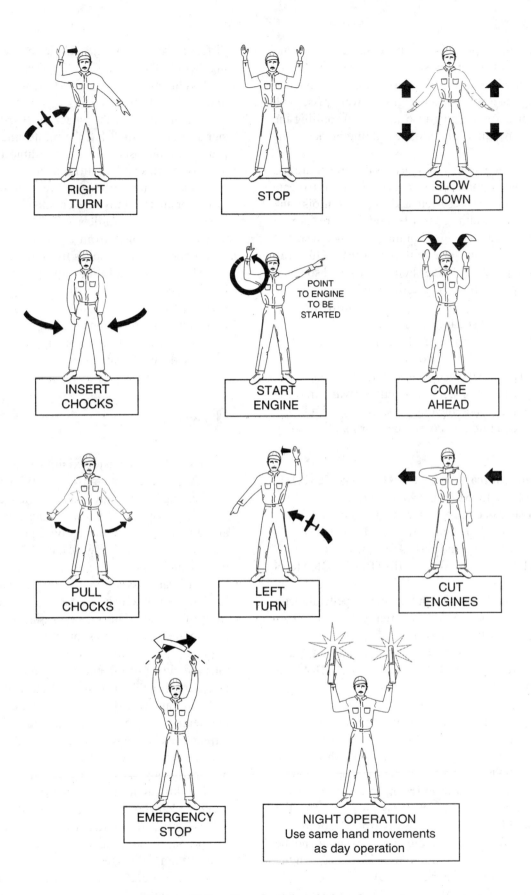

FIGURE 2-2.—Standard hand signals.

When hand propping is necessary, the ground surface near the propeller should be stable and free of debris. Unless a firm footing is available, consider relocating the airplane. Loose gravel, wet grass, mud, oil, ice, or snow might cause the person pulling the propeller through to slip into the rotating blades as the engine starts.

Both participants should discuss the procedure and agree on voice commands and expected action. To begin the procedure, the fuel system and engine controls (tank selector, primer, pump, throttle, and mixture) are set for a normal start. The ignition/magneto switch should be checked to be sure that it is OFF. Then the descending propeller blade should be rotated so that it assumes a position slightly above the horizontal. The person doing the hand propping should face the descending blade squarely and stand slightly less than one arm's length from the blade. If a stance too far away were assumed, it would be necessary to lean forward in an unbalanced condition to reach the blade. This may cause the person to fall forward into the rotating blades when the engine starts.

The procedure and commands for hand propping are:

- **Person out front** says, "GAS ON, SWITCH OFF, THROTTLE CLOSED, BRAKES SET."
- **Pilot seat occupant**, after making sure the fuel is ON, mixture is RICH, ignition/magneto switch is OFF, throttle is CLOSED, and brakes SET, says, "GAS ON, SWITCH OFF, CLOSED THROTTLE, BRAKES SET."
- **Person out front**, after pulling the propeller through to get the engine primed and ready to start, says, "BRAKES AND CONTACT."
- **Pilot seat occupant** checks the brakes SET and turns the ignition switch ON, then says, "BRAKES AND CONTACT."

The propeller is swung by forcing the blade downward rapidly, pushing with the palms of both hands. If the blade is gripped tightly with the fingers, the person's body may be drawn into the propeller blades should the engine misfire and rotate momentarily in the opposite direction. As the blade is pushed down, the person should step backward, away from the propeller. If the engine does not start, the propeller should not be repositioned for another attempt until it is certain the ignition/magneto switch is turned OFF.

The words CONTACT (mags ON) and SWITCH OFF (mags OFF) are used because they are significantly different from each other. Under noisy conditions or high winds, the words CONTACT and SWITCH OFF are less likely to be misunderstood than SWITCH ON and SWITCH OFF.

When removing the wheel chocks after the engine starts, it is essential that the pilot remember that the propeller is almost invisible. Incredible as it may seem, serious injuries and fatalities occur when people who have just started an engine walk or reach into the propeller arc to remove the chocks. Before the chocks are removed, the throttle should be set to idle and the chocks approached from the rear of the propeller. Never approach the chocks from the front or the side.

The procedures for hand propping should always be in accordance with the manufacturer's recommendations and checklist. Special starting procedures are used when the engine is already warm, very cold, or when flooded or vapor locked. There will also be a different starting procedure when an external power source is used.

TAXIING

The following basic taxi information is applicable to both nosewheel and tailwheel airplanes.

Taxiing is the controlled movement of the airplane under its own power while on the ground. Since an airplane is moved under its own power between the parking area and the runway, the pilot must thoroughly understand and be proficient in taxi procedures.

An awareness of other aircraft that are taking off, landing, or taxiing, and consideration for the right-of-way of others is essential to safety. When taxiing, the pilot's eyes should be looking outside the airplane, to the sides, as well as the front. The pilot must be aware of the entire area around the airplane to ensure that the airplane will clear all obstructions and other aircraft. If at any time there is doubt about the clearance from an object, the pilot should stop the airplane and have someone check the clearance. It may be necessary to have the airplane towed or physically moved by a ground crew.

It is difficult to set any rule for a single, safe taxiing speed. What is reasonable and prudent under some conditions may be imprudent or hazardous under others. The primary requirements for safe taxiing are positive control, the ability to recognize potential hazards in time to avoid them, and the ability to stop or turn where and when desired, without undue reliance on the brakes. Pilots should proceed at a cautious speed on congested

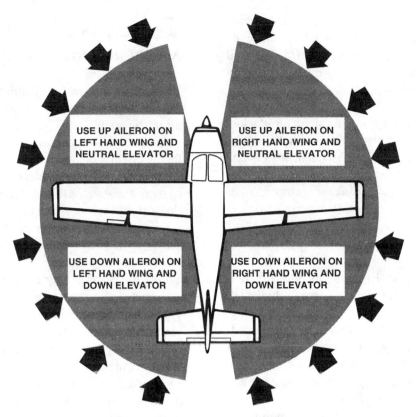

USE UP AILERON ON LEFT HAND WING AND NEUTRAL ELEVATOR

USE UP AILERON ON RIGHT HAND WING AND NEUTRAL ELEVATOR

USE DOWN AILERON ON LEFT HAND WING AND DOWN ELEVATOR

USE DOWN AILERON ON RIGHT HAND WING AND DOWN ELEVATOR

WIND DIRECTION INDICATED BY ARROWS

FIGURE 2-3.—Control positions during taxi.

or busy ramps. Normally, the speed should be at the rate where movement of the airplane is dependent on the throttle. That is, slow enough so when the throttle is closed the airplane can be stopped promptly. When yellow taxiway centerline stripes are provided, they should be observed unless necessary to clear airplanes or obstructions.

When taxiing, it is best to slow down before attempting a turn. Sharp, high-speed turns place undesirable side loads on the landing gear and may result in an uncontrollable swerve or a ground loop. This swerve is most likely to occur when turning from a downwind heading toward an upwind heading. In moderate to high-wind conditions, pilots will note the airplane's tendency to weathervane, or turn into the wind when the airplane is proceeding crosswind.

When taxiing at appropriate speeds in no-wind conditions, the aileron and elevator control surfaces have little or no effect on directional control of the airplane. The controls should not be considered steering devices and should be held in a neutral position. Their proper use while taxiing in windy conditions will be discussed later. [Figure 2-3]

Steering is accomplished with rudder pedals and brakes. To turn the airplane on the ground, the pilot should apply rudder in the desired direction of turn and use whatever power or brake that is necessary to control the taxi speed. The rudder pedal should be held in the direction of the turn until just short of the point where the turn is to be stopped. Rudder pressure is then released or opposite pressure is applied as needed.

More engine power may be required to start the airplane moving forward, or to start a turn, than is required to keep it moving in any given direction. When using additional power, the throttle should immediately be retarded once the airplane begins moving, to prevent excessive acceleration.

When first beginning to taxi, the brakes should be tested for proper operation as soon as the airplane is put in motion. Applying power to start the airplane moving forward slowly, then retarding the throttle and simultaneously applying pressure smoothly to both brakes does this. If braking action is unsatisfactory, the engine should be shut down immediately.

Downwind taxiing will usually require less engine power after the initial ground roll is begun, since the wind will be pushing the airplane forward. To avoid overheating the brakes when taxiing down wind, keep engine power to a minimum. Rather than continuously riding the brakes to control speed, it is better to apply brakes only occasionally. Other than sharp turns at low speed, the throttle should always be at idle before the brakes are applied. It is a common student error to taxi with a power setting that requires controlling taxi speed with the brakes. This is the aeronautical equivalent of driving an automobile with both the accelerator and brake pedals depressed.

When taxiing with a quartering headwind, the wing on the upwind side will tend to be lifted by the wind unless the aileron control is held in that direction (upwind aileron UP). Moving the aileron into the UP position reduces the effect of the wind striking that wing, thus reducing the lifting action. This control movement will also cause the downwind aileron to be placed in the DOWN position, thus a small amount of lift and drag on the downwind wing, further reducing the tendency of the upwind wing to rise.

When taxiing with a quartering tailwind, the elevator should be held in the DOWN position, and the upwind aileron, DOWN. Since the wind is striking the airplane from behind, these control positions reduce the tendency of the wind to get under the tail and the wing and to nose the airplane over.

The application of these crosswind taxi corrections helps to minimize the weathervaning tendency and ultimately results in making the airplane easier to steer.

Normally, all turns should be started using the rudder pedal to steer the nosewheel. To tighten the turn after full pedal deflection is reached; the brake may be applied as needed. When stopping the airplane, it is advisable to always stop with the nosewheel straight ahead to relieve any side load on the nosewheel and to make it easier to start moving ahead.

During crosswind taxiing, even the nosewheel-type airplane has some tendency to weathervane. However, the weathervaning tendency is less than in tailwheel-type airplanes because the main wheels are located farther aft, and the nosewheel's ground friction helps to resist the tendency. The nosewheel linkage from the rudder pedals provides adequate steering control for safe and efficient ground handling, and normally, only rudder pressure is necessary to correct for a crosswind.

TAXI CLEARANCES AT AIRPORTS WITH AN OPERATING CONTROL TOWER

Approval must be obtained prior to moving an aircraft onto the movement area during the hours an air traffic control (ATC) tower is in operation. Also, a clearance must be obtained prior to taxiing on a runway, taking off, or landing.

When an aircraft is cleared to taxi to an assigned runway, the absence of holding instructions authorizes the aircraft to cross all runways that the taxiway intersects, except the assigned takeoff runway. The pilot may not taxi onto or cross the assigned takeoff runway at any point.

At times, ATC may issue holding instructions or issue a specific taxi route. Anytime a pilot is unsure about a clearance; he or she should ask ATC for clarification. It is a good operating practice to always read back any clearance received by ATC. Pilots should always read back, in full, any clearance that includes a runway assignment or takeoff clearance. If operating at an unfamiliar airport, the pilot may request progressive taxi instructions from ATC.

Although ATC issues a taxi clearance, it is the pilot's responsibility to avoid collision with other aircraft. Therefore, the pilot should always be alert and scan the area during taxi operations.

BEFORE TAKEOFF CHECK

The before takeoff check is the systematic procedure for making a check of the engine, controls, systems, instruments, and avionics prior to flight. Normally, it is performed after taxiing to a position near the takeoff end of the runway. Taxiing to that position usually allows sufficient time for the engine to warm up to at least minimum operating temperatures. This ensures adequate lubrication and internal engine clearances before being operated at high-power settings. Many engines require that the oil temperature reach a minimum value as stated in the AFM/POH before high power is applied.

Air-cooled engines generally are closely cowled and equipped with pressure baffles that direct the flow of air to the engine in sufficient quantities for cooling in flight. On the ground, however, much less air is forced through the cowling and around the baffling. Prolonged ground operations may cause cylinder overheating long before there is an indication of rising oil temperature.

Cowl flaps, if available, should be set according to the AFM/POH.

Before beginning the before takeoff check, the airplane should be positioned clear of other aircraft. There should not be anything behind the airplane that might be damaged by the prop blast. To minimize overheating during engine runup, it is recommended that the airplane be headed as nearly as possible into the wind. After the airplane is properly positioned for the runup, it should be allowed to roll forward slightly so that the nosewheel or tailwheel will be aligned fore and aft.

During the engine runup, the surface under the airplane should be firm (a smooth, paved, or turf surface if possible) and free of debris. Otherwise, the propeller may pick up pebbles, dirt, mud, sand, or other loose objects and hurl them backwards. This damages the propeller and may damage the tail of the airplane. Small chips in the leading edge of the propeller form stress risers, or lines of concentrated high stress. These are highly undesirable and may lead to cracks and possible propeller blade failure.

While performing the engine runup, the pilot must divide attention inside and outside the airplane. If the parking brake slips, or if application of the toe brakes is inadequate for the amount of power applied, the airplane could move forward unnoticed if attention is fixed inside the airplane.

Each airplane has different features and equipment, and the before takeoff checklist provided by the airplane manufacturer or operator should be used to perform the runup.

AFTER-LANDING

During the after-landing roll, the airplane should be gradually slowed to normal taxi speed before turning off the landing runway. Any significant degree of turn at faster speeds could result in ground looping and subsequent damage to the airplane.

To give full attention to controlling the airplane during the landing roll, the after-landing check should be performed only after the airplane is brought to a complete stop clear of the active runway. There have been many cases of the pilot mistakenly grasping the wrong handle and retracting the landing gear, instead of the flaps, due to improper division of attention while the airplane was moving. However, this procedure may be modified if the manufacturer recommends that specific after-landing items be accomplished during landing rollout. For example, when performing a short-

field landing, the manufacturer may recommend retracting the flaps on rollout to improve braking. In this situation, the pilot should make a positive identification of the flap control and retract the flaps.

Clear of the Runway Checks

Because of different features and equipment in various airplanes, the after-landing checklist provided by the manufacturer should be used. Some of the items may include:

- Hold brakes ON.
- Identify landing flaps control and retract flaps.
- Open engine cowl flaps (if equipped).
- Recheck and set propeller control (if equipped) to FULL INCREASE.
- Set trim tabs for takeoff.

Parking

Unless parking in a designated, supervised area, the pilot should select a location and heading which will prevent the propeller or jet blast of other airplanes from striking the airplane broadside. Whenever possible, the airplane should be parked headed into the existing or forecast wind. After stopping on the desired heading, the airplane should be allowed to roll straight ahead enough to straighten the nosewheel or tailwheel.

Engine Shutdown Check

Finally, the pilot should always use the procedures in the manufacturer's checklist for shutting down the engine and securing the airplane. Some of the important items include:

- Set the parking brakes ON.
- Set throttle to IDLE or 1,000 RPM. If turbocharged, observe manufacturer's spool down procedure.
- Turn ignition switch OFF then ON at idle to check for proper operation of switch in the OFF position.
- Set propeller control (if equipped) to FULL INCREASE.
- Turn electrical units and radios OFF.
- Set mixture control to IDLE CUTOFF.
- Turn ignition switch to OFF when engine stops.
- Turn master electrical switch to OFF.
- Install control lock.

POSTFLIGHT

A flight is never complete until the engine is shut down and the airplane is secured. A pilot should consider this an essential part of any flight.

Securing and Servicing

After engine shutdown and deplaning passengers, the pilot should accomplish a postflight inspection. This includes checking the general condition of the aircraft. For a departure, the oil should be checked and fuel added if required. If the aircraft is going to be inactive, it is a good operating practice to fill the tanks to the top to prevent water condensation from forming.

When the flight is completed for the day, the aircraft should be hangared or tied down and the flight controls secured.

CHAPTER 3

TAKEOFFS AND CLIMBS

INTRODUCTION

This chapter discusses safe operations during taxi, takeoff, and climbs for tricycle landing gear (nosewheel-type) aircraft under normal conditions and maximum takeoff performance.

The takeoff and climb involves the movement of the airplane from its starting position on the runway to the point where a positive climb to a safe maneuvering altitude has been established. Since the takeoff requires both ground and inflight operation, the pilot must be able to use the controls during the transition from ground functions to inflight functions with maximum smoothness and coordination. Skill in these functions will improve the pilot's ability to control the airplane's direction of movement on and away from the runway.

TERMS AND DEFINITIONS

Although the takeoff and climb is one continuous maneuver, it will be divided into three separate steps for purposes of explanation: (1) the takeoff roll, (2) the lift-off, and (3) the initial climb after becoming airborne. [Figure 3-1]

• **Takeoff Roll (ground roll)**—the portion of the takeoff procedure during which the airplane is accelerated from a standstill to an airspeed that provides sufficient lift for it to become airborne.

• **Lift-off (rotation)**—the act of becoming airborne as a result of the wings lifting the airplane off the ground or the pilot rotating the nose up, increasing the angle of attack to start a climb.

• **Initial Climb**—begins when the airplane leaves the ground and a pitch attitude has been established to climb away from the takeoff area. Normally, it is considered complete when the airplane has reached a safe maneuvering altitude, or an en route climb has been established.

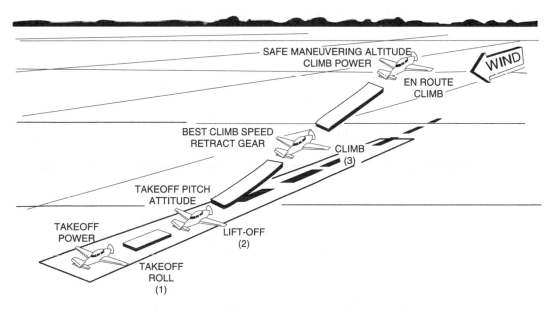

FIGURE 3-1.—Normal takeoff and climb.

PRIOR TO TAKEOFF

Before taxiing onto the runway or takeoff area, the pilot should ensure that the engine is operating properly and that all controls, including flaps and trim tabs, are set in accordance with the before takeoff checklist. In addition, the pilot must make certain that the approach and takeoff path is clear of other aircraft. At uncontrolled airports, pilots should announce their intentions on the common traffic advisory frequency (CTAF) assigned to that airport. When operating from an airport with an operating control tower, pilots must contact the tower operator and receive a takeoff clearance before taxiing onto the active runway.

It is not recommended to take off immediately behind another aircraft, particularly large, heavily loaded transport airplanes, because of the wake turbulence that is generated.

While taxiing onto the runway, the pilot can select ground reference points that are aligned with the runway direction as aids to maintaining directional control during the takeoff. These may be runway centerline markings, runway lighting, distant trees, towers, buildings, or mountain peaks.

NORMAL TAKEOFF

A normal takeoff is one in which the airplane is headed into the wind, or the wind is very light. Also, the takeoff surface is firm and of sufficient length to permit the airplane to gradually accelerate to normal lift-off and climb-out speed, and there are no obstructions along the takeoff path.

There are two reasons for making a takeoff as nearly into the wind as possible. First, the airplane's speed while on the ground is much less than if the takeoff were made down wind, thus reducing wear and stress on the landing gear. Second, a shorter ground roll and therefore much less runway length is required to develop the minimum lift necessary for takeoff and climb. Since the airplane depends on airspeed in order to fly, a headwind provides some of that airspeed, even with the airplane motionless, from the wind flowing over the wings.

Takeoff Roll

After taxiing onto the runway, the airplane should be carefully aligned with the intended takeoff direction,

and the nosewheel positioned straight, or centered. After releasing the brakes, the throttle should be advanced smoothly and continuously to takeoff power. An abrupt application of power may cause the airplane to yaw sharply to the left because of the torque effects of the engine and propeller. This will be most apparent in high horsepower engines. As the airplane starts to roll forward, the pilot should assure both feet are on the rudder pedals so that the toes or balls of the feet are on the rudder portions, not on the brake portions. [Figure 3-2] Engine instruments should be monitored during the takeoff roll for any malfunctions.

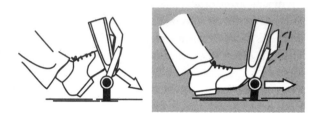

FIGURE 3-2.—Typical rudder and brake pedal.

In nosewheel-type airplanes, pressures on the elevator control are not necessary beyond those needed to steady it. Applying unnecessary pressure will only aggravate the takeoff and prevent the pilot from recognizing when elevator control pressure is actually needed to establish the takeoff attitude.

As speed is gained, the elevator control will tend to assume a neutral position if the airplane is correctly trimmed. At the same time, directional control should be maintained with smooth, prompt, positive rudder corrections throughout the takeoff roll. The effects of engine torque and P-factor at the initial speeds tend to pull the nose to the left. The pilot must use whatever rudder pressure and aileron needed to correct for these effects or for existing wind conditions to keep the nose of the airplane headed straight down the runway. The use of brakes for steering purposes should be avoided, since this will cause slower acceleration of the airplane's speed, lengthen the takeoff distance, and possibly result in severe swerving.

While the speed of the takeoff roll increases, more and more pressure will be felt on the flight controls, particularly the elevators and rudder. Since the tail surfaces (except "T" tails) receive the full effect of the propeller slipstream, they become effective first. As the speed continues to increase, all of the flight controls will gradually become effective enough to maneuver the airplane about its three axes. It is at this point, in the taxi to flight transition, that the airplane is being flown more than taxied. As this occurs, progressively smaller rudder deflections are needed to maintain direction.

The feel of resistance to the movement of the controls and as the airplane's reaction to such movements is the only real indicators of the degree of control attained. This feel of resistance is not a measure of the airplane's speed, but rather of its controllability. To determine the degree of controllability, the pilot must be conscious of the reaction of the airplane to the control pressures and immediately adjust the pressures as needed to control the airplane.

Lift-off

Since a good takeoff depends on the proper takeoff attitude, it is important to know how this attitude appears and how it is attained. The ideal takeoff attitude requires only minimum pitch adjustments shortly after the airplane lifts off to attain the speed for the best rate of climb speed (V_y). [Figure 3-3]

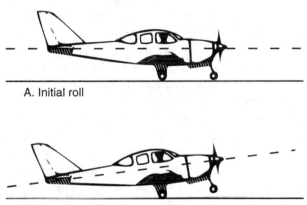

A. Initial roll

B. Takeoff attitude

FIGURE 3-3.—Initial roll and takeoff attitude.

Each type of airplane has a best pitch attitude for normal lift-off; however, varying conditions may make a difference in the required takeoff technique. A rough field, a smooth field, a hard surface runway, or a short or soft, muddy field, all call for a slightly different technique, as will smooth air in contrast to a strong, gusty wind. The different techniques for those other-than-normal conditions are discussed later in this chapter.

When all the flight controls become effective during the takeoff roll in a nosewheel-type airplane, back-elevator pressure should be gradually applied to raise the nosewheel slightly off the runway, thus establishing the takeoff or lift-off attitude. This is often referred to as "rotating." At this point, the position of the nose in relation to the horizon should be noted, then back elevator pressure applied as necessary to hold this attitude. The wings are to be kept level by applying aileron pressure as necessary.

The airplane is allowed to fly off the ground while in this normal takeoff attitude. Forcing it into the air by applying excessive back-elevator pressure would only result in an excessively high pitch attitude and may delay the takeoff. As discussed earlier, excessive and rapid changes in pitch attitude result in proportionate changes in the effects of torque, thus making the airplane more difficult to control.

Although the airplane can be forced into the air, this is considered an unsafe practice and should be avoided under normal circumstances. If the airplane is forced to leave the ground by using too much back-elevator pressure before adequate flying speed is attained, the wing's angle of attack may be excessive, causing the airplane to settle back to the runway or even to stall. On the other hand, if sufficient back-elevator pressure is not held to maintain the correct takeoff attitude after becoming airborne, or the nose is allowed to lower excessively, the airplane may also settle back to the runway. This would occur because the angle of attack is decreased and lift diminished to the degree where it will not support the airplane. It is important, then, to hold the correct attitude constant after rotation or lift-off.

Even as the airplane leaves the ground, the pilot must continue to be concerned with maintaining the wings in a level attitude, as well as holding the proper pitch attitude.

During takeoffs in a strong, gusty wind, it is advisable that an extra margin of speed be obtained before the airplane is allowed to leave the ground. A takeoff at the normal takeoff speed may result in a lack of positive control, or a stall, when the airplane encounters a sudden lull in strong, gusty wind, or other turbulent air currents. In this case, the pilot should allow the airplane to stay on the ground longer to attain more speed; then make a smooth, positive rotation to leave the ground.

Initial Climb

Upon lift-off, the airplane should be flying at approximately the pitch attitude that will allow it to accelerate to V_y. This is the speed at which the airplane will gain the most altitude in the shortest period of time.

If the airplane has been properly trimmed, some back-elevator pressure may be required to hold this attitude until the proper climb speed is established. On the other hand, relaxation of any back-elevator pressure before this time may result in the airplane settling, even to the extent that it contacts the runway.

The airplane will pick up speed rapidly after it becomes airborne. Once a positive rate of climb is established, the flaps and landing gear can be retracted (if equipped).

It is recommended that takeoff power be maintained until reaching an altitude of at least 500 feet above the surrounding terrain or obstacles. The combination of V_Y and takeoff power assures the maximum altitude gained in a minimum amount of time. This gives the pilot more altitude from which the airplane can be safely maneuvered in case of an engine failure or other emergency.

Since the power on the initial climb is fixed at the takeoff power setting, the airspeed must be controlled by making slight pitch adjustments using the elevators. However, the pilot should not stare at the airspeed indicator when making these slight pitch changes, but should, instead, watch the attitude of the airplane in relation to the horizon. It is better to first make the necessary pitch change and hold the new attitude momentarily, and then glance at the airspeed indicator as a check to see if the new attitude is correct. Due to inertia, the airplane will not accelerate or decelerate immediately as the pitch is changed. It takes a little time for the airspeed to change. If the pitch attitude has been over or under corrected, the airspeed indicator will show a speed that is more or less than that desired. When this occurs, the cross-checking and appropriate pitch-changing process must be repeated until the desired climbing attitude is established.

When the correct pitch attitude has been attained, it should be held constant while cross-checking it against the horizon and other outside visual references. The airspeed indicator should be used only as a check to determine if the attitude is correct.

After the recommended climb airspeed has been established, and a safe maneuvering altitude has been reached, the power should be adjusted to the recommended climb setting and the airplane trimmed to relieve the control pressures. This will make it much easier to hold a constant attitude and airspeed.

During initial climb, it is important that the takeoff path remain aligned with the runway to avoid the hazards of drifting into obstructions, or the path of another aircraft that may be taking off from a parallel runway.

CROSSWIND TAKEOFF

While it is usually preferable to take off directly into the wind whenever possible or practical, there will be many instances when circumstances or judgment will indicate otherwise. Therefore, the pilot must be familiar with the principles and techniques involved in crosswind takeoffs, as well as those for normal takeoffs. A crosswind will affect the airplane during takeoff much as it does in taxiing. With this in mind, it can be seen that the technique for crosswind correction during takeoffs closely parallels the crosswind correction techniques used in taxiing, previously explained in this handbook.

Takeoff Roll

The technique used during the initial takeoff roll in a crosswind is generally the same as used in a normal takeoff, except that the aileron control must be held INTO the crosswind. This raises the aileron on the upwind wing to impose a downward force on the wing to counteract the lifting force of the crosswind and prevents the wing from rising.

As the airplane is taxied into takeoff position, it is essential that the windsock and other wind direction indicators be checked so that the presence of a crosswind may be recognized and anticipated. If a crosswind is indicated, FULL aileron should be held into the wind as the takeoff roll is started. This control position should be maintained while the airplane is accelerating and until the ailerons start becoming sufficiently effective for maneuvering the airplane about its longitudinal axis.

With the aileron held into the wind, the takeoff path must be held straight with the rudder. [Figure 3-4] Normally, this will require applying downwind rudder pressure, since on the ground the airplane will tend to weathervane into the wind. When takeoff power is applied, torque or P-factor that yaws the airplane to the left may be sufficient to counteract the weathervaning tendency caused by a crosswind from the right. On the other hand, it may also aggravate the tendency to swerve left when the wind is from the left. In any case, whatever rudder pressure is required to keep the airplane rolling straight down the runway should be applied.

As the forward speed of the airplane increases and the crosswind becomes more and more of a relative headwind, the mechanical holding of full aileron into the wind should be reduced. It is when increasing

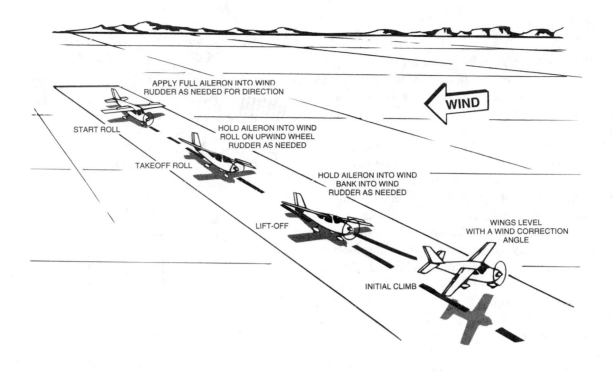

APPLY FULL AILERON INTO WIND
RUDDER AS NEEDED FOR DIRECTION

START ROLL

HOLD AILERON INTO WIND
ROLL ON UPWIND WHEEL
RUDDER AS NEEDED

TAKEOFF ROLL

HOLD AILERON INTO WIND
BANK INTO WIND
RUDDER AS NEEDED

LIFT-OFF

WINGS LEVEL
WITH A WIND CORRECTION
ANGLE

INITIAL CLIMB

WIND

FIGURE 3-4.—Crosswind takeoff roll and climb.

pressure is being felt on the aileron control that the ailerons are becoming more effective. As the aileron's effectiveness increases and the crosswind component of the relative wind becomes less effective, it will be necessary to gradually reduce the aileron pressure. The crosswind component effect does not completely vanish, so some aileron pressure will have to be maintained throughout the takeoff roll to keep the crosswind from raising the upwind wing. If the upwind wing rises, thus exposing more surface to the crosswind, a "skipping" action may result. [Figure 3-5] This is usually indicated by a series of very small bounces, caused by the airplane attempting to fly and then settling back onto the runway. During these bounces, the crosswind also tends to move the airplane sideways, and these bounces will develop into side skipping. This side skipping imposes severe side stresses on the landing gear and could result in structural failure.

It is important during a crosswind takeoff roll, to hold sufficient aileron into the wind not only to keep the upwind wing from rising but to hold that wing down so that the airplane will, immediately after lift-off, be slipping into the wind enough to counteract drift.

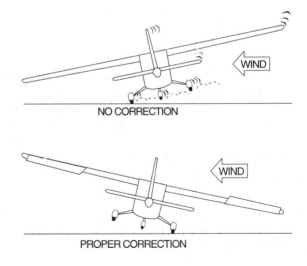

WIND

NO CORRECTION

WIND

PROPER CORRECTION

FIGURE 3-5.—Crosswind effect.

As the nosewheel is being raised off the runway, the holding of aileron control into the wind may result in the downwind wing rising and the downwind main wheel lifting off the runway first, with the remainder of the takeoff roll being made on that one main wheel. This is acceptable and is preferable to side skipping.

If a significant crosswind exists, the main wheels should be held on the ground slightly longer than in a normal takeoff so that a smooth but very definite lift-off can be made. This procedure will allow the airplane to leave the ground under more positive control so that it will definitely remain airborne while the proper amount of wind correction is being established. More importantly, this procedure will avoid imposing excessive side loads on the landing gear and prevent possible damage that would result from the airplane settling back to the runway while drifting.

As both main wheels leave the runway and ground friction no longer resists drifting, the airplane will be slowly carried sideways with the wind unless adequate drift correction is maintained by the pilot. Therefore it is important to establish and maintain the proper amount of crosswind correction prior to lift-off by applying aileron pressure toward the wind to keep the upwind wing from rising and applying rudder pressure as needed to prevent weathervaning.

Initial Climb

If proper crosswind correction is being applied, as soon as the airplane is airborne, it will be slipping into the wind sufficiently to counteract the drifting effect of the wind. [Figure 3-6] This slipping should be continued until the airplane has a positive rate of climb. At that time, the airplane should be headed toward the wind to establish just enough wind correction angle to counteract the wind and then the wings rolled level. The climb with this wind correction angle should be continued to follow a ground track aligned with the runway direction. The remainder of the climb technique is the same used for normal takeoffs and climbs.

SHORT-FIELD TAKEOFF AND CLIMB

Takeoffs and climbs from fields where the takeoff area is short or the available takeoff area is restricted by obstructions requires that the pilot operate the airplane at the limit of its takeoff performance

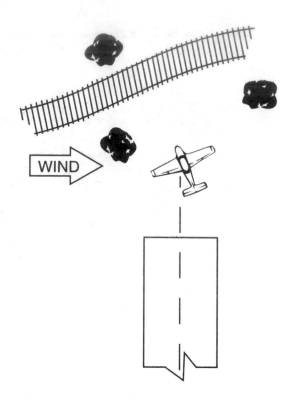

FIGURE 3-6.—*Takeoff flightpath.*

capabilities. To depart from such an area safely, the pilot must exercise positive and precise control of airplane attitude and airspeed so that takeoff and climb performance results in the shortest ground roll and the steepest angle of climb. [Figure 3-7]

The achieved result should be consistent with the performance section of the FAA-approved Airplane Flight Manual (AFM) and/or Pilot's Operating Handbook (POH). In all cases, the power setting, flap setting, airspeed, and procedures prescribed by the airplane's manufacturer should be followed.

In order to accomplish a maximum performance takeoff safely, the pilot must have adequate knowledge in the use and effectiveness of the best angle-of-climb speed (V_X) and the best rate-of-climb speed (V_Y) for the specific make and model of airplane being flown.

The speed for V_X is that which will result in the greatest gain in altitude for a given distance over the ground. It is usually slightly less than V_Y which provides the greatest gain in altitude per unit of time. The specific speeds to be used for a given airplane are stated in the FAA-approved AFM/POH.

Taking off from a short field requires the takeoff to be started from the very beginning of the takeoff area. At the field threshold, the airplane is aligned with the intended takeoff path. If the airplane manufacturer

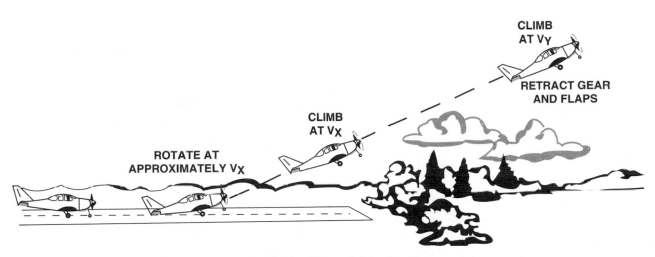

Figure 3-7.—Short-field takeoff.

recommends the use of flaps, they should be extended the proper amount before starting the takeoff roll. This permits the pilot to give full attention to the proper technique and the airplane's performance throughout the takeoff.

Takeoff power should be applied smoothly and continuously to accelerate the airplane as rapidly as possible; the airplane should be allowed to roll with its full weight on the main wheels and accelerated to the lift-off speed. As the takeoff roll progresses, the airplane's pitch attitude and angle of attack should be adjusted to that which results in the minimum amount of drag and the quickest acceleration. In nosewheel-type airplanes, this will involve little use of the elevator control, since the airplane is already in a low drag attitude.

The airplane should be smoothly and firmly lifted off, or rotated, by applying back-elevator pressure as approaching V_X. Since the airplane will accelerate more rapidly after lift-off, additional back-elevator pressure becomes necessary to hold a constant airspeed. After becoming airborne, a wings level climb should be maintained at V_X until the obstacles have been cleared or, if no obstacles are involved, until an altitude of at least 50 feet above the takeoff surface is attained. Thereafter, the pitch attitude may be lowered slightly, and the climb continued at V_Y until reaching a safe maneuvering altitude. Remember that an attempt to pull the airplane off the ground prematurely, or to climb too steeply, may cause the airplane to settle back to the runway or into the obstacles.

On short-field takeoffs, the flaps and landing gear should remain in takeoff position until clear of obstacles (or as recommended by the manufacturer) and V_Y has been established. It is generally unwise for the pilot to be looking in the cockpit or reaching for flap and landing gear controls until obstacle clearance is assured. When the V_Y has stabilized, the gear (if equipped) and then the flaps should be retracted. It is usually advisable to raise the flaps in increments to avoid sudden loss of lift and settling of the airplane. Next, reduce the power to the normal climb setting or as recommended by the aircraft manufacturer.

SOFT-FIELD TAKEOFF AND CLIMB

Takeoffs and climbs from soft fields require the use of operational techniques for getting the airplane airborne as quickly as possible to eliminate the drag caused by tall grass, soft sand, mud, and snow, and may or may not require climbing over an obstacle. These same techniques are also useful on a rough field where it is advisable to get the airplane off the ground as soon as possible to avoid damaging the landing gear.

Soft surfaces or long, wet grass usually reduces the airplane's acceleration during the takeoff roll so much that adequate takeoff speed might not be attained if normal takeoff techniques were employed.

The correct takeoff procedure at soft fields is quite different from that appropriate for short fields with firm, smooth surfaces. To minimize the hazards associated with takeoffs from soft or rough fields, support of the airplane's weight must be transferred as rapidly as possible from the wheels to the wings as the takeoff roll proceeds. Establishing and maintaining a relatively high angle of attack or nose-high pitch attitude as early as possible does this. Wing flaps may be lowered prior to starting the takeoff (if recommended by the manufacturer) to provide additional lift and to transfer

ACCELERATE   RAISE NOSEWHEEL   LIFT-OFF   LEVEL-OFF IN GROUND EFFECT   ACCELERATE IN GROUND EFFECT TO V_X OR V_Y

FIGURE 3-8.—Soft-field takeoff.

the airplane's weight from the wheels to the wings as early as possible.

Stopping on a soft surface, such as mud or snow, might bog the airplane down; therefore, it should be kept in continuous motion with sufficient power while lining up for the takeoff roll.

As the airplane is aligned with the takeoff path, takeoff power is applied smoothly and as rapidly as the powerplant will accept it without faltering. As the airplane accelerates, enough back-elevator pressure should be applied to establish a positive angle of attack and to reduce the weight supported by the nosewheel.

When the airplane is held at a nose-high attitude throughout the takeoff run, the wings will, as speed increases and lift develops, progressively relieve the wheels of more and more of the airplane's weight, thereby minimizing the drag caused by surface irregularities or adhesion. If this attitude is accurately maintained, the airplane will virtually fly itself off the ground. It may even become airborne at airspeed slower than a safe climb speed because of ground effect. This phenomenon produces an interim gain in lift during flight at very low altitude due to the effect the ground has on the flow pattern of the air passing along the wing. Ground effect is discussed in the following section. [Figure 3-8]

After becoming airborne, the nose should be lowered very gently with the wheels clear of the surface to allow the airplane to accelerate to V_Y or V_X if obstacles must be cleared. Extreme care must be exercised immediately after the airplane becomes airborne and while it accelerates, to avoid settling back onto the surface. An attempt to climb prematurely or too steeply may cause the airplane to settle back to the surface as a result of losing the benefit of ground effect. Therefore, it is recommended the airplane remain in ground effect until at least V_X is reached.

After a positive rate of climb is established, and the airplane has accelerated to V_Y, retract the landing gear and flaps, if equipped. If departing from an airstrip with wet snow or slush on the takeoff surface, the gear should not be retracted immediately. This allows for any wet snow or slush to be air-dried. In the event an obstacle must be cleared after a soft-field takeoff, the climb-out is performed at V_X until the obstacle has been cleared. After reaching this point, the pitch attitude is adjusted to V_Y and the gear and flaps are retracted. The power may then be reduced to the normal climb setting.

Ground Effect

Ground effect is a condition of improved performance encountered when the aircraft is operating near the ground. A change occurs in the three-dimensional flow pattern around the airplane because the vertical component of the airflow around the wing is restricted by the ground surface. This alters the wing's upwash, downwash, and wingtip vortices. [Figure 3-9]

While the aerodynamic characteristics of the tail surfaces and the fuselage are altered by ground effects, the principal effects due to proximity of the ground are the changes in the aerodynamic characteristics of the wing. As the wing encounters ground effect and is maintained at a constant lift coefficient, there is a reduction in the upwash, downwash, and the wingtip vortices.

In order for ground effect to be of significant magnitude, the wing must be quite close to the ground. One of the direct results of ground effect is the variation of induced drag with wing height above the ground at a constant lift coefficient. When the wing is at a height equal to its span, the reduction in induced drag is only 1.4 percent. However, when the wing is at a height equal to one-fourth its span, the reduction in induced drag is 23.5 percent and, when the wing is at a height equal to one-tenth its span, the reduction in induced drag is 47.6 percent. Thus, a large reduction in induced drag will take place only when the wing is very close to the ground. Because of this variation, ground effect is most usually recognized during the lift-off for takeoff or just prior to touchdown when landing.

During the takeoff phase of flight, ground effect produces some important relationships. The airplane

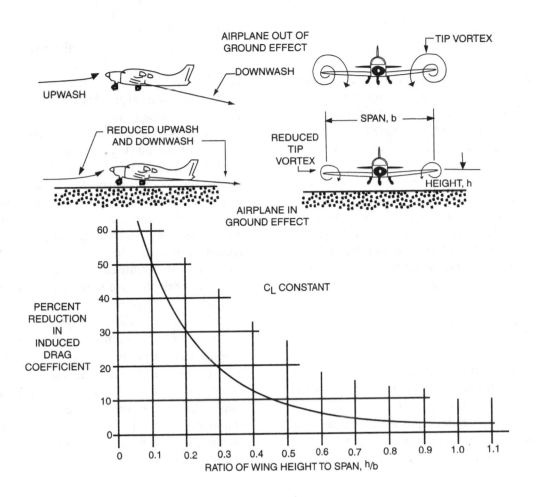

Figure 3-9.—Ground effect.

leaving ground effect after takeoff encounters just the reverse of the airplane entering ground effect during landing; i.e., the airplane leaving ground effect will:

• require an increase in the angle of attack to maintain the same lift coefficient;
• experience an increase in induced drag and thrust required;
• experience a decrease in stability and a noseup change in moment; and
• produce a reduction in static source pressure and increase in indicated airspeed.

These general effects should point out the possible danger in attempting takeoff prior to achieving the recommended lift-off speed. Due to the reduced drag in ground effect, the airplane may seem capable of takeoff well below the recommended speed. However, as the airplane rises out of ground effect with a lower-than-normal lift-off speed, the greater induced drag may result in very marginal initial climb performance.

In extreme conditions, such as high gross weight, high density altitude, and high temperature, lower-than-normal lift-off speed may permit the airplane to become airborne, but incapable of flying out of ground effect. In this case, the airplane may become airborne and then settle back to the runway. It is important not to force the airplane to become airborne before the recommended takeoff speed. The recommended takeoff speed is necessary to provide adequate initial climb performance. For this reason, it is imperative that a definite climb be established before retracting the landing gear or flaps.

REJECTED TAKEOFF

Emergency or abnormal situations can occur during a takeoff that will require a pilot to reject the takeoff while still on the runway. Circumstances such as a malfunctioning powerplant, inadequate acceleration, runway incursion, or air traffic conflict may be reasons for a rejected takeoff.

In the event a takeoff is rejected, the power should be reduced to idle and maximum braking applied while maintaining directional control. If it is necessary to shut down the engine due to a fire, the mixture control should be brought to the idle cutoff position and the magnetos turned off. In all cases, the manufacturer's emergency procedure should be followed.

NOISE ABATEMENT

Airplane noise problems have become a major concern at many airports throughout the country. Many local communities have pressured airports into developing specific operational procedures that will help limit airplane noise while operating over nearby areas. For years now, the FAA, airport managers, airplane operators, pilots, and special interest groups have been working together to minimize airplane noise for nearby sensitive areas. As a result, noise abatement procedures have been developed for many of these airports that include standardized profiles and procedures to achieve these lower noise goals.

Airports that have noise abatement procedures provide information to pilots, operators, air carriers, air traffic facilities, and other special groups that are applicable to their airport. These procedures are available to the aviation community by various means. Most of this information comes from; the Airport/Facility Directory, local and regional publications, printed handouts, operator bulletin boards, safety briefings, and local air traffic facilities.

At airports that use noise abatement procedures, reminder signs may be installed at the taxiway hold positions for applicable runways. These are to remind pilots to use and comply with noise abatement procedures on departure. If a pilot is not familiar with these procedures he should ask the tower or air traffic facility for the recommended procedures. In any case, pilots should be considerate of the surrounding community while operating their airplane to and from such an airport. This includes operating as quietly, yet safely as possible.

CHAPTER 4
BASIC FLIGHT MANEUVERS

INTRODUCTION

This chapter discusses integrated flight instruction, attitude flying concepts, and the basic flight maneuvers that all flying tasks and techniques are based on. When learning to fly, the basic fundamentals and maneuvers must be mastered before the more advanced maneuvers can be learned.

Basic flight maneuvers include the four fundamentals of flight: straight and level, turns, climbs, and descents. Controlled flight consists of either one, or a combination of these basic maneuvers. Proper control of an airplane is the result of the pilot knowing when and how to make pitch, bank, and power changes.

In flight training, control of the airplane is a matter of fixing the relationship of the nose and wingtips of the airplane to a specific position in relation to the horizon. As basic flying skills are developed through training and experience, the pilot will acquire an awareness of these references.

INTEGRATED FLIGHT INSTRUCTION

When introducing basic flight maneuvers to a beginning pilot, it is recommended that the integrated flight instruction method be used. When this type of instruction is used, training in the control of an airplane by outside visual references is integrated with instruction in the use of flight instruments. When beginning pilots use this technique, they achieve a more precise and competent overall piloting ability.

The use of this type of training does not, and is not intended to, prepare pilots for flight in instrument meteorological conditions (IMC). It does, however, provide basic instrument skills to be used in an emergency. This type of instruction also provides an excellent foundation for advanced training for those seeking to obtain an instrument rating.

When using the flight instruments, the responsibility to see and avoid other aircraft becomes more demanding.

ATTITUDE FLYING

Airplane control is composed of four components: pitch, bank, power control, and trim. [Figure 4-1]

• Pitch control is the control of the airplane about the lateral axis by using the elevator to raise or lower the nose.
• Bank control is control of the airplane about the longitudinal axis by use of the ailerons to attain a desired angle of bank.
• Power control is the control of power by use of the throttle to establish or maintain desired performance.

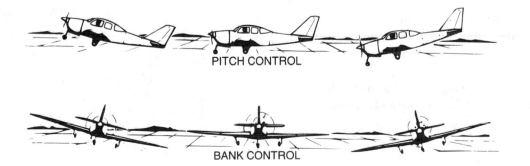

FIGURE 4-1.—Pitch and bank control.

• Trim control assists in holding an airplane in steady flight. The airplane should be trimmed by first applying control pressure to establish the desired attitude, and then adjusting the trim so that the airplane will maintain the attitude without control pressure in hands-off flight.

The following instruments are used as references for control of the airplane are attitude indicator, heading indicator, altimeter, airspeed indicator, vertical speed indicator (VSI), and turn coordinator.

• The attitude indicator shows both the pitch and bank attitude of the airplane.
• The heading indicator shows the airplane's direction of flight.
• The altimeter indicator shows the airplane's altitude and the need for a pitch change.
• The airspeed indicator shows the results of power and/or pitch changes by the airplane's speed.
• The VSI shows the rate of climb or descent.
• The turn coordinator shows the direction, rate, and quality of the turn.

Straight-and-Level Flight

Straight-and-level flight is a condition of flight in which a constant heading and altitude are maintained. It is accomplished by making small corrections for slight turns, descents, and climbs.

During straight-and-level flight, the pilot selects two or more outside visual reference points directly ahead of the airplane, such as towns, lakes, or distant clouds, and keeps the airplane's nose headed toward those objects. When using these references, a check of the heading indicator should be made frequently to determine that the airplane is maintaining flight in the desired direction.

Straight-and-level flight may also be accomplished by visually checking the relationship of the airplane's wingtips with the horizon. Both wingtips should be an equal distance above or below the horizon (depending on whether the airplane is a high-wing or low-wing type). Any necessary adjustments to bank should be made with the ailerons.

Observing the wingtips helps divert the pilot's attention from the airplane's nose and expands the area of visual scanning. [Figure 4-2]

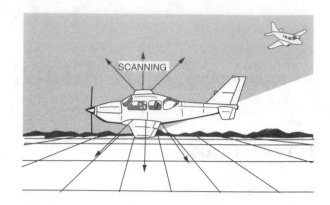

FIGURE 4-2.—Visual scanning.

The pitch attitude for level flight (constant altitude) is obtained by selecting some portion of the airplane's nose as a reference point, and then keeping that point in a fixed position relative to the horizon. That position should be cross-checked against the altimeter to determine whether or not the pitch attitude is correct. If altitude is being gained or lost, the nose attitude should be readjusted in relation to the horizon and then the altimeter rechecked to determine if altitude is now being maintained. The pitch information obtained from the attitude indicator will show the position of the nose relative to the horizon and will indicate the necessary corrections to return to level flight. [Figure 4-3]

For all practical purposes, the airspeed will remain constant in straight-and-level flight with a constant power setting. Practicing airspeed changes by increasing or decreasing the power will provide an excellent means of developing proficiency in maintaining straight-and-level flight at various speeds. Significant changes in airspeed will require changes in pitch attitude and trim to maintain altitude. Pronounced changes in pitch attitude and trim will also be necessary as the flaps and landing gear are extended or retracted.

Turns

A turn is a basic flight maneuver used to change or return to a desired heading. It involves close coordination of all three flight controls: aileron, rudder, and elevator. Since turns are a part of most other flight maneuvers, it is important to thoroughly understand the factors involved.

For purposes of this discussion, turns are divided into three classes: shallow turns, medium turns, and steep turns. [Figure 4-4]

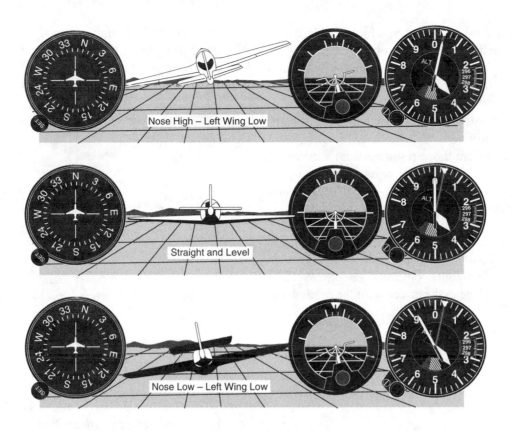

Nose High – Left Wing Low

Straight and Level

Nose Low – Left Wing Low

FIGURE 4-3.—Outside and instrument references.

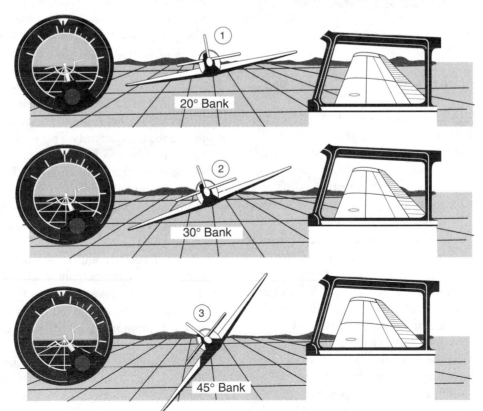

20° Bank

30° Bank

45° Bank

FIGURE 4-4.—Shallow, medium, and steep turns.

• Shallow turns are those in which the bank (less than approximately 20°) is so shallow that the inherent lateral stability of the airplane is acting to level the wings unless some aileron is applied to maintain the bank.

• Medium turns are those resulting from a degree of bank (approximately 20° to 45°) at which the airplane remains at a constant bank.

• Steep turns are those resulting from a degree of bank (45° or more) at which the "overbanking tendency" of an airplane overcomes stability, and the bank increases unless aileron is applied to prevent it.

Changing the direction of the wing's lift toward one side or the other causes the airplane to be pulled in that direction. Applying coordinated aileron and rudder to bank the airplane in the direction of the desired turn does this. [Figure 4-5]

FIGURE 4-5.—Unbalanced lift results in banking.

When an airplane is flying straight and level, the total lift is acting perpendicular to the wings and to the Earth. As the airplane is banked into a turn, the lift then becomes the resultant of two components. One, the vertical lift component, continues to act perpendicular to the Earth and opposes gravity. Second, the horizontal lift component (centripetal) acts parallel to the Earth's surface and opposes inertia (apparent centrifugal force). These two lift components act at right angles to each other, causing the resultant total lifting force to act perpendicular to the banked wing of the airplane. It is the horizontal lift component that actually turns the airplane—not the rudder. [Figure 4-6]

When applying aileron to bank the airplane, the lowered aileron (on the rising wing) produces a greater drag than the raised aileron (on the lowering wing). This increased aileron yaws the airplane toward the rising wing, or opposite to the direction of turn. To counteract this adverse yawing moment, rudder pressure

must be applied simultaneously with aileron in the desired direction of turn. This action is required to produce a coordinated turn.

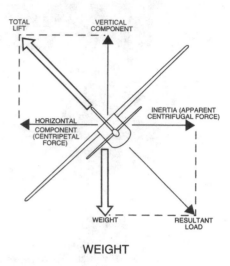

FIGURE 4-6.—Forces during a turn.

After the bank has been established in a medium banked turn, all pressure applied to the aileron may be relaxed. The airplane will remain at the selected bank with no further tendency to yaw since there is no longer a deflection of the ailerons. As a result, pressure may also be relaxed on the rudder pedals, and the rudder allowed to streamline itself with the direction of the slipstream. Rudder pressure maintained after the turn is established will cause the airplane to skid to the outside of the turn. If a definite effort is made to center the rudder rather than let it streamline itself to the turn, it is probable that some opposite rudder pressure will be exerted inadvertently. This will force the airplane to yaw opposite its turning path, causing the airplane to slip to the inside of the turn. The ball in the turn-and-slip indicator will be displaced off-center whenever the airplane is skidding or slipping sideways. In proper coordinated flight, there is no skidding or slipping. [Figure 4-7]

In all constant altitudes, constant airspeed turns, it is necessary to increase the angle of attack of the wing when rolling into the turn by applying up elevator. This is required because the total lift must be equal to the vertical component of lift plus the horizontal lift component.

To stop the turn, the wings are returned to level flight by the use of the ailerons and rudder applied in the opposite direction. To understand the relationship between airspeed, bank, and radius of turn, it should be noted that the rate of turn at any given true airspeed

SLIP   SKID   SLIP

FIGURE 4-7.—Indications of a slip and skid.

depends on the horizontal lift component. The horizontal lift component varies in proportion to the amount of bank. Therefore, the rate of turn at a given true airspeed increases as the angle of bank is increased. On the other hand, when a turn is made at a higher true airspeed at a given bank angle, the inertia is greater and the horizontal lift component required for the turn is greater, causing the turning rate to become slower. Therefore, at a given angle of bank, a higher true airspeed will make the radius of turn larger because the airplane will be turning at a slower rate.

When changing from a shallow bank to a medium bank, the airspeed of the wings on the outside of the turn increases in relation to the inside wing as the radius of turn decreases. The additional lift developed because of this increase in speed of the wing balances the inherent lateral stability of the airplane. At any given airspeed, aileron pressure is not required to maintain the bank. If the bank is allowed to increase from a medium to a steep bank, the radius of turn decreases further. The lift of the outside wing causes the bank to steepen and opposite aileron is necessary to keep the bank constant.

As the radius of the turn becomes smaller, a significant difference develops between the speed of the inside wing and the speed of the outside wing. The wing on the outside of the turn travels a longer circuit than the inside wing, yet both complete their respective circuits in the same length of time. Therefore, the outside wing travels faster than the inside wing, and as a result, it develops more lift. This creates an overbanking tendency that must be controlled by the use of the ailerons. Because the outboard wing is developing more lift, it also has more induced drag. This causes a slight slip during steep turns that must be corrected by use of the rudder. [Figure 4-8]

Sometimes during early training in steep turns, the nose may be allowed to get excessively low resulting in a significant loss in altitude. To recover, the pilot should first reduce the angle of bank with coordinated use of the rudder and aileron, then raise the nose of the airplane to level flight with the elevator. If recovery from an excessively nose-low steep bank condition is attempted by use of the elevator only, it will cause a steepening of the bank and could result in overstressing the airplane. Normally, small corrections for pitch during steep turns are accomplished with the elevator, and the bank is held constant with the ailerons.

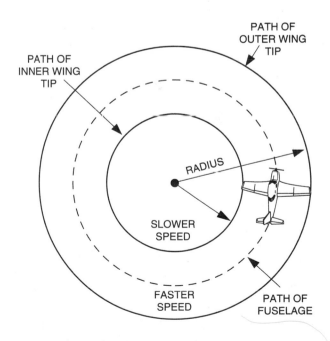

FIGURE 4-8.—Overbanking tendency during a steep turn.

To establish the desired angle of bank, the pilot should use outside visual reference points, as well as the bank indicator on the attitude indicator.

The best outside reference for establishing the degree of bank is the angle formed between the top of the engine cowling in relation to the horizon. Since on most light airplanes the engine cowling is fairly flat, its horizontal angle to the horizon will give some indication of the approximate degree of bank. Also, information obtained from the attitude indicator will show the angle of the wing in relation to the horizon.

The pilot's posture while seated in the airplane is very important, particularly during turns. It will affect the interpretation of outside visual references. At the beginning, the student may lean away from the turn in an attempt to remain upright in relation to the ground rather than ride with the airplane. This should be corrected immediately if the student is to properly learn to use visual references. [Figure 4-9]

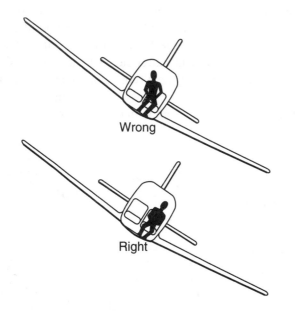

FIGURE 4-9.—Wrong and right posture while seated in the airplane.

Parallax error is common among students and experienced pilots. This error is a characteristic of airplanes that have side-by-side seats because the pilot is seated to one side of the longitudinal axis about which the airplane rolls. This makes the nose appear to rise when making a left turn and to descend when making right turns.

Beginning students should not use large aileron and rudder applications because this produces a rapid roll rate and allows little time for corrections before the

desired bank is reached. Slower (small control displacement) roll rates provide more time to make necessary pitch and bank corrections. As soon as the airplane rolls from the wings-level attitude, the nose should also start to move along the horizon, increasing its rate of travel proportionately as the bank is increased.

The following variations provide excellent guides:

• If the nose starts to move before the bank starts, rudder is being applied too soon.
• If the bank starts before the nose starts turning, or the nose moves in the opposite direction, the rudder is being applied too late.
• If the nose moves up or down when entering a bank, excessive or insufficient up-elevator is being applied.

As the desired angle of bank is established, aileron and rudder pressures should be relaxed. This will stop the bank from increasing because the aileron and rudder control surfaces will be neutral in their streamlined position. The up-elevator pressure should not be relaxed, but should be held constant to maintain a constant altitude. Throughout the turn the pilot should cross-check the airspeed indicator, and if the airspeed has decreased more than 5 knots, additional power should be used. The cross-check should also include outside references, altimeter, and VSI, which can help determine whether or not the pitch attitude is correct. If gaining or losing altitude, the pitch attitude should be adjusted in relation to the horizon, and then the altimeter and VSI rechecked to determine if altitude is being maintained.

During all turns, the ailerons, rudder, and elevator are used to correct minor variations in pitch and bank just as they are in straight-and-level flight.

The rollout from a turn is similar to the roll-in except the flight controls are applied in the opposite direction. Aileron and rudder are applied in the direction of the rollout or toward the high wing. As the angle of bank decreases, the elevator pressure should be relaxed as necessary to maintain altitude.

Since the airplane will continue turning as long as there is any bank, the rollout must be started before reaching the desired heading. The amount of lead required to rollout on the desired heading will depend on the degree of bank used in the turn. Normally, the lead is one half the degrees of bank. For example, if the bank is 30°, lead the rollout by 15°. As the wings become level, the control pressures should be smoothly relaxed so that the controls are neutralized as the airplane returns to straight-and-level flight. As the rollout is being completed, attention should be given to outside visual references, as well as the attitude and heading indicators to determine that the wings are being leveled and the turn stopped.

CLIMBS

Climbs and climbing turns are basic flight maneuvers used to gain altitude. When an airplane enters a climb, it changes its flightpath from level flight to an inclined plane or climb attitude. Weight for the first time is no longer acting in a direction perpendicular to the flightpath, but now acts in a rearward direction. This causes the total drag to increase requiring an increase in thrust (power) to balance the forces. An airplane can only sustain a climb angle when there is sufficient thrust to offset increased drag; therefore, climb is limited by the thrust available. [Figure 4-10]

A normal climb is made at a constant-pitch attitude and airspeed using the manufacturer's recommended climb power setting.

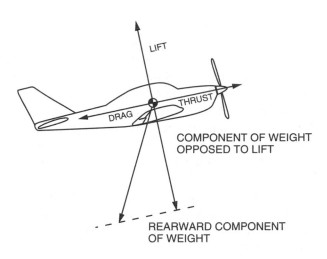

FIGURE 4-10.—*Thrust and drag during a climb.*

Like other maneuvers, climbs should be performed using both flight instruments and outside visual references. The normal climb speed that is recommended by the manufacturer should be used; this is usually the airplane's best rate-of-climb speed (V_Y). Manufacturers may also recommend a cruise climb speed that is usually higher than V_Y. A cruise climb provides a slightly less rate of climb, but a significant increase in speed. It also provides for better engine cooling and increased flight visibility over the nose. [Figure 4-11]

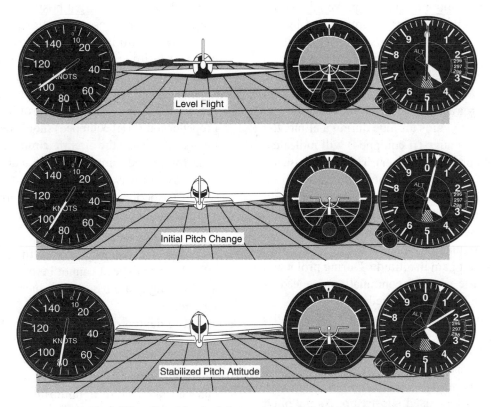

FIGURE 4-11.—*Outside and instrument references for a climb.*

As a climb is started, the airspeed will gradually diminish. This reduction in airspeed is gradual because of the initial momentum of the airplane. The thrust required to maintain straight-and-level flight at a given airspeed is not sufficient to maintain the same airspeed in a climb. Climbing flight requires more power than flying level because of the increased drag caused by gravity acting rearward. Therefore, power must be advanced to a higher-power setting to offset the increased drag.

The propeller effects at climb power are a primary factor. This is because airspeed is significantly slower than at cruising speed, and the airplane's angle of attack is significantly greater. Under these conditions, torque and asymmetrical loading of the propeller will cause the airplane to roll and yaw to the left. To counteract this, the right rudder must be used.

During the early practice of climbs and climbing turns, this may make coordination of the controls seem awkward (left climbing turn holding right rudder), but after a little practice this correction for propeller effects will become instinctive.

Trim is also a very important consideration during a climb. After the climb has been established, the airplane should be trimmed to relieve all pressures from the flight controls. If changes are made in the pitch attitude, power, or airspeed, the airplane should be retrimmed in order to relieve control pressures.

When performing a climb, the power should be advanced to the climb power recommended by the manufacturer. If the airplane is equipped with a controllable-pitch propeller, it will have not only an engine tachometer, but also a manifold pressure gauge. Normally, the flaps and landing gear (if retractable) should be in the retracted position to reduce drag.

As the airplane gains altitude during a climb, the manifold pressure gauge (if equipped) will indicate a loss in manifold pressure (power). This is because the same volume of air going into the engine's induction system gradually decreases in density as altitude increases. When the volume of air in the manifold decreases, it causes a loss of power. This will occur at the rate of approximately 1-inch of manifold pressure for each 1,000-foot gain in altitude. During prolonged climbs, the throttle must be continually advanced, if constant power is to be maintained.

To enter the climb, simultaneously advance the throttle and apply back-elevator pressure to raise the nose of the airplane to the proper position in relation to the horizon. As power is increased, the airplane's nose will rise due to increased download on the stabilizer. This is caused by increased slipstream. As the pitch attitude increases and the airspeed decreases, progressively more right rudder must be applied to compensate for propeller effects and to hold a constant heading.

After the climb is established, back-elevator pressure must be maintained to keep the pitch attitude constant. As the airspeed decreases, the elevators will try to return to their neutral or streamlined position, and the airplane's nose will tend to lower. Noseup elevator trim should be used to compensate for this so that the pitch attitude can be maintained without holding back-elevator pressure. Throughout the climb, since the power is fixed at the climb power setting, the airspeed is controlled by the use of elevator.

A cross-check of the airspeed indicator, attitude indicator, and the position of the airplane's nose in relation to the horizon will determine if the pitch attitude is correct. At the same time, a constant heading should be held with the wings level if a straight climb is being performed, or a constant angle of bank and rate of turn if a climbing turn is being performed.

To return to straight-and-level flight from a climb, it is necessary to initiate the level-off at approximately 10 percent of the rate of climb. For example, if the airplane is climbing at 500 feet per minute (FPM), leveling off should start 50 feet below the desired altitude. The nose must be lowered gradually because a loss of altitude will result if the pitch attitude is changed to the level flight position without allowing the airspeed to increase proportionately. [Figure 4-12]

After the airplane is established in level flight at a constant altitude, climb power should be retained temporarily so that the airplane will accelerate to the cruise airspeed more rapidly. When the speed reaches the desired cruise speed, the throttle setting and the propeller control (if equipped) should be set to the cruise power setting and the aircraft trimmed. After allowing time for engine temperatures to stabilize, adjust the mixture control as required.

In the performance of climbing turns, the following factors should be considered:

• With a constant power setting, the same pitch attitude and airspeed cannot be maintained in a bank as in a straight climb due to the increase in the total lift required.

• The degree of bank should not be too steep. A steep bank significantly decreases the rate of climb. The bank should always remain constant.

• It is necessary to maintain a constant airspeed and constant rate of turn in both right and left turns. The coordination of all flight controls is a primary factor.

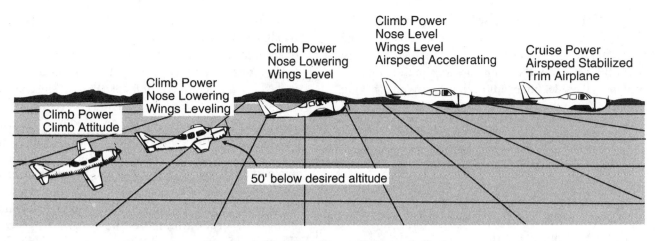

FIGURE 4-12.—Leveling off from a climb.

• At a constant power setting, the airplane will climb at a slightly shallower climb angle because some of the lift is being used to turn the airplane.

• Attention should be diverted from fixation on the airplane's nose and divided equally among inside and outside references.

There are two ways to establish a climbing turn. Either establish a straight climb and then turn, or enter the climb and turn simultaneously. Climbing turns should be used when climbing to the local practice area. Climbing turns allow better visual scanning, and it is easier for other pilots to see a turning aircraft.

In any turn, the loss of vertical lift and increased induced drag, due to increased angle of attack, becomes greater as the angle of bank is increased. So shallow turns should be used to maintain an efficient rate of climb.

DESCENTS

A descent, or glide, is a basic maneuver in which the airplane loses altitude in a controlled descent with little or no engine power. Forward motion is maintained by the component of weight acting along the flightpath, and the pilot balancing the forces of gravity and lift controls the descent rate. [Figure 4-13]

Although power-off descents are related to the practice of power-off accuracy landings, as will be covered in chapter 7, they have a specific purpose in simulated emergency landings. Descents must be performed with a high degree of proficiency because during approaches to landings, the pilot will be dividing his or her attention to details inside and outside the cockpit.

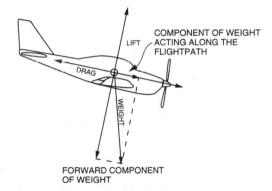

FIGURE 4-13.—Components acting on an airplane in a descent.

The glide ratio of an airplane is the distance the airplane will glide power-off from a given altitude. For instance, if an airplane travels 10,000 feet forward while descending 1,000 feet, its glide ratio is 10 to 1.

The glide ratio is affected by all four forces that act on an airplane (weight, lift, drag, and thrust). If all factors are in balance, the glide ratio will be constant. Although the effect of wind will not be covered in this section, it is an obvious factor that affects the gliding distance in relation to its movement over the ground. With a tailwind, the airplane will glide farther because of the higher groundspeed. With a headwind, the airplane will not glide as far because of the slower groundspeed.

Variations in weight do not affect the glide angle provided the pilot uses the correct airspeed. Since it is the lift over drag (L/D) ratio that determines the distance an airplane can glide, weight will not effect the distance. The glide ratio is based only on the relationship of the aerodynamic forces acting on the airplane. The only effect the weight will have is to vary the time that the airplane will glide. For example, if two airplanes having the same L/D ratio, but different weights, start a glide from the same altitude, the heavier airplane gliding at a higher airspeed will arrive at the touchdown point in a shorter time. Both airplanes will cover the same distance, only the lighter airplane will take a longer time. [Figure 4-14]

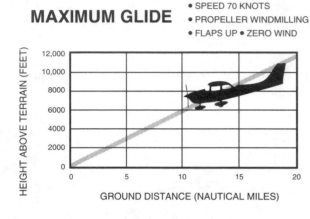

FIGURE 4-14.—Maximum glide chart.

Under various flight conditions, the drag factor may be changed through the operation of the landing gear and/or flaps. When the landing gear or the flaps are lowered, the drag is increased, and the airspeed will decrease unless the nose is lowered. As the nose is lowered, the glide angle increases and reduces the distance traveled. A power-off windmilling propeller also creates considerable drag and decreases the airplane's forward movement. In an emergency, the propeller may be changed to full high pitch (low RPM), which reduces the frontal area of the propeller blades, and reduces drag allowing the airplane to glide farther. The use of high pitch places an additional load on the engine at idle speeds and could cause the engine to stop. In addition, when the propeller blades are at high pitch, they are not ready to deliver maximum power if needed.

Although the propeller thrust of the airplane is normally dependent on the power output of the engine, the throttle is in the closed position during a glide, so the thrust is constant. In a power-off glide, the pitch attitude must be adjusted as necessary to maintain a constant airspeed.

The best speed to use for a glide is one that will result in the greatest glide distance for a given amount of altitude. The manufacturer determines this from the L/D max curve and usually provides this information in the Pilot's Operating Handbook (POH). Any change in the gliding airspeed will result in a proportionate change in the glide ratio. As the airspeed is reduced or increased from the optimum glide speed, the glide ratio is also changed. When below the optimum speed, the angle of descent will be greater and the airplane will not glide as far. For this reason, the pilot should never try to stretch a glide by reducing the airspeed below the airplane's recommended best glide speed. [Figure 4-15]

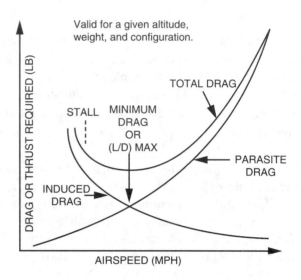

FIGURE 4-15. Lift/drag ratio.

Pilots should perform descents by reference to both flight instruments and outside visual references. [Figure 4-16]

To enter the glide, the pilot should close the throttle and advance the propeller control (if equipped) to low pitch (high RPM). A constant altitude should be held until the airspeed decreases to the recommended best glide speed, then the nose should be lowered to maintain that gliding speed. When the speed has stabilized, the airplane should be retrimmed.

When the approximate gliding pitch attitude is established, the airspeed indicator should be checked. If the airspeed is higher than the recommended speed, the nose is too low. If the airspeed is less than the recommended speed, the nose is too high, and the pitch attitude should be readjusted accordingly. When the proper glide has been established, flaps may be used.

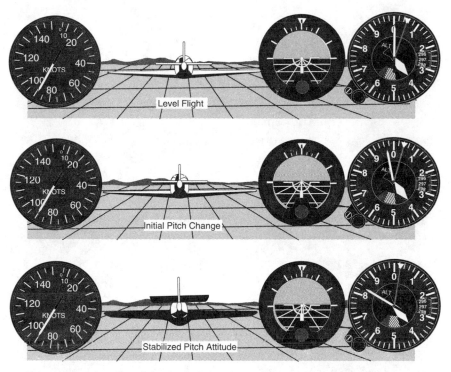

FIGURE 4-16.—*Outside and flight instrument references for a glide.*

The nose attitude will have to be lowered accordingly to maintain the desired glide speed. Again, the pitch attitude should be adjusted first, and then the airspeed checked to be sure that a constant airspeed is being maintained. It is always best to establish the proper flight attitude by establishing the visual reference first, then use the flight instruments as a secondary check.

In order to maintain the most efficient glide in a turn, more altitude will be sacrificed than in a straight glide since this is the only way speed can be maintained without power. Turning in a glide decreases the glide performance of the airplane to an even greater extent than a normal turn with power.

The level-off from a glide must be started before reaching the desired altitude. This is necessary because

of the airplane's downward inertia. The amount of lead depends upon the rate of descent and the pilot's control technique. With too little lead, there will be a tendency to descend below the selected altitude. For example, assuming a 500-FPM rate of descent, the altitude must be led by approximately 100 to 200 feet to level off at a higher airspeed than the glide speed. The higher the rate of descent, the greater the lead. At the selected lead point, the power should be advanced smoothly to the level flight cruise power setting. Since the nose will tend to rise due to increased slipstream over the stabilizer and the airspeed increases, the pilot should smoothly change the pitch attitude so that level flight is attained at the desired altitude. [Figure 4-17]

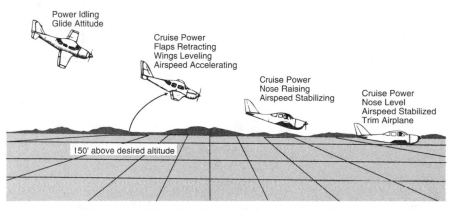

FIGURE 4-17.—*Leveling off from a descent.*

CHAPTER 5
SLOW FLIGHT, STALLS, AND SPINS

INTRODUCTION

This chapter provides the recommended procedures for the safe operation of an airplane at airspeeds less than cruise. The discussion includes slow flight; flight at minimum controllable airspeed; and information on stall and spin recognition, characteristics, and recovery.

SLOW FLIGHT

Slow flight can be defined as flight at any airspeed that is less than cruise airspeed. Flight instructors should have their students maneuver the airplane at airspeeds and in configurations that will be encountered during takeoffs, climbs, descents, go-around and approaches to landing. Flight should also be practiced at the slowest airspeed at which the airplane is capable of maintaining controlled flight without stalling, usually at 3 to 5 knots above stalling speed.

Maneuvering during slow flight

Maneuvering during slow flight demonstrates the flight characteristics and degree of controllability of an airplane at less than cruise speeds. The ability to determine the characteristic control responses of any airplane is of great importance to pilots. Pilot's must develop this awareness in order to avoid stalls in any airplane flown at the slower airspeeds which are characteristic during takeoffs, climbs, descents, go-arounds, and approaches to landing. Maintaining sufficient lift and adequate control of an airplane during performance maneuvers depends upon a certain minimum airspeed.

The objective of maneuvering during slow flight is to develop the pilot's sense of feel and ability to use the controls correctly, and to improve proficiency in performing maneuvers that require slow airspeeds. Maneuvering during slow flight should be performed using both instrument indications and outside visual reference. It is important that pilots form the habit of frequently referencing flight instruments for airspeed, altitude, and attitude indications while flying at slow speeds.

To begin the maneuver the throttle is gradually reduced from cruising position. While the airplane is losing airspeed, the position of the nose in relation to the horizon should be noted and should be raised as necessary to maintain altitude. [Figure 5-1] When the airspeed is below the maximum allowable for landing gear operation, the landing gear (if equipped with retractable gear) is extended and all gear-down checks performed. As the airspeed drops below the maximum allowable speed for flap operation, flaps are lowered and the pitch attitude adjusted to maintain altitude. Power and pitch attitude is now adjusted to maintain the altitude and airspeed desired.

During these changing flight conditions it is important to retrim the airplane as often as necessary to compensate for changes in control pressures. If too much speed is lost, or too little power is used, further

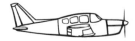 

FIGURE 5-1.— Flight at minimum controllable airspeed.

back pressure on the elevator control may result in a loss of altitude or a stall. When the desired pitch attitude and airspeed have been established, it is important to continually cross-check the, altimeter, and airspeed indicator, as well as outside references, to ensure that accurate control is being maintained.

When the attitude, airspeed, and power have been stabilized in straight flight, turns should be practiced to determine the airplane's controllability characteristics at this selected airspeed. During the turns, power and pitch attitude may need to be increased to maintain the airspeed and altitude. If a steep turn is made, the increase in angle of attack to maintain altitude may result in a stall. A stall may also occur as a result of abrupt or rough control movements when flying at slow flight. Abruptly raising the flaps during slow flight will also result in lift suddenly being lost, causing the airplane to lose altitude or perhaps stall.

Once flight at a selected airspeed is set up properly for level flight, a descent or climb at the selected airspeed, can be established by adjusting the power to maintain the desired airspeed, and simultaneously adjusting the pitch attitude as necessary to establish the desired rate of descent or climb.

Maneuvering during slow flight at minimum airspeed

Slow flight should also be practiced at just above stall speed. By definition, the term "flight at minimum airspeed" means a speed at which any further increase in angle of attack or load factor, or reduction in power will cause an immediate stall. This airspeed will depend upon various circumstances, such as the gross weight and CG location of the airplane and maneuvering load imposed by turns and pullups. Flight at minimum airspeed should include climbs, turns, and descents. Flight at minimum airspeed requires positive use of rudder and ailerons to counteract asymmetrical loading of the propeller, the action of the corkscrewing slipstream, and torque reaction. Rolling in and out of turns requires more rudder then rolling at normal airspeeds because of the greater displacement of the ailerons at minimum airspeed. A positive climb, however, may not be possible at altitude due to a lack of available power in excess of that required to maintain straight-and-level flight at the minimum airspeed. In some airplanes, an attempt to climb at such a slow airspeed may result in a loss of altitude, even with maximum power applied.

Flight at minimum airspeed will help pilots develop the ability to estimate the margin of safety above the stalling speed by the diminishing effectiveness of the flight controls.

STALLS

A stall occurs when the smooth airflow over the airplane's wing is disrupted, and the lift degenerates rapidly. This is caused when the wing exceeds its critical angle of attack. This can occur at any airspeed, in any attitude, with any power setting. [Figure 5-2]

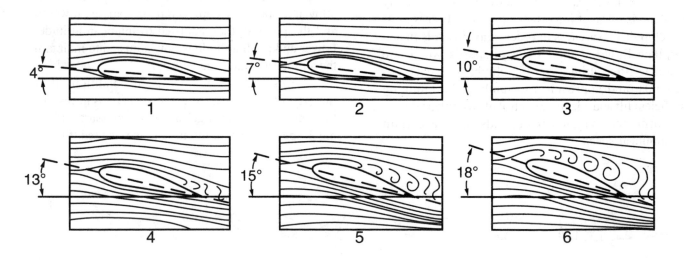

FIGURE 5-2.— Airflow around a wing at various angles of attack.

The practice of stall recovery and the development of awareness of stalls are of primary importance in pilot training. The objectives in performing intentional stalls are to familiarize the pilot with the conditions that produce stalls, to assist in recognizing an approaching stall, and to develop the habit of taking prompt preventive or corrective action.

Intentional stalls should be performed at an altitude that will provide adequate height above the ground for recovery and return to normal level flight. Though it depends on the degree to which a stall has progressed, most stalls require some loss of altitude during recovery. The longer it takes to recognize the approaching stall, the more complete the stall is likely to become, and the greater the loss of altitude to be expected.

Recognition of Stalls

Pilots must recognize the flight conditions that are conducive to stalls and know how to apply the necessary corrective action. They should learn to recognize an approaching stall by sight, sound, and feel. The following cues may be useful in recognizing the approaching stall:

• Vision is useful in detecting a stall condition by noting the attitude of the airplane. This sense can only be relied on when the stall is the result of an unusual attitude of the airplane. Since the airplane can also be stalled from a normal attitude, vision in this instance would be of little help in detecting the approaching stall.

• Hearing is also helpful in sensing a stall condition. In the case of fixed-pitch propeller airplanes in a power-on condition, a change in sound due to loss of revolutions per minute (RPM) is particularly noticeable. The lessening of the noise made by the air flowing along the airplane structure as airspeed decreases is also quite noticeable, and when the stall is almost complete, vibration and incident noises often increase greatly.

• Kinesthesia, or the sensing of changes in direction or speed of motion, is probably the most important and the best indicator to the trained and experienced pilot. If this sensitivity is properly developed, it will warn of a decrease in speed or the beginning of a settling or mushing of the airplane.

• The feeling of control pressures is also very important. As speed is reduced, the resistance to pressures on the controls becomes progressively less. Pressures exerted on the controls tend to become movements of the control surfaces. The lag between these movements and the response of the airplane becomes greater, until in a complete stall all controls can be moved with almost no resistance, and with little immediate effect on the airplane.

Several types of stall warning indicators have been developed to warn pilots of an approaching stall. The use of such indicators is valuable and desirable, but the reason for practicing stalls is to learn to recognize stalls without the benefit of warning devices.

Fundamentals of Stall Recovery

During the practice of intentional stalls, the real objective is not to learn how to stall an airplane, but to learn how to recognize an approaching stall and take prompt corrective action. [Figure 5-3] Though the recovery actions must be taken in a coordinated manner, they are broken down into three steps here for explanation purposes.

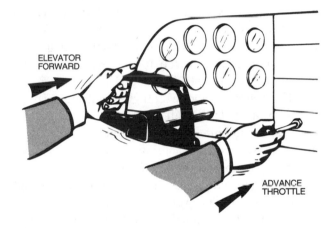

ELEVATOR FORWARD

ADVANCE THROTTLE

FIGURE 5-3.—Stall recognition and recovery.

First, at the indication of a stall, the pitch attitude and angle of attack must be decreased positively and immediately. Since the basic cause of a stall is always an excessive angle of attack, the cause must first be eliminated by releasing the back-elevator pressure that was necessary to attain that angle of attack or by moving the elevator control forward. This lowers the nose and returns the wing to an effective angle of attack. The amount of elevator control pressure or movement used depends on the design of the airplane, the severity of the stall, and the proximity of the ground. In some airplanes, a moderate movement of the elevator control—perhaps slightly forward of neutral—is enough, while in others a forcible push to the full forward position may be required. An excessive negative load on the wings caused by excessive forward movement of the elevator may impede, rather than hasten, the stall recovery. The object is to reduce the angle of attack but only enough to allow the wing to regain lift.

Second, the maximum allowable power should be applied to increase the airplane's speed and assist in reducing the wing's angle of attack. Generally, the throttle should be promptly, but smoothly, advanced to the maximum allowable power.

Although stall recoveries should be practiced without, as well as with the use of power, in most actual stalls the application of more power, if available, is an integral part of the stall recovery. Usually, the greater the power applied, the less the loss of altitude.

Maximum allowable power applied at the instant of a stall will usually not cause overspeeding of an engine equipped with a fixed-pitch propeller, due to the heavy air load imposed on the propeller at slow airspeeds. However it will be necessary to reduce the power as airspeed is gained after the stall recovery so the airspeed will not become excessive. When performing intentional stalls, the tachometer indication should never be allowed to exceed the red line (maximum allowable RPM) marked on the instrument.

Third, straight-and-level flight should be regained with coordinated use of all controls.

Practice in both power-on and power-off stalls is important because it simulates stall conditions that could occur during normal flight maneuvers. For example, the power-on stalls are practiced to show what could happen if the airplane were climbing at an excessively nose-high attitude immediately after takeoff or during a climbing turn. The power-off turning stalls are practiced to show what could happen if the controls are improperly used during a turn from the base leg to the final approach. The power-off straight-ahead stall simulates the attitude and flight characteristics of a particular airplane during the final approach and landing.

Usually, the first few practices should include only approaches to stalls, with recovery initiated as soon as the first buffeting or partial loss of control is noted. In this way, the pilot can become familiar with the indications of an approaching stall without actually stalling the airplane. Recovery should be practiced first without the addition of power, and then with the addition of power to determine how effective power will be in executing a safe recovery.

Stall accidents usually result from an inadvertent stall at a low altitude in which a recovery was not accomplished prior to contact with the surface. As a preventive measure, stalls should be practiced at an altitude which will allow recovery no lower than 1,500 feet AGL. To recover with a minimum loss of altitude requires an application of power, reduction in the angle of attack (lowering the airplane's pitch attitude), and termination of the descent without entering another stall.

Use of Ailerons/Rudder in Stall Recovery

Different types of airplanes have different stall characteristics. Most airplanes are designed so that the wings will stall progressively outward from the wing roots (where the wing attaches to the fuselage) to the wingtips. This is the result of designing the wings in a manner that the wingtips have less angle of incidence than the wing roots. Such a design feature causes the wingtips to have a smaller angle of attack than the wing roots during flight. [Figure 5-4]

Exaggerated view of wingtip washout

Figure 5-4.—Wingtip washout.

Exceeding the critical angle of attack causes a stall, and the wing roots of an airplane will exceed the critical angle before the wingtips, and the wing roots will stall first. The wings are designed in this manner so that aileron control will be available at high angles of attack (slow airspeed) and give the airplane more stable stalling characteristics.

When the airplane is in a stalled condition, the wingtips continue to provide some degree of lift, and the ailerons still have some control effect. During recovery from a stall, the return of lift begins at the tips and progresses toward the roots. Thus, the ailerons can be used to level the wings.

Using the ailerons requires finesse to avoid an aggravated stall condition. For example, if the right wing dropped during the stall and excessive aileron control were applied to the left to raise the wing, the aileron deflected downward (right wing) would produce a greater angle of attack (and drag), and possibly a more complete stall at the tip as the critical angle of attack is exceeded. The increase in drag created by the high angle of attack on that wing might cause the airplane to yaw in that direction. This adverse yaw could result in a spin unless directional control was maintained by rudder, and/or the aileron control sufficiently reduced.

Even though excessive aileron pressure may have been applied, a spin will not occur if directional (yaw) control is maintained by timely application of coordinated rudder pressure. Therefore, it is important that the rudder be used properly during both the entry and the recovery from a stall. The primary use of the rudder in stall recoveries is to counteract any tendency of the airplane to yaw or slip. The correct recovery technique would be to decrease the pitch attitude by applying forward-elevator pressure to break the stall, advancing the throttle to increase airspeed, and simultaneously maintaining directional control with coordinated use of the aileron and rudder.

Stall Characteristics

Because of engineering design variations, the stall characteristics for all airplanes cannot be specifically described; however, the similarities found in small general aviation training-type airplanes are noteworthy enough to be considered. It will be noted that the power-on and power-off stall warning indications will be different. The power-off stall will have less noticeable clues (buffeting, shaking) than the power-on stall. In the power-off stall, the predominant clue can be the elevator control position (full-up elevator against the stops) and a high descent rate. When performing the power-on stall, the buffeting will likely be the predominant clue that provides a positive indication of the stall. For the purpose of airplane certification, the stall warning may be furnished either through the inherent aerodynamic qualities of the airplane, or by a stall warning device that will give a clear distinguishable indication of the stall. Most airplanes are equipped with a stall warning device.

The factors that affect the stalling characteristics of the airplane are balance, bank, pitch attitude, coordination, drag, and power. The pilot should learn the effect of the stall characteristics of the airplane being flown and the proper correction. It should be reemphasized that a stall can occur at any airspeed, in any attitude, or at any power setting, depending on the total number of factors affecting the particular airplane.

A number of factors may be induced as the result of other factors. For example, when the airplane is in a nose-high turning attitude, the angle of bank has a

tendency to increase. This occurs because with the airspeed decreasing, the airplane begins flying in a smaller and smaller arc. Since the outer wing is moving in a larger radius and traveling faster than the inner wing, it has more lift and causes an overbanking tendency. At the same time, because of the decreasing airspeed and lift on both wings, the pitch attitude tends to lower. In addition, since the airspeed is decreasing while the power setting remains constant, the effect of torque becomes more prominent, causing the airplane to yaw.

During the practice of power-on turning stalls, to compensate for these factors and to maintain a constant flight attitude until the stall occurs, aileron pressure must be continually adjusted to keep the bank attitude constant. At the same time, back-elevator pressure must be continually increased to maintain the pitch attitude, as well as right-rudder pressure increased to keep the ball centered and to prevent adverse yaw from changing the turn rate. If the bank is allowed to become too steep, the vertical component of lift decreases and makes it even more difficult to maintain a constant-pitch attitude.

Whenever practicing turning stalls, a constant pitch-and-bank attitude should be maintained until the stall occurs. Whatever control pressures are necessary should be applied even though the controls appear to be crossed (aileron pressure in one direction, rudder pressure in the opposite direction). During the entry to a power-on turning stall to the right, in particular, the controls will be crossed to some extent. This is due to right-rudder pressure being used to overcome torque and left aileron pressure being used to prevent the bank from increasing.

Approaching Stalls—Power-On or Power-Off

An approaching stall is one in which the airplane is approaching a stall but is not allowed to completely stall. This stall maneuver is primarily for practice in retaining (or regaining) full control of the airplane immediately upon recognizing that it is almost in a stall or that a stall is likely to occur if timely preventive action is not taken.

The practice of these stalls is of particular value in developing the pilot's sense of feel for executing maneuvers in which maximum airplane performance is required. These maneuvers require flight with the airplane approaching a stall, and recovery initiated before a stall occurs. As in all maneuvers that involve significant changes in altitude or direction, the pilot must ensure that the area is clear of other air traffic before executing the maneuver.

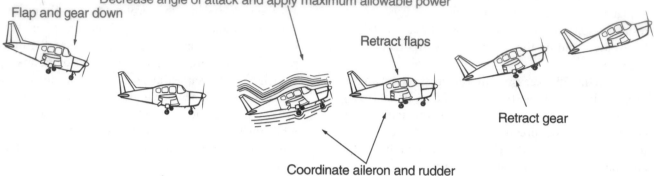

Flap and gear down

Decrease angle of attack and apply maximum allowable power

Retract flaps

Retract gear

Coordinate aileron and rudder

FIGURE 5-5.—Power-off stall.

These stalls may be entered and performed in the attitudes and with the same configuration of the basic full stalls or other maneuvers described in this chapter. However, instead of allowing a complete stall, when the first buffeting or decay of control effectiveness is noted, the angle of attack must be reduced immediately by releasing the back-elevator pressure and applying whatever additional power is necessary. Since the airplane will not be completely stalled, the pitch attitude needs to be decreased only to a point where minimum controllable airspeed is attained or until adequate control effectiveness is regained.

The pilot must promptly recognize the indication of a stall and take timely, positive control action to prevent a stall.

Power-Off Stalls

The practice of power-off stalls is usually performed with normal landing approach conditions in simulation of an accidental stall occurring during landing approaches. Airplanes equipped with flaps and/ or retractable landing gear should be in the landing configuration. Airspeed in excess of the normal approach speed should not be carried into a stall entry since it could result in an abnormally nose-high attitude. Before executing these practice stalls, the pilot must be sure the area is clear of other air traffic.

After extending the landing gear, applying carburetor heat (if applicable), and retarding the throttle to idle (or normal approach power), the airplane should be held at a constant altitude in level flight until the airspeed decelerates to that of a normal approach. The

airplane should then be smoothly nosed down into the normal approach attitude to maintain that airspeed. Wing flaps should then be extended and pitch attitude adjusted to maintain the airspeed.

When the approach attitude and airspeed have stabilized, the airplane's nose should be smoothly raised to an attitude that will induce a stall. [Figure 5-5] Directional control should be maintained with the rudder, the wings held level by use of the ailerons, and a constant-pitch attitude maintained with the elevator until the stall occurs. The stall will be recognized by clues, such as full-up elevator, high descent rate, uncontrollable nosedown pitching, and possible buffeting.

Recovering from the stall should be accomplished by reducing the angle of attack, releasing back-elevator pressure, and advancing the throttle to maximum allowable power. Right-rudder pressure is necessary to overcome the engine torque effects as power is advanced and the nose is being lowered.

The nose should be lowered as necessary to regain flying speed and returned to straight-and-level flight attitude. After establishing a positive rate of climb, the flaps and landing gear are retracted, as necessary, and when in level flight, the throttle should be returned to cruise power setting. After recovery is complete, a climb or go-around procedure should be initiated, as the situation dictates, to assure a minimum loss of altitude.

Recovery from power-off stalls should also be practiced from shallow banked turns to simulate an inadvertent stall during a turn from base leg to final approach. During the practice of these stalls, care should be taken that the turn continues at a uniform rate until

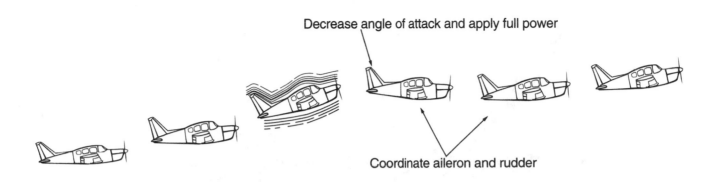

FIGURE 5-6.—Power-on stall.

the complete stall occurs. If the power-off turn is not properly coordinated while approaching the stall, wallowing may result when the stall occurs. If the airplane is in a slip, the outer wing may stall first and whip downward abruptly. This does not affect the recovery procedure in any way; the angle of attack must be reduced, the heading maintained, and the wings leveled by coordinated use of the controls. In the practice of turning stalls, no attempt should be made to stall the airplane on a predetermined heading. However, to simulate a turn from base to final approach, the stall normally should be made to occur within a heading change of approximately 90°.

After the stall occurs, the recovery should be made straight ahead with minimum loss of altitude, and accomplished in accordance with the recovery procedure discussed earlier.

Recoveries from power-off stalls should be accomplished both with, and without, the addition of power, and may be effected either just after the stall occurs, or after the nose has pitched down through the level flight attitude.

Power-On Stalls

Power-on stall recoveries are practiced from straight climbs, and climbing turns with 15 to 20° banks, to simulate an accidental stall occurring during takeoffs and climbs. Airplanes equipped with flaps and/or retractable landing gear should normally be in the takeoff configuration; however, power-on stalls should also be practiced with the airplane in a clean configuration (flaps and/or gear retracted) as in departure and normal climbs. [Figure 5-6]

After establishing the takeoff or climb configuration, the airplane should be slowed to the normal lift-off speed while clearing the area for other air traffic. When the desired speed is attained, the power should be set at takeoff power for the takeoff stall or the recommended climb power for the departure stall while establishing a climb attitude. The purpose of reducing the airspeed to lift-off airspeed before the throttle is advanced to the recommended setting is to avoid an excessively steep noseup attitude for a long period before the airplane stalls.

After the climb attitude is established, the nose is then brought smoothly upward to an attitude obviously impossible for the airplane to maintain and is held at that attitude until the full stall occurs. In most airplanes, after attaining the stalling attitude, the elevator control must be moved progressively further back as the airspeed decreases until, at the full stall, it will have reached its limit and cannot be moved back any farther.

Recovery from the stall should be accomplished by immediately reducing the angle of attack by positively releasing back-elevator pressure and smoothly advancing the throttle to maximum allowable power. In this case, since the throttle is already at the climb power setting, the addition of power will be relatively slight.

The nose should be lowered as necessary to regain flying speed with the minimum loss of altitude. Then, the airplane should be returned to the normal straight-and-level flight attitude, and when in normal level flight, the throttle should be returned to cruise power setting.

The pilot must recognize instantly when the stall has occurred and take prompt action to prevent a prolonged stalled condition.

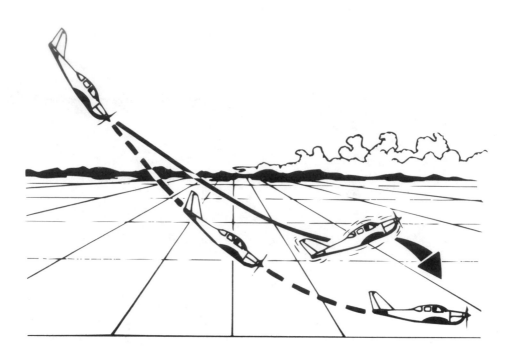

Figure 5-7.—Secondary stall.

Secondary Stall

This stall is called a secondary stall since it may occur after a recovery from a preceding stall. It is caused by attempting to hasten the completion of a stall recovery before the airplane has regained sufficient flying speed. When this stall occurs, the back-elevator pressure should again be released just as in a normal stall recovery. When sufficient airspeed has been regained, the airplane can then be returned to straight-and-level flight. [Figure 5-7]

This stall usually occurs when the pilot uses abrupt control input to return to straight-and-level flight after a stall or spin recovery.

Accelerated Stalls

Though the stalls just discussed normally occur at a specific airspeed, the pilot must thoroughly understand that all stalls result solely from attempts to fly at excessively high angles of attack. During flight, the angle of attack of an airplane wing is determined by a number of factors, the most important of which are the airspeed, the gross weight of the airplane, and the load factors imposed by maneuvering.

At the same gross weight, airplane configuration, and power setting, a given airplane will consistently stall at the same indicated airspeed if no acceleration is involved. The airplane will, however, stall at a higher indicated airspeed when excessive maneuvering loads are imposed by steep turns, pullups, or other abrupt changes in its flightpath. Stalls entered from such flight situations are called "accelerated maneuver stalls," a term, which has no reference to the airspeeds involved. [Figure 5-8]

Stalls which result from abrupt maneuvers tend to be more rapid, or severe, than the unaccelerated stalls, and because they occur at higher-than-normal airspeeds, they may be unexpected by an inexperienced pilot. Failure to take immediate steps toward recovery when an accelerated stall occurs may result in a complete loss of flight control, notably, power-on spins.

This stall should never be practiced with wing flaps in the extended position due to the lower "G" load limitations in that configuration.

Accelerated maneuver stalls should not be performed in any airplane, which is prohibited from such maneuvers by its type certification restrictions or Airplane Flight Manual (AFM) and/or Pilot's Operating Handbook (POH). If they are permitted, they should be performed with a bank of approximately 45°, and in no case at a speed greater than the airplane manufacturer's recommended airspeeds or the design maneuvering speed specified for the airplane. The design maneuvering speed is the maximum speed at which the airplane can be stalled or full available aerodynamic control will not exceed the airplane's limit load factor.

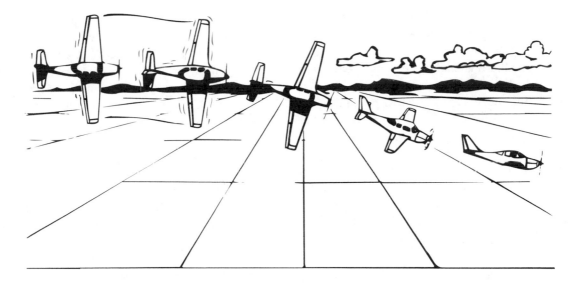

FIGURE 5-8.—Accelerated stall.

At or below this speed, the airplane will usually stall before the limit load factor can be exceeded. Those speeds must not be exceeded because of the extremely high structural loads that are imposed on the airplane, especially if there is turbulence. In most cases, these stalls should be performed at no more than 1.2 times the normal stall speed.

The objective of demonstrating accelerated stalls is not to develop competency in setting up the stall, but rather to learn how they may occur and to develop the ability to recognize such stalls immediately, and to take prompt, effective recovery action. It is important that recoveries are made at the first indication of a stall, or immediately after the stall has fully developed; a prolonged stall condition should never be allowed.

An airplane will stall during a coordinated steep turn exactly as it does from straight flight, except that the pitching and rolling actions tend to be more sudden. If the airplane is slipping toward the inside of the turn at the time the stall occurs, it tends to roll rapidly toward the outside of the turn as the nose pitches down because the outside wing stalls before the inside wing. If the airplane is skidding toward the outside of the turn, it will have a tendency to roll to the inside of the turn because the inside wing stalls first. If the coordination of the turn at the time of the stall is accurate, the airplane's nose will pitch away from the pilot just as it does in a straight flight stall, since both wings stall simultaneously.

An accelerated stall demonstration is entered by establishing the desired flight attitude, then smoothly, firmly, and progressively increasing the angle of attack until a stall occurs. Because of the rapidly changing flight attitude, sudden stall entry, and possible loss of altitude, it is extremely vital that the area be clear of other aircraft and the entry altitude be adequate for safe recovery.

This demonstration stall, as in all stalls, is accomplished by exerting excessive back-elevator pressure. Most frequently it would occur during improperly executed steep turns, stall and spin recoveries, and pullouts from steep dives. The objectives are to determine the stall characteristics of the airplane and develop the ability to instinctively recover at the onset of a stall at other-than-normal stall speed or flight attitudes. An accelerated stall, although usually demonstrated in steep turns, may actually be encountered any time excessive back-elevator pressure is applied and/or the angle of attack is increased too rapidly.

From straight-and-level flight at maneuvering speed or less, the airplane should be rolled into a steep level flight turn and back-elevator pressure gradually applied. After the turn and bank are established, back-elevator pressure should be smoothly and steadily increased. The resulting apparent centrifugal force will push the pilot's body down in the seat, increase the wing loading, and decrease the airspeed. After the airspeed reaches the design maneuvering speed or within 20 knots above the unaccelerated stall speed, back-elevator pressure should be firmly increased until a definite stall occurs. These speed restrictions must be observed to prevent exceeding the load limit of the airplane.

When the airplane stalls, recovery should be made promptly, by releasing sufficient back-elevator pressure and increasing power to reduce the angle of attack. If an uncoordinated turn is made, one wing may tend to drop suddenly, causing the airplane to roll in that direction. If this occurs, power must be added, the excessive back-elevator pressure released, and the airplane returned to straight-and-level flight with coordinated control pressure.

The pilot should recognize when the stall is imminent and take prompt action to prevent a completely stalled condition. It is imperative that a prolonged stall, excessive airspeed, excessive loss of altitude, or spin be avoided.

Cross-Control Stall

The objective of a cross-control stall demonstration maneuver is to show the effect of improper control technique and to emphasize the importance of using coordinated control pressures whenever making turns. This type of stall occurs with the controls crossed—aileron pressure applied in one direction and rudder pressure in the opposite direction.

In addition, when excessive back-elevator pressure is applied, a cross-control stall may result.

This is a stall that is most apt to occur during a poorly planned and executed base-to-final approach turn, and often is the result of overshooting the centerline of the runway during that turn. Normally, the proper action to correct for overshooting the runway is to increase the rate of turn by using coordinated aileron and rudder. At the relatively low altitude of a base-to-final approach turn, improperly trained pilots may be apprehensive of steepening the bank to increase the rate of turn, and rather than steepening the bank, they hold the bank constant and attempt to increase the rate of turn by adding more rudder pressure in an effort to align it with the runway.

The addition of inside rudder pressure will cause the speed of the outer wing to increase therefore, creating greater lift on that wing. To keep that wing from rising and to maintain a constant angle of bank, opposite aileron pressure needs to be applied. The added inside rudder pressure will also cause the nose to lower in relation to the horizon. Consequently, additional back-elevator pressure would be required to maintain a constant-pitch attitude. The resulting condition is a turn with rudder applied in one direction, aileron in the opposite direction, and excessive back-elevator pressure—a pronounced cross-control condition.

Since the airplane is in a skidding turn during the cross-control condition, the wing on the outside of the turn speeds up and produces more lift than the inside wing; thus, the airplane starts to increase its bank. The down aileron on the inside of the turn helps drag that wing back, slowing it up and decreasing its lift, which requires more aileron application. This further causes the airplane to roll. The roll may be so fast that it is possible the bank will be vertical or past vertical before it can be stopped.

For the demonstration of the maneuver, it is important that it be entered at a safe altitude because of the possible extreme nosedown attitude and loss of altitude that may result.

Before demonstrating this stall, the pilot should clear the area for other air traffic while slowly retarding the throttle. Then the landing gear (if retractable gear) should be lowered, the throttle closed, and the altitude maintained until the airspeed approaches the normal glide speed. Because of the possibility of exceeding the airplane's limitations, flaps should not be extended. While the gliding attitude and airspeed are being established, the airplane should be retrimmed. When the glide is stabilized, the airplane should be rolled into a medium-banked turn to simulate a final approach turn that would overshoot the centerline of the runway. During the turn, excessive rudder pressure should be applied in the direction of the turn but the bank held constant by applying opposite aileron pressure. At the same time, increased back-elevator pressure is required to keep the nose from lowering.

All of these control pressures should be increased until the airplane stalls. When the stall occurs, recovery is made by releasing the control pressures and increasing power as necessary to recover.

In a cross-control stall, the airplane often stalls with little warning. The nose may pitch down, the inside wing may suddenly drop, and the airplane may continue to roll to an inverted position. This is usually the beginning of a spin. It is obvious that close to the ground is no place to allow this to happen.

Recovery must be made before the airplane enters an abnormal attitude (vertical spiral or spin); it is a simple matter to return to straight-and-level flight by coordinated use of the controls. The pilot must be able to recognize when this stall is imminent and must take immediate action to prevent a completely stalled condition. It is imperative that this type of stall not occur during an actual approach to a landing, since recovery may be impossible prior to ground contact due to the low altitude.

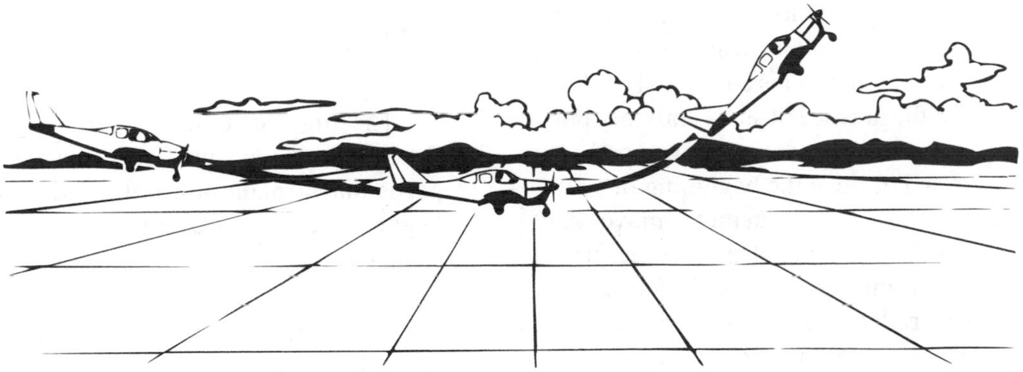

FIGURE 5-9.—Elevator trim stall.

Elevator Trim Stall

The elevator trim stall maneuver shows what can happen when full power is applied for a go-around and positive control of the airplane is not maintained. Such a situation may occur during a go-around procedure from a normal landing approach or a simulated forced-landing approach, or immediately after a takeoff. The objective of the demonstration is to show the importance of making smooth power applications, overcoming strong trim forces and maintaining positive control of the airplane to hold safe flight attitudes, and using proper and timely trim techniques. [Figure 5-9]

At a safe altitude and after ensuring that the area is clear of other air traffic, the pilot should slowly retard the throttle and extend the landing gear (if retractable gear). One-half to full flaps should be lowered, the throttle closed, and altitude maintained until the airspeed approaches the normal glide speed. When the normal glide is established, the airplane should be trimmed for the glide just as would be done during a landing approach (noseup trim).

During this simulated final approach glide, the throttle is then advanced smoothly to maximum allowable power as would be done in a go-around procedure. The combined forces of thrust, torque, and back-elevator trim will tend to make the nose rise sharply and turn to the left.

When the throttle is fully advanced and the pitch attitude increases above the normal climbing attitude and it is apparent that a stall is approaching, adequate forward pressure must be applied to return the airplane to the normal climbing attitude. While holding the airplane in this attitude, the trim should then be adjusted to relieve the heavy control pressures and the normal go-around and level-off procedures completed.

The pilot should recognize when a stall is approaching, and takes prompt action to prevent a completely stalled condition. It is imperative that a stall not occur during an actual go-around from a landing approach.

SPINS

A spin may be defined as an aggravated stall that results in what is termed "autorotation" wherein the airplane follows a downward corkscrew path. As the airplane rotates around a vertical axis, the rising wing is less stalled than the descending wing creating a rolling, yawing, and pitching motion. The airplane is basically being forced downward by gravity, rolling, yawing, and pitching in a spiral path. [Figure 5-10]

The autorotation results from an unequal angle of attack on the airplane's wings. The rising wing has a decreasing angle of attack, where the relative lift increases and the drag decreases. In effect, this wing is less stalled. Meanwhile, the descending wing has an increasing angle of attack, past the wing's critical angle of attack (stall) where the relative lift decreases and drag increases.

A spin is caused when the airplane's wing exceeds its critical angle of attack (stall) with a side slip or yaw acting on the airplane at, or beyond, the actual stall. During this uncoordinated maneuver, a pilot may not be aware that a critical angle of attack has been exceeded until the airplane yaws out of control toward the lowering wing. If stall recovery is not initiated immediately, the airplane may enter a spin.

If this stall occurs while the airplane is in a slipping or skidding turn, this can result in a spin entry and rotation in the direction that the rudder is being applied, regardless of which wingtip is raised.

Many airplanes have to be forced to spin and require considerable judgment and technique to get the spin started. These same airplanes that have to be forced to spin, may be accidentally put into a spin by mishandling the controls in turns, stalls, and flight at minimum controllable airspeeds. This fact is additional evidence of the necessity for the practice of stalls until the ability to recognize and recover from them is developed.

Often a wing will drop at the beginning of a stall. When this happens, the nose will attempt to move (yaw) in the direction of the low wing. This is where use of the rudder is important during a stall. The correct amount of opposite rudder must be applied to keep the nose from yawing toward the low wing. By maintaining directional control and not allowing the nose to yaw toward the low wing, before stall recovery is initiated, a spin will be averted. If the nose is allowed to yaw during the stall, the airplane will begin to slip in the direction of the lowered wing, and will enter a spin. An airplane must be stalled in order to enter a spin; therefore, continued practice in stalls will help the pilot develop a more instinctive and prompt reaction in recognizing an approaching spin. It is essential to learn to apply immediate corrective action any time it is apparent that the airplane is nearing spin conditions. If it is impossible to avoid a spin, the pilot should immediately execute spin recovery procedures.

FIGURE 5-10.—Two-turn spin.

SPIN PROCEDURES

The flight instructor should demonstrate spins. Special spin procedures or techniques required for a particular airplane are not presented here. Before beginning any spin operations, the following items should be reviewed:

• The airplane's AFM/POH limitations section, placards, or type certification data, to determine if the airplane is approved for spins.
• Weight and balance limitations.
• Recommended entry and recovery procedures.
• The requirements for parachutes. It would be appropriate to review a current Title 14 of the Code of Federal Regulations (14 CFR) part 91 for the latest parachute requirements.

A thorough airplane preflight should be accomplished with special emphasis on excess or loose items that may affect the weight, CG, and controllability of the airplane. Slack or loose control cables (particularly rudder and elevator) could prevent full anti-spin control deflections and delay or preclude recovery in some airplanes.

Prior to beginning spin training, the flight area, above and below the airplane, must be clear of other air traffic. This may be accomplished while slowing the airplane for the spin entry. All spin training should be initiated at an altitude high enough for a completed recovery at or above 1,500 feet AGL.

It may be appropriate to introduce spin training by first practicing both power-on and power-off stalls, in a clean configuration. This practice would be used to familiarize the student with the airplane's specific stall and recovery characteristics. Care should be taken with the handling of the power (throttle) in entries and during spins. Carburetor heat should be applied according to the manufacturer's recommendations.

There are four phases of a spin: entry, incipient, developed, and recovery.

Entry Phase

The entry phase is where the pilot provides the necessary elements for the spin, either accidentally or intentionally. The entry procedure for demonstrating a spin is similar to a power-off stall. During the entry, the power should be reduced slowly to idle, while simultaneously raising the nose to a pitch attitude that will ensure a stall. As the airplane approaches a stall, smoothly apply full rudder in the direction of the desired spin rotation while applying full back (up) elevator to the limit of travel. Always maintain the ailerons in the neutral position during the spin procedure unless AFM/POH specifies otherwise.

Incipient Phase

The incipient phase is from the time the airplane stalls and rotation starts until the spin has fully developed. This change may take up to two turns for most aircraft. Incipient spins that are not allowed to develop into a steady-state spin are the most commonly used in the introduction to spin training and recovery techniques. In this phase, the aerodynamic and inertial forces have not achieved a balance. As the incipient spin develops, the indicated airspeed should be near or below stall airspeed, and the turn-and-slip indicator should indicate the direction of the spin.

The incipient spin recovery procedure should be commenced prior to the completion of 360° of rotation. The pilot should apply full rudder opposite the direction of rotation. If the pilot is not sure of the direction of the spin, check the turn-and-slip indicator; it will show a deflection in the direction of rotation.

Developed Phase

The developed phase occurs when the airplane's angular rotation rate, airspeed, and vertical speed are stabilized while in a flightpath that is nearly vertical. This is where airplane aerodynamic forces and inertial forces are in balance, and the attitude, angles, and self-sustaining motions about the vertical axis are constant or repetitive. The spin is in equilibrium.

Recovery Phase

The recovery phase occurs when the angle of attack of the wings decreases below the critical angle of attack and autorotation slows. Then the nose steepens and rotation stops. This phase may last for a quarter turn to several turns.

To recover, control inputs are initiated to disrupt the spin equilibrium by stopping the rotation and stall. To accomplish spin recovery, the manufacturer's recommended procedures should be followed. In the absence of the manufacturer's recommended spin recovery procedures and techniques, the following spin recovery procedures are recommended.

Step 1—REDUCE THE POWER (THROTTLE) TO IDLE. Power aggravates the spin characteristics. It usually results in a flatter spin attitude and increased rotation rates.

Step 2—POSITION THE AILERONS TO NEUTRAL. Ailerons may have an adverse effect on spin recovery. Aileron control in the direction of the spin may speed up the rate of rotation and delay the recovery. Aileron control opposite the direction of the spin may cause the down aileron to move the wing deeper into the stall and aggravate the situation. The best procedure is to ensure that the ailerons are neutral.

Step 3—APPLY FULL OPPOSITE RUDDER AGAINST THE ROTATION. Make sure that full (against the stop) opposite rudder has been applied.

Step 4—APPLY A POSITIVE AND BRISK, STRAIGHT FORWARD MOVEMENT OF THE ELEVATOR CONTROL FORWARD OF THE NEUTRAL TO BREAK THE STALL. This should be done immediately after full rudder application. The forceful movement of the elevator will decrease the excessive angle of attack and break the stall. The controls should be held firmly in this position. When the stall is "broken," the spinning will stop.

Step 5—AFTER SPIN ROTATION STOPS, NEUTRALIZE THE RUDDER. If the rudder is not neutralized at this time, the ensuing increased airspeed acting upon a deflected rudder will cause a yawing or skidding effect.

Slow and overly cautious control movements during spin recovery must be avoided. In certain cases it has been found that such movements result in the airplane continuing to spin indefinitely, even with anti-spin inputs. A brisk and positive technique on the other hand, results in a more positive spin recovery.

Step 6—BEGIN APPLYING BACK-ELEVATOR PRESSURE TO RAISE THE NOSE TO LEVEL FLIGHT. Caution must be used not to apply excessive back-elevator pressure after the rotation stops. Excessive back-elevator pressure can cause a secondary stall and result in another spin. Care should be taken not to exceed the "G" load limits and airspeed limitations during recovery. If the flaps and/or retractable landing gear are extended prior to the spin, they should be retracted as soon as possible after spin entry.

It is important to remember that the above-spin recovery procedures and techniques are recommended for use only in the absence of the manufacturer's procedures. Before any pilot attempts to begin spin training, he or she must be familiar with the procedures provided by the manufacturer for spin recovery.

The most common problems in spin recovery include, pilot confusion as to the direction of spin rotation, and whether the maneuver is a spin versus spiral. If the airspeed is increasing, the airplane is no longer in a spin but in a spiral.

AIRCRAFT LIMITATIONS

The official sources for determining if the spin maneuver IS APPROVED or NOT APPROVED for a specific airplane are:

• Type Certificate Data Sheets or the Aircraft Specifications.
• The limitation section of the FAA-approved AFM/POH. The limitation sections may provide additional specific requirements for spin authorization, such as limiting gross weight, CG range, and amount of fuel.
• On a placard located in clear view of the pilot in the airplane, NO ACROBATIC MANEUVERS INCLUDING SPINS APPROVED. In airplanes placarded against spins, there is no assurance that recovery from a fully developed spin is possible.

WEIGHT AND BALANCE REQUIREMENTS

With each airplane that is approved for spinning, the weight and balance requirements are important for safe performance and recovery from the spin maneuver. Pilots must be aware that just minor weight or balance changes can affect the airplane's spin recovery characteristics. Such changes can either alter or enhance the spin maneuver and/or recovery characteristics. For example, if the addition of weight in the aft baggage compartment, or additional fuel, may still permit the airplane to be operated within CG, it could seriously affect the spin and recovery characteristics.

An airplane that may be difficult to spin intentionally in the Utility Category (restricted aft CG and reduced weight) could have less resistance to spin entry in the Normal Category (less restricted aft CG and increased weight). This situation is due to the airplane being able to generate a higher angle of attack and load factor. Furthermore, an airplane that is approved for spins in the Utility Category, but loaded in the Normal Category, may not recover from a spin that is allowed to progress beyond the incipient phase.

CHAPTER 6

GROUND REFERENCE AND PERFORMANCE MANEUVERS

INTRODUCTION

This chapter describes the flight training maneuvers and related factors that are useful in developing pilot skills. Although most of these maneuvers are not performed in normal everyday flying, the elements and principles are applicable to performance of customary pilot operations. They aid the pilot in analyzing the effect of wind and other forces acting on the airplane and in developing a fine control touch, coordination, and division of attention for accurate and safe maneuvering of the airplane. The pilot should acquire a thorough understanding of the factors involved and the procedures recommended in this chapter.

MANEUVERING BY REFERENCE TO GROUND OBJECTS

Ground track or ground reference maneuvers are performed at a relatively low altitude while applying wind drift correction as needed to follow a predetermined track or path over the ground. They are designed to develop the ability to control the airplane, and to recognize and correct for the effect of wind while dividing attention among other matters. This requires planning ahead of the airplane, maintaining orientation in relation to ground objects, flying appropriate headings to follow a desired ground track, and being cognizant of other air traffic in the immediate vicinity.

The altitude should be low enough to easily recognize drift, but in no case lower than 500 feet above the highest obstruction. The altitude flown should be approximately 600 to 1,000 feet above the ground (the altitude usually required for airport traffic patterns). During these maneuvers, pilots should be alert for available forced-landing fields. The area chosen should be away from communities, livestock, or groups of people to prevent possible annoyance or hazards to others. Due to the altitudes at which these maneuvers are performed, there is little time available to search for a suitable field for landing in the event the need arises.

Drift and Ground Track Control

Whenever any object is free from the ground, it is affected by the medium with which it is surrounded. This means that a free object will move in whatever direction and speed that the medium moves.

For example, if a power boat crossing a river and the river were still, the boat could head directly to a point on the opposite shore and travel on a straight course to that point without drifting. However, if the river were flowing swiftly, the water current would have to be considered. That is, as the boat progresses forward with its own power, it must also move upstream at the same rate the river is moving it downstream. This is accomplished by angling the boat upstream sufficiently to counteract the downstream flow. If this is done, the boat will follow the desired track across the river from the departure point directly to the intended destination point. Should the boat not be headed sufficiently upstream, it would drift with the current and run aground at some point downstream on the opposite bank. [Figure 6-1]

As soon as an airplane becomes airborne, it is free of ground friction. Its path is then affected by the air mass in which it is flying; therefore, the airplane (like the boat) will not always track along the ground in the exact direction that it is headed. When flying with the longitudinal axis of the airplane aligned with a road, it

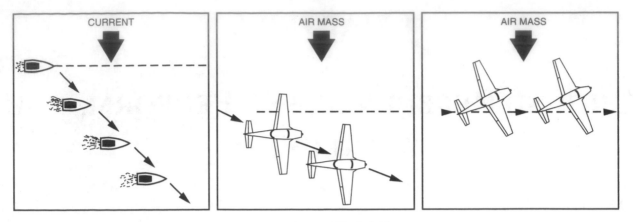

FIGURE 6-1.—Wind drift.

may be noted that the airplane gets closer to or farther from the road without any turn having been made. This would indicate that the air mass is moving sideward in relation to the airplane. Since the airplane is flying within this moving body of air (wind), it moves or drifts with the air in the same direction and speed, just like the boat moved with the river current. [Figure 6-1]

When flying straight and level and following a selected ground track, the preferred method of correcting for wind drift is to head the airplane (wind correction angle) sufficiently into the wind to cause the airplane to move forward into the wind at the same rate the wind is moving it sideways. Depending on the wind velocity, this may require a large wind correction angle or one of only a few degrees. When the drift has been neutralized, the airplane will follow the desired ground track. [Figure 6-1]

To understand the need for drift correction during flight, consider a flight with a wind velocity of 30 knots from the left and 90° to the direction the airplane is headed. After 1 hour, the body of air in which the airplane is flying will have moved 30 nautical miles (NM) to the right. Since the airplane is moving with this body of air, it too will have drifted 30 NM to the right. In relation to the air, the airplane moved forward, but in relation to the ground, it moved forward as well as 30 NM to the right.

There are times when the pilot needs to correct for drift while in a turn. [Figure 6-2] Throughout the turn the wind will be acting on the airplane from constantly changing angles. The relative wind angle and speed govern the time it takes for the airplane to progress through any part of a turn. This is due to the constantly changing groundspeed. When the airplane

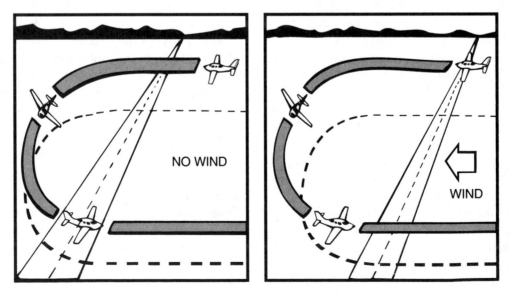

FIGURE 6-2.—Effect of wind during a turn.

is headed into the wind, the groundspeed is decreased; when headed down wind, the groundspeed is increased. Through the crosswind portion of a turn, the airplane must be turned sufficiently into the wind to counteract drift. To follow a desired circular ground track, the wind correction angle must be varied in a timely manner because of the varying groundspeed as the turn progresses. The faster the groundspeed, the faster the wind correction angle must be established; the slower the groundspeed, the slower the wind correction angle may be established. It can be seen then that the steepest bank and fastest rate of turn should be made on the downwind portion of the turn and the shallowest bank and slowest rate of turn on the upwind portion.

The principles and techniques of varying the angle of bank to change the rate of turn and wind correction angle for controlling wind drift during a turn are the same for all ground track maneuvers involving changes in direction of flight.

When there is no wind, it should be simple to fly along a ground track with an arc of exactly 180° and a constant radius because the flightpath and ground track would be identical. This can be demonstrated by approaching a road at a 90° angle and, when directly over the road, rolling into a medium-banked turn, then maintaining the same angle of bank throughout the 180° of turn. [Figure 6-2]

To complete the turn, the rollout should be started at a point where the wings will become level as the airplane again reaches the road at a 90° angle and will be directly over the road just as the turn is completed. This would be possible only if there were absolutely no wind and if the angle of bank and the rate of turn remained constant throughout the entire maneuver.

If the turn were made with a constant angle of bank and a wind blowing directly across the road, it would result in a constant radius turn through the air. However, the wind effects would cause the ground track to be distorted from a constant radius turn or semicircular path. The greater the wind velocity, the greater would be the difference between the desired ground track and the flightpath. To counteract this drift, the flight path can be controlled by the pilot in such a manner as to neutralize the effect of the wind, and cause the ground track to be a constant radius semicircle can control the flightpath.

The effects of wind during turns can be demonstrated after selecting a road, railroad, or other ground reference that forms a straight line parallel to the wind. Fly into the wind directly over and along the line and then make a turn with a constant medium angle of bank for 360° of turn. [Figure 6-3] The airplane will return to a point directly over the line but slightly down wind from the starting point, the amount depending on the wind velocity and the time required to complete the turn. The path over the ground will be an elongated circle, although in reference to the air it is a perfect circle. Straight flight during the upwind segment after completion of the turn is necessary to bring the airplane back to the starting position.

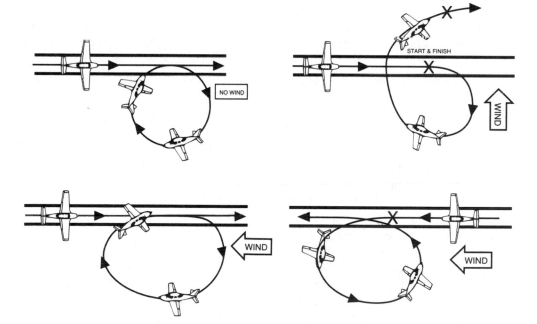

FIGURE 6-3.—Effect of wind during turns.

A similar 360° turn may be started at a specific point over the reference line, with the airplane headed directly down wind. In this demonstration, the effect of wind during the constant banked turn will drift the airplane to a point where the line is reintercepted, but the 360° turn will be completed at a point down wind from the starting point.

Another reference line which lies directly crosswind may be selected and the same procedure repeated, showing that if wind drift is not corrected the airplane will, at the completion of the 360° turn, be headed in the original direction but will have drifted away from the line a distance dependent on the amount of wind.

From these demonstrations, it can be seen where and why it is necessary to increase or decrease the angle of bank and the rate of turn to achieve a desired track over the ground. The principles and techniques involved can be practiced and evaluated by the performance of the ground track maneuvers discussed in this chapter.

Rectangular Course

The rectangular course is a training maneuver in which the ground track of the airplane is equidistant from all sides of a selected rectangular area on the ground. While performing the maneuver, the altitude and airspeed should be held constant.

Like those of other ground track maneuvers, one of the objectives is to develop division of attention between the flightpath and ground references, while controlling the airplane and watching for other aircraft in the vicinity. Another objective is to develop recognition of drift toward or away from a line parallel to the intended ground track. This will be helpful in recognizing drift toward or from an airport runway during the various legs of the airport traffic pattern.

For this maneuver, a square or rectangular field, or an area bounded on four sides by section lines or roads (the sides of which are approximately a mile in length), should be selected well away from other air traffic. [Figure 6-4] The airplane should be flown parallel to and at a uniform distance about one-fourth to one-half mile away from the field boundaries, not above the boundaries. For best results, the flightpath should be positioned outside the field boundaries just far enough that they may be easily observed from either pilot seat by looking out the side of the airplane. If an attempt is made to fly directly above the edges of the field, the pilot will have no usable reference points to start and complete the turns. The closer the track of the airplane is to the field boundaries, the steeper the bank necessary at the turning points. Also, the pilot should be able to see the edges of the selected field while seated in a normal position and looking out the side of the airplane during either a left-hand or right-hand course. The distance of the ground track from the edges of the field should be the same regardless of whether the course is flown to the left or right. All turns should be started when the airplane is abeam the corner of the field boundaries, and the bank normally should not exceed 45°. These should be the determining factors in establishing the distance from the boundaries for performing the maneuver.

Although the rectangular course may be entered from any direction, this discussion assumes entry on a downwind.

On the downwind leg, the wind is a tailwind and results in an increased groundspeed. Consequently, the turn onto the next leg is entered with a fairly fast rate of roll-in with relatively steep bank. As the turn progresses, the bank angle is reduced gradually because the tailwind component is diminishing, resulting in a decreasing groundspeed.

During and after the turn onto this leg (the equivalent of the base leg in a traffic pattern), the wind will tend to drift the airplane away from the field boundary. To compensate for the drift, the amount of turn will be more than 90°.

The rollout from this turn must be such that as the wings become level; the airplane is turned slightly toward the field and into the wind to correct for drift. The airplane should again be the same distance from the field boundary and at the same altitude, as on other legs. The base leg should be continued until the upwind leg boundary is being approached. Once more the pilot should anticipate drift and turning radius. Since drift correction was held on the base leg, it is necessary to turn less than 90° to align the airplane parallel to the upwind leg boundary. This turn should be started with a medium bank angle with a gradual reduction to a shallow bank as the turn progresses. The rollout should be timed to assure paralleling the boundary of the field as the wings become level.

While the airplane is on the upwind leg, the next field boundary should be observed as it is being approached, to plan the turn onto the crosswind leg. Since the wind is a headwind on this leg, it is reducing the airplane's groundspeed and during the turn onto the crosswind leg will try to drift the airplane toward the field. For this reason, the roll-in to the turn must be slow and the bank relatively shallow to counteract this effect. As the turn progresses, the headwind component

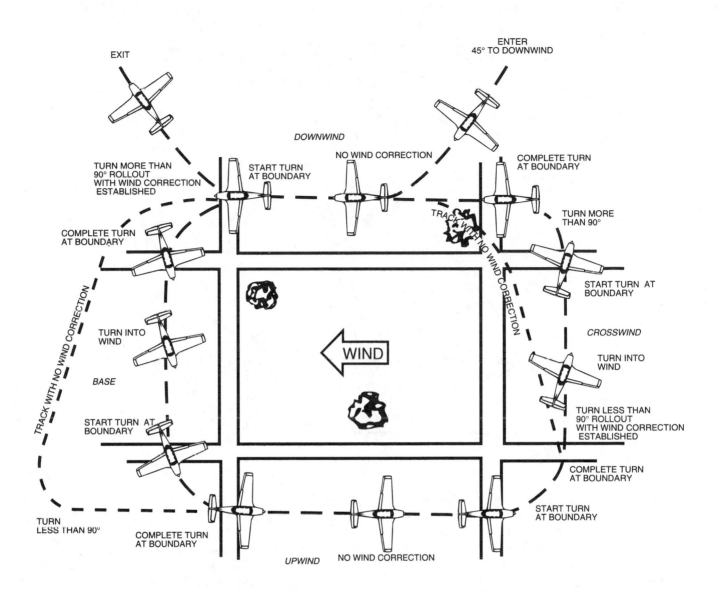

Figure 6-4.—Rectangular course.

decreases, allowing the groundspeed to increase. Consequently, the bank angle and rate of turn is increased gradually to assure that upon completion of the turn the crosswind ground track will continue the same distance from the edge of the field. Completion of the turn with the wings level should be accomplished at a point aligned with the upwind corner of the field.

Simultaneously, as the wings are rolled level, the proper drift correction is established with the airplane turned into the wind. This requires that the turn be less than a 90° change in heading. If the turn has been made properly, the field boundary will again appear to be one-fourth to one-half mile away. While on the crosswind leg, the wind correction angle should be

adjusted as necessary to maintain a uniform distance from the field boundary.

As the next field boundary is being approached, the pilot should plan the turn onto the downwind leg. Since a wind correction angle is being held into the wind and away from the field while on the crosswind leg, this next turn will require a turn of more than 90°. Since the crosswind will become a tailwind, causing the groundspeed to increase during this turn, the bank initially should be medium and progressively increased as the turn proceeds. To complete the turn, the rollout must be timed so that the wings become level at a point aligned with the crosswind corner of the field just as the longitudinal axis of the airplane again becomes

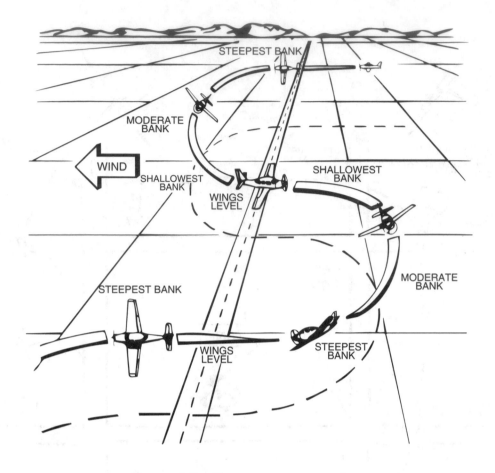

FIGURE 6-5.—S-turns across a road.

parallel to the field boundary. The distance from the field boundary should be the same as from the other sides of the field.

Usually, drift should not be encountered on the upwind or the downwind leg, but it may be difficult to find a situation where the wind is blowing exactly parallel to the field boundaries. This would make it necessary to use a slight wind correction angle on all the legs. It is important to anticipate the turns to correct for groundspeed, drift, and turning radius. When the wind is behind the airplane, the turn must be faster and steeper; when it is ahead of the airplane, the turn must be slower and shallower. These same techniques apply while flying in airport traffic patterns.

S-Turns Across a Road

An S-turn across a road is a practice maneuver in which the airplane's ground track describes semicircles of equal radii on each side of a selected straight line on the ground. [Figure 6-5] The straight line may be a road, fence, railroad, or section line that lies perpendicular to the wind, and should be of sufficient length for making a series of turns. A constant altitude should be maintained throughout the maneuver.

The objectives are to develop the ability to compensate for drift during turns, orient the flightpath with ground references, and divide the pilot's attention. The maneuver consists of crossing the road at a 90° angle and immediately beginning a series of 180° turns of uniform radius in opposite directions, recrossing the road at a 90° angle just as each 180° turn is completed.

To accomplish a constant radius ground track requires a changing roll rate and angle of bank to establish the wind correction angle. Both will increase or decrease as groundspeed increases or decreases.

The bank must be steepest when beginning the turn on the downwind side of the road and must be shallowed gradually as the turn progresses from a downwind heading to an upwind heading. On the upwind side, the turn should be started with a relatively shallow bank and then gradually steepened as the airplane turns from an upwind heading to a downwind heading.

In this maneuver, the airplane should be rolled from one bank directly into the opposite just as the reference line on the ground is crossed.

Before starting the maneuver, a straight ground reference line or road that lies 90° to the direction of the wind should be selected, then the area checked to ensure that no obstructions or other aircraft are in the immediate vicinity. The road should be approached from the upwind side, at the selected altitude on a downwind heading. When directly over the road, the first turn should be started immediately. With the airplane headed down wind, the groundspeed is greatest and the rate of departure from the road will be rapid; so the roll into the steep bank must be fairly rapid to attain the proper wind correction angle. This prevents the airplane from flying too far from the road and from establishing a ground track of excessive radius.

During the latter portion of the first 90° of turn when the airplane's heading is changing from a downwind heading to a crosswind heading, the groundspeed becomes less and the rate of departure from the road decreases. The wind correction angle will be at the maximum when the airplane is headed directly crosswind.

After turning 90°, the airplane's heading becomes more and more an upwind heading, the groundspeed will decrease, and the rate of closure with the road will become slower. If a constant steep bank were maintained, the airplane would turn too quickly for the slower rate of closure, and would be headed perpendicular to the road prematurely. Because of the decreasing groundspeed and rate of closure while approaching the upwind heading, it will be necessary to gradually shallow the bank during the remaining 90° of the semicircle, so that the wind correction angle is removed completely and the wings become level as the 180° turn is completed at the moment the road is reached.

At the instant the road is being crossed again, a turn in the opposite direction should be started. Since the airplane is still flying into the headwind, the groundspeed is relatively slow. Therefore, the turn will have to be started with a shallow bank so as to avoid an excessive rate of turn that would establish the maximum wind correction angle too soon. The degree of bank should be that which is necessary to attain the proper wind correction angle so the ground track describes an arc the same size as the one established on the downwind side.

Since the airplane is turning from an upwind to a downwind heading, the groundspeed will increase and after turning 90°, the rate of closure with the road will increase rapidly. Consequently, the angle of bank and rate of turn must be progressively increased so that the airplane will have turned 180° at the time it reaches the road. Again, the rollout must be timed so the airplane is in straight-and-level flight directly over and perpendicular to the road.

Throughout the maneuver a constant altitude should be maintained, and the bank should be changing constantly to effect a true semicircular ground track.

Often there is a tendency to increase the bank too rapidly during the initial part of the turn on the upwind side, which will prevent the completion of the 180° turn before recrossing the road. This is apparent when the turn is not completed in time for the airplane to cross the road at a perpendicular angle. To avoid this error, the pilot must visualize the desired half circle ground track, and increase the bank during the early part of this turn. During the latter part of the turn, when approaching the road, the pilot must judge the closure rate properly and increase the bank accordingly, so as to cross the road perpendicular to it just as the rollout is completed.

Turns Around a Point

In this training maneuver, the airplane is flown in two or more complete circles of uniform radii or distance from a prominent ground reference point using a maximum bank of approximately 45° while maintaining a constant altitude. Its objective, as in other ground reference maneuvers, is to help the pilot develop the ability to subconsciously control the airplane while dividing attention between the flightpath and ground references and watching for other air traffic in the vicinity.

The factors and principles of drift correction that are involved in S-turns are also applicable in this maneuver. As in other ground track maneuvers, a constant radius around a point will, if any wind exists, require a constantly changing angle of bank and angles of wind correction. The closer the airplane is to a direct downwind heading where the groundspeed is greatest, the steeper the bank and the faster the rate of turn required to establish the proper wind correction angle. The more nearly it is to a direct upwind heading where the groundspeed is least, the shallower the bank and the slower the rate of turn required to establish the proper wind correction angle. It follows, then, that throughout the maneuver the bank and rate of turn must be gradually varied in proportion to the groundspeed.

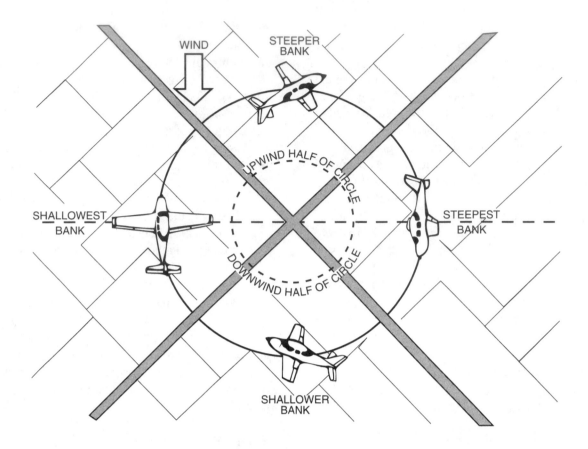

FIGURE 6-6.—*Turns around a point.*

The point selected for turns around a point should be prominent, easily distinguished by the pilot, and yet small enough to present precise reference. [Figure 6-6] Isolated trees, crossroads, or other similar small landmarks are usually suitable.

To enter turns around a point, the airplane should be flown on a downwind heading to one side of the selected point at a distance equal to the desired radius of turn. In a high-wing airplane, the distance from the point must permit the pilot to see the point throughout the maneuver even with the wing lowered in a bank. If the radius is too large, the lowered wing will block the pilot's view of the point.

When any significant wind exists, it will be necessary to roll into the initial bank at a rapid rate so that the steepest bank is attained abeam of the point when the airplane is headed directly down wind. By entering the maneuver while heading directly down wind, the steepest bank can be attained immediately. Thus, if a maximum bank of 45° is desired, the initial bank will be 45° if the airplane is at the correct distance from the point. Thereafter, the bank is shallowed gradually until the point is reached where the airplane is headed directly up wind. At this point, the bank should be gradually steepened until the steepest bank is again attained when heading down wind at the initial point of entry.

Just as S-turns require that the airplane be turned into the wind in addition to varying the bank, so do turns around a point. During the downwind half of the circle, the airplane's nose is progressively turned toward the inside of the circle; during the upwind half, the nose is progressively turned toward the outside. The downwind half of the turn around the point may be compared to the downwind side of the S-turn across a road; the upwind half of the turn around a point may be compared to the upwind side of the S-turn across a road.

As the pilot becomes experienced in performing turns around a point and has a good understanding of the effects of wind drift and varying of the bank angle and wind correction angle as required, entry into the maneuver may be from any point. When entering this maneuver at any point, the radius of the turn should be carefully selected, taking into account the wind velocity and groundspeed so that an excessive bank is not required later on to maintain the proper ground track.

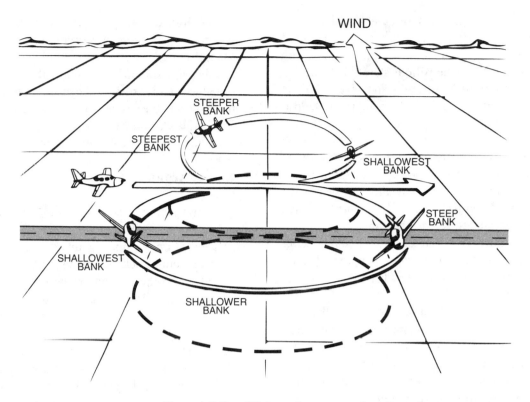

FIGURE 6-7.—Eights along a road.

Eights Along a Road

An eight along a road is a maneuver in which the ground track consists of two complete adjacent circles of equal radii on each side of a straight road or other reference line on the ground. The ground track resembles a figure 8. [Figure 6-7] Like the other ground reference maneuvers, its objective is to develop division of attention while compensating for drift, maintaining orientation with ground references, and maintaining a constant altitude.

Although eights along a road may be performed with the wind blowing parallel to the road or directly across the road, for simplification purposes, only the latter situation is explained since the principles involved in either case are common.

A reference line or road which is perpendicular to the wind should be selected and the airplane flown parallel to and directly above the road. Since the wind is blowing across the flightpath, the airplane will require some wind correction angle to stay directly above the road during the initial straight and level portion. Before starting the maneuver, the area should be checked to ensure clearance of obstructions and avoidance of other aircraft.

Usually, the first turn should be made toward a downwind heading starting with a medium bank. Since the airplane will be turning more and more directly down wind, the groundspeed will be gradually increasing and the rate of departing the road will tend to become faster. Thus, the bank and rate of turn is increased to establish a wind correction angle to keep the airplane from exceeding the desired distance from the road when 180° of change in direction is completed. The steepest bank is attained when the airplane is headed directly down wind.

As the airplane completes 180° of change in direction, it will be flying parallel to and using a wind correction angle toward the road with the wind acting directly perpendicular to the ground track. At this point, the pilot should visualize the remaining 180° of ground track required to return to the same place over the road from which the maneuver started.

While the turn is continued toward an upwind heading, the wind will tend to keep the airplane from reaching the road, with a decrease in groundspeed and rate of closure. The rate of turn and wind correction angle is decreased proportionately so that the road will be reached just as the 360° turn is completed. To accomplish this, the bank is decreased so that when headed directly up wind, it will be at the shallowest angle. In the last 90° of the turn, the bank may be varied to correct any previous errors in judging the returning rate and closure rate. The rollout should be timed so that the airplane will be straight and level over the starting point, with enough drift correction to hold it over the road.

After momentarily flying straight and level along the road, the airplane is then rolled into a medium bank turn in the opposite direction to begin the circle on the upwind side of the road. The wind will still be decreasing the groundspeed and trying to drift the airplane back toward the road; therefore, the bank must be decreased slowly during the first 90° change in direction in order to reach the desired distance from the road and attain the proper wind correction angle when 180° change in direction has been completed.

As the remaining 180° of turn continues, the wind becomes more of a tailwind and increases the airplane's groundspeed. This causes the rate of closure to become faster; consequently, the angle of bank and rate of turn is increased further to attain sufficient wind correction angle to keep the airplane from approaching the road too rapidly. The bank will be at its steepest angle when the airplane is headed directly down wind.

In the last 90° of the turn, the rate of turn should be reduced to bring the airplane over the starting point on the road. The rollout must be timed so the airplane will be straight and level, turned into the wind, and flying parallel to and over the road.

Eights Across a Road

This maneuver is a variation of eights along a road and involves the same principles and techniques. The primary difference is that at the completion of each loop of the figure eight, the airplane should cross an intersection of roads or a specific point on a straight road. [Figure 6-8] The loops should be across the road and the wind should be perpendicular to the road. Each time the road is crossed, the crossing angle should be the same and the wings of the airplane should be level. The eights also may be performed by rolling from one bank immediately to the other, directly over the road.

Eights Around Pylons

This training maneuver is an application of the same principles and techniques of correcting for wind drift as used in turns around a point and the same objectives as other ground track maneuvers. In this case, two points or pylons on the ground are used as references, and turns around each pylon are made in opposite directions to follow a ground track in the form of a figure 8. [Figure 6-9] The pattern involves flying down wind between the pylons and up wind outside of the pylons. It may include a short period of straight-and-level flight while proceeding diagonally from one pylon to the other.

The pylons selected should be on a line 90° to the direction of the wind and should be in an area away from communities, livestock, or groups of people, to avoid possible annoyance or hazards to others. The area selected should be clear of hazardous obstructions and other air traffic. Throughout the maneuver a constant altitude of at least 500 feet above the ground should be maintained.

The eight should be started with the airplane on a downwind heading when passing between the pylons. The distance between the pylons and the wind velocity will determine the initial angle of bank required to maintain a constant radius from the pylons during each turn. The steepest banks will be necessary just after

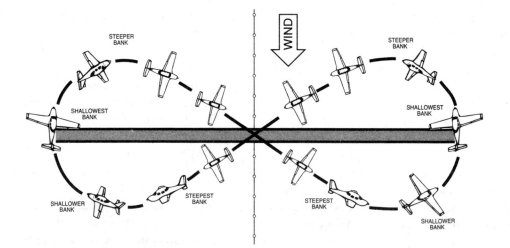

FIGURE 6-8.—Eights across a road.

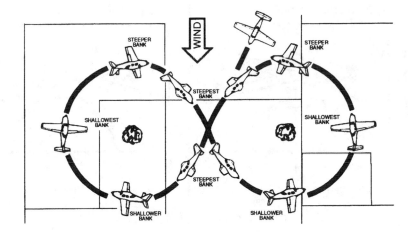

FIGURE 6-9.—Eights around pylons.

each turn entry and just before the rollout from each turn where the airplane is headed down wind and the groundspeed is greatest; the shallowest banks will be when the airplane is headed directly up wind and the groundspeed is least.

The rate of bank change will depend on the wind velocity, the same as it does in S-turns and turns around a point, and the bank will be changing continuously during the turns. The adjustment of the bank angle should be gradual from the steepest bank to the shallowest bank as the airplane progressively heads into the wind, followed by a gradual increase until the steepest bank is again reached just prior to rollout. If the airplane is to proceed diagonally from one turn to the other, the rollout from each turn must be completed on the proper heading with sufficient wind correction angle to ensure that after brief straight-and-level flight, the airplane will arrive at the point where a turn of the same radius can be made around the other pylon. The straight-and-level flight segments must be tangent to both circular patterns.

Eights-on-Pylons (Pylon Eights)

The eights-on-pylons is an advanced training maneuver that provides practice in developing coordination skills while the pilot's attention is directed at maintaining a pivotal position on a selected pylon.

This training maneuver also involves flying the airplane in circular paths, alternately left and right, in the form of a figure 8 around two selected points or pylons on the ground. In this case, no attempt is made to maintain a uniform distance from the pylon. Instead, the airplane is flown at such an altitude and airspeed that a line parallel to the airplane's lateral axis, and extending from the pilot's eye, appears to pivot on each of the pylons. [Figure 6-10] The altitude that is appropriate for the airplane being flown is called the

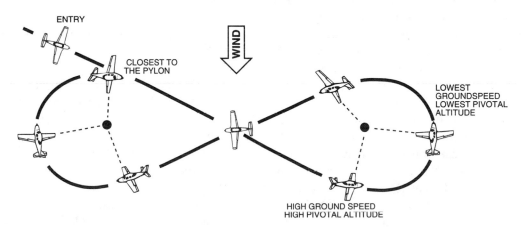

FIGURE 6-10.—Eights-on-pylons.

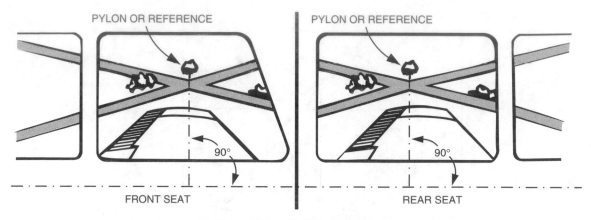

PYLON OR REFERENCE

90°

FRONT SEAT

PYLON OR REFERENCE

90°

REAR SEAT

FIGURE 6-11.—Pylon position.

pivotal altitude and is governed by the groundspeed. While not truly a ground track maneuver as were the preceding maneuvers, the objective is similar—to develop the ability to maneuver the airplane accurately while dividing one's attention between the flightpath and the selected points on the ground.

In explaining the performance of eights-on-pylons, the term "wingtip" is frequently considered as being synonymous with the proper reference line, or pivot point on the airplane. This interpretation is not always correct. High-wing, low-wing, sweptwing, and taper-wing airplanes, as well as those with tandem or side-by-side seating, will all present different angles from the pilot's eye to the wingtip. [Fig. 6-11] Therefore, in the correct performance of eights-on-pylons, as in other maneuvers requiring a lateral reference, the pilot should use a sighting reference line that, from eye level, parallels the lateral axis of the airplane.

The sighting point or line, while not necessarily on the wingtip itself, may be positioned in relation to the wingtip (ahead, behind, above, or below), but even then it will differ for each pilot, and from each seat in the airplane. This is especially true in tandem (fore and aft) seat airplanes. In side-by-side type airplanes, there will be very little variation in the sighting lines for different persons if those persons are seated so that the eyes of each are at approximately the same level.

An explanation of the pivotal altitude is also essential. There is a specific altitude at which, when the airplane turns at a given groundspeed, a projection of the sighting reference line to the selected point on the ground will appear to pivot on that point. Since different airplanes fly at different airspeeds, the groundspeed will be different. [Figure 6-12] Therefore, each airplane will have its own pivotal altitude. The pivotal altitude does not vary with the angle of bank

being used unless the bank is steep enough to affect the groundspeed. A rule of thumb for estimating pivotal altitude in calm wind is to square the true airspeed and divide by 15 for miles per hour (MPH) or 11.3 for knots.

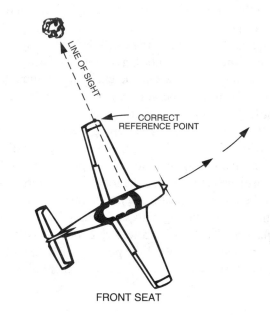

LINE OF SIGHT

CORRECT REFERENCE POINT

FRONT SEAT

FIGURE 6-12.—Looking parallel to the lateral axis.

Distance from the pylon affects the angle of bank. At any altitude above that pivotal altitude, the projected reference line will appear to move rearward in a circular path in relation to the pylon. Conversely, when the airplane is below the pivotal altitude, the projected reference line will appear to move forward in a circular path.

To demonstrate this, the airplane is flown at normal cruising speed , and at an altitude estimated to be below the proper pivotal altitude, and then placed in a medium-banked turn. It will be seen that the projected reference line of sight appears to move forward along the ground as the airplane turns.

A climb is then made to an altitude well above the pivotal altitude, and when the airplane is again at normal cruising speed, it is placed in a medium-banked turn. At this higher altitude, the projected reference line of sight now appears to move backward across the ground in a direction opposite that of flight.

After the high altitude extreme has been demonstrated, the power is reduced, and a descent at cruising speed begun in a continuing medium bank around the pylon. The apparent backward travel of the projected reference line with respect to the pylon will slow down as altitude is lost, stop for an instant, then start to reverse itself, and would move forward if the descent were allowed to continue below the pivotal altitude.

The altitude at which the line of sight apparently ceased to move across the ground was the pivotal altitude. If the airplane descended below the pivotal altitude, power should be added to maintain airspeed while altitude is regained to the point at which the projected reference line moves neither backward nor forward but actually pivots on the pylon. In this way the pilot can determine the pivotal altitude of the airplane. [Figure 6-13]

The pivotal altitude is critical and will change with variations in groundspeed. Since the headings throughout the turns continually vary from directly down wind to directly up wind, the groundspeed will constantly change. This will result in the proper pivotal altitude varying slightly throughout the eight. Therefore, adjustment is made for this by climbing or descending, as necessary, to hold the reference line or point on the pylons. This change in altitude will be dependent on how much the wind affects the groundspeed.

Before beginning the maneuver, select two points on the ground along a line which lies 90° to the direction of the wind. The area in which the maneuver is to be performed should be checked for obstructions and any other air traffic, and it should be located where a disturbance to groups of people, livestock, or communities will not result.

The selection of proper pylons is of importance to good eight-on-pylons. They should be sufficiently prominent to be readily seen by the pilot when completing the turn around one pylon and heading for the next, and should be adequately spaced to provide time for planning the turns and yet not cause unnecessary straight-and-level flight between the pylons. Approximately 3 to 5 seconds of straight-and-level flight should be sufficient for checking the area properly before entering the next turn.

For uniformity, the eight is usually begun by flying diagonally crosswind between the pylons to a point down wind from the first pylon so that the first turn can be made into the wind.

As the airplane approaches a position where the pylon appears to be just ahead of the wingtip, the turn should be started by lowering the upwind wing to place the pilot's line of sight reference on the pylon. As the turn is continued, the line of sight reference can be held on the pylon by gradually increasing the bank. The reference line should appear to pivot on the pylon. As the airplane heads into the wind, the groundspeed decreases; consequently, the pivotal altitude is lower and the airplane must descend to hold the reference line on the pylon. As the turn progresses on the upwind side of the pylon, the wind becomes more of a crosswind and drifts the airplane closer to the pylon. Since a constant distance from the pylon is not required on this maneuver, no correction to counteract drifting should be applied. Therefore, with the airplane drifting closer to the pylon, the angle of bank is increased to hold the reference line on the pylon.

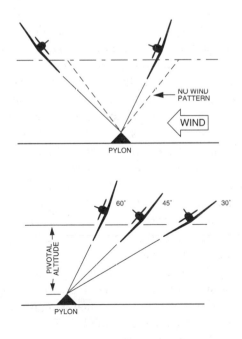

FIGURE 6-13.—Determining proper pivotal altitude of the airplane.

If the reference line appears to move ahead of the pylon, the pilot should increase altitude. If the reference line appears to move behind the pylon, the pilot should decrease altitude. Varying rudder pressure to yaw the airplane and force the wing and reference line forward or backward to the pylon is a dangerous technique and must not be attempted.

As the airplane turns toward a downwind heading, the rollout from the turn should be started to allow the airplane to proceed diagonally to a point on the downwind side of the second pylon. The rollout must be completed in the proper wind correction angle to correct for wind drift, so that the airplane will arrive at a point down wind from the second pylon the same distance it was from the first pylon at the beginning of the maneuver.

Upon reaching that point, a turn is started in the opposite direction by lowering the upwind wing to again place the pilot's line of sight reference on the pylon. The turn is then continued just as in the turn around the first pylon but in the opposite direction.

The most common error in attempting to hold a pylon is incorrect use of the rudder. When the projection of the reference line moves forward with respect to the pylon, many pilots will tend to press the inside rudder to yaw the wing backward. When the reference line moves behind the pylon, they will press the outside rudder to yaw the wing forward. The rudder is to be used only as a coordination control.

PERFORMANCE MANEUVERS

Performance maneuvers are useful in developing a high degree of pilot skill. Although most of these maneuvers are not performed during everyday flying, they aid the pilot in analyzing the forces acting on the airplane and in developing a fine control touch, coordination, and division of attention for accurate and safe maneuvering of the airplane. Therefore, the pilot should acquire a thorough understanding of the factors involved and the techniques recommended.

Steep Turns

The objective of the maneuver is to develop smoothness, coordination, orientation, division of attention, and control techniques while executing high performance turns.

The steep turn maneuver consists of a turn in either direction, using a bank angle between 45 to 60°. This will cause an overbanking tendency during which maximum turning performance is attained and relatively high load factors are imposed. Because of the high load factors imposed, these turns should be performed at an airspeed does not exceed the airplane's design that maneuvering speed (V_A). The principles of an ordinary steep turn apply, but as a practice maneuver the steep turns should be continued until 360° or 720° of turn have been completed. [Figure 6-14]

An airplane's maximum turning performance is its fastest rate of turn and its shortest radius of turn, that change with both airspeed and angle of bank. Each airplane's turning performance is limited by the amount of power its engine is developing, its limit load factor (structural strength), and its aerodynamic characteristics.

The limiting load factor determines the maximum bank which can be maintained without stalling or exceeding the airplane's structural limitations. In most small planes, the maximum bank has been found to be approximately 50 to 60°.

The pilot should realize the tremendous additional load that is imposed on an airplane as the bank is increased beyond 45°. During a coordinated turn with a 70° bank, a load factor of approximately 3-G's is placed on the airplane's structure. Most general aviation type airplanes are stressed for approximately 3.8-G's.

Regardless of the airspeed or the type of airplanes involved, a given angle of bank in a turn, during which altitude is maintained will always produce the same load factor. Pilots must be aware that an additional load factor increases the stalling speed at a significant rate— stalling speed increases with the square root of the load factor. For example, a light plane that stalls at 60 knots in level flight will stall at nearly 85 knots in a 60° bank. The pilot's understanding and observance of this fact is an indispensable safety precaution for the performance of all maneuvers requiring turns.

Before starting the steep turn, the pilot should ensure that the area is clear of other air traffic since the rate of turn will be quite rapid. After establishing the manufacturer's recommended entry speed or the design maneuvering speed, the airplane should be smoothly rolled into a selected bank angle between 45 to 60°. As the turn is being established, back-elevator pressure should be smoothly increased to increase the angle of attack. This provides the additional wing lift required to compensate for the increasing load factor.

After the selected bank angle has been reached, the pilot will find that considerable force is required on the elevator control to hold the airplane in level flight—

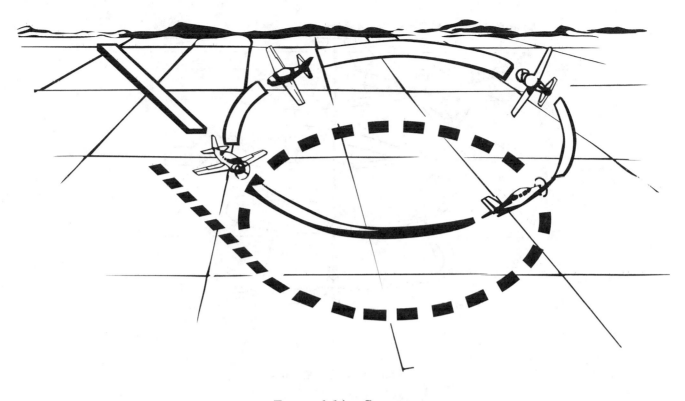

FIGURE 6-14.—Steep turns.

to maintain altitude. Because of this increase in the force applied to the elevators, the load factor increases rapidly as the bank is increased. Additional back-elevator pressure increases the angle of attack, which results in an increase in drag. Consequently, power must be added to maintain the entry altitude and airspeed.

Eventually, as the bank approaches the airplane's maximum angle, the maximum performance or structural limit is being reached. If this limit is exceeded, the airplane will be subjected to excessive structural loads, and will lose altitude, or stall. The limit load factor must not be exceeded, to prevent structural damage.

During the turn, the pilot should not stare at any one object. To maintain altitude, as well as orientation, requires an awareness of the relative position of the nose, the horizon, the wings, and the amount of bank. The pilot who references the aircraft's turn by watching only the nose will have trouble holding altitude constant; on the other hand, the pilot who watches the nose, the horizon, and the wings can usually hold altitude within a few feet. If the altitude begins to increase, or decrease, relaxing or increasing the back-elevator pressure will be required as appropriate. This may also require a power adjustment to maintain the selected airspeed. A small increase or decrease of 1 to 3° of bank angle may be used to control small altitude deviations. All bank angle changes should be done with coordinated use of aileron and rudder.

The rollout from the turn should be timed so that the wings reach level flight when the airplane is exactly on the heading from which the maneuver was started. While the recovery is being made, back-elevator pressure is gradually released and power reduced, as necessary, to maintain the altitude and airspeed.

Steep Spiral

A steep spiral is nothing more than a constant gliding turn, during which a constant radius around a point on the ground is maintained similar to the maneuver, turns around a point. The radius should be such that the steepest bank will not exceed 60°. The objective of the maneuver is to improve pilot techniques for power-off turns, wind drift control, planning, orientation, and division of attention. This spiral is not only a valuable flight training maneuver, but it has practical application in providing a procedure for dissipating altitude while remaining over a selected spot in preparation for landing, especially for emergency forced landings.

Sufficient altitude must be obtained before starting this maneuver so that the spiral may be continued through a series of at least three 360° turns.

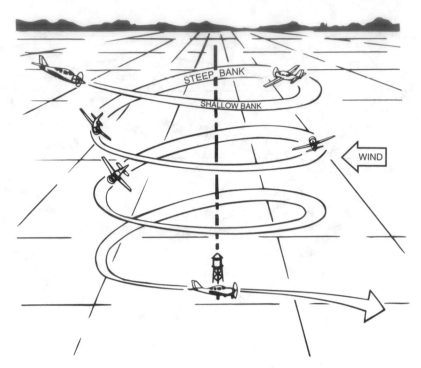

FIGURE 6-15.—Steep spiral.

[Figure 6-15] The maneuver should not be continued below 1,000 feet above the surface unless performing an emergency landing in conjunction with the spiral.

Operating the engine at idle speed for a prolonged period during the glide may result in excessive engine cooling or spark plug fouling. The engine should be cleared periodically by briefly advancing the throttle to normal cruise power, while adjusting the pitch attitude to maintain a constant airspeed. Preferably, this should be done while headed into the wind to minimize any variation in groundspeed and radius of turn.

After the throttle is closed and gliding speed is established, a gliding spiral should be started and a turn of constant radius maintained around the selected spot on the ground. This will require correction for wind drift by steepening the bank on downwind headings and shallowing the bank on upwind headings, just as in the maneuver turns around a point. During the descending spiral, the pilot must judge the direction and speed of the wind at different altitudes and make appropriate changes in the angle of bank to maintain a uniform radius.

A constant airspeed should also be maintained throughout the maneuver. Failure to hold the airspeed constant will cause the radius of turn and necessary angle of bank to vary excessively. On the downwind side of the maneuver, the steeper the bank angle the lower the pitch attitude must be to maintain a given airspeed. Conversely, on the upwind side, as the bank angle becomes shallower, the pitch attitude must be raised to maintain the proper airspeed. This is necessary because the airspeed tends to change as the bank is changed from shallow to steep to shallow.

During practice of the maneuver, the pilot should execute three turns and roll out toward a definite object or on a specific heading. During the rollout, smoothness is essential, and the use of controls must be so coordinated that no increase or decrease of speed results when the straight glide is resumed.

Chandelle

The objective of this maneuver is to develop the pilot's coordination, orientation, planning, and feel for maximum performance flight, and to develop positive control techniques at varying airspeeds and attitudes.

A chandelle is a climbing turn beginning from approximately straight-and-level flight, and ending at the completion of 180° of turn in a wings-level, nose-high attitude at the minimum controllable airspeed. [Figure 6-16] The maneuver demands that the maximum flight performance of the airplane be obtained; the airplane should gain the most altitude possible for a given degree of bank and power setting without stalling. Since numerous atmospheric variables beyond control of the pilot will affect the specific amount of altitude gained, the altitude gain is not a criterion of the quality of the maneuver.

CHANDELLE

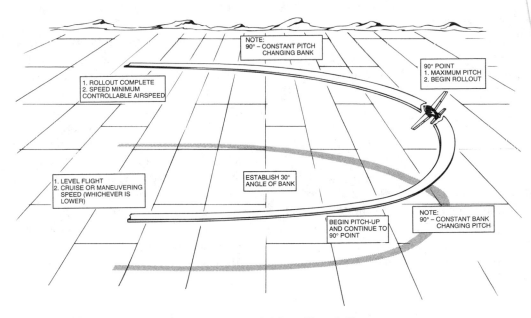

FIGURE 6-16.—Chandelle.

Prior to starting a chandelle, the flaps and gear (if retractable) should be in the UP position, power set to cruise condition, and the airspace behind and above clear of other air traffic. The maneuver should be entered from straight and level and at any speed no greater than the maximum entry speed recommended by the manufacturer—in most cases not above the airplane's design maneuvering speed.

After the appropriate airspeed and power setting have been established, the chandelle is started by smoothly entering a coordinated turn with an angle of bank appropriate for the airplane being flown. Normally, this angle of bank should not exceed approximately 30°. After the appropriate bank is established, a climbing turn should be started by smoothly applying back-elevator pressure to increase the pitch attitude at a constant rate and to attain the highest pitch attitude as 90° of turn is completed. As the climb is initiated in airplanes with fixed-pitch propellers, full throttle may be applied, but is applied gradually so that the maximum allowable RPM is not exceeded. In airplanes with constant-speed propellers, power may be left at the normal cruise setting.

Once the bank has been established, the angle of bank should remain constant until 90° of turn is completed. Although the degree of bank is fixed during this climbing turn, it may appear to increase and, in fact, actually will tend to increase if allowed to do so as the maneuver continues.

When the turn has progressed 90° from the original heading, the pilot should begin rolling out of the bank at a constant rate while maintaining a constant-pitch attitude. Since the angle of bank will be decreasing during the rollout, the vertical component of lift will increase slightly. For this reason, it may be necessary to release a slight amount of back-elevator pressure in order to keep the nose of the airplane from rising higher.

As the wings are being leveled at the completion of 180° of turn, the pitch attitude should be noted by checking the outside references and the attitude indicator. This pitch attitude should be held momentarily while the airplane is at the minimum controllable airspeed. Then the pitch attitude may be gently reduced to return to straight-and-level cruise flight.

Since the airspeed is constantly decreasing throughout the maneuver, the effects of engine torque become more and more prominent. Therefore, right-rudder pressure is gradually increased to control yaw and maintain a constant rate of turn and to keep the airplane in coordinated flight. The pilot should maintain coordinated flight by the feel of pressures being applied on the controls and by the ball instrument of the turn-and-slip indicator. If coordinated flight is being maintained, the ball will remain in the center of the race.

To roll out of a left chandelle, the left aileron must be lowered to raise the left wing. This creates more drag than the aileron on the right wing, resulting in a tendency for the airplane to yaw to the left. With the low airspeed at this point, torque effect tries to make the airplane yaw to the left even more. Thus, there are two forces pulling the airplane's nose to the left—aileron drag and torque. To maintain coordinated flight, considerable right-rudder pressure is required during the rollout to overcome the effects of aileron drag and torque.

In a chandelle to the right, when control pressure is applied to begin the rollout, the aileron on the right wing is lowered. This creates more drag on that wing and tends to make the airplane yaw to the right. At the same time, the effect of torque at the lower airspeed is causing the airplane's nose to yaw to the left. Thus, aileron drag pulling the nose to the right and torque pulling to the left, tend to neutralize each other. If excessive left-rudder pressure is applied, the rollout will be uncoordinated.

The rollout to the left can usually be accomplished with very little left rudder, since the effects of aileron drag and torque tend to neutralize each other. Releasing some right rudder, which has been applied to correct for torque, will normally give the same effect as applying left-rudder pressure. When the wings become level and the ailerons are neutralized, the aileron drag disappears. Because of the low airspeed and high power, the effects of torque become the more prominent force and must continue to be controlled with rudder pressure.

A rollout to the left is accomplished mainly by applying aileron pressure. During the rollout, right-rudder pressure should be gradually released, and left rudder applied only as necessary to maintain coordination. Even when the wings are level and aileron pressure is released, right-rudder pressure must be held to counteract torque and hold the nose straight.

Lazy Eight

The objective of the lazy eight is to develop the pilot's feel for varying control forces, and the ability to plan and remain oriented while maneuvering the airplane with positive, accurate control. It requires constantly changing control pressures necessitated by changing combinations of climbing and descending turns at varying airspeeds. This is a maneuver often used to develop and demonstrate the pilot's mastery of the airplane in maximum performance flight situations.

This maneuver derives its name from the manner in which the extended longitudinal axis of the airplane is made to trace a flight pattern in the form of a figure 8 lying on its side (a lazy 8). [Figure 6-17]

A lazy eight consists of two 180° turns, in opposite directions, while making a climb and a descent in a symmetrical pattern during each of the turns. At no time throughout the lazy eight is the airplane flown straight and level; instead, it is rolled directly from one bank to the other with the wings level only at the moment the turn is reversed at the completion of each 180° change in heading.

As an aid to making symmetrical loops of the 8 during each turn, prominent reference points should be selected on the horizon. The reference points selected should be 45°, 90°, and 135° from the direction in which the maneuver is begun.

Prior to performing a lazy eight, the airspace behind and above should be clear of other air traffic. The maneuver should be entered from straight-and-level flight at normal cruise power and at the airspeed recommended by the manufacturer or at the airplane's design maneuvering speed.

The maneuver is started from level flight with a gradual climbing turn in the direction of the 45° reference point. The climbing turn should be planned and controlled so that the maximum pitchup attitude is reached at the 45° point. The rate of rolling into the bank must be such as to prevent the rate of turn from becoming too rapid. As the pitch attitude is raised, the airspeed decreases, causing the rate of turn to increase. Since the bank also is being increased, it too causes the rate of turn to increase. Unless the maneuver is begun with a slow rate of roll, the combination of increasing pitch and increasing bank will cause the rate of turn to be so rapid that the 45° reference point will be reached before the highest pitch attitude is attained.

At the 45° point, the pitch attitude should be at maximum and the angle of bank continuing to increase. Also, at the 45° point, the pitch attitude should start to decrease slowly toward the horizon and the 90° reference point. Since the airspeed is still decreasing, right-rudder pressure will have to be applied to counteract torque.

As the airplane's nose is being lowered toward the 90° reference point, the bank should continue to increase. Due to the decreasing airspeed, a slight amount of opposite aileron pressure may be required to prevent the bank from becoming too steep. When the airplane completes 90° of the turn, the bank should be at the maximum angle (approximately 30°), the airspeed should be at its minimum (5 to 10 knots above stall speed), and the airplane pitch attitude should be passing through level flight. It is at this time that an imaginary line, extending from the pilot's eye and parallel to the longitudinal axis of the airplane, passes through the 90° reference point.

LAZY EIGHT

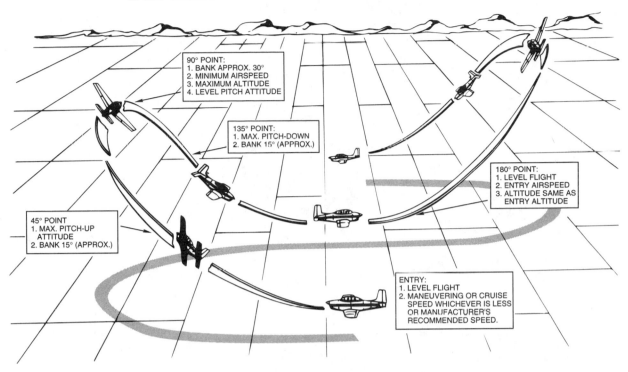

90° POINT:
1. BANK APPROX. 30°
2. MINIMUM AIRSPEED
3. MAXIMUM ALTITUDE
4. LEVEL PITCH ATTITUDE

135° POINT:
1. MAX. PITCH-DOWN
2. BANK 15° (APPROX.)

180° POINT:
1. LEVEL FLIGHT
2. ENTRY AIRSPEED
3. ALTITUDE SAME AS ENTRY ALTITUDE

45° POINT
1. MAX. PITCH-UP ATTITUDE
2. BANK 15° (APPROX.)

ENTRY:
1. LEVEL FLIGHT
2. MANEUVERING OR CRUISE SPEED WHICHEVER IS LESS OR MANUFACTURER'S RECOMMENDED SPEED.

FIGURE 6-17. Lazy eight.

Lazy eights normally should be performed with no more than approximately a 30° bank. Steeper banks may be used, but control touch and technique must be developed to a much higher degree than when the maneuver is performed with a shallower bank.

The pilot should not hesitate at this point but should continue to fly the airplane into a descending turn so that the airplane's nose describes the same size loop below the horizon as it did above. As the pilot's reference line passes through the 90° point, the bank should be decreased gradually, and the airplane's nose allowed to continue lowering. When the airplane has turned 135°, the nose should be in its lowest pitch attitude. The airspeed will be increasing during this descending turn, so it will be necessary to gradually relax rudder and aileron pressure and to simultaneously raise the nose and roll the wings level. As this is being accomplished, the pilot should note the amount of turn remaining and adjust the rate of rollout and pitch change so that the wings become level and the original airspeed is attained in level flight just as the 180° point is reached. Upon returning to the starting altitude and the 180° point, a climbing turn should be started immediately in the opposite direction toward the selected reference points

to complete the second half of the eight in the same manner as the first half.

Due to the decreasing airspeed, considerable right-rudder pressure is gradually applied to counteract torque at the top of the eight in both the right and left turns. The pressure will be greatest at the point of lowest airspeed.

More right-rudder pressure will be needed during the climbing turn to the right than in the turn to the left because more torque correction is needed to prevent yaw from decreasing the rate of turn. In the left climbing turn, the torque will tend to contribute to the turn; consequently, less rudder pressure is needed. It will be noted that the controls are slightly crossed in the right climbing turn because of the need for left aileron pressure to prevent overbanking and right rudder to overcome torque.

The correct power setting for the lazy eight is that which will maintain the altitude for the maximum and minimum airspeeds used during the climbs and descents of the eight. Obviously, if excess power were used, the airplane would have gained altitude when the maneuver is completed, if insufficient power were used, altitude would have been lost.

CHAPTER 7

AIRPORT TRAFFIC PATTERNS, APPROACHES, AND LANDINGS

INTRODUCTION

This chapter explains the methods and factors that affect safety and the flow of air traffic, approaches, and landings at airports. This chapter also discusses the traffic pattern, approaches, and landings for both normal and abnormal circumstances. This chapter also provides the recommended procedures for a proper pattern approach and landing, so that pilots may better understand the factors that will influence their judgment and performance.

AIRPORT TRAFFIC PATTERNS AND OPERATIONS

Just as roads and streets are needed in order to utilize automobiles, airports or airstrips are needed to utilize airplanes. Every flight begins and ends at an airport or other suitable landing field. For that reason, it is essential that the pilot learn the traffic rules, traffic procedures, and traffic pattern layouts that may be in use at various airports.

When an automobile is driven on congested city streets, it can be brought to a stop to give way to conflicting traffic; however, an airplane can only be slowed down. Consequently, specific traffic patterns and traffic control procedures have been established at designated airports. The traffic patterns provide specific routes for takeoffs, departures, arrivals, and landings. The exact nature of each airport traffic pattern is dependent on the runway in use, wind conditions, obstructions, and other factors.

Control towers and radar facilities provide a means of adjusting the flow of arriving and departing aircraft, and render assistance to pilots in busy terminal areas. Airport lighting and runway marking systems are used frequently to alert pilots to abnormal conditions and hazards, so arrivals and departures can be made safely.

Airports vary in complexity from small grass or sod strips to major terminals having many paved runways and taxiways. Regardless of the type of airport, the pilot must know and abide by the rules and general operating procedures applicable to the airport being used. These rules and procedures are based not only on logic or common sense, but also on courtesy, and their objective is to keep air traffic moving with maximum safety and efficiency. The use of any traffic pattern, service, or procedure does not alter the responsibility of pilots to see and avoid other aircraft.

Airport Traffic Patterns

To assure that air traffic flows into and out of an airport in an orderly manner, an airport traffic pattern is established appropriate to the local conditions, including the direction and placement of the pattern, the altitude to be flown, and the procedures for entering and leaving the pattern. Unless the airport displays approved visual markings indicating that turns should be made to the right, the pilot should make all turns in the pattern to the left.

When operating at an airport with an operating control tower, the pilot receives, by radio, a clearance to approach or depart, as well as pertinent information about the traffic pattern. If there is not a control tower, it is the pilot's responsibility to determine the direction of the traffic pattern, to comply with the appropriate traffic rules, and to display common courtesy toward other pilots operating in the area.

The pilot is not expected to have extensive knowledge of all traffic patterns at all airports, but if the pilot is familiar with the basic rectangular pattern, it will be easy to make proper approaches and departures from most airports, regardless of whether they have control towers. At airports with operating control

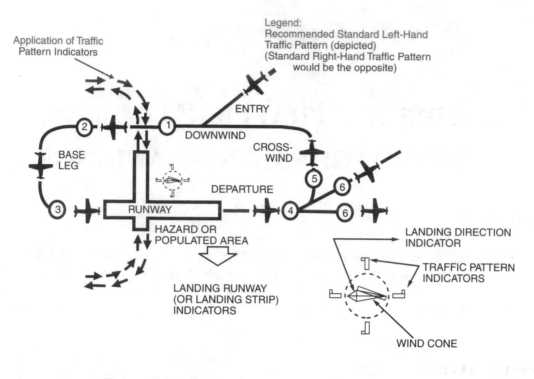

FIGURE 7-1.—Standard rectangular traffic pattern.

towers, the tower operator may instruct pilots to enter the traffic pattern at any point or to make a straight-in approach without flying the usual rectangular pattern. Many other deviations are possible if the tower operator and the pilot work together in an effort to keep traffic moving smoothly. Jets or heavy airplanes will frequently be flying wider and/or higher patterns than lighter airplanes, and in many cases will make a straight-in approach for landing.

Compliance with the basic rectangular traffic pattern reduces the possibility of conflicts at airports without an operating control tower. It is imperative that the pilot form the habit of exercising constant vigilance in the vicinity of airports even though the air traffic appears to be light.

The standard rectangular traffic pattern is illustrated in Figure 7-1. The traffic pattern altitude is usually 1,000 feet above the elevation of the airport surface. The use of a common altitude at a given airport is the key factor in minimizing the risk of collisions at airports without operating control towers.

It is recommended that while operating in the traffic pattern at an airport without an operating control tower the pilot maintain an airspeed that conforms with the limits established by Title 14 of the Code of Federal Regulations (14 CFR) part 91 for such an airport: no more than 200 knots (230 miles per hour (MPH). In

any case, the speed should be adjusted, when practicable, so that it is compatible with the speed of other airplanes in the pattern.

When entering the traffic pattern at an airport without an operating control tower, inbound pilots are expected to observe other aircraft already in the pattern and to conform to the traffic pattern in use. If other aircraft are not in the pattern, then traffic indicators on the ground and wind indicators must be checked to determine which runway and traffic pattern direction should be used. Many airports have L-shaped traffic pattern indicators displayed with a segmented circle adjacent to the runway. The short member of the L shows the direction in which the traffic pattern turns should be made when using the runway parallel to the long member. These indicators should be checked while at a distance well away from any pattern that might be in use, or while at a safe height well above generally used pattern altitudes. When the proper traffic pattern direction has been determined, the pilot should then proceed to a point well clear of the pattern before descending to the pattern altitude.

When approaching an airport for landing, the traffic pattern should be entered at a 45° angle to the downwind leg, headed toward a point abeam of the midpoint of the runway to be used for landing. Arriving airplanes should be at the proper traffic pattern altitude before entering the pattern, and should stay clear of the traffic flow until established on the entry leg. Entries into traffic patterns while descending create specific collision hazards and should always be avoided.

The entry leg should be of sufficient length to provide a clear view of the entire traffic pattern, and to allow the pilot adequate time for planning the intended path in the pattern and the landing approach.

The downwind leg is a course flown parallel to the landing runway, but in a direction opposite to the intended landing direction. This leg should be approximately 1/2 to 1 mile out from the landing runway, and at the specified traffic pattern altitude. During this leg, the before landing check should be completed and the landing gear extended if retractable. Pattern altitude should be maintained until abeam the approach end of the landing runway. At this point, power should be reduced and a descent begun. The downwind leg continues past a point abeam the approach end of the runway to a point approximately 45° from the approach end of the runway, and a medium bank turn is made onto the base leg.

The base leg is the transitional part of the traffic pattern between the downwind leg and the final approach leg. Depending on the wind condition, it is established at a sufficient distance from the approach end of the landing runway to permit a gradual descent to the intended touchdown point. The ground track of the airplane while on the base leg should be perpendicular to the extended centerline of the landing runway, although the longitudinal axis of the airplane may not be aligned with the ground track when it is necessary to turn into the wind to counteract drift. While on the base leg, the pilot must ensure, before turning onto the final approach, that there is no danger of colliding with another aircraft that may be already on the final approach.

The final approach leg is a descending flightpath starting from the completion of the base-to-final turn and extending to the point of touchdown. This is probably the most important leg of the entire pattern, because here the pilot's judgment and procedures must be the sharpest to accurately control the airspeed and descent angle while approaching the intended touchdown point. The various aspects are thoroughly explained later in this chapter.

As stipulated in 14 CFR part 91, aircraft while on final approach to land or while landing, have the right-of-way over other aircraft in flight or operating on the surface. When two or more aircraft are approaching an airport for the purpose of landing, the aircraft at the lower altitude has the right-of-way. Pilots should not take advantage of this rule to cut in front of another aircraft that is on final approach to land, or to overtake that aircraft.

The upwind leg is a course flown parallel to the landing runway, but in the same direction to the intended landing direction. The upwind leg continues past a point abeam of the departure end of the runway to where a medium bank 90° turn is made onto the crosswind leg.

The upwind leg is also the transitional part of the traffic pattern when on the final approach and a go-around is initiated and climb attitude is established. When a safe altitude is attained, the pilot should commence a shallow bank turn to the upwind side of the airport. This will allow better visibility of the runway for departing aircraft.

The departure leg of the rectangular pattern is a straight course aligned with, and leading from, the takeoff runway. This leg begins at the point the airplane leaves the ground and continues until the 90° turn onto the crosswind leg is started.

On the departure leg after takeoff, the pilot should continue climbing straight ahead until reaching a point beyond the departure end of the runway and within 300 feet of traffic pattern altitude or 500 feet above ground level (AGL). If leaving the pattern, the pilot should continue straight ahead, or depart by making a 45° left turn (right turn for a right-hand pattern).

The crosswind leg is the part of the rectangular pattern that is horizontally perpendicular to the extended centerline of the takeoff runway and is entered by making approximately a 90° turn from the upwind leg. On the crosswind leg, the airplane proceeds to the downwind leg position.

Since in most cases the takeoff is made into the wind, the wind will now be approximately perpendicular to the airplane's flightpath. As a result, the airplane will have to be turned or headed slightly into the wind while on the crosswind leg to maintain a ground track that is perpendicular to the runway centerline extension.

Additional information on airport operations can be found in the Aeronautical Information Manual (AIM).

NORMAL APPROACH AND LANDING

A normal approach and landing involves the use of procedures for what is considered a normal situation; that is, when engine power is available, the wind is light or the final approach is made directly into the wind, the final approach path has no obstacles, and the landing surface is firm and of ample length to gradually bring the airplane to a stop. The selected landing point should be beyond the runway's approach threshold but within the first one-third portion of the runway.

The factors involved and the procedures described for the normal approach and landing also have applications to the other-than-normal approaches and landings which are discussed later in this chapter. This being the case, the principles of normal operations are explained first and must be understood before proceeding to the more complex operations. So that the pilot may better understand the factors that will influence judgment and procedures, that last part of the approach pattern and the actual landing will be divided into five phases: the base leg, the final approach, the roundout, the touchdown, and the after-landing roll.

Base Leg

The placement of the base leg is one of the more important judgments made by the pilot in any landing approach. The pilot must accurately judge the altitude and distance from which a gradual descent will result in landing at the desired spot. The distance will depend on the altitude of the base leg, the effect of wind, and the amount of wing flaps used. When there is a strong wind on final approach or the flaps will be used to produce a steep angle of descent, the base leg must be positioned closer to the approach end of the runway than would be required with a light wind or no flaps. Normally, the landing gear should be extended and the before landing check completed prior to reaching the base leg.

After turning onto the base leg, the pilot should start the descent with reduced power and airspeed of approximately 1.4 V_{SO}. (V_{SO}—the stalling speed with power off, landing gears and flaps down.) For example, if V_{SO} is 60 knots, the speed should be 1.4 times 60, or 84 knots. Landing flaps may be partially lowered, if desired, at this time. Full flaps are not recommended until the final approach is established and the landing assured. Drift correction should be established and maintained to follow a ground track perpendicular to the extension of the centerline of the runway on which the landing is to be made. Since the final approach and landing will normally be made into the wind, there will be somewhat of a crosswind during the base leg. This requires that the airplane be angled sufficiently into the wind to prevent drifting farther away from the intended landing spot.

The base leg should be continued to the point where a medium to shallow-banked turn will align the airplane's path directly with the centerline of the landing runway. This descending turn should be completed at a safe altitude that will be dependent upon the height of the terrain and any obstructions along the ground track. The turn to the final approach should also be sufficiently above the airport elevation to permit a final approach long enough for the pilot to accurately estimate the resultant point of touchdown, while maintaining the proper approach airspeed. This will require careful planning as to the starting point and the radius of the turn. Normally, it is recommended that the angle of bank not exceed a medium bank because the steeper the angle of bank, the higher the airspeed at which the airplane stalls. Since the base-to-final turn is made at a relatively low altitude, it is important that a stall not occur at this point. If an extremely steep bank is needed to prevent overshooting the proper final approach path, it is advisable to discontinue the approach, go around, and plan to start the turn earlier on the next approach rather than risk a hazardous situation.

Final Approach

After the base-to-final approach turn is completed, the longitudinal axis of the airplane should be aligned with the centerline of the runway or landing surface, so that drift (if any) will be recognized immediately. On a normal approach, with no wind drift, the longitudinal axis should be kept aligned with the runway centerline throughout the approach and landing. (The proper way to correct for a crosswind will be explained under the section, Crosswind Approach and Landing. For now, only an approach and landing where the wind is light or straight down the runway will be discussed.)

After aligning the airplane with the runway centerline, the final flap setting should be completed and the pitch attitude adjusted as required for the desired rate of descent. Slight adjustments in pitch and power may be necessary to maintain the descent attitude and the desired approach airspeed. In the absence of the manufacturer's recommended airspeed, a speed equal to 1.3 V_{SO} should be used. If V_{SO} is 60 knots, the speed should be 78 knots. When the pitch attitude and airspeed have been stabilized, the airplane should be retrimmed to relieve the pressures being held on the controls.

The descent angle should be controlled throughout the approach so that the airplane will land in the center of the first third of the runway. The descent angle is affected by all four fundamental forces that act on an airplane (lift, drag, thrust, and weight). If all the forces are constant, the descent angle will be constant in a no-wind condition. The pilot can control these forces by adjusting the airspeed, attitude, power, and drag (flaps or forward slip).

The wind also plays a prominent part in the gliding distance over the ground; naturally, the pilot does not have control over the wind but may correct for its effect on the airplane's descent by appropriate pitch and power adjustments.

Considering the factors that affect the descent angle on the final approach, for all practical purposes at a given pitch attitude there is only one power setting for one airspeed, one flap setting, and one wind condition. A change in any one of these variables will require an appropriate coordinated change in the other controllable variables. For example, if the pitch attitude is raised too high without an increase of power, the airplane will settle very rapidly and touch down short of the desired spot. For this reason, never try to stretch a glide by applying back-elevator pressure alone to reach the desired landing spot. This will shorten the gliding distance if power is not added simultaneously. The proper angle of descent and airspeed should be maintained by coordinating pitch attitude changes and power changes.

The objective of a good final approach is to descend at an angle and airspeed that will permit the airplane to reach the desired touchdown point at an airspeed which will result in minimum floating just before touchdown. To accomplish this, it is essential that both the descent angle and the airspeed be accurately controlled. Since on a normal approach the power setting is not fixed as in a power-off approach, the power should be adjusted, as necessary, to control the airspeed, and the pitch attitude adjusted simultaneously to control the descent angle or to attain the desired altitudes along the approach path. By lowering the nose and reducing power to keep approach airspeed constant, a descent at a higher rate can be made to correct for being too high in the approach. This is one reason for performing approaches with partial power; if the approach is too high, merely lower the nose and reduce the power. When the approach is too low, add power and raise the nose. On the other hand, if the approach is extremely high or low, it is advisable to execute a go-around. This procedure is explained later in this chapter.

Adjusting the descent through the use of the landing flaps may also vary the lift/drag factors. [Figures 7-2 and 7-3] When the flaps are lowered, the airspeed will decrease unless the power is increased

or the pitch attitude lowered. After starting the final approach, the pilot must then estimate where the airplane will land through discerning judgment of the descent angle. If it appears that the airplane is going to overshoot or land slightly beyond the desired spot, more flaps may be used if not fully extended or the power reduced further, and the pitch attitude lowered. This will result in a steeper approach. If the spot is being undershot and a shallower approach is needed, the power and the pitch attitude should be increased to readjust the descent angle and the airspeed. Never retract the flaps to correct for undershooting since that will suddenly decrease the lift and cause the airplane to sink even more rapidly.

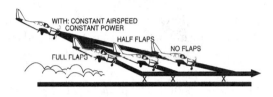

FIGURE 7-2.—*Effect of flaps on the landing point.*

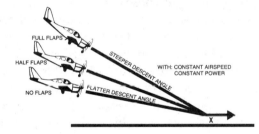

FIGURE 7-3.—*Effect of flaps on the approach angle.*

The airplane must be retrimmed on the final approach to compensate for the change in aerodynamic forces. With the reduced power and with a slower airspeed, the airflow produces less lift on the wings and less downward force on the horizontal stabilizer, resulting in a significant nosedown tendency. The elevator must then be trimmed more nose up.

It will be found that the roundout, touchdown, and landing roll are much easier to accomplish when they are preceded by a proper final approach with precise control of airspeed, attitude, power, and drag resulting in a stabilized descent angle.

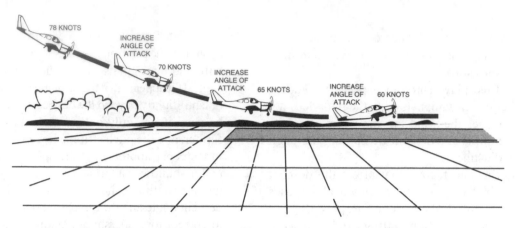

FIGURE 7-4.—Changing angle of attack during roundout.

Estimating Height and Movement

During the approach, roundout, and touchdown vision is of prime importance. To provide a wide scope of vision and to foster good judgment of height and movement, the pilot's head should assume a natural, straight-ahead position. The pilot's visual focus should not be fixed on any one side or any one spot ahead of the airplane, but should be changing slowly from a point just over the airplane's nose to the desired touchdown zone and back again, while maintaining a deliberate awareness of distance from either side of the runway within the pilot's peripheral field of vision.

Accurate estimation of distance is, besides being a matter of practice, dependent upon how clearly objects are seen; it requires that the vision be focused properly in order that the important objects stand out as clearly as possible.

Speed blurs objects at close range. For example, most everyone has noted this in an automobile moving at high speed. Nearby objects seem to merge together in a blur, while objects farther away stand out clearly. The driver subconsciously focuses the eyes sufficiently far ahead of the automobile to see objects distinctly.

The distance at which the pilot's vision is focused should be proportionate to the speed at which the airplane is traveling over the ground. Thus, as speed is reduced during the roundout, the distance ahead of the airplane at which it is possible to focus should be brought closer accordingly.

If the pilot attempts to focus on a reference that is too close or looks directly down, the reference will become blurred, and the reaction will be either too abrupt or too late. In this case, the pilot's tendency will be to overcontrol, roundout high, and make full-stall drop-in landings. When the pilot focuses too far ahead, accuracy in judging the closeness of the ground is lost

and the consequent reaction will be too slow since there will not appear to be a necessity for action, this will result in the airplane flying into the ground, nose first. The change of visual focus from a long distance to a short distance requires a definite time interval and even though the time is brief, the airplane's speed during this interval is such that the airplane travels an appreciable distance, both forward and downward toward the ground.

If the focus is changed gradually, being brought progressively closer as speed is reduced, the time interval and the pilot's reaction will be reduced, and the whole landing process smoothed out.

Roundout (Flare)

The roundout is a slow, smooth transition from a normal approach attitude to a landing attitude. When the airplane, in a normal descent, approaches within what appears to be 10 to 20 feet above the ground, the roundout or flare should be started, and once started should be a continuous process until the airplane touches down on the ground.

As the airplane reaches a height above the ground where a timely change can be made into the proper landing attitude, back-elevator pressure should be gradually applied to slowly increase the pitch attitude and angle of attack. This will cause the airplane's nose to gradually rise toward the desired landing attitude. The angle of attack should be increased at a rate that will allow the airplane to continue settling slowly as forward speed decreases.

When the angle of attack is increased, the lift is momentarily increased, which decreases the rate of descent. [Figure 7-4] Since power normally is reduced to idle during the roundout, the airspeed will also gradually decrease. This will cause lift to decrease

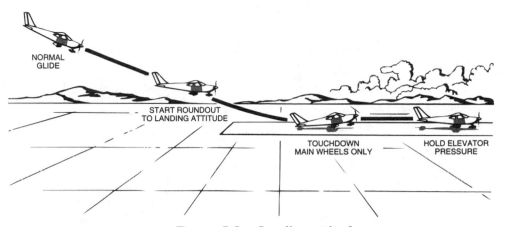

NORMAL GLIDE

START ROUNDOUT TO LANDING ATTITUDE

TOUCHDOWN MAIN WHEELS ONLY

HOLD ELEVATOR PRESSURE

FIGURE 7-5.—*Landing attitude.*

again, and it must be controlled by raising the nose and further increasing the angle of attack. During the roundout, the airspeed is being decreased to touchdown speed while the lift is being controlled so the airplane will settle gently onto the landing surface. The roundout should be executed at a rate that the proper landing attitude and the proper touchdown airspeed are attained simultaneously just as the wheels contact the landing surface.

The rate at which the roundout is executed depends on the airplane's height above the ground, the rate of descent, and the pitch attitude. A roundout started excessively high must be executed more slowly than one from a lower height to allow the airplane to descend to the ground while the proper landing attitude is being established. The rate of rounding out must also be proportionate to the rate of closure with the ground. When the airplane appears to be descending very slowly, the increase in pitch attitude must be made at a correspondingly slow rate.

The pitch attitude of the airplane in a full-flap approach is considerably lower than in a no-flap approach. To attain the proper landing attitude before touching down, the nose must travel through a greater pitch change when flaps are fully extended. Since the roundout is usually started at approximately the same height above the ground regardless of the degree of flaps used, the pitch attitude must be increased at a faster rate when full flaps are used; however, the roundout should still be executed at a rate proportionate to the airplane's downward motion.

Once the actual process of rounding out is started, the elevator control should not be pushed forward. If too much back-elevator pressure has been exerted, this pressure should be either slightly relaxed or held constant, depending on the degree of the error. In some cases, it may be necessary to advance the throttle

slightly to prevent an excessive rate of sink, or a stall, all of which would result in a hard drop-in landing.

It is recommended that the pilot form the habit of keeping one hand on the throttle throughout the approach and landing, should a sudden and unexpected hazardous situation require an immediate application of power.

Touchdown

The touchdown is the gentle settling of the airplane onto the landing surface. The roundout and touchdown should be made with the engine idling, and the airplane at minimum controllable airspeed, so that the airplane will touch down on the main gear at approximately stalling speed. As the airplane settles, the proper landing attitude is attained by application of whatever back-elevator pressure is necessary.

Some pilots may try to force or fly the airplane onto the ground without establishing the proper landing attitude. The airplane should never be flown on the runway with excessive speed. It is paradoxical that the way to make an ideal landing is to try to hold the airplane's wheels a few inches off the ground as long as possible with the elevators. In most cases, when the wheels are within 2 or 3 feet off the ground, the airplane will still be settling too fast for a gentle touchdown; therefore, this descent must be retarded by further back-elevator pressure. Since the airplane is already close to its stalling speed and is settling, this added back-elevator pressure will only slow up the settling instead of stopping it. At the same time, it will result in the airplane touching the ground in the proper landing attitude, and the main wheels touching down first so that little or no weight is on the nosewheel. [Figure 7-5]

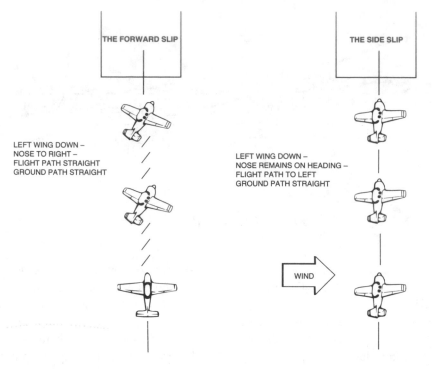

THE FORWARD SLIP

LEFT WING DOWN –
NOSE TO RIGHT –
FLIGHT PATH STRAIGHT
GROUND PATH STRAIGHT

THE SIDE SLIP

LEFT WING DOWN –
NOSE REMAINS ON HEADING –
FLIGHT PATH TO LEFT
GROUND PATH STRAIGHT

WIND

FIGURE 7-6.—*Forward and side slip.*

After the main wheels make initial contact with the ground, back-elevator pressure should be held to maintain a positive angle of attack for aerodynamic braking, and to hold the nosewheel off the ground until the airplane decelerates. As the airplane's momentum decreases, back-elevator pressure may be gradually relaxed to allow the nosewheel to gently settle onto the runway. This will permit steering with the nosewheel. At the same time, it will cause a low angle of attack and negative lift on the wings to prevent floating or skipping, and will allow the full weight of the airplane to rest on the wheels for better braking action.

It is extremely important that the touchdown occur with the airplane's longitudinal axis exactly parallel to the direction in which the airplane is moving along the runway. Failure to accomplish this imposes severe sideloads on the landing gear. To avoid these side stresses, the pilot should not allow the airplane to touch down while turned into the wind or drifting.

Slips

Basically there are two types of slips, a forward slip and a side slip. [Figure 7-6] A forward slip can be used to increase the airplane's descent angle without increasing airspeed. This could prove useful in making an emergency landing or in landing in an area with obstructions. A pilot should not use a slip to lose altitude because of poor planning.

To perform a forward slip, one wing should be lowered and at the same time opposite rudder applied to prevent the airplane from turning in the direction of the lowered wing. In this situation, the nose of the airplane will be pointed away from the runway, but the flightpath will be aligned with the runway. Once an acceptable altitude has been attained, the slip may be discontinued.

A sideslip is commonly used when performing a crosswind landing to counteract wind drift. A sideslip is the same as a forward slip except in a sideslip the airplane's longitudinal axis remains parallel to the original flightpath and is aligned with the runway.

Before performing slips, the Airplane's Flight Manual (AFM) and/or Pilot's Operating Handbook (POH) should be checked to see if any restrictions apply.

Go-Arounds (Rejected Landings)

Occasionally, it may be advisable for safety reasons to discontinue the landing approach and make another approach under more favorable conditions. Situations, such as air traffic control (ATC) requirements, extremely low base-to-final turns, overshooting turns, low final approaches, overtaking another airplane on the approach, wake turbulence from a preceding airplane, or unexpected appearance of hazards on the runway are examples of hazardous conditions that would demand initiating a go-around.

The need to discontinue an approach or landing may arise at any point in the approach or landing phase. Obviously, the most critical go-around landing is the one that is started when very close to the ground. Therefore, it is important that the earlier an unsafe situation is recognized, the safer the go-around/rejected landing will be.

A safe go-around can be accomplished if an early go-around decision is made, a sound plan is followed, and procedures are performed properly. When the decision is made to discontinue an approach, go around, or reject a landing, smoothly apply maximum allowable power, level the airplane's wings and transition to a climb pitch attitude that will slow or stop the descent. After the descent has been stopped, landing flaps should be partially retracted and set as recommended by the manufacturer. In the absence of such a procedure, the flaps should be positioned to an approach or takeoff setting.

Caution must be used in retracting the flaps. Depending on the airplane's altitude and airspeed, it may be wise to retract the flaps in small increments to allow time for the airplane to accelerate properly as they are being raised. A sudden and complete retraction of the flaps at a very low airspeed could cause a loss of lift resulting in the airplane settling into the ground.

Unless otherwise specified in the airplane's operating manual, it is recommended that the flaps be retracted (at least partially) before retracting the landing gear.

After a positive rate of climb is established, the landing gear can be retracted. It is important to accelerate to the best angle-of-climb speed, or greater, as quickly as possible and retract the remaining flaps. These speeds will provide for best climb performance.

Since the airplane has been trimmed for the approach (a low power and airspeed condition), application of maximum allowable power will require considerable control pressures to maintain a climb pitch attitude. This addition of power will tend to raise the airplane's nose suddenly and veer to the left. Forward elevator pressure must be anticipated and applied to stop the nose at a proper climb pitch attitude. Right-rudder pressure also must be increased to counteract torque and P-factor, and to keep the nose from turning left. The pilot must hold the airplane at this proper pitch attitude, regardless of the amount of control pressure required.

While holding the airplane in a takeoff or climb pitch attitude, the pilot should quickly retrim the airplane to relieve any adverse control pressures. Additional trim adjustment may be necessary to relieve control pressures as the airspeed increases. Later, more precise trim adjustments can be made when flight conditions are stabilized.

On airplanes that produce high control pressures when using maximum power on go-arounds, pilots should use caution when reaching for the flap handle to retract the flaps. Airplane control may become critical during this high workload phase.

It is advisable to retract the landing gear only after the initial or rough trim has been accomplished and when it is certain the airplane will remain airborne and not contact the surface. During the initial part of an extremely low go-around, the airplane may mush onto the runway and bounce. This situation is not particularly dangerous if takeoff pitch attitude and directional control is maintained. The airplane will be approaching safe flying speed rapidly and the higher power will cushion any secondary touchdown.

If the pitch attitude is increased excessively to prevent the airplane from settling onto the runway, this may cause the airplane to stall. This would be more likely if no trim correction is made and the flaps remain fully extended. Do not attempt to retract the landing gear until after some initial trim adjustment has been made and a positive rate of climb is established.

After a positive rate of climb is established and the landing gear is retracted, the airplane should be allowed to accelerate to the best angle (V_x) or to the best rate-of-climb speed (V_y) before the final flap retraction is accomplished.

From this point on, the go-around procedure is similar with that for a normal climb after takeoff. If there is a conflict with departing traffic when at a safe altitude, it is recommended that a shallow banked turn be made away from the runway to keep the traffic in sight. The go-around should be completed parallel to the runway (upwind leg). This will provide better visibility and clearance from such traffic.

If operating at an airport with parallel runways, use caution when making a clearing turn away from the runway. It will be important to listen for traffic advisories and check for conflicting traffic on the parallel runway.

Tower communications and UNICOM advise should only be made up when the airplane is cleared and under positive control. Proceed on this upwind leg to again rejoin the traffic pattern crosswind leg for another approach and landing.

After-Landing Roll

The landing process must never be considered complete until the airplane decelerates to the normal taxi speed during the landing roll or has been brought to a complete stop when clear of the landing area. Many accidents have occurred as a result of pilots abandoning their vigilance and positive control after getting the airplane on the ground.

The pilot must be alert for directional control difficulties immediately upon and after touchdown due to the ground friction on the wheels. The friction creates a pivot point on which a moment arm can act.

Loss of directional control may lead to an aggravated, uncontrolled, tight turn on the ground, or a ground loop. The combination of centrifugal force acting on the center of gravity (CG) and ground friction of the main wheels resisting it during the ground loop may cause the airplane to tip or lean enough for the outside wingtip to contact the ground. This may even impose a sideward force which could collapse the landing gear.

The rudder serves the same purpose on the ground as it does in the air—it controls the yawing of the airplane. The effectiveness of the rudder is dependent on the airflow, which depends on the speed of the airplane. As the speed decreases and the nosewheel has been lowered to the ground, the steerable nose provides more positive directional control.

The brakes of an airplane serve the same primary purpose as the brakes of an automobile—to reduce speed on the ground. In airplanes they may also be used as an aid in directional control when more positive control is required than could be obtained with rudder or nosewheel steering alone.

To use brakes, on an airplane equipped with toe brakes, the pilot should slide the toes or feet up from the rudder pedals to the brake pedals. If rudder pressure is being held at the time braking action is needed, that pressure should not be released as the feet or toes are being slid up to the brake pedals, because control may be lost before brakes can be applied.

During the ground roll, the airplane's direction of movement can be changed by carefully applying pressure on one brake or uneven pressures on each brake in the desired direction. Caution must be exercised when applying brakes to avoid overcontrolling.

The ailerons serve the same purpose on the ground as they do in the air—they change the lift and drag components of the wings. During the after-landing roll, they should be used to keep the wings level in much the same way they were used in flight. If a wing starts to rise, aileron control should be applied toward that wing to lower it. The amount required will depend on speed because as the forward speed of the airplane decreases, the ailerons will become less effective. Procedures for using ailerons in crosswind conditions are explained further in this chapter, in the crosswind landings section.

After the airplane is on the ground, back-elevator pressure may be gradually relaxed to place normal weight on the nosewheel to aid in better steering.

If available runway permits, the speed of the airplane should be allowed to dissipate in a normal manner. Once the airplane has slowed sufficiently and has turned on to the taxiway and stopped, the pilot should retract the flaps and clean up the airplane. Too many accidents have occurred as a result of the pilot unintentionally operating the landing gear control and retracting the gear instead of the flap control when the airplane was still rolling. The habit of positively identifying both of these controls, before actuating them, should be formed from the very beginning of flight training and continued in all future flying activities.

Hydroplaning

When there is a film of water on a runway, the airplane ground controllability and braking efficiency can be seriously affected. As the speed of the airplane and depth of the water increase, the water layer builds up an increasing resistance to displacement, resulting in the formation of a wedge of water beneath the tire. This progressively lifts the tire, decreasing the area in contact with the runway and causes the airplane to hydroplane on the film of water. In this condition, the tires no longer contribute to directional control and braking action is nil.

There are basically three types of hydroplaning they are dynamic, viscous, and reverted rubber.

Dynamic
Dynamic hydroplaning occurs when there is standing water on the runway surface. Water about one-tenth of an inch deep acts to lift the tire off the runway as explained above.

Viscous
Viscous hydroplaning is due to the viscous properties of water. A thin film of fluid no more than one-thousandth of an inch in depth cannot be penetrated by the tire and the tire rolls on top of this film. This can occur at a much lower speed than dynamic

hydroplaning, but requires a smooth or smooth-acting surface.

Reverted Rubber

Reverted rubber hydroplaning requires a prolonged locked wheel skid, reverted rubber, and a wet runway surface. The reverted rubber acts as a seal between the tire and the runway, and delays water exit from the tire footprint area. The water heats and is converted to steam and the steam supports the tire off the runway.

Data obtained during hydroplaning tests have shown the minimum dynamic hydroplaning speed of a tire to be 8.6 times the square root of the tire pressure in pounds per square inch (PSI). For an airplane with a main tire pressure of 24 pounds, the calculated hydroplaning speed would be approximately 42 knots. It is important to note that the calculated speed referred to above is for the start of dynamic hydroplaning. Once hydroplaning has started, it may persist to a significantly slower speed depending on the type being experienced.

Pilots should always be alert to the possibility of standing water on a runway if it has recently rained. It is important to note that smooth surfaces and ungrooved runways do not promote drainage, as well as other runways. A pilot should always consider the type of runway, its width and length, as well as any other pertinent factors when the possibility of hydroplaning exists. If a landing is questionable, divert to another airport.

Lowering the nosewheel on a wet runway of adequate length will reduce angle of attack and stabilize the airplane during rollout. Therefore, it is important to have the nose tire tracking as soon as possible. Also retracting the flaps as soon as possible will improve traction; however, this should be done with caution, especially if operating a retractable gear airplane. Above all, use good judgment and follow recommendations provided by the manufacturer.

CROSSWIND APPROACH AND LANDING

Many runways or landing areas are such that landings must be made while the wind is blowing across rather than parallel to the landing direction. All pilots should be prepared to cope with these situations when they arise. The same basic principles and factors involved in a normal approach and landing apply to a crosswind approach and landing; therefore, only the additional procedures required for correcting for wind drift are discussed here.

Crosswind landings are a little more difficult to perform than crosswind takeoffs, mainly due to different problems involved in maintaining accurate control of the airplane while its speed is decreasing rather than increasing as on takeoff.

There are two usual methods of accomplishing a crosswind approach and landing—the crab method and the wing-low method. Although the crab method may be easier for the pilot to maintain during final approach, it requires a high degree of judgment and timing in removing the crab immediately prior to touchdown. The wing-low method is recommended in most cases although a combination of both methods may be used.

Crosswind Final Approach

The crab method is executed by establishing a heading (crab) toward the wind with the wings level so that the airplane's ground track remains aligned with the centerline of the runway. This crab angle is maintained until just prior to touchdown, when the longitudinal axis of the airplane must be aligned with the runway to avoid sideward contact of the wheels with the runway. If a long final approach is being flown, the pilot may use the crab method until just before the roundout is started and then smoothly change to the wing-low method for the remainder of the landing.

The wing-low method will compensate for a crosswind from any angle, but more important, it enables the pilot to simultaneously keep the airplane's ground track and longitudinal axis aligned with the runway centerline throughout the final approach, roundout, touchdown, and after-landing roll. This prevents the airplane from touching down in a sideward motion and imposing damaging side loads on the landing gear.

To use the wing-low method, the pilot aligns the airplane's heading with the centerline of the runway, notes the rate and direction of drift, and then promptly applies drift correction by lowering the upwind wing. [Figure 7-7] The amount the wing must be lowered depends on the rate of drift. When the wing is lowered, the airplane will tend to turn in that direction. It is then necessary to simultaneously apply sufficient opposite rudder pressure to prevent the turn and keep the airplane's longitudinal axis aligned with the runway. In other words, the drift is controlled with aileron, and the heading with rudder. The airplane will now be side slipping into the wind just enough that both the resultant flightpath and the ground track are aligned with the runway. If the crosswind diminishes, this crosswind correction is reduced accordingly, or the airplane will begin slipping away from the desired approach path.

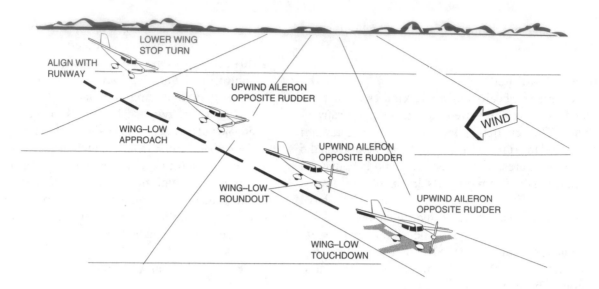

FIGURE 7-7.—Crosswind approach and landing.

To correct for strong crosswind, the slip into the wind is increased by lowering the upwind wing a considerable amount. As a consequence, this will result in a greater tendency of the airplane to turn. Since turning is not desired, considerable opposite rudder must be applied to keep the airplane's longitudinal axis aligned with the runway. In some airplanes, there may not be sufficient rudder travel available to compensate for the strong turning tendency caused by the steep bank. If the required bank is such that full opposite rudder will not prevent a turn; the wind is too strong to safely land the airplane on that particular runway with those wind conditions. Since the airplane's capability will be exceeded, it is imperative that the landing be made on a more favorable runway either at that airport or at an alternate airport.

Flaps can and should be used during most approaches since they tend to have a stabilizing effect on the airplane. The degree to which flaps should be extended will vary with the airplane's handling characteristics, as well as the wind velocity.

Crosswind Roundout (Flare)

Generally, the roundout can be made like a normal landing approach, but the application of a crosswind correction is continued as necessary to prevent drifting.

Since the airspeed decreases as the roundout progresses, the flight controls gradually become less effective. As a result, the crosswind correction being held will become inadequate. When using the wing-low method, it is necessary to gradually increase the deflection of the rudder and ailerons to maintain the proper amount of drift correction.

Do not level the wings; keep the upwind wing down throughout the roundout. If the wings are leveled, the airplane will begin drifting and the touchdown will occur while drifting. Remember, the primary objective is to land the airplane without subjecting it to any side loads that result from touching down while drifting.

Crosswind Touchdown

If the crab method of drift correction has been used throughout the final approach and roundout, the crab must be removed the instant before touchdown by applying rudder to align the airplane's longitudinal axis with its direction of movement. This requires timely and accurate action. Failure to accomplish this will result in severe side loads being imposed on the landing gear.

If the wing-low method is used, the crosswind correction (aileron into the wind and opposite rudder) should be maintained throughout the roundout, and the touchdown made on the upwind main wheel.

During gusty or high-wind conditions, prompt adjustments must be made in the crosswind correction to assure that the airplane does not drift as the airplane touches down.

As the forward momentum decreases after initial contact, the weight of the airplane will cause the downwind main wheel to gradually settle onto the runway.

In those airplanes having nosewheel steering interconnected with the rudder, the nosewheel may not be aligned with the runway as the wheels touch down because opposite rudder is being held in the crosswind correction. To prevent swerving in the direction the nosewheel is offset, the corrective rudder pressure must be promptly relaxed just as the nosewheel touches down.

Crosswind After-Landing Roll

Particularly during the after-landing roll, special attention must be given to maintaining directional control by the use of rudder or nosewheel steering, while keeping the upwind wing from rising by the use of aileron.

When an airplane is airborne, it moves with the air mass in which it is flying regardless of the airplane's heading and speed. When an airplane is on the ground, it is unable to move with the air mass (crosswind) because of the resistance created by ground friction on the wheels.

Characteristically, an airplane has a greater profile or side area, behind the main landing gear than forward of it does. With the main wheels acting as a pivot point and the greater surface area exposed to the crosswind behind that pivot point, the airplane will tend to turn or weathervane into the wind.

Wind acting on an airplane during crosswind landings is the result of two factors. One is the natural wind, which acts in the direction the air mass is traveling, while the other is induced by the movement of the airplane and acts parallel to the direction of movement. Consequently, a crosswind has a headwind component acting along the airplane's ground track and a crosswind component acting 90° to its track. The resultant or relative wind is somewhere between the two components. As the airplane's forward speed decreases during the after-landing roll, the headwind component decreases and the relative wind has more of a crosswind component. The greater the crosswind component, the more difficult it is to prevent weathervaning.

While the airplane is decelerating during the after-landing roll, more and more aileron is applied to keep the upwind wing from rising. Since the airplane is slowing down, there is less airflow around the ailerons and they become less effective. At the same time, the relative wind is becoming more of a crosswind and exerting a greater lifting force on the upwind wing.

When the airplane is coming to a stop, the aileron control must be held fully toward the wind.

Turbulent Air Approach and Landing

Power-on approaches at airspeed slightly above the normal approach speed should be used for landing in turbulent air. This provides for more positive control of the airplane when strong horizontal wind gusts, or up and down drafts, is experienced.

Like other power-on approaches (when the pilot can vary the amount of power), the angle of descent is controlled primarily by pitch adjustments, and the airspeed is controlled primarily by changes in power. A coordinated combination of both pitch and power adjustments is usually required. As in most other landing approaches, the proper approach attitude and airspeed require a minimum roundout and should result in little or no floating during the landing.

To maintain good control, the approach in turbulent air with gusty crosswind may require the use of partial wing flaps. With less than full flaps, the airplane will be in a higher pitch attitude. Thus, it will require less of a pitch change to establish the landing attitude, and the touchdown will be at a higher airspeed to ensure more positive control. The speed should not be so excessive that the airplane will float past the desired landing area.

One procedure is to use the normal approach speed plus one-half of the wind gust factors. If the normal speed is 70 knots, and the wind gusts increase 15 knots, airspeed of 77 knots is appropriate. In any case, the airspeed and the amount of flaps should be as the airplane manufacturer recommends.

An adequate amount of power should be used to maintain the proper airspeed throughout the approach, and the throttle retarded to idling position only after the main wheels contact the landing surface. Care must be exercised in closing the throttle before the pilot is ready for touchdown. In this situation, the sudden or premature closing of the throttle may cause a sudden increase in the descent rate that could result in a hard landing.

Landings from power approaches in turbulence should be such that the touchdown is made with the airplane in approximately level flight attitude. The pitch attitude at touchdown should be only enough to prevent the nosewheel from contacting the surface before the main wheels have touched the surface.

SHORT-FIELD APPROACH AND LANDING

Short-field approaches and landings require the use of procedures for the approaches and landings at fields with a relatively short landing area or where an approach is made over obstacles that limit the available landing area. As in short-field takeoffs, it is one of the most critical of the maximum performance operations. It requires that the pilot fly the airplane at one of its crucial performance capabilities while close to the ground in order to safely land within confined areas. This low-speed type of power-on approach is closely related to the performance of flight at minimum controllable airspeeds.

To land within a short-field or a confined area, the pilot must have precise, positive control of the rate of descent and airspeed to produce an approach that will clear any obstacles, result in little or no floating during the roundout, and permit the airplane to be stopped in the shortest possible distance. [Figure 7-8]

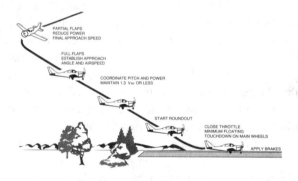

FIGURE 7-8.—Short-field approach and landing.

The procedures for landing in a short-field or for landing approaches over 50-foot obstacles, as recommended in the AFM/POH, should be used. These procedures generally involve the use of full flaps, and the final approach started from an altitude of at least 500 feet higher than the touchdown area. In the absence of the manufacturer's recommended approach speed, a speed of not more than 1.3 V_{SO} should be used—in an airplane that stalls at 60 knots with power off, and flaps and landing gear extended, the approach speed should not be higher than 78 knots. In gusty air, no more than one-half the gust factor should be added. An excessive amount of airspeed could result in a touchdown too far from the runway threshold or an after-landing roll that exceeds the available landing area.

After the landing gear and full flaps have been extended, the pilot should simultaneously adjust the power and the pitch attitude to establish and maintain the proper descent angle and airspeed.

Since short-field approaches are power-on approaches, the pitch attitude is adjusted, as necessary, to establish and maintain the desired rate or angle of descent, and power is adjusted to maintain the desired airspeed. A coordinated combination of both pitch and power adjustments is usually required. When this is done properly, very little change in the airplane's pitch attitude is necessary to make corrections in the angle of descent, and only small power changes are needed to control the airspeed.

If it appears that the obstacle clearance is excessive and touchdown will occur well beyond the desired spot, leaving insufficient room to stop, power may be reduced while lowering the pitch attitude to increase the rate of descent. If it appears that the descent angle will not ensure safe clearance of obstacles, power should be increased while simultaneously raising the pitch attitude to decrease the rate of descent. Care must be taken to avoid an excessively low airspeed. If the speed is allowed to become too slow, an increase in pitch and application of full power may only result in a further rate of descent. This occurs when the angle of attack is so great and creating so much drag that the maximum available power is insufficient to overcome it. This is generally referred to as operating in the region of reverse command or operating on the back side of the power curve.

Because the final approach over obstacles is made at a steep approach angle and close to the airplane's stalling speed, the initiation of the roundout or flare must be judged accurately to avoid flying into the ground, or stalling prematurely and sinking rapidly. A lack of floating during the flare, with sufficient control to touch down properly, is one verification that the approach speed was correct.

Touchdown should occur at the minimum controllable airspeed with the airplane in approximately the pitch attitude that will result in a power-off stall when the throttle is closed. Care must be exercised to avoid closing the throttle rapidly before the pilot is ready for touchdown, as closing the throttle may result in an immediate increase in the rate of descent and a hard landing.

Upon touchdown, the airplane should be held in this positive pitch attitude as long as the elevators remain effective. This will provide aerodynamic braking by the wings.

Immediately upon touchdown, and closing the throttle, the brakes should be applied evenly and firmly to minimize the after-landing roll. The airplane should be stopped within the shortest possible distance consistent with safety.

SOFT-FIELD APPROACH AND LANDING

Landing on fields that are rough or have soft surfaces, such as snow, sand, mud, or tall grass requires unique procedures. When landing on such surfaces, the pilot must control the airplane in a manner that the wings support the weight of the airplane as long as practical, to minimize drag and stresses imposed on the landing gear by the rough or soft surface.

The approach for the soft-field landing is similar to the normal approach used for operating into long, firm landing areas. The major difference between the two is that, during the soft-field landing, the airplane is held 1 to 2 feet off the surface as long as possible to dissipate the forward speed sufficiently to allow the wheels to touch down gently at minimum speed.

The use of flaps during soft-field landings will aid in touching down at minimum speed and is recommended whenever practical. In low-wing airplanes, the flaps may suffer damage from mud, stones, or slush thrown up by the wheels. If flaps are used, it is generally inadvisable to retract them during the after-landing roll because the need for flap retraction is usually less important than the need for total concentration on maintaining full control of the airplane.

The final approach airspeed used for short-field landings is equally appropriate to soft-field landings, but there is no reason for a steep angle of descent unless obstacles are present in the approach path. Touchdown on a soft or rough field should be made at the lowest possible airspeed with the airplane in a nose-high pitch attitude.

In nosewheel-type airplanes, after the main wheels touch the surface, the pilot should hold sufficient back-elevator pressure to keep the nosewheel off the ground until it can no longer aerodynamically be held off the field surface. At this time, the pilot should gently lower the nosewheel to the surface. A slight addition of power during and immediately after touchdown usually will aid in easing the nosewheel down.

The use of brakes on a soft field is not needed and should be avoided as this may tend to impose a heavy load on the nose gear due to premature or hard contact with the landing surface, causing the nosewheel to dig in. The soft or rough surface itself will provide sufficient reduction in the airplane's forward speed. Often it will be found that upon landing on a very soft field, the pilot will need to increase power to keep the airplane moving and from becoming stuck in the soft surface.

POWER-OFF ACCURACY APPROACHES

Power-off accuracy approaches are approaches and landings made by gliding with the engine idling, through a specific pattern to a touchdown beyond and within 200 feet of a designated line or mark on the runway. The objective is to instill in the pilot the judgment and procedures necessary for accurately flying the airplane, with out power, to a safe landing.

The ability to estimate the distance an airplane will glide to a landing is the real basis of all power-off accuracy approaches and landings. This will largely determine the amount of maneuvering that may be done from a given altitude. In addition to the ability to estimate distance, it requires the ability to maintain the proper glide while maneuvering the airplane.

With experience and practice, altitudes up to approximately 1,000 feet can be estimated with fair accuracy, while above this level the accuracy in judgment of height above the ground decreases, since all features tend to merge. The best aid in perfecting the ability to judge height above this altitude is through the indications of the altimeter and associating them with the general appearance of the earth.

The judgment of altitude in feet, hundreds of feet, or thousands of feet is not as important, as the ability to estimate gliding angle and its resultant distance. The pilot who knows the normal glide angle of the airplane can estimate with reasonable accuracy, the approximate spot along a given ground path at which the airplane will land, regardless of altitude. The pilot, who also has the ability to accurately estimate altitude, can judge how much maneuvering is possible during the glide, which is important to the choice of landing areas in an actual emergency.

The objective of a good final approach is to descend at an angle that will permit the airplane to reach the desired landing area, and at an airspeed that will result in minimum floating just before touchdown. To accomplish this, it is essential that both the descent angle and the airspeed be accurately controlled.

Unlike a normal approach when the power setting is variable, on a power-off approach the power is fixed at the idle setting. Pitch attitude rather than power is adjusted to control the airspeed. This will also change the glide or descent angle. By lowering the nose to

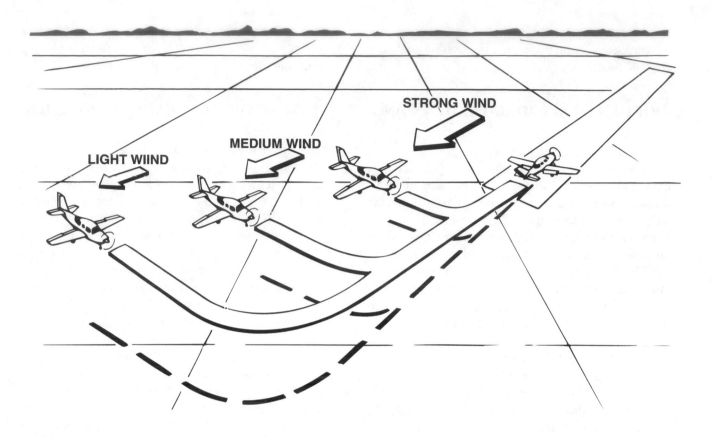

FIGURE 7-9.—Plan the base leg for wind conditions.

keep the approach airspeed constant, the descent angle will steepen. If the airspeed is too high, raise the nose, and when the airspeed is too low, lower the nose. If the pitch attitude is raised too high, the airplane will settle rapidly due to a slow airspeed and insufficient lift. For this reason, never try to stretch a glide to reach the desired landing spot.

Uniform approach patterns, such as the 90°, 180°, or 360° power-off approaches are described in the following sections. Practice in these approaches provides the pilot with a basis on which to develop judgment in gliding distance and in planning an approach.

The basic procedure in these approaches involves closing the throttle at a given altitude, and gliding to a key position. This position, like the pattern itself, must not be allowed to become the primary objective, it is merely a convenient point in the air from which the pilot can judge whether the glide will safely terminate at the desired spot. The selected key position should be one that is appropriate for the available altitude and the wind condition. From the key position, the pilot must constantly evaluate the situation.

It must be emphasized that, although accurate spot touchdowns are important, safe and properly executed approaches and landings are vital. The pilot must never sacrifice a good approach or landing just to land on the desired spot.

90° Power-Off Approach

The 90° power-off approach is made from a base leg and requires only a 90° turn onto the final approach. The approach path may be varied by positioning the base leg closer to or father out from the approach end of the runway according to wind conditions. [Figure 7-9]

The glide from the key position on the base leg through the 90° turn to the final approach is the final part of all accuracy landing maneuvers.

The 90° power-off approach usually begins from a rectangular pattern at approximately 1,000 feet above the ground or at normal traffic pattern altitude. The airplane should be flown onto a downwind leg at the same distance from the landing surface as in a normal

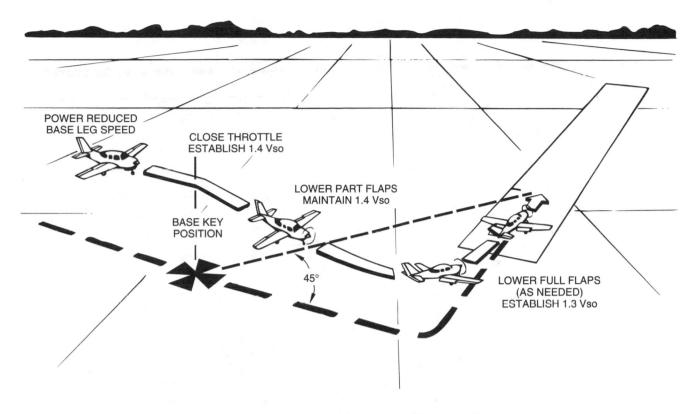

POWER REDUCED
BASE LEG SPEED

CLOSE THROTTLE
ESTABLISH 1.4 Vso

LOWER PART FLAPS
MAINTAIN 1.4 Vso

BASE KEY
POSITION

45°

LOWER FULL FLAPS
(AS NEEDED)
ESTABLISH 1.3 Vso

FIGURE 7-10.—90° power-off approach.

traffic pattern. The before landing checklist should be completed on the downwind leg, including extension of the landing gear if the airplane is equipped with retractable gear.

After a medium-banked turn onto the base leg is completed, the throttle should be retarded slightly and the airspeed allowed to decrease to the normal base-leg speed. [Figure 7-10] On the base leg, the airspeed, wind drift correction, and altitude should be maintained while proceeding to the 45° key position. At this position, the intended landing spot will appear to be on a 45° angle from the airplane's nose.

The pilot can determine the strength and direction of the wind from the amount of crab necessary to hold the desired ground track on the base leg. This will help in planning the turn onto the final approach and in lowering the correct amount of flaps.

At the 45° key position, the throttle should be closed completely, the propeller control (if equipped) advanced to the full increase RPM position, and altitude maintained until the airspeed decreases to the manufacturer's recommended glide speed. In the absence of a recommended speed, use 1.4 V_{SO}. When this airspeed is attained, the nose should be lowered to maintain the gliding speed and the controls retrimmed.

The base-to-final turn should be planned and accomplished so that upon rolling out of the turn the airplane will be aligned with the runway centerline. When on final approach, the wing flaps are lowered and the pitch attitude adjusted, as necessary, to establish the proper descent angle and airspeed (1.3 V_{SO}), then the controls retrimmed. Slight adjustments in pitch attitude or flaps setting may be necessary to control the glide angle and airspeed. However, NEVER TRY TO STRETCH THE GLIDE OR RETRACT THE FLAPS to reach the desired landing spot. The final approach may be made with or without the use of slips.

After the final approach glide has been established, full attention is then given to making a good, safe landing rather than concentrating on the selected landing spot. The base leg position and the flap setting already determined the probability of landing on the spot. In any event, it is better to execute a good landing 200 feet from the spot than to make a poor landing precisely on the spot.

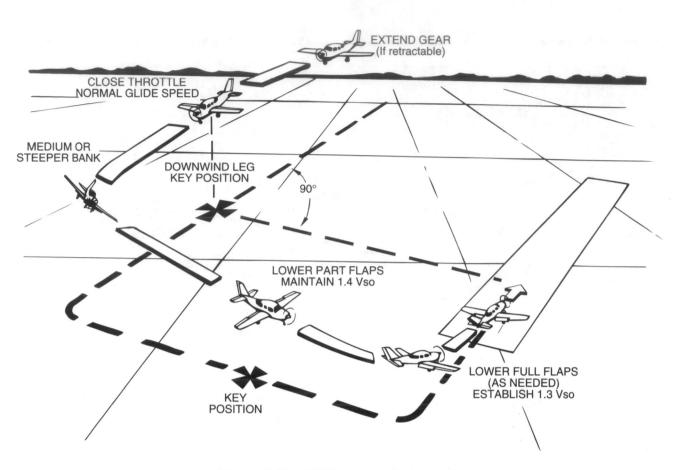

FIGURE 7-11.—180° power-off approach.

180° Power-Off Approach

The 180° power-off approach is executed by gliding with the power off from a given point on a downwind leg to a preselected landing spot. [Figure 7-11] It is an extension of the principles involved in the 90° power-off approach just described. Its objective is to further develop judgment in estimating distances and glide ratios, in that the airplane is flown without power from a higher altitude and through a 90° turn to reach the base leg position at a proper altitude for executing the 90° approach. The 180° power-off approach requires more planning and judgment than the 90° power-off approach.

In the execution of 180° power-off approaches, the airplane is flown on a downwind heading parallel to the landing runway and the landing gear extended (if retractable). The altitude from which this type of approach should be started will vary with the type of airplane, but it should usually not exceed 1,000 feet above the ground, except with large airplanes. Greater accuracy in judgment and maneuvering is required at higher altitudes.

When abreast of or opposite the desired landing spot, the throttle should be closed and altitude maintained while decelerating to the manufacturer's recommended glide speed, or 1.4 V_{so}. The point at which the throttle is closed is the downwind key position.

The turn from the downwind leg to the base leg should be a uniform turn with a medium or slightly steeper bank. The degree of bank and amount of this initial turn will depend upon the glide angle of the airplane and the velocity of the wind. Again, the base leg should be positioned as needed for the altitude, or wind condition—position the base leg to conserve or dissipate altitude so as to reach the desired landing spot.

The turn onto the base leg should be made at an altitude high enough and close enough to permit the airplane to glide to what would normally be the base key position in a 90° power-off approach.

Although the key position is important, it must not be overemphasized nor considered as a fixed point on the ground. Many inexperienced pilots may gain a conception of it as a particular landmark, such as a tree, crossroad, or other visual reference, to be reached at a certain altitude. This will result in a mechanical

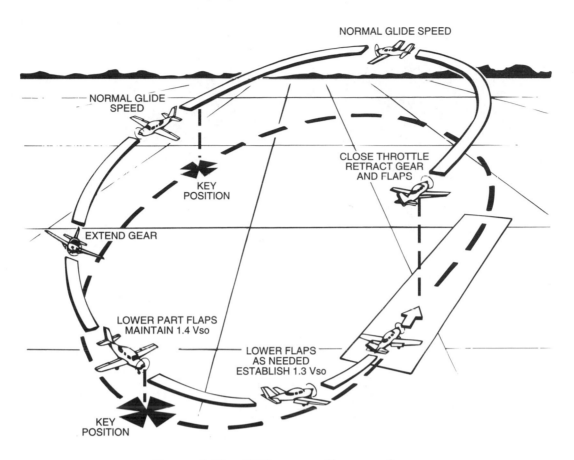

NORMAL GLIDE SPEED

NORMAL GLIDE SPEED

KEY POSITION

CLOSE THROTTLE RETRACT GEAR AND FLAPS

EXTEND GEAR

LOWER PART FLAPS MAINTAIN 1.4 Vso

LOWER FLAPS AS NEEDED ESTABLISH 1.3 Vso

KEY POSITION

FIGURE 7-12.—360° power-off approach.

conception and leave the pilot at a total loss any time such objects are not present. Both altitude and geographical location should be varied as much as is practical to eliminate any such conception. After reaching the base key position, the approach and landing are the same as in the 90° power-off approach.

360° Power-Off Approach

The 360° power-off approach is one in which the airplane glides through a 360° change of direction to the preselected landing spot. The entire pattern is designed to be circular, but the turn may be shallowed, steepened, or discontinued at any point to adjust the accuracy of the flightpath.

The 360° approach is started from a position over the approach end of the landing runway or slightly to the side of it, with the airplane headed in the proposed landing direction and the landing gear and flaps retracted. [Figure 7-12]

It is usually initiated from approximately 2,000 feet or more above the ground—where the wind may vary significantly from that at lower altitudes. This must be

taken into account when maneuvering the airplane to a point from which a 90° or 180° power-off approach can be completed.

After the throttle is closed over the intended point of landing, the proper glide speed should immediately be established, and a medium banked turn made in the desired direction so as to arrive at the downwind key position opposite the intended landing spot. At or just beyond the downwind key position, the landing gear should be extended if the airplane is equipped with retractable gear. The altitude at the downwind key position should be approximately 1,000 to 1,200 feet above the ground.

After reaching that point, the turn should be continued to arrive at a base leg key position, at an altitude of about 800 feet above the terrain. Flaps may be used at this position, as necessary, but full flaps should not be used until established on the final approach.

The angle of bank can be varied as needed throughout the pattern to correct for wind conditions and to align the airplane with the final approach. The turn-to-final should be completed at a minimum altitude of 300 feet above the terrain.

CHAPTER 8
FAULTY APPROACHES AND LANDINGS

INTRODUCTION

This chapter discusses the factors contributing to faulty approaches and landings and describes the appropriate actions for making recoveries. A thorough knowledge of these factors is invaluable to the pilot in preventing landing accidents.

The explanations of approaches and landings up to this point have been devoted mainly to normal situations, in which the landings were ideally executed. In addition to occasional errors in judgment during some part of the approach and landing, numerous variables, such as traffic, wind shift, or wind gusts create situations requiring corrections or recoveries to assure a safe landing. Pilot skill in anticipation of, recognition of, and recovery from abnormal situations is equal in importance to normal approach and landing skills.

FINAL APPROACHES

Low Final Approach

When the base leg is too low, insufficient power is used, landing flaps are extended prematurely, or the velocity of the wind is misjudged, sufficient altitude may be lost, which will cause the airplane to be well below the proper final approach path. When it is realized the runway will not be reached unless appropriate action is taken, power must be applied immediately to maintain the airspeed while the pitch attitude is raised to increase lift and stop the descent. When the proper approach path has been intercepted, the correct approach attitude should be reestablished and the power reduced. DO NOT increase the pitch attitude without increasing the power, since the airplane will decelerate rapidly and may approach the critical angle of attack and stall. DO NOT retract the flaps, this will suddenly decrease lift and cause the airplane to sink more rapidly. If there is any doubt about the approach being safely completed, it is advisable to EXECUTE AN IMMEDIATE GO-AROUND.

High Final Approach

When the final approach is too high, lower the flaps as required. Further reduction in power may be necessary, and lowering the nose simultaneously to maintain approach airspeed and increase the rate of descent. When the proper approach path has been intercepted, adjust the power as required. When increasing the descent rate, care must be taken not to descend at an excessively high rate. If a high-sink rate is continued close to the surface, it may be difficult to slow to a proper rate prior to ground contact. A go-around should be initiated if the descent rate becomes excessive.

Slow Final Approach

When the airplane is flown at a slower-than-normal airspeed on the final approach, the pilot's judgment of the rate of sink (descent) and the height of roundout will be difficult. During an excessively slow approach, the wing is operating near the critical angle of attack and, depending on the pitch attitude changes and control usage, the airplane may stall or sink rapidly, contacting the ground with a hard impact.

Whenever a slow-speed approach is noted, the pilot should apply power to accelerate the airplane and increase the lift to reduce the sink rate and to prevent a stall. This should be done while still at a high enough altitude to reestablish the correct approach airspeed and attitude. If too slow and too low, it is best to EXECUTE A GO-AROUND.

Use of Power

Power can be used effectively during the approach and roundout to compensate for errors in judgment. Power can be added to accelerate the airplane to increase lift without increasing the angle of attack; thus,

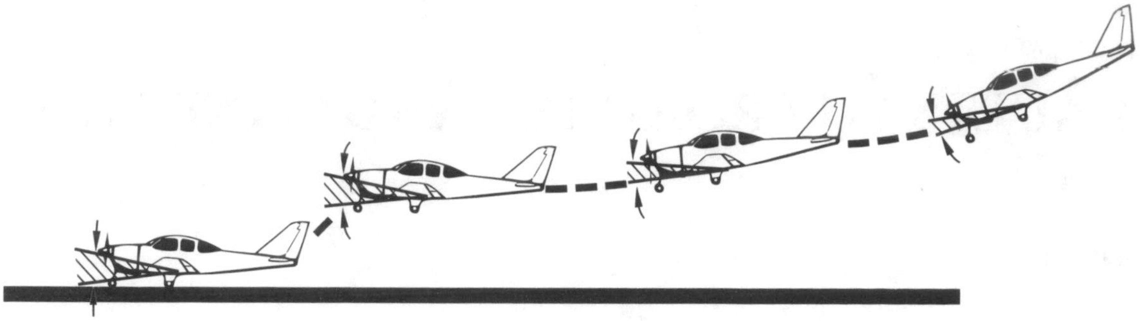

FIGURE 8-1.—Rounding out too high.

the descent can be slowed to an acceptable rate. If the proper landing attitude has been attained and the airplane is only slightly high, the landing attitude should be held constant and sufficient power applied to help ease the airplane onto the ground. After the airplane has touched down, it will be necessary to close the throttle so the additional thrust and lift will be removed and the airplane will stay on the ground.

ROUNDOUT (FLARE)

High Roundout

Sometimes when the airplane appears to temporarily stop moving downward, the roundout has been made too rapidly and the airplane is flying level, too high above the runway. Continuing the roundout would further reduce the airspeed, resulting in an increase in angle of attack to the critical angle. This would result in the airplane stalling and dropping hard onto the runway. To prevent this, the pitch attitude should be held constant until the airplane decelerates enough to again start descending. Then the roundout can be continued to establish the proper landing attitude. This procedure should only be used when there is adequate airspeed. It may be necessary to add a slight amount of power to keep the airspeed from decreasing excessively and to avoid losing lift too rapidly.

Although back-elevator pressure may be relaxed slightly, the nose should not be lowered any perceptible amount to make the airplane descend when fairly close to the runway unless some power is added momentarily. The momentary decrease in lift that would result from lowering the nose and decreasing the angle of attack may be so great that the airplane might contact the ground with the nosewheel first, which could collapse.

When the proper landing attitude is attained, the airplane is approaching a stall because the airspeed is decreasing and the critical angle of attack is being approached, even though the pitch attitude is no longer being increased. [Figure 8-1]

It is recommended that a GO-AROUND be executed any time it appears the landing is uncertain.

Late or Rapid Roundout

Starting the roundout too late or pulling the elevator control back too rapidly to prevent the airplane from touching down prematurely can impose a heavy load factor on the wing and cause an accelerated stall.

Suddenly increasing the angle of attack and stalling the airplane during a roundout is a dangerous situation since it may cause the airplane to land extremely hard on the main landing gear, and then bounce back into the air. As the airplane contacts the ground, the tail will be forced down very rapidly by the back-elevator pressure and by inertia acting downward on the tail.

Recovery from this situation requires prompt and positive application of power prior to occurrence of the stall. This may be followed by a normal landing if sufficient runway is available—otherwise the pilot should EXECUTE A GO-AROUND immediately.

If the roundout is late, the nosewheel may strike the runway first, causing the nose to bounce upward. No attempt should be made to force the airplane back onto the ground; a GO-AROUND should be executed immediately.

Floating During Roundout

If the airspeed on final approach is excessive, it will usually result in the airplane floating. [Figure 8-2] Before touchdown can be made, the

FIGURE 8-2.—Floating during roundout.

airplane may be well past the desired landing point and the available runway may be insufficient. When diving an airplane on final approach to land at the proper point, there will be an appreciable increase in airspeed. The proper touchdown attitude cannot be established without producing an excessive angle of attack and lift. This will cause the airplane to gain altitude or balloon.

Any time the airplane floats, judgment of speed, height, and rate of sink must be especially sharp. The pilot must smoothly and gradually adjust the pitch attitude as the airplane decelerates to touchdown speed and starts to settle, so the proper landing attitude is attained at the moment of touchdown. The slightest error in judgment and timing will result in either ballooning or bouncing.

Since prolonged floating utilizes considerable runway length, it should be avoided especially on short runways or in strong crosswinds. If a landing cannot be made on the first third of the runway, or the airplane drifts sideways, the pilot should EXECUTE A GO-AROUND.

Ballooning During Roundout

If the pilot misjudges the rate of sink during a landing and thinks the airplane is descending faster than it should, there is a tendency to increase the pitch attitude and angle of attack too rapidly. This not only stops the descent, but actually starts the airplane climbing. This climbing during the roundout is known as ballooning. [Figure 8-3] Ballooning can be dangerous because the height above the ground is increasing and the airplane may be rapidly approaching a stalled condition. The altitude gained in each instance will depend on the airspeed or the speed with which the pitch attitude is increased.

When ballooning is slight, a constant landing attitude should be held and the airplane allowed to gradually decelerate and settle onto the runway. Depending on the severity of ballooning, the use of throttle may be helpful in cushioning the landing. By adding power, thrust can be increased to keep the airspeed from decelerating too rapidly and the wings from suddenly losing lift, but throttle must be closed immediately after touchdown. Remember that torque will be created as power is applied; therefore, it will be necessary to use rudder pressure to keep the airplane straight as it settles onto the runway.

When ballooning is excessive, it is best to EXECUTE A GO-AROUND IMMEDIATELY; DO NOT ATTEMPT TO SALVAGE THE LANDING. Power must be applied before the airplane enters a stalled condition.

The pilot must be extremely cautious of ballooning when there is a crosswind present because the crosswind correction may be inadvertently released or it may become inadequate. Because of the lower airspeed after ballooning, the crosswind affects the airplane more. Consequently, the wing will have to be

FIGURE 8-3.—Ballooning during roundout.

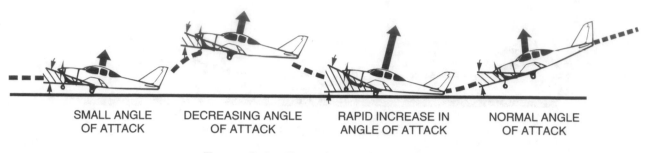

SMALL ANGLE
OF ATTACK

DECREASING ANGLE
OF ATTACK

RAPID INCREASE IN
ANGLE OF ATTACK

NORMAL ANGLE
OF ATTACK

FIGURE 8-4.—Bouncing during touchdown.

lowered even further to compensate for the increased drift. It is imperative that the pilot makes certain that the appropriate wing is down and that directional control is maintained with opposite rudder. If there is any doubt, or the airplane starts to drift, EXECUTE A GO-AROUND.

TOUCHDOWN

Bouncing During Touchdown

When the airplane contacts the ground with a sharp impact as the result of an improper attitude or an excessive rate of sink, it tends to bounce back into the air. Though the airplane's tires and shock struts provide some springing action, the airplane does not bounce like a rubber ball. Instead, it rebounds into the air because the wing's angle of attack was abruptly increased, producing a sudden addition of lift. [Figure 8-4]

The abrupt change in angle of attack is the result of inertia instantly forcing the airplane's tail downward when the main wheels contact the ground sharply. The severity of the bounce depends on the airspeed at the moment of contact and the degree to which the angle of attack or pitch attitude was increased.

Since a bounce occurs when the airplane makes contact with the ground before the proper touchdown attitude is attained, it is almost invariably accompanied by the application of excessive back-elevator pressure. This is usually the result of the pilot realizing too late that the airplane is not in the proper attitude and attempting to establish it just as the second touchdown occurs.

The corrective action for a bounce is the same as for ballooning and similarly depends on its severity. When it is very slight and there is no extreme change in the airplane's pitch attitude, a follow-up landing may be executed by applying sufficient power to cushion the subsequent touchdown, and smoothly adjusting the pitch to the proper touchdown attitude.

In the event a very slight bounce is encountered while landing with a crosswind, crosswind correction must be maintained while the next touchdown is made. Remember that since the subsequent touchdown will be made at a slower airspeed, the upwind wing will have to be lowered even further to compensate for drift.

Extreme caution and alertness must be exercised any time a bounce occurs, but particularly when there is a crosswind. Inexperienced pilots will almost invariably release the crosswind correction. When one main wheel of the airplane strikes the runway, the other wheel will touch down immediately afterwards, and the wings will become level. Then, with no crosswind correction as the airplane bounces, the wind will cause the airplane to roll with the wind, thus exposing even more surface to the crosswind and drifting the airplane more rapidly.

When a bounce is severe, the safest procedure is to EXECUTE A GO-AROUND IMMEDIATELY. No attempt to salvage the landing should be made. Full power should be applied while simultaneously maintaining directional control, and lowering the nose to a safe climb attitude. The go-around procedure should be continued even though the airplane may descend and another bounce may be encountered. It would be extremely foolish to attempt a landing from a bad bounce since airspeed diminishes very rapidly in the nose-high attitude, and a stall may occur before a subsequent touchdown could be made.

Porpoising

In a bounced landing that is improperly recovered, the airplane comes in nose first setting off a series of motions that imitate the jumps and dives of a porpoise—

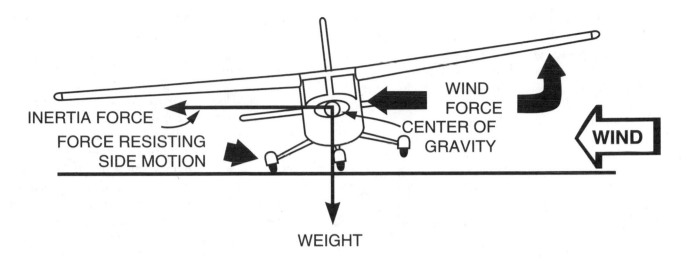

FIGURE 8-5.—Drifting during touchdown.

hence the name. The problem is improper aircraft attitude at touchdown, sometimes caused by inattention, not knowing where the ground is, mistrimming or forcing the aircraft onto the runway.

Ground effect decreases elevator control effectiveness and increases the effort required to raise the nose. Not enough elevator or stabilator trim can result in a nose-low contact with the runway and a porpoise develops.

Porpoising can also be caused by improper airspeed control. Usually, if an approach is too fast, the airplane floats and the pilot tries to force it on the runway when the airplane still wants to fly. A gust of wind, a bump in the runway, or even a slight tug on the control wheel will send the aircraft aloft again.

The corrective action for a porpoise is the same as for a bounce and similarly depends on its severity. When it is very slight and there is no extreme change in the airplane's pitch attitude, a follow-up landing may be executed by applying sufficient power to cushion the subsequent touchdown, and smoothly adjusting the pitch to the proper touchdown attitude.

When a porpoise is severe, the safest procedure is to EXECUTE A GO-AROUND IMMEDIATELY. No attempt to salvage the landing should be made. Full power should be applied while simultaneously maintaining directional control, and lowering the nose to a safe climb attitude.

Wheelbarrowing

When a pilot permits the aircraft weight to become concentrated about the nosewheel during the takeoff or landing roll, a condition know as wheelbarrowing will occur. Wheelbarrowing may cause loss of directional control during the landing roll because braking action is ineffective, and the airplane tends to swerve or pivot on the nosewheel, particularly in crosswind conditions. One of the most common causes of wheelbarrowing during the landing roll is a simultaneous touchdown of the main and nosewheel with excessive speed followed by application of forward pressure on the elevator control. Usually, the situation can be corrected by smoothly applying back-elevator pressure. However, if wheelbarrowing is encountered and runway and other conditions permit, it may be advisable to promptly initiate a go-around. Wheelbarrowing will not occur if the pilot achieves and maintains the correct landing attitude, touches down at the proper speed, and gently lowers the nosewheel while losing speed on rollout. If the pilot decides to stay on the ground rather than attempt a go-around or if he or she should lose directional control, then close the throttle, and smoothly but firmly rotate to the landing attitude. Raise the flaps to reduce lift and to increase the load on the main wheels for better braking action.

Hard Landing

When the airplane contacts the ground during landings, its vertical speed is instantly reduced to zero. Unless provisions are made to slow this vertical speed and cushion the impact of touchdown, the force of contact with the ground may be so great it could cause structural damage to the airplane.

The purpose of pneumatic tires, shock absorbing landing gears, and other devices is to cushion the impact and to increase the time in which the airplane's vertical descent is stopped. The importance of this cushion may be understood from the computation that a 6-inch free fall on landing is roughly equal, to a 340-foot-per-minute descent. Within a fraction of a second, the airplane must be slowed from this rate of vertical descent to zero, without damage.

During this time, the landing gear together with some aid from the lift of the wings must supply whatever force is needed to counteract the force of the airplane's inertia and weight. The lift decreases rapidly as the airplane's forward speed is decreased, and the force on the landing gear increases by the impact of touchdown. When the descent stops, the lift will be practically zero, leaving the landing gear alone to carry both the airplane's weight and inertia force. The load imposed at the instant of touchdown may easily be three or four times the actual weight of the airplane depending on the severity of contact.

Touchdown in a Drift or Crab

At times the pilot may correct for wind drift by crabbing on the final approach. If the roundout and touchdown are made while the airplane is drifting or in a crab, it will contact the ground while moving sideways. This will impose extreme side loads on the landing gear, and if severe enough, may cause structural failure.

The most effective method to prevent drift in primary training aircraft is the wing-low method. This technique keeps the longitudinal axis of the airplane aligned with both the runway and the direction of motion throughout the approach and touchdown.

There are three factors that will cause the longitudinal axis and the direction of motion to be misaligned during touchdown: drifting, crabbing, or a combination of both.

If the pilot has not taken adequate corrective action to avoid drift during a crosswind landing, the main wheels' tire tread offers resistance to the airplane's sideward movement in respect to the ground. Consequently, any sidewise velocity of the airplane is abruptly decelerated, with the result that the inertia force is as shown in Figure 8-5. This creates a moment around the main wheel when it contacts the ground, tending to overturn or tip the airplane. If the windward wingtip is raised by the action of this moment, all the weight and shock of landing will be borne by one main wheel. This could cause structural damage.

Not only are the same factors present that are attempting to raise a wing, but the crosswind is also acting on the fuselage surface behind the main wheels,

tending to yaw (weathervane) the airplane into the wind. This often results in a ground loop.

Ground Loop

A ground loop is an uncontrolled turn during ground operation that may occur while taxiing or taking off, but especially during the after-landing roll. Drift or weathervaning does not always cause a ground loop although these things may cause the initial swerve. Careless use of the rudder, an uneven ground surface, or a soft spot that retards one main wheel of the airplane may also cause a swerve. In any case, the initial swerve tends to make the airplane ground loop, whether it is a tailwheel-type or nosewheel-type. [Figure 8-6]

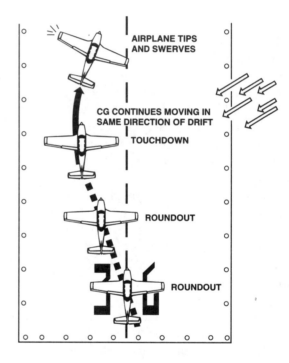

FIGURE 8-6.—Start of a ground loop.

Nose-wheel type airplanes are somewhat less prone to ground loop. Since the center of gravity (CG) is located forward of the main landing gear on these airplanes, any time a swerve develops, centrifugal force acting on the CG will tend to stop the swerving action.

If the airplane touches down while drifting or in a crab, the pilot should apply aileron toward the high wing and stop the swerve with the rudder. Brakes should be used to correct for turns or swerves only when the rudder is inadequate. The pilot must exercise caution when applying corrective brake action because it is very easy to overcontrol and aggravate the situation.

If brakes are used, sufficient brake should be applied on the low-wing wheel (outside of the turn) to stop the swerve. When the wings are approximately level, the new direction must be maintained until the airplane has slowed to taxi speed or has stopped.

Wing Rising After Touchdown

When landing in a crosswind, there may be instances when a wing will rise during the after-landing roll. This may occur whether or not there is a loss of directional control, depending on the amount of crosswind and the degree of corrective action.

Any time an airplane is rolling on the ground in a crosswind condition, the upwind wing is receiving a greater force from the wind than the downwind wing. This causes a lift differential. Also, as the upwind wing rises, there is an increase in the angle of attack, which increases lift on the upwind wing, rolling the aircraft down wind.

When the effects of these two factors are great enough, the upwind wing may rise even though directional control is maintained. If no correction is applied, it is possible that the upwind wing will rise sufficiently to cause the downwind wing to strike the ground.

In the event a wing starts to rise during the landing roll, the pilot should immediately apply more aileron pressure toward the high wing and continue to maintain direction. The sooner the aileron control is applied, the more effective it will be. The further a wing is allowed to rise before taking corrective action, the more airplane surface is exposed to the force of the crosswind. This diminishes the effectiveness of the aileron.

CHAPTER 9

FLIGHT BY REFERENCE TO INSTRUMENTS

INTRODUCTION

This chapter provides guidance in developing the ability to maneuver the airplane for limited periods by reference to flight instruments and in following instructions from Air Traffic Control (ATC), when outside visual references are lost due to flight into instrument meteorological conditions (IMC). In an emergency situation, this ability could save the pilot's life and those of the passengers, but intentional ventures into even marginal weather might eventually end in a serious accident.

BASIC INSTRUMENT TRAINING

During basic instrument training, pilots must understand that emergency use of flight instruments does not prepare them for unrestricted operations in instrument weather conditions. It is intended for emergency use only. Only those trained and certified as instrument pilots should attempt intentional flight in such conditions. Persons interested in pursuing a comprehensive instrument flying program should study the material in AC 61-27, Instrument Flying Handbook, and other pertinent publications, and complete a suitable instrument flying training course under the guidance of a certificated instrument flight instructor.

Accident investigations reveal that, as a related factor, weather continues to be cited more frequently than any other in general aviation accidents. The data also shows that weather-involved accidents are more likely to result in fatal injury than accidents not involving weather. Low ceilings, rain, and fog continue to head the list in the fatal, weather-involved general aviation accidents. The pilot involvement in this type of accident is usually the result of inadequate preflight preparation and/or planning, continued visual flight rules (VFR) flight into adverse weather conditions, and attempted operation beyond the pilot's experience/ability level. In far too many cases, it was determined that the pilot did not obtain a preflight weather briefing. It appears logical to assume that if an adequate preflight briefing had been obtained, unexpected weather conditions would not have been encountered and many of the accidents would not have occurred.

All pilots should be somewhat conservative in judging their own capabilities and should use every means available to avoid weather situations that overtax one's ability.

If inadvertently caught in poor weather conditions, the VFR pilot should, in addition to maintaining control of the airplane, notify the nearest Federal Aviation Administration (FAA) facility by radio, and follow their instructions. Calmness, patience, and compliance with those instructions represent the best chance for survival.

The Senses During Instrument Flight

The only way a pilot can control an airplane safely in a low-visibility environment is by using and trusting flight instruments. The orientation senses are not designed to cope with flight when clouds, fog, haze, dust, darkness, or other phenomena obscure external visual references, unless visual reference is transferred to the flight instruments. When the visual sense is provided with reference points, such as the Earth's horizon or the flight instruments, there usually is not a problem with airplane attitude control since the visual sense overrides the other senses.

It is in situations where visual references, such as the ground and horizon are obscured that trouble develops, especially for pilots who lack training, experience, and proficiency in instrument flight. The vestibular sense (motion sensing by the inner ear) in particular tends to confuse the pilot. Because of inertia, the sensory areas of the inner ear cannot detect slight changes in the attitude of the airplane, nor can they accurately sense attitude changes that occur at a uniform rate over a period of time. On the other hand, false sensations often are generated; leading the pilot to believe the attitude of the airplane has changed when, in fact, it has not. These false sensations result in the pilot experiencing spatial disorientation.

FIGURE 9-1.—Straight-and-level flight.

When a disoriented pilot actually does make a recovery from a turn, bank, climb, or descent, there is a very strong tendency to feel that the airplane has entered a turn, bank, climb, or descent in the opposite direction. These false sensations may lead to the well-known "graveyard spiral."

All pilots should be aware of these illusions and their consequences. Flight instructors should provide each student with an opportunity to experience these sensations under controlled conditions.

Basic Instrument Flight

The use of an airplane equipped with flight instruments and an easy means of simulating instrument flight conditions, are needed for training in flight by reference to instruments.

Instruction in attitude control by reference to instruments should be conducted with the use of all available instruments in the airplane. When an attitude indicator is provided, its use as the primary reference for the control of the attitude of the airplane should be emphasized.

From the beginning of instruction in maneuvering the airplane by reference to instruments, three important actions should be stressed. First, a person cannot feel control pressure changes with a tight grip on the controls. Relaxing and learning to control with the eyes and the brain instead of only the muscles usually takes considerable conscious effort.

Second, attitude changes should be smooth and small, yet with positive pressure. No attitude changes should be made unless the instruments show a need for change.

Third, with the airplane properly trimmed, all control pressure should be released momentarily when one becomes aware of tenseness. The airplane is inherently stable and, except in turbulent air, will maintain approximate straight-and-level flight if left alone.

It must be reemphasized that the following procedures are intended only for an emergency while extracting one's self from an inadvertent entry into IMC. The main goal is not precision instrument flying; rather, it is to help the VFR pilot keep the airplane under adequate control until suitable visual references are regained.

Straight-and-Level Flight

To maintain straight-and-level flight, the pilot must keep the airplane's wings level with the horizon. Any degree of bank (in coordinated flight) will result in a deviation from straight flight, and a change in the airplane's heading. Using the attitude indicator, straight flight is simplified by merely keeping the wings of the representative airplane level with the representative or artificial horizon. [Figure 9-1] This is accomplished by applying the necessary coordinated aileron and rudder pressures.

The needle of a turn indicator or the representative wings on a turn coordinator will deflect whenever the airplane is turning and will be centered or level when the airplane is in straight flight. They also can be used to maintain straight flight by applying coordinated aileron and rudder pressures, as needed; to keep the needle centered or the turn coordinator's airplane wings level.

Regardless of which of these instruments is being used, the heading indicator should be checked frequently to determine whether a straight flightpath is actually being maintained. This is particularly true when flying in turbulent air since every little gust may bank the airplane and make it turn.

Pitch Attitude

At the same time that straight flight is being maintained, the pilot must also control the pitch attitude to keep the airplane level—no gain or loss of altitude. This can be accomplished by referencing several instruments. They are the attitude indicator, altimeter, and vertical speed indicator (VSI).

The attitude indicator will show the airplane pitch attitude in relation to the horizon. The altimeter tells when a constant altitude is being maintained or if the flight altitude is changing. The VSI will indicate the rate at which altitude is changing. Either of these instruments shows the pilot whether a change in pitch attitude is needed and approximately how much. [Figure 9-1]

Level flight requires the airplane's nose be raised or lowered in relation to the horizon. This can be done by reference to the attitude indicator, by applying elevator pressure to adjust the representative airplane in relation to the horizon bar. The application of elevator pressure should be very slight to prevent overcontrolling. It must be emphasized that turn coordinators provide NO PITCH INFORMATION even though they have an appearance similar to attitude indicators.

In lieu of using an attitude indicator, the VSI may be used. If the instrument shows a climb or descent, the pilot should apply only sufficient elevator pressure to start the pointer moving toward the zero indication, since there is a certain amount of lag in the indication. Trying to obtain an immediate zero indication usually results in overcontrolling. When the pointer stabilizes again, additional pressure, if needed, can be added in increments to get a zero indication and gradually stop the climb or descent. Only after the vertical speed is zero and the altimeter remains constant should an attempt be made to return to the original altitude.

In the case of an airplane having neither attitude indicator nor VSI, the airspeed indicator can be used like the VSI to maintain level flight. Remember though that it, too, lags somewhat as a result of the time required for the airplane to accelerate and decelerate after a pitch change is made.

Pilots must be cautioned not to chase the pointers on the instruments when flight through turbulent air produces erratic movements.

Descents

When unexpected adverse weather is encountered by the VFR pilot, the most likely situation is being trapped in or above a broken or solid layer of clouds or haze, requiring that a descent be made to an altitude where the pilot can reestablish visual reference to the ground. Generally, the descent should be made in straight flight.

A descent can be made at a variety of airspeeds and vertical speeds by reducing power, adding drag (gear and flaps), and lowering the nose to a predetermined attitude. Before beginning the descent, it is recommended that first the descent airspeed and the desired heading are established while holding the wings level. In addition, the landing gear and flaps should be positioned, as appropriate, to help in maintaining the desired rate of descent, or a fast rate of descent, as desired. Establishing the desired configuration before starting the descent will permit a more stabilized descent and require less division of attention once the descent is started. Rather than attempting to maintain a specific rate of descent, it is recommended that only a constant airspeed be maintained.

The following method for entering a descent is effective either with or without an attitude indicator. First, the airspeed is reduced to the desired airspeed by reducing power while maintaining straight-and-level

FIGURE 9-2.—Descents.

flight. When the descent speed is established, a further reduction in power is made, and simultaneously the nose is lowered to maintain a constant airspeed. [Figure 9-2] A rule of thumb would be 100 RPM or 1 inch of manifold pressure reduction in power for each 100 feet per minute (FPM) rate of descent desired. The power should remain at a fixed (constant) setting and deviations in airspeed corrected by making pitch changes. Rapid throttle movements to control airspeed only adds to the pilot's workload.

If an attitude indicator is available, the pitch attitude can be adjusted by reference to the representative airplane and the artificial horizon, and then checking the airspeed indicator to determine if the attitude is correct. Using a half a bar width or one bar width below the artificial horizon will help establish a proper pitch attitude. Deviations from the desired airspeed should be corrected by adjusting the pitch attitude. If there is not an attitude indicator available and the airspeed is too high or too low, the pilot should apply sufficient elevator pressure to start the airspeed pointer moving toward the desired airspeed, since it takes a little time for the airspeed to stabilize. Trying to nail down the airspeed immediately will result in overcontrolling the airplane. Additional pressure can then be added, as necessary, to attain the desired airspeed.

In any case, the pilot should not be concerned with slight deviations in airspeed. The main objective is to descend at a safe airspeed, well above the stall, but not more than the airplane's design maneuvering speed.

While descending, directional control should be maintained by referencing the directional instruments as described for straight-and-level flight. Pilots are cautioned against "chasing" the instrument pointers.

If any thought is given to the matter before starting the flight, the pilot will have a rough idea of the height of obstructions and terrain in the vicinity of the descent. Before starting the descent, a decision must be made regarding the minimum altitude to which the descent will be made.

Climbs

When adverse weather is encountered, a climb by referencing flight instruments is required primarily to assure clearance of obstructions or terrain. It may sometimes be advisable to climb to a clear area above a layer of fog, haze, or low clouds.

As in straight descents, the climb should be made at a constant airspeed—one that is well above the stall and results in a positive climb. The power setting and pitch attitude determines the airspeed.

FIGURE 9-3.—Climb.

The attitude indicator provides the greatest help in visualizing the pitch attitude. To enter a constant airspeed climb from cruising airspeed (the most likely entry speed), the nose of the representative airplane is raised in relation to the artificial horizon to the approximate climbing attitude, approximately a half to one bar width. [Figure 9-3] Only a small amount of back-elevator pressure should be added to initiate and maintain the climb attitude. The power setting may be advanced to climb power simultaneously with the pitch change, or, after the pitch change is established and the airspeed approaches the desired climb speed.

If there is not an attitude indicator available, the pilot should apply sufficient elevator pressure to start the airspeed pointer moving toward the desired climb airspeed and to cause the altimeter to show an upward trend. Because of inertia, speed will not be reduced immediately to the climb speed. The pilot must give the airspeed time to stabilize, then should apply whatever additional elevator pressure is needed to attain and maintain the desired airspeed. During the climb, the power should remain at a fixed (constant) setting and deviation in airspeed should be corrected by making pitch changes. Making throttle adjustments to correct for airspeed are unnecessary and burdensome.

As in descents during the emergency use of flight instruments, maintaining a precise airspeed is not important. The primary objective is to keep the airplane climbing—and not allow a stall to occur.

While climbing, the directional instruments should be scanned to detect any lapse of directional control just as in straight-and-level flight and straight descents. Unless a specific heading is required, slight deviations in headings, particularly in gusty air, should be of little concern—just keep the wings as level as possible.

Turns to Headings

When encountering adverse weather conditions, it is advisable for the pilot to use radio navigation aids, or to obtain directional guidance from ATC facilities. This usually requires that turns are made and/or specific headings be maintained.

When making turns in adverse weather conditions, nothing is gained by maneuvering the airplane faster than the pilot's ability to keep up with the changes that occur in the flight instrument indications. It is advisable to limit all turns to no more than a standard rate. A standard rate turn is one during which the heading changes 3° per second. On most turn indicators, this is

FIGURE 9-4.—Turns to headings.

shown when the needle is deflected one needle width; on turn coordinators, this is shown when the wingtip of the representative airplane is opposite the standard rate marker.

The rate at which a turn should be made is dictated generally by the amount of turn desired—a slow turn for small changes (less than 30°) in heading, a faster turn (up to a standard rate) for larger changes (more than 30°) in heading. [Figure 9-4]

Before starting the turn to any new heading, the pilot should hold the airplane straight and level and determine what direction the turn will be made. Then, based upon the amount of turn needed to reach the new heading, the rate or angle of bank should be decided upon. A rule of thumb would be to use 5° of bank for a 5° change of heading. When using the turn indicator, the needle should be deflected one needle width; when using a turn coordinator, the representative airplane's wings should not be banked more than the standard marker.

Using the attitude indicator, the pilot should roll into the turn using coordinated aileron and rudder pressure in the direction of the desired turn to establish the desired bank angle. The amount and direction of the bank will be shown by the angle formed between the wings of the representative airplane and the line representing the horizon. If only a turn indicator is available, control pressures should be applied until the needle is deflected

the desired amount; then the bank angle or turn needle deflection should be maintained until just before the desired heading is reached. Throughout the turn, the pitch attitude and altitude must be controlled as previously described.

While making turns for large heading changes, there may be a tendency to gain or lose altitude. If the bank is controlled adequately, the altitude deviation usually will be only slight. The pilot should not be concerned about small deviations that can be corrected after the rollout; however, if the bank becomes too steep, altitude may be lost rapidly. In this case, the bank should be shallowed rather than adding more back-elevator pressure.

As long as the airplane is in a coordinated bank, it will continue to turn. The rollout to a desired heading must be started before the heading is reached; therefore, it is important to refer to the heading indicator to determine the progress being made toward the desired heading, and when the rollout should be started.

At approximately 10° before reaching the desired heading (less lead for small heading changes) coordinated aileron and rudder pressures should be applied to roll the wings level and stop the turn. This is accomplished best by referencing the attitude indicator. If only a turn indicator or turn coordinator is available, the needle should be centered or the representative wings leveled as appropriate. Failure to roll out exactly on the desired heading should not cause great alarm—final corrections can be made after the airplane is in straight-and-level flight and the pilot is assured of having positive control. Remember that the airplane's nose will tend to rise as the wings are being returned to the level attitude. Sufficient forward elevator pressure must be applied to maintain a constant altitude.

Once again, the pilot is cautioned against chasing the pointers on the instruments. The pointers should be allowed to settle down and then make adjustments as needed.

Unusual Flight Attitudes

When outside visual references are inadequate or lost, the non-instrument rated pilot is apt to unintentionally let the airplane enter an unusual attitude. This involves an excessively nose-high attitude in which the airplane may be approaching a stall, or an extremely steep bank that may result in a steep downward spiral.

Since such attitudes are not intentional, they are often unexpected, and the reaction of an inexperienced or inadequately trained pilot is usually instinctive rather than intelligent and deliberate. However, with practice,

the techniques for a rapid and safe recovery from these critical attitudes can be learned.

During instruction flights, the pilot should be instructed to take their hands and feet off the controls and to close their eyes. The instructor should then put the airplane into a critical attitude. The attitude may be an approach to a stall, or a well developed spiral dive. At this point, the pilot should be told to open their eyes, take the controls, and effect a recovery by referencing the flight instruments. IN ALL CASES, recoveries should be made to straight-and-level flight.

When an unusual attitude is noted on the flight instruments, the immediate problem is to recognize what the airplane is doing and decide how to return it to straight-and-level flight as quickly as possible. [Figure 9-5]

Nose-high attitudes are shown by the rate and direction of movement of the altimeter, vertical speed, and airspeed indicator, as well as the immediately recognizable indication on the attitude indicator. Nose-low attitudes are shown by the same instruments, but pointer movement is in the opposite direction.

Since many critical attitudes involve a rather steep bank, it is important to determine the direction of the

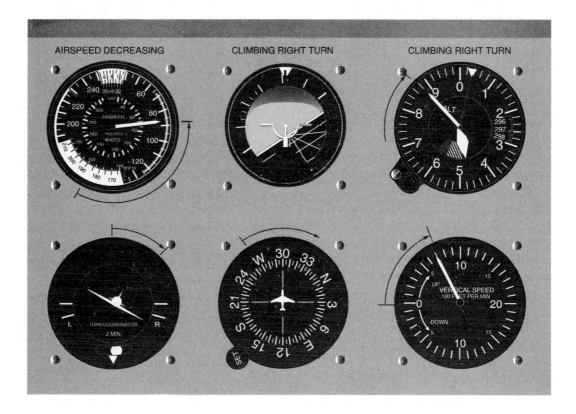

FIGURE 9-5.—Unusual attitude.

turn. This can be accomplished best by referencing the attitude indicator. In the absence of an attitude indicator, it will be necessary in the recovery to refer to the turn needle or turn coordinator to determine the direction of turn. Coordinated aileron and rudder pressure should be applied to level the wings of the representative airplane and center the turn needle.

Unlike the control applications in normal maneuvers, larger control movements in recoveries from critical attitudes may be necessary to bring the airplane under control. Nevertheless, such control applications must be smooth, positive, and prompt. To avoid aggravating the critical attitude with a control application in the wrong direction, the initial interpretation of the instruments must be accurate. Once the airplane is returned to approximately straight-and-level flight, control movements should be limited to small adjustments.

If the airspeed is decreasing rapidly and the altimeter indication is increasing faster than desired, the airplane's nose is too high. To prevent a stall from occurring, it is important to lower the nose as quickly as possible while simultaneously increasing power to prevent a further loss of airspeed. If an attitude indicator is available, the representative airplane should be lowered in relation to the artificial horizon by applying positive forward elevator pressure. If there is not an attitude indicator available, sufficient forward pressure should be applied to stop the movement of the pointers on the altimeter and airspeed indicators.

After the airplane has been returned to straight-and-level flight and the airspeed returns to normal, the power can be reduced to the normal setting.

If the airspeed is increasing rapidly and the altimeter indication is decreasing faster than desired, the airplane's nose is too low. To prevent losing too much altitude or exceeding the speed limitations of the airplane, power must be reduced and the nose must be raised. With the higher-than-normal airspeed, it is vital to raise the nose smoothly to avoid overstressing the airplane. Back-elevator pressure must not be applied too suddenly. If the airplane is in a steep bank while descending, the wings should be leveled before attempting to raise the nose. Increasing back-elevator pressure before the wings are leveled will tend to increase the bank and only further aggravate the situation, leading to what is called a "graveyard spiral." Furthermore, excessive G loads may be imposed, resulting in structural failure.

During initial training, students should be required to make the recovery from a nose-low spiral attitude by taking actions in the following sequence: (1) reduce the power; (2) level the wings; and (3) raise the nose.

After proficiency is attained, all recovery actions may be taken simultaneously.

To level the wings, coordinated aileron and rudder pressure should be applied until the wings of the representative airplane are approximately parallel to the horizon bar on the attitude indicator. If only a turn indicator or turn coordinator is available, pressures should be applied to center the needle or to level the wings of the representative airplane as appropriate. Then smooth back-elevator pressure will be necessary to bring the representative airplane on the attitude indicator up to the horizon bar. Remember that the turn coordinator provides NO PITCH INFORMATION. If an attitude indicator is not available, sufficient back-elevator pressure must be applied to start the airspeed pointer moving toward a lower airspeed and to stop the movement of the altimeter pointer. After the airplane is in level flight and the airspeed returns to normal, the power can be adjusted to the normal setting. If considerable altitude has been lost, a gradual climb to the original altitude may be necessary to ensure safe terrain clearance.

USE OF NAVIGATION SYSTEMS

VFR flights should begin in good weather conditions. Most often it is after the flight progresses from good weather into deteriorating weather and the pilot continues in the hope that conditions will improve that the need for navigational help arises. Since the area from which the pilot came is where the good weather was, naturally it is advisable to turn around and head back to that area when deteriorating weather is first encountered. In most cases, there will be some type of navigation system available to help the pilot return to the good weather area. Unless hopelessly disoriented, the pilot should determine the location and transmitting frequency of a VOR or NDB (automatic direction finder (ADF)) or program a global positioning system (GPS) or long range navigation (LORAN) coordinate that can be used for guiding the airplane back to the better weather area.

When a VOR is chosen, the omnireceiver should be tuned to the assigned frequency of the selected VOR station. After the station is identified, the omnibearing selector (OBS) should be turned until the TO/FROM indicator shows TO and the course deviation needle is centered.

The OBS then will then indicate the magnetic course to fly directly to the station. The airplane should then be turned to the corresponding magnetic heading, and heading adjustments made as required to follow the course to the station.

If an NDB is used, the ADF receiver should be tuned to the frequency of the selected NDB and the station positively identified. Then the airplane should be turned until the ADF pointer is on the nose position of the instrument. Keeping the pointer on this position will result in the airplane flying to the station although the ground track may be slightly curved due to a crosswind.

When using a GPS or LORAN, the pilot may program in an airport, VOR station, ADF station, or a known position to be in visual flying conditions. Using the direct key function, the unit will determine a direct route from the airplane's present position to the fix. The unit will indicate the course to be flown to the fix. The airplane should then be turned to the corresponding heading, and adjustments to the heading made as required to follow the course to the station. The use of navigation systems when in unfavorable weather conditions requires additional division of attention while attempting to maintain control of the airplane. The pilot's main concern is airplane control.

USE OF RADAR SERVICES

All pilots should be aware of radar equipped ATC facilities that provide assistance and navigation services, provided the airplane has appropriate communications equipment, is within radar coverage, and can be radar identified. This will allow radar facilities to vector a pilot to a nearby airport or to an area of good weather. The term "vector" simply means the heading to fly to reach a certain location. In this way, the pilot only needs to communicate and follow instructions while giving almost full attention to flying the airplane.

There are certain terms in the use of transponders that the pilot must understand. When instructed to SQUAWK a certain code (number), the pilot should first ensure that the transponder is set to the specified 4-digit number and turned ON (not standby). If told to IDENT, the pilot should press the button marked as such on the transponder. When told to SQUAWK MAYDAY (the emergency position), the transponder should be set to 7700.

To obtain assistance by radio and apply it effectively, some preparation and training is necessary. All pilots should become familiar with the appropriate emergency procedures. The actual use of designated emergency radio frequencies for training exercises is not permitted, but FAA facilities are often able to provide practice orientation and radar guidance procedures using their regular communications frequencies.

When a pilot is in doubt about the airplane's position, or feels apprehensive about the safety of the flight, there should be no hesitation to ask for help. That is the first means of declaring an emergency— use the radio transmitter and ask for help. If in actual distress, and help is needed immediately, the pilot should transmit the word MAYDAY several times before transmitting the emergency message. This will get immediate attention from all who hear.

Since frequent communications may be necessary, it is recommended that the microphone be continually held in the hand. This will eliminate the need to take the eyes away from the flight instruments every time the microphone is removed from or replaced in its receptacle. After some practice, loosely holding the mike in one hand should not create any difficulty in using the flight controls. It is important though, that the mike button not be depressed accidentally, which would block the frequency and prevent the reception of further assistance. The initial request for assistance can be made on the regular communications frequency of the facility, or on the emergency frequency, 121.5 MHz, especially designated for such messages. The designated emergency very high frequency (VHF), 121.5 MHz, is available on radios installed in general aviation airplanes. This is usually the best frequency on which to transmit and receive because all radar facilities, control towers, and Flight Service Stations (FSS's) monitor this frequency. Regardless of which frequency is used, it is essential that the pilot not change frequency unless instructed to do so by the operator or unless absolutely necessary.

If unable to establish communication with a radar facility, the pilot should call any control tower or FSS. The request will then be relayed immediately to the appropriate radar facility. The pilot must remember, though, that VHF transmissions follow line of sight; therefore, the higher the altitude, the better the chance of obtaining service. Effectiveness of radar service will depend on terrain conditions and altitude.

When the pilot request radar services, the operator will ask if the airplane is in VFR or instrument flight rules (IFR) weather conditions, the amount of fuel remaining, the altitude, and the heading. Also, the operator should be informed whether the pilot is instrument rated. If the airplane is in IFR weather conditions, the pilot will be informed of the minimum safe altitude and the current local altimeter setting will be provided.

When the airplane's position has been determined, the radar operator will specify the direction to turn and the magnetic heading to be flown. (i.e., TURN LEFT, HEADING ZERO ONE ZERO, FOR RADAR VECTORS TO LENAWEE COUNTY AIRPORT, REPORT AIRPORT IN SIGHT.)

Pilots should understand clearly that authorization to proceed in accordance with such radar navigational assistance does not constitute authorization for the pilot to violate the Code of Federal Regulations (CFR's).

To avoid possible hazards resulting from being vectored into IFR conditions, a VFR pilot in difficulty should keep the controller advised of the weather conditions the airplane is operating in and along the course ahead.

If the airplane has already encountered IFR conditions, the controller will inform the pilot of the minimum safe altitude. If the airplane is below the minimum safe altitude and sufficiently accurate position information has been received or radar identification is established, a heading or VOR radial on which to climb to reach the minimum safe altitude will be furnished.

CHAPTER 10

NIGHT OPERATIONS

INTRODUCTION

This chapter introduces night operations. It includes a brief description of night visual perceptions, suggested pilot equipment, airplane lighting and equipment, airport lighting, and night-flight operations.

Night operations differ from daylight operations only by the fact that vision is restricted at night. As confidence is gained through experience, many pilots prefer night operations over day operations because the air is usually smoother, and generally, there is less air traffic to contend with.

NIGHT VISION

Generally, most pilots are poorly informed about night vision. Human eyes never function as effectively at night as the eyes of animals with nocturnal habits, but if humans learn how to use their eyes correctly and know their limitations, night vision can be improved significantly. There are several reasons for training to use the eyes correctly.

One reason is the mind and eyes act as a team for a person to see well; both team members must be used

effectively. The construction of the eyes is such that to see at night they are used differently than during the day. Therefore, it is important to understand the eye's construction and how the eye is affected by darkness.

Innumerable light-sensitive nerves, called "cones" and "rods," are located at the back of the eye or retina, a layer upon which all images are focused. These nerves connect to the cells of the optic nerve, which transmits messages directly to the brain. The cones are located in the center of the retina, and the rods are concentrated in a ring around the cones. [Figure 10-1]

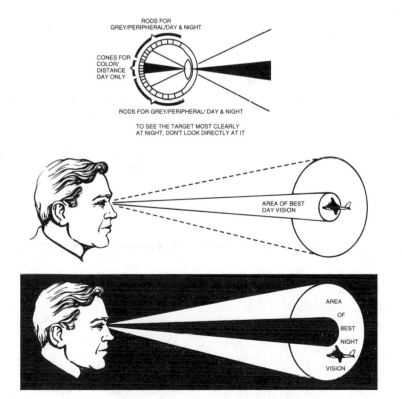

FIGURE 10-1.—Rods and cones.

The function of the cones is to detect color, details, and faraway objects. The rods function when something is seen out of the corner of the eye or peripheral vision. They detect objects, particularly those that are moving, but do not give detail or color—only shades of gray. Both the cones and the rods are used for vision during daylight.

Although there is not a clear-cut division of function, the rods make night vision possible. The rods and cones function in daylight and in moonlight, but in the absence of normal light, the process of night vision is placed almost entirely on the rods.

The fact that the rods are distributed in a band around the cones and do not lie directly behind the pupils makes off-center viewing (looking to one side of an object) important during night flight. During daylight, an object can be seen best by looking directly at it, but at night a scanning procedure to permit off-center viewing of the object is more effective. Therefore, the pilot should consciously practice this scanning procedure to improve night vision.

The eye's adaptation to darkness is another important aspect of night vision. When a dark room is entered, it is difficult to see anything until the eyes become adjusted to the darkness. Most everyone has experienced this after entering a darkened movie theater. In this process, the pupils of the eyes first enlarge to receive as much of the available light as possible. After approximately 5 to 10 minutes, the cones become adjusted to the dim light and the eyes become 100 times more sensitive to the light than they were before the dark room was entered. Much more time, about 30 minutes, is needed for the rods to become adjusted to darkness, but when they do adjust, they are about 100,000 times more sensitive to light than they were in the lighted area. After the adaptation process is complete, much more can be seen, especially if the eyes are used correctly.

After the eyes have adapted to the dark, the entire process is reversed when entering a lighted room. The eyes are first dazzled by the brightness, but become completely adjusted in a very few seconds, thereby losing their adaptation to the dark. Now, if the dark room is reentered, the eyes again go through the long process of adapting to the darkness.

The pilot before and during night flight must consider the adaption process of the eyes. First, the eyes should be allowed to adapt to the low level of light and then they should be kept adapted. After the eyes have become adapted to the darkness, the pilot should avoid exposing them to any bright white light that will cause

temporary blindness and could result in serious consequences.

Temporary blindness, caused by an unusually bright light, may result in illusions or after images until the eyes recover from the brightness. The brain creates these illusions reported by the eyes. This results in misjudging or incorrectly identifying objects, such as mistaking slanted clouds for the horizon or populated areas for a landing field. Vertigo is experienced as a feeling of dizziness and imbalance that can create or increase illusions. The illusions seem very real and pilots at every level of experience and skill can be affected. Recognizing that the brain and eyes can play tricks in this manner is the best protection for flying at night.

Good eyesight depends upon physical condition. Fatigue, colds, vitamin deficiency, alcohol, stimulants, smoking, or medication can seriously impair vision. Keeping these facts in mind and taking adequate precautions should safeguard night vision.

In addition to the principles previously discussed, the following items will aid in increasing night vision effectiveness:

• Adapt the eyes to darkness prior to flight and keep them adapted. About 30 minutes is needed to adjust the eyes to maximum efficiency after exposure to a bright light.
• If oxygen is available, use it during night flying. Keep in mind that a significant deterioration in night vision can occur at cabin altitudes as low as 5,000 feet.
• Close one eye when exposed to bright light to help avoid the blinding effect.
• Do not wear sunglasses after sunset.
• Move the eyes more slowly than in daylight.
• Blink the eyes if they become blurred.
• Concentrate on seeing objects.
• Force the eyes to view off center.
• Maintain good physical condition.
• Avoid smoking, drinking, and using drugs that may be harmful.

NIGHT ILLUSIONS

In addition to night vision limitations, pilots should be aware that night illusions could cause confusion and concerns during night flying. The following discussion covers some of the common situations that cause illusions associated with night flying.

On a clear night, distant stationary lights can be mistaken for stars or other aircraft. Even the northern lights can confuse a pilot and indicate a false horizon. Certain geometrical patterns of ground lights, such as a freeway, runway, approach, or even lights on a moving train can cause confusion. Dark nights tend to eliminate reference to a visual horizon. As a result, pilots need to rely less on outside references at night and more on flight and navigation instruments.

Visual autokinesis can occur when a pilot stares at a single light source for several seconds on a dark night. The result is that the light will appear to be moving. The autokinesis effect will not occur if the pilot expands the visual field. It is a good procedure not to become fixed on one source of light.

Distractions and problems can result from a flickering light in the cockpit, anticollision light, strobe lights, or other aircraft lights and can cause flicker vertigo. If continuous, the possible physical reactions can be nausea, dizziness, grogginess, unconsciousness, headaches, or confusion. The pilot should try to eliminate any light source causing blinking or flickering problems in the cockpit.

A black-hole approach occurs when the landing is made from over water or non-lighted terrain where the runway lights are the only source of light. Without peripheral visual cues to help, pilots will have trouble orientating themselves relative to Earth. The runway can seem out of position (downsloping or upsloping) and in the worse case, results in landing short of the runway. If an electronic glide slope or visual approach slope indicator (VASI) is available, it should be used. If navigation aids (NAVAID's) are unavailable, careful attention should be given to using the flight instruments to assist in maintaining orientation and a normal approach. If at any time the pilot is unsure of his or her position or attitude, a go-around should be executed.

Bright runway and approach lighting systems, especially where few lights illuminate the surrounding terrain, may create the illusion of less distance to the runway. In this situation, the tendency is to fly a higher approach. Also, when flying over terrain with only a few lights, it will make the runway recede or appear farther away. With this situation, the tendency is common to fly a lower-than-normal approach. If the runway has a city in the distance on higher terrain, the tendency will be to fly a lower-than-normal approach. A good review of the airfield layout and boundaries before initiating any approach will help the pilot maintain a safe approach angle.

Illusions created by runway lights result in a variety of problems. Bright lights or bold colors advance the runway, making it appear closer.

Night landings are further complicated by the difficulty of judging distance and the possibility of confusing approach and runway lights. For example, when a double row of approach lights joins the boundary lights of the runway, there can be confusion where the approach lights terminate and runway lights begin. Under certain conditions, approach lights can make the aircraft seem higher in a turn to final, than when its wings are level.

PILOT EQUIPMENT

Before beginning a night flight, carefully consider personal equipment that should be readily available during the flight. At least one reliable flashlight is recommended as standard equipment on all night flights. A D-cell size flashlight with a bulb switching mechanism that can be used to select white or red light is preferable. The white light used while performing the preflight visual inspection of the airplane, and the red light is used when performing cockpit operations. Since the red light is nonglaring, it will not impair night vision. Some pilots prefer two flashlights, one with a white light for preflight, and the other a penlight type with a red light. The latter can be suspended by a string from around the neck to ensure the light is always readily available. One word of caution; if a red light is used for reading an aeronautical chart, the red features of the chart will not show up. Remember to place a spare set of batteries in the flight kit.

Aeronautical charts are essential for night cross-country flight and, if the intended course is near the edge of the chart, the adjacent chart should also be available. The lights of cities and towns can be seen at surprising distances at night, and if this adjacent chart is not available to identify those landmarks, confusion could result. Regardless of the equipment used, organization of the cockpit eases the burden on the pilot and enhances safety.

AIRPLANE EQUIPMENT AND LIGHTING

Title 14 of the Code of Federal Regulations (14 CFR) part 91 specifies the basic minimum airplane equipment required for night flight. This equipment includes only basic instruments, lights, electrical energy source, and spare fuses.

The standard instruments required for instrument flight under 14 CFR part 91 are a valuable asset for aircraft control at night. An anticollision light system, including a flashing or rotating beacon and position lights, is required airplane equipment. Airplane position lights are arranged similar to those of boats and ships. A red light is positioned on the left wingtip, a green light on the right wingtip, and a white light on the tail. [Figure 10-2]

This arrangement provides a means by which pilots can determine the general direction of movement of other airplanes in flight. If both a red and green light of another aircraft were observed, the airplane would be flying toward the pilot, and could be on a collision course.

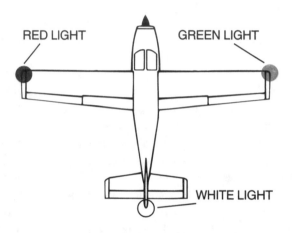

FIGURE 10-2.—Position lights.

Landing lights are not only useful for taxi, takeoffs, and landings, but also provide a means by which airplanes can be seen at night by other pilots. The Federal Aviation Administration (FAA) has initiated a voluntary pilot safety program called "operation lights on." The lights on idea is to enhance the "see and be seen" concept of averting collisions both in the air and on the ground, and to reduce the potential for bird strikes. Pilots are encouraged to turn on their landing lights when operating within 10 miles of an airport. This is for both day and night, or in conditions of reduced visibility. This should also be done in areas where flocks of birds may be expected.

Although turning on aircraft lights supports the see and be seen concept, pilots should not become complacent about keeping a sharp lookout for other aircraft. Most aircraft lights blend in with the stars or the lights of the cities at night and go unnoticed unless a conscious effort is made to distinguish them from other lights.

AIRPORT AND NAVIGATION LIGHTING AIDS

The lighting systems used for airports, runways, obstructions, and other visual aids at night are other important aspects of night flying.

Lighted airports located away from congested areas can be identified readily at night by the lights outlining the runways. Airports located near or within large cities are often difficult to identify in the maze of lights. It is important not to only know the exact location of an airport relative to the city, but also to be able to identify these airports by the characteristics of their lighting pattern.

Aeronautical lights are designed and installed in a variety of colors and configurations, each having its own purpose. Although some lights are used only during low ceiling and visibility conditions, this discussion includes only the lights that are fundamental to visual flight rules (VFR) night operation.

It is recommended that prior to a night flight, and particularly a cross-country night flight, the pilot check the availability and status of lighting systems at the destination airport. This information can be found on aeronautical charts and in the Airport/Facility Directory. The status of each facility can be determined by reviewing pertinent Notices to Airmen (NOTAM's).

A rotating beacon is used to indicate the location of most airports. The beacon rotates at a constant speed, thus producing what appears to be a series of light flashes at regular intervals. These flashes may be one or two different colors that are used to identify various types of landing areas. For example:

• Lighted civilian land airports—alternating white and green.
• Lighted civilian water airports—alternating white and yellow.
• Lighted military airports—alternating white and green, but are differentiated from civil airports by dual peaked (two quick) white flashes, then green.

Beacons producing red flashes indicate obstructions or areas considered hazardous to aerial navigation. Steady burning red lights are used to mark obstructions on or near airports and sometimes to supplement flashing lights on en route obstructions. High intensity flashing white lights are used to mark some supporting structures of overhead transmission lines that stretch across rivers, chasms, and gorges. These high intensity lights are also used to identify tall structures, such as chimneys and towers.

As a result of the technological advancements in aviation, runway lighting systems have become quite sophisticated to accommodate takeoffs and landings in various weather conditions. However, the pilot whose flying is limited to VFR only needs to be concerned with the following basic lighting of runways and taxiways.

The basic runway lighting system consists of two straight parallel lines of runway-edge lights defining the lateral limits of the runway. These lights are aviation white, although aviation yellow may be substituted for a distance of 2,000 feet from the far end of the runway to indicate a caution zone. At some airports, the intensity of the runway-edge lights can be adjusted to satisfy the individual needs of the pilot. The length limits of the runway are defined by straight lines of lights across the runway ends. At some airports, the runway threshold lights are aviation green, and the runway end lights are aviation red.

At many airports, the taxiways are also lighted. A taxiway-edge lighting system consists of blue lights that outline the usable limits of taxi paths.

PREPARATION AND PREFLIGHT

Night flying requires that pilots be aware of, and operate within, their abilities and limitations. Although careful planning of any flight is essential, night flying demands more attention to the details of preflight preparation and planning.

Preparation for a night flight should include a thorough review of the available weather reports and forecasts with particular attention given to temperature/dewpoint spread. A narrow temperature/dewpoint spread may indicate the possibility of ground fog. Emphasis should also be placed on wind direction and speed, since its effect on the airplane cannot be as easily detected at night as during the day.

On night cross-country flights, appropriate aeronautical charts should be selected, including the appropriate adjacent charts. Course lines should be drawn in black to be more distinguishable.

Prominently lighted checkpoints along the prepared course should be noted. Rotating beacons at airports, lighted obstructions, lights of cities or towns, and lights from major highway traffic all provide excellent visual checkpoints. The use of radio navigation aids and communication facilities add significantly to the safety and efficiency of night flying.

All personal equipment should be checked prior to flight to ensure proper functioning. It is very disconcerting to find, at the time of need, that a flashlight, for example, does not work.

All airplane lights should be turned ON momentarily and checked for operation. Position lights can be checked for loose connections by tapping the light fixture. If the lights blink while being tapped, further investigation to determine the cause should be made prior to flight.

The parking ramp should be examined prior to entering the airplane. During the day, it is quite easy to see stepladders, chuckholes, wheel chocks, and other obstructions, but at night it is more difficult. A check of the area can prevent taxiing mishaps.

STARTING, TAXIING, AND RUNUP

After the pilot is seated in the cockpit and prior to starting the engine, all items and materials to be used on the flight should be arranged in such a manner that they will be readily available and convenient to use.

Extra caution should be taken at night to assure the propeller area is clear. Turning the rotating beacon ON, or flashing the airplane position lights will serve to alert persons nearby to remain clear of the propeller. To avoid excessive drain of electrical current from the battery, it is recommended that unnecessary electrical equipment be turned OFF until after the engine has been started.

After starting and before taxiing, the taxi or landing light should be turned ON. Continuous use of the landing light with RPM power settings normally used for taxiing may place an excessive drain on the airplane's electrical system. Also, overheating of the landing light could become a problem because of inadequate airflow to carry the heat away. Landing lights should be used as necessary while taxiing. When using landing lights, consideration should be given to not blinding other pilots. Taxi slowly, particularly in congested areas. If taxi lines are painted on the ramp or taxiway, these lines should be followed to ensure a proper path along the route.

The before takeoff and runup should be performed using the checklist. During the day, forward movement of the airplane can be detected easily. At night, the airplane could creep forward without being noticed unless the pilot is alert for this possibility. Hold or lock the brakes during the runup and be alert for any forward movement.

FIGURE 10-3.—Establish a positive climb.

TAKEOFF AND CLIMB

Night flying is very different from day flying and demands more attention of the pilot. The most noticeable difference is the limited availability of outside visual references. Therefore, flight instruments should be used to a greater degree in controlling the airplane. This is particularly true on night takeoffs and climbs. The cockpit lights should be adjusted to a minimum brightness that will allow the pilot to read the instruments and switches and yet not hinder the pilot's outside vision. This will also eliminate light reflections on the windshield and windows.

After ensuring that the final approach and runway are clear of other air traffic, or when cleared for takeoff by the tower, the landing lights and taxi lights should be turned ON and the airplane lined up with the centerline of the runway. If the runway does not have centerline lighting, use the painted centerline and the runway-edge lights. After the airplane is aligned, the heading indicator should be noted or set to correspond to the known runway direction. To begin the takeoff, the brakes should be released and the throttle smoothly advanced to maximum allowable power. As the airplane accelerates, it should be kept moving straight ahead between and parallel to the runway-edge lights.

The procedure for night takeoffs is the same as for normal daytime takeoffs except that many of the runway visual cues are not available. Therefore, the flight instruments should be checked frequently during the takeoff to ensure the proper pitch attitude, heading, and airspeed is being attained. As the airspeed reaches the normal lift-off speed, the pitch attitude should be adjusted to that which will establish a normal climb. This should be accomplished by referring to both outside visual references, such as lights, and to the flight instruments. [Figure 10-3]

After becoming airborne, the darkness of night often makes it difficult to note whether the airplane is getting closer to or farther from the surface. To ensure the airplane continues in a positive climb, be sure a climb is indicated on the attitude indicator, vertical speed indicator (VSI), and altimeter. It is also important to ensure the airspeed is at best climb speed.

Necessary pitch and bank adjustments should be made by referencing the attitude and heading indicators. It is recommended that turns not be made until reaching a safe maneuvering altitude.

Although the use of the landing lights provides help during the takeoff, they become ineffective after the airplane has climbed to an altitude where the light beam no longer extends to the surface. The light can cause distortion when it is reflected by haze, smoke, or fog that might exist in the climb. Therefore, when the landing light is used for the takeoff, it may be turned off after the climb is well established provided other traffic in the area does not require its use for collision avoidance.

ORIENTATION AND NAVIGATION

Generally, at night it is difficult to see clouds and restrictions to visibility, particularly on dark nights or under overcast. The pilot flying under VFR must exercise caution to avoid flying into clouds or a layer of fog. Usually, the first indication of flying into restricted visibility conditions is the gradual disappearance of lights on the ground. If the lights begin to take on an appearance of being surrounded by a halo or glow, the pilot should use caution in attempting further flight in that same direction. Such a halo or glow around lights on the ground is indicative of ground fog. Remember that if a descent must be made through fog, smoke, or haze in order to land, the horizontal visibility is considerably less when looking through the restriction than it is when looking straight down through it from above. Under no circumstances should a VFR night-flight be made during poor or marginal weather conditions unless both the pilot and aircraft are certificated and equipped for flight under instrument flight rules (IFR).

The pilot should practice and acquire competency in straight-and-level flight, climbs and descents, level turns, climbing and descending turns, and steep turns. Recovery from unusual attitudes should also be practiced, but only on dual flights with a flight instructor. The pilot should also practice these maneuvers with all the cockpit lights turned OFF. This blackout training is necessary if the pilot experiences an electrical or instrument light failure. Training should also include using the navigation equipment and local NAVAID'S.

In spite of fewer references or checkpoints, night cross-country flights do not present particular problems if preplanning is adequate, and the pilot continues to monitor position, time estimates, and fuel consumed. NAVAIDS, if available, should be used to assist in monitoring en route progress.

Crossing large bodies of water at night in single-engine airplanes could be potentially hazardous, not only from the standpoint of landing (ditching) in the water, but also because with little or no lighting the horizon blends with the water, in which case, depth perception and orientation become difficult. During poor visibility conditions over water, the horizon will become obscure, and may result in a loss of orientation. Even on clear nights, the stars may be reflected on the water surface, which could appear as a continuous array of lights, thus making the horizon difficult to identify.

Lighted runways, buildings, or other objects may cause illusions to the pilot when seen from different altitudes. At an altitude of 2,000 feet, a group of lights on an object may be seen individually, while at 5,000 feet or higher, the same lights could appear to be one solid light mass. These illusions may become quite acute with altitude changes and if not overcome could present problems in respect to approaches to lighted runways.

APPROACHES AND LANDINGS

When approaching the airport to enter the traffic pattern and land, it is important that the runway lights and other airport lighting be identified as early as possible. If the airport layout is unfamiliar to the pilot, sighting of the runway may be difficult until very close-in due to the maze of lights observed in the area. The pilot should fly toward the rotating beacon until the lights outlining the runway are distinguishable. To fly a traffic pattern of proper size and direction, the runway threshold and runway-edge lights must be positively identified. Once the airport lights are seen, these lights should be kept in sight throughout the approach.

Distance may be deceptive at night due to limited lighting conditions. A lack of intervening references on the ground and the inability of the pilot to compare the size and location of different ground objects cause this. This also applies to the estimation of altitude and speed. Consequently, more dependence must be placed on flight instruments, particularly the altimeter and the airspeed indicator.

When entering the traffic pattern, allow for plenty of time to complete the before landing checklist. If the heading indicator contains a heading bug, setting it to the runway heading will be an excellent reference for the pattern legs.

Every effort should be made to maintain the recommended airspeeds and execute the approach and landing in the same manner as during the day. A low, shallow approach is definitely inappropriate during a night operation. The altimeter and VSI should be constantly cross-checked against the airplane's position along the base leg and final approach.

After turning onto the final approach and aligning the airplane midway between the two rows of runway-edge lights, the pilot should note and correct for any wind drift. Throughout the final approach, pitch and power should be used to maintain a stabilized approach.

Flaps should be used the same as in a normal approach. Usually, halfway through the final approach, the landing light should be turned on. Earlier use of the landing light may be necessary because of "Operation Lights ON" or for local traffic considerations. The landing light is sometimes ineffective since the light beam will usually not reach the ground from higher altitudes. The light may even be reflected back into the pilot's eyes by any existing haze, smoke, or fog. This disadvantage is overshadowed by the safety considerations provided by using the "Operation Lights On" procedure around other traffic.

The roundout and touchdown should be made in the same manner as in day landings. At night, the judgment of height, speed, and sink rate is impaired by the scarcity of observable objects in the landing area. The inexperienced pilot may have a tendency to round out too high until attaining familiarity with the proper height for the correct roundout. To aid in determining the proper roundout point, continue a constant approach descent until the landing lights reflect on the runway and tire marks on the runway can be seen clearly. At this point the roundout should be started smoothly and the throttle gradually reduced to idle as the airplane is touching down. [Figure 10-4] During landings without the use of landing lights, the roundout may be started when the runway lights at the far end of the runway first appear to be rising higher than the nose of the airplane. This demands a smooth and very timely roundout, and requires that the pilot feel for the runway surface using power and pitch changes, as necessary, for the airplane to settle slowly to the runway. Blackout landings should always be included in night pilot training as an emergency procedure.

NIGHT EMERGENCIES

Perhaps the pilot's greatest concern about flying a single-engine airplane at night is the possibility of a complete engine failure and the subsequent emergency landing. This is a legitimate concern, even though continuing flight into adverse weather and poor pilot judgment account for most serious accidents.

If the engine fails at night, several important procedures and considerations to keep in mind are:

• Maintain positive control of the airplane and establish the best glide configuration and airspeed. Turn the airplane towards an airport or away from congested areas.

FIGURE 10-4.—Roundout when tire marks are visible.

• Check to determine the cause of the engine malfunction, such as the position of fuel selectors, magneto switch, or primer. If possible, the cause of the malfunction should be corrected immediately and the engine restarted.
• Announce the emergency situation to Air Traffic Control (ATC) or UNICOM. If already in radio contact with a facility, do not change frequencies, unless instructed to change.
• If the condition of the nearby terrain is known, turn towards an unlighted portion of the area. Plan an emergency approach to an unlighted portion.
• Consider an emergency landing area close to public access if possible. This may facilitate rescue or help, if needed.
• Maintain orientation with the wind to avoid a downwind landing.

• Complete the before landing checklist, and check the landing lights for operation at altitude and turn ON in sufficient time to illuminate the terrain or obstacles along the flightpath. The landing should be completed in the normal landing attitude at the slowest possible airspeed. If the landing lights are unusable and outside visual references are not available; the airplane should be held in level-landing attitude until the ground is contacted.

• After landing, turn off all switches and evacuate the aircraft as quickly as possible.

CHAPTER 11

NAVIGATION SYSTEMS

INTRODUCTION

This chapter reviews very high frequency (VHF) omnidirectional range (VOR) navigation, and discusses area navigation (RNAV), long range navigation (LORAN), and global positioning systems (GPS). For basic elements of planning and executing a cross-country and using a VOR and automatic direction finder (ADF), refer to AC 61-23, Pilot's Handbook of Aeronautical Knowledge.

VOR NAVIGATION

For decades the VOR has been the mainstay of radio navigation. VOR, VOR/distance measuring equipment (DME), and very high frequency omnidirectional range/military tactical air navigation (VORTAC) symbols are shown on aeronautical charts in blue, with an adjacent frequency and Morse Code identifier. Additional Flight Service Station (FSS) communication frequencies and other symbols may also be present.

The VOR system is present in three slightly different navigation aids (NAVAID's): VOR, VOR/DME, and VORTAC. By itself it is known as a VOR, and it provides magnetic bearing information to and from the station. When DME is also installed with a VOR, the NAVAID is referred to as a VOR/DME. When military tactical air navigation (TACAN) equipment is installed with a VOR, the NAVAID is known as a VORTAC. DME is always an integral part of a VORTAC. Regardless of the type of NAVAID utilized (VOR, VOR/DME or VORTAC), the VOR indicator behaves the same. Unless otherwise noted, in this section, VOR, VOR/DME and VORTAC NAVAID's will all be referred to hereafter as VOR's.

The blue shaded lines drawn between VOR's on aeronautical charts are victor, or low altitude, airways. The magnetic bearing of each radial that comprises an airway is shown near the VOR. The letter V followed by V 4, V 71, V 159, etc. identifies the airways. Victor airways are Class E airspace and extend vertically up to but not including 18,000 feet mean sea level (MSL).

VOR's offer simplicity of operation and are found in almost any airplane with an electrical system. Their signals are highly resistant to atmospheric disturbances. A drawback of VOR navigation is that the signal, like all VHF transmissions, is limited to line-of-sight— reception distance decreases as altitude decreases. Depending upon airplane altitude and the VOR's service volume, ranges from 25 to 130 nautical miles (NM) can be expected. The Airport/Facility Directory classifies service volume of VOR's as T (terminal), L (low), or H (high).

To properly utilize the VOR for navigation, the frequency of the station is first selected. The three-letter Morse Code identifier may be heard by enabling the unit's identification (IDENT) feature. This audible code should be compared with the one on the aeronautical chart for positive identification. If the OFF flag is displayed and no identifier is received, or if the letters T-E-S-T (— • • • • —) are present as an identifier, the station is unusable for navigation. Assuming that the station is operating properly, the pilot may now use the VOR indicator for navigation.

Each VOR indicator is composed of several elements: the omnibearing selector (OBS); the course index; the TO-FROM indicator; and the course deviation indicator (CDI), sometimes referred to as the Left-Right needle, or the needle. [Figure 11-1] The OBS, also known as the course selector, permits the selection of any course either to or from the VOR. The course selected is shown in the course index. The TO-FROM indicator indicates whether the selected course, if intercepted and flown, would take the airplane to or from the VOR. When a valid signal is not being received, the TO-FROM indicator will show OFF. Some course indicators use a separate OFF flag for this purpose. The CDI shows the relationship of the airplane to the selected course. With proper sensing, a left deflected CDI indicates that the selected course lies to the left of the airplane; a right deflected CDI indicates that the selected course lies to the right. A centered needle shows on course.

FIGURE 11-1.—VOR indicator.

The CDI displays angular deviation from the selected course. Full-scale CDI deflection is 10° on either side of the course, or 20° from full-scale left to full-scale right. The actual distance off course is dependent upon the distance from the station. Each dot of deviation equals 200 feet of linear deviation at 1 NM from the VOR, 400 feet at 2 NM, etc.

A VOR can be used to track to a station or track from a station. It can also be used for orientation in determining position in relation to a station. To track to a VOR, the pilot should tune and identify the desired station as previously described. The OBS should be turned until the CDI centers with a TO indication. The airplane should now be turned to a heading that approximates the course displayed in the course index. The needle should be kept centered with small heading corrections.

As the VOR is approached, the course will become increasingly sensitive and tracking it will require greater attention. Station passage will be indicated by the TO-FROM indicator momentarily displaying OFF, then switching to FROM. [Figure 11-2] As the TO-FROM flag momentarily displays OFF, it will be accompanied by full-scale oscillations of the needle as the airplane passes directly over the VOR.

As the VOR is crossed, the pilot may continue to fly an outbound course that is the same as the inbound course, or an entirely new outbound course may be selected. If the outbound course is the same as the inbound course, the pilot need only continue to track as before. The only difference will be a TO-FROM indicator that shows FROM.

If the pilot wishes to select a new outbound course, the OBS should be turned to select the outbound course just prior to station passage. The airplane should then be turned to a heading that will intercept the new course.

VOR's are oriented in relation to magnetic north. Electronically, VOR's provide an infinite number of radials. For most purposes in air navigation, however, 360 radials are assumed—one for each degree of azimuth. Proper definition and terminology here can save a lot of confusion later. Any radial, e.g., the 360°

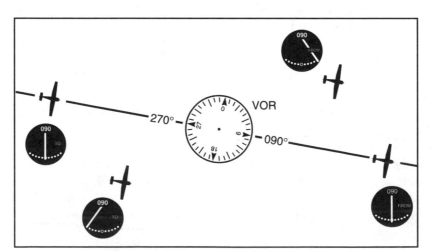

FIGURE 11-2.—VOR tracking TO and FROM.

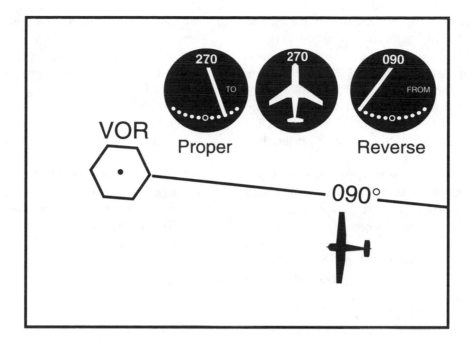

FIGURE 11-3.— Proper and reverse sensing.

radial, the 090° radial, etc., is a line of magnetic bearing that extends from the VOR. Pilots may track either outbound or inbound on any radial. When tracking from a VOR, the outbound course will be the same as the radial. When tracking to a VOR, the pilot is tracking inbound on a radial, and the inbound course will be the reciprocal of the radial.

To use a VOR for orientation, the pilot should select, tune, and identify the station as previously described. Using the OBS, the CDI should be centered with a FROM indication. The airplane is located on the radial displayed in the course index. Pilots should note that as the OBS is turned, the CDI will also center with a TO indication. The course shown with a TO indication is the reciprocal of the radial that the airplane is located on. For any given position of the airplane, the CDI will center on two courses. One course, if intercepted and flown, will take the airplane from the VOR. The other, if intercepted and flown, will take the airplane to the VOR. These two courses are reciprocals of one another.

The TO-FROM indicator does not tell the pilot whether the airplane is actually proceeding to or from the station at that moment. The VOR course indicator responds to and displays airplane position, not heading, in relation to the selected course. It is up to the pilot to put the airplane on an appropriate heading that will track the course.

There is an aspect called reverse sensing that must be guarded against when tracking with a VOR. [Figure 11-3] Reverse sensing occurs when the heading being flown is essentially opposite the selected course. With reverse sensing, the CDI needle deflects away from the selected course, the reverse of what is desired. Pilots can prevent reverse sensing by ensuring that the magnetic heading of the airplane is always approximately in agreement with the course being tracked. If the heading and selected course are approximately reciprocals of each other, reverse sensing occurs.

Distance measuring equipment (DME) is an ultra high frequency (UHF) navigational aid present with VOR/DME's and VORTAC's. It measures, in NM, the slant range distance of an airplane from a VOR/DME or VORTAC (both hereafter referred to as a VORTAC). Although DME equipment is very popular, not all airplanes are DME equipped.

To utilize DME, the pilot should select, tune, and identify a VORTAC, as previously described. The DME receiver, utilizing what is called a "paired frequency" concept, automatically selects and tunes the UHF DME frequency associated with the VHF VORTAC frequency selected by the pilot. This process is entirely transparent to the pilot. After a brief pause, the DME display will show the slant range distance to or from the VORTAC. Slant range distance is the direct distance between the airplane and the VORTAC, and is therefore affected by airplane altitude. (Station passage directly over a VORTAC from an altitude of 6,076 feet above ground level (AGL) would show approximately 1.0 NM on the DME.) DME is a very useful adjunct to VOR navigation. A VOR radial alone merely gives line of position information. With DME, a pilot may precisely locate the airplane on that line (radial).

Most DME receivers also provide groundspeed and time-to-station modes of operation. The groundspeed is displayed in knots (NM per hour). The time-to-station mode displays the minutes remaining to VORTAC station passage, predicated upon the present groundspeed. Groundspeed and time-to-station information is only accurate when tracking directly to or from a VORTAC. DME receivers typically need a minute or two of stabilized flight directly to or from a VORTAC before displaying accurate groundspeed or time-to-station information.

Some DME installations have a hold feature that permits a DME signal to be retained from one VORTAC while the course indicator displays course deviation information from an ILS or another VORTAC.

VOR/DME RNAV

Area navigation (RNAV) permits electronic course guidance on any direct route between points established by the pilot. While RNAV is a generic term that applies to a variety of navigational aids, such as LORAN-C, GPS, and others, this section will deal with VOR/DME-based RNAV. VOR/DME RNAV is not a separate ground-based NAVAID, but a method of navigation using VOR/DME and VORTAC signals specially processed by the airplane's RNAV computer. [Figure 11-4] In this section, the term "VORTAC" also includes VOR/DME NAVAID's.

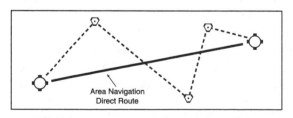

FIGURE 11-4.— Flying an RNAV course.

In its simplest form, VOR/DME RNAV allows the pilot to electronically move VORTAC's around to more convenient locations. Once electronically relocated,

they are referred to as waypoints. These waypoints are described as a combination of a selected radial and distance within the service volume of the VORTAC to be used. These waypoints allow a straight course to be flown between almost any origin and destination, without regard to the orientation of VORTAC's or the existence of airways.

While the capabilities and methods of operation of VOR/DME RNAV units differ, there are basic principals of operation that are common to all. Pilots are urged to study the manufacturer's operating guide and receive instruction prior to the use of VOR/DME RNAV or any unfamiliar navigational system. Operational information and limitations should also be sought from placards and the supplement section of the Airplane Flight Manual (AFM) and/or Pilot's Operating Handbook (POH).

VOR/DME-based RNAV units operate in at least three modes: VOR, En Route, and Approach. A fourth mode, VOR Parallel, may also be found on some models. The units need both VOR and DME signals to operate in any RNAV mode. If the NAVAID selected is a VOR without DME, RNAV mode will not function.

In the VOR (or non-RNAV) mode, the unit simply functions as a VOR receiver with DME capability. [Figure 11-5] The unit's display on the VOR indicator is conventional in all respects. For operation on established airways or any other ordinary VOR navigation, the VOR mode is used.

FIGURE 11-5.—RNAV controls.

To utilize the unit's RNAV capability, the pilot selects and establish a waypoint or a series of waypoints to define a course. To operate in any RNAV mode, the unit needs both radial and distance signals; therefore, a VORTAC (or VOR/DME) needs to be selected as a NAVAID. To establish a waypoint, a point somewhere within the service range of a VORTAC is defined on the basis of radial and distance. Once the waypoint is entered into the unit and the RNAV En Route mode is selected, the CDI will display course guidance to the waypoint, not the original VORTAC. DME will also display distance to the waypoint. Many units have the capability to store several waypoints, allowing them to be programmed prior to flight, if desired, and called up in flight.

RNAV waypoints are entered into the unit in magnetic bearings (radials) of degrees and tenths (i.e., 275.5°) and distances in nautical miles and tenths (i.e., 25.2 NM). When plotting RNAV waypoints on an aeronautical chart, pilots will find it difficult to measure to that level of accuracy, and in practical application, it is rarely necessary. A number of flight planning publications publish airport coordinates and waypoints with this precision and the unit will accept those figures. There is a subtle, but important difference in CDI operation and display in the RNAV modes.

In the RNAV modes, course deviation is displayed in terms of linear deviation. In the RNAV En Route mode, maximum deflection of the CDI typically represents 5 NM on either side of the selected course, without regard to distance from the waypoint. In the RNAV Approach mode, maximum deflection of the CDI typically represents 1 1/4 NM on either side of the selected course. There is no increase in CDI sensitivity as the airplane approaches a waypoint in RNAV mode.

The RNAV Approach mode is used for instrument approaches. Its narrow scale width (one-quarter of the En Route mode) permits very precise tracking to or from the selected waypoint. In visual flight rules (VFR) cross-country navigation, tracking a course in the Approach mode is not desirable because it requires a great deal of attention and soon becomes tedious.

A fourth, lesser-used mode on some units is the VOR Parallel mode. This permits the CDI to display linear (not angular) deviation as the airplane tracks to and from VORTAC's. It derives its name from permitting the pilot to offset (or parallel) a selected course or airway at a fixed distance of the pilot's choosing, if desired. The VOR Parallel mode has the same effect as placing a waypoint directly over an existing VORTAC. Some pilots select the VOR Parallel mode when utilizing the navigation (NAV) tracking function of their autopilot for smoother a course following near the VORTAC.

Confusion is possible when navigating an airplane with VOR/DME-based RNAV, and it is essential that the pilot become familiar with the equipment installed. It is not unknown for pilots to operate inadvertently in one of the RNAV modes when the operation was not intended by overlooking switch positions or annunciators. The reverse has also occurred with a pilot neglecting to place the unit into one of the RNAV modes by

overlooking switch positions or annunciators. As always, the prudent pilot is not only familiar with the equipment used, but never places complete reliance in just one method of navigation when others are available for cross-check.

LORAN-C NAVIGATION

Long Range Navigation, version C (LORAN-C) is another form of RNAV, but one that operates from chains of transmitters broadcasting signals in the low frequency (LF) spectrum. World Aeronautical Chart (WAC), Sectional Charts, and VFR Terminal Area Charts do not show the presence of LORAN-C transmitters. Selection of a transmitter chain is either made automatically by the unit, or manually by the pilot using guidance information provided by the manufacturer. LORAN-C is a highly accurate, supplemental form of navigation typically installed as an adjunct to VOR and ADF equipment. Databases of airports, NAVAID's and Air Traffic Control (ATC) facilities are frequently features of LORAN-C receivers.

LORAN-C is an outgrowth of the original LORAN-A developed for navigation during World War II. The LORAN-C system is used extensively in maritime applications. It experienced a dramatic growth in popularity with pilots with the advent of the small, panel-mounted LORAN-C receivers available at relatively low cost. These units are frequently very sophisticated and capable, with a wide variety of navigational functions.

With high levels of LORAN-C sophistication and capability, a certain complexity in operation is an unfortunate necessity. Pilots are urged to read the operating handbooks and to consult the supplements section of the AFM/POH prior to utilizing LORAN-C for navigation. Many units offer so many features that the manufacturers often publish two different sets of instructions: one, a brief operating guide and two, in-depth operating manual.

While coverage is not global, LORAN-C signals are suitable for navigation in all of the conterminous United States, and parts of Canada and Alaska. Several foreign countries also operate their own LORAN-C systems. In the United States, the U.S. Coast Guard operates the LORAN-C system. LORAN-C system status is available from: USCG Navigation Center, Alexandria, VA (703) 313-5900.

LORAN-C absolute accuracy is excellent—typically less than .25 NM. Repeatable accuracy, or the ability to return to a waypoint previously visited, is even better. While LORAN-C is a form of RNAV, it differs significantly from VOR/DME-based RNAV. It operates in a 90 – 110 KHz frequency range and is based upon measurement of the difference in arrival times of pulses of radio frequency (RF) energy emitted by a chain of transmitters hundreds of miles apart.

Within any given chain of transmitters, there is a master station, and from three to five secondary stations. LORAN-C units must be able to receive at least a master and two secondary stations to provide navigational information. Unlike VOR/DME-based RNAV, where the pilot must select the appropriate VOR/DME or VORTAC frequency, there is not a frequency selection in LORAN-C. The most advanced units automatically select the optimum chain for navigation. Other units rely upon the pilot to select the appropriate chain with a manual entry.

After the LORAN-C receiver has been turned on, the unit must be initialized before it can be used for navigation. While this can be accomplished in flight, it is preferable to perform this task, which can take several minutes, on the ground. The methods for initialization are as varied as the number of different models of receivers. Some require pilot input during the process, such as verification or acknowledgment of the information displayed.

Most units contain databases of navigational information. Frequently, such databases contain not only airport and NAVAID locations, but also extensive airport, airspace, and ATC information. While the unit will operate with an expired database, the information should be current or verified to be correct prior to use. The pilot can update some databases, while others require removal from the aircraft and the services of an avionics technician.

VFR navigation with LORAN-C can be as simple as telling the unit where the pilot wishes to go. The course guidance provided will be a great circle (shortest distance) route to the destination. Older units may need a destination entered in terms of latitude and longitude, but recent designs only need the identifier of the airport or NAVAID. The unit will also permit database storage and retrieval of pilot defined waypoints. LORAN-C signals follow the curvature of the Earth and are generally usable hundreds of miles from their transmitters.

The LORAN-C signal is subject to degradation from a variety of atmospheric disturbances. It is also susceptible to interference from static electricity buildup on the airframe and electrically "noisy" airframe equipment. Flight in precipitation or even dust clouds can cause occasional interference with navigational guidance from LORAN-C signals. To minimize these effects, static wicks and bonding straps should be installed and properly maintained.

LORAN-C navigation information is presented to the pilot in a variety of ways. All units have self-contained displays, and some elaborate units feature built-in moving map displays. Some installations can also drive an external moving map display, a conventional VOR indicator, or a horizontal situation indicator (HSI). Course deviation information is presented as a linear deviation from course—there is no increase in tracking sensitivity as the airplane approaches the waypoint or destination. Pilots must carefully observe placards, selector switch positions, and annunciator indications when utilizing LORAN-C because aircraft installations can vary widely. The pilot's familiarity with unit operation through AFM/POH supplements and operating guides cannot be overemphasized.

LORAN-C Notices To Airmen (NOTAM's) should be reviewed prior to relying on LORAN-C for navigation. LORAN-C NOTAM's will be issued to announce outages for specific chains and transmitters. Pilots may obtain LORAN-C NOTAM's from FSS briefers only upon request.

The prudent pilot will never rely solely on one means of navigation when others are available for backup and cross-check. Pilots should never become so dependent upon the extensive capabilities of LORAN-C that other methods of navigation are neglected.

GLOBAL POSITIONING SYSTEM (GPS)

The global positioning system (GPS) is a satellite-based radio navigation system of increasing popularity among pilots. Its RNAV guidance is worldwide in scope. There are no symbols for GPS on aeronautical charts as it is a space-based system with global coverage. At the present time, GPS is an extremely accurate, supplemental form of navigation.

Development of the system is underway so that GPS will be capable of providing the primary means of electronic navigation. Portable and yoke mounted units are proving to be very popular in addition to those permanently installed in the airplane. Extensive navigation databases are common features in aircraft GPS receivers.

The GPS is a satellite radio navigation and time dissemination system developed and operated by the U.S. Department of Defense (DOD). Civilian interface and GPS system status is available from the U.S. Coast Guard.

It is not necessary to understand the technical aspects of GPS operation to use it in VFR/instrument flight rules (IFR) navigation. It does differ significantly from conventional, ground-based electronic navigation, and awareness of those differences is important. Awareness of equipment approvals and limitations is critical to the safety of flight. The GPS system is composed of three major elements:

1. The space segment is composed of a constellation of 26 satellites orbiting approximately 10,900 NM above the earth. The operational satellites are often referred to as the GPS constellation. The satellites are not geosynchronous but instead orbit the earth in periods of approximately 12 hours. Each satellite is equipped with highly stable atomic clocks and transmits a unique code and navigation message. Transmitting in the UHF range means that the signals are virtually unaffected by weather although they are subject to line-of-sight limitations. The satellites must be above the horizon (as seen by the receiver's antenna) to be usable for navigation.

2. The control segment consists of a master control station at Falcon AFB, Colorado Springs, CO, five monitor stations, and three ground antennas. The monitor stations and ground antennas are distributed around the Earth to allow continual monitoring and communications with the satellites. Updates and corrections to the navigational message broadcast by each satellite are uplinked to the satellites as they pass over the ground antennas.

3. The user segment consists of all components associated with the GPS receiver, ranging from portable, hand-held receivers to receivers permanently installed in the aircraft. The receiver matches the satellite's coded signal by shifting its own identical code in a matching process to precisely measure the time of arrival. Knowing the speed the signal traveled (approximately 186,000 miles per second) and the exact broadcast time, the distance traveled by the signal can be inferred from its arrival time.

To solve for its location, the GPS receiver utilizes the signals of at least four of the best positioned satellites to yield a three dimensional fix (latitude, longitude, and altitude). A two dimensional fix (latitude and longitude only) can be determined with as few as three satellites.

GPS receivers have extensive databases. Databases are provided initially by the receiver manufacturer and updated by the manufacturer or a designated data agency.

A wide variety of GPS receivers with extensive navigation capabilities are available. Panel mounted units permanently installed in the aircraft may be used for VFR and may also have certain IFR approvals. Portable hand-held and yoke mounted GPS receivers are also popular although these are limited to VFR use. Not all GPS receivers on the market are suited for air navigation. Marine, recreational, and surveying units, for example, are not suitable for aircraft use. As with LORAN-C receivers, GPS unit features and operating procedures vary widely. The pilot must be familiar with the manufacturer's operating guide. Placards, switch positions, and annunciators should be carefully observed.

Initialization of the unit will require several minutes and should be accomplished prior to flight. If the unit has not been operated for several months or if it has been moved to a significantly different location (by several hundred miles) while off, this may require several additional minutes. During initialization, the unit will make internal integrity checks, acquire satellite signals, and display the database revision date. While the unit will operate with an expired database, the database should be current, or verified to be correct, prior to relying on it for navigation.

VFR navigation with GPS can be as simple as selecting a destination (an airport, VOR, NDB, intersection, or pilot defined waypoint) and placing the unit in the navigation mode. Course guidance provided will be a great circle route (shortest distance) direct to the destination. Many units provide advisory information about special use airspace and minimum safe altitudes, along with extensive airport data, and ATC services and frequencies. Users having prior experience with LORAN-C receivers will note many similarities in the wealth of navigation information available although the technical principles of operation are quite different.

All GPS receivers have integral (built into the unit) navigation displays and some feature integral moving map displays. Some panel mounted units will drive a VOR indicator, HSI, or even an external moving map display. GPS course deviation is linear—there is not an increase in tracking sensitivity as the airplane approaches a waypoint. Pilots must carefully observe placards, selector switch positions, and annunciator indications when utilizing GPS as installations and approvals can vary widely.

The integral GPS navigation display (like most LORAN-C units) uses several additional navigational terms beyond those used in NDB and VOR navigation. Some of these terms, whose abbreviations vary among manufacturers, are shown below. The pilot should consult the manufacturer's operating guide for specific definitions.

NOTAM's should be reviewed prior to relying on GPS for navigation. GPS NOTAM's will be issued to announce outages for specific GPS satellites by pseudorandom noise code (PRN) and satellite vehicle number (SVN). Pilots may obtain GPS NOTAM's from FSS briefers only upon request.

When using any sophisticated and highly capable navigation system, such as LORAN-C or GPS, there is a strong temptation to rely almost exclusively on that unit, to the detriment of using other techniques of position keeping. The prudent pilot will never rely on one means of navigation when others are available for cross-check and backup.

RADAR SERVICES

Radar is a device that detects objects that reflect back transmitted pulses. The reflected pulses are electronically processed to obtain information regarding distance and azimuth. The Federal Aviation Administration (FAA) uses two types of radar systems: primary and secondary.

A primary radar system is one in which a minute portion of a radio pulse transmitted from a site is reflected by an object and then received back at the same site for processing and display at an ATC facility. With this type of system, large aircraft reflect better than small ones, and close aircraft reflect better than distant ones. Even the structure of the aircraft (wood, fabric, aluminum, or composite) affects the strength of the reflected radio pulse.

A secondary radar system is one in which the aircraft responds to a radio pulse (an interrogation) from a site with a distinctive transmission from its transponder. This reply transmission, rather than the directly reflected signal, is received at the site for processing and display. Secondary radar is typically used in conjunction with primary radar at most locations although some sites are only equipped with secondary radar. Secondary radar can only display the returns of transponder equipped aircraft. This secondary radar is sometimes referred to as the air traffic control radar beacon system (ATCRBS).

There are primarily two different types of ATC radar facilities available: terminal radar approach control facilities (TRACON's) and air route traffic control centers (ARTCC's). Both facilities can provide radar monitoring (flight following) and radar navigational guidance (vectors).

A terminal radar approach control (TRACON) is a terminal radar facility whose primary job is separating and sequencing aircraft arriving, departing, or transitioning the area. They serve all Class B and Class C airspaces and are also found at other high activity airports. Certain major military airports have like facilities that provide similar services.

Air route traffic control centers (ARTCC's) are widely spaced, en route radar facilities whose areas of coverage typically encompass several states. "Centers" are the controlling agency for all Class A airspace, but their radar coverage also extends to much lower altitudes. Although their primary function is separation of en route IFR traffic, radar services to VFR aircraft are provided on a workload permitting basis.

Pilots must keep several factors in mind when receiving radar services. First, ATC radar does not necessarily display all aircraft in the vicinity. Pilots must never relax vigilance for other air traffic, even when in radar contact. Secondly, ATC radar does not display clouds or other restrictions to visibility (although some primary radar systems will display significant precipitation). The pilot is always responsible for maintaining VFR visibility and cloud separation criteria. In addition, pilots are also responsible for terrain and obstruction clearance and wake turbulence avoidance. If an assigned heading or altitude compromises these responsibilities, pilots are expected to advise the controller so that an alternate clearance or instruction can be issued. Finally, radar frequencies, both primary and secondary, are limited to line-of-sight propagation paths. In fringe or marginal coverage areas, climbing to a higher altitude will assist detection.

Even when not operating in Class A (IFR only), B, or C airspace, pilots are encouraged to use radar services whenever they are available. There may be occasions when routine radar monitoring or radar vectors are not available due to frequent congestion, controller workload, equipment limitations, or other factors.

CHAPTER 12

EMERGENCY OPERATIONS

INTRODUCTION

This chapter discusses some of the considerations for system and equipment malfunctions. It covers emergency situations, such as descents, emergency approaches, and emergency landings. It also covers general guidelines for actual emergency situations.

The Airplane Flight Manual (AFM) and/or Pilot's Operating Handbook (POH) for each airplane contains information pertinent to most emergency procedures and the safe operation of the airplane. Manufacturers also provide the checklists that complement the procedures. The owner/operator is responsible for keeping the checklists and the latest information available in the airplane for easy reference in case of an emergency. Some emergency procedures for engine failure on takeoff or inflight fire should be committed to memory and practiced so that response is timely and accurate.

SYSTEMS AND EQUIPMENT MALFUNCTIONS

Throughout each phase of flight training, several types of typical emergencies or system and equipment malfunctions will be simulated. These situations will be introduced in flight at safe altitudes to provide a better understanding of the procedures and options available.

A few emergency conditions will be discussed below. This information is general in nature, and is not intended to be used in lieu of specific procedures recommended by the manufacturer.

Engine Fire On Start

When an engine is primed excessively before starting, especially with cold temperatures, an induction fire may occur during start. When this occurs, the pilot should continue cranking the engine and shut off the fuel. This will normally draw the fire into the intake manifold. If the fire does not extinguish, exit the airplane. If operating from an airport with an operating control tower, advise the tower of the fire and where the airplane is located if time permits.

Smoke/Fire In Flight

If a pilot experiences smoke in the cabin during flight, it may be controlled by identifying and shutting down the faulty system. Heaters and all electrical equipment should be turned OFF. Smoke may be removed by opening windows or emergency exits. If the smoke intensifies, the exits and windows should be closed. After the smoke has been removed from the cabin, electrical equipment may be turned ON one item at a time until the faulty system is identified. If the source of the smoke is determined to be an upholstery fire, the fire extinguisher (if available) should be used in an attempt to put it out. Smoke entering the cabin from the engine compartment is indicative of either a heater or engine fire. In all cases the pilot should follow the manufacturer's checklist, if one is provided.

With the use of modern installation techniques and materials, the probability of an engine fire occurring is remote. A good preflight of the airplane can reduce the possibility of engine fire by detecting conditions that could contribute to a fire. An extensive preflight inspection should be given to the engine compartment. Leaks in the fuel system, oil system, or exhaust system can lead to an inflight fire. Fire in flight must be immediately controlled. It is easily identified by an open flame or smoke coming from the engine compartment or the rapid discoloration of paint on the engine cowling. Fuel to the engine must be immediately cut OFF and boost pumps must be shut OFF. If the manufacturer provides a checklist for an engine fire, it must be followed. The principle concern of engine fire is major structural damage. Such an occurrence requires that a landing be made as quickly as possible. An emergency descent should be made, and if possible, Air Traffic Control (ATC) notified of the emergency. If the fire and flames are visible during the descent, attempt to slip away from the fire as much as possible. For example, if the fire is observed on the left side, consider slipping to the right. This may help move the fire away from the airplane.

Emergency Descents

An emergency descent is a maneuver for descending as rapidly as possible to a lower altitude or to the ground for an emergency landing. The need for this maneuver may result from an uncontrollable fire, a sudden loss of cabin pressurization, or any other situation demanding an immediate and rapid descent. The objective is to descend the airplane as soon and as rapidly as possible, within the structural limitations of the airplane. Simulated emergency descents should be made in a turn to check for other air traffic below and to look around for a possible emergency landing area. A radio call announcing descent intentions may be appropriate to alert other aircraft in the area. When initiating the descent, a bank of approximately 30 to 45° should be established to maintain positive load factors ("G" forces) on the airplane.

Emergency descent training should be performed as recommended by the manufacturer, including the configuration and airspeeds. Except when prohibited by the manufacturer, the power should be reduced to idle, and the propeller control (if equipped) should be placed in the low pitch (or high revolutions per minute (RPM)) position. This will allow the propeller to act as an aerodynamic brake to help prevent an excessive airspeed buildup during the descent. The landing gear and flaps should be extended as recommended by the manufacturer. This will provide maximum drag so that the descent can be made as rapidly as possible, without excessive airspeed. The pilot should not allow the airplane's airspeed to pass the never exceed speed (V_{NE}), the maximum gear extended speed (V_{LE}), or the maximum flap extended speed (V_{FE}), as applicable. In the case of an engine fire, a high airspeed descent could blow out the fire. However, the weakening of the airplane structure is a major concern and descent at low airspeed would place less stress on the airplane. If the descent is conducted in turbulent conditions, the pilot must also comply with the maneuvering speed (V_A) limitations. The descent should be made at the maximum allowable airspeed consistent with the procedure used. This will provide increased drag and therefore the loss of altitude as quickly as possible. The recovery from an emergency descent should be initiated at a high enough altitude to ensure a safe recovery back to level flight or a precautionary landing.

When the descent is established and stabilized during training and practice, the descent should be terminated. In airplanes with piston engines, prolonged practice of emergency descents should be avoided to prevent excessive cooling of the engine cylinders.

Partial Power Loss

When experiencing a partial power loss in flight, consider maintaining an airspeed that will provide the best airplane performance available. This airspeed will be approximately best glide speed.

If the power available will provide a climb at this airspeed, the pilot should climb to a more advantageous altitude. However, the pilot must consider that the engine may not continue to run very long in this condition. A decision on where to land must be made and continually updated as the flight progresses. If at this airspeed, the airplane is descending, an emergency landing will be imminent. A suitable landing area should be selected while sufficient altitude remains to allow for necessary maneuvering. In any case, an emergency exists, and should be declared and handled accordingly. Declaring an emergency with ATC will provide for priority handling.

Complete Power Loss

When a complete power loss occurs in flight in a single-engine airplane, the pilot must maintain control, stabilize the airplane in best glide attitude, and follow the engine failure checklist. If power is not restored and the engine is still turning, a last resort action may be attempted by unlocking the primer and pulling it out to allow fuel to be drawn into the cylinders. If this does not restore some power, close the primer.

If a complete power loss occurs in flight in an airplane with a controllable-pitch propeller, positioning the propeller to high pitch (low RPM) can extend the glide. This option may be available provided the engine is windmilling (turning) and the propeller governor is producing oil pressure.

Landing Gear Emergencies

Prior to starting the engine when the master switch is turned ON, check to see if the landing gear position light(s) are illuminated. If the landing gear lights are not visible, be sure the navigation lights are turned OFF. In some airplanes the landing gear lights are dimmed for night operations and appear to be OFF during daylight.

If the landing gear fails to retract on takeoff, leave the gear in the DOWN position and return for a landing.

If during an approach to landing, the pilot extends the landing gear and it fails to extend, leave the traffic pattern and climb to a safe altitude to analyze the problem.

The first step in determining whether the landing gear is down would be to check the gear down light bulb by testing it or replacing it with another bulb. If the problem is not the bulb, recycle the landing gear. If recycling the gear is unsuccessful, close the throttle and check for the gear warning horn. In many cases the problem is only an inoperative microswitch on the landing gear. Also, slowing the airplane below maneuvering speed and yawing from side to side or applying up-elevator control sometimes will force the landing gear down into the locked position. In any procedure involving rapid control input, care must be taken not to overstress the airplane.

If a decision is made to make a gear-up landing, follow the manufacturer's recommended procedures outlined in the checklist. In the absence of an emergency checklist, proceed as follows:

- Seat belts and shoulder harness secure.
- Normal approach.
- Throttle closed.
- Fuel OFF.
- Ignition OFF.
- Full flaps, for slowest touchdown speed.
- After landing is assured, master switch OFF.
- Land as normally and slowly as possible.

Inadvertent Door Opening on Takeoff or In Flight

When a cabin or baggage door opens suddenly after takeoff, the pilot must maintain control of the airplane, remain in the traffic pattern, fly a normal approach, and land as soon as possible. Although a cabin door will not open very far or cause a serious problem, the sudden noise is startling. Some loose cabin items may be drawn out of the airplane.

If an airplane baggage door opens, the pilot must maintain adequate airspeed to ensure proper control. Additional airspeed may be used on final approach and in the roundout to ensure adequate control is available until touchdown.

Always follow the instructions in the AFM/POH, if provided.

Split Flap Condition

An unexpected rolling motion may occur when the flaps are lowered. This rolling condition may have resulted from an asymmetrical flap condition.

In this situation follow the instructions in the AFM/POH, if provided. If information is not provided and the airplane is controllable, it may be best not to make an attempt to raise the flaps, but to land as soon as possible. An attempt to raise the flaps may possibly aggravate the situation. If the airplane is not controllable, then an attempt should be made to raise the flaps.

EMERGENCY APPROACHES AND LANDINGS (ACTUAL)

In spite of the remarkable reliability of present-day airplane engines, the pilot should always be prepared to cope with emergencies that may involve an emergency landing caused by partial or complete engine failure.

A study by the National Transportation Safety Board (NTSB) reveals several factors that may interfere with a pilot's ability to act promptly and properly when faced with such an emergency:

- **Reluctance to Accept the Emergency Situation.** A pilot whose mind is allowed to become paralyzed at the thought that the airplane will be on the ground in a short time, regardless of what is done, is severely handicapped in the handling of the emergency. An unconscious desire to delay this dreaded moment may lead to errors, such as failure to lower the nose to maintain flying speed, delay in the selection of the most suitable touchdown area within reach, and indecision in general.

- **Desire to Save the Airplane.** A pilot who has been conditioned to expect to find a relatively safe landing area whenever the instructor closes the throttle for a simulated emergency landing may ignore all basic rules of airmanship to avoid a touchdown in terrain where airplane damage is unavoidable. The desire to save the airplane, regardless of the risks involved, may be influenced by the pilot's financial stake in the airplane and the certainty that an undamaged airplane implies no bodily harm. There are times when a pilot should be more interested in sacrificing the airplane so that all occupants can safely walk away from it.

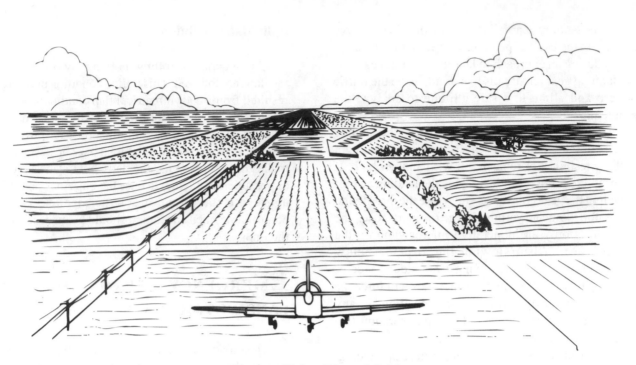

FIGURE 12-1.—Plowed field.

• **Undue Concern About Getting Hurt.** Fear is a vital part of our self-preservation mechanism. When fear leads to panic, we invite what we want to avoid the most. The survival records favor the pilot who maintains their composure and knows how to apply the general concepts and procedures that have been developed throughout the years.

A competent pilot is constantly on the alert for the nearest emergency landing field. Naturally, the perfect forced-landing field is an established airport, or a hard-packed, long, smooth field with out high obstacles on the approach end. These ideal conditions may not be readily available, so the best available field must be selected. Cultivated fields are usually satisfactory, and plowed fields are acceptable if the landing is made parallel to the furrows. [Figure 12-1] In any case, fields with large boulders, ditches, or other features that present a hazard during the landing should be avoided. A landing with the landing gear retracted may be advisable in soft or snow-covered fields to eliminate the possibility of the airplane nosing over, or damaging the gear, as a result of the wheels digging in.

Several factors must be considered in determining whether a field is of adequate length. When landing on a level field into a strong headwind, the distance required for a safe landing would naturally be much less than the distance required for landing with a tailwind. If it is impossible to land directly into the wind because maneuvering to an upwind approach would place the airplane at a dangerously low altitude, or a suitable field into the wind is not available, then the landing should be made crosswind or downwind. [Figure 12-2] A large field that is crosswind, or even downwind, may be safer than a smaller field that is directly into the wind. Whenever possible the pilot should select a field that is wide enough to allow extending the base leg and delaying the turn onto the final approach to correct for any error in planning. [Figure 12-3]

The direction and speed of the wind are important factors during any landing, particularly in an emergency landing, since the wind affects the airplane's gliding distance over the ground, the path over the ground during the approach, the groundspeed at which the airplane contacts the ground, and the distance the airplane rolls after the landing. All these effects should be considered during the selection of a field.

As a general rule, all landings should be made with the airplane headed into the wind, but this cannot be a hard and fast rule since many other factors may make it inadvisable in an actual emergency landing. The following are examples of such factors.

• Insufficient altitude may make it inadvisable or impossible to attempt to maneuver into the wind.

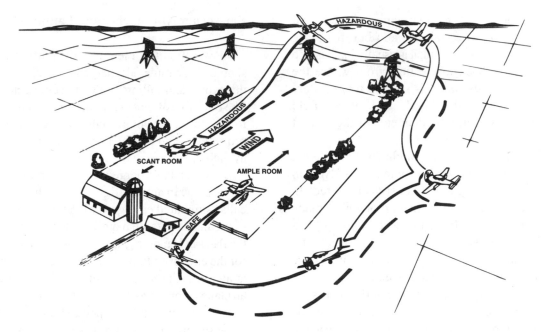

FIGURE 12-2.— Use good judgment in choosing direction.

• Ground obstacles may make landing into the wind impractical or inadvisable because they shorten the effective length of the available field.

• Distance from a suitable field up wind from the present position may make it impossible to reach the field from the altitude the engine failure occurs.

• The best available field may be downhill and at such an angle to the wind that a downwind landing uphill would be preferable and safer.

The altitude available is, in many ways, the controlling factor in the successful accomplishment of

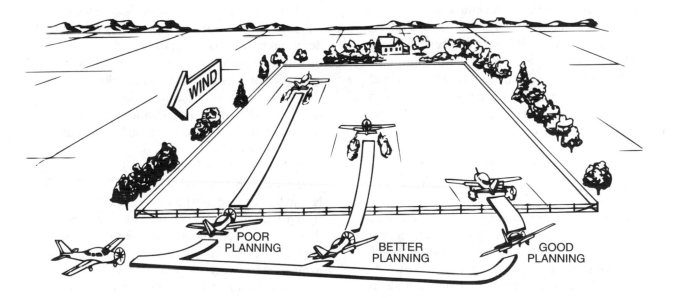

FIGURE 12-3.—Extended base leg.

an emergency landing. If an actual engine failure should occur immediately after takeoff and before a safe maneuvering altitude is attained, it is usually inadvisable to attempt to turn back to the field from where the takeoff was made. Instead, it is safer to immediately establish the proper glide attitude, and select a field directly ahead or slightly to either side of the takeoff path.

The decision to continue straight ahead is often a difficult to make unless the problems involved in attempting to turn back are seriously considered. In the first place, the takeoff was in all probability made into the wind. To get back to the takeoff field, a downwind turn must be made. This increases the groundspeed and rushes the pilot even more in the performance of procedures and in planning the landing approach. Secondly, the airplane will be losing considerable altitude during the turn and might still be in a bank when the ground is contacted, resulting in the airplane cartwheeling (which would be a catastrophe for the occupants, as well as the airplane). After turning down wind the apparent increase in groundspeed could mislead the pilot into attempting to prematurely slow down the airplane and cause it to stall. On the other hand, continuing straight ahead or making a slight turn allows the pilot more time to establish a safe landing attitude, and the landing can be made as slowly as possible, but more importantly, the airplane can be landed while under control.

Concerning the subject of turning back to the runway following an engine failure on takeoff, the pilot should determine the minimum altitude an attempt of such a maneuver would be made in a particular airplane. Experimentation at a safe altitude should give the pilot an approximation of height lost in a descending 180° turn at idle power. By adding a safety factor of about 25 percent, the pilot should arrive at a practical decision height. The ability to make a 180° turn does not necessarily mean that the departure runway can be reached in a power-off glide; this depends on the wind, the distance traveled during the climb, the height reached, and the glide distance of the airplane without power.

When an emergency landing is imminent, wind direction and speed should always be considered, but the main objective is to complete a safe landing in the best field available. This involves getting the airplane on the ground in as near a normal landing attitude as possible without striking obstructions. If the pilot gets the airplane on the ground under control, it may sustain damage, but the occupants will probably get no worse than a shaking up.

Emergency Approaches and Landings (Simulated)

From time to time on dual flights, the instructor should give simulated emergency landings by retarding the throttle and calling "simulated emergency landing." The objective of these simulated emergency landings is to develop the pilot's accuracy, judgment, planning, procedures, and confidence when little or no power is available.

A simulated emergency landing may be given with the airplane in any configuration. When the instructor calls "simulated emergency landing," the pilot should immediately establish a glide attitude and ensure that the flaps and landing gear are in the proper configuration for the existing situation. When the proper glide speed is attained, the nose should then be lowered and the airplane trimmed to maintain that speed.

A constant gliding speed should be maintained because variations of gliding speed nullify all attempts at accuracy in judgment of gliding distance and the landing spot. The many variables, such as altitude, obstruction, wind direction, landing direction, landing surface and gradient, and landing distance requirements of the airplane will determine the pattern and approach procedures to use.

Utilizing any combination of normal gliding maneuvers, from wings level to spirals, the pilot should eventually arrive at the normal key position at a normal traffic pattern altitude for the selected landing area. From this point on, the approach will be as nearly as possible a normal power-off approach. [Figure 12-4]

With the greater choice of fields afforded by higher altitudes, the inexperienced pilot may be inclined to delay making a decision, and with considerable altitude in which to maneuver, errors in maneuvering and estimation of glide distance may develop.

All pilots should learn to determine the wind direction and estimate its speed from the windsock at the airport, smoke from factories or houses, dust, brush fires, and windmills.

Once a field has been selected, the student pilot should always be required to indicate it to the instructor. Normally, the student should be required to plan and fly a pattern for landing on the field first elected until the instructor terminates the simulated emergency landing. This will give the instructor an opportunity to explain and correct any errors; it will also give the student an opportunity to see the results of the errors. However, if the student realizes during the approach that a poor field has been selected—one that would obviously result in disaster if a landing were to be

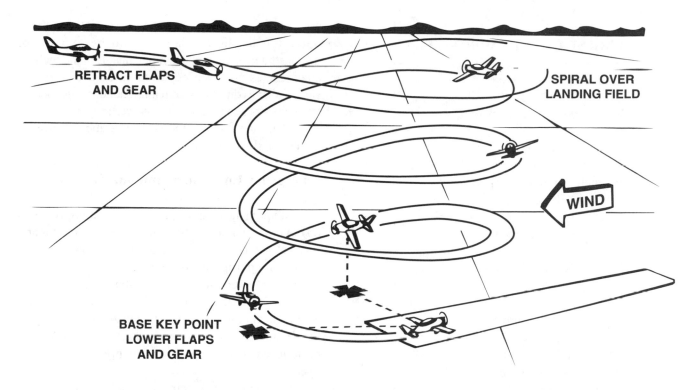

FIGURE 12-4.— Remain over intended landing area.

made—and there is a more advantageous field within gliding distance, a change to the better field should be permitted. The hazards involved in these last-minute decisions, such as excessive maneuvering at very low altitudes, should be thoroughly explained by the instructor.

Slipping the airplane, using flaps, varying the position of the base leg, and varying the turn onto final approach should be stressed as ways of correcting for misjudgment of altitude and glide angle.

Eagerness to get down is one of the most common faults of inexperienced pilots during simulated emergency landings. In giving way to this, they forget about speed and arrive at the edge of the field with too much speed to permit a safe landing. Too much speed may be just as dangerous as too little; it results in excessive floating and overshooting the desired landing spot. It should be impressed on the students that they cannot dive at a field and expect to land on it.

During all simulated emergency landings, the engine should be kept warm and cleared. During a simulated emergency landing, either the instructor or the student should have complete control of the throttle. There should be no doubt as to who has control since many near accidents have occurred from such misunderstandings.

Every simulated emergency landing approach should be terminated as soon as it can be determined whether a safe landing could have been made. In no case should it be continued to a point where it creates an undue hazard or an annoyance to persons or property on the ground.

In addition to flying the airplane from the point of simulated engine failure to where a reasonable safe landing could be made, the student should also be taught certain emergency cockpit procedures. The habit of performing these cockpit procedures should be developed to such an extent that, when an engine failure actually occurs, the student will check the critical items that would be necessary to get the engine operating again while selecting a field and planning an approach. Combining the two operations—accomplishing emergency procedures and planning and flying the approach—will be difficult for the student during the early training in emergency landings.

There are definite steps and procedures to be followed in a simulated emergency landing. Although they may differ somewhat from the procedures used in an actual emergency, they should be learned thoroughly by the student, and each step called out to the instructor. The use of a checklist is strongly recommended. Most airplane manufacturers provide a checklist of the appropriate items. [Figure 12-5]

ENGINE FAILURE DURING FLIGHT

Engine Failure
Airspeed — Glide
Fuel Selector — Fullest Tank
Fuel Pump — ON
Mixture — RICH
Carb Heat — ON
Magneto Switch — BOTH
Flaps — UP
Gear — UP
Seat Belts — Fastened

EMERGENCY LANDING

Airspeed
Mixture — Idle Cutoff
Fuel Shutoff Valve — OFF
Ignition Switch — OFF
Flaps — As Required
Master Switch — OFF
Doors — Unlatch Prior to Touchdown

FIGURE 12-5.— Sample emergency checklist.

Critical items to be checked should include the position of the fuel tank selector, the quantity of fuel in the tank selected, the fuel pressure gauge to see if the electric fuel pump is needed, the position of the mixture control, the position of the magneto switch, and the use of carburetor heat. Many actual emergency landings have been made and later found to be the result of the fuel selector valve being positioned to an empty tank while the other tank had plenty of fuel. It may be wise to change the position of the fuel selector valve even though the fuel gauge indicates fuel in all tanks because fuel gauges can be inaccurate. Many actual emergency landings could have been prevented if the pilots had developed the habit of checking these critical items during flight training to the extent that it carried over into later flying.

Instruction in emergency procedures should not be limited to simulated emergency landings caused by power failures. Other emergencies associated with the operation of the airplane should be explained, demonstrated, and practiced if practicable. Among these emergencies are such occurrences as fire in flight, electrical or hydraulic system malfunctions, unexpected severe weather conditions, engine overheating, imminent fuel exhaustion, and the emergency operation of airplane systems and equipment.

Emergency Equipment and Survival Gear

Although the Code of Federal Regulations (CFR's) do not require that specific emergency equipment and survival gear be carried on board small airplanes during flight, it is appropriate to have a few basic items in the event of an emergency situation. Items, such as a first aid kit, flashlight, container of water, knife, matches, additional clothing, and signaling devices could be part of a basic survival kit. The contents of such a kit can be tailored to the conditions or preference of the operator.

When a pilot is planning a cross-country flight, the need for appropriate emergency equipment, clothing, and survival gear should always be included in this preparation. Some of the en route environmental conditions and factors that should be considered are:

• Type of terrain or surface to be overflown and potential for a safe emergency landing, i.e., mountains, level, remote, civilized, and water. If the route appears to be especially hazardous, a modified route should be seriously considered.
• Type of climate and temperature conditions expected, such as hot and dry or wet and cold. Supplemental clothing and water should be available if any of these conditions are expected in extreme.
• Type of emergency communications needed. This may include the use of a battery powered, hand held transceiver or a portable cellular phone.

After all these conditions and factors are considered, a better decision can be made as to what additional emergency equipment and survival gear should be included for the flight.

CHAPTER 13

TRANSITION TO DIFFERENT AIRPLANES AND SYSTEMS

INTRODUCTION

This chapter provides guidance and a recommended structured training program for a pilot transitioning to other airplanes that have different flight characteristics, performance capabilities, operating procedures, and systems from those airplanes that the pilot has previously flown. A conscientious application of the training recommended for each airplane group will result in a more knowledgeable, competent, and safer pilot.

GENERAL

Airplane size alone is not the most important consideration on whether training is needed. Airplanes are as different as people are, and the only safe transition is to receive differences training. The following areas are considered important elements of a proper transition to a different airplane.

- Engage a qualified and authorized flight instructor or checkout pilot, as required.
- Review and understand the Airplane Flight Manual (AFM) and/or Pilot's Operating Handbook (POH).
- Study engine and flight controls, engine and flight instruments, fuel management controls, wing flaps and landing gear controls and indicators, and avionics equipment.
- Review checklists for normal, abnormal, and emergency procedures.
- Practice slow flight; stalls; maximum performance maneuver techniques; and normal, crosswind, short-field, and soft-field takeoffs and landings, as well as normal and emergency operating procedures.
- Receive training in takeoffs, landings, and flight maneuvers with the airplane fully loaded or simulated fully loaded. This may include performance affected by higher-than-standard temperatures (density altitude). Most four place and larger airplanes handle quite differently when loaded to near maximum gross weight, as compared with operation with only two occupants in the pilot seats. Weight and balance calculations should be made for various loading conditions.

- When making a transition to any airplane, it is advisable to utilize a ground and flight training syllabus. A generic syllabus that can be adapted to most airplane checkouts is included at the end of this chapter for both ground training and flight training.

TRANSITION TO DIFFERENT MAKE AND/OR MODEL AIRPLANES

When a pilot has an opportunity to transition from one make and model airplane to another make or model, within the same class (single-engine land to single-engine land), specialized training is recommended. Although an authorized flight instructor is not required by the regulations to conduct this different make or model checkout (except in the case of high performance and complex or to a tailwheel or conventional gear airplane for the first time), it is important to remember that a well qualified instructor, or pilot with extensive experience in that particular make or model, should be utilized to provide this training.

The amount of time spent on each phase of training should be adequate to achieve satisfactory performance in each phase of ground and flight training. It is important that a comprehensive and realistic training program be conducted to ensure that a pilot can operate the new type of airplane safely.

High Performance/Complex Airplanes

Transition to a high performance or complex airplane can be demanding for most pilots without previous experience. These airplanes normally have increased performance and require additional planning, judgment, and skills. Therefore, it is important for a pilot to receive appropriate training before attempting to fly this type of airplane.

A high performance airplane is defined as an airplane with an engine of more than 200 horsepower. A complex airplane is defined as an airplane equipped with a retractable landing gear, wing flaps, and a controllable propeller. For a seaplane to be considered complex, it is required to have wing flaps and a controllable propeller.

Many high performance/complex airplanes have rather sophisticated systems and procedures that require additional knowledge and skills to operate safely. This may require additional ground and flight training in specific areas to ensure that proper understanding and skills have been achieved.

All complex and most high performance airplanes are equipped with a controllable propeller. This kind of propeller will require basic power management rules and procedures. Therefore, pilots must have a thorough understanding of the relationship between recommended manifold pressure and the requirements for engine or propeller revolutions per minute (RPM). Pilots must be cautioned not to exceed the recommended power.

When transitioning to a high performance or complex airplane, there are certain regulatory requirements that must be met. Title 14 of the Code of Federal Regulations (14 CFR) part 61 requires that no person can act as pilot in command of a high performance or complex airplane unless that person has met certain additional requirements. These requirements include evidence that a person has received and logged ground and flight training from an authorized flight instructor in that type airplane, simulator, or flight training device that is representative of that airplane.

To meet these regulatory requirements, it is important to train with an authorized flight instructor. Upon satisfactory completion of instruction, the flight instructor certifying the pilot is proficient to operate a high performance or complex airplane will make an endorsement in the pilot's logbook.

AIRPLANE SYSTEMS

When upgrading to complex airplanes, a pilot may encounter systems that are not ordinarily installed in other airplanes. A discussion on anti-icing/deicing pressurization and oxygen is included in this chapter.

Anti-icing/Deicing Equipment

Anti-icing/deicing equipment consists of a combination of different systems. These may be classified as either anti-icing or deicing, depending upon the function. The presence of anti-icing and deicing equipment, even though it may appear elaborate and complete, does not necessarily mean that the airplane is approved for flight in icing conditions. The AFM/POH, placards, and even the manufacturer should be consulted for specific determination of approvals and limitations.

Anti-icing equipment is provided to prevent ice from forming on certain protected surfaces. Anti-icing equipment includes heated pitot tubes, heated or non-icing static ports and fuel vents, propeller blades with electrothermal boots or alcohol slingers, windshields with alcohol spray or electrical resistance heating, windshield defoggers, and heated stall warning lift detectors. On many turboprop engines, the lip surrounding the air intake is heated either electrically or with bleed air.

Deicing equipment is generally limited to pneumatic boots on the wing and tail leading edges. Deicing equipment is installed to remove ice that has already formed on protected surfaces. Upon pilot actuation, the boots inflate with air from the pneumatic pumps to break off accumulated ice. After a few seconds of inflation, they are deflated back to their normal position with the assistance of a vacuum. The pilot monitors the buildup of ice, and cycles the boots whenever the ice accumulation reaches a certain AFM/POH-specified thickness (one-half inch is typical).

Other equipment may include an alternate induction air source and an alternate static system source. Ice tolerant antennas may also be installed.

In the event of impact ice accumulating over normal engine air induction sources, carburetor heat (carbureted engines) or alternate air (fuel-injected engines) should be selected. A loss of engine RPM with fixed-pitch propellers and a loss of manifold pressure can detect ice buildup on normal indication sources with constant-speed propellers. On some fuel-injected engines, an alternate air source is automatically activated with blockage of the normal air source.

An alternate static system provides an alternate source of static air for the pitot-static system in the unlikely event that the primary static source becomes blocked. In nonpressurized airplanes, most alternate static sources are plumbed to the cabin. On pressurized airplanes, they are usually plumbed to a (nonpressurized) baggage compartment. The pilot activates the alternate static source by opening a valve or a fitting in the cockpit. Upon activation, the airspeed indicator, altimeter, and the vertical speed indicator (VSI) will be affected and will read somewhat in error. A correction table is frequently provided in the AFM/POH.

Anti-icing/deicing equipment only eliminates ice from the protected surfaces. Significant ice accumulation may form on unprotected areas, even with the proper use of anti-ice and deice systems. Flight at high angles of attack or even normal climb speeds will permit significant ice accumulation on lower wing surfaces that are unprotected. Many AFM/POH's mandate minimum speeds to be maintained in icing conditions. Degradation of all flight characteristics and large performance losses can be expected with ice accumulation. Pilots should not rely upon the stall warning devices for adequate stall warning when ice accumulates.

Ice will accumulate unevenly on the airplane. It will add weight and drag (primarily drag), and decrease thrust and lift. Even wing shape can affect ice accumulation; thin, airfoil sections are more prone to ice accumulation than thick, highly-cambered sections. For this reason certain surfaces, such as the horizontal stabilizer, are more prone to icing than the wing. With ice accumulations, landing approaches should be made with a minimum wing flap setting (flap extension increases the angle of attack of the horizontal stabilizer) and with an added margin of airspeed. Sudden and large configuration and airspeed changes should be avoided.

Unless otherwise recommended in the AFM/POH, the autopilot should be used only briefly in icing conditions. Continuous use of the autopilot will mask trim and handling changes that will occur with ice accumulation. Without this control feel, the pilot may not be aware of ice accumulation building to hazardous levels. The autopilot will suddenly disconnect when it reaches design limits, and the pilot may find the airplane has assumed unsatisfactory handling characteristics.

Even with deicing equipment, the prudent pilot will avoid icing conditions to the maximum extent practicable, and avoid extended flight in any icing conditions.

PRESSURIZED AIRPLANES

When an airplane is flown at a high altitude, it consumes less fuel for a given airspeed than it does for the same speed at a lower altitude. In other words, the airplane is more efficient at a high altitude. In addition, bad weather and turbulence may be avoided by flying in the relatively smooth air above the storms. Because of the advantages of flying at high altitudes, many modern general aviation-type airplanes are being designed to operate in that environment. It is important that pilots transitioning to such sophisticated equipment be familiar with at least the basic operating principles.

A cabin pressurization system accomplishes several functions in providing adequate passenger comfort and safety. It maintains a cabin pressure altitude of approximately 8,000 feet at the maximum designed cruising altitude of the airplane, and prevents rapid changes of cabin altitude that may be uncomfortable or cause injury to passengers and crew. In addition, the pressurization system permits a reasonably fast exchange of air from the inside to the outside of the cabin. This is necessary to eliminate odors and to remove stale air.

Pressurization of the airplane cabin is an accepted method of protecting occupants against the effects of hypoxia. Within a pressurized cabin, occupants can be transported comfortably and safely for long periods of time, particularly if the cabin altitude is maintained at 8,000 feet or below, where the use of oxygen equipment is not required. The flight crew in this type of airplane must be aware of the danger of accidental loss of cabin pressure and must be prepared to deal with such an emergency whenever it occurs.

In the typical pressurization system, the cabin, flight compartment, and baggage compartments are incorporated into a sealed unit that is capable of containing air under a pressure higher than outside atmospheric pressure. On aircraft powered by turbine engines, bleed air from the engine compressor section is used to pressurize the cabin. Superchargers may be used on older model turbine powered airplanes to pump air into the sealed fuselage. Piston-powered airplanes may use air supplied from each engine turbocharger through a sonic venturi (flow limiter). Air is released from the fuselage by a device called an outflow valve. The outflow valve, by regulating the air exit, provides a constant inflow of air to the pressurized area.

To understand the operating principles of pressurization and air-conditioning systems, it is necessary to become familiar with some of the related terms and definitions, such as:

• **Aircraft altitude**—the actual height above sea level at which the airplane is flying.
• **Ambient temperature**—the temperature in the area immediately surrounding the airplane.
• **Ambient pressure**—the pressure in the area immediately surrounding the airplane.
• **Cabin altitude**—used to express cabin pressure in terms of equivalent altitude above sea level.
• **Differential pressure**—the difference in pressure between the pressure acting on one side of a wall and the pressure acting on the other side of the wall. In aircraft air-conditioning and pressurizing systems, it is the difference between cabin pressure and atmospheric pressure.

The cabin pressure control system provides cabin pressure regulation, pressure relief, vacuum relief, and the means for selecting the desired cabin altitude in the isobaric and differential range. In addition, dumping of the cabin pressure is a function of the pressure control system. A cabin pressure regulator, an outflow valve, and a safety valve are used to accomplish these functions.

The cabin pressure regulator controls cabin pressure to a selected value in the isobaric range and limits cabin pressure to a preset differential value in the differential range. When the airplane reaches the altitude at which the difference between the pressure inside and outside the cabin is equal to the highest differential pressure for which the fuselage structure is designed, a further increase in airplane altitude will result in a corresponding increase in cabin altitude. Differential control is used to prevent the maximum differential pressure, for which the fuselage was designed, from being exceeded. This differential pressure is determined by the structural strength of the cabin and often by the relationship of the cabin size to the probable areas of rupture, such as window areas and doors.

The cabin air pressure safety valve is a combination pressure relief, vacuum relief, and dump valve. The pressure relief valve prevents cabin pressure from exceeding a predetermined differential pressure above ambient pressure. The vacuum relief prevents ambient pressure from exceeding cabin pressure by allowing external air to enter the cabin when ambient pressure exceeds cabin pressure. The cockpit control switch actuates the dump valve. When this switch is positioned to ram, a solenoid valve opens, causing the valve to dump cabin air to atmosphere.

The degree of pressurization and the operating altitude of the aircraft are limited by several critical design factors. Primarily the fuselage is designed to withstand a particular maximum cabin differential pressure.

Several instruments are used in conjunction with the pressurization controller. The cabin differential pressure gauge indicates the difference between inside and outside pressure. This gauge should be monitored to assure that the cabin does not exceed the maximum allowable differential pressure. A cabin altimeter is also provided as a check on the performance of the system. In some cases, these two instruments are combined into one. A third instrument indicates the cabin rate of climb or descent. A cabin rate-of-climb instrument and a cabin altimeter are illustrated in Figure 13-1.

FIGURE 13-1.—Cabin pressurization instruments.

Decompression is defined as the inability of the airplane's pressurization system to maintain its designed pressure differential. This can be caused by a malfunction in the pressurization system or structural damage to the airplane. Physiologically, decompressions fall into two categories, they are:

• **Explosive Decompression**—Explosive decompression is defined as a change in cabin pressure faster than the lungs can decompress; therefore, it is possible that lung damage may occur. Normally, the time required to release air from the lungs without restrictions, such as masks, is 0.2 seconds. Most authorities consider any decompression that occurs in less than 0.5 seconds as explosive and potentially dangerous.
• **Rapid Decompression**—Rapid decompression is defined as a change in cabin pressure where the lungs can decompress faster than the cabin; therefore, there is no likelihood of lung damage.

During an explosive decompression, there may be noise, and for a split second, one may feel dazed. The cabin air will fill with fog, dust, or flying debris. Fog occurs due to the rapid drop in temperature and the change of relative humidity. Normally, the ears clear automatically. Air will rush from the mouth and nose due to the escape of air from the lungs, and may be noticed by some individuals.

The primary danger of decompression is hypoxia. Unless proper utilization of oxygen equipment is accomplished quickly, unconsciousness may occur in a very short time. The period of useful consciousness is considerably shortened when a person is subjected to a rapid decompression. This is due to the rapid reduction of pressure on the body—oxygen in the lungs is exhaled rapidly. This in effect reduces the partial pressure of oxygen in the blood and therefore reduces the pilot's effective performance time by one-third to one-fourth its normal time. For this reason, the oxygen mask should be worn when flying at very high altitudes (35,000 feet or higher). It is recommended that the crewmembers select the 100 percent oxygen setting on the oxygen regulator at high altitude if the airplane is equipped with a demand or pressure demand oxygen system.

Another hazard is being tossed or blown out of the airplane if near an opening. For this reason, individuals near openings should wear safety harnesses or seatbelts at all times when the airplane is pressurized and they are seated.

Another potential hazard during high altitude decompressions is the possibility of evolved gas decompression sicknesses. Exposure to wind blasts and extremely cold temperatures are other hazards one might have to face.

Rapid descent from altitude is necessary if these problems are to be minimized. Automatic visual and aural warning systems are included in the equipment of all pressurized airplanes.

OXYGEN SYSTEMS

Most high altitude airplanes come equipped with some type of fixed oxygen installation. If the airplane does not have a fixed installation, portable oxygen equipment must be readily accessible during flight. The portable equipment usually consists of a container, regulator, mask outlet, and pressure gauge. Aircraft oxygen is usually stored in high pressure system containers of 1,800 – 2,200 pounds per square inch (PSI). When the ambient temperature surrounding an oxygen cylinder decreases, pressure within that cylinder will decrease because pressure varies directly with temperature if the volume of a gas remains constant. If a drop in indicated pressure on a supplemental oxygen cylinder is noted, there is no reason to suspect depletion of the oxygen supply, which has simply been compacted due to storage of the containers in an unheated area of the aircraft. High pressure oxygen containers should be marked with the PSI tolerance (i.e., 1,800 PSI) before filling the container to that pressure. The containers should be supplied with aviation oxygen only, which is 100 percent pure oxygen. Industrial oxygen is not intended for breathing and may contain impurities, and medical oxygen contains water vapor that can freeze in the regulator when exposed to cold temperatures. To assure safety, oxygen system periodic inspection and servicing should be done.

An oxygen system consists of a mask and a regulator that supplies a flow of oxygen dependent upon cabin altitude. Regulators approved for use up to 40,000 feet are designed to provide zero percent cylinder oxygen and 100 percent cabin air at cabin altitudes of 8,000 feet or less, with the ratio changing to 100 percent oxygen and zero percent cabin air at approximately 34,000 feet cabin altitude. Regulators approved up to 45,000 feet are designed to provide 40 percent cylinder oxygen and 60 percent cabin air at lower altitudes, with the ratio changing to 100 percent at the higher altitude. Pilots should avoid flying above 10,000 feet without oxygen during the day and above 8,000 feet at night.

Pilots should be aware of the danger of fire when using oxygen. Materials that are nearly fireproof in ordinary air may be susceptible to burning in oxygen. Oils and greases may catch fire if exposed to oxygen, and cannot be used for sealing the valves and fittings of oxygen equipment. Smoking during any kind of oxygen equipment use is prohibited. Before each flight, the pilot should thoroughly inspect and test all oxygen equipment. The inspection should include a thorough examination of the aircraft oxygen equipment, including available supply, an operational check of the system, and assurance that the supplemental oxygen is readily accessible. The inspection should be accomplished with clean hands and should include a visual inspection of the mask and tubing for tears, cracks, or deterioration; the regulator for valve and lever condition and positions; oxygen quantity; and the location and functioning of oxygen pressure gauges, flow indicators and connections. The mask should be donned and the system should be tested. After any oxygen use, verify that all components and valves are shut off.

Masks

There are numerous types of oxygen masks in use that vary in design detail. It would be impractical to discuss all of the types in this handbook. It is important that the masks used be compatible with the particular oxygen system involved. Crew masks are fitted to the user's face with a minimum of leakage. Crew masks usually contain a microphone. Most masks are the oronasal-type, which covers only the mouth and nose.

Passenger masks may be simple, cup-shaped rubber moldings sufficiently flexible to obviate individual fitting. They may have a simple elastic head strap or the passenger may hold them to the face.

All oxygen masks should be kept clean. This reduces the danger of infection and prolongs the life of the mask. To clean the mask, wash it with a mild soap and water solution and rinse it with clear water. If a microphone is installed, use a clean swab, instead of running water, to wipe off the soapy solution. The mask should also be disinfected. A gauze pad that has been soaked in a water solution of Merthiolate can be used to swab out the mask. This solution should contain one-fifth teaspoon of Merthiolate per quart of water. Wipe the mask with a clean cloth and air dry.

Diluter Demand Oxygen Systems

Diluter demand oxygen systems supply oxygen only when the user inhales through the mask. An automix lever allows the regulators to automatically mix cabin air and oxygen or supply 100 percent oxygen, depending on the altitude. The demand mask provides a tight seal over the face to prevent dilution with outside air and can be used safely up to 40,000 feet. A pilot who has a beard or mustache should be sure it is trimmed in a manner that will not interfere with the sealing of the oxygen mask. The fit of the mask around the beard or mustache should be checked on the ground for proper sealing.

Pressure Demand Oxygen Systems

Pressure demand oxygen systems are similar to diluter demand oxygen equipment, except that oxygen is supplied to the mask under pressure at cabin altitudes above 34,000 feet. Pressure demand regulators also create airtight and oxygen-tight seals, but they also provide a positive pressure application of oxygen to the mask face piece that allows the user's lungs to be pressurized with oxygen. This feature makes pressure demand regulators safe at altitudes above 40,000 feet. Some systems may have a pressure demand mask with the regulator attached directly to the mask, rather than mounted on the instrument panel or other area within the flight deck. The mask-mounted regulator eliminates the problem of a long hose that must be purged of air before 100 percent oxygen begins flowing into the mask.

Continuous Flow Oxygen System

Continuous flow oxygen systems are usually provided for passengers. The passenger mask typically has a reservoir bag, which collects oxygen from the continuous flow oxygen system during the time when the mask user is exhaling. The oxygen collected in the reservoir bag allows a higher inspiratory flow rate during the inhalation cycle, which reduces the amount of air dilution. Ambient air is added to the supplied oxygen during inhalation after the reservoir bag oxygen supply is depleted. The exhaled air is released to the cabin.

Servicing Of Oxygen Systems

Certain precautions should be observed whenever aircraft oxygen systems are to be serviced. Before servicing any aircraft with oxygen, consult the specific aircraft service manual to determine the type of equipment required and procedures to be used. Oxygen system servicing should be accomplished only when the aircraft is located outside of the hangars. Personal cleanliness and good housekeeping are imperative when working with oxygen. Oxygen under pressure and petroleum products creates spontaneous results when they are brought in contact with each other. Service people should be certain to wash dirt, oil, and grease (including lip salves and hair oil) from their hands before working around oxygen equipment. It is also essential that clothing and tools are free of oil, grease, and dirt. Aircraft with permanently installed oxygen tanks usually require two persons to accomplish servicing of the system. One should be stationed at the service equipment control valves, and the other stationed where he or she can observe the aircraft system pressure gauges. Oxygen system servicing is not recommended during aircraft fueling operations or while other work is performed that could provide a source of ignition. Oxygen system servicing while passengers are on board the aircraft is not recommended.

Physiological Altitude Limits

The response of human beings to increased altitude varies with each individual. People who are in poor health will be affected at a much lower altitude than people who are in good physical condition. Without supplementary oxygen, most people will begin to experience a reduction in night vision or general visual acuity at approximately 5,000 feet. At an altitude of approximately 10,000 feet, a person will begin to display measurable deterioration in mental abilities and physical dexterity after a period of several hours. At 18,000 feet, the mental deterioration may result in unconsciousness, and the time of useful consciousness (TUC) is generally about 15 minutes. At 25,000 feet, the TUC for most people is about 3 - 10 minutes. At altitudes above 25,000 feet, the TUC decreases very rapidly, becoming only a few seconds at 40,000 feet. If a person is breathing 100 percent oxygen, the partial pressure of oxygen in the lungs at 34,000 feet is the same as that for a person breathing air at sea level. At 40,000 feet, a person breathing 100 percent oxygen will have the same partial pressure of oxygen in the lungs as a person breathing air at 10,000 feet. Therefore, 34,000 feet is the highest altitude a person would be provided complete protection from the effects of hypoxia, and 40,000 feet is the highest altitude 100 percent oxygen will provide reasonable protection for the limited period of time needed to descend to a safe altitude.

Regulatory Requirements

Title 14 of the Code of Federal Regulations (14 CFR) part 91 requires that the minimum flightcrew on civil aircraft of U.S. registry be provided with and use supplemental oxygen at cabin pressure altitudes above 12,500 feet mean sea level (MSL) up to and including 14,000 feet MSL for the portion of the flight that is at these altitudes for more than 30 minutes. The required minimum flightcrew must be provided with and use supplemental oxygen at all times when operating an aircraft above 14,000 feet MSL. At cabin pressure altitudes above 15,000 feet MSL, all occupants of the aircraft must be provided with supplemental oxygen.

14 CFR part 91 also requires pressurized aircraft to have at least a 10-minute additional supply of supplemental oxygen for each occupant at flight altitudes above FL 250 in the event of decompression. At flight altitudes above FL 350, one pilot at the controls of the airplane must wear and use an oxygen mask that is secured and sealed. The oxygen mask must supply oxygen at all times or must automatically supply oxygen when the cabin pressure altitude of the airplane exceeds 14,000 feet MSL. An exception to this regulation exists for two-pilot crews that operate at or below FL 410. One pilot does not need to wear and use an oxygen mask if both pilots are at the controls and each pilot has a quick donning type of oxygen mask that can be placed on the face with one hand from the ready position and be properly secured, sealed, and operational within 5 seconds. If one pilot of a two-pilot crew is away from the controls, then the pilot that is at the controls is required to wear and use an oxygen mask that is secured and sealed.

CHAPTER 14

TRANSITION TO A MULTIENGINE AIRPLANE

INTRODUCTION

This chapter discusses the factors involved in the operation of multiengine airplanes. This involves normal and emergency procedures during ground and flight operations.

MULTIENGINE PERFORMANCE CHARACTERISTICS

The term "multiengine" as used here pertains to the propeller driven airplane having a maximum certificated gross weight of less than 12,500 pounds, and which has two reciprocating airplane engines mounted on the wings.

From the transitioning pilot's point of view, the basic difference between a multiengine and single-engine airplane is the potential problem involving engine failure. The information that follows is confined to that one basic difference.

Before the subject of operating procedures in multiengine airplanes can be thoroughly discussed, there are several terms that need to be reviewed. V-speeds, such as V_{XSE}, V_{YSE}, V_{SSE}, and V_{MC} are the new speeds the multiengine pilot needs to know in addition to the other V-speeds that are common to both multiengine and single-engine airplanes. The airspeed indicator in multiengine airplanes is marked (in addition to other normally marked speeds) with a red radial line at the minimum controllable airspeed (V_{MC}) with the critical engine inoperative and a blue radial line at the best rate-of-climb airspeed (V_{YSE}) with one engine inoperative. [Figure 14-1]

- V_R—Rotation speed. The speed at which rotation is initiated during takeoff.
- V_{LOF}—Lift-off speed.
- V_X—Best angle-of-climb speed. At this speed, the airplane will gain the greatest height for a given distance of forward travel. This speed is used for obstacle clearance with all engines operating.

FIGURE 14-1.—Airspeed indicator markings for a multiengine airplane.

- V_{XSE}—Best angle-of-climb speed (single-engine). At this speed, the airplane will gain the greatest height for a given distance of forward travel. This speed is used for obstacle clearance with one engine inoperative.
- V_Y—Best rate-of-climb speed. This speed will provide the maximum altitude gain for a given period of time with all engines operating.
- V_{YSE}—Best rate-of-climb speed (single-engine). This speed will provide the maximum altitude gain for a given period of time with one engine inoperative.
- V_{SSE}—Intentional one-engine-inoperative speed. The speed above both V_{MC} and stall speed selected by the manufacturer to provide a margin of lateral and directional control when one engine is suddenly rendered inoperative. Intentional failing of one engine below this speed is not recommended.

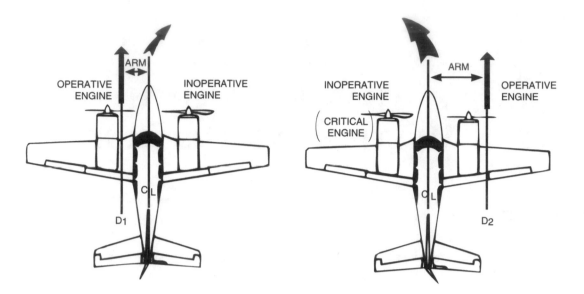

FIGURE 14-2.—Forces created during single-engine operation.

- **V$_{MC}$**—Minimum control speed. The minimum flight speed at which the airplane is controllable with a bank of not more than 5° into the operating engine when one engine suddenly becomes inoperative and the remaining engine is operating at takeoff power.
- **V$_{MCA}$**—Minimum control speed with one engine inoperative (in flight). The minimum airspeed in flight at which directional control can be maintained, when one engine is suddenly made inoperative. V$_{MCA}$ is a function of engine thrust that varies with altitude and temperature.
- **V$_{MCG}$**—Minimum control speed with one engine inoperative (on the ground). The minimum airspeed on the ground at which directional control can be maintained, when one engine is suddenly made inoperative, using only aerodynamic controls. V$_{MCG}$ is a function of engine thrust that varies with altitude and temperature.

THE CRITICAL ENGINE

P-factor is present in multiengine airplanes just as it is in single-engine airplanes. Remember that P-factor is caused by the dissimilar thrust of the rotating propeller blades when in certain flight conditions. It is the result of the downward moving blade having a greater angle of attack than the upward moving blade when the relative wind striking the blades is not aligned with the thrust line (as in a nose-high attitude).

In most U.S. designed multiengine airplanes, both engines rotate to the right (clockwise) when viewed from the rear, and both engines develop an equal amount of thrust. At low airspeed and high-power conditions, the downward moving propeller blade of each engine develops more thrust than the upward moving blade. This asymmetric propeller thrust or P-factor, results in a center of thrust at the right side of each engine as indicated by lines D1 and D2 in Figure 14-2. The turning (or yawing) force of the right engine is greater than the left engine since the center of thrust (D2) is much farther away from the centerline (CL) of the fuselage because it has a longer leverage arm. When the right engine is operative and the left engine is inoperative, the turning (or yawing) force is greater than in the opposite situation of an operative left engine and an inoperative right engine. In other words, directional control is more difficult when the left engine (the critical engine) is suddenly made inoperative.

Some multiengine airplanes are equipped with engines turning in opposite directions; that is, the left engine and propeller turn clockwise and the right engine and propeller turn counterclockwise. With this arrangement, the thrust line of either engine is the same distance from the centerline of the fuselage, so there will be no difference in yaw effect between loss of left or right engine. In this case, there is not an engine designated as critical.

V_{MC} FOR CERTIFICATION

V_{MC} for airplane certification is based on the critical engine becoming inoperative and windmilling, up to 5° of bank towards the operative engine, takeoff power on operative engine, landing gear up, flaps in takeoff position, maximum gross weight, and most rearward center of gravity (CG).

Under some conditions of weight and altitude, a stall can be encountered at speeds above V_{MC} as established by the certification procedure described above, in which event the stall speed is regarded as the limit of effective directional control.

The Code of Federal Regulations (CFR's) under which the airplane was certificated stipulate that at V_{MC} the certificating test pilot must be able to:

• Stop the turn that results when the critical engine is suddenly made inoperative within 20° of the original heading, using maximum rudder deflection, and not more than 5° of bank into the operative engine.
• After recovery, maintain the airplane in straight flight with not more than a 5° of bank towards the operating engine. This does not mean that the airplane is required to be able to climb or even hold altitude. It only means that the heading can be maintained.

V_{MC}—Minimum Control Airspeed

The principle of V_{MC} is that at any airspeed less than V_{MC}, with up to 5° of bank towards the operative engine (bank depends on manufacturer), air flowing along the rudder is such that the application of rudder forces cannot overcome the asymmetrical yawing forces caused by takeoff power on one engine and a powerless windmilling propeller on the other. The demonstration of V_{MC} is discussed in a later section of this chapter.

When one engine fails, the pilot must overcome the asymmetrical thrust (except on airplanes with centerline thrust) created by the operating engine by setting up a counteracting moment with the rudder. When the rudder is fully deflected, its yawing power will depend on the velocity of airflow across the rudder, which in turn is dependent on the airspeed. As the airplane decelerates, it will reach a speed below which the rudder moment will no longer balance the thrust moment and directional control will be lost.

During single-engine flight, the large rudder deflection required to counteract the asymmetric thrust also results in a lateral lift force on the vertical fin. This lateral lift represents an unbalanced side force on the airplane that must be counteracted by allowing the airplane to accelerate sideways until the lateral drag caused by the sideslip equals the rudder lift force.

In this case, the wings will be level, the ball in the turn-and-slip indicator will be centered, and the airplane will be in a moderate sideslip toward the inoperative engine. Flight tests have shown that holding the ball of the turn-and-slip indicator in the center while maintaining heading with wings level drastically increases V_{MC} as much as 20 knots in some airplanes. Banking toward the operative engine reduces V_{MC}, whereas decreasing the bank angle away from the operative engine increases V_{MC} at the rate of approximately 3 knots per degree of bank angle.

Flight tests have also shown that the high drag caused by the wings level, ball centered configuration can reduce single-engine climb performance by as much as 300 feet per minute (FPM), which is just about all that is available at sea level in a nonturbocharged multiengine airplane.

The sideslipping method has several major disadvantages.

• The relative wind blowing on the inoperative engine side of the vertical fin tends to increase the asymmetric moment caused by the failure of one engine.
• The resulting sideslip severely degrades stall characteristics.
• The greater rudder deflection required to balance the extra moment and the sideslip drag cause a significant reduction in climb and/or acceleration capability.

Banking into the operating engine and using a component of the airplane weight to counteract the rudder induced side force lowers V_{MC}, by increasing the slip angle. The resulting stable yawing moment reduces the rudder deflection required. In a one-engine inoperative condition in stabilized flight with a 5° bank into the operating engine, the pilot cannot choose the sideslip angle without using a calibrated sideslip vane or yaw string. At zero sideslip, the ball will have a large deflection toward the operating engine. In unaccelerated flight, the ball is really a bank indicator and does not give information about sideslip angle. A pilot cannot intentionally fly the airplane at the minimum drag condition of zero sideslip (or minimum sideslip) without an indicator, such as a yaw string. The ball position can be determined for any airplane by using a yaw string during single-engine training and the ball position noted for zero slip.

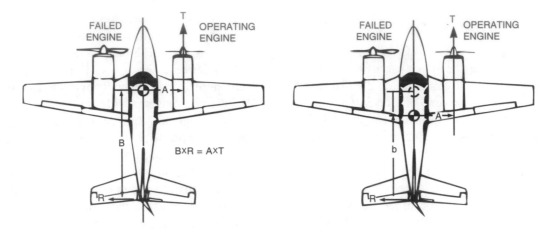

FIGURE 14-3.—Effect of CG location on yaw.

The correct procedure for flying at zero slip is wings banked into the operating engine, the ball deflected toward the operative engine as determined by a yaw string. The amount of bank varies with the type of airplane, weight, and density altitude. This will maximize single-engine performance for best climb performance, and stall characteristics will not be degraded. When zero slip bank angle is exceeded, performance is degraded. The magnitude of these effects will vary from airplane to airplane, but the principles are applicable in all cases. A bank limitation of up to 5° during V_{MC} demonstration is applicable only to certification tests of the airplane, and is not intended as a limit in training or testing a pilot's ability to extract maximum performance from the airplane. Single-engine flight with the ball centered is never a correct configuration and, in fact, will degrade performance and result in unsafe stall characteristics.

For an airplane with nonturbocharged engines, V_{MC} decreases as altitude is increased. Consequently, directional control can be maintained at a lower airspeed than at sea level. The reason for this is that since power decreases with altitude the thrust moment of the operating engine becomes less, thereby lessening the need for the rudder's yawing force. Since V_{MC} is a function of power (which decreases with altitude), it is possible for the airplane to reach a stall speed prior to the loss of directional control.

It must be understood that there is a certain density altitude above which the stalling speed is higher than the single-engine minimum control speed. This maneuver can still be effectively performed by limiting rudder travel or by limiting the power setting to less than takeoff power. Before flight demonstrations, the significance of the single-engine minimum control speed,

including the results of attempting flight below this speed with one engine inoperative, the recognition of the imminent loss of control, and the recovery procedures involved should be orally emphasized.

V_{MC} is greater when the CG is at the rearmost allowable position. Since the airplane rotates around its CG, the moments are measured using that point as a reference. A rearward CG would not affect the thrust moment, but would shorten the arm to the center of the rudder's horizontal lift, which would mean that a higher force (airspeed) would be required to counteract the engine inoperative yaw. Figure 14-3 shows an exaggerated view of the effects of a rearward CG.

Generally, the CG range of most multiengine airplanes is short enough so that the effect on the V_{MC} is relatively small, but it is a factor that should be considered. Many pilots only consider the rear CG of their multiengine airplanes as a factor for pitch stability, not realizing that it could affect the controllability with one engine inoperative.

While in straight-and-level flight, the airplane weight will not affect V_{MC}; however, banking into the operating engine creates a horizontal component of lift. This component pulls the airplane into the operating engine, counteracting adverse yaw, requiring less rudder deflection. The heavier the airplane, the stronger the horizontal component of lift, and the lower V_{MC} becomes.

There are many multiengine pilots who think that the only control problem experienced in flight below V_{MC} is a yaw toward the inoperative engine. With full power applied to the operative engine, as the airspeed drops below V_{MC}, the airplane tends to roll, as well as yaw into the inoperative engine. This tendency becomes greater as the airspeed is further reduced. Since this tendency must be counteracted by aileron control, the yaw condition is aggravated by aileron yaw (the down aileron creates more drag than the up aileron). If a stall should occur in this condition, a violent roll into the inoperative (dead) engine may be experienced. Such an event occurring close to the ground could be disastrous. This may be avoided by maintaining airspeed above V_{SSE} at all times during single-engine operations. If the airspeed should fall below V_{SSE} and approach V_{MC}, then power must be reduced on the operative engine and the airplane must be banked at least 5° toward the operative engine.

PERFORMANCE

Many pilots erroneously believe that because an airplane has two engines, it will continue to perform at least half as well with only one engine operating. There is nothing in Title 14 of the Code of Federal Regulations (14 CFR) part 23, governing the certification of multiengine airplanes which requires an airplane to maintain altitude while in the takeoff configuration and with one engine inoperative. In fact, many of the current multiengine airplanes are not required to do this with one engine inoperative in any configuration, even at sea level. This is of major significance in the operation of multiengine airplanes certified under 14 CFR part 23. With regard to performance (but not controllability) in the takeoff or landing configuration, the multiengine airplane is, in concept, merely a single-engine airplane with its power divided into two individual units.

When one engine fails on a multiengine airplane, performance is not halved, but is reduced by approximately 80 percent. The performance loss is greater than 50 percent because an airplane's climb performance is a function of the thrust horsepower which is in excess of that required for level flight. When power is increased in both engines in level flight and the airspeed is held constant, the airplane will start climbing. The rate of climb depends on the power added (which is power in excess of that required for straight-and-level flight). When one engine fails, however, it not only loses power, but the drag increases considerably because of asymmetric thrust, and the operating engine then carries the full burden alone. This leaves very little excess power for climb performance.

For example, an airplane that has an all-engine rate of climb of 1,860 FPM and a single-engine rate of climb of 190 FPM would lose almost 90 percent of its climb performance when one engine fails.

FACTORS IN TAKEOFF PLANNING

Pilots of multiengine airplanes will plan the takeoff in sufficient detail to be able to take immediate action if one engine fails during the takeoff process. They will be thoroughly familiar with the airplane's performance capabilities and limitations, including accelerate/stop distance, as well as the distance available for takeoff, and will include such factors in their plan of action.

If it has been determined that the airplane cannot maintain altitude with one engine inoperative (considering the gross weight and density altitude), an immediate landing may have to be made in the most suitable area available when an engine fails on lift-off. The competent pilot will not make an attempt to maintain altitude at the expense of a safe airspeed.

Also consider the surrounding terrain, obstructions, and nearby landing areas so that a definite direction of flight can be established immediately if an engine fails at a critical point during the climb after takeoff. It is imperative that the takeoff and climb path be planned so that all obstacles between the point of takeoff and the available areas of landing can be cleared if one engine suddenly becomes inoperative.

In addition, a competent pilot knows that the multiengine airplane has to be flown with precision if maximum takeoff performance and safety are to be obtained. For example, the airplane must lift off at a specific airspeed, accelerate to a definite climbing airspeed, and climb with maximum allowable power on both engines to a safe single-engine maneuvering altitude. In the meantime, if an engine fails, a different airspeed must be attained immediately. This airspeed must be held precisely because only at this airspeed will the pilot be able to obtain maximum performance from the airplane. To understand the factors involved in proper takeoff planning, a further explanation of this critical speed follows, beginning with the lift-off.

The airplane can be controlled satisfactorily while firmly on the ground when one engine fails prior to reaching V_{MC} during the takeoff roll. This is possible by closing both throttles, by proper use of rudder and brakes, and with many airplanes, by use of nosewheel steering. If the airplane is airborne at less than V_{MC}, however, and suddenly loses all power on one engine, it cannot be controlled satisfactorily. On normal takeoffs, follow the manufacturer's recommended rotation speed (V_R) or lift-off speed (V_{LOF}). If speeds are not published, use a minimum speed of V_{MC} plus 5 knots before lift-off. Lift-off should never take place

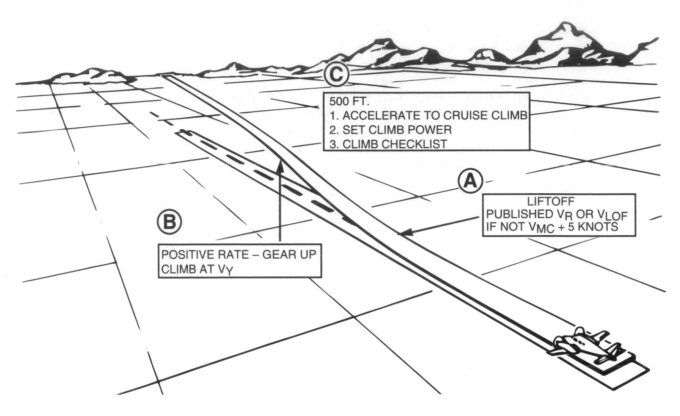

FIGURE 14-4.—Normal takeoff procedure.

until the airspeed reaches and exceeds V_{MC}. From this point, an efficient climb procedure should be followed. [Figure 14-4]

An efficient climb procedure is one in which the airplane leaves the ground above V_{MC}, accelerates quickly to V_Y (best rate-of-climb speed) and climbs at V_Y. The climb at V_Y should be made with both engines set to maximum takeoff power until reaching a safe single-engine maneuvering altitude (minimum of approximately 500 feet above field elevation or as dictated by airplane performance capability and/or local obstacles). At this point, power may be reduced to climb power, and the desired en route climb speed may then be established. The following discussion explains why V_Y is recommended for the initial climb.

When an engine fails on takeoff below V_Y speed with no bank angle correction, V_{MC} could be 15 to 20 knots above published. This will occur because published V_{MC} is based up to a maximum of 5° of bank into the operating engine. Tests have shown that V_{MC} increases approximately 3 knots for each degree of bank less than 5. With no bank when the engine initially fails, the higher speed of V_Y will allow the pilot time to increase the bank angle up to 8° or higher, if necessary, to maintain control of the airplane and establish V_{YSE}.

By increasing the bank angle above 5°, the pilot lowers V_{MC} even more than published V_{MC}, but is sacrificing climb performance. During an initial engine failure, this will help maintain control. Once control and airspeed are established, bank angle can be reduced to as little as 2 to 3° of bank to increase climb performance.

Extremes in takeoff technique may suggest hold it down to accelerate the airplane to near cruise speed before climbing, or pull it off below V_{MC} and climb as steeply as possible. If one considers the possibility of an engine failure somewhere during the takeoff, neither of these procedures makes much sense for the following reasons. Remember that drag increases as the square of the speed, so for any increase in speed over and above the best rate-of-climb speed (V_Y) the greater the drag and the less climb performance the airplane will have. At 123 knots the drag is approximately one and one-half times greater than it is at 100 knots. At 141 knots the drag is doubled, and at 200 knots the drag is approximately four times as great as at 100 knots. While the drag is increasing as the square of the velocity (V x V), the power required to maintain a velocity increases as the cube of that velocity (V x V x V).

In the event of engine failure, a pilot who uses excessive speed on takeoff will suddenly discover that all energy produced by the engines has been converted into speed. Some pilots believe that the excess speed can always be converted to altitude, but this theory is invalid. Available power is only wasted in accelerating the airplane to an unnecessary speed. Also, experience has shown that an unexpected engine failure so surprises the inexperienced pilot that proper reactions are extremely lagging. By the time the initial shock wears off and the pilot is ready to take control of the situation, the excess speed has dissipated and the airplane is still barely off the ground. From this low altitude, the pilot would still have to climb, with an engine inoperative, to whatever height is needed to clear all obstacles and return to the approach end of the runway. Excess speed cannot be converted readily to the altitude or distance necessary to reach a landing area safely.

In contrast, an airplane will fly in level flight much easier than it will climb. Therefore, if the total energy of both engines is initially converted to enough height above the ground to permit clearance of all obstacles while in level flight (safe maneuvering altitude), the problem is much simpler in the event an engine fails. If some extra height is available, it can usually be traded for airspeed or gliding distance when needed.

Simply stated, altitude is more essential to safety after takeoff than excess airspeed. On the other hand, trying to gain height too fast in the takeoff can also be very dangerous because of control problems. If the airplane has just become airborne and the airspeed is at or below V_{MC} when an engine fails, the pilot could avoid a serious accident by retarding both throttles immediately. If this action is not taken immediately, the pilot will be unable to control the airplane.

Consequently, the pilot should always keep one hand on the control wheel (when not operating hand controlled nose steering) and the other hand on the throttles throughout the takeoff roll. The airplane should remain on the ground until adequate speed is reached so that a smooth transition to the proper climb speed can be made. THE AIRPLANE SHOULD NEVER LEAVE THE GROUND BEFORE V_{MC} IS REACHED. Preferably, V_{MC} + 5 knots should be attained.

If an engine fails before leaving the ground, it is advisable to discontinue the takeoff and STOP. If an engine fails after lift-off, the pilot will have to decide immediately whether to continue flight, or to close both throttles and land. However, waiting until the engine failure occurs is not the time for the pilot to plan the correct action. The action has to be planned before the airplane is taxied onto the runway. The plan of action must consider the density altitude, length of the runway,

weight of the airplane, and the airplane's accelerate/stop distance, and accelerate/go distance under these conditions. Only on the basis of these factors can the pilot decide what course to follow if an engine should fail. When the flight crew consists of two pilots, the pilot in command will brief the second pilot on what course of action will be taken should the need arise.

To reach a safe single-engine maneuvering altitude as safely and quickly as possible, the climb with all engines operating has to be made at the proper airspeed. That speed should provide for:

- Good control of the airplane in case an engine fails.
- Quick and easy transition to the single-engine best rate-of-climb speed if one engine fails.
- A fast rate of climb to attain an altitude that permits adequate time for analyzing the situation and making decisions.

To make a quick and easy transition to the single-engine best rate-of-climb speed in case an engine fails, the pilot should climb at a speed greater than V_{YSE}. If an engine fails at less than V_{YSE}, it would be necessary for the pilot to lower the nose to increase the speed to V_{YSE} in order to obtain the best climb performance. If the airspeed is considerably less than this speed, it might be necessary to lose valuable altitude to increase the speed to V_{YSE}. Another factor to consider is the loss of airspeed that may occur because of erratic pilot technique after a sudden, unexpected power loss. Consequently, the normal initial two-engine climb speed should not be less than V_Y.

In summary, the initial climb speed with both engines operating should permit an attainment of a safe single-engine maneuvering altitude as quickly as possible. In the event of a sudden power loss on one engine, it should also provide time to roll 5 to 8° of bank into the operative engine for good control capabilities, identify and feather inoperative engine, and establish V_{YSE}. The only speed that meets all of these requirements for a normal takeoff is the best rate-of-climb speed (V_Y) with both engines operating.

ACCELERATE/STOP DISTANCE

The accelerate/stop distance is the total distance required to accelerate the multiengine airplane to a specified speed, and assuming failure of an engine at the instant that speed is attained, to bring the airplane to a stop on the remaining runway.

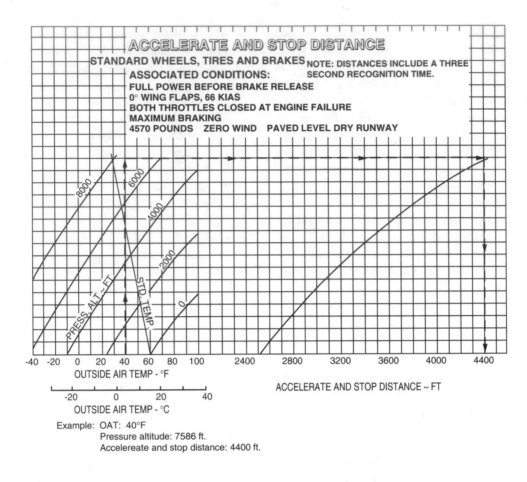

Example: OAT: 40°F
      Pressure altitude: 7586 ft.
      Accelereate and stop distance: 4400 ft.

FIGURE 14-5.—Accelerate/stop distance.

To determine accelerate stop distance for takeoff, a pilot has to consider the runway length, field elevation, density altitude, and the airplane's gross weight. (For simplification purposes, the following additional factors will not be discussed here: obstruction, height, headwind component, runway slope, and runway contaminants, such as rubber, soot, water, ice, and snow.)

Using the chart in Figure 14-5 and with a temperature of 40 °F, a calm wind at a pressure altitude of 7,586 feet, a gross weight of 4,570 pounds, and all engines operating, the airplane being flown requires 4,400 feet to accelerate to 66 KIAS and then be brought to a stop.

The most critical time for a one-engine inoperative condition in a multiengine airplane is during the 2 or 3-second period immediately following lift-off while the airplane is accelerating to climb-out speed. Although most multiengine airplanes are controllable at a speed close to the single-engine minimum control speed, the performance is often so far below optimum that continued flight following takeoff might be marginal or impossible.

If one engine fails prior to reaching V_{MC}, there is no choice but to close both throttles and bring the airplane to a stop. If engine failure occurs just after lift-off, the pilot has to decide immediately to land or to continue the takeoff and accelerate to V_{YSE}, if that particular airplane has single-engine climb capability.

To determine climb performance, a pilot has to consider the field elevation, density altitude, obstruction height, and the airplane's gross weight. Climb performance is based on conditions specified on the chart in Figure 14-6. If these conditions are not met after lift-off, the airplane may not climb as depicted in the chart.

In this example, using the chart in Figure 14-6 with a temperature of 50 °F, at a pressure altitude of 10,000 feet, and a gross weight of 4,570 pounds, two-engine rate of climb would be 1,200 FPM versus one-engine rate of climb of 100 FPM.

If the decision is made to continue the takeoff, the airplane has to be able to gain altitude with one engine inoperative. This requires acceleration to V_{YSE} if obstacles are not involved, or to V_{XSE} if obstacles are a

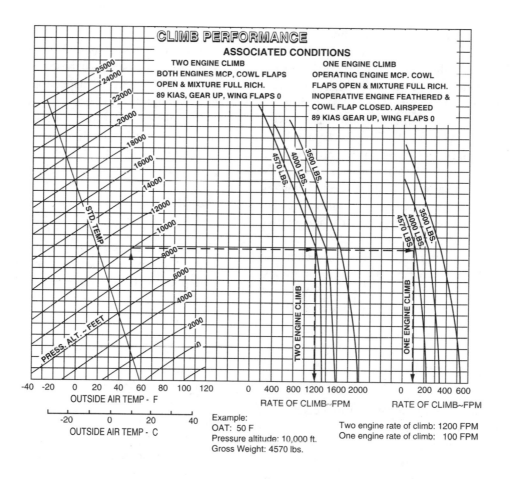

Example:
OAT: 50 F
Pressure altitude: 10,000 ft.
Gross Weight: 4570 lbs.

Two engine rate of climb: 1200 FPM
One engine rate of climb: 100 FPM

FIGURE 14-6.—Climb performance.

factor. At high density altitudes and at gross weight, a successful continuation of the takeoff is extremely improbable.

The flightpaths illustrated in Figure 14-7 indicate an area of decision. An engine failure in this area demands an immediate decision. Beyond this decision area, the airplane, within the limitations of single-engine climb performance, can usually be maneuvered to a landing at the departure airport.

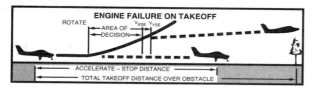

FIGURE 14-7.—Area of decision.

PROPELLER FEATHERING

When an engine fails in flight, the movement of the airplane through the air tends to keep the propeller rotating, much like a windmill. Since the failed engine is no longer delivering power to the propeller to produce thrust, but instead is absorbing energy to overcome friction and compression of the engine, the drag of the windmilling propeller is significant and causes the airplane to yaw toward the failed engine. [Figure 14-8] Most multiengine airplanes are equipped with full feathering propellers to minimize that yawing tendency.

FIGURE 14-8.—Windmilling propeller creates drag.

The blades of a feathering propeller may be positioned by the pilot to such a high angle that they are streamlined in the direction of flight. In this feathered position, the blades act as powerful brakes to assist engine friction and compression in stopping the windmilling rotation of the propeller. This is of particular advantage in case of a damaged engine, since further damage caused by a windmilling propeller can be eliminated, and a feathered prop creates the least possible drag on the airplane and reduces the yawing tendency. As a result, multiengine airplanes are easier to control in flight when the propeller of an inoperative engine is feathered.

Feathering of propellers for training and checkout purposes should be performed only when conditions, altitudes, and locations allow a safe landing on an established airport in the event of difficulty in unfeathering the propeller.

USE OF TRIM TABS

The trim tabs in a multiengine airplane serve the same purpose as in a single-engine airplane, but their function is usually more important to safe and efficient flight. This is because of the greater control forces, weight, power, asymmetrical thrust with one engine inoperative, range of operating speeds, and range of center-of-gravity location. In some multiengine airplanes, it taxes the pilot's strength to overpower an improperly set elevator trim tab on takeoff or go-around. Many fatal accidents have occurred when pilots took off or attempted a go-around with the airplane trimmed full noseup for the landing configuration. Therefore, prompt retrimming of the elevator trim tab in the event of an emergency go-around from a landing approach is essential to the success of the flight. Multiengine airplanes should be retrimmed in flight for each change of attitude, airspeed, power setting, and loading. Without such changes, constant application of firm forces on the flight controls is necessary to maintain any desired flight attitude.

PREFLIGHT PREPARATION

The increased complexity of multiengine airplanes demands the conduct of a more systematic inspection of the airplane before entering the cockpit, and the use of a more complete and appropriate checklist for each ground and flight operation. Preflight visual inspections

of the exterior of the airplane should be conducted in accordance with the manufacturer's operating manual. The procedures set up in these manuals usually provide for a comprehensive inspection, item by item in an orderly sequence, to be covered on a complete check of the airplane. The transitioning pilot should have a thorough briefing in this inspection procedure, and should understand the reason for checking each item.

CHECKLIST

All multiengine airplanes are provided with checklists, which can be very brief or extremely comprehensive. A pilot, who desires to operate a multiengine airplane safely, should use the checklist pertinent to that particular airplane. A checklist is normally divided under separate headings for common operations, such as preflight, before starting, starting, before takeoff, takeoff, cruise climb, cruise, descent, in range, before landing, landing, system malfunctions, and emergency procedures including single-engine operations. Multiengine airplanes have many more controls, switches, instruments, and indicators. Failure to position or check any of these items may have more serious results than would a similar error in a single-engine airplane. Only definite procedures, systematically planned and executed, can ensure safe and efficient operation. The cockpit checklist provided by the manufacturer should be used, with only those modifications made necessary by subsequent alterations or additions to the airplane and its equipment.

In airplanes that require a copilot, or in which a second pilot is available, it is a good practice for the second pilot to read the checklist. The pilot in command should check each item by actually touching the control or device and repeating the instrument reading or prescribed control position in question, under the careful observation of the pilot calling out the items on the checklist. [Figure 14-9] Even when a copilot is not present, the pilot should form the habit of touching, pointing to, or operating each item as it is read from the checklist.

In the event of an inflight emergency, the pilot should be sufficiently familiar with emergency procedures to instinctively take immediate action to prevent more serious situations. However, as soon as circumstances permit, the emergency checklist should be reviewed to ensure that all required items have been checked.

FIGURE 14-9.—Teamwork in a multiengine airplane.

TAXIING

Although ground operation of multiengine airplanes may differ in some respects from the operation of single-engine airplanes, the taxiing procedures also vary somewhat between those airplanes with a nosewheel and those with a tailwheel-type landing gear. With either of these landing gear arrangements, the difference in taxiing multiengine airplanes that is most obvious to a transitioning pilot is the capability of using power differential between individual engines to assist in directional control.

Tailwheel-type multiengine airplanes are usually equipped with tailwheel locks that can be used to advantage for taxiing in a straight line especially in a crosswind. The tendency to weathervane can also be neutralized to a great extent in these airplanes by using more power on the upwind engine, with the tailwheel lock engaged and the brakes used as necessary.

On nosewheel-type multiengine airplanes, the brakes and throttles are mainly used to control the momentum, and steering is done principally with the steerable nosewheel. The steerable nosewheel is usually actuated by the rudder pedals, or in some airplanes by a separate hand operated steering mechanism.

No airplane should be pivoted on one wheel when making sharp turns because this can damage the landing gear, tires, and even the airport pavement. All turns should be made with the inside wheel rolling, even if only slightly.

Brakes may be used to start and stop turns while taxiing. When initiating a turn, the brakes should be used cautiously to prevent overcontrolling the turn. Brakes should be used as lightly as practicable while taxiing to prevent undue wear and heating of the brakes and wheels, and possible loss of ground control. When brakes are used repeatedly or constantly, they tend to heat to the point that they may either lock or fail completely. Also, tires may be weakened or blown out by extremely hot brakes. Abrupt use of brakes in multiengine, as well as single-engine airplanes is evidence of poor pilot technique; it not only abuses the airplane, but may even result in loss of control.

Due to the greater weight of multiengine airplanes, effective braking is particularly essential. Therefore, as the airplane begins to move forward when taxiing is started, the brakes should be tested immediately by depressing each brake pedal. If the brakes are weak, taxiing should be discontinued and the engines shut down. Looking outside the cockpit while taxiing becomes more important in multiengine airplanes. Since these airplanes are usually somewhat heavier, larger, and more powerful than single-engine airplanes, they often require more time and distance to accelerate or stop, and provide a different perspective for the pilot. While it is usually not necessary to make S-turns to observe the taxiing path, additional vigilance is necessary to avoid obstacles, other aircraft, or bystanders.

NORMAL TAKEOFFS

There is virtually little difference between a takeoff in a multiengine airplane and one in a single-engine airplane. The controls of each class of airplane are operated the same; the multiple throttles of the multiengine airplane normally are treated as one compact power control and can be operated simultaneously with one hand.

In the interest of safety, it is important that the pilot have a plan of action to cope with engine failure during takeoff. In a multi-pilot crew, the flying pilot should brief the crew on his or her plan of action for normal and abnormal procedures and their individual responsibilities. This briefing consists of at least the following: minimum control speed (V_{MC}), rotation speed (V_R), lift-off speed (V_{LOF}), single-engine best rate-of-climb speed (V_{YSE}), all-engine best rate-of-climb speed (V_Y), and what procedures will be followed if an engine failure occurs prior to V_{MC} and after V_{MC}. The multiengine pilot's primary concern on all takeoffs is the attainment of the single-engine minimum control speed plus 5 knots prior to lift-off. Until this speed is achieved, directional control of the airplane in flight may be impossible after the failure of an engine, unless power is reduced immediately on the operating engine.

If an engine fails before the single-engine minimum control speed is attained, THE PILOT HAS NO CHOICE BUT TO CLOSE BOTH THROTTLES, ABANDON THE TAKEOFF, AND DIRECT COMPLETE ATTENTION TO BRINGING THE AIRPLANE TO A SAFE STOP ON THE GROUND.

The multiengine pilot's second concern on takeoff is the attainment of the best rate-of-climb speed (V_Y) in the least amount of time. This is the airspeed that will provide the greatest rate of climb with both engines operating. In the event of an engine failure, the single-engine best rate-of-climb speed must be held. This will provide the best rate of climb when operating with one engine inoperative and propeller feathered (if possible), or the slowest rate of descent with the proper bank angle toward the operating engine. When takeoff is made over obstructions, the best angle-of-climb speed should be maintained until the obstacles are passed then the best rate of climb maintained.

The single-engine minimum control speed and the single-engine best rate-of-climb speed are published in the Airplane Flight Manual (AFM) and/or Pilot's Operating Handbook (POH).

If the crew consists of two pilots, the flying pilot will brief the other pilot on takeoff procedures prior to takeoff. Otherwise, a single pilot operator should mentally review the emergency procedures before takeoff.

After runup and the "Before Takeoff" checks have been completed, the airplane should be taxied into takeoff position and aligned with the runway. If the airplanes is a tailwheel-type, the tailwheel lock (if installed) should be engaged only after the airplane has been allowed to roll straight a few feet along the intended takeoff path to center the tailwheel.

Next, both throttles should be advanced simultaneously to takeoff power, and directional control maintained by the use of the steerable nosewheel and the rudder. Brakes should be used for directional control only during the initial portion of the takeoff roll when the rudder and steerable nosewheel are ineffective. During the initial takeoff roll, the engine instruments should be monitored.

As the takeoff progresses, flight controls should be used, as necessary, to compensate for wind conditions. Follow the manufacturer's recommended rotation speed (V_R) or lift-off speed (V_{LOF}). If speeds are not published, use a minimum speed of V_{MC} plus 5 knots before lift-off. After lift-off, the airplane should be allowed to accelerate to the all-engine best rate-of-climb speed (V_Y). If an engine should fail, the airplane will immediately lose airspeed and this will allow a buffer between V_{YSE} and V_Y.

The landing gear may be raised as soon as practicable with a positive rate of climb, but not before reaching the point from which a safe landing can no longer be made on the remaining portion of the runway. The flaps (if used) should be retracted as directed in the AFM/POH.

CROSSWIND TAKEOFFS

Crosswind takeoffs are performed in multiengine airplanes in basically the same manner as those in single-engine airplanes. During the initial takeoff roll, less power may be used on the downwind engine to overcome the tendency of the airplane to weathervane. Full power should be applied to both engines as the airplane accelerates to a speed where rudder control is effective. The airplane should accelerate to a slightly higher-than-normal takeoff speed, and then a positive lift-off should be made to prevent possible settling back to the runway while drifting. When clear of the ground, a coordinated turn should be made into the wind to correct for drift.

SHORT-FIELD OR OBSTACLE CLEARANCE TAKEOFF

If it is necessary to take off over an obstacle or from a short field, the procedures should be altered slightly. For example, the initial climb speed that should provide the best angle of climb for obstacle clearance is V_X rather than V_Y. However, V_X in some multiengine airplanes is below V_{MC}. In this case, if the climb were made at V_X and a sudden power failure occurred on one engine, the pilot would not be able to control the airplane unless power were reduced on the operating engine. This would create an impossible situation because it would not be likely that the airplane could clear an obstacle with one engine inoperative and the other at some reduced power setting. In any case, if an engine fails and the climb is to be continued over an obstacle, V_{XSE} must be established if maximum performance is to be obtained.

Generally, the short-field or obstacle clearance takeoff will be much the same as a normal takeoff using the manufacturer's recommended flap settings, power settings, and speeds. However, if the published best angle-of-climb speed (V_X) is less than $V_{MC} + 5$, then it is recommended that no less than $V_{MC} + 5$ be used.

During the takeoff roll as the airspeed reaches the best angle-of-climb speed, or V_{MC} + 5, whichever is higher, the airplane should be rotated to establish a pitch attitude that will cause the airplane to lift off and climb at that specified speed. At an altitude of approximately 50 feet or after clearing the obstacle, the pitch attitude can be lowered gradually to allow the airspeed to increase to the all-engine best rate-of-climb speed. Upon reaching safe maneuvering altitude, the airplane should be allowed to accelerate to normal or en route climb speed and the power controls reduced to the normal climb power settings.

STALLS

As with single-engine airplanes, the pilot should be familiar with the stall and minimum controllability characteristics of the multiengine airplane being flown. The larger and heavier airplanes have slower responses in stall recoveries and in maneuvering at slow speeds due to their greater weight. The practice of stalls in multiengine airplanes should be performed at altitudes sufficiently high to allow recoveries to be completed at least 3,000 feet above the ground or as recommended by the manufacturer.

It usually is inadvisable to execute stalls in multiengine airplanes because of their relatively high wing loading; therefore, practice should be limited to approaches to stalls with recoveries initiated at the first physical indication of an approaching stall. As a general rule, stalls in multiengine airplanes are not necessarily violent or hazardous.

The pilot should become familiar with approaching stalls entered with various flap settings, power settings, landing gear positions, and bank angles. It should be noted that the extension of the landing gear will cause little difference in the stalling speed, but it will cause a more rapid loss of speed in approaching to a stall.

For power-off stalls, the airplane can be configured for landing. After a rate of descent is established that is consistent with landing, power should be reduced to or near idle. This usually results in a level attitude stall.

Power-on stalls should be entered with both engines set at approximately 65 percent power. Takeoff power may be used after slowing to lift-off airspeed. Stalls in airplanes with relative low power loading using maximum climb power usually result in an excessive nose-high attitude and make the recovery more difficult.

Because of possible loss of control, stalls with one engine inoperative or at idle power and the other engine developing effective power, should not be practiced by applicants for multiengine class ratings. The same procedures used in the recognition and avoidance of stalls of single-engine airplanes apply to stalls in multiengine airplanes. The transitioning pilot has to be familiar with the characteristics that announce an approaching stall, the indicated airspeed at which it occurs, and the proper procedure for recovery.

The increase in pitch attitude for stall entries should be gradual to prevent momentum from carrying the airplane into an abnormally high noseup attitude with a resulting deceptively low indicated airspeed at the time the stall occurs. It is recommended that the rate-of-pitch change result in a 1-knot-per second decrease in airspeed. In all stall recoveries, the controls should be used very smoothly, avoiding abrupt pitch changes. Because of high gyroscopic stresses, this is particularly true in airplanes with extensions between the engines and propellers.

EMERGENCY DESCENT

When it is necessary to descend as rapidly as feasible, such as in the case of an inflight fire, follow the manufacturer's recommended procedures. When specific procedures are not published, the following procedures may be used and modified, as required.

1.	Props	Max RPM
2.	Throttles	Closed
3.	Airspeed	Max Gear Down Speed or Max Flap Approach Speed (whichever is lower)
4.	Landing Gear	Down
5.	Flaps	Approach

The maneuvering speed (V_A) may be used as descent airspeed but should not be higher than maximum gear down speed or flap approach speed if flaps are used. During practice emergency descents, careful consideration should be given to the operating temperature of the engines. Rapid descents with throttles closed will cause the engines to cool rapidly and possibly cause cylinder damage. In practice, some power should be left on to prevent the engines from cooling rapidly.

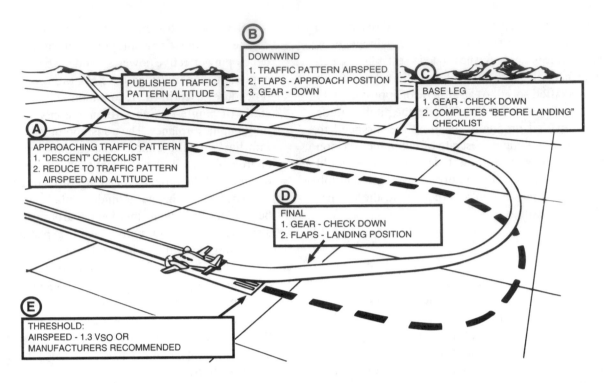

FIGURE 14-10.—Normal two-engine approach and landing.

APPROACHES AND LANDINGS

Multiengine airplanes characteristically have steeper gliding angles because of their relatively high wing loading, and greater drag of wing flaps and landing gear when extended. For this reason, power is normally used throughout the approach to shallow the approach angle and prevent a high rate of sink.

The accepted procedure for making stabilized landing approaches is to reduce the power to a predetermined setting during the arrival descent, so the appropriate landing gear extension speed will be attained in level flight as the downwind leg of the approach pattern is entered. [Figure 14-10] With this power setting, the extension of the landing gear will further reduce the airspeed to the desired traffic pattern airspeed. The manufacturer's recommended speed should be used throughout the pattern. When practicable, the speed should be compatible with other air traffic in the traffic pattern. When within the maximum speed for flap extension, the flaps may be partially lowered, if desired, to aid in reducing the airspeed to traffic pattern speed. The angle of bank should normally not exceed 30° while turning onto the legs of the traffic pattern.

The landing checklist should be completed by the time the airplane is on base leg so that the pilot may direct full attention to the approach and landing. In a power approach, the airplane should descend at a stabilized rate, allowing the pilot to plan and control the approach path to the point of touchdown. Further extension of the flaps and slight adjustment of power and pitch should be accomplished, as necessary, to establish and maintain a stabilized approach path. Power and pitch changes during approaches should in all cases, be smooth and gradual.

The airspeed of the final approach should be as recommended by the manufacturer. If a recommended speed is not furnished, the airspeed should not be less than the single-engine best rate-of-climb speed (V_{YSE}) until the landing is assured. This is the minimum speed a single-engine go-around can be made if necessary. IN NO CASE SHOULD THE APPROACH SPEED BE LESS THAN THE CRITICAL ENGINE INOPERATIVE MINIMUM CONTROL SPEED. If an engine should fail suddenly and it is necessary to make a go-around from a final approach at less than this speed, a loss of control could occur. As a rule of thumb, after the wing flaps are extended the final approach speed should be gradually reduced to 1.3 times the power-off stalling speed (1.3 V_{SO}).

The roundout or flare should be started at a sufficient altitude to allow a smooth transition from the approach to the landing attitude. The touchdown should be smooth, with the airplane touching down on the main wheels and in a tail-low attitude, with or without power as desired. Although airplanes with nosewheels should touch down in a tail-low attitude, it should not be so low as to drag the tail on the runway. On the other hand, since the nosewheel is not designed to absorb the impact of the full weight of the airplane, level or nose-low attitudes must be avoided.

Directional control on the rollout should be accomplished primarily with the rudder and the steerable nosewheel, with discrete use of the brakes applied only as necessary for crosswinds or other factors.

CROSSWIND LANDINGS

Crosswind landing procedures in multiengine airplanes are similar to those in single-engine airplanes. The only significant difference lies in the fact that because of the greater weight, more positive drift correction must be maintained before the touchdown.

The two basic methods of making crosswind landings, the slipping approach (wing low) and the crabbing approach, may be combined. These are discussed in the chapter on Approaches and Landings.

The essential factor in all crosswind landing procedures is touching down without drift, with the heading of the airplane parallel to its direction of motion. This will result in minimum side loads on the landing gear.

SHORT-FIELD LANDING

Short-field landing procedures are similar to those in a normal approach and landing. Approach with full flaps at the recommended short-field approach speed. If a recommended speed is not furnished, after landing is assured and the wing flaps are extended, a rule of thumb is $1.2 \times V_{SO}$, but not less than V_{MC} for safety. Immediately after touchdown, raise the flaps, apply the back-elevator pressure and apply brakes.

GO-AROUND PROCEDURE

The complexity of multiengine airplanes makes a knowledge of and proficiency in emergency go-around

procedures particularly essential for safe piloting. The emergency go-around during a landing approach is inherently critical because it is usually initiated at a very low altitude and airspeed with the airplane's configuration and trim adjustments set for landing.

Unless absolutely necessary, the decision to go around should not be delayed to the point where the airplane is ready to touch down. [Figure 14-11] The more altitude and time available to apply power, establish a climb, retrim, and set up a go-around configuration, the easier and safer the maneuver becomes. When the pilot has decided to go around, immediate action should be taken without hesitation, while maintaining positive control and accurately following the manufacturer's recommended procedures.

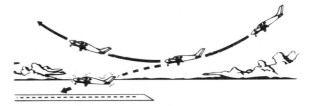

FIGURE 14-11.—Make a timely decision to go around or land.

Go-around procedures vary with different airplanes, depending on their weight, flight characteristics, flap and retractable gear systems, and flight performance. Specific procedures must be learned by the transitioning pilot from the AFM/POH, which should always be available in the cockpit.

There are several general go-around procedures that apply to most airplanes.

• When the decision to go around is reached, takeoff power should be applied immediately and the descent stopped by adjusting the pitch attitude to avoid further loss of altitude.

• The flaps should be retracted in accordance with the procedure prescribed in the AFM/POH.

• After a positive rate of climb is established, the landing gear should be retracted, best rate-of-climb airspeed (V_Y) obtained and maintained, and the airplane trimmed for this climb. Any remaining flaps are then retracted. The procedure for a normal takeoff climb should then be followed.

At any time the airspeed is faster than the flaps-up stalling speed, the flaps may be retracted completely without losing altitude if simultaneously the angle of attack is increased sufficiently. At slow airspeeds, retracting the flaps prematurely or suddenly can cause a stall or an unanticipated loss of altitude. Rapid or premature retraction of the flaps should be avoided on go-arounds, especially when close to the ground, because of the careful attention and exercise of precise pilot technique necessary to prevent a sudden loss of altitude. Generally, retracting the flaps only halfway or to the specified approach setting decreases the drag a relatively greater amount than it decreases the lift.

The AFM/POH should be consulted regarding landing gear and flap retraction procedures. In some installations, simultaneous retraction of the gear and flaps may increase the flap retraction time, and full flaps create more drag than the extended landing gear.

ENGINE INOPERATIVE EMERGENCIES

The operating and flight characteristics of multiengine airplanes with one engine inoperative are excellent. Multiengine airplanes can be controlled and maneuvered safely as long as sufficient airspeed is maintained. However, to utilize the safety and performance characteristics effectively, the pilot has to have a sound understanding of the single-engine performance and the limitations resulting from an unbalance of power.

A pilot checking out for the first time in any multiengine airplane should practice and become thoroughly familiar with the control and performance problems that result from the failure of one engine during any flight condition. Practice should be continued as long as the pilot engages in flying a multiengine airplane so that corrective action will be instinctive, and the ability to control airspeed, heading, and altitude will be retained.

The feathering of a propeller should be demonstrated and practiced during training in all airplanes equipped with propellers that can be feathered and unfeathered safely in flight. If the airplane used is not equipped with feathering propellers, one engine should be secured (shut down) in accordance with the procedures in the AFM/POH. All training in multiengine airplanes involving engine shut down, regardless if the propeller can be feathered or not, must be accomplished at an altitude that will allow for a safe landing at an established airport if an actual emergency develops.

ENGINE INOPERATIVE PROCEDURES

The following procedures are recommended to develop in the transitioning pilot the habit of using proper procedures and proficiency in coping with an inoperative engine.

At a safe altitude (minimum 3,000 feet above terrain) and within landing distance of a suitable airport, an engine may be shut down with the mixture control or fuel selector. At lower altitudes, however, shut down should be simulated by reducing power by adjusting the throttle to the zero thrust setting. The following procedures should then be followed:

1. Fly the airplane — Maintain control, V_{YSE}, heading, bank into operating engine.
2. Power — Increase or leave as set for takeoff.
3. Drag (reduce) — Props, gear, or flaps—pilots choice based on conditions and airplane.
4. Identify — Idle foot inoperative engine.
5. Verify — With throttle or other means.
6. Feather — Inoperative engine propeller.
7. Checklist — Start from the top.

In all cases, the airplane manufacturer's recommended procedure for single-engine operation should be followed. The general procedures listed above are not intended to replace or conflict with any procedure established by the manufacturer of any airplane. It can be used effectively for general training purposes and to emphasize the importance of maintaining aircraft control and reducing drag.

The pilot must be proficient in the control of heading, airspeed, and altitude; in the prompt identification of a power failure; and in the accuracy of shutdown and restart procedures as prescribed in the AFM/POH.

There is not a better way to develop skill in single-engine emergencies than by continued practice. The fact that the procedures of single-engine operation are mastered thoroughly at one time during a pilot's career is no assurance of being able to cope successfully with a single-engine emergency unless review and practice are continued. Some engine inoperative emergencies may be so critical that there may not be a safety margin for lack of skill or knowledge. It is essential that the multiengine pilot take proficiency training periodically from a competent flight instructor.

The pilot should practice and demonstrate the effects (on single-engine performance) of various configurations of gear, flaps, and both; the use of carburetor heat; and the failure to feather the propeller on an inoperative engine. Each configuration should be maintained at single-engine best rate-of-climb speed long enough to determine its effect on the climb (or sink) achieved. Prolonged use of carburetor heat, if equipped, at high-power settings should be avoided.

V$_{MC}$ DEMONSTRATIONS

Every multiengine airplane checkout should include a demonstration of the airplane's single-engine minimum control speed. The single-engine minimum control speed given in the AFM/POH or other manufacturer's published limitations is determined during the original airplane certification under conditions specified in the CFR's. These conditions are normally not duplicated during pilot training or testing because they consist of the most adverse situations for airplane-type certification purposes. Prior to a pilot checkout, a thorough discussion of the factors affecting single-engine minimum control speed is essential.

The V$_{MC}$ demonstrations should be performed at an altitude that will allow the maneuver to be completed no lower than 3,000 feet above ground level (AGL) or the manufacturer's recommended altitude, whichever is higher. One demonstration should be made while holding the wings level and the ball centered, and another demonstration should be made while banking the airplane at least 5° toward the operating engine to establish zero sideslip. These maneuvers will demonstrate the single-engine minimum control speed for the existing conditions and will emphasize the necessity of banking into the operative engine. An attempt should not be made to duplicate V$_{MC}$, as determined for airplane certification.

After the propellers are set to high revolutions per minute (RPM), the landing gear is retracted, and the flaps are in the takeoff position, the airplane should be placed in a climb attitude and an airspeed at or above the intentional one-engine inoperative speed (V$_{SSE}$). With both engines developing as near rated takeoff power as possible, power on the critical engine (usually the left) should then be reduced to idle (windmilling, not shut down). After this is accomplished, the airspeed should be reduced at approximately 1 knot per second with the elevators until directional control can no longer be maintained. At this point, recovery should be initiated by simultaneously reducing power sufficiently on the operating engine and reducing the angle of attack by lowering the nose of the airplane to accelerate to V$_{SSE}$. Under no circumstances should an attempt be made to fly at a speed below V$_{MC}$ with only one engine operating. Should indications of a stall occur prior to reaching this point, recovery should be initiated immediately by reducing the angle of attack and power on the operating engine to control roll and increase airspeed to V$_{SSE}$. The demonstration should then be accomplished with the rudder travel limited at a higher airspeed.

ENGINE FAILURE BEFORE LIFT-OFF (REJECTED TAKEOFF)

When an engine fails during the takeoff roll before becoming airborne, it is advisable to close both throttles immediately and employ maximum braking, while maintaining directional control. In training, the recommended procedure to simulate an engine failure on takeoff is to close the mixture on one engine before 50 percent V$_{MC}$. This provides a safety factor for the instructor pilot and more time for the training pilot to make a proper decision. If the training pilot fails to recognize the emergency promptly, the instructor pilot can close the mixture on the running engine and bring the airplane safely to a stop. Also, during training, to save wear and tear on the airplane, the training pilot may announce maximum braking rather than actually using maximum braking when remaining runway length is adequate.

ENGINE FAILURE AFTER LIFT-OFF

If after becoming airborne an engine should fail prior to having reached the single-engine best rate-of-climb speed (V$_{YSE}$), the same procedure used for engine failure before lift-off should be followed. This is recommended because an immediate landing is usually inevitable because of the altitude loss required to increase the speed to V$_{YSE}$.

The pilot must have determined before takeoff what altitude, airspeed, and airplane configuration must exist

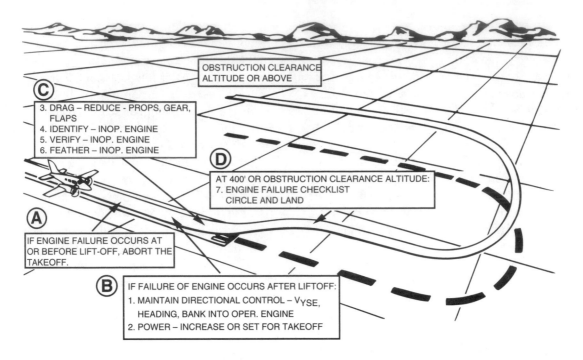

FIGURE 14-12.—Engine failure during takeoff procedures.

to permit the flight to continue in the event of an engine failure. The pilot should also be ready to accept the fact that if engine failure occurs before these required factors are established, both throttles must be closed and the situation treated the same as an engine failure on a single-engine airplane. If it has been predetermined that the single-engine rate of climb under existing circumstances will be at least 50 FPM at 1,000 feet above the airport, and that at least the single-engine best angle-of-climb speed has been attained, the pilot may decide to continue the takeoff. If the airspeed is below the single-engine best angle-of-climb speed (V_{XSE}) and the landing gear has not been retracted, the takeoff should be abandoned immediately.

If the single-engine best angle-of-climb speed (V_{XSE}) has been obtained and the landing gear is in the retract cycle, the pilot should climb at the single-engine best angle-of-climb speed (V_{XSE}) to clear any obstructions. The pilot should hold 5 to 8° of bank into the operating engine and stabilize the airspeed at the single-engine best rate-of-climb speed (V_{YSE}) while identifying, verifying, and feathering the inoperative engine propeller, then, retract the flaps.

When the decision is made to continue the flight, the single-engine best rate-of-climb speed should be attained and maintained with the inoperative engine feathered. [Figure 14-12] Even if altitude cannot be maintained, it is best to continue to hold that speed because it would result in the slowest rate of descent and provide the most time for executing the emergency landing. After the decision is made to continue flight and a positive rate of climb is attained, the landing gear should be retracted as soon as practical.

If the airplane is barely able to maintain altitude and airspeed, a turn requiring a bank greater than 15° should not be attempted. When such a turn is made under these conditions, both lift and airspeed will decrease. It is advisable to continue straight ahead whenever possible, until reaching a safe maneuvering altitude and V_{YSE}. At that time, a steeper bank may be made safely in either direction. There is nothing wrong with banking toward a "inoperative" engine if a safe speed and zero sideslip are maintained.

When an engine fails after becoming airborne, the pilot should hold the heading with the rudder and simultaneously roll into a bank of 5 to 8° toward the operating engine. The more bank used initially will lower V_{MC} and help maintain control with no or very little climb performance. With the airplane under control and the proper airspeed attained for climb, the bank angle can be reduced to establish zero slip to increase climb performance. Without a yaw indicator, 2° to 3° of bank and one-half ball deflection is recommended for maximum performance.

The best way to identify the inoperative engine is to note the direction of yaw and the rudder pressure required to maintain heading. To counteract the asymmetrical thrust, extra rudder pressure will have to be exerted on the operating engine side. To aid in identifying the failed engine, some pilots use the expression "Dead Foot Dead Engine." Never rely on tachometer or manifold pressure readings to determine which engine has failed. After power has been lost on an engine, the tachometer will often indicate the correct RPM and the manifold pressure gauge will indicate the approximate atmospheric pressure or above.

Experience has shown that the biggest problem is not in identifying the inoperative engine, but rather in the pilot's actions after the inoperative engine has been identified. In other words, a pilot may identify the inoperative engine and then attempt to shut down the wrong one, resulting in no power at all. To avoid this mistake, the pilot should verify that the inoperative engine has been identified by retarding the throttle of the suspected engine before shutting it down.

When demonstrating or practicing procedures for engine failure on takeoff, the feathering of the propeller and securing of the engine should be simulated rather than actually performed, so that the engine may be available for immediate use if needed. All other settings should be made just as in an actual power failure.

ENGINE FAILURE EN ROUTE

Normally, when an engine failure occurs while en route in cruising flight, the situation is not as critical as when an engine fails on takeoff. With the more leisurely circumstances, the pilot should take time to determine the cause of the failure and to correct the condition, if possible. If the condition cannot be corrected, the single-engine procedure recommended by the manufacturer should be accomplished and a landing made as soon as practical.

A primary error during engine failure is the pilot's tendency to perform the engine inoperative identification and shutdown too quickly, resulting in improper identification or incorrect shutdown procedures. The element of surprise generally associated with actual engine failure may result in confused and hasty reactions.

When an engine fails during cruising flight, the pilot's main problem is to maintain sufficient altitude to be able to continue flight to the nearest suitable point of landing. This is dependent on the density altitude, gross weight of the airplane, and elevation of the terrain and obstructions. When the airplane is above its single-engine service ceiling, altitude will be lost. The single-engine service ceiling is the maximum density altitude at which the single-engine best rate-of-climb speed will produce 50 FPM rate of climb. This ceiling is determined by the manufacturer on the basis of the airplane's maximum gross weight, flaps and landing gear retracted, the critical engine inoperative, and the propeller feathered.

Although engine failure while en route in normal cruise conditions may not be critical, it is a recommended practice to add maximum available power to the operating engine before securing or shutting down the failed engine. If it is determined later that maximum available power on the operating engine is not needed to maintain altitude, it is a simple matter to reduce the power. Conversely, if maximum available power is not applied, the airspeed may decrease much farther and more rapidly than expected. This condition could present a serious performance problem, especially if the airspeed should drop below V_{YSE}.

The altitude should be maintained if it is within the capability of the airplane. If the airplane is not capable of maintaining altitude with an engine inoperative under existing circumstances, the airspeed should be maintained at the single-engine best rate-of-climb speed (V_{YSE}) so as to conserve altitude as long as possible to reach a suitable landing area.

After the failed engine is shut down and everything is under control (including heading and altitude), it is recommended that the pilot communicate with the nearest ground facility to let them know the flight is being conducted with one engine inoperative. Federal Aviation Administration (FAA) facilities are able to give valuable assistance if needed, particularly when the flight is conducted under instrument flight rules (IFR) or a landing is to be made at a tower controlled airport. Good judgment dictates that a landing be made at the nearest suitable airport rather than continuing flight.

During single-engine practice using zero thrust power settings, the engine may cool to temperatures considerably below the normal operating range. This factor requires caution when advancing the power at the termination of single-engine practice. If the power is advanced rapidly, the engine may not respond and an actual engine failure may be encountered. This is particularly important when practicing single-engine approaches and landings. A good procedure is to slowly advance the throttle to approximately one-half power, then allow it to respond and stabilize before advancing to higher power settings. This procedure also results in less wear on the engines.

Restarts after feathering require the same amount of care, primarily to avoid engine damage. Following the restart, the engine power should be maintained at the idle setting or slightly above until the engine is sufficiently warm and is receiving adequate lubrication.

ENGINE INOPERATIVE APPROACH AND LANDING

Essentially, a single-engine approach and landing is the same as a normal approach and landing. Long, flat approaches with high-power output on the operating engine and/or excessive threshold speed that results in floating and unnecessary runway use should be avoided. Due to variations in the performance and limitations of many multiengine airplanes, a specific flightpath or procedure can not be proposed that would be adequate in all single-engine approaches. In most multiengine airplanes, a single-engine approach can be accomplished with the flightpath and procedures almost identical to a normal approach and landing. The multiengine manufacturers include a recommended single-engine landing procedure in the AFM/POH.

During the checkout, the transitioning pilot should perform approaches and landings with the power of one engine set to simulate the drag of a feathered propeller (zero thrust), or if feathering propellers are not installed, the throttle of the simulated failed engine set to idle. With the inoperative engine feathered or set to zero thrust, normal drag is considerably reduced, resulting in a longer landing roll. Allowances should be made accordingly for the final approach and landing.

The final approach speed should not be less than V_{YSE} until the landing is assured; thereafter, it should be at the speed commensurate with the flap position until beginning the roundout for landing. Under normal conditions, the approach should be made with full flaps; however, neither full flaps nor the landing gear should be extended until the landing is assured. When more drag is required, the landing gear should be the first option if it does not conflict with the manufacturer's recommended procedure. With full flaps, the approach speed should be $1.3 \, V_{SO}$ or as recommended by the manufacturer.

The pilot should be particularly judicious in lowering the flaps. Once they have been extended, it may not be possible to retract them in time to initiate a go-around. Most of the multiengine airplanes are not capable of making a single-engine go-around with full flaps. Each make and model of airplane must be operated in accordance with the manufacturer's recommended procedures.

CHAPTER 15

TRANSITION TO TAILWHEEL AIRPLANES

INTRODUCTION

This chapter discusses the procedures for the safe operation of tailwheel-type airplanes sometimes referred to as conventional gear. The focus will be on the operational differences that occur during ground operations, takeoffs, and landings.

LANDING GEAR

The main landing gear forms the principal support of the airplane on the ground. The tailwheel also supports the airplane, but steering and directional control are its primary functions. With the tailwheel-type airplane, the two main struts are attached to the airplane slightly ahead of the airplane's center of gravity (CG).

The rudder pedals are the primary directional controls while taxiing. Steering with the pedals may be accomplished through the forces of airflow or propeller slipstream acting on the rudder surface, or through a mechanical linkage to the steerable tailwheel. Initially, the pilot should taxi with the heels of the feet resting on the cockpit floor and the balls of the feet on the bottom of the rudder pedals. The feet should be slid up onto the brake pedals only when it is necessary to depress the brakes. This permits the simultaneous application of rudder and brake whenever needed. The brakes are used primarily to stop the airplane at a desired point, to slow the airplane, or as an aid in making a sharp controlled turn. Whenever used, they must be applied smoothly, evenly, and cautiously at all times.

TAXIING

When beginning to taxi, the brakes should be tested immediately for proper operation. This is done by first applying power to start the airplane moving slowly forward, then retarding the throttle and simultaneously applying pressure smoothly to both brakes. If braking action is unsatisfactory, the engine should be shut down immediately.

To turn the airplane on the ground, the pilot should apply rudder in the desired direction of turn and use whatever power or brake that is necessary to control the taxi speed. The rudder should be held in the direction of the turn until just short of the point where the turn is to be stopped, then the rudder pressure released or slight opposite pressure applied as needed.

While taxiing, the pilot will have to anticipate the movements of the airplane and adjust rudder pressure accordingly. Since the airplane will continue to turn slightly even as the rudder pressure is being released, the stopping of the turn must be anticipated and the rudder pedals neutralized before the desired heading is reached. In some cases, it may be necessary to apply opposite rudder to stop the turn, depending on the taxi speed.

The presence of moderate to strong headwinds and/or a strong propeller slipstream makes the use of the elevator necessary to maintain control of the pitch attitude while taxiing. This becomes apparent when considering the lifting action that may be created on the horizontal tail surfaces by either of those two factors. The elevator control should be held in the aft position to hold the tail down.

When taxiing in a quartering headwind, the wing on the upwind side will usually tend to be lifted by the wind unless the aileron control is held in that direction (upwind aileron UP). Moving the aileron into the UP position reduces the effect of wind striking that wing, thus reducing the lifting action. This control movement will also cause the opposite aileron to be placed in the DOWN position, thus creating drag and possibly some lift on the downwind wing, further reducing the tendency of the upwind wing to rise.

When taxiing with a quartering tailwind, the elevator should be held in the DOWN or NEUTRAL position, and the upwind aileron down. Since the wind is striking the airplane from behind, these control positions reduce the tendency of the wind to get under the tail and the wing possibly causing the airplane to nose over. The application of these crosswind taxi corrections also helps to minimize the weathervaning tendency and ultimately result in making the airplane easier to steer.

An airplane with a tailwheel has a tendency to weathervane or turn into the wind while it is being taxied. The tendency of the airplane to weathervane is greatest while taxiing directly crosswind; consequently, directional control is somewhat difficult. Without brakes, it is almost impossible to keep the airplane from turning into any wind of considerable velocity since the airplane's rudder control capability may be inadequate to counteract the crosswind. In taxiing down wind the tendency to weathervane is increased, due to the tailwind decreasing the effectiveness of the flight controls. This requires a more positive use of the rudder and the brakes, particularly if the wind velocity is above that of a light breeze.

Unless the field is soft, or very rough, it is best when taxiing down wind to hold the elevator control in neutral or slightly forward. Even on soft fields, the elevator should be raised only as much as is absolutely necessary to maintain a safe margin of control in case there is a tendency of the airplane to nose over.

On most tailwheel-type airplanes, directional control while taxiing is facilitated by the use of a steerable tailwheel, which operates along with the rudder. The tailwheel steering mechanism remains engaged when the tailwheel is operated through an arc of 16 to 18° each side of neutral and then automatically becomes full swiveling when turned to a greater angle. The airplane may be pivoted within its own length, if desired, yet is fully steerable for slight turns while taxiing forward. While taxiing, the steerable tailwheel should be used for making normal turns and the pilot's feet kept off the brake pedals to avoid unnecessary wear on the brakes.

Since a tailwheel-type airplane rests on the tailwheel as well as the main landing wheels, it assumes a nose-high attitude when on the ground. In most cases this places the engine cowling high enough to restrict the pilot's vision of the area directly ahead of the airplane. Consequently, objects directly ahead of the airplane are difficult, if not impossible, to see. To observe and avoid colliding with any objects or hazardous surface conditions, the pilot should alternately turn the nose from one side to the other—that is zigzag, or make a series of short S-turns while taxiing forward. This should be done slowly, smoothly, positively, and cautiously.

NORMAL TAKEOFF ROLL

After taxiing onto the runway, the airplane should be carefully aligned with the intended takeoff direction, and the tailwheel positioned straight, or centered. In airplanes equipped with a locking device, the tailwheel should be locked in the centered position. After releasing the brakes, the throttle should be smoothly and continuously advanced to takeoff power. As the airplane starts to roll forward, the pilot should slide both feet down on the rudder pedals so that the toes or balls of the feet are on the rudder portions, not on the brake portions.

An abrupt application of power may cause the airplane to yaw sharply to the left because of the torque effects of the engine and propeller. Also, precession will be particularly noticeable during takeoff in a tailwheel-type airplane if the tail is rapidly raised from a three point to a level flight attitude. The abrupt change of attitude tilts the horizontal axis of the propeller, and the resulting precession produces a forward force on the right side (90° ahead in the direction of rotation), yawing the airplane's nose to the left. The amount of force created by this precession is directly related to the rate the propeller axis is tilted when the tail is raised. With this in mind, the throttle should always be advanced smoothly and continuously to prevent any sudden swerving.

Smooth, gradual advancement of the throttle is very important in tailwheel-type airplanes, since peculiarities in their takeoff characteristics are accentuated in proportion to the rapidity the takeoff power is applied.

As speed is gained, the elevator control will tend to assume a neutral position if the airplane is correctly trimmed. At the same time, directional control should be maintained with smooth, prompt, positive rudder corrections throughout the takeoff roll. The effects of torque and P-factor at the initial speeds tend to pull the nose to the left. The pilot must use what rudder pressure is needed to correct for these effects or for existing wind conditions to keep the nose of the airplane headed straight down the runway. The use of brakes for steering purposes should be avoided, since they will cause slower acceleration of the airplane's speed, lengthen the takeoff distance, and possibly result in severe swerving.

When the elevator trim is set for takeoff, on application of maximum allowable power, the airplane will (when sufficient speed has been attained) normally assume the correct takeoff pitch attitude on its own—the tail will rise slightly. This attitude can then be maintained by applying slight back elevator pressure. If the elevator control is pushed forward during the takeoff roll to prematurely raise the tail, its effectiveness will rapidly build up as the speed increases, making it necessary to apply back-elevator pressure to lower the tail to the proper takeoff attitude. This erratic change in attitude will delay the takeoff and lead to directional control problems. Rudder pressure must be used promptly and smoothly to counteract yawing forces so that the airplane continues straight down the runway.

While the speed of the takeoff roll increases, more and more pressure will be felt on the flight controls, particularly the elevators and rudder. Since the tail surfaces receive the full effect of the propeller slipstream, they become effective first. As the speed continues to increase, all of the flight controls will gradually become effective enough to maneuver the airplane about its three axes. It is at this point, in the taxi to flight transition, that the airplane is being flown more than taxied. As this occurs, progressively smaller rudder deflections are needed to maintain direction.

TAKEOFF

Since a good takeoff depends on the proper takeoff attitude, it is important to know how this attitude appears and how it is attained. The ideal takeoff attitude requires only minimum pitch adjustments shortly after the airplane lifts off to attain the speed for the best rate of climb.

The tail should first be allowed to rise off the ground slightly to permit the airplane to accelerate more rapidly. At this point, the position of the nose in relation to the horizon should be noted, then elevator pressure applied as necessary to hold this attitude. The wings are kept level by applying aileron pressure as necessary.

The airplane may be allowed to fly off the ground while in normal takeoff attitude. Forcing it into the air by applying excessive back-elevator pressure would result in an excessively high pitch attitude and may delay the takeoff. As discussed earlier, excessive and rapid changes in pitch attitude result in proportionate changes in the effects of torque, making the airplane more difficult to control.

Although the airplane can be forced into the air, this is considered an unsafe practice and should be avoided under normal circumstances. If the airplane is forced to leave the ground by using too much back-elevator pressure before adequate flying speed is attained, the wing's angle of attack may be excessive, causing the airplane to settle back to the runway or even to stall. On the other hand, if sufficient back-elevator pressure is not held to maintain the correct takeoff attitude after becoming airborne, or the nose is allowed to lower excessively, the airplane may also settle back to the runway. This occurs because the angle of attack is decreased and lift is diminished to the degree where it will not support the airplane. It is important, to hold the attitude constant after rotation or lift-off.

As the airplane leaves the ground, the pilot must continue to maintain straight flight, as well as holding the proper pitch attitude. During takeoffs in strong, gusty wind, it is advisable that an extra margin of speed be obtained before the airplane is allowed to leave the ground. A takeoff at the normal takeoff speed may result in a lack of positive control, or a stall, when the airplane encounters a sudden lull in strong, gusty wind, or other turbulent air currents. In this case the pilot should hold the airplane on the ground longer to attain more speed, then make a smooth, positive rotation to leave the ground.

CROSSWIND TAKEOFF

It is important to establish and maintain the proper amount of crosswind correction prior to lift-off; that is, apply aileron pressure toward the wind to keep the upwind wing from rising and apply rudder pressure as needed to prevent weathervaning.

As the tailwheel is raised off the runway, the holding of aileron control into the wind may result in the downwind wing rising and the downwind main wheel lifting off the runway first, with the remainder of the takeoff roll being made on one main wheel. This is acceptable and is preferable to side skipping.

If a significant crosswind exists, the main wheels should be held on the ground slightly longer than in a normal takeoff so that a smooth but definite lift-off can be made. This procedure will allow the airplane to leave the ground under more positive control so that it will definitely remain airborne while the proper amount of drift correction is being established. More importantly, it will avoid imposing excessive side loads on the landing gear and prevent possible damage that would result from the airplane settling back to the runway while drifting.

As both main wheels leave the runway, and ground friction no longer resists drifting, the airplane will be slowly carried sideways with the wind until adequate drift correction is maintained.

SHORT-FIELD TAKEOFF

Wing flaps should be lowered prior to takeoff if recommended by the manufacturer. Takeoff power should be applied smoothly and continuously, (there should be no hesitation) to accelerate the airplane as rapidly as possible. As the takeoff roll progresses, the airplane's pitch attitude and angle of attack should be adjusted to that which results in the minimum amount of drag and the quickest acceleration. The tail should be allowed to rise off the ground slightly, then held in this tail-low flight attitude until the proper lift-off or rotation airspeed is attained. For the steepest climb-out and best obstacle clearance, the airplane should be allowed to roll with its full weight on the main wheels and accelerated to the lift-off speed.

SOFT-FIELD TAKEOFF

Wing flaps may be lowered prior to starting the takeoff (if recommended by the manufacturer) to provide additional lift and transfer the airplane's weight from the wheels to the wings as early as possible. The airplane should be taxied onto the takeoff surface without stopping on a soft surface. Since stopping on a soft surface, such as mud or snow, might bog the airplane down. The airplane should be kept in continuous motion with sufficient power while lining up for the takeoff roll.

As the airplane is aligned with the proposed takeoff path, takeoff power is applied smoothly and as rapidly as the powerplant will accept it without faltering. The tail should be kept low to maintain the inherent positive angle of attack and to avoid any tendency of the airplane to nose over as a result of soft spots, tall grass, or deep snow.

When the airplane is held at a nose-high attitude throughout the takeoff run, the wings will, as speed increases and lift develops, progressively relieve the wheels of more and more of the airplane's weight, thereby minimizing the drag caused by surface irregularities or adhesion. If this attitude is accurately maintained, the airplane will virtually fly itself off the ground. The airplane should be allowed to accelerate to climb speed in ground effect.

TOUCHDOWN

The touchdown is the gentle settling of the airplane onto the landing surface. The roundout and touchdown should be made with the engine idling, and the airplane at minimum controllable airspeed, so that the airplane will touch down at approximately stalling speed. As the airplane settles, the proper landing attitude must be attained by applying whatever back-elevator pressure is necessary. The roundout and touchdown should be timed so that the wheels of the main landing gear and tailwheel touch down simultaneously (three-point landing). This requires proper timing, technique, and judgment of distance and altitude. [Figure 15-1]

When the wheels make contact with the ground, the elevator control should be carefully eased fully back to hold the tail down and to keep the tailwheel on the ground. This provides more positive directional control of the airplane equipped with a steerable tailwheel, and prevents any tendency for the airplane to nose over. If the tailwheel is not on the ground, easing back on the elevator control may cause the airplane to become airborne again because the change in attitude will increase the angle of attack and produce enough lift for the airplane to fly.

It is extremely important that the touchdown occur with the airplane's longitudinal axis exactly parallel to the direction the airplane is moving along the runway. Failure to accomplish this not only imposes severe sideloads on the landing gear, but imparts groundlooping (swerving) tendencies. To avoid these side stresses or a ground loop, the pilot must never allow the airplane to touch down while in a crab or while drifting.

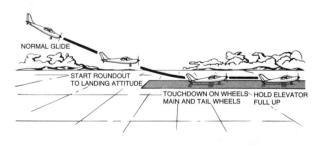

FIGURE 15-1.—Tailwheel touchdown.

AFTER-LANDING ROLL

The landing process must never be considered complete until the airplane decelerates to the normal taxi speed during the landing roll or has been brought to a complete stop when clear of the landing area. The pilot must be alert for directional control difficulties immediately upon and after touchdown due to the ground friction on the wheels. The friction creates a pivot point on which a moment arm can act. This is because the CG is behind the main wheels. [Figure 15-2]

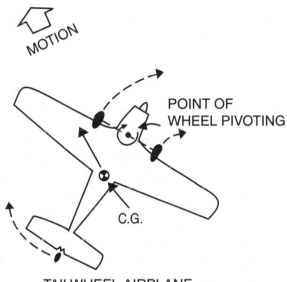

MOTION

POINT OF WHEEL PIVOTING

C.G.

TAILWHEEL AIRPLANE

FIGURE 15-2—Effect of CG on directional control.

Any difference between the direction the airplane is traveling and the direction it is headed will produce a moment about the pivot point of the wheels, and the airplane will tend to swerve. Loss of directional control may lead to an aggravated, uncontrolled, tight turn on the ground, or a ground loop. The combination of inertia acting on the CG and ground friction of the main wheels resisting it during the ground loop may cause the airplane to tip or lean enough for the outside wingtip to contact the ground, and may even impose a sideward force that could collapse the landing gear. The aircraft can ground loop late in the after-landing roll because rudder effectiveness decreases with the decreasing flow of air along the rudder surface as the airplane slows. As the airplane speed decreases and the tailwheel has been lowered to the ground, the steerable tailwheel provides more positive directional control.

To use the brakes, the pilot should slide the toes or feet up from the rudder pedals to the brake pedals. If rudder pressure is being held at the time braking action is needed, that pressure should not be released as the feet or toes are being slid up to the brake pedals, because control may be lost before brakes can be applied. During the ground roll, the airplane's direction of movement may be changed by carefully applying pressure on one brake or uneven pressures on each brake in the desired direction. Caution must be exercised, when applying brakes to avoid overcontrolling.

If a wing starts to rise, aileron control should be applied toward that wing to lower it. The amount required will depend on speed because as the forward speed of the airplane decreases, the ailerons will become less effective.

The elevator control should be held back as far as possible and as firmly as possible, until the airplane stops. This provides more positive control with tailwheel steering, tends to shorten the after-landing roll, and prevents bouncing and skipping.

If available runway permits, the speed of the airplane should be allowed to dissipate in a normal manner by the friction and drag of the wheels on the ground. Brakes may be used if needed to help slow the airplane. After the airplane has been slowed sufficiently and has been turned onto a taxiway or clear of the landing area, it should be brought to a complete stop. Only after this is done should the pilot retract the flaps and perform other checklist items.

CROSSWIND LANDING

If the crab method of drift correction has been used throughout the final approach and roundout, the crab must be removed before touchdown by applying rudder to align the airplane's longitudinal axis with its direction of movement. This requires timely and accurate action. Failure to accomplish this results in severe sideloads being imposed on the landing gear and imparts ground looping tendencies.

If the wing-low method is used, the crosswind correction (aileron into the wind and opposite rudder) should be maintained throughout the roundout, and the touchdown made on the upwind main wheel.

During gusty or high-wind conditions, prompt adjustments must be made in the crosswind correction to assure that the airplane does not drift as the airplane touches down.

As the forward momentum decreases after initial contact, the weight of the airplane will cause the downwind main wheel to gradually settle onto the runway.

An adequate amount of power should be used to maintain the proper airspeed throughout the approach, and the throttle should be retarded to idling position after the main wheels contact the landing surface. Care must be exercised in closing the throttle before the pilot is ready for touchdown, because the sudden or premature closing of the throttle may cause a sudden increase in the descent rate that could result in a hard landing.

CROSSWIND AFTER-LANDING ROLL

Particularly during the after-landing roll, special attention must be given to maintaining directional control by the use of rudder and tailwheel steering, while keeping the upwind wing from rising by the use of aileron. Characteristically, an airplane has a greater profile, or side area, behind the main landing gear than forward of it. [Figure 15-3] With the main wheels acting as a pivot point and the greater surface area exposed to the crosswind behind that pivot point, the airplane will tend to turn or weathervane into the wind. This weathervaning tendency is more prevalent in the tailwheel-type because the airplane's surface area behind the main landing gear is greater than in nosewheel-type airplanes.

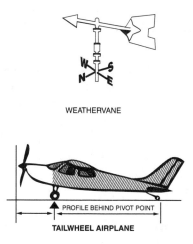

FIGURE 15-3—*Weathervaning tendency.*

Pilots should be familiar with the crosswind component of each airplane they fly, and avoid operations in wind conditions that exceed the capability of the airplane, as well as their own limitations.

While the airplane is decelerating during the after-landing roll, more aileron must be applied to keep the upwind wing from rising. Since the airplane is slowing down, there is less airflow around the ailerons and they become less effective. At the same time, the relative wind is becoming more of a crosswind and exerting a greater lifting force on the upwind wing. Consequently, when the airplane is coming to a stop, the aileron control must be held fully toward the wind.

WHEEL LANDING

Landings from power approaches in turbulence or in crosswinds should be such that the touchdown is made with the airplane in approximately level flight attitude. The touchdown should be made smoothly on the main wheels, with the tailwheel held clear of the runway. This is called a "wheel landing" and requires careful timing and control usage to prevent bouncing. These wheel landings can be best accomplished by holding the airplane in level flight attitude until the main wheels touch, then immediately but smoothly retarding the throttle, and holding sufficient forward elevator pressure to hold the main wheels on the ground. The airplane should never be forced onto the ground by excessive forward pressure.

If the touchdown is made at too high a rate of descent as the main wheels strike the landing surface, the tail is forced down by its own weight. In turn, when the tail is forced down, the wing's angle of attack increases resulting in a sudden increase in lift and the airplane may become airborne again. Then as the airplane's speed continues to decrease, the tail may again lower onto the runway. If the tail is allowed to settle too quickly, the airplane may again become airborne. This process, often called "porpoising," usually intensifies even though the pilot tries to stop it. The best corrective action is to execute a go-around procedure.

SHORT-FIELD LANDING

Upon touchdown, the airplane should be firmly held in a three-point attitude. This will provide aerodynamic braking by the wings. Immediately upon touchdown, and closing the throttle, the brakes should be applied evenly and firmly to minimize the after-landing roll. The airplane should be stopped within the shortest possible distance consistent with safety.

SOFT-FIELD LANDING

The tailwheel should touch down simultaneously with or just before the main wheels, and should then be held down by maintaining firm back-elevator pressure throughout the landing roll. This will minimize any tendency for the airplane to nose over and will provide aerodynamic braking. The use of brakes on a soft field is not needed because the soft or rough surface itself will provide sufficient reduction in the airplane's forward speed. Often it will be found that upon landing on a very soft field, the pilot will need to increase power to keep the airplane moving and from becoming stuck in the soft surface.

GROUND LOOP

A ground loop is an uncontrolled turn during ground operation that may occur while taxiing or taking off, but especially during the after-landing roll. It is not always caused by drift or weathervaning although these things may cause the initial swerve. Careless use of the rudder, an uneven ground surface, or a soft spot that retards one main wheel of the airplane may also cause a swerve. In any case, the initial swerve tends to cause the airplane to ground loop.

Due to the characteristics of an airplane equipped with a tailwheel, the forces that cause a ground loop increase as the swerve increases. The initial swerve develops inertia and this, acting at the CG (which is located behind the main wheels), swerves the airplane even more. If allowed to develop, the force produced may become great enough to tip the airplane until one wing strikes the ground.

If the airplane touches down while drifting or in a crab, the pilot should apply aileron toward the high wing and stop the swerve with the rudder. Brakes should be used to correct for turns or swerves only when the rudder is inadequate. The pilot must exercise caution when applying corrective brake action because it is very easy to overcontrol and aggravate the situation. If brakes are used, sufficient brake should be applied on the low-wing wheel (outside of the turn) to stop the swerve. When the wings are approximately level, the new direction must be maintained until the airplane has slowed to taxi speed or has stopped.

CHAPTER 16
TRANSITION TO SEAPLANES

INTRODUCTION

This chapter introduces seaplane flying, and provides a general review for experienced seaplane pilots. It contains general explanations of commonly accepted techniques and procedures for operating seaplanes on the water, with special emphasis on procedures that are different from landplane flying.

The explanations herein apply to single-engine and multiengine seaplanes typical of those used in general aviation operations. For information regarding the operation of airplanes approved as seaplanes, reference should be made to that airplane's Airplane Flight Manual (AFM) and/or Pilot's Operating Handbook (POH) and the manufacturer's recommendations. In addition to material contained herein, there are numerous commercially produced publications relating to water operations that contain additional valuable information. All this information used collectively with good training and practice will result in a safe and pleasurable experience during water-based operations.

A ground and flight training syllabus is included at the end of this chapter for use in preparing pilots for seaplane class rating certification, or transitioning to other types of seaplanes.

TERMS AND DEFINITIONS

Pilots who operate airplanes may already be familiar with some of the nomenclature associated with operating seaplanes. However, there are several new important float and hull terms that seaplane pilots need to be familiar with. They are listed here and shown in Figures 16-1 and 16-2.

- **Seaplane**—an airplane that can take off from, and land on water.
- **Amphibians**—seaplanes that can be operated from both land and water.

- **Afterbody Length**—length from step, to stern of float or hull.
- **Beam**—float or hull width, at its widest point.
- **Bilge**—lowest point or area inside a float or hull where water collects.
- **Bow**—front end of the floats or hull.
- **Bracing Wires**—steel wires with threaded ends to tighten and rig floats.
- **Bulkhead**—structural upright partitions separating the compartments of the floats or hull.
- **Bumper**—rubber bumper installed on the bow of float or hull.

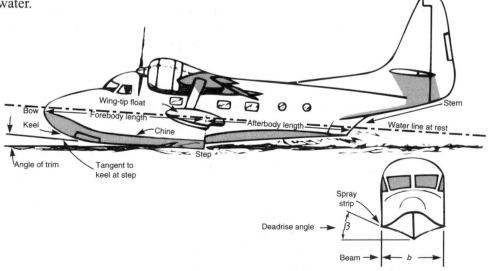

FIGURE 16-1.—Hull components.

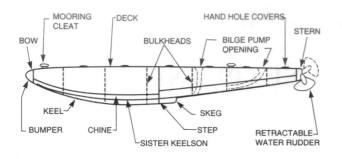

FIGURE 16-2.—Float components.

- **Center of Buoyancy**—average point of support on the float or hull.
- **Chine**—the intersection of the bottom and the side of a float or hull.
- **Deadrise Angle**—angle of rise in "V" design of the float or hull.
- **Forebody Length**—length from step, to bow of the float or hull.
- **Keel**—structural member extending from below the bumper, along the length of the bottom of the float or hull to the step.
- **Mooring Cleat**—metal fitting with projecting ends on which a rope can be fastened.
- **Sister Keelson**—additional longitudinal structural members, fastened on the outside skin for additional strength.
- **Skeg**—fitting installed at step where keel terminates.
- **Spreader Bars**—aerodynamic tubing attached to the inner portion of each float to establish a predetermined length between the floats.
- **Spray Strip or Rail**—an extrusion or surface extending horizontally from where the hull bottom and sides join, to minimize water spray.
- **Step**—a longitudinal break in the keel line approximately midway down the float or hull.
- **Water Line**—longitudinal line or position on the float or hull when the seaplane is at rest in water.
- **Wingtip Float**—flotation unit attached to outer wing structure to keep the hull seaplane level in the water.

GENERAL

The operation of an airplane on water is somewhat different than operating one on land. This is because of the widely varying and constantly changing conditions of the water surface. However, operating a seaplane should not be more difficult than operating a landplane, if a pilot acquires the essential knowledge and skills required for safe water flying operations.

When a pilot transitions to a seaplane, additional training is required. Ground and flight training must be received and logged, and a class rating practical test must be passed, prior to initial operations as pilot in command. This training will require the use of an authorized flight instructor to conduct such training and attest to the competency of a pilot prior to taking the practical test.

CHARACTERISTICS OF WATER

A competent seaplane pilot must be knowledgeable in the characteristics of water to understand its effects on the seaplane. Water is a fluid, and although it is much heavier than air, it behaves in a manner similar to air.

Since it is a fluid, water seeks its own level and, if not disturbed, lies flat and glassy. It will change, however, if disturbed by forces, such as winds, undercurrents, and objects traveling on its surface creating waves or movements.

Because of its weight, water can exert a tremendous force. This force, a result of resistance, produces drag as the water flows around or under an object being propelled throughout or on its surface. The force of drag imposed by the water increases as the square of the speed. This means that as the speed of the object traveling on the water is doubled, the force exerted is four times as great.

Forces created when operating an airplane on water are more complex than those created on land. When a landplane's wheels contact the ground, the force of friction or drag acts at a fixed point on the airplane. However, the water forces act along the entire length of a seaplane's floats or hull with the center of pressure constantly changing depending upon the pitch attitude, dynamic float or hull motion, and action of the waves.

Since the surface condition of water varies constantly, it is important that the pilot be able to recognize and understand the effects of the various conditions of the water surface.

Under calm wind conditions, a waveless water surface is perhaps the most dangerous to the seaplane pilot and requires precise piloting techniques. Glassy water presents a uniform mirrorlike appearance from above, and with out visual references to judge height, it can be extremely deceptive. Also, if waves are decaying and setting up certain patterns, or if clouds are reflected from the water surface, distortions result that are even

Terms Used by U.S. Weather Service	Velocity mph	Estimating Velocities on Land	Estimating Velocities on Sea	
Calm	Less than 1	Smoke rises vertically	Sea like a mirror	Check your glassy water technique before water flying under these conditions.
Light Air	1 - 3	Smoke drifts; wind vanes unmoved.	Ripples with the appearance of scales are formed but without foam crests.	
Light Breeze	4 - 7	Wind felt on face; leaves rustle; ordinary vane moves by wind.	Small wavelets, still short but more pronounced; crests have a glassy appearance and do not break.	
Gentle Breeze	8 - 12	Leaves and small twigs in constant motion; wind extends light flag	Large wavelets; crests begin to break. foam of glassy appearance. (Perhaps scattered whitecaps.)	Ideal water flying characteristics in protected water.
Moderate Breeze	13 - 18	Dust and loose paper raised; small branches are moved.	Small waves, becoming longer; fairly frequent whitecaps.	
Fresh Breeze	19 - 24	Small trees in leaf begin to sway; crested wavelets form in inland water.	Moderate waves; taking a more pronounced long form; many whitecaps are formed. (Chance of some spray.)	This is considered rough water for seaplanes and small amphibians, especially in open water.
Strong Breeze	25 - 31	Large branches in motion; whistling heard in telegraph wires; umbrellas used with difficulty.	Large waves begin to form; white foam crests are more extensive everywhere. (Probably some spray.)	
Moderate Gale	32 - 38	Whole trees in motion; inconvenience felt in walking against the wind.	Sea heaps up and white foam from breaking waves begins to be blown in streaks along the direction of the wind.	This type of water condition is for emergency only in small aircraft in inland waters and for the expert pilot.

FIGURE 16-3.—Surface wind force table.

more confusing for inexperienced, as well as experienced pilots.

Wave conditions on the surface of the water are a very important factor in seaplane operations. Wind provides the force that generates waves, and the velocity of the wind governs the size of the waves or the roughness of the water surface. [Figure 16-3]

Calm water resists wave motion until a wind velocity of about 2 knots is attained, then patches of ripples are formed. If the wind velocity increases to 4 knots, the ripples change to small waves that continue to persist for some time even after the wind stops blowing. If this gentle breeze diminishes, the water viscosity dampens the ripples and the surface promptly returns to a flat and glassy condition.

As the wind velocity increases above 4 knots, the water surface becomes covered with a complicated pattern of waves; the characteristics vary continuously between wide limits. This is referred to as the generating area. This generating area remains disarranged as long as the wind velocity is increasing. With a further increase in wind velocity, the waves become larger and travel faster. When the wind reaches a constant velocity and remains constant, waves develop into a series of equidistant parallel crests of the same height.

An object floating on the water surface, where simple waves are present, will show that the water itself does not actually move along with waves. The floating object will describe a circle in a vertical plane, moving upward as the crest approaches, forward and downward as the crest passes, and backward as the trough between the waves passes. After the passage of each wave, the object stays at almost the same point it started. Consequently, the actual movement of the object is a vertical circle whose diameter is equal to the height of the wave. This theory must be slightly modified, because the friction of the wind will cause a slow downwind flow of water resulting in drift. Therefore, a nearly submerged object, such as a float or hull, will slowly drift with the waves.

When the wind increases to a velocity of 12 knots, waves will no longer maintain smooth curves. The waves will break at their crest and create foam—whitecaps. When the wind decreases, the whitecaps disappear; however, lines or streaks form, which can be used as an accurate indication of the path of the wind. Generally, it will be found that waves generated by wind velocities up to 10 knots do not reach a height of more than 1 foot.

A great amount of wind energy is needed to produce large waves. When the wind ceases, the energy in the wave persists and is reduced only by a very slight internal friction in the water. As a result, the wave patterns continue for long distances from their source and diminish at a barely perceptible rate. These waves are known as swells, and gradually lengthen, become less high, but increase in speed.

If the wind changes direction during the diminishing process, an entirely separate wave pattern will form which is superimposed on the swell. These patterns are easily detected by the pilot from above, but are difficult to see from the surface.

Islands, shoals, and tidal currents also affect the size of waves. An island with steep shores and sharply pointed extremities allows the water at some distance from the shore to pass with little disturbance or wave motion. Normally, this creates a glassy surface on the lee side. Wind gusts on glassy water will appear as dark patches.

If the island has rounded extremities, a shallow slope and outlying shoals where the water shallows and then becomes deep again, the waves will break and slow down. This breaking will cause a considerable loss of wave height on the lee side of the shoal; however, if the water is too deep above the shoal, the waves will not break.

When waves are generated in nonflowing water and travel into moving water, such as a current, they undergo important changes. If the current is moving in the same direction as the waves, they increase in speed and length but lose their height. If the current is moving opposite to the waves, they will decrease in speed and length, but will increase in height and steepness. This explains "tidal rips" which are formed where strong streams run against the waves. A current traveling at 6 miles per hour (MPH) will break almost all waves traveling against it. When waves break, a considerable loss in wave height occurs to the leeward side of the breaking.

Another characteristic of water that should be mentioned is the ability of water to provide buoyancy and cause some objects to float on the surface. Some of these floating objects can be seen from the air, while others are partially submerged and difficult to see. Consequently, seaplane pilots must constantly be aware

of the possibility of floating debris and avoid striking these objects during operations on the water.

CHARACTERISTICS OF SEAPLANES

The seaplane is ordinarily understood to be a conventional landplane equipped with separate floats instead of wheels. On the flying boat type, the hull serves the dual purpose of providing buoyancy in the water and space for the pilot, crew, and passengers. The float type is the more common seaplane, particularly those with relatively low horsepower engines. Most of these seaplanes are of the twin-float variety.

Though there are considerable differences between handling a seaplane and a hull type on the water, the theory on which the procedures and techniques are based on similar. With few exceptions, the explanations given here for one type may be considered to apply to the other.

In the air, the seaplane is operated and controlled in much the same manner as the landplane. The only major difference is the installation of floats instead of wheels. Because of the float's greater weight, replacing wheels with floats increases the airplane's empty weight and decreases its useful load. Floats also increase drag and reduce performance.

On many seaplanes, the directional stability will be affected to some extent by the installation of the floats. This is caused by the length of the floats and the location of their mass in relation to the airplane's center of gravity (CG). To help restore directional stability, an auxiliary fin(s) is often added to the tail. The pilot will also find that less aileron pressure is needed to hold the seaplane in a slip, and holding some rudder pressure during inflight turns is usually required. This is due to the water rudder being connected to the air rudder or rudder pedals by cables and springs which tend to prevent the air rudder from streamlining in a turn.

Research and experience have improved float and hull designs throughout the years. The primary consideration in float and hull construction is the use of sturdy, lightweight material, designed hydrodynamically and aerodynamically for optimum performance.

All floats and hulls being used have multiple watertight compartments. This makes the seaplane virtually unsinkable, and prevents the entire float or hull from becoming filled with water in the event it is ruptured at any point.

Both the lateral and longitudinal lines of a float or hull are designed to achieve a maximum lifting force by diverting the water and the air downward. The forward bottom portion of the float (and hull) is designed very much like the bottom surface of a speedboat. The rearward portion differs significantly from a speedboat.

A speedboat is designed for traveling at an almost constant-pitch angle and the contour of the entire bottom is constructed in a continuous straight line. A scaplane float or hull must be designed to permit the seaplane to be rotated or pitched up to increase the wing's angle of attack and gain the most lift for takeoffs and landings. The underside of the float or hull has a sudden break in its longitudinal lines at the point around where the seaplane rotates into the lift-off attitude. This break, called a "step," also provides a means of interrupting the capillary or adhesive properties of the water. The water can then flow freely behind the step, resulting in minimum surface friction so the seaplane can lift out of the water.

The steps are located slightly behind the airplane's CG, at the point where the main wheels of a landplane are located. If the steps were located too far aft or forward of this point, it would be difficult, to rotate the seaplane into a pitchup attitude prior to planing (rising partly out of the water while moving at a high speed) or lift-off.

Although steps are necessary, the sharp break along the float's or hull's underside causes structural stress concentration, and inflight produces considerable drag because of the eddying turbulence it creates in the airflow.

SEAPLANE BASES/LANDING AREAS

Some states and cities have very liberal laws regarding the operation of seaplanes on their lakes and waterways, while other states and cities may impose restrictions. It is recommended that before operating a seaplane on public waters, the Parks and Wildlife Department of the state, the State Aeronautics Department, or the Flight Standards District Office (FSDO's) nearest the site of the planned operation be contacted concerning the local requirements. In any case, seaplane pilots should always avoid creating a nuisance in any area, particularly in congested marine areas or near swimming or boating facilities.

The location of established seaplane bases/landing areas is symbolized on aeronautical charts by depicting an anchor inside a circle. They are also listed in Airport/ Facility Directories. The facilities provided at seaplane bases/landing areas vary greatly, but most include a hard surface ramp for launching, servicing facilities, and an area for mooring or hangaring seaplanes. Many marinas designed for boats also provide a seaplane facility.

In some cases seaplane operations are conducted in bush country where regular or emergency facilities are limited or nonexistent. The terrain and waterways are often hazardous, and any servicing must be the pilot's responsibility. Prior to operating in the bush, it is recommended that seaplane pilots obtain advice from Federal Aviation Administration (FAA) appointed Accident Prevention Counselors or other well qualified seaplane pilots who are familiar with the area.

SAFETY RULES FOR SEAPLANES

Title 14 of the Code of Federal Regulations (14 CFR) part 91 contains the right-of-way rules for operating seaplanes on water.

In addition to these operating rules, the United States Coast Guard (USCG) manual (M16672.2C), Navigation Rules, International-Inland applies to all vessels navigating upon the high seas and certain inland waters. The Inland rules apply to all public or private vessels operating upon the inland waters of the U.S., high seas, and certain inshore waters. The USCG has jurisdiction over operations on the high seas and certain inland waters.

It is strongly recommended that seaplane pilots acquire copies of the pertinent rules, become thoroughly familiar with their contents, and comply with the requirements during all operations.

In the interest of safety, it is particularly important that seaplane pilots become familiar with NAVIGATION AIDS, such as buoys, day and night beacons, light and sound signals, and steering and sailing rules.

Safety Equipment for Seaplanes

The safety equipment requirements for seaplanes are included in 14 CFR part 91. These are minimum requirements only, and are specifically for those who operate seaplanes for hire over water, and beyond power-off gliding distance from shore. This section requires that for such operations, approved flotation gear must be readily available to each occupant and at least one pyrotechnic signaling device is required to be available. Although this requirement does not apply to flight operations, it is highly recommended.

Additional safety and personal equipment considerations should be reviewed prior to each flight. Equipment requirements should be tailored to meet the needs of potential problems for each type of flight and destination environment.

PREFLIGHT INSPECTION

The preflight inspection should begin with a review of the existing local weather, destination weather, and water conditions. This weather evaluation should include the windspeed and direction to determine their effects on takeoffs, landings, and water operations.

The preflight inspection of a seaplane is similar to a landplane. The major difference is the checking of floats or hull components. In all cases, the preflight recommendations from the AFM/POH should be used.

If the seaplane is in the water when the preflight inspection is conducted, the pilot should first note how the seaplane is sitting in the water. If the sterns of the floats are very low in the water, or one wing is low, consideration should be given to how the seaplane is loaded. Also, if lower than normal for a given load, a rear compartment may have a leak.

During preflight, special attention should be paid to the propeller, floats or hull, and empennage components. These are the areas that take most of the abuse. If discrepancies are noted, a certified mechanic should check them.

Floats and hulls should be inspected for obvious or apparent defects and damage. This would include loose rivets, corrosion, separation of seams, punctures, and general condition of the metal skin. When floats or hull are out of the water, bilges should be checked for trapped water and leaks.

Because of the rigidity of the float installation, fittings and adjacent structures should be checked for cracks, defective welds, proper attachment, alignment, and safetying. All hinged points should be examined for wear and corrosion, particularly if the seaplane is operated in salt water. If water rudders are installed, they should be inspected for condition and proper movement.

It is important to check each compartment of the floats or hull for any accumulation of water before flight. Even a small amount of water, such as a cup full, is not unusual and can occur from condensation or normal leakage. All water should be removed before flight, because this water may critically affect the location of the seaplane's CG and performance.

If an excessive amount of water is found, a thorough search for the leak should be made. If drain plugs and inspection plates are installed, a systematic method of removing and reinstalling these plugs and plates securely should be used. It is extremely important to ensure that all drain plugs and inspection plates are securely in place before launching the seaplane. It is recommended that each plug and plate be counted and placed in a receptacle upon removal and counted again when reinstalled.

If near freezing temperatures are encountered, float compartments, and water rudders should be inspected for ice. Airframe icing, resulting from water spray during a takeoff or landing, should also be considered.

Part of the preflight inspection should include a cabin inspection. All support items must be secured, such as ropes, anchors, and paddles prior to takeoff. Flotation gear should be available for each occupant and appropriate survival gear should be on board.

Safety Briefing

After boarding the passengers, the pilot in command must ensure that a thorough passenger safety briefing is accomplished and understood. This includes the procedures for evacuation, the use of flotation gear, and the location and operation of regular and emergency exits. All passengers are required to be familiar with the operation of safety belts and shoulder harnesses (if installed), and in particular, can unfasten their safetybelts and shoulder harnesses, if an emergency event occurs on the water.

TAXIING

One of the major differences between the operation of a seaplane and a landplane is the method of maneuvering the aircraft on the surface. The landplane will usually remain motionless with the engine idling, particularly with the brakes applied, but a seaplane, since it is free-floating, will invariably move in some direction, depending upon the forces exerted by wind, water currents, propeller thrust, and inertia. Because a seaplane does not have brakes, it is important that the pilot be familiar with the existing wind and water conditions, effectively plan the course of action, and mentally stay ahead of the aircraft.

There are three positions or attitudes a seaplane can be moved about on the water, they are the idling position, the plowing position, and the planing or step taxi position. [Figure 16-4]

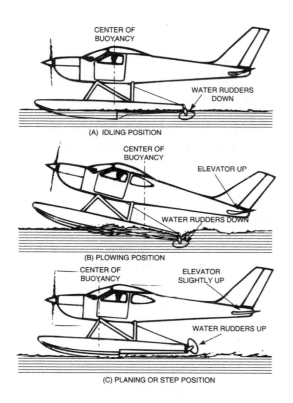

FIGURE 16-4. —Taxiing positions.

Idling Position

When taxiing with the engine idling or up to approximately 1,000 revolutions per minute (RPM), the seaplane will remain in what is considered a displacement condition similar to being at rest on the water. This is the idling position. The recommended taxi speed is usually below 6 or 7 knots so the propeller will not pick up water spray that causes serious erosion of the propeller blades. In calm or light wind conditions, the elevator control should be held full back to raise the seaplane's nose and further reduce the possibility of water spray on the propeller, and to improve overall maneuverability of the seaplane. This is particularly true if it is equipped with water rudders because more rudder area is kept in the water. Since seaplanes do not have brakes, it is especially important to taxi at this slow speed in congested or confined areas because inertia forces build up rapidly, making the seaplane vulnerable to serious damage even in minor collisions.

Plowing Position

When the power is increased significantly above idling, the seaplane will usually assume a noseup or plowing position. Most seaplane experts do not recommend the plowing position for taxiing, except in rough water when it would be desirable to raise the propeller clear of the spray, or when turning the seaplane down wind during strong wind conditions. To attain this position, full power should be applied and the elevator control held in the full aft position. Seaplanes that have a high thrust line will tend to nosedown upon application of power, in which case it is imperative that the elevator control be held in the full aft position. The plowing position is brought about by the combination of the propeller slipstream striking the elevator and the hydrodynamic force of water exerted on the underside of the float's or hull's bow. After the plowing position is attained, the power should be reduced to maintain the proper speed.

Planing or Step Position

During the planing or step position the water rudder is in the up position. The position is best attained by holding the elevator control full aft and advancing the throttle to full power. As the seaplane accelerates, it will then gradually assume a nose-high pitch attitude, raising the bow of the float or hull and causing the weight of the seaplane to be transferred toward the aft portion of the float or hull. At the time the seaplane attains its highest pitch attitude, back-elevator pressure should be gradually relaxed, causing the weight to be transferred from the aft portion of the float or hull onto the step area. This can be compared to a speedboat's occupants moving forward in the boat to aid in attaining a planing attitude. In the seaplane the pilot does essentially the same thing by use of aerodynamics (elevators). As a result of aerodynamic and hydrodynamic lifting, the seaplane is raised higher in the water, allowing the floats or hull to ride on top of rather than in the water.

The entire process of planing a seaplane is similar to that of water skiing. The skier cannot make the transition from a submerged condition to that of being supported on the surface of the water unless a sufficiently high speed is attained and maintained.

As further acceleration takes place, the flight controls become more responsive just as in the landplane and elevator deflection must be reduced in order to hold the required planing/pitch attitude. This, of course, is accomplished by further relaxing back pressure, increasing forward pressure, or using forward elevator trim depending on the aircraft flight characteristics.

Throughout the acceleration, the transfer of weight and the hydrodynamic lifting of the float or hull may be seen from the cockpit. When the seaplane is taxiing slowly, the water line is quite high on the floats or hull as compared to on the step. At slow taxi speeds, a small wake is created close to the bow of the float or hull and moves outward at a very shallow angle. As acceleration commences, the wake starts to move from the bow aft toward the step area and the wake now turns into an outward spray pattern. As speed and lifting action increase, the spray pattern continues to move aft toward the step taxi position and increases in intensity, i.e., slow-speed spray may be approximately 1 foot outboard compared to about a 20-foot outboard spray at higher speed on the step taxi position. Some seaplane pilots use the spray pattern as an additional visual reference in aiding them in determining when the seaplane has accelerated sufficiently to start easing it over onto the step.

After the planing position has been attained, proper control pressures must be used to control the proper pitch attitude/trim angle. Usually, this will be maintained with slight back-elevator pressure. As for the amount of pressure to be held, the beginner will find a very thin line between easing off back-elevator pressure too much or too little. It can perhaps best be described as finding the slippery spot on the float or hull. With too much back-elevator pressure, acceleration rate decreases. Not enough back-elevator pressure or too much forward pressure also decreases acceleration rate. So that fine line or slippery spot is a position between not enough or too much back-elevator pressure.

If the pilot does not want to take off and just wants to continue to taxi on the step, a reduction in power should be initiated at approximately the time the seaplane is eased over onto the step. Power requirements to maintain the proper speed with wind, load, and current action will vary. More power will be required taxiing into the wind or an upcurrent or with a heavy load; however, 65 to 70 percent of maximum power can be used as a starting point.

From either the plowing or on the step position, if power is reduced to idle, the seaplane will decelerate quite rapidly and eventually assume the displacement or idle position. Care must be taken to use proper flight control pressures during the acceleration phase because weight is now being transferred toward the bow and drag is increasing; hence, some aircraft have a nose-over tendency. This is controllable by the proper use of the elevator controls.

Turns On Water

If water rudders have the proper amount of movement, a seaplane can be turned within a radius less than the span of the wing during calm conditions or a light breeze. Water rudders are usually more effective at slow speeds because they are acting in comparatively undisturbed water. At high speeds, the stern of the float churns the adjacent water, causing the water rudder to become less efficient. Because of the high speed, the water's impact on the rudders may tend to force them to swing up or retract.

Particular attention should always be given to the risks involved in making turns in a strong wind or at high speeds. Any seaplane will tend to weathervane into a strong wind if the controls are not positioned to prevent it. In a single-engine seaplane, the rudder should be applied, as necessary, to control the turn while aileron is held into the wind. On multiengine seaplanes, this tendency can be overcome through the use of differential power, including using a higher setting on the upwind side. The rate at which the seaplane turns when it weathervanes is directly proportional to the speed of the crosswind. When taxiing down wind or crosswind, the seaplane will swing into the wind as soon as the flight controls are neutralized or power is reduced.

During a high speed taxiing turn, centrifugal force tends to tip the seaplane toward the outside of the turn. [Figure 16-5]

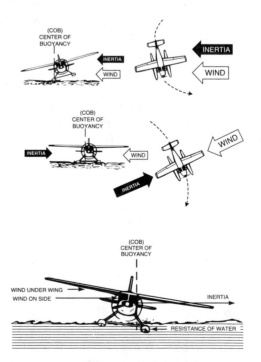

FIGURE 16-5.— Effect of wind.

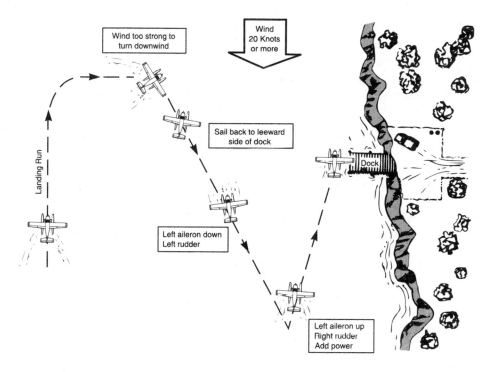

Wind too strong to turn downwind

Wind 20 Knots or more

Sail back to leeward side of dock

Dock

Left aileron down Left rudder

Landing Run

Left aileron up Right rudder Add power

FIGURE 16-6.—Taxiing in strong wind.

When turning from a downwind heading to an upwind heading, the wind force striking the fuselage and the under side of the wing increases the tendency for the seaplane to lean to the outside of the turn. If an abrupt turn is made, the combination of these two forces may be sufficient to tip the seaplane to the extent that the outside wing drags in the water, and may even tip the seaplane onto its back. The further the seaplane tips, the greater the effect of the wind, since more wing area on the windward side is exposed to the wind force. As a general rule when operating with a surface wind, avoid step turns from down wind to up wind.

When making a turn into the wind from a crosswind condition, the air rudder may be neutralized and the seaplane allowed to weathervane into the wind. If taxiing directly down wind, a turn into the wind may be started by deflecting the air rudder in the same direction that the turn is desired. As soon as the seaplane begins to turn, the rudder should be neutralized; if the wind is strong, some opposite rudder may be needed during the turn. The amount of opposite rudder depends upon the rate at which the seaplane turns. The greater the amount of opposite rudder, the slower the rate of turn. Normally, the power should be reduced to idle when the turn begins because with the power on, the left turning tendency of the seaplane may become excessive. Short bursts of power are best for turning in a small radius, but sustained excessive power causes a buildup of speed and a larger turning radius.

The seaplane tends to use its center of buoyancy (COB) as a pivot point wherever it may be. Center of buoyancy moves laterally, as well as forward and aft. Each object in water has a point of COB. In a twin-float installation, the effects of wind, power and flight controls are shared by the two floats and the average COB is free to move significantly.

The COB, or average point of support, moves aft when the seaplane is placed in a noseup or plowing position. This position exposes to the wind a considerable amount of float and fuselage side area forward of the COB. When taxiing crosswind in this position, many seaplanes will show a tendency to turn down wind because of the wind force on the exposed area of the float and the fuselage. For this reason, it is sometimes helpful to place the seaplane in a noseup position when turning down wind, particularly if the wind velocity is high. Under high-wind conditions, the throttle may be used as a turning device by increasing the power to cause a noseup position when turning down wind, and decreasing power to allow the seaplane to weathervane into the wind.

Sailing

Occasions often arise when it is advisable to move the seaplane backward or to one side because wind or water conditions or limited space make it impractical to attempt a turn. [Figures 16-6 and 16-7] In this situation, particularly if there is a significant wind, the seaplane can be sailed into a space which to an inexperienced pilot might seem extremely cramped. Even if the wind is calm and the space is inadequate for making a normal turn, a paddle (which should be part of every seaplane's equipment) may be used to propel the seaplane or to turn the nose in the desired direction.

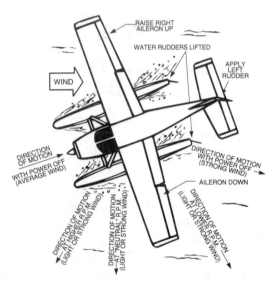

FIGURE 16-7.—Sailing procedures.

In light wind conditions with the engine idling or shut down, the seaplane will naturally weathervane into the wind and then sail in the direction the tail is pointed. With a stronger wind and a slight amount of power, the seaplane will usually sail down wind toward the side in which the nose is pointed. Rudder and aileron can be deflected to create drag on the appropriate side to control the direction of movement. Positioning the controls for the desired direction of motion in light or strong winds is illustrated in Figure 16-6. Lowering the wing flaps and opening the cabin doors will increase the air resistance and add to the effect of the wind; however, the effect of the air rudder may be reduced in this configuration. Since water rudders have little or no effect in controlling direction while sailing, they should be lifted.

With the engine shut down, most seaplanes will sail backward and toward the side to which the nose is pointed, much as a sailboat tacks, regardless of wind

velocity because the hull does not provide as much keel (side area) as floats do in proportion to the size of the seaplane. To sail directly backward in a seaplane having a hull, the controls should be released and the wind allowed to steer the seaplane.

Sailing is an essential part of seaplane operation. Since each type of seaplane has its own minor peculiarities, depending on the design of the floats or hull, it should be practiced until thorough familiarization with that particular type is gained.

During initial seaplane training, sailing should be practiced in large bodies of water, such as lakes or bays, but sufficiently close to a prominent object in order to evaluate performance. Where there are strong tides or a rapidly flowing current, such as in rivers, care must be taken in observing the relative effect of both the wind and the water current. Often the force of the current will be equal to or greater than the force of the wind.

Before taxiing into a confined area, the effect of wind and the current should be considered carefully. Otherwise, the seaplane may be carried into obstructions with resulting damage to the wings, tail surfaces, floats, hull, or other parts of the seaplane. Generally, with a seaplane of average size and power at idle, a water current of 5 knots will more than offset a wind velocity of 25 knots. This means that the seaplane will move against the wind.

BEFORE TAKEOFF

If powerplant checks are not accomplished while on the beach, ramp, or tethered, extra planning and spacing will be required to accomplish them prior to takeoff. When accomplished while taxiing, the pilot must ensure the path will be free of hazards or other watercraft when operating at a higher power setting. Powerplant checks can be accomplished while positioning for takeoff. The remainder of the checks, including takeoff configuration and briefing, should be completed prior to commencing the takeoff.

TAKEOFFS

Unlike landplane operations at airports, seaplane operations are often conducted on water areas that other activities are permitted. The seaplane pilot is constantly confronted with floating objects, some of which are almost submerged and difficult to see. These include swimmers, skiers, and a variety of watercraft. Before beginning the takeoff, it is advisable to taxi along the intended takeoff path to check for the presence of any hazardous objects or obstructions. Thorough scrutiny should be given to the area to assure not only that it is clear, but that it will remain clear throughout the takeoff. Operators of motorboats and sailboats often do not realize the hazard resulting from moving their vessels into the takeoff path of a seaplane.

During a takeoff, hydrodynamic or water drag becomes the major part of the forces resisting acceleration. This resistance reaches its peak at a speed of about 27 knots, and just before the floats or hulls are placed into a planing attitude. [Figure 16-8]

The point of greatest resistance is referred to as the "hump" because the increasing and decreasing effect of water drag causes a hump in the resisting curve. After the hump is passed and the seaplane is traveling on the step, water resistance decreases.

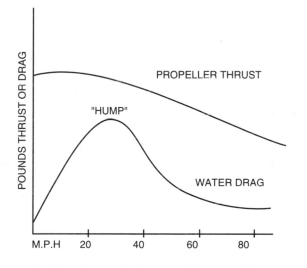

FIGURE 16-8.—Water drag on takeoff.

Several factors greatly increase the water drag or resistance. These primarily include weight or loading of the aircraft and water conditions. With glassy water conditions, air bubbles do not slide under the floats or hull as they do during a choppy water condition. In extreme cases, the drag may exceed the available thrust and prevent the seaplane from becoming airborne. This is particularly true when operating in areas with high density altitudes (high elevation/high temperatures) with lower performance seaplanes. For this reason, the pilot should also practice takeoffs using only partial power to simulate the long takeoff run usually needed when operating at water areas where the density altitude is high and/or the seaplane is heavily loaded.

There are five basic types of seaplane takeoffs. These include normal, glassy water, rough water, confined area, and crosswind (discussed in combination crosswind landings).

A seaplane pilot is required to be competent in these takeoffs to achieve seaplane class rating certification.

Each type of seaplane takeoff may be divided further into four distinct phases, they are the displacement phase, the hump or plowing phase, the planing or on the step phase, and the lift-off phase. During takeoff the water rudder is in the up position.

The first three phases were previously described in the section on taxiing. The lift-off is merely transferring support of the seaplane from the floats or hull to the wings by applying back-elevator pressure. This results in the seaplane lifting off the water and becoming airborne.

Normal Takeoffs

Because the seaplane is not supported on a solid surface and the float or one side of the hull can be forced deeper into the water, right aileron control is usually required to offset the effect of torque when full power is applied during takeoff.

The spray pattern for each particular seaplane should also be considered during takeoff. During acceleration the water is increasingly sprayed upward, outward, and rearward from the bow portion of the floats or hull, and on some seaplanes will be directed into the propeller, eventually causing erosion of the blades. This water spray is greater during the hump phase. The spray can be reduced during takeoff, by first increasing the planing speed about 10 knots, then opening the throttle as rapidly as practical. This method shortens the time that propellers are exposed to the spray. The best technique must be learned through experience with each particular seaplane. Bear in mind that a rough water condition creates more spray than does smooth water.

A glassy water takeoffs in a low-powered seaplane loaded to its maximum authorized weight presents a difficult, but not necessarily dangerous, problem. Under these conditions, the seaplane may assume a plowing or noseup position, but may not unstick or get on the step because of the adhesive action of smooth water. Always plan ahead and consider the possibility of aborting the takeoff. If these conditions are not too excessive, the takeoff can be accomplished using the following procedure.

After the bow has risen to the highest point in the plowing position with full back-elevator pressure, decreasing back-elevator pressure should lower the bow. The bow will drop if the seaplane has attained enough speed to be on the verge of attaining the step position. After a few seconds, the bow will rise again. At the instant it starts to rise, the rebound should be caught by again applying firm back-elevator pressure, and as soon as the bow reaches its maximum height, the entire routine should be repeated. After several repetitions, it will be noted that the bow attains greater height and that the speed is increasing. If the elevator control is then pushed well forward and held there, the seaplane will slowly flatten out on the step and the controls may then be eased back to the neutral position.

Whenever the water is glassy smooth, a takeoff can be made with less difficulty by making the takeoff run across the wakes created by motorboats. If boats are not operating in the area, it is possible to create wakes by taxiing the seaplane in a circle and then taking off across these self-made wakes.

On seaplanes with twin floats, water drag can be reduced by applying sufficient aileron pressure to raise the wing and lift one float out of the water after the seaplane is on the step. By allowing the seaplane to turn slightly in the direction the aileron is being held rather than holding opposite rudder to maintain a straight course, considerable aerodynamic drag can be eliminated, aiding acceleration and lift-off. When using this technique, great care must be exercised to not lift the wing to the extent that the opposite wing strikes the water. Naturally, this would result in serious consequences.

Rough Water Takeoffs

In most cases an experienced seaplane pilot can safely take off in rough water, but a beginner should not attempt to take off if the waves are high. Using the proper procedures during rough water operation lessens the abuse of the floats, as well as the entire seaplane.

Rough water takeoffs require the throttle to be opened to takeoff power just as the bow is rising on a wave. This prevents the bow from digging into the water and helps keep the spray from the propeller. Slightly more back-elevator pressure should be applied to the elevator than on a smooth water takeoff. This raises the bow to a higher angle.

After planing has begun, the seaplane will bounce from one wave crest to the next, raising the nose higher with each bounce, and each successive wave will be struck with increasing severity. To correct this situation

and to prevent a stall, smooth elevator pressures should be used to set up a fairly constant-pitch attitude that will allow the aircraft to skim across each successive wave as speed increases. Remember, in waves, the length of the float is very important. It is important that control pressure be maintained to prevent the bow from being pushed under the water surface or stubbing its toe, which could result in capsizing the seaplane. A takeoff in rough water is accomplished within a short time because if there is sufficient wind to make the water rough, the wind will also be strong enough to produce aerodynamic lift earlier and enable the seaplane to become airborne quickly.

With respect to water roughness, one condition that seaplane pilots should be aware of is the effect of a strong water current flowing against the wind. For example, if the velocity of the current is moving at 10 knots, and the wind is blowing at 15 knots, the relative velocity between the water and the wind is 25 knots. In other words, the waves will be as high as those produced in still water by a wind of 25 knots.

The advisability of canceling a proposed flight because of rough water depends upon the size of the seaplane, wing loading, power loading, and most important, the pilot's ability. As a general rule, if the height of the waves from trough to crest is more than 20 percent of the length of the floats, takeoffs should not be attempted except by the most experienced and expert seaplane pilots.

Confined Area Takeoffs

If operating from a small body of water, an acceptable technique may be to begin the takeoff run while headed down wind, and then turning to complete the takeoff into the wind. This may be done by planing the seaplane while on a downwind heading, then making a step turn into the wind to complete the takeoff. Caution must be exercised when using this technique since wind and centrifugal force will be acting in the same direction and could result in the seaplane tipping over.

Porpoising

Porpoising in a seaplane is much like the antics of a dolphin. It is a rhythmic pitching and heaving while in the water. Porpoising is a dynamic instability of the seaplane and may occur when the seaplane is moving across the water while on the step during takeoff or landing. It occurs when the angle between the float or hull and the water surface exceeds the upper or lower limit of the seaplane's pitch angle. Improper use of the elevator, resulting in attaining too high or too low a pitch (trim angle), sets off a cyclic oscillation which steadily increases in amplitude unless the proper trim angle or pitch attitude is reestablished.

A seaplane will travel smoothly across the water while on the step, so long as the floats or hull remains within a moderately tolerant range of trim angles. If the trim angle is held too low during planing, water pressure in the form of a small crest or wall is built up under the bow or forward part of the floats or hull. As the seaplane's forward speed is increased to a certain point, the bow of the floats or hull will no longer remain behind this crest, and is abruptly forced upward as the seaplane rides over the crest. As the crest passes the step and on to the stern or aft portion of the floats or hull, the bow abruptly drops into a low position. This again builds a crest or wall of water in front of the bow resulting in another oscillation. Each oscillation becomes increasingly severe, and if not corrected will cause the seaplane to nose into the water, resulting in extensive damage or possible capsizing. Porpoising can also cause a premature lift-off with an extremely high angle of attack, resulting in a stall or being in the area of reverse command and unable to climb over obstructions.

Porpoising will occur during the takeoff run if the trim angle is not properly controlled with proper elevator pressure just after passing through the hump speed, or when the highest trim angle before the planing attitude is attained—if up elevator is held too long and the angle reaches the upper limits. On the other hand, if the seaplane is nosed down too sharply, the lower trim range can be entered and will also result in porpoising. Usually, porpoising does not start until a degree or two after the seaplane has passed into the critical trim angle range, and does not cease until a degree or two after the seaplane has passed out of the critical range.

If porpoising does occur, it can be stopped by applying timely back-elevator pressure on the elevator control to prevent the bow of the floats or hull from digging into the water. The back-elevator pressure must be applied and maintained until porpoising is damped. If porpoising is not damped by the time the second oscillation occurs, it is recommended that the power be reduced to idle and elevator control held firmly back so the seaplane will settle into the water with no further instability.

The correct trim angle for takeoff, planing, and landing applicable to each type of seaplane must be learned by the pilot and practiced until there is no doubt as to the proper angles for the various maneuvers.

LANDINGS

In comparison, the land surfaces of all airports are of firm, static matter, whereas the surface of water is changing continually as a fluid. Floating obstacles and various activities frequently present on the water surface may present serious hazards during seaplane landings. For these reasons, it is advisable to circle the area of intended landing and examine it thoroughly for obstructions, such as buoys or floating debris, and to note the direction of movement of any boats that may be operating at the intended landing site.

Most established seaplane bases are equipped with a wind sock to indicate wind direction, but if one is not available the wind can still be determined prior to landing. The following are a few of the methods used to determine the wind direction.

If there are not strong tides or water currents, boats lying at anchor will weathervane and automatically point into the wind. It is also true that sea gulls and other water fowl usually land facing the wind. Smoke, flags, and the set of sails on sailboats also provide the pilot with a fair approximation of wind direction. If there is an appreciable wind velocity, streaks parallel to the wind are formed on the water. During strong winds, these streaks form distinct white lines. However, wind direction cannot always be determined from these streaks alone. If there are white caps or foam on top of the waves, the foam appears to move into the wind. This illusion is caused by the waves moving under the foam.

In seaplanes equipped with retractable landing gear (amphibians), it is extremely important to make certain that the wheels are in the retracted position when landing on water. Wherever possible, a visual check of the wheels themselves is recommended, in addition to checking the landing gear position indicating devices. A wheels-down landing on water is almost certain to capsize the seaplane, and is far more serious than landing the seaplane wheels-up on land. The water rudder should also be in the retracted position during landings.

The landing approach procedure in a seaplane is very similar to that of a landplane and is governed to a large extent by pilot preference, wind, and water conditions.

Under normal conditions a seaplane can be landed either power-off or power-on. Power-on landings are recommended in most cases, because this technique gives the pilot more positive control of the seaplane and provides a means for correcting errors in judgment during the approach and landing. So that the slowest possible airspeed can be maintained, the power-on landing should be accomplished with maximum flaps extended. The seaplane should be trimmed to the manufacturer's recommended approach speed, and the approach made similar to that of a landplane.

Touchdown on the water should be made in a pitch attitude that is correct for taxiing on the step, or perhaps a slightly higher attitude. [Figure 16-9] This attitude will result in the floats or hull first contacting the water at a point aft of the step. Once water contact is made, the throttle should be closed and back-elevator pressure gradually applied. The application of back-elevator pressure reduces the tendency for the seaplane to nosedown and the bows to dig in due to increased drag of the floats as they contact the water. The faster the speed a seaplane is landed, the more water drag is encountered, resulting in a greater nosedown attitude after touchdown. If the seaplane has a tendency to nosedown excessively with full flaps extended, it is recommended that subsequent approaches and landings be made with less flaps. Remember, the objective is to land the seaplane at the slowest possible speed in a slightly noseup attitude.

FIGURE 16-9.—Touchdown attitude.

After contacting the water, gradually increase back-elevator pressure. It may be desirable at times to remain on the step after touchdown. To do so, merely add sufficient power and maintain the planing attitude immediately after touchdown.

Flat, calm, glassy water is perhaps the most deceptive condition that a seaplane pilot will experience. The calmness of the water has a psychological effect in that it tends to overly relax the pilot when there should be special alertness. This surface condition is frequently the most dangerous for seaplane operation.

The mirrorlike appearance of smooth water looks the most inviting and easy to land on, but as many pilots have suddenly learned, adequate depth perception may be lacking. Even experienced pilots misjudge height above the water, making timely roundouts difficult. This results in either flying bow first into the water or stalling the seaplane at too great a height above the water. When the water is crystal clear and glassy, pilots often attempt to judge height by using the bottom of the lake as a reference, rather than the water surface.

An accurately set altimeter may be used as an aid in determining the height above the glassy water. A more effective means is to make the approach and landing near the shoreline so it can be used as a reference for judging height above the water. Another method is to cross the shoreline on final approach at the lowest possible safe altitude so that a height reference is maintained within a few feet of the water surface.

Glassy water landings should always be made power-on, and the need for this type of landing should be recognized in ample time to set up the proper final approach.

During the final approach, the seaplane should be flown at the best nose-high attitude, using flaps as required or as recommended by the manufacturer. A power setting and pitch attitude should be established that would result in a rate of descent not to exceed 150 feet per minute (FPM) and at airspeed approximately 10 knots above stall speed. With a constant-power setting and a constant-pitch attitude, the airspeed will stabilize and remain so if no changes are made. The power or pitch should be changed only if the airspeed or rate of descent deviates from that desired. Throughout the approach the seaplane performance should be closely monitored by cross-checking the instruments until contact is made with the water.

Upon touchdown, back-elevator pressure should be applied, as necessary, to maintain the same pitch attitude. Throttle should be reduced or closed only after the pilot is sure that the aircraft is firmly on the water. Several indications should be used. A slight deceleration force will be felt. A slight downward pitching moment will be seen. The sound of water spray striking the floats, hull, or other parts of the aircraft will be heard.

All three cues should be used because accidents have resulted from reducing the power rapidly after initially touching the water. To the pilot's surprise a skip had taken place and it was found when the power was cut, the aircraft was 10 to 15 feet in the air and not on the water, resulting in a stall and substantial damage.

Maintaining a noseup, wings-level attitude, at the correct speed and a small rate of descent, are imperative for a successful glassy water landing. All aspects of this approach and landing should be considered prior to its execution. This type of approach and landing will usually consume considerable landing distance. Landing near unfamiliar shorelines increases the possibility of encountering submerged objects and debris.

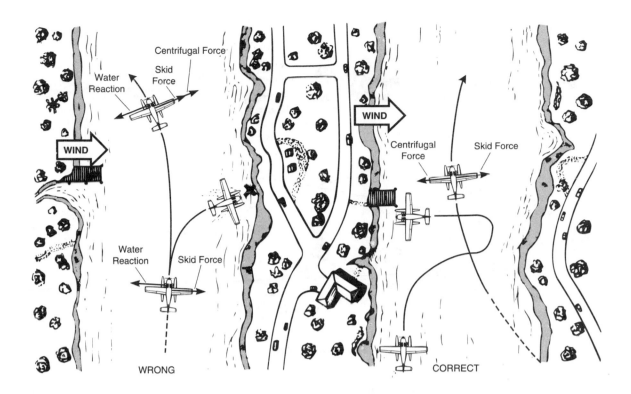

FIGURE 16-10.—Crosswind landing technique.

It is impractical to describe an ideal rough water procedure because of the varying conditions of the surface. In most instances, the approach is made the same as for any other water landing. It may be better to level off just above the water surface and increase the power sufficiently to maintain a rather flat attitude until conditions appear to be more acceptable, and then reduce the power to touchdown. If severe bounces occur, power should be increased and a search made for a more ideal landing spot.

It is recommended that night water landings in seaplanes be avoided, since they can be extremely dangerous due to the difficulty or almost impossibility of seeing objects in the water. If it becomes necessary to land at night in a seaplane, serious consideration should be given to landing at a lighted airport. An emergency landing can be made on land in seaplanes with little or no damage to the floats or hull. Touchdown should be made with the keel of the floats or hull as nearly parallel to the surface as possible. After touchdown, full back-elevator pressure must be applied and additional power applied to lessen the rapid deceleration and noseover tendency. Do not worry about getting stopped with additional power after touchdown. It will stop! The power is applied only for increasing elevator effectiveness.

Crosswind Techniques

Because of restricted or limited areas of operation, it is not always possible to take off or land the seaplane directly into the wind. Such restricted areas may be canals or narrow rivers; therefore, skill must be acquired in crosswind techniques to enhance the safety of seaplane operation.

The forces developed by crosswinds during takeoffs or landings on water are almost the same as those developed during similar operations on land. Directional control is more difficult because of the more yielding properties of water, less surface friction, and lack of nosewheel, tailwheel, or brakes. Though water surface is more yielding than solid land, a seaplane does not have shock absorbing capability, so all the shock is absorbed by the hull or floats and transmitted to the aircraft structure.

As shown in Figure 16-10, a crosswind tends to push the seaplane sideways. The drifting force, acting through the seaplane's CG, is opposed by the water reacting on the area of the floats or hull in contact with the water. This results in a tendency to weathervane into the wind. Once this weathervaning has started, the turn continues and is further aggravated by the addition of inertia (centrifugal force) acting outward from the

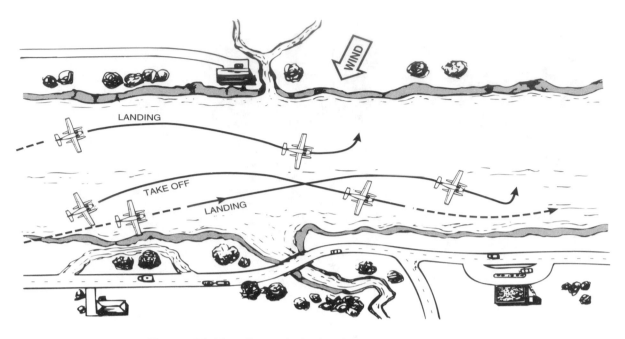

FIGURE 16-11.—Crosswind takeoff and landing technique.

turn, which again is opposed by the water reaction on the floats or hull. If strong enough, the combination of the wind and inertia may tip the seaplane to the point where the downwind float will submerge and subsequently the wingtip may strike the water and capsize the seaplane. This is known as a waterloop, which is similar to a ground loop on land.

Because of the lack of clear reference lines for directional guidance, such as are found on airport runways, it is difficult to quickly detect sidedrift on water. Early detection of sidedrift is not really essential because the seaplane takeoff and landing can be made without maintaining a straight line while in contact with the water. A turn should be made toward the downwind side after landing. This will allow the seaplane to dissipate its forward speed prior to its weathervaning into the wind. By doing this, inertia while weathervaning will be kept to a minimum and better aircraft control will result with less turnover tendency.

One technique sometimes used to compensate for crosswinds during water operations is the same as that used on land—by lowering the upwind wing while holding a straight course with rudder. This creates a slip into the wind to offset the drifting tendency. The upwind wing is held in the lowered position throughout the touchdown and until completion of the landing.

Another technique used to compensate for crosswinds is the downwind arc method. Using this method, the pilot creates a sideward force (inertia) that will offset the crosswind force. This is accomplished by steering the seaplane in a downwind arc. The pilot merely plans an arced path and follows this arc to produce sufficient inertia so that the seaplane will lean outward against the wind force. During the run, the pilot can adjust the rate of turn by varying rudder pressure, thereby increasing or decreasing the centrifugal force to compensate for a changing wind force.

It is quite simple to plan sufficient curvature of the takeoff path to cancel out strong crosswinds, even on very narrow rivers. The takeoff is started at the lee side of the river with the seaplane heading slightly into the wind. The takeoff path is then gradually made in an arc away from the wind and the lift-off is accomplished on the downwind edge of the river. This pattern also allows for more climb-out space into the wind. [Figure 16-11]

It should be noted that the greatest degree of the downwind arc is during the time the seaplane is traveling at slower speeds during a takeoff or landing. At faster speeds, the crosswind effect lessens considerably, and at very slow speeds the seaplane can weathervane into the wind with no ill effect.

Unless the current is extremely swift, crosswind or calm wind takeoffs and landings in rivers or tidal flows should be made in the same direction as the current. This reduces the water forces on the floats or hull of the seaplane.

Again, experience will play an important part in successful seaplane operation during crosswinds. It is essential that all seaplane pilots have thorough knowledge and skill in these maneuvers.

Skipping

Skipping is a form of instability that may occur when landing with excessive speed at a noseup trim angle. This noseup attitude places the seaplane at the upper trim limit of stability, and causes the seaplane to enter a cyclic oscillation when touching the water, resulting in the seaplane skipping across the surface. This action may be compared to skipping flat stones across the water.

Skipping can also occur by crossing a boat wake while fast taxiing on the step or during a takeoff. Sometimes the new seaplane pilot will confuse a skip with a porpoise. Pilot's body feelings can quickly determine whether a skip or porpoise has been encountered. A skip will give the body vertical "G" forces similar to bouncing a landplane. The porpoise is a rocking chair type forward and aft motion feeling.

Correction for skipping is made by first increasing back pressure on the elevator control and adding sufficient power to prevent the floats from contacting the water. Then pressure on the elevator is adjusted to attain the proper trim angle, and the power gradually reduced to allow the seaplane to settle gently onto the water.

Skipping will not continue increasing its oscillations, as in porpoising, because of the lack of forward thrust with reduced power.

ANCHORING, MOORING, DOCKING, AND BEACHING

Anchoring the seaplane is the easiest method of securing it on the water surface after a flight. The area selected should be out of the way of moving vessels, and in water deep enough to ensure that the seaplane will not be left high and dry during low tide. The length of the anchor line should be approximately seven times the depth of the water. After dropping anchor with the seaplane headed into the wind, allow the seaplane to drift backward so the anchor is set. To determine that the anchor is holding the seaplane at the desired location, select two fixed objects nearby or on shore that are lined up, and check to assure that these objects remain aligned. If they do not, it means that the seaplane is drifting and dragging the anchor on the bottom.

The effects of a wind shift must be considered, and sufficient room should be allowed so the seaplane can swing around without striking other anchored vessels or nearby obstacles.

If anchoring the seaplane overnight or for longer periods of time, an additional, heavier anchor should be used. This anchor should be dropped about twice as far ahead as the first anchor and about 30° to one side of the seaplane.

Mooring a seaplane eliminates the problem of the anchor dragging. A permanent mooring installation consists of a firmly implanted anchor or heavy weight connected by a wire or chain to a floating buoy.

A mooring should be approached at a very low speed and straight into the wind. To avoid the possibility of overrunning the mooring, the engine should be shut down early and the seaplane allowed to coast to the mooring. The engine can always be started again if needed for better positioning. Never straddle the buoy with a twin-float installation. Always approach the buoy on the outside of the float to avoid damage to the propeller and underside of the fuselage. It is recommended that initial contact with the mooring be made with a boathook or a person standing on the deck of one float.

If a person is on the float, the seaplane should be taxied right or left of the mooring so that the float the person is standing on is brought directly alongside the buoy. A short line, which has one end already secured to a strut, can then be secured to the mooring.

It is very important to exercise extreme caution whenever a person is assisting in securing the seaplane. Numerous accidents have been caused by the helper being struck by the propeller.

The procedure for docking is essentially the same as used for mooring. Properly planning the approach to the dock under existing conditions, and skill in handling the seaplane in congested areas are essential to successful docking. Bear in mind that a seaplane is fragile and striking an obstruction could result in extensive damage to the seaplane.

Beaching the seaplane is easy. Success in beaching depends primarily upon the type and firmness of the shoreline. Inspect the beach before using it. If this is impossible, the approach to the beach should be made at an oblique angle so that the seaplane can be turned out into deeper water in the event the beach is not satisfactory. The hardest packed sand is usually found near the water's edge and becomes softer further from the water's edge where it is dry. Mud bottoms are usually not desirable for beaching.

Ground Training Syllabus

1. **Aeronautical Decision Making (ADM)**

2. **Seaplane Overview**

3. **Safety/Emergency Equipment**

   a. Float/Pontoon Servicing/Repairing
   b. Seat Belts and Shoulder Harness
   c. Emergency Exits
   d. Fire Extinguishers
   e. Survival Gear
   f. Water Navigation/Right-of-Way Rules
   g. Other

4. **Airplane Flight Manual (AFM) and/or Pilot's Operating Handbook (POH)**

   a. General Information
   b. Airplane Systems

      (1) Electrical
      (2) Hydraulic
      (3) Brake
      (4) Fuel and Oil
      (5) Oxygen
      (6) Other

   c. Engine

      (1) Turbocharger
      (2) Propeller Systems

   d. Limitations
   e. Normal/Abnormal Procedures
   f. Emergency Procedures
   g. Weight and Balance

   h. Performance Data (takeoff, cruise, and landing)
   i. Supplements

5. **Preflight Inspection**

6. **Cockpit Familiarization**

   a. Instruments
   b. Controls
   c. Avionics
   d. Lighting
   e. Checklists

7. **Servicing**

8. **Specific Flight Characteristics Peculiar to the Seaplane**

9. **Other**

Flight Training Syllabus

1. **Preflight Inspection**

2. **Water Operations**

    a. Engine Start
    b. Taxiing
    c. Turns
    d. Sailing
    e. Before Takeoff Checks

3. **Takeoffs**

    a. Rejected
    b. Normal
    c. Crosswind
    d. Glassy Water
    e. Rough Water
    f. Maximum Performance

4. **Landings**

    a. Normal
    b. Crosswind
    c. Glassy Water
    d. Rough Water
    e. Maximum Performance
    f. Go-Around
    g. Landing Area Reconnaissance

5. **Flight Maneuvers**

    a. Slow Flight
    b. Power-off Stalls (Approach and Landing)
    c. Power-on Stalls (Takeoff and Departure)
    d. Steep Turns
    e. Control by Reference to Instruments
    f. Other

6. **Navigation**

    a. VHF
    b. LF
    c. GPS
    d. LORAN

7. **Normal/Abnormal Procedures**

    a. Hydraulic System Failures/Malfunctions
    b. Electrical System Failure/Malfunctions
    c. Landing Gear System Failure/ Malfunctions
    d. Flap System Failure/Malfunctions
    e. Partial Flooded Float

8. **Emergency Procedures**

    a. Power Failure
    b. Other

9. **Securing Seaplane**

    a. Anchoring
    b. Mooring
    c. Docking

10. **Postflight Procedures**

11. **Debriefing and Documentation**

CHAPTER 17

TRANSITION TO SKIPLANES

INTRODUCTION

This chapter introduces pilots to the procedures required in the operation of skiplanes. Since most skiplane operations and training are conducted in single-engine airplanes with a tailwheel/conventional gear configuration, this information will be based on operating skiplanes of this type.

To assist pilots in transitioning to skiplanes, a ground and flight training syllabus is included at the end of this chapter for reference by flight instructors or other pilots conducting transition or recurrent skiplane training.

TERMS AND DEFINITIONS

• **Skis**—A device used for traveling over snow or ice. A long, wide surface is desirable for a fresh fall of light, powdery snow. A narrow sharp blade is best for smooth ice. What is needed for airplanes, is a compromise that works well under most conditions. Most airplane skis are made from aluminum or wood, with the undersides covered in a polyethylene, which helps prevent sticking to the surface.

Ski Types

• **Wheel Replacement**—wheels are removed and ski boards are substituted. [Figure 17-1]
• **Clamp On**—skis that attach to the tires and benefit from the additional shock absorbing qualities of the tires.
• **Roll On or Full Board**—similar to the clamp on type except the tires are bypassed and do not carry side or torque loads. Only the tire cushioning effect is retained with this installation. These plain ski types provide for snow only operations.

• **Retractable Ski**—can be extended into place for snow operations or retracted for non-snow operations. This is accomplished by either a hydraulic pump or crank.
• **Combination (Penetration) Ski**—the wheel extending down partially below the ski. This also allows the skiplane to be operated from both snow and non-snow surfaces. This type of ski gives poor ground clearance on non-snow surfaces and causes extra drag when on snow. [Figure 17-2]

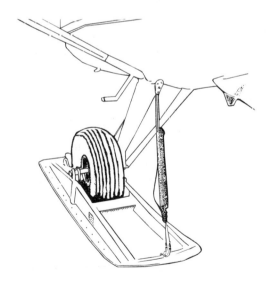

FIGURE 17-2.—Combination ski.

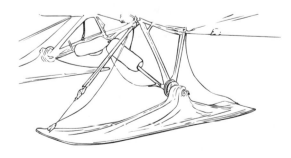

FIGURE 17-1.—Plain ski.

Types of Snow

- **Powder Snow**—dry snow in which the water content and ambient temperature are low.
- **Wet Snow**—contains high moisture and is of low quality and is associated with warmer temperatures near the freezing point.
- **Granular Snow**—wet snow that has had a temperature drop causing the snow to ball up.

Types of Ice

- **Glaze Ice**—snow that has been packed down and frozen to a solid ice pack, or frozen snow.
- **Glare Ice**—a smooth sheet of ice that is exceedingly slippery with no deformities, cracks, or other irregularities in the surface. This ice lacks any kind of traction, with a near zero coefficient of friction.
- **Clear Ice**—ice that forms smoothly over a surface with a transparent appearance.

Surface Environments

- **Glaciers**—sloping snow or ice packs.
- **Frozen Lakes**—frozen bodies of water with snow cover or just ice covered lakes.
- **Tundra**—a large area of grass clumps supporting snow cover.

GENERAL

A skiplane configuration affects the overall operation and performance of an airplane in several different ways. It will affect ground handling, takeoff, landing, and flight operations. Some manufacturers provide recommended procedures and performance data in the Airplane Flight Manual (AFM) and/or Pilot's Operating Handbook (POH).

Although Title 14 of the Code of Federal Regulations (14 CFR) part 61 does not require specific pilot training and authorization to operate skiplanes, it is important for pilots to train with a qualified skiplane flight instructor.

Since most skiplane pilots will be operating in a wide variety of conditions, such as landing on frozen or snow-covered lakes, and sloping glaciers, with varying quality of snow, it is important to know how performance will be affected. Pilots should use the performance data provided by the manufacturer.

Preflight

Before departing on any trip, it is important to properly preflight. Even if only flying in the local area, good preflight planning enhances the safety of the flight.

A good preflight should include a review of the proposed and possible alternate routes; terrain; local, en route, and destination weather; fuel requirements; destination facilities; weight and balance; and takeoff and landing distance requirements.

A complete weather briefing and a flight plan filed with appropriate remarks should be completed for each leg. For local flights, always advise someone at home of the area of operation and the expected time of return if a flight plan is not filed.

Include good Aeronautical Decision Making (ADM) procedures, such as running a personal minimums checklist, and think PAVE (Pilot, Aircraft, Environment, and External Pressures), during the preflight phase.

Equipment

Before a skiplane pilot departs on a flight, whether it is a local or cross-country flight, it is imperative that survival equipment that is appropriate for the conditions is carried on board. Some countries and states (such as Alaska) have laws that require all certain survival equipment to be on board. Even for local flights, this equipment is required. Every occupant should be dressed for a long walk, which should include adequate boots or rubber bottom shoes and an arctic parka.

If a pilot is forced to land at an unplanned destination, or if the engine will not restart after landing at a remote location, the survival gear and clothing should keep the pilot and passengers alive until help arrives.

There are other items that should be on board in addition to basic survival equipment. If a pilot is planning for an overnight stay away from an airport, or the skiplane is routinely parked outside, wing covers and non-sticking fuselage covers would be desirable. In the event of precipitation, these covers will prevent the buildup of frost and snow and simplify the preflight and departure.

When temperatures are going to be cold (below 0° F), a pilot may need to carry an engine cover and catalytic heater to prewarm the engine compartment. Oil can also be drained into a bucket and kept indoors. It is also practical to check the destination for hangar space and preheating equipment.

The wearing of sunglasses is highly recommended, even on cloudy days. Pilots can be blinded by the brightness of the snow, and the glare can destroy a pilot's depth perception.

GROUND OPERATIONS

It is important to always conduct a thorough preflight. If a skiplane has been sitting outside overnight or longer, the most important preflight issues are to insure that the skiplane is ice/frost free and that the skis are not frozen to the ground. Often times while sitting on the ground, precipitation may fall and cover the aircraft. Temperatures on the ground may be slightly colder than in the air above the surface. Even though the precipitation is unfrozen, the aircraft can be below freezing and may have a coating of clear ice and be frozen to the ground. Now, the airplane must be completely de-iced.

When parked on ice or snow, the skis may be difficult to free. Normally, during the day the temperatures may approach the melting point and this would easily free them. But as night approaches, temperatures may drop well below freezing and again bind the skis to the surface. Sometimes the friction heat generated during taxi, or after the last landing, causes the ski bottoms to melt the snow underneath. Then when the temperature lowers again, they become frozen to the surface.

If the frozen surface will support the wheels, and the skis are the retractable type, the pilot can place the skis in the UP position. Next, the pilot should dig the snow out from around the skis and leave it in that condition until the following morning. This helps prevent the skis from freezing to the surface. Should the surface not be substantial enough to support the wheels, use a board or other strong, flat material to support the wheels.

When parking in remote areas, sometimes a pilot has to be creative. For example, when in the back woods, burlap bags or fir, pine, or spruce boughs, even saplings, laid perpendicular to the ski bottoms, can be used to make a parking bed. A pilot may even consider applying a light coat of clean motor oil to the polypropylene ski surface before departing and landing on a remote snow-covered surface.

During the preflight, it is important to check the main skis for proper tension on the limiting cables, springs, and bungies. Ensure that all the clamping bolts, cotter keys or diaper pins are in place. If equipped with retractable skis, check for adequate fluid and leaks. Ensure all hardware on the skis are in place and secure. Also, check the tailwheel spring and tail ski for security, cracks, and signs of failure. Without a tail ski, the entire tailwheel and rudder assembly can be easily damaged.

During fuel sump checks, sometimes moisture can freeze a drain valve open. This may cause the remaining fuel to drain out and the drain valve could freeze shut. If there is ice inside the fuel tank, it can break loose and block the outlet port and cause engine fuel starvation. If the manufacturer recommends the use of anti-icing additives for the fuel system during cold weather operations, strict adherence to ratio and mixing instructions is required.

Tire pressure should be checked frequently, particularly when using clamp-on, roll-on, or combination skis. This is especially important if moving a skiplane from a warm hangar to cold temperatures outdoors.

Wing and tail surfaces must be checked to ensure they are frost free. Any frost, ice, and snow destroys lift and also can cause aileron or elevator flutter. Flutter can cause serious control and/or structural problems.

Preheating

For most skiplane operations, it will be necessary to adequately preheat the aircraft before startup and departure. This will include preheating the engine, battery, and the cockpit instruments. Sometimes engine oil may require heating separately.

Check the manufacturer's recommendation on engines when ambient temperatures are below freezing. The engine compartment and battery temperatures should also be heated to at least 30 °F, before attempting a battery start.

Batteries require special consideration. In cold climates a strong, fully charged battery is needed. With just a little cold soaking, the engine may require three times the usual amperage to start the engine.

Another consideration is the electrolyte freezing point. A newly charged battery is almost freeze proof since the electrolyte's specific gravity is at a proper level. Conversely, with a weak battery the specific gravity will have dropped enough to cause the battery to freeze at temperatures below freezing. If a new battery is depleted by an unsuccessful start, it may freeze. Later, when the engine is started, and the battery is partially frozen and receiving a charge, it could explode.

Engine Start

An engine start should not be attempted until the engine and/or ambient temperatures are in the proper range, or preheating has been completed. Engine starting using recommended multi-viscosity oils may be possible at lower ambient temperatures. After start, a proper warmup should be completed prior to a runup and high-power settings.

Runup

If a skiplane is parked in heavily crusted snow or glaze ice, with skis still frozen, an engine start and runup may be done in the parking area. This procedure should be considered only if the area behind the skiplane is clear. A runup in place will be possible with the skis still frozen. If during the runup, one ski becomes unstuck, the runup should be aborted.

If skis are still stuck after the runup, it may take outside assistance to rock the skiplane and free the skis, one at a time. When outside assistance is not available, a solo pilot can sometimes add power while operating the elevators and rudder to free the skis.

If parked on glare ice, the pilot may want to leave the skiplane tied down for start and runup. Otherwise chocks, sandbags, or even rocks can be placed under the nose of each ski prior to runup.

If tiedowns or ski blocking is not available, the runup can be accomplished while taxiing when clear of obstacles or other hazards.

Taxiing

Directional control comes from tail ski steering and from prop wash across the rudder. Taxiing and turning a skiplane normally requires more maneuvering room and space to turn than a non-ski plane. Frequently, the use of power and forward elevator control is often helpful. The goal is to lighten the tail to help the turn and not put the skiplane on its nose.

Taxiing in strong crosswinds can be difficult. Skiplanes tend to weathervane into the wind. Taxiing in a skid or weathervaned into the wind is normal in some crosswind operations. Drifting sideways in turns is also normal. Preplan the taxi track so as to remain in the clear to miss drifts, ridges, or other obstructions.

When taxiing in crosswinds on glare ice, if possible, it is advisable to have a wing walker at each wingtip to help with turns and line up for takeoff.

As a general rule, power settings and taxi speeds should be kept as slow as possible on ice, or crusted snow. On loose or powder snow, a pilot should add enough power to keep moving and even step taxi. This is a float plane term and means just below takeoff speed. Otherwise, the skiplane can sink down into the soft or powder snow and may stop moving.

At some snow-covered airports, airport managers or FBOs will spray red or purple dye onto taxiways and snow banks to visually aid pilots. They may even implant pine boughs at regular intervals in the snow to help define taxiways and runways, and mark hazardous areas. These helpful aids simplify ground operations and improve safety.

Takeoffs

Since skiplanes operate from varied types of surfaces, it is important to remember that many takeoff areas can generate unforeseen hazards; therefore, it is important to always plan for the unexpected.

If the takeoff surface condition is unknown, it is advisable to walk or taxi the full length of the takeoff area and back to check the surface for hazards and help pack the snow. It is better to discover any irregularities before attempting a takeoff than to experience unknown hazards at high speeds during takeoff.

Most takeoff distances are greater on snow than on cleared runways and other hard surfaces. On wet or powder snow, a pilot may need two or three times the normal distance. Beware of frost or crusted snow accumulation on skis. If contamination has accumulated, it must be cleaned off prior to takeoff. Such contamination increases the drag and weight, which results in a greater takeoff distance.

Select a takeoff direction that will provide an adequate distance to lift-off and clear any obstructions. Use headwinds or a downhill slope for takeoff when possible to ensure best performance. When turning into headwinds keep moving and turning in a wide arc. A quick turn can result in a ground loop.

Plan and configure for a soft-field takeoff. Soft-field procedures are recommended because the glare of snow or ice may hide possible hazards. Undetected drifts or soft sticky spots can cause sudden deceleration and even a possible nose over.

When lining up to depart, have the skiplane configured properly and keep moving. Do not stop before adding takeoff power because the skiplane may settle into soft snow and limit acceleration. If this happens, it may be necessary to taxi the takeoff path again to pack the snow.

Crosswind takeoffs require the standard procedures and techniques. Beware that the skiplane may be sliding in a crab during takeoff acceleration. On glaze ice an increase in lateral drift may be seen on takeoff.

Off airport landing sites

There are a number of factors that must be considered when operating from glaciers. There can be many hidden hazards.

The first consideration is the condition of the snow and the quality of the pack. If planning to land on a new area, always drag the glacier downhill to see if it will support the airplane. Fly with the skis on the surface, just touching the snow, as slowly as possible above a stall speed. This will assist in determining the snow condition. If unsure of the pack, and it is not on a ridge or the crest of an ice fall, look for a gentle slope and land up the slope or hill. This situation will give the requirement of a headwind on a downslope takeoff.

If the slope angle of the landing area is very steep, always view the area for the possibility of an avalanche. This is where a small valley forms on a glacier and the snow meets below the apex. This will usually give the best pack and sturdiest conditions for landing up the valley. Avoid landing near the bottom of the valley because ice falls may exist and provide rough and unusable terrain.

Glaciers are very deceptive. It is advisable to train with an experienced glacier pilot and become comfortable before departing alone. Just a few clouds overhead can totally change the picture the pilot sees of the area of intended landing so extreme caution must be used.

Snow-covered frozen lakes can provide a number of obstacles. Wind drifts, formed by the wind, can freeze moisture into solid ridges on the lake. These ridges can be so rough that they can damage or destroy the landing gear and skiplane. The best plan is to land parallel to ridge rows, even if there is a slight crosswind. Another option is to find a lee area (protected area), where wind drifts do not reside and land in this area.

Other problems that may be encountered are beaver dams, houses, or other hidden obstructions on the lake that have been covered with snow and have become invisible to the pilot, especially in flat lighting situations. A condition known as "overflow" which can be found on frozen lakes with or without snow cover will present problems on landing and takeoffs. The overflow is water, in a liquid state, that is cooled below its freezing point.

The moment a ski or any other part of the aircraft touches this super cooled water, it freezes solid. As the water freezes, it will provide a rapid deceleration. Thin ice also creates a problem because it is not always obvious. It will be thick enough to support a layer of snow or other material, but not an aircraft.

Lakes that are frozen without snow cover are better for observing obstacles. Major obstacles encountered are spider holes. These are ports formed by escaping air from under the ice, forming a weak hole or bubble at the surface. These may or may not support the plane. Pilots should avoid running over these if at all possible. Clear ice, under certain conditions, can be extremely slick and will not allow directional control once the aerodynamic controls become ineffective due to the loss of airflow. This becomes critical in crosswind landing conditions.

Tundra is probably the least desirable surface since most of the above hazards can exist. Tundra is composed, typically, of small clumps of grass that can support snow and make ridge lines invisible. They also hide obstacles and cover holes that may be too weak to support skiplanes. Unless a tundra area is well known, avoiding it should be considered.

Lighting

There are three operational lighting conditions that skiplane pilots will have to deal with routinely. They are flat lighting, white out, and nighttime. The implications of nighttime are obvious, and in the interest of safety, night operations from unlighted air strips are not recommended.

Flat lighting is an overcast or broken sky condition with intermittent sunlight, hills, valleys, and snow mounds, taking on varying shades of white, and may appear taller, shorter, or wider than they really are. This indirect lighting alters a pilot's depth perception. When this occurs pilots may not recognize that their depth perception is impaired, and this can cause serious consequences when operating skiplanes near hilly terrain. When a condition of "flat lighting" is encountered, flight operations should be avoided or discontinued, especially at an unfamiliar strip.

White out can occur when flying in a valley and both walls are obscured by snow or fog. Clear sky conditions can exist, but references can not be established. Reference to attitude gyro instruments will help when this condition is encountered.

Takeoffs and landings should not be attempted under flat lighting or whiteout conditions.

Landings

Landing a skiplane is easy compared to landing with wheels; however, for off-airport landings, there are a few extra precautions that have to be taken. A pilot should be careful in choosing a landing site. Once the landing is completed, an evaluation should be done for a safe departure.

Upon arriving at a prospective landing site, a pass(es) should be made over the landing site to determine landing direction, and to determine if a safe approach and landing can be completed. A trial landing should be accomplished to determine the best approach, subsequent departure, and quality of the surface.

To perform the trial landing, the pilot should plan and configure for a soft-field landing with a stable approach. Then perform a gentle soft-field touchdown, controlled with power, while remaining at near takeoff speed for approximately 600 to 800 feet, and initiating a go-around.

A trial landing is very helpful in determining the quality of the snow surface and looking for possible hazards. The pilot should be prepared to go around at anytime the landing does not appear normal or a hazard is detected.

When landing on a level surface, and the wind can be determined, the landing should be made into the wind. If landing on a slope, an uphill landing is recommended.

If landing on solid ice without the benefit of snow, it is better to land with the wheels extended through the skis to improve the ground handling characteristic. Solid or clear ice surfaces will require a greater landing distance and more area to maneuver when slowing down.

Under bright sun conditions and without brush or trees for contrast, the glare may restrict a pilot's vision and make it difficult to identify snow drifts and hazards. Depth perception can also be impaired with glare conditions; therefore, it is recommended that pilots plan a soft-field landing when landing off airports.

After touchdown on soft snow, the pilot should anticipate using additional power to keep the skiplane moving while taxiing to a suitable parking area and to turn the skiplane around. The pilot should taxi slowly after landing to allow the skis to cool down prior to stopping. Warm skis will eventually cool and could possibly freeze to the surface while parked.

Plan for extra distance to stop when landing on ice, for there is no braking action. Also, allow for extra room for turns.

Parking/Postflight

Skiplanes do not have any parking brakes and will slide on inclines or sloping surfaces. In this event, it is most desirable to park perpendicular to the incline. Be prepared to block or chock the skis to prevent movement.

If the skiplane is to remain parked for a considerable amount of time, support the skis away from the snow to prevent them from sticking or freezing. If available, place tree boughs or other materials under the skis to help prevent them from freezing to the surface.

When parking on a hill, pilots should consider the proper position of the fuel selector valve. Typically, the uphill tank should be selected to prevent fuel from transferring to the lower wing and subsequently venting overboard.

Limitations and Restrictions

The AFM/POH skiplane supplement may provide limitations including limiting airspeeds for operation with skis inflight and for other wheel/ski configurations. These speeds may be different than a normal landing gear configuration, depending on the type of ski, tension of the springs, and/or bungies holding the nose of the skis up.

EMERGENCY OPERATIONS

When operating a skiplane, it is important to carry an adequate survival kit. A good rule of thumb is to carry what is needed to be comfortable. An excellent resource for putting a survival kit together is the Alaska Supplement. It is also important to note the summer and winter differences.

Ski Tuck

There is a possibility when skis are not rigged properly, or when a pilot exceeds recommended airspeeds, that a ski will tuck down and give a momentary downward rotation of the nose of the aircraft. This is generally caused by spring or bungie tension not being sufficient to hold ski tips up. The pitching and yawing will get your undivided attention. The immediate fix is to reduce power and reduce the speed of the aircraft. When the air loads are decreased below the tension of the spring of bungie, the ski will pitch back into place and the control problem will go away. The proper fix is to get a maintenance shop to correctly adjust the spring or bungie tension and then not exceed the speed limits on the skis.

A precautionary landing may be necessary for events, such as a broken ski cable or broken hydraulic line. If a ski cable breaks, the ski will reposition. This can develop into an asymmetrical drag situation, similar to a large speed brake. This condition is controllable; however, it will take skill to maintain control. A landing should be made as soon as practical.

The pilot will need to slow the skiplane to maneuvering speed or slightly below, so the ski will trail correctly. If possible ensure the skis are both in the UP position (for a pavement landing) and land on pavement. Avoid a snow landing if possible because the condition of the skis is unknown.

With a broken hydraulic line, the pilot may have a condition of one ski up and one ski down. Again, the aircraft is controllable with proper rudder and braking technique.

Minimum Survival Equipment

1. Food for each occupant sufficient to sustain life for 2 weeks.
2. One ax or hatchet.
3. One first aid kit.
4. One pistol, revolver, or shotgun and ammunition.
5. One small gill net and an assortment of tackle, such as hooks, flies, lines, and sinkers, etc.
6. One knife.
7. Two small boxes of matches.
8. One mosquito headnet for each occupant.
9. Two small signaling devices in a sealed metal container.

From October 15 - April 1 (in addition to above)

1. One pair of snow shoes.
2. One sleeping bag.
3. One wool blanket for each occupant over four.

SKIPLANE TRANSITION SYLLABUS

Ground Training

1. **Airplane Overview** ✓

2. **Use of Safety Equipment**

   a. Emergency Exits ✓
   b. Seat Belts and Shoulder Harness
   c. Other

3. **Review of AFM/POH (and supplements) or Owner's Manual to include:**

   a. General Information
   b. Limitations
   c. Procedures (including skiplane supplement)
   d. Emergency Procedures
   e. Modifications/Ski Systems*

*Focus on the mechanics of the skis and how, if any, it affects the handling of the aircraft while on the ground and in the air.

   f. Weight and Balance Limitations
   g. Performance Data (takeoff, cruise, and landing)

4. **En Route Emergency Procedures**

5. **Emergency and Survival Equipment**

6. **Cockpit Familiarization**

7. **Snow Environment**

   a. Types of Snow
   b. Hazardous Conditions

8. **Servicing**

9. **Problems/Pilot Errors Common to the Specific Airplane**

Flight Training

1. **Aeronautical Decision Making (ADM)**

2. **Preflight Inspection and Preheat**

   a. Remove Ice/Frost
   b. Free Skiplane

3. **Ground Operations**

   a. Engine Start
   b. Taxiing

      (1) Turning under Power
      (2) Maneuvering under Power
      (3) Avoiding Ski Tuck

   c. Before Takeoff Checks

4. **Takeoffs, Landings, and Go-Arounds**

   a. Normal and Crosswind Snow Takeoffs

      (1) Wind Drifts
      (2) Aborts

   b. Normal and Crosswind (Soft Field) Snow Landings
   c. Trial Landings
   d. Go-Around Procedures

5. **Flight Maneuvers**

   a. Inflight Maneuvering
   b. Slow Flight
   c. Power-Off Stalls
   d. Power-On Stalls
   e. Control by Reference to Instruments
   f. Other

6. **Parking/Postflight Procedures**

7. **Other Procedures**

   a. Emergency Procedures
   b. Abnormal Procedures
   c. Ski Tuck

8. **Debriefing and Documentation**

CHAPTER 18
AERONAUTICAL DECISION MAKING

INTRODUCTION

Throughout pilot training, safety, and good Aeronautical Decision Making (ADM) should be emphasized. Some of the basic concepts of ADM are presented in this chapter to provide an understanding of the ADM process.

GENERAL

Many aeronautical decisions are made easily—like flying on a beautiful day when the weather is perfect. However, some decisions can be more difficult—like whether to turn back when the clouds start closing in and visibility drops. When this happens, the decisions made on whether to continue the flight, turn back or deviate to an alternate airport, or fly higher or lower, will become critical to ensuring that the flight is completed safely. All too often many flights end in tragedy because of a bad decision that placed the aircraft in a situation that exceeded the capabilities of the pilot, aircraft, or both. This does not have to happen if a pilot recognizes the importance of timely decision making and takes some of the steps outlined below to ensure that he or she makes the best decisions possible under the circumstances.

Most pilots usually think good judgment is only acquired through years of experience. The general aviation private pilot, who flies for pleasure or occasional personal business, will probably fly a small percentage of the hours that a professional pilot will fly over the course of a flying career. A pilot cannot rely simply upon experience as a teacher of good judgment. It is important to learn how to deal with decision making in general and to learn strategies that will lead to effective judgment in a wide variety of situations.

TYPES OF DECISIONS

It is important to recognize that there are two general types of decisions. Decisions that are tied to time constraints and those that are not. In a time constraint decision, a solution is required almost immediately. An example might be an engine failure near the ground. For the most part, a pilot is trained to recognize events like this that require immediate action.

Usually, when time is not a constraint, time is available to gather information and consider alternative courses of action. For example, when planning a flight, a pilot has access to an extensive array of information sources, such as weather, airport conditions, and aircraft performance. A pilot should examine the sources until he or she is confident that all the information needed to make the flight has been examined.

A study conducted by NASA revealed that 80 percent of the errors that led to an incident occurred during the preflight phase, while the incidents occurred later during the flight.

It seems obvious that a large number of accidents and incidents could be avoided, if a pilot were to perform better preflight planning. Flight planning is similar to an open-book test in school—all the information needed is available, if a pilot knows where to look. Decision aids are tools that can be used to ensure all relevant information is considered. The appropriate flight planning, followed by the operation of the aircraft within a pilot's capabilities, will ensure a safe flight. Good examples of decision making tools are the various checklists that are provided by the manufacturers of aircraft. There are checklist, for guiding our preflight inspection of the aircraft, starting the engine(s), setting up the radios, and preparing for takeoff and landing. They are inexpensive, effective, and enhance safety. Checklists provide an effective means of solving the most human of frailties—forgetting. If a pilot follows a checklist, those temporary memory lapses need not have an impact on the flight. The sequence of operations and the critical information required is all recorded for a pilot to use.

EFFECTIVENESS OF ADM

The effectiveness of ADM and the safety of general aviation depend on several factors:

•   The knowledge required to understand the situation, the information available, and the possible options.
•   The skills required to execute a decision.
•   Understanding how to make decisions effectively, including how to search for information and when to stop searching and choose a course of action.
•   The self-awareness to recognize when hazardous attitudes are influencing decisions and possessing the self-discipline to overcome those attitudes.

The first two factors, knowledge and skills, will be addressed during the ground and flight training. The knowledge required to understand weather conditions, calculate fuel requirements, use of checklists, and other items required for flight planning will be explained. Flight instructors will also teach how to put preflight planning into action. This will start a pilot on a path toward making good aeronautical decisions based on the limitations of the aircraft, weather conditions, and the pilot's experience level. This will also help a pilot develop a positive attitude toward safety and risk management. Having a positive attitude means always considering the potential safety implications of decisions.

Progressive decision making recognizes that changes are constantly taking place, and that a pilot should be continually assessing the outcome. For example, more weather information about alternate airports will allow the pilot to judge the quality of the decision and to recognize when it is time to modify that outcome in the face of new information. A pilot with this progressive decision making strategy may make changes rapidly based on the information at hand. The pilot should continue to seek more information about the situation so the plan may be refined and modified if necessary.

Flexibility and the capability to modify actions as new information is obtained are very desirable features of decision making. What this means, in simplest terms, is always having a way out.

The other factor that was mentioned earlier that would affect the quality and safety of a pilot's decisions is attitude. Attitude is one of those aspects of human nature that is hard to define precisely, but we know it when we see it. It is an overall approach to life. It is something in the way people talk and act that makes us

think that they are reckless, safe, liberal, conservative, serious, happy-go-lucky, or any one of a number of other adjectives. They have a certain style of responding to life's events that is relatively consistent and which they tend to apply in many situations.

Think for a moment about the stereotypical image of pilots portrayed in popular films—particularly those from several years ago. Films deal in images and an image like that is much easier to portray than the reality. There is a lot of truth to the old adage, "There arc old pilots and there are bold pilots, but there are no old, bold pilots." Flying is a wondrous adventure, but it is not the place for boldness, thrill seeking, complacence, or lack of dedication to doing the best one can.

A series of studies conducted a few years ago identified five attitudes among pilots that were particularly hazardous. These attitudes are:

•   **Antiauthority**—This attitude is found in people who do not like anyone telling them what to do. Flying is governed by many regulations established for the safety of all, so pilots with this hazardous attitude may rebel against authority by deliberately breaking rules intended for safety.
•   **Impulsivity**—This is the attitude of people who frequently feel the need to do something—anything—immediately. They do the first thing that comes to mind, without thinking about what the best alternative might be.
•   **Invulnerability**—Many people feel that accidents happen to others, but never to them. They know accidents can happen, and they know that anyone can be affected, but they never really feel or believe they will be personally involved. A pilot with this attitude is more likely to take chances and increase risk.
•   **Macho**—A pilot who is always trying to prove that he or she is better than anyone else is thinking, "I can do it—I'll show them." All pilots are equally susceptible to this hazardous attitude which can lead to taking risks to impress others.
•   **Resignation**—Pilots who think, "What's the use?" do not see themselves as being able to make a great deal of difference in what happens. They blame whatever happens on luck. Instead of seeking out information and making positive decisions, they just drift along making no changes and hoping for the best.

Having these attitudes can contribute to poor pilot judgment, since they tend to push the pilot toward making decisions that involve more risk. Recognizing that these hazardous attitudes exist is the first step in neutralizing them in the decision making process. Before dismissing these attitudes as belonging to someone else, realize that everyone has these attitudes to some degree. At one time or another all pilots have acted impulsively or in a macho fashion to demonstrate their aviation skills to others.

Pilots should be aware of these attitudes and constantly examine their actions to see if they are falling prey to their influences. This will help a pilot improve the quality of his or her actions.

Developing good decision making skills will allow pilots to fly securely in the knowledge that they are controlling risk and ensuring safety. Figure 18-1 provides some useful antidotes for hazardous attitudes.

Minimum Personal Checklist

Proper planning will allow a pilot to make better decisions and to have a safer flight. Figure 18-2 provides a sample checklist to assist a pilot in the planning and decision making process. It can be revised and updated to meet the needs of individual pilots.

HAZARDOUS ATTITUDE	ANTIDOTE
Antiauthority: Don't tell me	Follow the rules. They are usually right.
Impulsivity: Do something quickly.	Not so fast. Think first.
Invulnerability: It won't happen to me.	It could happen to me.
Macho: I can do it.	Taking chances is foolish.
Resignation: What's the use?	I'm not helpless. I can make a difference.

FIGURE 18-1.—Hazardous attitude antidotes.

PILOT

Experience/Recency
Takeoff/landings................ __6__ In the last __60__ days

Hours in make/model............. __1__ In the last __60__ days

Instrument approaches.......... __6__ In the last
(simulated or actual) __30__ days

Instrument flight hours........... __1__ In the last
(simulated or actual) __60__ days

Terrain and airspace...........................familiar

Physical Condition
Sleep...................................... __8__ In the last
24 hours

Food and water...................... In the last
__4__ hours

Alcohol................................. None in the last
__12__ hours

Drugs or medication.............. None in the last
__12__ hours

Stressful events..................... None in the last
__1__ days

Illnesses................................ None in the last
__1__ days

AIRCRAFT

Fuel Reserves (Cross-Country)
VFR Day.............................. __1__ hours
Night........................... __1__ hours
IFR Day.............................. __1__ hours
Night........................... __1__ hours

Experience in Type
Takeoffs/landings.................. __6__ In the last
in aircraft type __60__ days

Aircraft Performance
Establish that you have additional performance available over that required. Consider the following:

* Gross weight
* Load distribution
* Density altitude
* Performance chart

Aircraft Equipment

Avionics......................familiar with equipment (including autopilot and GPS systems)

COM/NAV...................equipment appropriate to flight

Charts........................ current

Clothing..................... suitable for preflight and flight

Survival gear.............. appropriate for flight and terrain

FIGURE 18-2. —Minimum personal checklists.

ENVIRONMENT

Airport Conditions
Crosswind.................. _____% of max POH
Runway length........... _____% more than POH

Weather
Reports and forecasts............not more than
   in aircraft type   _____hours old
Icing conditions.....................within aircraft/pilot
                   capabilities

Weather for VFR
Ceiling   Day............................_____feet
           Night........................._____feet
Visibility   Day............................_____miles
           Night........................._____miles

Weather for IFR

Precision Approaches
Ceiling.................._____feet above min.
Visibility................._____mile(s) above min.

Non-Precision Approaches
Ceiling.................._____feet above min.
Visibility................._____mile(s) above min.

Missed Approaches
No more than........ _3__before diverting

Takeoff Minimums
Ceiling................._200_ feet
Visibility................._1__mile(s)

EXTERNAL PRESSURES

Trip Planning .
Allowance for delays............... _____minute

Diversion or Cancellation Alternate Plans
Notification of person(s) you are meeting

Passengers briefed on diversion or cancellation plans and alternatives

Modification or cancellation of car rental, resturant, or hotel reservations

Arrangement of alternative transportation (Airline, car, etc.)

Personal Equipment
Credit card and telephone numbers available for alternate plans

Appropriate clothing or personal needs (eye wear, medication...) in the event of an unexpected stay

Figure 18-2. —Minimum personal checklists, continued.

Index